What the Bible teaches

EXODUS

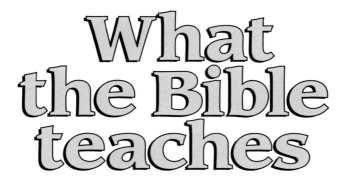

EXODUS

John Grant

GENERAL EDITOR   **W. S. STEVELY**

JOHN RITCHIE LTD
CHRISTIAN PUBLICATIONS

ISBN 1 904064 26 4

WHAT THE BIBLE TEACHES
© 2004 John Ritchie Ltd.
40 Beansburn, Kilmarnock, Scotland

Typeset by John Ritchie Ltd.
Printed by The Bath Press, Avon, England.

CONTENTS

Page

CONTRIBUTOR

JOHN GRANT

John Grant was born in Glasgow, Scotland into a Christian
family. At eighteen years of age he was received into assembly
fellowship in Kilmacolm, Renfrewshire. In 1990 he left secular
employment to engage "full time" in the preaching of the
gospel and the teaching of the Word of God, and has laboured
throughout the United Kingdom, North America, and the Far
East. He has been the editor of the Believer's Magazine since
1999, and is the author of "Living for God" and the John Ritchie
"Family Series".

ABBREVIATIONS

AV	Authorised Version (known in USA as King James Version)
JND	New Translation by J. N. Darby
Newberry	The AV as edited by Thomas Newberry; also known as "The Englishman's Bible"
RSV	Revised Standard Version (revision of the American Standard Version)
RV	Revised Version, 1885 (published in England, revision of the AV)
Septuagint	The ancient translation of the Old Testament into Greek. Often quoted in the New Testament
TWOT	Theological Wordbook of the Old Testament
YLT	Young's Literal Translation

PREFACE

The publishers have commissioned this Old Testament series of commentaries to complement the completed set of New Testament commentaries issued under the general title "What the Bible Teaches". Together they seek to provide an accessible and useful tool for the study of, and meditation on, Scripture.

While there is no shortage of commentaries currently available on the various books of the Old Testament it was felt that there was no complete series that sought simply to apply the message of Genesis through to Malachi to the concerns of believers today.

The authors of these volumes are not scholars of the original languages and rely on others for guidance on the best modern views of word meanings and similar matters. However, all the authors share the conviction that the Bible in its entirety is the Word of God. They believe it to be reliable, accurate, and intended "for our learning" (Rom 15.4). This view has been explained further by the Editor in a short series of articles that appeared in "The Believer's Magazine", also published by John Ritchie Ltd., in 1999.

The two Testaments fit together so that principles and illustrations from the Old are brought to bear on issues that arise on nearly every page of the New. Knowledge of the Old is therefore an indispensable aid to the proper understanding of the New. In particular the Lord Jesus can be seen in prophecy and picture again and again. He, Himself, as described in the Gospels, is an exemplar of this approach to the Old Testament through His constant reference to people and incidents whose histories are recorded for us, and to those prophetic statements that applied to Him.

Given this understanding of the nature and purpose of the Scriptures, the main lessons of the books are considered and applied to our circumstances today by authors experienced in preaching and teaching the Word of God.

Since no attempt is being made to produce an academic series the technical apparatus has been kept to a minimum. Where authors have judged it of value attention is drawn to linguistic and other issues. Transliteration, where appropriate, is accompanied by reference to the numerical system devised by Strong to allow the reader without knowledge of the original languages to gain access to the various lexical aids which have adopted this system. For clarity, numerical references to New Testament words only are given in italics, following the practice used in Strong's Concordance.

The system of transliteration generally used is that adopted by the

Theological Wordbook of the Old Testament (TWOT), edited by Harris, Archer and Waltke, and published by Moody Press, Chicago, 1980. However, there are occasions when account has been taken of the commonly recognised English spelling of some Hebrew words.

References to Scripture without attribution are taken from the Authorised (King James) Version. Where other translations are quoted the source is indicated.

Biblical measurements are usually given in cubits. For ease of calculation the general assumption has been adopted that 1 cubit = 18 inches/46cms.

When utilised, Notes are placed at the end of the relevant chapter, and in the Introduction and Chapter 25.1-9 these are numbered consecutively. In the other expository chapters the existence of a Note is shown by [†], and the Note itself indicates the verse(s) to which it applies.

Since the commentaries do not necessarily follow a verse-by-verse approach, and to save space and cost, the text of Scripture is not included. It is assumed that all readers have available a copy of the Bible.

The complete Old Testament is expected to be covered in around fifteen to eighteen volumes. These will not appear in the order in which they are found in the Scriptures but simply in order of completion by the authors commissioned for the series.

W. S. STEVELY

BIBLIOGRAPHY

1. History
Edersheim, Alfred. *Bible History: Old Testament.* Massachusetts: Hendrickson Publishers, Inc., 2001.
  An easily read history dealing with each book in the Old Testament and providing helpful historical background.
Johnson, P. *The Civilisation of Ancient Egypt.* London: Weidenfeld & Nicholson, 1978.
  A fascinating, well illustrated examination of the civilisation of Ancient Egypt. A good introduction to the subject.
Rohl, David. *A Test of Time.* London: Arrow Books, Ltd., 1995.
  Provides a well-developed argument for an alternative dating overview of the history of Egypt. Interesting to read his reasoning for agreeing with certain key biblical passages.
Siliotti, Alberto. *Egypt: Splendours of an Ancient Civilisation.* London: Thames and Hudson, Ltd., 1966.
  Very pictorial, but helpful in giving a taste of the greatness of Ancient Egypt.

2. Commentaries
Baxter, J. Sidlow. *Explore the Book, Vol. 1.* London: Marshall, Morgan & Scott, 1951.
  One of a well-known series providing an excellent basic introduction to each book.
Brown, William. *The Tabernacle.* Massachusetts: Hendrickson Publishers, Inc., 1996.
  A reprinted work containing some fine devotional teaching. Despite being written in the late 19th century, the language is easy to follow.
Bush, George. *Commentary on Exodus.* Grand Rapids: Kregel Publications, 1993.
  Written in the nineteenth century with much detail. In some parts somewhat dated, but nevertheless a full commentary. The print style and approach to writing do not make this an easy book to read.
Chadwick, G. A. *The Expositor's Bible – The Book of Exodus.* London: Hodder and Stoughton, 1890.
  A standard exposition of the text with useful comments.
Coates, C. A. *An Outline of the Book of Exodus.* London: Stow Hill Bible and Tract Depot.
  Most useful for the devotional nature of the writing which gives insights not usually available in a standard commentary on the text. It is necessary, however, to be careful in accepting some of the views put forward.

Currid, John D. *Exodus: Volume 1.* Darlington: Evangelical Press, 2000.
A recent addition to the works on Exodus; useful for the freshness of approach.

Darby, J. N. *Synopsis of the Books of the Bible, Vol. 1: Exodus.* London: Stow Hill Bible and Tract Depot, 1957. Several Reprints.
A most useful tool for those seeking to gain an overview of the Word of God. More recent editions have been successfully reformatted to make the text more readable.

Darby, J. N. *Collected Writings of J. N. Darby: Volume XIX.* London: G. Morrish.
Further help from the prolific writings of Mr. Darby. Always useful, although his style of writing requires considerable concentration from the reader.

Dennett, Edward. *Typical Teachings of Exodus.* Oak Park: Bible Truth Publishers.
A small volume which is written in the style of brethren of the mid-nineteenth century. It is, however, not a difficult book to read, and has much to commend it.

Edersheim, Alfred. *The Life and Times of Jesus the Messiah.* Grand Rapids: Wm. B. Eerdman's Publishing Co., 1981.
A standard well-known work dealing in detail with the subject. An invaluable scholarly reference book providing much background detail of great interest.

Halley, Henry. *Bible Handbook.* USA: Zondervan Publishing House, 1959.
Another standard handbook of value.

Jamieson, Fausset, and Brown. *A Commentary on the Whole Bible.* USA: Zondervan Publishing House.
As with all commentaries on the complete Bible, this book suffers from the need to deal superficially with the subject. It is, nevertheless, a valuable tool, but does require care in accepting all the views expressed.

Keil, C. F. & Delitzsch, F. *Commentary on the Old Testament, The Pentateuch: Exodus.* Massachusetts: Hendrickson Publishers, Inc., 1996.
A well-known, detailed reference book which gives a most helpful exposition of the text. A must for all who study the Old Testament more than superficially.

Law, Henry. *Christ is All - The Gospel of the Old Testament - Exodus.* London: Hamilton, Adams & Co., 1856.
A delightful little volume, written in the mid-nineteenth century, which is devotional and makes much of the Lord Jesus from the text. Well worth reading to enjoy the richness of language employed. One of a series of companion volumes.

Mackintosh, C. H. *Notes on the Book of Exodus.* USA: Loizeaux Brothers, Inc., 1972. Several Reprints.
The writings of C. H. Mackintosh have become recognised as a standard work, necessary for all who commence reading the Pentateuch. Despite

the fact that they originate in the nineteenth century the style is not dated and is not difficult to follow. Essential reading!

Merrill, E. H. *Bible Knowledge Key Word Study: Genesis-Deuteronomy.* Colorado Springs: Cook Communication Ministries, 2003.
A new series which discusses the meaning of key words in the text. Very useful for those who are interested in this most helpful level of study. A good back-up for those who use TWOT.

Meyer, F. B. *Devotional Commentary on Exodus.* Grand Rapids: Kregel Publications, 1978.
Meyer's commentaries are well-known and devotional in content. They are not verse by verse commentaries but deal with single verses or groups of verses in a most useful manner.

Page, John B. D. *Christ and Solomon's Temple.* Glasgow: Gospel Tract Publications, 1994.
Solomon's Temple has been less considered than the Tabernacle, but this volume by one who has made a life-time study of the subject is a welcome tool. Written in a readable style.

Raven, C. H. *God's Sanctuary.* Kilmarnock: John Ritchie, Ltd., 1991.
A small proportion of the views expressed may not be shared by all, but they are carefully put forward and worthy of consideration.

Smith, J. E. *The Promised Messiah.* Nashville: Thomas Nelson, 1993.
Covers the Old Testament prophecies concerning the Messiah and is presented in a very acceptable format. Useful insight is given to each of the prophecies, emphasising to the reader that the Old Testament is filled with Christ.

Soltau, Henry. *The Tabernacle, The Priesthood, and The Offerings.* Grand Rapids: Kregel Publications, 1994.

Soltau, Henry. *The Holy Vessels and Furniture of the Tabernacle.* Grand Rapids: Kregel Publications, 1994.
These are two classic volumes, well presented and illustrated, from a reliable writer.

Stallan, F. E. *Things Written Afore Time.* Kilmarnock: John Ritchie Ltd., 1990.
A careful exposition of each verse in the Old Testament which is quoted in the New Testament. Reliable and readable, it provides helpful insight into the text.

Strong, James. *The Tabernacle of Israel.* Grand Rapids: Kregel Publications, 1987.
A small volume which, although dealing with spiritual truth to be found in the Tabernacle, considers the practical issues in its construction.

White, Frank H. *Christ in the Tabernacle.* London: S. W. Partridge and Co., 1907.
A fine, easily read, devotional commentary which is rich in appreciation of the Lord.

INTRODUCTION

To Hebrew speaking Jews the second book of the Pentateuch is named "And these (are) the names", at times shortened to *shemoth*, "the names", a title derived, as is the custom in all the first five books of Scripture, from its opening words. It was not until the third and second centuries BC that the title "*Exodos*" was used by the Jews of Alexandria who translated the Hebrew Scriptures into Greek. The Greek word has been taken, only slightly changed, into the English language. Its meaning is "departure", "emigration", or "going out", an ideal title to describe a book dealing with the departure of the Israelites from Egypt.

The account of the departure of a captive nation to a new country, and the surrounding circumstances, would rank at any time with the heroic tales of history. For an entire nation to leave where they had lived for centuries, survive as a people for forty wilderness years, and then take possession of a land which was already populated by powerful and warlike nation tribes is a feat which has not been equalled. Even today it is accepted that Moses is a textbook example for those who seek to lead. Although outwith the scope of this volume, the military strategy of Joshua in taking possession of Canaan is acknowledged as superb in planning and execution, based on principles which still hold true.

Typical Teaching in Exodus

Exodus, however, is much more than a historical account alone. That it is historically accurate is not in doubt. Paul, when writing about events that took place during the journey to Canaan states clearly that "all these things happened" (1 Cor 10.11). However, the book must be looked at, not only historically, but also typically. Those who regard the historical records of the Old Testament as being irrelevant to this present age lose much of the teaching of the Word of God. Indeed, it can be asserted that a lack of knowledge of the Old Testament is a serious deficiency when it comes to seeking an understanding of New Testament teaching. The Old Testament and the New Testament stand as one book and the full enjoyment of their teaching is only obtained when both are studied and seen to complement each other perfectly. When Paul wrote to Timothy and reminded him that "from a child thou hast known the holy scriptures, which are able to make thee wise unto salvation through faith which is in Christ Jesus" (2 Tim 3.15), he was referring to the Old Testament Scriptures. When he later stated that "All scripture is given by inspiration of God" (2 Tim 3.16), he was including the New Testament Scriptures, then being written, with the Old Testament.

The principle of seeking truth for today from the Old Testament is established in the New Testament. The Epistle to the Romans makes much of the lessons drawn from the life of Abraham (see for example Rom 4);

the journeys of the Children of Israel through the wilderness are the source from which Paul draws lessons for the assembly at Corinth (1 Cor 10); the account in Genesis of the two sons of Abraham, Isaac and Ishmael, is used by Paul when writing to the Galatians (Gal 4.21-31); the Tabernacle is the basis of much of the teaching in the Epistle to the Hebrews. These few examples confirm the value of the Old Testament narrative for today.

The departure of the Israelites from Egypt, and the forty years during which they were in the wilderness, were purposed by God to teach lessons regarding redemption and the means by which men and women can secure and maintain a relationship with God. The narrative reveals, in graphic detail, lessons that are relevant today. Those who wish to understand God's ways, and to know Him, cannot ignore the book of Exodus. Therein is set out the way of salvation, and the provision which God has made for those who are delivered from the kingdom of darkness.

Just as the Epistle to the Romans sets out the doctrine of the gospel, so this book introduces the reader, through historical events with typical meaning, to the same salvation. This is the book of redemption, describing the servitude of the people, the interest of God in their sufferings and groaning, the work of God in bringing about their deliverance, and the great truth of salvation effected by blood. But the narrative does not end there! Deliverance from the penalty of sin has been brought about, but at the Red Sea there is deliverance from the power of Egypt, a symbol of the power of sin. Israel travel into the wilderness where lessons have to be learned in the school of God. Such an account cannot fail to grip the heart of all Christians who have a desire to get to know God in a closer way.

The failings of this redeemed people are not overlooked. Their complaints and murmurings are noted, as is the Lord's response to their ingratitude. The lessons to be learned from these failures are vital for Christian life. Paul states that these things happened "for ensamples: and they are written for our admonition, upon whom the ends of the world are come" (1 Cor 10.11). As the history of this nation of redeemed slaves is detailed, the thought may arise that believers today could not fail as they failed. The stark warning, however, is, "Wherefore let him that thinketh he standeth take heed lest he fall" (1 Cor 10.12). Believers in this present age are subject to temptations as strong as those which faced Israel, but have examples in the Word of God from which they can find guidance. In the book of Exodus is presented a grand panorama of truth relevant to the lives of all those who desire to serve the God and Father of our Lord Jesus Christ.

Authorship
The language used
As with the other four books of the Pentateuch, credit for authorship of most, if not all of the text, has been given to Moses. (The closing verses of Deuteronomy may have been added by another writer to complete the

history of Moses). This has been challenged on the basis that alphabetic writing of the necessary sophistication had not come into being during the "early days of civilisation" in which Moses lived. The Egyptian system of hieroglyphics (picture language) was certainly in use,[1] but this could not possibly convey the beauty of the Hebrew language nor give the shades of meaning which Hebrew allows the author to impart. Since the original documents are not available, there cannot be established with complete certainty the language which was used. It is, however, clear that Moses would know the Egyptian script and be able to use it to the full. He was brought up in the palace of Pharaoh and was "learned in all the wisdom of the Egyptians" (Acts 7.22). The written language of Egypt was not so unsophisticated that it was able only to convey simple ideas, and, although unlikely, Moses could have written this book in Egyptian before translating it into the language of the Hebrews. The writing would have been on clay tablets or on leather or papyrus, writing materials that were in general use at that time.

R. K. Harrison confirms this in his *Introduction to the Old Testament* where he states: "There can no longer be any doubt from archaeological sources that writing was a feature of life in Syria and Palestine from the earliest occupational periods. Certainly by the time of Moses there were several well established means of linguistic expression for the purpose of transmitting written communication".

However, even in the days of Joseph the language used by Jacob and his sons was different from the language of Egypt.[2] Added to this is the fact that writing and literature amongst the Hebrews did exist in the times of Moses. The "book of the wars of the Lord" (Num 21.14)[3] is an example of this. After the defeat of Amalek, Moses is told by Jehovah to "Write this for a memorial in a book" (17.14). It is likely that a people as tenacious as the Israelites, with the hope of returning to the land promised to their fathers, would retain the use of their own language and have a written alphabet. Having left Egypt they would emphasise their nationhood in this way. It appears to be a reasonable proposition, therefore, that this book was written in the language of the Hebrews and that writing skills to make this possible did exist in the time of Moses.

The author

Having established that it was possible for Moses to write this book, the evidence which confirms him as the author must now be considered. The information within Exodus itself does not provide a full answer. We know that Moses "wrote all the words of the Lord" (24.4), and that at times he was commanded by Jehovah to write an account of what had taken place (17.14; 34.27), but there is no signature of Moses over the complete work. External evidence, however, is more compelling. The Lord Jesus says of Moses that "he wrote of me" (Jn 5.46). This established that Moses did write some of the Old Testament Scriptures, for His listeners were exhorted to "Search the scriptures" (Jn 5.39). The two who met the Saviour on the road to Emmaus heard Him, "beginning at Moses and all the prophets" (Lk 24.27), expound unto them in all the Scriptures the things concerning Himself. He commenced at the writings of Moses, which indicates that these were at the beginning of the Scriptures. Finally, the Lord Jesus refers to Exodus as "the book of Moses" (Mk 12.26). Clearly this establishes Moses as the writer.

Some object to this conclusion on the basis that the book is written in the third person, even when reference is made to Moses. Such an objection barely merits consideration. The use of the third person is not only an acceptable form in the recording of such a history; it was commonly used at that time, the inscriptions on tombs and pyramids being examples. Above all such objection, believers accept the word of the Lord Jesus in Mark 12.

Who better to write the book than the man who had been appointed by the Lord to lead the people? There was no part of this history, right up until his death, in which he did not play a prominent part. He had an understanding of the hearts of the people and the motives which moved them in their behaviour, often in disobedience to the God who had so blessed them. He understood also the feelings of the Lord regarding this people. The Lord was pleased to say that Moses "is faithful in all mine house", and that He spoke to him "mouth to mouth, even apparently, and not in dark speeches (openly, and not in riddles, JND)". He had the privilege of beholding "the similitude of the Lord (the form of Jehovah, JND)" (Num 12.7-8). He stands as one of the giants of the Old Testament, his name being found in nineteen of its books, but his influence being seen throughout all thirty-nine. He is one of the small number to whom the Lord refers as "my servant". The last mention of him in the Old Testament reminds the nation that the Law and teaching which he brought to them still stood: "Remember ye the law of Moses my servant, which I commanded unto him in Horeb for all Israel, with the statutes and judgments" (Mal 4.4).

Beyond the human author, however, the book of Exodus is, as are all the books in the Bible, the Word of God. This commentary is written on the basis that what Moses wrote was God's Word.

The Duration of the Captivity

The first mention of the captivity of the Israelites in Egypt (Gen 15.13) indicates that the period of their sojourn in that land would be 400 years. The exact number of years is given as 430 (Ex 12.40). This is confirmed by Stephen in his defence before the High Priest (Acts 7.6) when, quoting the Scripture mentioned above, he states that the period of bondage would be 400 years. Some doubt has been raised due to the comment of Paul; "the covenant, that was confirmed before of God in Christ, the law, which was four hundred and thirty years after, cannot disannul" (Gal 3.17). If the exodus took place 430 years after the giving of the covenant to Abraham (Gen 15) the Israelites must have been in Egypt for the shorter period of about 215 years as there were 215 years from the call of Abraham until Jacob went down to Egypt:

From the call of Abraham to the birth of Isaac -
25 years (Gen 12.4 & 21.5)

From the birth of Isaac until the birth of Jacob -
60 years (Gen 25.26)

From the birth of Jacob until his arrival in Egypt -
130 years (Gen 47.9)
Total - 215 years.

It is unlikely, however, that a shorter period of 215 years would be sufficient to cover all that took place during Israel's bondage and the increase in numbers from twelve brethren to 600,000 men. With reference to Galatians 3.17 it has been noted that "Paul is not concerned here with the exact duration of the interval between the intimation to Abraham of God's purpose to bless the world through him, and the giving of the law at Sinai immediately after the Exodus...The number of years cannot have been less than four hundred and thirty in either case. That the period was a considerable one is all the argument requires".[4] This, however, is suggesting that on this occasion Paul uses a degree of inexactitude which is out of character.

One possible and more satisfactory way of looking at Galatians 3 is that Paul is referring to the time between Jacob entering Egypt (see Gen 46.1-3) and the exodus. "On the day following the last repetition of the promise orally (Gen 46.1-6), at Beer-sheba, Israel passed into Egypt", and it is from that day "that the interval of four hundred thirty years [*sic*] between it and the law is to be counted" (Jamieson, Fausset, and Brown). For 215 years the patriarchal family was in the place where the covenant was given, enjoying the land which, one day, would be theirs. The Law, which came 430 years after the land was left behind by Jacob and his family, cannot annul that covenant. The weight of evidence, therefore, indicates that the Israelites were in Egypt for 430 years.

The Land of Egypt

"Mizraim" (4714) is the name by which the land of Egypt is known in Scripture. The meaning is "Double Strip", or "Two Lands",[5] referring to the fertile land which is to be found on the banks of the Nile. These two strips of land were essential for the life of the nation. On their fertility the Egyptians depended for food, and such was their regard for the river that they looked on the annual flood as being provided by a god. It was to this rich soil the Egyptians referred when they called their land "Kemi" (Black Land).

The name Mizraim is first found in Scripture as that given to one of the sons of Ham (Gen 10.6) who was a son of Noah. The Psalmist refers to

Egypt as "the land of Ham" (Ps 105.23,27) confirming that the family of Ham spread southward and occupied this territory.

The first mention of the name as that of a country is when Abram left Canaan due to the famine and went down to Egypt (Gen 12.10). While there he told a lie regarding Sarai and also gave Lot a taste for the things of Egypt that later would be one of the factors in drawing him to live in Sodom, which appeared to him to be "like the land of Egypt" (Gen 13.10).

The History of Egypt
The writings of Manetho

Most of the written history of ancient Egypt comes from the writings of Manetho, an Egyptian priest in the temple of Heliopolis, who lived about 300 BC. His *History of Egypt* has become accepted as the best available record of Egyptian civilisation for the period which it covers. No complete edition of this work survives, but it is known because sections of it are quoted in the works of others, including those of Josephus. It should be noted, however, that the *History of Egypt* was written long after the power of Egypt had declined and when its grandeur was part of history. All of the sources available to Manetho are not known, and there are difficulties in reconciling some of his narrative with facts which have been established. His accounts of the exploits and achievements of some of the Pharaohs are clearly mythical, but this work still remains the only written archive covering the rise and fall of one of the greatest civilisations of history.

Manetho arbitrarily divided the successive sovereigns into 31 dynasties, a dynasty usually being one family. Although doubt has been cast on the "old accepted chronology" which he gives, current scholars have, for convenience sake, preserved these dynasties, which are grouped together into eight or nine periods called "Kingdoms". These kingdoms are identified by the governmental structure of the country resulting from the degree of authority exercised by the central power. Between the end of one kingdom and the beginning of the next there were times of upheaval which are known as "Intermediate Periods".

It is very difficult to date the various kingdoms and dynasties with accuracy. The timescales which the Egyptians used were based on the reigns of the pharaohs, and they would refer to the eighth year of one pharaoh or the tenth year of another pharaoh. There was, however, no "beginning date" to which all other dates were referred, and this makes it impossible to relate these dates with confidence to a stated chronology. Manetho's chronology places the rise of the Egyptian state at about 3000 BC but this is at variance with Bible chronology if it is accepted that the Flood took place about 2400-2500 BC.

The dates quoted below to define the periods in the history of Egypt are those used by Manetho. It is outwith the scope of this book to consider these issues in detail, but the dates are included to let the reader understand the relative position of each period or kingdom. No accuracy is claimed for the dates; indeed the data on which they are based is fragmentary and unreliable. They are included only to give some indication of the relationship of one era to another, although even that is open to doubt.

Early Dynastic Period

Before the state came into being, Egypt was divided into forty-two regions (*nomes*), which were ruled by local princes. Twenty-two of these were grouped together to form the kingdom of Upper (Red) Egypt, which consisted mainly of the area of the Nile delta, and twenty of them were grouped together to form the kingdom of Lower (White) Egypt. This view of the country, consisting of two separate regions, was held even after the two kingdoms were united by Menes (who may have been Narmer, a somewhat mythical figure whose existence is problematic), a prince from the south, who added the northern kingdom to his realm. He is reputed to have made his capital in Memphis approximately ten miles south of the present capital city of Cairo. This was on the old border of the southern and northern kingdoms. This period is known as the *Archaic* or *Early Dynastic Period,* during which the first and second dynasties ruled, and the rule of the pharaohs commenced. The title "Pharaoh" (6547) comes from the ancient Egyptian *per a'o* meaning "Great House", signifying that this was he who ruled from the palace.

The Old Kingdom

Following this, the era known as the *Old Kingdom* commenced and spanned a period of about 500 years from around 2700 BC. The third to the sixth dynasties ruled at this time. The pharaohs received the double crown of Upper and of Lower Egypt and at that time were given an "official name" in addition to the name which was given them at birth. They usually added a number of other names to commemorate great victories or show their devotion to other deities which were considered to be worthy of honour. The Step Pyramid of Djoser (a pharaoh of the third dynasty), built during this early era, is claimed to be the most ancient building to be found in Egypt. Although this pyramid was different in design from those which followed (it was a tiered structure) this marked the beginning of the pyramid building age. Before this the kings had been buried in *mastabas*, mud brick burial chambers, but an architect and builder, Imhotep, constructed this first stone built burial chamber. Under a *mastaba* he dug deep down into the rock and created passageways and the burial vault. Over the *mastaba* the pyramid was erected.

During the fourth dynasty, pyramid building reached its peak with the development of the true pyramid. These structures did not stand alone. They were the centre of a group of buildings consisting of mortuary temples, *mastabas* for relatives and friends of the monarchs, and other temples and buildings with religious significance. While there was in the heart of man an understanding that death was not the end of existence, it is sad to contemplate these elaborate and costly preparations for the "afterlife" which achieved nothing. They stand today empty and forlorn.

Pharaoh Khufu (or Kheops) constructed the largest pyramid at Giza, and for his son Khafre (Khephren) he built the second largest. The Sphinx, which has the face of Khafre and the body of a lion crouches to guard the pyramid precincts. This great pyramid is the only one of the seven wonders of the ancient world standing today. It was built with 2,300,000 blocks of limestone each with an average weight of 2 tons.[6] It was originally 146.6 metres (481ft) high although it has lost its top 9.25 metres (30ft) over the centuries. Until the 19th century it was the highest man-made building still in existence. The Tower of Babel may have been higher but there is no record of its height. The area of the base is so great that the cathedrals of Florence, Milan, St Paul's, Westminster Abbey, and St Peter's in Rome could be accommodated in it with some space left over.[7] Even today, controversy rages as to how a project of this magnitude could have been undertaken and completed with such skill. Sir Flinders Petrie, the archaeologist who measured the pyramid, stated that "neither needle or hair" could be inserted into the joints between the blocks of limestone. Errors in the lengths and angles of the building can be "covered with one's thumb". Herodotus states that 100,000 men were employed in its construction for a period of twenty years. An enterprise like this must have been a great strain on the state exchequer. It may be for this reason that later kings were much more modest in the size of their tombs.

It is worthy of note that some of these buildings may have been constructed before Abram went down to Egypt (Gen 12.10). As Abram was known in the court of Pharoah he would have seen the great edifices before time and robbers ravished them. Such majesty and beauty did not affect the heart of the man who had left the glory of Ur of the Chaldees at the call of God, although it did give rise to desires for the things of Egypt in the heart of his nephew, Lot. When Lot saw the well watered plain of Jordan, in which were situated Sodom and Gomorrah, it appeared to him, as has already been noted, to be "like the land of Egypt" (Gen 13.10), and there he decided to make his home.

Ruling such a huge empire required skill and organisation. A civil service had to be put in place. Canals and dams were built, and warehouses were constructed to house the harvests. The land was surveyed and a system of taxation was introduced. Distribution of the harvest required an efficient infrastructure, and all this was in addition to the grand building projects undertaken.

The finances of the realm were under the control of chancellors who carried responsibility for the two Treasuries, one for Upper and the other for Lower Egypt. The Controller of the Grain Warehouses was a position of power as was the Controller of the Royal Household. Scribes were necessary to keep communication flowing over such a vast territory, and they became a powerful group in the kingdom. The science of mathematics was well understood, and this industrious people mastered the complex calculations necessary for such projects as pyramid building.

The First Intermediate Period

Gradually, however, the authority of the monarchy decreased. With the death of Pepi II, who is reputed to have ruled for ninety-four years, power fell into the hands of local princes. For a period of 100-200 years, known as the *First Intermediate Period,* civil war and violence gripped the nation. This was one of the darkest periods in Egyptian history. The social fabric suffered and agriculture declined. Famine was not unknown. Grave robbers emptied and destroyed much of the content of the pyramids built during the Old Kingdom. The roads, such as they were, threatened danger and robbery to those who travelled. The gold mines in the south, which had fed the appetite of the Old Kingdom for wealth, were not worked with the discipline which had marked them in the past. The system of tax collection collapsed, and the exchequer suffered as a result. For a prolonged period the Nile flood failed. The pharaohs who sought to impose rule on this disorderly society were weak and ineffective. They are said to comprise the seventh to the commencement of the eleventh dynasties, and their rule was restricted mainly to small areas of the country.

The Middle Kingdom

The *Middle Kingdom* began when Metuhotep II (one of four pharaohs who bore this name) of the eleventh dynasty took control and united the country. The eleventh and the twelfth dynasties are placed at this time. The great temple built by Metuhotep III as a burial chamber on the banks of the Nile was the first in the Valley of the Kings. No matter how cleverly the builders and architects of the pyramids sought to protect the burial chambers, the tomb robbers succeeded in pillaging them. The move to the Valley of the Kings and the ingenious and complicated devices used to defeat the avarice of the tomb robbers proved to be as ineffective as those employed at the construction of the pyramids.

In the Nile delta much work was carried out at this time to reclaim large areas of marshland. Thousands of acres became productive after canals and a drainage system were in place and a large lake, Lake Moeris, was created.

Literature flourished. What has come to light shows that the writings of the Egyptians at this time reached a peak of style and content which has correctly been regarded as "classic". In later years scribes looked back on this period with nostalgia and used its writings as copybook examples of good practice.

It appears that the monarchs of this era did not have the absolute authority of the pharaohs of the Old Kingdom. They could no longer count on a population that was as subservient to the "God-King" as in the way in which society had been ordered in the past. There appears to have been the first stirrings of individualism. Indeed, one of the great pharaohs of the period, Ammenemes I, the founder of the twelfth dynasty, was assassinated in his palace. There were attempts to enforce totalitarian government but without any great degree of success. The nobles had to be kept in a contented mood, but it must not be thought that Egypt was in any way democratic. The pharaohs still held enormous power even although it had been somewhat diluted.

The Middle Kingdom lasted for about four hundred years from approximately 2040 BC. The borders were enlarged northwards almost into Canaan and extended considerably to the south. Trade flourished, and merchants undertook trading expeditions to the kingdoms of the south. Once again, however, a decline set in and a further period of unrest began. At times the overflow of the Nile was so great that seed planting was ineffective, causing hardship that led to civil unrest.

The Second Intermediate Period

The *Second Intermediate Period* began as the country went through a further period of transition. This was the era of the thirteenth to the seventeenth dynasties. It was at this time that the Hyksos invaders from Asia entered the country and conquered it by the use of chariots and horses, previously unknown to the Egyptians. They gave Egypt the sixteenth dynasty and were known as the "Shepherd Kings". Written history claimed that these invaders oppressed the people, but there is evidence that their rule was in some ways benevolent. It was, however, an affront to Egyptian pride that foreign rulers held power.

The New Kingdom

The Hyksos were driven out by Amosis, a Theban prince, who created the *New Kingdom*, during which the eighteenth, nineteenth, and twentieth dynasties ruled, and which commenced about 1600 BC. It is known as the Empire Age, and saw Egypt at the height of its international power. Further extension of its borders took place. Egyptian armies stood on the Euphrates in the north, and marched deep into the Sudan in the south. Despite this, the Egyptians were reluctant colonisers. The military thrust outward was the result of the shame of having been ruled by the occupying Hyksos power. It was an attempt to preserve the frontiers of Egypt from further incursions. Living outside of the home state was not a coveted aim. The thought of dying there was repugnant, and being buried there was unacceptable.

There was an era of building and art which was never again equalled. The Temple of Karnak was extended on many occasions. The Colossos of Memnon and parts of Luxor are all evidences of the greatness and glory of this period of Egyptian history. Under the Pharaoh Tuthmosis III Egypt became the leading world power. During his reign the four obelisks which are known today as Cleopatra's Needles, and which are now to be found in London, New York, Istanbul, and Rome were erected. In later years pharaohs such as Rameses II, known as Rameses the Great, continued to assert Egyptian hegemony, but by the end of his reign Egyptian prestige was declining, and 1070 BC is considered to mark the end of the New Kingdom.

The Third Intermediate Period

Following the fall of the New Kingdom there was the *Third Intermediate Period* (1070-712 BC). Once again the country was divided into Upper and Lower Egypt. The twenty-first to the twenty-fourth dynasties ruled, and Sheshonk, the first Pharaoh of the twenty-second dynasty may be Shishak, king of Egypt who "came up against Jerusalem: And...took away the treasures of the house of the Lord, and the treasures of the king's house" (1 Kings 14.25,26) in the days of Rehoboam.[8]

The Late Period

The *Late Period* (712-332 BC) covered the era when momentous events were taking place. The twenty-fifth to the thirtieth dynasties held power. Josiah was defeated in battle by Pharaoh Necho, who, fearing the might of Babylon which had destroyed Nineveh, was marching against Carchemish, a city which stood on the banks of the Euphrates and was the gateway to Asia (2 Chr 35.20-24). After the death of Josiah, Egypt was able to exercise control over Judah for a short time (2 Chr 36.1-4), but her days as an independent world power were over. Jerusalem fell to the Babylonians and the Times of the Gentiles were ushered in by the fall and captivity of Judah. The Persians invaded (525 BC), but after some time the Egyptians threw off this yoke. When the Persian Artaxerxes III, however, reconquered Egypt he commenced the thirtieth dynasty, and the once mighty empire was never again to be ruled by a prince of native Egyptian blood. It was not until the revolution of AD 1952, which brought General Neguib to power, that Egypt was once again ruled by a government with an Egyptian at its head.

The Pharaoh of the Exodus

It is not possible with confidence to identify which Pharaoh ruled at the time of the exodus. It seems probable that it took place during the era of the New Kingdom or the Third Intermediate Period. As Scripture does not provide this information it may be regarded as superfluous to the study of the book itself.

What is certain is that in the days of Moses Egypt was a world power renowned for its architecture, military might, advanced infrastructure, and social order. The buildings that are still standing today are a mute testimony to the advanced skills of its architects and builders. From a natural standpoint it represented the best of the world that then was. Its social structure was based on religion, and this had been developed over the centuries to become a sophisticated system of idolatry backed up by astrology and other black arts. This religion had changed to meet the different circumstances of passing generations, but it remained a testimony to the darkness of the Egyptian people as a whole to the knowledge of God. It is therefore little wonder that in Egypt is seen a picture of the world under the sway of the Adversary. Thrusting, powerful, self confident, proud, developing the leading technologies of the day, at times seemingly impregnable but blind to spiritual truth, conscious of a life after death but leaning on hopeless schemes and teachings that had proved unsupportable. In such an environment the Hebrews lived, Amram and Jochebed saw their family increase, and Moses spent the first forty years of his life.

The Religion of Egypt
The religion of Egypt was wholly idolatrous. The form which this idolatry took went though many phases. In early days there were local deities, and these formed the basis of a complex web of myths and legends which developed over the centuries, new gods being added as the system became more sophisticated. Animals and insects were often deified. The worship of the sun and the worship of the god who brought the annual flood to the River Nile, together with other deities, flourished. In the closing years of the New Kingdom foreign deities such as Baal and Astarte were introduced.

The pyramids and tombs prove that the Egyptians had a keen sense of life after death. The great effort and expense which went into the preparation of the burial chambers which would be sealed, never again to be seen (this purpose was thwarted by the tomb robbers), is evidence of the importance which they placed on the after-life. The pyramids were, in effect, intended to be a court which would function after death. Thus food was left, furniture was installed, and gold and precious artefacts were sealed in with the dead. In some of the early tombs the retainers of the monarch appeared to be buried in tombs surrounding that of the pharaoh. It is not known whether these courtiers and retainers were put to death when the monarch died or whether the bodies of others who had died at the same time as the king were placed there to form such a court. What is clear is the belief that life continued after death.

The priesthood, centred on On, in the north, asserted that Ra, the sun god, crossed the skies each day in a boat and that at night the moon and the stars embarked on the same journey. The problem of what happened to the sun during the night was overcome by teaching that it passed through the underworld (the Det). Similarly the stars undertook that journey during the day. Others taught that the goddess Nut consumed the sun each evening and gave birth to it again each morning.

Osiris, who was probably a petty king with only local authority, predating the mythical Menes, was gradually deified and became the head of another cult. Other "gods" were brought into this family. Osiris was believed to be the son of the earth god Geb and the goddess Nut. He held sway over all the earth but was murdered by his brother, Seth. The wife of Osiris, Isis by name, brought her husband's body back to Egypt where she gave birth to her son, Horus. Later in the "narrative" Horus sought to avenge his father's death, and in the struggle with Seth lost an eye. Nevertheless he was victorious and had his eye restored by the god Thoth. So Seth represents all that is evil and Horus represents what is good. He (Horus) is pictured as having the body of a man and the head of a falcon.

Throughout the turmoil of her history the land of Egypt has been continually dependent on the River Nile. In summer much rain falls on the great lakes situated in the highlands of Ethiopia. These rains, together with the water from the melting snows, flow into the Nile, which rapidly rises, and floods. This took place each year in the month of June and the river could rise about 7 metres (22.75 ft) in the south of the country and 5 metres (16.25 ft) in the north around the area where Cairo is now situated. The water then was about twenty times its usual volume. The Nile flood was the most important part of the year for the Egyptians. It marked the beginning of the year. In September the waters abated and it was possible to sow in the wet soil. After about four months, harvest could be taken in and then, until the floods returned, the ground lay fallow. The higher the flood, the greater the potential harvest. Clearly, during the seven fat years when Joseph gathered the harvest into storehouses the river rose to great heights, but in the lean years the flood failed to rise to a height that guaranteed a useful harvest.

Today the annual rise and fall of the river has been controlled by reservoirs so that regular irrigation of the land is possible. Apart from the effect on the harvest, the river water filtered into the soil and replenished the water table. As a result there was an abundance of deep wells round which houses could be placed and trees grown. Such were the benefits which came from this river that the Egyptians called the god of the flood Hapy, who is represented as a bearded man with a part female body and a large abdomen to portray the fertility and generous bounty which came from the river.

Other "gods" are Bes, who protected from evil, Khnum, who gave life and created the first man on a potter's wheel, Thoth, already named in connection with Horus, who was the lord of magic, knowledge, and wisdom, and Hathor, the mother of Horus, the goddess of love, seduction, and music.

But the religious life of the nation at times went through periods of turmoil. During the reign of Akhenaten (Amenophis IV) there took place a religious revolution. Details are difficult to uncover, but the evidence available indicates that the ascension to the throne of this monarch led to the establishment of the worship of Aten, a sun god, as the supreme deity. A new capital city, planned and designed by Akhenaten, was built further south, to which he gave the name Akhetaten, meaning "Horizon of the Aten". To this city there came the *nouveau riche* and others who were promoted by the king to positions of power. The impression is left of a divided nation, for, after the death of Akhenaten the new capital was abandoned and the worship of the old deities resumed with vigour, as the priestly caste reasserted its authority. For archaeologists, the abandoned capital has become a rich source of artefacts throwing light on daily life at that time.

Religion and the state were closely linked. Each pharaoh "acquired" divinity at the coronation ceremony. He became one of the favoured who joined the divine world at this time, and after death he acquired full deity.   Such a religious system kept the people in bondage and darkness. The priests held great power, being viewed as the guardians of the "mysteries" which were not open to the "laity". Pharaoh's power was enhanced by his being the possessor of the ultimate "mysteries". These teachings may have been watered down somewhat in later dynasties, but appear to have been accepted during the time of the Old Kingdom.

There was, therefore, a closely interwoven social structure of which religion was the centre. Mystique, priest craft, wizardry, and idolatry were its pillars. It left the people in darkness and hopelessness, the hallmark of all religious systems which have the god of this age at their head.

The Chronology of the Book

We have already noted that the Israelites spent 430 years in Egypt. The opening eight verses of the book, therefore, cover a period of approximately 350 years. Following that it is not possible to put an accurate time span on the subsequent events of ch.1 (one year has been assumed), but from ch.2 the dates can be defined with reasonable certainty. There is no doubt about the two blocks of forty years.

Up until the birth of Moses[9]	1 year
From Moses' birth until the flight to Midian	40 years
From the flight to Midian until the return to Egypt	40 years
From the return to Egypt until the exodus	1 year
From the exodus until the Tabernacle was reared	1 year
Total	83 years

The year which commenced with the exodus and ended with the rearing of the Tabernacle was one of great activity for Israel. The stated dates in Exodus are:-

	CHAPTER	YEAR	MONTH	DAY
Passover	12.1ff	1	1	14
Arrival at Wilderness of Sin	16.1	1	2	15
Arrival at Wilderness of Sinai[10]	19.1	1	3	1
The Tabernacle set up	40.17ff	2	1	1

The Route of the Exodus

The stages recorded in the book of Exodus are:-

Stage 1 *Exodus 12.37* *From Rameses to Succoth.*
Six hundred thousand men, besides women and children leave Egypt by this route.

Stage 2 *Exodus 13.20* *From Succoth to Etham.*
The Lord goes before them in a pillar of cloud by day and a pillar of fire by night.

Stage 3 *Exodus 14.2* *Turn and encamp before Pi-hahiroth between Migdol and the sea over against Baal-zephon.*
They turn to encamp beside the sea. Pharaoh sees this as an opportunity to re-capture them as they will be trapped between his armies and the sea. The people are fearful and complain. The angel of God moves between the Israelites and the Egyptians to provide defence for His people. The Red Sea is then crossed.

Stage 4 *Exodus 15.22* *From the Red Sea into the Wilderness of Shur, to Marah.*
After three days they find no water. When water is found at Marah it proves to be bitter. The water is made sweet by the tree being placed in it.

Stage 5 *Exodus 15.27* *From Marah to Elim.*
At Elim they find plenty of water.

Stage 6 *Exodus 16.1* *From Elim into the Wilderness of Sin.*
Complaint is made that they do not have sufficient food. The manna is given.

Stage 7 *Exodus 17.1* *From Wilderness of Sin to Rephidim.*
Once again there is a lack of water which leads to further complaints. At this stage the rock is smitten and water is given.

Stage 8 *Exodus 19.1* *From Rephidim into the Wilderness of Sinai.*
Here the Law is given and the Tabernacle is reared.

The Number who Travelled

According to 12.37 the number of adult males who left Egypt was about 600,000. This is confirmed in 38.26 when the more exact figure of 603,550 over the age of twenty is given. The total number of males of all ages is not given and therefore only an estimate is possible. This has been put at between 1,000,000 and 1,100,000.[11] In total, therefore, it can be assumed that in excess of 2,000,000 men, women and children crossed the Red Sea.

It has been argued that this must be excessive because such a great

number would strike fear into any enemy; no attack would be made on a
nation of such size. This reasoning, however, ignores the size and power
of the enemies of Israel. It does not take into account that the people led
by Moses were freed slaves regarded as homeless wanderers who had no
history of military prowess. They were untried in battle, and their life in
Egypt suggested that they were not given to struggle and resistance.

Further objections have been raised on the basis of the requirements to
feed so many in the wilderness. Even if we believe that the Sinai was more
productive than it is today, and there is no evidence to support such a
claim, we must accept that the feeding of the Israelites could present a
problem. They were not spread throughout the peninsula but gathered in
one area. Such objections, however, are easily overcome when we recall
that their staple diet consisted of manna, which was given from the Lord.
The nature of their surroundings did not affect the quantity of food that
was available to them.

OUTLINE OF THE BOOK

CHAPTERS 1-18   REDEMPTION FROM EGYPT
Chapters 1-4   Preparation for deliverance
Chapter 1   *The scene is set.*
   Conditions in Egypt and the persecution of the Israelites.
   The three plans of Pharaoh to destroy all the male children of the
   Israelites.
Chapter 2   *The birth and early life of Moses.*
   The plan of Amram and Jochebed to preserve their second son.
   Moses' early life.
   Moses' hasty attempt to become the deliverer of Israel.
Chapters 3-4   *The call of Moses.*
   Moses' flight to Midian and his marriage to Zipporah.
   Moses' forty years as a shepherd in the employ of Jethro, his father-
   in-law.
   The call to Moses from the Burning Bush.
   The five objections raised by Moses and the Lord's replies.

Chapters 5-10   Confrontation with Pharaoh
Chapter 5   *Persecution increases.*
   Moses and Aaron make their request to Pharaoh as a result of which
   the burdens of the Israelites are made heavier.
Chapter 6   *Promises from the Lord re-stated.*
   Despite the Israelites now refusing to listen to Moses the commission
   to deliver the nation is re-stated.
Chapters 7-10   *Plagues on Egypt.*
   First cycle of three plagues (7.17-8.19):
      Water turns to blood

Frogs fill the land
Dust becomes lice.
Second cycle of three plagues (8.20-9.12):
Swarms of flies
Death of the cattle of the Egyptians
Boils break out upon man and beast.
Third cycle of three plagues (9.13-10.29):
Thunder, hail, and fire
Locusts fill the land
Darkness over the land.

Chapters 11-14 **Salvation by being sheltered under the blood**
Chapters 11-13 *The Passover and flight from Egypt.*
Chapter 14 *The crossing of the Red Sea.*

Chapters 15-18 **Education in the ways of God**
Chapter 15.1-21 *Praise - the Song of Redemption.*
Chapters 15.22-18.27 *Problems on the journey.*
No water in the Wilderness of Shur (15.22)
Bitter water at Marah (15.23-26)
Water and palm trees at Elim (15.27)
The giving of the manna (16.1-36)
The smiting of the rock (17.1-7)
The battle with Amalek (17.8-16)
Jethro's advice to Moses (18.1-27).

CHAPTERS 19-40 **RELATIONSHIP WITH JEHOVAH**
Chapters 19-23 **The giving of the Law**
Chapter 19 *The Prelude to the giving of the Law.*
Chapters 20-23 *The Precepts.*
The Ten Commandments and sundry laws.

Chapter 24 **The presentation of the Law**
The Covenant is read to the people and the glory of the Lord appears.

Chapters 25-40 **The Sanctuary for the people**
Chapters 25-31 *Instructions on the construction of the Tabernacle and the consecration of the priests.*
These are received by Moses while on the mount with God.
Chapter 32 *Idolatry in the Camp.*
Moses breaks the two tablets of the Law.
Chapters 33-34 *The covenant is confirmed.*
Chapters 35-39 *The construction of the Tabernacle.*
Chapter 40 *The Tabernacle is reared and is filled with the glory of the Lord.*

Notes

1 The key to understanding the ancient Egyptian language was found in the Rosetta Stone, discovered in the town of Rosetta near the mouth of the Nile by M. Boussard, a scholar who accompanied Napoleon's expedition to Egypt (1798-1799). It is now in the British Museum. The inscriptions on the stone are in Greek, Egyptian Hieroglyphic, and Egyptian Demotic (a simpler form of Egyptian writing which was introduced about 800 BC). The writing was a decree by Ptolemy V, Epiphanes, dated about 200 BC and written in these three languages. As Greek is a known language it was possible to compare the Greek text with the others and determine the meaning of the Hieroglyphic and Demotic scripts. After four years of intensive labour (1888-92) Champollion, another French scholar, using the Greek text in this way as a key, was able to read the ancient writing.

2 Joseph's brothers assumed that the Egyptian potentate before them was unable to understand their speech (Gen 42.23). Among the many problems which Joseph faced when he arrived as a slave in Egypt was the need to learn the Egyptian language.

3 "Nothing is known of this book but what appears here. If it should seen strange that a book of this description should be already in existence, we must remember that amongst the multitudes of Israel there must in the nature of things have been some "poets" in the then acceptation of the word." (Whitelaw, *The Pulpit Commentary*).

4 W. E. Vine, *The Epistle to the Galatians*.

5 See "Egypt" in TWOT at 1235. It is possible that the "Two Lands" referred to Northern and Southern Egypt.

6 P. Johnston, *The Civilization of Ancient Egypt*.

7 P. A. Clayton, *Chronicle of the Pharaohs*.

8 The accuracy of this is disputed by David Rohl in *A Test of Time*.

9 It may have taken only one year for Pharaoh to see the failure of his policy of persecution recorded in ch.1. Up to five years has been suggested as a more likely period.

10 Differences exist as to whether in Exodus 19.1 "the same day" indicates the first day of the third month - see Keil & Delitzsch. As the chronology above is not affected by this, the first day of the month is assumed.

11 See Keil & Delitzsch.

EXODUS 1

The Scene is Set

Verses 1-7: Introduction

Exodus commences with the Children of Israel serving Pharaoh as slaves, and ends with them serving the Lord as a redeemed people. At the beginning of the book they are building the treasure houses of Egypt, but after they have been redeemed through the blood of the lamb they build a house for God in the wilderness. They travel from the house of bondage (13.3) to the house of the Lord their God (23.19). From groaning under the whip they move to worship, and from sighing to singing under the gracious guidance of Jehovah.

As the book is opened, Egypt is introduced in a different light from that in which it is seen at the end of the book of Genesis. It was not the right place for Abraham, but in the days of Joseph it is presented as a place of preservation for the Children of Israel. Now, however, it is a dangerous, godless, idolatrous place. The cause of this change is that there arose a new king who "knew not Joseph" (v.8). Under this new Pharaoh the rulers revealed themselves to be bitterly opposed to the Children of Israel, and this is how Egypt is presented from this point on through the Word of God. Even in the book of the Revelation the character of the city where the bodies of the two witnesses lie is called "Sodom and Egypt" (Rev 11.8). The Israelites are, therefore, seen to be prisoners and slaves in the world, and Exodus is the book of their redemption. It portrays vividly the ways of God in salvation, and the blessed condition of those who are covered by the blood and who know redemption from the penalty and the power of sin.

Egypt, therefore, is a picture of the world. Abraham erred in going down there, and when he left he probably brought Hagar with him, as she was an Egyptian (Gen 16.1). As was noted in the Introduction, memories of that journey were left with Lot, and when he looked on the well-watered plain of Jordan he saw it "even as the garden of the Lord, like the land of Egypt" (Gen 13.10). The influence of Egypt on Abraham's family, therefore, was not good. But why is it, then, that Joseph and his family are found in Egypt? The answer is that at the end of Genesis Joseph is the ruler over Egypt. This completes the book which commenced with man's rebellion against God, and in so doing gives us a picture of the day when the Lord Jesus will reign over this world in His millennial kingdom. Genesis, which commences with man forfeiting his right to have dominion over the earth ends with God's appointed man ruling. This brief interlude at the end of Genesis, when Egypt is seen in this way, is introduced to remind us that the world that is so opposed to God will one day be subdued under His rule.

Exodus, therefore, must be of interest to all who have known the redeeming power of the blood of the Cross. There is, in picture form, in the history of Israel, a series of lessons relating to the truths of the gospel. To grasp the spiritual significance of the lessons will establish believers in the faith by increasing understanding of what takes place in the life when the gospel is believed. The change in the condition of the Israelites reflects that which God brings into the lives of believers today. In this history are clearly set out the great facts of redemption and sanctification, worship and service which must be understood by those who seek to serve God.

First, it must be noted that God is fulfilling His purpose. This is not a new history that is beginning, but the continuation of the record of the dealings of God with mankind which commenced in the book of Genesis. The words "now", or "and" at the beginning of v.1, and these opening verses, form the link between the two books. The writer is indicating that Exodus is a continuation of Genesis. The practice of opening a book in this way, connecting it with the book which has gone before, is found in the Pentateuch and other historical books.[†] In the writings of Moses this can be understood since these are the writings of one man. He is opening merely another chapter in the narrative. When it is used, however, by writers linking back to books which were written by others, their belief that they were writing what would form part of a single work can be perceived.

From this one can discover the inexorable march of the purpose of God. Genesis was but the beginning, and now the grand history of God's dealings with His creation continues. No force or power can prevent Him completing His purpose. The Fall did not stop it, the sin of men before the Flood could not stop it, the Tower of Babel could not stop it, and even the death of the patriarchs could not stop it. Exodus is one part of the unfolding panorama of God's dealings with mankind.

The promises given to Abraham and Jacob

In fulfilling His purpose, however, God is faithful to His promises. The promises which He made to Abraham were quite specific.

Genesis 12.2	"I will make of thee a great nation".
Genesis 12.7	"Unto thy seed will I give this land".
Genesis 15.7	"I am the Lord that brought thee out of Ur of the Chaldees, to give thee this land to inherit it".
Genesis 15.13-14	"Know of a surety that thy seed shall be a stranger in a land that is not theirs, and shall serve them; and they shall afflict them four hundred years; And also that nation, whom they shall serve, will I judge: and afterward shall they come out with great substance".
Genesis 17.8	"And I will give unto thee, and to thy seed after thee, the land wherein thou art a stranger, all

Genesis 22.17

the land of Canaan, for an everlasting possession".

"In blessing I will bless thee, and in multiplying I will multiply thy seed as the stars of the heaven, and as the sand which is upon the sea shore".

In addition to this, as Jacob travelled towards Egypt he received a promise from the Lord: "Fear not to go down into Egypt; for I will there make of thee a great nation. I will go down with thee into Egypt; and I will also surely bring thee up again" (Gen 46.3,4). The promises of God could, therefore, be summarised as follows.

1. They would go to a land that was not theirs, that is, Egypt.
2. The Lord would go down with them to Egypt.
3. In Egypt the children of Israel would be strangers. They would not merge with the Egyptians, but remain as a separate people for whom Egypt was not home.
4. They would serve the Egyptians and be oppressed by them for four hundred years.
5. Their numbers would multiply greatly.
6. God would judge the Egyptian nation for oppressing them.
7. They would leave Egypt with great wealth.
8. They would return to Canaan and take possession of that land.

These opening verses of the book provide the bridge between when the promises were given and the time when they are about to be fulfilled.

The number of Jacob's family

The eleven sons of Jacob who came with him down into Egypt are named individually. Joseph's name is omitted because he was in Egypt already. Seventy souls of Jacob's family are noted as being in Egypt when Jacob arrived there. In Genesis 46.26 the number is given as sixty-six but this excludes Jacob, Joseph, Mannaseh and Ephraim as it is clearly stated that sixty-six came *with* Jacob, and at that time Joseph and his two sons were already in Egypt. In Acts 7.14 Stephen states that seventy-five of the family were in Egypt, a number arrived at by taking the seventy noted in Exodus and adding five grandchildren mentioned in the Septuagint from which he quotes. It should be noted, however, that it is expressly stated in Genesis 46.26 that the wives of Jacob's sons were not included in this number.

There is a sense of dignity in their being named the "children of Israel", linking them with the one who was a prince with God. To the Egyptians they must have appeared to be no different from the many who had come seeking food, their family link with Joseph being the only outstanding feature about them. Before God, however, they were the children of Israel, possessed of the distinction of such a name. Not even their disgraceful conduct towards their brother Joseph diminished their standing. So it is in the ways of God. Believers today have the privilege of being "saints" and "sons of God". Conduct will at times fall far short of such a standing, but in Christ that standing is secure. Sin takes its toll and always robs those who engage in it; it has not to be practised lightly; it brings the chastening hand of God to those who so act, but the position of dignity before the Lord into which salvation brings individuals cannot be lost.

The eleven sons who came with Jacob to join Joseph (the first son of Rachel) are listed in the order of their mothers: first the sons of Leah, Jacob's first wife (Reuben, Simeon, Levi, Judah, Issachar, and Zebulun), then the second son of Rachel, Jacob's second wife (Benjamin), followed by the sons of Jacob's two handmaidens, Bilhah (Dan and Naphtali) and Zilpah (Gad and Asher). Not one son is therefore overlooked. God's grace and faithfulness towards this family is clearly displayed.

The increase in the family

Hundreds of years have passed since Jacob arrived in Egypt, and he, Joseph, and the whole of that generation, to whom the story of the events leading up to the arrival of the family of Joseph in Egypt would be well known, have long since died. The Israelites became a despised but feared people. God had not forgotten them, and their numbers grew in the land. Now the time was drawing near for the Lord to bring to pass His promise that they would leave Egypt. This did not depend on the faithfulness of the Israelites, nor on their remembrance of the word of God. It depended entirely on God's faithfulness. No matter what these people may have done in the intervening years, God will now commence the work of deliverance, for He will keep His word.

There is enough evidence to suggest that many of the Children of Israel had forgotten, if they ever had known, that their deliverance from Egypt had been long foretold. The many years in this foreign land had left them with only dim memories of the great promises given to their fathers. Many of them had adopted some of the idolatrous ways of their Egyptian masters. When they moved out into the wilderness, they showed, at a low point in their dealings with God, that they knew much about the worship practised by the Egyptians and were not slow in making the golden calf. Joshua reminds them in later years that their fathers served other gods in Egypt (Josh 24.14).

The clear evidence that God still cared for them is seen in the growth in their numbers. They multiplied and grew, and the verbs and adverbs used in v.7 indicate the rate of increase which took place. They "increased abundantly, and multiplied, and waxed exceeding mighty". Their presence was seen everywhere and "the land was filled with them", yet during this period it appears that they lived peacefully beside the Egyptians and did not threaten them. Their extraordinary fruitfulness was directly the result of the work of Jehovah among them as their rate of increase must have been higher than that of the Egyptians.

Verse 8: The New Pharaoh

Having noted the remarkable increase in the number of the Israelites, the story of the book begins. In v.8 a second change of circumstance in Egypt is introduced. Not only was the population mix dramatically changed, but also there arose a new king. The change in population is followed by a change on the throne. This king "knew not Joseph". In view of this he based his rule on principles different from those which were in place in the reigns of earlier monarchs. It is probable that he represented a new dynasty. How different he was from those who had gone before him is seen in this absence of knowledge of Joseph. This ruler governed a country that owed so much to Joseph, and yet he did not know of the "Saviour of the World".† There need be no surprise at this because nations act in the same way today. When there is a time of great need, be it in war or in famine, nations will turn to God for national days of prayer and other means of invoking the blessing of God. When the crisis passes God is soon forgotten.

This Pharaoh would not have been the choice of Israel if they had had any influence in the selection of a monarch. He "arose" to prominence and took the ascendancy over other claimants to the reins of government because it was the will of God that he should be on the throne. Moses, as instructed by the Lord, clearly declares to another Pharaoh that he had been "raised...up" by God (9.16). Doubtless Pharaoh would scoff at the suggestion that the God of the Hebrews had this power, and the Egyptians would treat such a claim with disdain, but the feelings of men do not alter the truth. The Lord brought this Pharaoh to the throne, as He did with those who followed. This is quite in keeping with the teaching of the New Testament where in Romans 13.1 it is taught that the powers that be are ordained of God. The mistake should not be made of thinking that this can only be true of those powers that do not oppress their people. When Paul wrote to the Romans, Nero was on the throne. He was a murderous tyrant, and yet his being in power was ordained of God.

The problem which this presents is, "Why does God not only allow, but raise up godless and, in many cases, wicked and evil men to rule?". Many who have suffered under the scourge of such men have asked this question. The answer is that He is working everything out according to His purpose, and the powers that be are there to bring this about. Rulers might be preferred who are honest, competent, with the interest of all the people at heart, and with the ability to satisfy all the people. God, however, sometimes raises up powers of a different character, because, although it may not seem so on the surface, they are all working out what He desires. The current dealings of God with nations and with individuals can be difficult to understand, particularly if they are accompanied by suffering and oppression. Looking back after the events there are times when the will of God can be discerned in these circumstances, and at other times an understanding of them must be left until eternity. All nations are sinful,

and in order for the judgment of God to be seen to be righteous their sin
has to be allowed to be shown. Nevertheless, this does not diminish the
responsibility of men to behave justly. If God works through wicked men
to fulfil His purpose, He does not thereby condone their sin. The wonder
is that the wisdom of God is such that He is working His own purpose
through them.

This problem exercised the mind of the prophet Habakkuk when he
learned that judgment on sinful Judah would come by the action of the
Chaldeans whom he states to be even more sinful than Judah (Hab 1.12-
17). How is it possible for the Lord to use such a people? The answer is
that the Chaldeans will in turn be judged for their sin (Hab 2.5-20). Their
actions will bring judgment on God's rebellious people, but they will also
endure the judgment of God for the sins which they have committed.
Righteousness will always prevail when God is working.

It must be noted, however, that the persecution which Pharaoh
introduced led directly to the preservation of Moses and his education
and upbringing in the court. Little did the king realise that the actions
which he took to suppress Israel led to his daughter arranging the
education of the one who would ultimately lead Israel out of Egypt. Had
that persecution never taken place, the babe would not have been laid in
the basket and placed in the river, the daughter of Pharaoh would not
have found him, and Moses would not have been brought up in the court.

A strange lesson is learned here about the dealings of the Adversary. No
matter how bitter is his hatred of God, his actions always rebound on him.
They never achieve the end for which he is working. His attack on Adam
and Eve brought about the Fall, but led to the work of redemption, a work
which he cannot destroy. The capture of the Ark (1 Sam 5-6) led to a display
of the power of the Lord over the false deities of the Philistines.

Verses 9-14: The First Plan of Pharaoh - Enslave the Israelites
Concern over the Israelites

What, then, about the first directive of the King? Pharaoh acted out of
fear. He had a great dread that, should an enemy attack Egypt, the Israelites
could rise and take sides with the enemy. He may have had armies and
chariots, but he still felt fear of those potential "fifth columnists" among
them. He used the only wisdom that he had at his disposal, the wisdom of
the world, and determined that the way to deal with this threat was to
enslave them and thus, he considered, weaken them. The "good days" for
Israel in Egypt were over. They were now organised as a nation of oppressed
serfs working on the land and building the treasure cities of Egypt.

Pharaoh could only think as unregenerate men think; he had no
knowledge of the wisdom which is from above. The third chapter of the
Epistle of James deals with two different kinds of wisdom and it is
appropriate at this point to consider the differences between them. The
wisdom that does not descend from above is earthly, sensual, and devilish,

producing envy, strife that manifests itself in tumult, disorder, and every evil work. Barnes comments: "There is learning, shrewdness, tact, logical skill, subtle and skilful argumentation–'making the worse appear the better reason;' but all this is often connected with a spirit so narrow, bigoted, and contentious, as to show clearly that it has not its origin in heaven" (*Commentary on the New Testament*). The wisdom that is from above produces that which is "peaceable, gentle, and easy to be intreated, full of mercy and good fruits, without partiality, and without hypocrisy" (Jas 3.17). Pharaoh, the monarch who ruled them, displayed the wisdom that is earthly; Moses, who led them out of Egypt, displayed the wisdom that is from above. "The fear of the Lord is the beginning of wisdom" (Ps 110.10) is a truth that all would do well to heed.

Throughout the history of the nation of Israel there have been many attempts to ensure that it did not continue. This is the first on record. If Israel could be brought to nothing there would not be born the One in whom all the nations of the earth would be blessed. The Adversary had been a silent listener when the promises were made to the patriarchs. Now he is working to frustrate these promises. It may seem surprising that he will seek to overturn the declared purpose of God, but there is madness about everything that he does. How else could he have attempted to ascend and be like the most High (Is 14.14)?

The plan put into effect

The tasks allocated to the children of Israel were twofold. First, there was the building of the cities of Pithom and Raamses. Second, they were made to labour in the field. Taskmasters† were set over them who made them serve with rigour. So great was their suffering that Moses uses this rare word "rigour" (6531), which means "to break", or "to crush". Israel were instructed never to rule over servants with "rigour" (Lev 25.43,46,53) because in Egypt they had experienced what it was to have the whip and the rod applied to them without restraint to increase their productivity. The building projects were huge. Treasure cities, the purpose of which was to store oil, wine, other provisions, and weapons, were built from nothing. These were large warehouse cities in which the rich produce of the land could be hoarded, and where arms were kept against the possibility of revolt or invasion. This society was of the same nature as the farmer who boasted that "I will pull down my barns, and built greater" (Lk 12.18), the boast of those who felt that they were "rich, and increased with goods" (Rev 3.17).

The labour of the Israelites in the field was most probably the tending of herds and the sowing and harvesting of crops. The annual Nile flood added to the difficulties of this as care would be required to ensure that cattle were not lost when the flood came, and that homes and other buildings were saved from being washed away. Josephus (*The Antiquities of the Jews*, Book II, ch.9, sect 1) suggests that their work in the field also included the building of irrigation canals. In the scorching heat of eastern days they carried the clay, transported the bricks, dug into the soil, and felt the stroke of the rod and the lash of the whip. Truly this was a life of rigour.

It should not be thought strange that the Israelites failed to rise up in revolt against their oppressors. The Egyptians had the weapons and tools to enslave. The government was in their hands and they were organised and determined as they set about the task. The purpose was to slow up the growth of their unwanted "guests" by so afflicting them that they lost heart, and in their reduced physical condition would bear fewer children. The death of many of them under the whip would be an added factor in their enfeeblement.

According to the wisdom of the world it seemed to be a plan that could not fail, and so it must have been with disappointment and astonishment that the Egyptians saw the number of Israelites continuing to increase. They learned that God chooses the foolish things of the world to confound the wise (1 Cor 1.27). This people who were regarded as weak and foolish were used, as they continued to multiply, to bring to nothing the counsels of the wise of this world. In response, the harshness of the bondage was increased. This only led to an even greater increase in the number of the slaves. And so the circle continued. Egyptian bondage increased, resulting in increased fruitfulness among the slaves. Indeed it is clear that the increase in fruitfulness was directly related to the increase in bondage for "the more they afflicted them, the more they multiplied and grew" (v.12). God confounded the evil purposes of men.

Not only Pharaoh, but also many godless oppressors since, have found to their cost that persecution, rather than stamping out God's work, leads to its growth. The persecution of the church, which is recorded in the Acts of the Apostles, produced the same results. The scattering of persecuted believers (Acts 11.19) was but sowing the seed in areas where previously the gospel had never been preached. As a result, a great many believed and the enemies of the gospel were thwarted in their plan.

Verses 15-21: The Second Plan of Pharaoh - Kill the Male Children at Birth
The plan put into practice

Having failed in persecuting the Israelites, Pharaoh now turns to another plan. If he cannot reduce the number of births, he will seek to ensure that sons do not survive. So the command is given to the midwives to kill the male children. By this means, after a number of years, the Israelites would have few or even no men amongst them and they would therefore cease to exist as a nation. Two Hebrew midwives are mentioned, but there must have been many to deal with all the Israelites. The two mentioned were probably the chief of the midwives who acted in a supervisory role over those who were present at the birth of children. It was to them that this angry monarch turned to enlist their help in carrying out his second plan. His scheme is simple but murderous. It should not cause surprise because Satan "was a murderer from the beginning" (Jn 8.44) and Pharaoh is revealing that it is the Adversary who is behind this vicious campaign of brutal persecution. The words of the Lord Jesus to the Jews can be said of Pharaoh; "Ye are of your father the devil, and the lusts of your father ye will do" (Jn 8.44). In Genesis the character of the devil was revealed in this way when Cain murdered his brother Abel, but now it was mass murder that he promoted. When the Hebrew women gave birth, girls were to be preserved, but male children were to be put to death. The plan, if put into practice, would soon have brought suspicion upon the midwives. It would be observed that the male children were all failing to survive birth. Pharaoh would see no problem in this, as, even if the plan were made known, he would still expect them to carry it out. At each birth the mother would have the added anxiety of knowing that if the child were a boy he would not survive. The cruel and murderous heart of Pharaoh is further exposed. He cares little if the scheme is seen to emanate from the palace, and, like the devil, he has no thought for the well-being of those who serve him.

The actions of the midwives

These midwives were named Shiphrah (8236) meaning "Beauty", and Puah (6326) meaning "Glittering, splendid light". They were well named, for their example casts its glittering beauty and brilliance over a dark period, and they must be regarded as two of the great women of the Bible, receiving the commendation that they "feared God". Putting their own lives at risk, they determined to obey God rather than men. Such a course of action at this time required courage and determination. God blessed them because of the fear that they had for Him, but to them, at the time of their defiance of Pharaoh, the future was unknown. Their fear and reverence for God was greater than any fear of Pharaoh.

The fear of God is not much spoken of today among Christians. Some argue that as believers of this era are not under the Law the grace of God has removed any need for them to fear Him. But these two Hebrew midwives were not yet under the Law, which was not given until the Israelites had left Egypt more than eighty years later. The fear of the Lord is not, therefore, linked with the Law alone, but involves the reverential fear and honour that must be felt for God. It is true that access into His presence is a privilege enjoyed by believers, but this must never be mistaken as a basis for claiming the right to show familiarity in His presence. John was the disciple who leaned on Jesus' breast and is noted as "the disciple whom Jesus loved". When, on the Isle of Patmos, John saw the Saviour now glorified, he fell down at His feet as dead. He was told not to fear, that is not to feel terror in His presence, but John did not show undue familiarity. Peter exhorts, "Fear God" (1 Pet 2.17); Solomon begins his proverbs with "The fear of the Lord is the beginning of knowledge" (Prov 1.7).

These midwives understood that their actions must reflect this fear of the Lord else they would not prosper.

When asked why male children were surviving, the midwives replied that the Hebrew mothers gave birth more quickly than the Egyptian mothers and so the children were born before the midwives could attend the birth. There may have been some truth in this, as the Hebrew women spent much of their time in harsh conditions and hard physical work. It was at most, however, only part of the truth.

Questions raised by the actions of the midwives

This raises two interesting questions. The first is that, although Romans 13 teaches subjection to the higher powers (v.1) and that "Whosoever...resisteth the power, resisteth the ordinance of God" (v.2), it is clear that at times it is necessary to say that "We ought to obey God rather than men" (Acts 5.29). When is it permissible to take this stand? It must be clear that there is no question here, or in any other Scripture, of seeking to overthrow the government of the day. When Peter and the other apostles answered that they would obey God and not men, they were stating that they would not heed the instruction to refrain from preaching and teaching in Jerusalem. This message was no threat to the Roman power. When believers have to take this stand today it must be to ensure that the preaching of the gospel and the teaching of the Word of God is not silenced, and that Christians are not forced to behave in a way that is contrary to Scripture. Believers should not be known for preaching a message of revolution. The actions of Pharaoh did not lead these godly women, or any other of the Israelites, to seek the overthrow of the authorities.

The second question is why the midwives gave Pharaoh the excuse regarding the speed with which the Hebrew women gave birth. It is encouraging to observe that those who did much for God were not perfect individuals. They had fears and concerns which at times led them to make mistakes. Faced with the fear of punishment from Pharaoh, and anxious about what might happen to the Hebrew male children if they (the midwives) were put to death for their disobedience, they prepared this excuse for the ears of the monarch.

They should not be held in disrepute because of this. How many believers down through the centuries have acted in the same way when faced with such difficulties? They have at heart the preservation of God's people and the furtherance of the gospel. Rather than bring greater problems into the lives of the persecuted they do not tell the whole truth. This passage shows the care and consideration that God has for his servants even when they falter in moments of extreme pressure. It is also testimony to the accuracy of the record that this failure is noted. If this had not been the Word of God such failures might have been omitted in an attempt to honour those who had done so much for Israel.

It is remarkable that the king was prepared to listen to their story. Perhaps he was not familiar with Hebrew society, but he could well have given instructions that greater haste was to be made to have the children put to death. He might well have asked why it was that they did not tell him this when he first put the plan to them. They were experienced midwives and this apparent difficulty had not been raised with him previously. It is clear that as they stood before Pharaoh they were under the protecting hand of God, and He delivered them from the wrath of the king.

But what would have taken place if they had boldly announced that they would not obey? Certainly such an intrepid statement is not always wise, but when summoned to appear again before the king to explain the failure of the plan they could have given an honest answer. The result of such an action cannot be guessed. What would have been learned was the course of action that God would have taken to preserve them and the children. By acting as they did the reader is denied that lesson.

Reward to the midwives

The compensation for the midwives is now described. God dealt well with them and made them houses (vv.20-21). The compensation is twofold. They had the joy of seeing the fruitfulness of their work, for "the people multiplied, and waxed very mighty". Israel was now more fruitful than ever, and the midwives could rightly rejoice that the hand of God had been with them as they hazarded their lives to bring this about. In addition to this joyful evidence of God's blessing, they were blessed personally. God made them houses in that he gave them families. Thus blessed with families of their own they received an abiding place in the history of Israel.

Verse 22: The Third Plan of Pharaoh - Drown the Male Children in the Nile
The detail of the plan

With the second plan having failed Pharaoh adopted a third. He was not easily deflected from the course that he had taken. Failure did not blunt his determination to have this people destroyed. The Egyptian population at large was charged with the responsibility of being rid of the Israelites. They were required to ensure that any male child born to an Israelite mother was cast into the River Nile. The full extent of the hatred felt by the Egyptians is seen here in that the whole nation was enlisted in this vile enterprise. No exceptions were made. Egyptian civilisation at this time was the most advanced of the day. There have been left many evidences of the workmanship of these people. Their architecture, art, writings, government, and wealth are all well known. Yet they were prepared to stoop to the cruellest and lowest acts of genocide to achieve what they perceived to be for their benefit. Advances in civilisation do not change the human heart, and the

Egyptians showed that they were a nation who did not pull back from such cruelty. Through history there has been a parallel growth of man's achievements and his cruelty.

The reason for the failure of the third plan

The first plan of Pharaoh failed because the people continued to multiply despite the persecution which they suffered. The second plan of Pharaoh failed because the midwives feared God. Why did the third plan fail? The next chapter shows that it was put into practice, because Moses' parents found it necessary to hide him in order to keep him alive. There was clearly no lack of zeal on the part of the Egyptians, but it is equally clear that the male Israelite children in Egypt were not all slain. It may be that the size of the task was too great for its successful execution. There were also, no doubt, other parents like Amram and Jochebed who hid their children. It could also be that not all the Egyptians were prepared to murder the young. Perhaps there dawned on these oppressors the realisation that they had need of these people to be their slaves and that murdering the young was too extreme a policy to pursue. Over all this, however, was the purpose of God in preserving the seed of Abraham. Although the murder of the young may have been abandoned,[†] persecution was carried on for many years. Eighty years later, when Moses was called by God to go back to Egypt, the lash of the slave master was still being felt.

Despite all this the Israelites continued to increase in number. Seven times over this is emphasised. They "were fruitful", "increased abundantly", "multiplied", "waxed exceeding mighty", and "the land was filled with them" (v.7); "they multiplied and grew" (v.12); they "multiplied and waxed very mighty" (v.20). Nothing could stop them.

One final important fact must not be missed. In the second and third plans of Pharaoh it is the male children who are singled out for attention. Without male children there would ultimately be no men in the nation of Israel, and the women of Israel would have been given as wives to men of other nations. Here there is a further attempt to corrupt the "seed of the woman" so that the promised Deliverer could not be born.

The Methods of the Adversary Today
Persecution

Satan's methods have not changed since this cruel program of infanticide. Down through the ages, persecution has often been the main tool used in working against believers. Over the past century in Eastern Europe and elsewhere in the world, governments have sought to stamp out Christian testimony.

Smother new life before it develops

If persecution does not achieve the desired results, Satan seeks to prevent souls being born again by placing his own agents at the point of birth and ensuring that the life which has been created is smothered before it can grow. If the two midwives had carried out the command they would have been Pharaoh's agents in the birth chamber. The midwives would have appeared to be at one with the Israelites and present to preserve life, but would in truth have been agents of Pharaoh. For this reason there must be an awareness of those who assert that they are preachers of the gospel and teachers of the Scriptures, but who do not hold to the teachings of the Word of God. These false teachers can ensure that any sign of spiritual life is smothered, never to grow and be of value for God.

Drowning in the river of the world

Pharaoh's third plan is also still in use. Where persecution does not prevent fruitfulness, and when new life cannot be smothered at birth, it is the desire of the enemy to drown that life in the river of death, the river of the world. How many believers have found themselves in this situation! Saved and going on well for God with progress which is clearly seen, suddenly they are overwhelmed and drowned in the world. The Egyptians worshipped the River Nile flood. A believer submerged in what the world worships, the river of the world, will lose any usefulness in the service of God.

How sad it is to see that at the time when Paul was preparing to "be offered", knowing that "the time of my departure is at hand", there was another man who had served with him but was about to depart to Thessalonica "having loved this present world (age, JND)" (2 Tim 4.6,10). As others were being sent away in the service of the gospel, Demas expressed his desire to go to Thessalonica, but Paul well understood that this was not out of a desire to serve the Lord, but due to the love of this present age which had drawn his heart away. He was in danger of being drowned in the river of the world. As no further mention is made of him it is not possible to tell whether he recovered. This is sad when it is considered that he was once a "fellow-labourer" of Paul, along with Mark and Luke (Col 4.14; Phm v.24). "His motive for forsaking Paul seems to have been love of worldly ease, safety, and the comforts at home, and disinclination to brave danger with Paul" (Jamieson, Fausset, and Brown).

Egypt

Having examined the actions of this evil monarch what can be learned about the Egypt over which he ruled? Remember that this was the civilisation that is one of the most highly regarded in history.

It was a kingdom of darkness

There was little to brighten the days of these poor slaves as they went about the building of the treasure cities. Every day was one of oppression, and rather than there being any alleviation of their condition it grew worse.

In writing to the Colossians Paul tells them that before they were saved they were held under the power of darkness (Col 1.13). The master who held them in his thrall was the Adversary. This was Satan's kingdom and they well remembered the harshness of his rule. Thus these Israelites, languishing in their misery and slavery, are a picture of all those who have never yet known redemption.

It was a place of hopelessness
There appeared to be no way out of this misery. As slaves, they had no resources to call their own. They were, therefore, unable to mount any successful rebellion against the Egyptians. Clearly their treatment at the hands of the taskmasters had weakened them considerably, and therefore they would have had few reserves of physical strength. As these slaves looked ahead through the years of their lives they could see no light. There appeared to be no hope, no release from the rigour of bondage. The despair which must have gripped their hearts would further darken their days.

It was a place of sorrow
How many tears were shed and hearts broken in these years of misery? Parents weeping for their children and brothers and sisters sorrowing for their loved ones were the common experiences of every day. Even should the male children not be murdered in the way commanded by Pharaoh, many would perish under the strokes of harsh slave drivers.

It was a place of idolatry
The worship of the true God was not to be found here. Egypt had a highly developed system of idolatry. The priests had created a god for every circumstance that they could imagine, and the religious system was an important part of the life of Egyptian society. Despite the presence of Joseph, and then the Israelites, the idols had not been put away. Rather the system had been developed and enhanced. It is not surprising that the worship of Jehovah was unknown to the Egyptians. Pharaoh spoke the truth when he declared to Moses, "Who is the Lord…I know not the Lord" (5.2).

It was a place of outward beauty
Amidst all the misery and sadness, the Egyptians were building a society which is regarded today as one of the most advanced cultures of history. This is the paradox of the condition of mankind. When God is rejected there is an attempt to build on earth that which is beautiful and an ideal place in which to live. Cain and his descendants did this in Genesis 4. He was the first city builder and many have followed in his footsteps. This exterior beauty, however, was only a covering for sin. History attests to the fact that cruelty in Egypt did not stop with persecuting Israelites.

It was a place of wealth

The task given to the Israelite slaves was to build store cities. It has already been noted that these cities were repositories for produce and armaments. The hearts of the Egyptians were also set on the accumulation of wealth, and to this they applied all their skills, their science, and their military might. Looking around the ruins today, the folly of such ambition is seen. This civilisation was eventually reduced to powerless servitude under the hand of foreigners. The slaves, however, who suffered under their hands were the forefathers of a nation which has yet to see its days of greatest glory. The wisdom of serving the living and the true God is seen in this. Those who are redeemed by the blood look forward to a glorious future; those who enjoy no such redemption know only ruin and loss, no matter how great, proud, and glorious they appear to be today.

It was a place of overwhelming power

No nation could oppose the Egyptians successfully at this time. Their military might was overwhelming, and by it they were able to dominate the world stage. What great nations were unable to achieve, the Israelites would see accomplished at the Red Sea. So it is with the power of darkness. It is great and wields mighty influence, but those who have been redeemed by the blood of the Lamb have seen its power broken.

Notes

1 Leviticus, Numbers, Joshua, Judges, Ruth, Samuel, Kings, Ezra, Nehemiah, and Esther all open in this way.

8 Zaphnath-paaneah, the name given to Joseph in Genesis 41.45, has been translated as "The Revealer of Secrets", or "The Saviour of the World".

11 The taskmasters were "lords of tribute", or "lords of service" (8269, 4522). These were overseers of forced labour who were responsible for obtaining the maximum service from the slave workers of Egypt.

22 Proof of the failure of this policy is the fact that there were many male Israelites under eighty years of age at the time of the exodus. This can be verified from the numbering of the people in the opening chapters of the book of Numbers.

EXODUS 2

Moses' Birth and Early Life

At the end of the previous chapter the activities of Pharaoh against the Israelites reached their high water mark. The murder of young children was the ultimate form of persecution, and human reasoning would judge the plight of the Israelites to be hopeless. There was no one to whom they could turn for help, and they had no power to bring about their own deliverance. If they were to leave Egypt it could only be by the power of God. By this means God was teaching them, as He still teaches, that human strength, independent of Him, is useless. How often does He bring the oppressed to the point when it has to be recognised that the situation without God is hopeless! This causes them to cry to Him and when He is then seen at work there is cause to praise Him for His goodness.

But God does use men and women, doing His work through them, to bring about His triumphs. Servants of God arise from the most improbable backgrounds. Not always from the families of the great, but from humble origins. Samuel, David, and John Baptist all confirm this. How encouraging it is, therefore, for all who wish to serve God, to realise that a humble family background is no bar to His service. Equally, God can use members of a godly family which has been prominent in His service. Jehoshaphat had a godly and prominent father, and Timothy, from an obscure family, had the benefit of a godly mother and grandmother.

The Tribe of Levi

In Egypt God was about to work. In the midst of such a background of fear, the Israelites went about their daily lives. Levi had been associated with Simeon in the sad incident concerning their sister Dinah (Gen 34). "Ye have troubled me to make me to stink among the inhabitants of the land, among the Canaanites and the Perizzites" (Gen 34.30), was the censure of their father. Jacob never forgot this, and when he blessed his sons in Genesis 49 he linked Simeon and Levi together, declaring his abhorrence at what they had done: "Simeon and Levi are brethren; instruments of cruelty are in their habitations...I will divide them in Jacob, and scatter them in Israel" (Gen 49.5,7). The history of the tribe of Simeon shows this to have been an accurate prediction. They numbered 59,300 at the beginning of the wilderness journey (Num 1.22-23), and 22,200 at the end of it (Num 26.12-14). There is no mention of Simeon in the blessing of the tribes in Deuteronomy 33. The tribe of Levi, however, was not numbered, as they were appointed to be over the Tabernacle and all its vessels (Num 1.47-50). They rose from their state of shame, even although, as Jacob had foretold, no territory was given to them and they were scattered in forty-eight cities throughout the land of Canaan (Josh 21.1-42). This was the tribe chosen to be the servants of the priests, and who were charged with the keeping of the Tabernacle. But not only were they to be servants; the priestly family also came from the tribe of Levi. How was such a change of circumstances brought about?

The ready response of the sons of Levi in standing by the side of Moses when Israel sinned in worshipping the golden calf, and the action which they took on that day, led to the blessing of the Lord being on them (32.25-29). That sorry event, when Israel sank into idolatry, a critical time in the life of the nation, and the steadfastness of Levi, was an important step in the restoration of the nation. It is no surprise, therefore, to learn that the story of the salvation of the Israel, even at this early stage, involved the tribe of Levi. The events surrounding the worship of the golden calf took place, however, after Israel had left Egypt. The choice of the tribe of Levi for the birth of Moses could not, therefore, be on the basis of the response when the Levites heeded the call of Moses: "Who is on the Lord's side?" (32.26). These later actions but confirmed the choice which the Lord had made in His sovereignty. It is worthy of note that "Levi" means "United". It has already been observed that Levi was united with Simeon. How complete became the break between the two tribes when Phinehas, the son of Aaron, a Levite, slew Zimri, a prince of Simeon, over the sin committed in Shittim (Num 25.14). Clearly, however, the sovereignty of God was at work in the land of Egypt and Levi was chosen to be the tribe from whom the deliverer would come. Levi would rise in the service of God, whereas Simeon was divided and dispersed.

The wisdom of God is seen in such a choice. The priests and Levites could never claim that their privileged position was due to the faithfulness of their fathers, nor even to the faithfulness of Levi, the father of the tribe. There was nothing in them that commended them for such an honour, emphasising that in His service the Lord so works that "no flesh should glory in his presence" (1 Cor 1.29). So it is today as "God hath chosen the foolish things of the world to confound the wise; and God hath chosen the weak things of the world to confound the things that are mighty; And base things of the world, and things which are despised, hath God chosen, yea, and things which are not, to bring to nought things that are" (1 Cor 1.27-28).

Verses 1-4: The Birth of Moses
Moses' parents
The narrative now narrows down to one family. A man, unnamed at this point, took a wife. They were both of the tribe of Levi, and, at the time of their betrothal and at their marriage, there was nothing to mark them out as being the future parents of the leader who would deliver Israel from bondage. As has been noted, great servants of God can rise from insignificant backgrounds. But the Lord had put his hand on this family! In stating the fact of the marriage, the assertion of the purity of the relationship is made, the events that follow confirming that this was a godly family.

The parents of Moses were named Amram, his father, who had three brothers, Izhar, Hebron, and Uzziel (1 Chr 23.12), and Jochebed (Ex 6.20; Num 26.59), his mother. They were descended from Kohath the son of Levi, and thus were of the branch of the tribe of Levi that in later days would be given responsibility for carrying the Ark and the vessels of the Holy Place (Num 3.27-32). Their son Aaron became the first High Priest of Israel. The honour of being responsible for the principal vessels of the Tabernacle may well have been given to the Kohathites because of their relationship to Moses and Aaron. Jochebed was the aunt of Amram (Num 26.59). When the Law was given such a union was forbidden (Lev 18.12), but no prohibition had yet been given when they entered into marriage. No assumption as to age can be made from the fact that Jochebed was Amram's aunt. Average life span was longer and made it possible for Jochebed to be of an age similar to Amram, although even today, without such exceptional life spans, it is still possible.

The birth of Moses

The record of their marriage is followed immediately by the account of the birth of their son. It is clear, however, that a number of years had intervened. Moses was not the first child. Aaron had already been born to them some three years before the birth of Moses. Confirmation of this is given from the ages of the two brothers when, years later, they stood before Pharaoh. At that time Moses was aged eighty and Aaron was eighty-three (7.7). A sister, Miriam, had also been born, and she was the eldest child in the family. At the birth of Moses she had come to an age, possibly between twelve and fifteen years, when she could accept the responsibility of watching over the ark of bulrushes, and engage in conversation with the daughter of Pharaoh.

As Aaron had reached three years of age at the time of the birth of Moses, the edict of Pharaoh must have been enforced after his birth. There is no record of an attempt to hide him, and if his life had been at risk arrangements would have been made to hide both brothers. The murderous project of destroying the male children was at its height. That Aaron is not mentioned here is because Moses is central to the unfolding story. Amram and Jochebed were now confronted with a decision that they had not faced in the past. Should they allow the birth of their second son to be known and, as a result, see him drowned in the Nile? They determined that this would not take place, and steps were taken to preserve the life of the child.

As Jochebed looked at her son she saw that he was "fair to God" (Acts 7.20, AV margin). This is confirmed in Hebrews 11.23 where he is described as "a proper child". This goes beyond his physical appearance which would be sturdy and attractive, but suggests also that he was fair in the sight of God. His mother had the Lord before her as she looked on the babe, and was concerned that he should be pleasing to Him. It may be that, Hannah like, Jochebed had in her heart the need to provide a deliverer for the nation, and desired that this child should be set apart by the Lord for that purpose.

Since the creation of man it has been the intent of Satan to destroy that which is pleasing to God. To achieve this completely his purpose was to ensure that it was not possible for the Lord Jesus to be born. It has already been observed in chapter one of this commentary that this was his intent. Coates comments: "God's object is to bring in Christ, and to give Him a place in the faith and affections of His people, and this the enemy resists to the utmost of his power". Behind these events this evil plan was being worked out.

Decisions were made regarding the future of the babe. Although the Exodus account emphasises the part that Jochebed took, for every step here is attributed to her, Hebrews reveals that the decision was made by both parents. Stephen in his defence before the Council emphasises that the child was brought up in "his father's house" (Acts 7.20). Father and mother were united in their resolve, but the prominence given to his mother here may suggest that she took the initiative and personally undertook all the tasks necessary to preserve the life of her newly born son.

They were fearless in their endeavour, for "they were not afraid of the king's commandment" (Heb 11.23), and were prepared to put their lives at risk to preserve the child. Despite this, however, the three months during which the child was hidden in the home must have been a time of anxiety. The cry of the child put it at risk, and Jochebed would spend many hours ensuring that Moses was comfortable and quiet. Above all, God was watching over that little slave family in Egypt. The deliverance of Israel would be the work of this child, preserved and protected from the world by these godly parents.

Moses hidden in the ark

After three months it was no longer possible to keep the child in the house. Discovery would certainly be the outcome. But what was to be the means of preserving life? There is surely significance in the fact that although the parents chose to place their child in the Nile, the river of death to the Israelites, they also sought to preserve his life. The principle here is of the utmost importance. The river could not be avoided, but they worked to ensure that he was kept safe in it. Is this not a work in which godly parents have been engaged throughout the ages? They live with the knowledge that their children cannot be hidden from the world in later life, so they seek to ensure that when the day comes to leave home and enter that world, which is death to those who succumb to it, they are prepared and fitted to survive it. The ark must be placed in the river, but the river must never be in the ark else it will end the life of the child.

The ark of bulrushes, daubed with slime and pitch to make it watertight, was prepared, and the child was placed among the reeds and water plants which grew along the riverbank.† An ark of bulrushes must not be considered a poor vessel in which to place a child. Vessels made of this material sailed the seas and of them Isaiah writes: "That sendeth ambassadors by the sea, even in vessels of bulrushes upon the waters" (18.2). The warm Egyptian weather made it possible for this to be a safe hiding place. Miriam was given the task of watching the scene so that the family would be aware of anything that might befall the babe. God is sovereign. The river that the Egyptians used to destroy the male children of Israel was the same river which was used of God to preserve the life of Moses.

The task that faced these godly parents seemed to be impossible. Without faith it would be considered that although the child could be hidden for a short time in the river, it would not be long before he would have to be taken back into a more suitable hiding place. It may be, as will be seen, that Jochebed had considered this very carefully. At that point they were waiting to see how, in the words of Paul, God would use the "weak things of the world to confound the things which are mighty" (1 Cor 1.27).

Verses 5-9: The Discovery of Moses

The ark had not been placed in a secluded, lonely part on the river side. It was where the daughter of Pharaoh came to wash herself. It may be that she also used other parts of the river for this purpose, but clearly this was an accessible area. It could be that as this was a place for those of royal blood to come, Hebrew slaves would not normally be found there. Did Moses' mother choose this place deliberately, knowing that the daughter of Pharaoh would come along, possibly to perform her religious ablutions? When this royal entourage appeared, the ark was seen. It was not the crying of the child that attracted the attention of Pharaoh's daughter - "she saw the ark among the flags (the reeds, RSV)". The ark was, therefore, not so hidden that it was impossible to see, but even if hidden from the bank of the river, those who were bathing in its waters could see it. The immediate action of Miriam in offering to find a nurse for the child suggests that this situation had been foreseen and that the family had agreed a course of action. Credit, however, must be given to Miriam for the initiative that she used.

It would appear that Moses' parents had been careful in their plans and had asked the Lord for guidance. Amram and Jochebed were acting in faith when they hid the child in the home (Heb 11.23), and the same faith was evident as they placed him in the Nile. If they had acted without faith, the last place where they would have put Moses was where an Egyptian could find him. Faith acted contrary to human reasoning and God honoured it.

How remarkable to see, once again, the sovereignty of God in all this. This has already been observed in connection with the use of the Nile, but the use of the family of Pharaoh is another example. This family that was responsible for the attempt to destroy the Israelites is the same family used of God for their deliverance. Over all the plans and schemes of men He sits supreme and will raise up and cast down whom He will in the fulfilment of His purpose.

As the ark was opened the baby was weeping, and this moved the heart of the princess with compassion. She knew that this was one of the Hebrews' children, but the sight of the weeping babe so touched her that the life of the child was preserved. Doubtless she understood the relationship between Miriam, the child, and the nurse whom Miriam brought to her, but God overruled in every detail.

Blessing to Moses' parents

What blessing did Moses' parents enjoy because they had faith in God and did not trust to man's devices in seeking to preserve the life of their second son?

1. They were allowed to bring up their child in their own home. The happiness and the harmony of the home was not destroyed, and for years they enjoyed the presence of the child in their midst. What a blessing this was when around them there were grieving parents whose children had been cast into the Nile.

2. Moses' mother was paid wages to bring up the child. Once again the sovereignty of God can be traced. The nation which oppressed the Hebrews paid for the bringing up of their deliverer. Thus the needs of the child and the family were met.

3. Their son was free from the bondage of slavery. He was never required to work under the scourge of the taskmasters' whip. The servitude under which the Hebrews suffered was not to be his.

It is remarkable that the presence of Moses in their home did not bring jealousy from other parents who had lost their children. Those who knew them would understand that Moses was their own child, but God still took care of them. It may be that the feelings which were aroused by the preservation of Moses led in part to the refusal of the Israelites, in later years, to let Moses intervene in their affairs (v.14).

Influence in the house

The nursing of the child must have taken place over a considerable time. It has been reckoned that, with the longer nursing periods at that time, Moses' mother would have him a number of years. This early period is vital to the development of a child and during it the mother has the responsibility of shaping the growth of the child physically, mentally, and spiritually. It is unbecoming for a mother to leave this privilege willingly to others. Modern thinking is that a mother can continue her "career" and use others to bring up the child. This is to be avoided, and any material benefit that accrues is valued at nothing compared to what is lost.

During these formative years Moses learned from his mother of the God of Abraham, Isaac, and Jacob. He was taught that he was a Hebrew. She fulfilled her responsibility in ensuring that his young mind was filled with great truths which would never leave him. What a privilege it was for her to be able to do this! It is an honour for any mother to be given the responsibility of bringing up a child and leaving impressions of godly living.

The name of the mother of David, king of Israel, is not known but she left with him impressions of godliness. In later life he refers to himself as "the son of thine handmaid" (Ps 86.16), conscious of a mother who looked continually to the Lord to ensure that she was aware of every indication of His will, and obeyed it.

Verses 10-14: Moses in the Palace

The day came, however, when Moses had to be taken to the palace to be brought into the family of Pharaoh's daughter. What sadness there would be in the home that day, but also contentment that the child had been committed into the care of the Lord. It was in the palace that he was given the name "Moses". He would never be allowed to forget the goodness of God in saving him from drowning in the Nile. Even the name by which he would be known was given by the family of Pharaoh.† Now the child was secure under the protecting care of the highest family in the land.

It has previously been observed that the river which was chosen to destroy Israel was that by the use of which Moses was preserved. In His dealings with the forces of evil "He that sitteth in the heavens shall laugh: the Lord shall have them in derision" (Ps 2.4).

Life in the palace was very different from life in the humble home of his parents. He was now treated as one of noble rank and would enjoy all the luxury and honour which went with this high position in the land. He had the privilege of being educated as a prince, and training in the art of government and in the skills of war became a familiar part of his days.

Moses made great progress and he became "learned in all the wisdom of the Egyptians, and was mighty in words and deeds" (Acts 7.22). The wisdom of Egypt was famed throughout the world. Moses, being an active young man, applied this wisdom and became renowned for his words and actions. Such a man had before him a glittering life at the centre of the then most powerful nation on earth. However, in the record of Moses' life his time in the palace is passed over in a few verses. Accounts by other authors would have described in great detail the life enjoyed there, the feats which he carried out, and the wealth which was at his disposal. Not so in the divine record. Of far greater importance are the dealings of God with him. This is a lesson to be learned in these days of materialism when great emphasis is laid on material gain and progress in the world. It must always be remembered that spiritual life is where gain is made for eternity. Everything else passes with time.

The first decision he made

Moses made two decisions at this time which show how effectively his mother had instructed her son. When he reached maturity he refused to be called "the son of Pharaoh's daughter" (Heb 11.24). This was a position of great honour and dignity which would have made him a member of Pharaoh's family. All the wealth, rank, honour and glory enjoyed by the family of Pharaoh were within his grasp. Rarely can anyone have had so much set before him and been faced with such a choice. He was being offered the greatest wealth and the highest honour which the world could then set before him. He stood at the crossroads, looking on one side at the greatest prize earth could provide, and on the other at persecuted slaves with nothing but a promise from God.

Had he accepted what Egypt could have given, even greater dignity in the realm would have followed, and the prospects for his future looked outstanding. Arguing that it was the Lord who had placed him in this position of great privilege, and asserting that he would use his rank to alleviate the condition of the Hebrews, could have been the basis for justifying such a decision. "Might it not be therefore that he should occupy it, and use the influence connected with it, on behalf of his downtrodden brethren?" (Dennett). It would be very attractive to consider that he could bring to bear all the power and influence of the monarchy to help the Hebrews and deliver them from the taskmaster. Circumstances seemed to point to this, and a lesser man would have been content to enjoy the luxuries of court life, thankful to be able to accept without question that this was the place which been planned for him "by the Lord".

Yet Moses refused. The question is why he did so. The decision was not merely a negative one. The reason given is that he did this "by faith" (Heb 11.24). Circumstances alone are no guide to the will of the Lord. Faith looks at the unseen and takes into account matters which the world cannot understand and of which it has no knowledge. What compelled Abraham to leave the sophisticated, comfortable society of Ur of the Chaldees and commence a journey to an unknown destination? It was the same faith as that which motivated Moses. He looked beyond the present attractive offer and by faith realised that there was something far greater than promotion in Egypt. Had he accepted this elevation to membership of the royal house he could have worked tirelessly to improve the conditions under which the Israelites laboured, but still they would have been under Pharaoh's power and still they would have laboured as slaves in Egypt. Moses would never have known the trouble and affliction of leading the nation, but neither would the Lord have spoken to him "face to face, as a man speaketh unto his friend" (33.11), nor would he have seen the display of the glory of the Lord manifested. Just as the disciples, had they remained on the shore and refused to follow the Lord Jesus into the boat, would have avoided the fear which overwhelmed them as they sailed into the storm, but also would have lost the opportunity of seeing the Master at work as He "rebuked the wind, and said unto the sea, Peace, be still" (Mk 4.39), so Moses had lessons to learn which would have been lost to a prince, no matter how exalted, in Egypt.

It is clear that Moses knew of his origins. That the Israelites would leave Egypt and go back to the land promised to them would be known to him, and was a far greater attraction than all the wealth and power which Egypt could bestow. He would have known of the revelation regarding the length of the captivity in Egypt (Gen 15.13), and realised that the time for the fulfilment of this was drawing near. So Moses esteemed "the reproach of Christ greater riches than the treasures in Egypt" (Heb 11.26). He knew that there was a reward for following the Lord, and to that he gave himself with vigour.

Comments in Hebrews

What is involved in "the reproach of Christ"? It is to be reviled and treated with contempt. It is to be treated as He was treated. As far as Moses was concerned it was to be identified with the Israelites. So closely, in later years, did Moses become identified with the God whom he served that, when he returned to Egypt after forty years, he was treated with the same contempt with which they treated the God of Israel and which later was displayed against the Lord. This was not only a shame on Egypt, for which they would pay, but it was a credit to Moses. Today believers are exhorted to "go forth therefore unto him without the camp, bearing his reproach" (Heb 13.13).

The writer to the Hebrews states two things on which Moses turned his back: "pleasures" and "treasures" (Heb 11.25-26). These are what men and women seek today, and to which they devote their lives to achieve their aims. Christians should have completely different priorities, and Moses stands as a beacon, displaying a right attitude to the society around him. This cannot have been a light decision for him to make. The pull of Egypt would be very strong and the temptation to go in for a life of pleasure, the possession of wealth, and to have all that he desired would be carefully weighed and all the issues duly considered. But, by faith, the right decision was made, and Moses, in a critical life-changing moment, chose to suffer affliction with the people of God. He was not unaware of the implications of his choice. He knew that it would mean giving up the luxury that was his. He knew that it would lead to affliction and trouble. He knew also that it was God's way.

The example of Moses is one that all believers would do well to follow. A good education and suitable employment are necessary today, but the pursuit of these aims should not blind the mind to the greater aim of pleasing the Lord and serving Him wholeheartedly. This requires right decisions to be made, but the Lord is the rewarder of all those who put their trust in Him. Those who gave their lives over to the service of the Lord did not find that this pathway in life simply evolved with little decision on their part. It was not that they had no other options in life and were forced into this service. Neither did they look around them and consider this to be the easiest life to pursue. All believers who have determined to serve the Lord by giving Him of their time, energy, and resources have stood at the crossroads of life, with the options before them. Blessed indeed are those who have decided that they would serve the Lord by putting Him first and giving their lives into His hands. This alone is the pathway of satisfaction and fulfilment.

The second decision he made

The second decision of Moses, made when he was forty years of age (Acts 7.23), was to go and visit his brethren. It has already been noted that he was aware that these despised slaves were his brethren. Now he determined to visit them and see the burdens that they carried and the oppressions that they suffered. He considered the time had come for action to deliver the Israelites from their bondage and so, on seeing an Egyptian smiting a Hebrew, he slew the Egyptian. There is no indication that the Egyptian was one of the taskmasters, but such a view would accord with the account. This would make the act a crime against one of the officers of Pharaoh which would make Moses' position precarious.

Before Moses buried the Egyptian he was careful to look this way and that to ensure that no one, apart from the Hebrew whom he was helping, would see the action. How much better if, rather than looking on men, he had kept his eyes on the God of Israel. The body was buried in the sand, and Moses, probably satisfied with his day's work, returned to his Egyptian home. He had defended the one who was being wronged. That night must have been one of suppressed excitement. At last he had done what he had been considering for some time. At last he had struck a blow for the deliverance of those who were oppressed. Now the slaves would recognise who was to deliver them.

The second recorded visit to the Hebrews took place on the next day[†] (see also Acts 7.26). This shows how close had become his interest in the Hebrews. The previous visit was not merely the result of sudden impulse. Again he returned to visit "his brethren" and saw two of them struggling together. If the Egyptian had been in the wrong on the previous day, it was clear to Moses which of the two Hebrews was in the wrong on this occasion. As he urged the wrongdoer to cease, the reply that he received struck fear into his heart. The deed of yesterday was clearly common knowledge amongst the Hebrews. Rather than being received as a deliverer, he was regarded as having no right to be involved in these matters. The slaves of Egypt would not follow this man.

The problem which Moses had created is one that is all too common. He had a desire to do the work of the Lord, considered that it was in accord with the will of God for this work to commence now, and deemed that he was fitted to do it. However, he acted in his own way and in his own time. There was no waiting on the Lord to learn His will and to wait His time. Moses' actions were disastrous. It is still the case that good motives, and a wish to work for the Lord, must be backed up with a desire to wait His time and to move in the way which He determines. This cannot be done without prayerful, patient waiting in His presence. It is important not to run ahead of God, neither come behind Him, but wait on Him. If that is done He will clearly show us what to do and when to do it.

What a contrast there is here between the faith that caused him to refuse to be called the son of Pharaoh's daughter and his behaviour as he visited his brethren. It can hardly be thought that a man with such faith would act in this way. The warning to us is most solemn. It is possible to act on faith and yet quickly to be overcome by the impulses of the flesh. Even more solemn it is to consider that this was done in what Moses perceived to be the service of the Lord. Care has to be exercised at all times, and the principle to be enjoyed by Israel in a coming day must guide our actions today, that "he that believeth shall not make haste" (Is 28.16).

Verses 15-22: Fleeing to Midian

Moses did not immediately flee from Egypt. He waited, hoping that word of this act might not come to the ears of Pharaoh. Perhaps he made this the subject of prayer that his progress towards becoming the deliverer of the people might not come to an end as a result of his impetuous action. He may even have thought that there was no danger of this taking place, as the Lord would preserve him. It must, therefore, have dismayed him to learn, not only that Pharaoh had received news of the slaying of the Egyptian, but also that he was determined to have Moses put to death. The would-be deliverer was now forced to flee Egypt.

As he fled he was doubtless confused in mind. Why had the Lord allowed this to take place when he could have led the Israelites out of bondage? Why should they suffer further when he could have brought an end to their oppression? Was this not the time for them to return to the land of which he had heard so much from his mother? The questions would rise constantly in his mind, and at that time there appeared to be no answer. How many have felt as Moses felt, when the door of service which they thought was opening was firmly closed? How often has it been imagined that the pathway ahead has been marked out clearly by God, only to find it blocked completely? The reason may be as it was with Moses. Further preparation is needed to carry out the service on which the heart has been set. Moses had as much, if not more, to learn in the forty years which lay ahead of him, as he had learned in his first forty years.

The Midianites

The Midianites were descendants of Abraham through Keturah (Gen 25.2,4). They were a rich and powerful people. Some of them lived in cities (Num 31.10), with others probably leading a nomadic existence. Those who occupied the region into which Moses had come would appear to have had a settled life there. On reaching Midian, Moses sat by a well, no doubt tired and weary after the mental and physical strain of the past weeks. He had arrived at the area on the west coast of the Arabian peninsula, which was the east coast of the Red Sea. The well was a gathering point, and refreshment was available for the weary traveller. It was a good spot to choose in order to meet the inhabitants of that place. He was dressed as an Egyptian, so no one was in any doubt as to the area from which he had come. To that well there came the seven daughters of Reuel, who is also called Jethro, one of the chiefs of Midian. The paths of the Midianites and the sons of Jacob had crossed already when Joseph's brothers sold him into the hands of Midianitish merchantmen (Gen 37.28).

Introduction to Jethro and his family

Jethro was the priest of Midian. The worship of the true God was carried on in this area. This man, although he did not have the revelation that was given to Abraham, Isaac, Jacob, and Joseph, nevertheless worshipped their God, proof that the worship of the true God in these days was not confined to the sons of Abraham.

As Moses watched the seven women filling the troughs to water their flocks, they were interrupted by shepherds who forced them away and used the water which the women had drawn to supply their own flocks. The impetuous nature of Moses, which had led him into such trouble, must have caused him to consider taking control of the situation and drive the shepherds themselves away to enable the women to water their sheep. Already, however, Moses is learning to control his impetuosity. There is no record of a confrontation with the shepherds, only that Moses helped the women to water their flock. It is clear (v.19) that Moses had to refill the troughs before the sheep could be cared for, but this he did with helpful courtesy.

Shepherding was an occupation which was an abomination to the Egyptians (Gen 46.34). Moses must have been aware, however, that "his brethren" the Hebrews kept sheep, but nevertheless this prince from Egypt is being taught the need of humility and meekness. It would humble him to be "reduced" to watering sheep, and the first signs are already visible of the meekness that would become one of the outstanding features of his leadership (Num 12.3). The change from being one of the chief princes in Egypt to helping a few women water sheep at a Midianitish well was great indeed, but a necessary part in the education of the servant of God.

This meeting at the well had far reaching consequences for Moses. The servant of Abraham met Rebekah, the wife of Isaac, at a well. Jacob met Rachel, his wife, at a well, and Moses met Zipporah, his wife, at this well. When his daughters returned early to Jethro, showing the remarkable fact that Moses was able to carry out the task effectively and at a faster rate than could these seven women, his interest was aroused. How have they come back so soon today? Moses had been left at the well, because he would not force his company on anyone. He would not arrive uninvited at the house of Jethro, but the invitation soon came and he was welcomed into the home. Jethro obviously was a hospitable, courteous man whose treatment of his daughters stands in favourable and stark contrast to the behaviour of Laban to Rachel and Leah, his daughters, who became the wives of Jacob. This home was one in which Moses was content to stay for many years.

Life with Jethro

It has not to be supposed that Moses had given up all thoughts of delivering the people. When the call came to do so there was a becoming reluctance on his part to jump to the task without raising the questions which had formed in his mind over the years. Impetuosity was then a thing of the past. Over these years in Midian "he endured, as seeing him who is invisible" (Heb 11.27). Such perseverance was his from the moment he refused to be called the son of Pharaoh's daughter. With steadfast purpose he lived through these years, keeping before him the One who is invisible. He knew that there was One who was greater than Pharaoh and that He would be faithful to His promises. He may not have appreciated the fact, but he was now waiting on God's time. It has already been noted that there may have been some confusion in Moses' mind as Egypt was left behind, but there was still an underlying faith that things would work out for the deliverance of the people.

In course of time the marriage of Moses and Zipporah took place and a child, Gershom (1647), meaning, "a stranger, or foreigner" was born.[†] The name means that Moses never forgot that neither Midian nor Egypt was his home and that he was stranger, no matter how kind was his new-found family, how loving his wife, or how much enjoyment and satisfaction his son gave him. And so, miles away from his suffering people, Moses learned the art of shepherding. Little did he realise how valuable this was to be to him in years to come, not only in the shepherding skills which he acquired, but in the knowledge which he gained of the wilderness on the east side of the Red Sea.

Preparation for the service of God is often carried out without an awareness that God is working in the life. As David was tending his sheep he little knew that he was being fitted to sit on the throne of Israel as the shepherd/king. The young Samuel at Shiloh was yet to understand that God had chosen him to bring about revival in the nation. As Daniel and his companions left Jerusalem on the journey to Babylon they could not have known that this disaster was to provide them with the opportunity to serve the God of Israel. Young Timothy, as he sat at the knee of his mother and grandmother, would have no understanding that the Scriptures which he was being taught were a part of his preparation for service in the furtherance of the gospel. So it is today. The current problems and difficulties of life may make little sense, yet it may be that He is preparing us for an as yet unknown future service.

The way of God with Moses has been seen in the lives of many of His servants. Moses was set aside in Midian, not because he was unsuitable for service, but because he had a further lesson to learn. It would take many years to bring him to the point where he was ready to serve as God required. The lesson is that he must wait until it is seen clearly that God alone is acting. If the early attempts by Moses to deliver the people had gone ahead, and even if he had been able to effect some kind of partial deliverance, it would have been recorded in history as the work of Moses. He might have been remembered as a powerful leader such as Alexander the Great, or Napoleon, but how valueless this would have been. The more excellent way is to accept that God has laid the servant aside to learn the further lessons which He teaches during this period, and to wait until He works and the work is seen as His alone. In God's time Moses had the great privilege of acting as God's servant carrying out God's work in God's way with God's power and, as a result, seeing the fruit at first hand. Anything less than this is a poor, second rate substitute.

Verses 23-25: Life in Egypt

The phrase "in process of time" (1992, 3117, 7227) means "during (or, in the course of) those many days". Indication is thus given of the length of time during which the Hebrews suffered under this Pharaoh. Quite apart from the number of days, the phrase drives home the fact that periods of persecution do not pass quickly. Each day, with its grinding labour, was slow in passing. The same truth is seen in the description of the time between the return of the Ark to the house of Abinadab in the hill and the revival being brought about under the leadership of Samuel. It is recorded "that the time was long; for it was twenty years" (1 Sam 7.2). What a contrast this is with Jacob when he was serving Laban with the prospect of having Rachel to wife at the end of seven years. These years "seemed unto him but a few days, for the love he had to her" (Gen 29.20). Truly the circumstances in the days determine whether they are regarded as long or short, many or few. At least forty years of oppression had passed and these days were many, not only in the sense of the number of them, but also in the sense that they passed slowly.

The death of the Pharaoh who had inflicted such suffering on the Israelites may have given them hope that their groaning would soon be over. It might be that the new Pharaoh would look with greater sympathy upon them. This, however, was a false hope, but they were not forgotten. There was no compassion in the heart of the new Pharaoh, but their sighs and groans reached to heaven and God heard the cries of His people. He kept His promises and, although there seemed little around them to encourage optimism, they would be fulfilled. With that they could have encouraged themselves.

All during those "many days" Moses worked as a shepherd. It is not known how much contact he had with Egypt or his family during these years, but in Midian he was "a stranger" (Acts 7.29 - *3941*). He did not settle down there and was never regarded as being completely integrated into the society of the Midianites. This is confirmed by the fact that, unlike Jacob (Gen 30.25-36), he never asked to have a flock or household of his own. This he surely would have done if he had contemplated permanent residence by moving away from the immediate vicinity of Jethro's home area in order to establish his independent status. After forty years he was still keeping the flock of his father-in-law. If the days and years were long for Israel, they must have been likewise for Moses. In the deserted areas, leading and feeding sheep, there would be plenty of time for thought and consideration of life's journey so far. It does seem that Moses realised that the story was not yet fully told and that God still had a work for him to do.

Comparison with the Perfect Servant

In Deuteronomy 18.15 Moses tells the people that "The Lord thy God will raise up unto thee a Prophet from the midst of thee, of thy brethren, like unto me; unto him ye shall hearken". This prophet to whom he refers is the Lord Jesus Christ. It should be noted, however, that although Moses said that he would be "like unto me" there are significant differences, some of which are seen in these early days. Note three of these.

1. *The commencement of their service.* Moses was too early. Forty years were to pass before God's time came, but the Saviour appeared publicly at exactly the right time, as John Baptist was preaching by the River Jordan.

2. *Attitude to the task ahead.* Moses made mistakes in his service, but the Saviour made no mistakes.

3. *The time in the wilderness.* In the forty years which lay ahead of him Moses would continue his education in the school of God. How invaluable to him would be all that he learned as he shepherded the sheep. The long hours of solitude gave him time to meditate and consider the lessons from the past. The Lord Jesus required no such time of education. His time in the wilderness was not to be taught lessons without which He was unfit to serve. It was the time for showing the Adversary that he was a defeated foe and that the Saviour would triumph over him.

Notes

3 The use of the word "ark" reminds us of the preservation of Noah and his family in the Flood. It was a chest of rushes made of the papyrus, or paper reed, which grew plentifully in the Nile at that time. These reeds could grow to a height of 3 metres (10 ft) and were used in building small boats for the navigation of the river. The reeds were bound together with bitumen which came from the Dead Sea. The application of pitch made the little craft watertight.

10 Moses (4872), or *Mosheh*, from the verb MASHA means "to draw out", referring to the drawing out of the child from the Nile. The name was probably Hebrew in origin, given because Pharaoh's daughter knew him to be a Hebrew child. However, the Egyptian for "boy child" is similar in sound and it may be that she used this name to satisfy both the Hebrew and Egyptian interest in the child.

13 "When he went out the next day" (RSV).

22 See note on Moses' family at 18.3.

EXODUS 3

The Call of Moses

Forty years have passed since the arrival of Moses in the land of Midian. There is no record in Scripture of the events of those years. Forty, however, is the number of testing and education. The Israelites were forty years in their journey from Egypt to Canaan. The Lord Jesus was forty days and nights in the wilderness. So Moses had a forty-year period of testing and education before he commenced the forty-year period of public service.

He learned dependence on God and there, away from the influences of the palace, he came to know God in a way that would not have been possible if he had remained in Egypt. As the years wore on his faith would be tried. It has already been noted that his flight to Midian did not signal the end of his desire to deliver the Israelites. As months and years slipped past, however, he must have wondered when, if ever, that day would come. This impetuous man who had lacked patience is now being taught the necessity of patient waiting on the Lord. God deals with His servants in this way to bring them to an end of themselves. He teaches them that they have no resources apart from Him, and that without Him they can achieve nothing. Any self-confidence reduces their usefulness in His service.

> That I am nothing, Thou art all,
> I would be daily taught.
> (Johann C. Lavater)

It should not seem surprising that Moses records nothing of what took place during this period. "It could not but be a severe trial of his faith to find year after year elapsing, and the prime and vigour of his age apparently wearing away, while no tokens from above indicted that the great work of his vocation was any nearer at hand" (Bush). Yet despite this, nothing is known of the turmoil of mind that he must have suffered and the attacks of the Adversary that he must have endured. Doubtless he was often assailed by the thought that his life had been wasted when he could have been a man of influence for good if he had remained in Pharaoh's court. Those who have "lost" their lives for the sake of the Lord Jesus will be attacked in this way. As in the servant Gospel of Mark there are no details of the temptations in the wilderness, simply the statement that they took place (Mk 1.13), so Moses is silent on the detail of these years. Private preparation alone with God is necessary for all His servants, and there are dealings with God that are not for others to share.

Verses 1-6: The Call from the Bush
Moses the shepherd
After hundreds of years of waiting God was about to speak again, not in

the great centres of world government, not to the mighty, but to a shepherd alone in the desert. What a foretaste this is of the coming of the forerunner of the Good Shepherd: "Now in the fifteenth year of the reign of Tiberius Caesar, Pontius Pilate being governor of Judaea, and Herod being tetrarch of Galilee, and his brother Philip tetrarch of Ituraea and of the region of Trachonitis, and Lysanias the tetrarch of Abilene, Annas and Caiaphas being the high priests, the word of God came unto John the son of Zacharias in the wilderness" (Lk 3.1-2).

Before consideration is given to what took place when Moses saw the burning bush it must be noted how Moses was occupied. "Now Moses kept the flock of Jethro his father in law, the priest of Midian". The verb "kept" (7462) means to feed and act as a shepherd towards the flock. Moses took the responsibility of shepherding the flock very seriously. The sheep were not neglected. Although others looking on would consider him to be in much diminished circumstances, he did not allow this to affect the quality of his work. The man who was to shepherd Israel through the wilderness learned the art of shepherding in Midian. Forty years was long enough for him to be well tried and proven in the care of the flock.

The education of Moses was therefore in two distinct parts. In Egypt he was taught lessons on government and leadership, but the art of shepherding could never have been learned there. It was necessary for him to be in a place where sheep were to be found in plenty. How gracious is the Lord to Moses. Even his impetuous failure in Egypt is used to bring him to the place where his education was continued. For Moses, all things were working together for good, even although it may have been difficult to perceive this as the events unfolded.

Apart from Midian, however, there were other areas where he could have learned the skills of shepherding the sheep, but it was through this region that he was to lead the people. These were the mountains and valleys through which they would travel; Moses would shepherd the flock of Israel through the same land where he had shepherded the flock of Jethro. There is an important principle in this of which all shepherds of the flock must be aware. Sheep can only be led with confidence through ways which the shepherds know well and which they have experienced themselves. The valleys and the mountain tops, the dark days and the light days, all the experiences of life through which the Lord has led are, for the shepherd, training for the day when the flock will be led over the same paths. Leadership cannot be effective when it is beyond the spiritual experience of those who lead.

After long years the time of testing and preparation for the task ahead is completed. It is true that the time of education is never over, for those who serve Him do not stop learning in the school of God. However, for Moses the lessons fitting him to commence this particular service are now past.

When God called

Let it be noted when and where the call from the Lord took place. In the backside of the desert, during a day which had commenced like every other day, God spoke and Moses was ready for the call when it came. There had been no early warnings that morning to prepare him for this, the past forty years had been preparation. There had been no trumpet sound to wake Moses as the dawn arrived, no special miraculous word that today God was to speak. It was in the ordinary round of duties, which he was fulfilling faithfully, during a day like hundreds which had gone before that God intervened, and the course of Moses' life was changed completely. Similarly, it was a night like every other night when Samuel heard the call, "Samuel, Samuel". In later years there was nothing remarkable about David's day until suddenly, without warning, he was summoned into the presence of Samuel to be anointed king of Israel. In the Gospel narrative, the business of tax gathering was as it had been on so many days until the Master passed by and called Matthew to leave all and follow Him. Blind Bartimaeus would not have regarded the day as being different in any way until he heard the "Son of David" pass by. The call of God must be heeded at all times. If there is a desire to serve Him it is necessary to wait on Him. Until He lets His will be made known the servant must move on quietly carrying out the responsibilities lying to hand.

Where God called
In his search for pasture for the sheep, Moses had led them to the backside of the wilderness, to a mountain in Horeb. The "backside" (310) is "behind" the wilderness. Pasture was not always readily to be found and the search led Moses a great distance into the desert. He had travelled using what pasture could be found, but now he was at the boundary, out in the extremities of where it was possible to venture. It cannot fail to be noticed that he led (5090) the flock and the flock did not lead him. It was the responsibility of the shepherd to seek out pastures for the flock and this Moses did just as the Psalmist knew that the Lord does this for His flock: "Give ear, O Shepherd of Israel, thou that leadest Joseph like a flock" (Ps 80.1). His purpose in travelling so far through the desert to this area was that here was to be found *suitable* pasture. Keil & Delitzsch comment: "Moses drove the sheep from Jethro's home as far as Horeb, so that he passed through a desert with the flock before he reached the pasture land of Horeb…*Horeb* is called the Mount of God by anticipation, with reference to the consecration which it subsequently received through the revelation of God upon its summit. The supposition that it had been a holy locality even before the calling of Moses, cannot be sustained. Moreover, the name is not restricted to one single mountain, but applies to the central group of mountains in the southern part of the peninsula (19.1). Hence the spot where God appeared to Moses cannot be precisely determined".

Those who shepherd the flock of God today must be aware of this responsibility. It is their duty to ensure that the flock is led in pastures where the food is plentiful and suitable for their growth. To leave the flock to feed on their own is but to encourage wandering and to result in poorly fed, spiritually malnourished sheep, and shepherds who do not know where the flock is feeding. Peter exhorts the elders to "Feed the flock of God which is among you, taking the oversight thereof, not by constraint, but willingly; not for filthy lucre, but of a ready mind" (1 Pet 5.2). Paul had this shepherd care before him when he exhorted the elders of the assembly at Ephesus to "Take heed therefore unto yourselves, and to all the flock, over the which the Holy Ghost hath made you overseers to feed the church of God" (Acts 20.28).

This shepherd was prepared to go anywhere, and exhaust himself with long hours of travel, to ensure that the sheep would not go hungry. He came to the mountain called the Mount of God, because, as has been noted by Keil & Delitzsch, not only now, but also in later years, God would use this area and in some cases this same mountain to reveal Himself. In the life of Moses and others it would be place of particular significance.

1. As Moses journeyed back to Egypt he would meet Aaron on the "mount of God" (4.27).

2. Water would gush from the smitten rock when Moses stood upon Horeb and smote it (17.6).

3. Moses, Aaron and Hur stood on the hill while Joshua led Israel in battle against the Amalekites (17.8-16). This was still in the area of Horeb where the water had come from the smitten rock.

4. Moses would meet Jethro and be reunited with his wife Zipporah, after the Israelites left Egypt, when Moses was "encamped at the mount of God" (18.5).

5. In this area the Law would be given as Moses "went up into the mount of God" (24.13).

6. It was to this mountain that Elijah would come in despair, and hear the word of the Lord: "What doest thou here Elijah?" (1 Kings 19.8-9).

The mount is identified as Horeb (Dryness), indicating that in the main this was a bleak, dry area, and emphasising the difficulties faced by the shepherd in finding suitable pasture for the flock, although clearly in Horeb there were areas where suitable pasture could be found.

The burning bush

The sight that met Moses was that of a burning thorn bush. Such a bush, which probably was a type of acacia shrub, small and without the magnificence of a great tree, was common in that area. It may be that to Moses the sight of a burning bush was not altogether unusual, but this bush commanded his attention because there was something remarkable to be seen. The flames were not devouring the bush. As he looked on it there is no indication that initially he considered the fire of itself to be anything but a natural phenomenon. His interest was aroused to turn aside to see how this thorn bush could be surviving the flame. Under normal conditions it would soon turn to ashes, but these were not normal, natural conditions. God was there. What was the significance of the bush burning but not being consumed? Two suggestions have been made.

1. The fire speaks to us of the holiness of God. "Our God is a consuming fire" (Heb 12.29), were words which would turn the mind of Hebrew Christians to this passage of Scripture. This little bush was able to exist even in the heat of the flame. So there can be conditions when the Lord can dwell in the midst, amongst those who would be considered to be at risk of being devoured in judgment by the presence of a holy God. But just as the Lord enabled the bush to survive, so He will bring about conditions that will make it possible for those with whom He dwells, not only to survive, but also to enjoy His presence. It is not suggested that Moses understood all this as he looked at the thorn bush, but knowledge of later events allows the reader to see these lessons, and, doubtless, in years to come Moses would look back and understand the significance of the thorn bush that was not consumed by the flame.

2. As Egypt is likened to an "iron furnace" (Deut 4.20), the burning thorn bush represents the Israelites suffering in the furnace of affliction down in Egypt, yet not being consumed. This has been seen clearly in the continued multiplication of the people despite the persecution that they endured under the taskmasters. Bush states: "They were in a furnace of fire, and in themselves but as briars and thorns compared with those that kindled it. But they were nevertheless not destroyed; nay, they were still flourishing; the nation continued to shoot forth vigorous branches, and a numerous offspring surrounded them in spite of their enemies".

Whereas there is truth in both of these conclusions it appears that the former better fits the circumstances. Moses, in later years speaking of the blessings bestowed by the Lord on Joseph, remembers "the good will of him that dwelt in the bush"(Deut 33.16). The fire would appear, therefore, to indicate the presence of the Lord and not the furnace of affliction. This is the first recorded revelation of the Lord to Moses, and He does not come with the glory, thunders and lightnings which were revealed later as the Law was given. He appears in a humble thorn bush and the fire that was burning in it would be of a size to be contained within this bush. Moses will learn the lesson that the Lord had chosen a people who were not amongst the great and powerful of earth, but who were insignificant to other nations, just as the thorn bush was a humble shrub. With such a nation He was pleased to dwell.

Who appeared to Moses?

The next question to be settled is who appeared to Moses in the bush. It has already been indicated that it was the Lord who spoke, but this must be substantiated. Just as Peter never forgot the Mount of Transfiguration to which he referred many years later as the "holy mount" (2 Pet 1.18), so years later Moses revealed that he had never forgotten what took place before the bush. Moses knew that it was Lord who was in the bush. The truth of this is confirmed in these verses.

1. It was the angel of the Lord who appeared to him in the flame of fire (v.2).

2. It was the Lord who saw that he turned aside (v.4).

3. It was God who spoke to him (v.4).

The angel of the Lord is identified as God Himself. The call of this servant was not to be delegated to any angel or other created being. The high and holy calling to which he would devote the remaining forty years of his life came from the Lord directly and through no person or agency, no matter how glorious or worthy. So with believers today who are the "called of Jesus Christ" (Rom 1.6). It is He who has issued the great commission and still calls men and women into His glorious service. Let it never be undervalued.

Moses turned aside to see the great sight. It is probable that he did not yet realise the meaning of what he saw. Even yet there was no indication of the presence of God, but he did recognise that this was a great sight; it was something out of the ordinary, demanding further investigation. What Moses would have lost if he had continued on his way and had failed to take time to stop and consider what he saw! It is possible to be so busy and concerned with the problems of life that believers do not turn aside when the Lord is speaking. There may be no sensitivity to the fact that the circumstances which He orders demand that time is taken to consider them more closely.

It had been many years since there was noted in Scripture such a direct revelation of God. The last recorded instance had been when Jacob was encouraged to go down to Egypt (Gen 46.1-4), and now, after more than 400 years, God is about to speak once more to an individual openly, this time to encourage him to lead the people out of land to which Jacob had travelled.

The initial greeting

Consider what Moses heard. Here he is introduced into the presence of God, and immediately the Lord speaks He reveals His compassion. As he turns aside to see the great sight Moses hears his name called: "Moses, Moses". It is not often in Scripture that He uses the double call of a name, "Abraham, Abraham" (Gen 22.11); "Jacob, Jacob" (Gen 46.2); "Samuel, Samuel (1 Sam 3.10)"; "Martha, Martha (Lk 10.41)" etc are also times when it was used; its use here is therefore significant. It brings an added note of consideration and care. There is tenderness in this manner of addressing an individual. It is intended to attract attention, and to cause Moses to listen carefully to what is about to be said. As the Speaker is acting out of love and compassion, the grace of God is seen in His manner of addressing His servant, and this loving concern will be the foundation of the commission given to Moses, not a spirit of fear or intimidation.

The reply of Moses confirms his willingness to hear the voice of God. "Here am I", are the words of one who is before God with no prior conditions; he is willing to listen and ready to hear what the Lord has to say to him. May all be willing to cry, "Here am I", when the call of God is heard. It is probable that Moses understood immediately who was speaking to him, but the instruction to take his shoes off certainly confirmed that he was meeting God. The command here was twofold. First, he had to ensure that he came no closer to the bush. This was no place for the satisfaction of idle curiosity. As God spoke to him, the tumult of emotions in his heart could have caused him to rush forward to be as close as possible to the Lord. Impetuosity in the presence of God is an even greater danger than in the presence of the Egyptian oppressor.

Second, a lesson can be learned from Moses' unshod feet. The sandals that covered the soles of his feet had to be discarded in the presence of God. This act is common in the east in showing respect for a host when entering his house. The priests who served in the Tabernacle wore no shoes on their feet. It was the means commanded to show reverence in the presence of God. The fact that God would dwell with His people did not reduce His holiness; His presence demanded reverence, even when the meeting place was alone in the desert. No one else was present to see the burning bush and to witness the momentous meeting which was about to take place, but there must still be reverence in the presence of God. We should note that Moses went even further than the divine command, and hid his face, for he was afraid to look upon God.

In today's easygoing society God is often approached and addressed in a most casual manner. The excuse for this is often that salvation has brought us near to God and that saints are in such a close relationship with Him that there need no longer be old fashioned "formality". This reasoning ignores that fact that those who come into His presence are still dealing with a holy God, and that such familiarity is neither seen nor taught in the New Testament. No one was closer to the Lord Jesus than John, the beloved disciple. He leaned on His breast and is presented in Scripture as the "disciple whom Jesus loved". As an old man, on the Isle of Patmos he saw the Lord and fell down before Him as dead. There was no undue familiarity, only reverential, loving awe at His majesty.

Now the Lord brings to the attention of Moses His faithfulness. The words which came to his ears must have caused him to wonder. This God was the God of Abraham, Isaac, and Jacob, and Moses was well aware of the history of these great giants of the past. But "the God of thy father"? These words show that there is the continuing care of God over His people in Egypt. Indeed, the singular noun "father" may lead us to believe that it was Moses' father, Amram, who is spoken of here. If that is so it is of interest to consider that he was not one of the great men of the past, nor are the details of his life or of his dealings with God recorded in Scripture. He was an ordinary man going about his daily business, a humble man who made no claims to greatness. Our God is not only the God of the great, but also the God of the humble. What an encouragement to us. Our lives, which at times seem so mundane and ordinary, are under the scrutiny of heaven, and God is pleased to associate Himself with those who live in this quiet way. Amram was a man of faith (Heb 11.23), and he was prepared to show by his works that his faith was genuine. May all therefore heed the instruction, "Seekest thou great things for thyself? seek them not" (Jer 45.5), and rather show that faith is the basis of all our actions. That will give Him pleasure.

But above that there is impressed on Moses the faithful dealings of God with the Israelites down the centuries. When Stephen speaks of this incident (Acts 7.32) he uses the plural "fathers", indicating that the noun "father" in this chapter is used in the sense of a collective singular. It may be, therefore, that the patriarchs Abraham, Isaac, and Jacob are in view when the Lord said, "The God of thy father". The God who had preserved the patriarchs, who had spoken to them and guided them, was the same God with whom Moses and his present generation would now have dealings. Perhaps the use of the singular was to convey both meanings to Moses. The God of his father was the God of the patriarchs.

How often is it felt that God is different today from what He was to past generations? Great men of God were raised up to do mighty works for God. Some seemed to come to a knowledge of God far beyond any knowledge of Him which others could ever hope to have. Has God changed? The answer given to Moses, which remains the same today, is that He has not. He can be known as intimately as He was to past generations and His work can be seen in lives in the present, not exactly as He did in others, for He deals with us all individually, but just as powerfully. Moses was about to learn that the God who did great things in the past could still do them in his day.

Verses 7-10: The Commission from the Bush

The commission from the Lord to Moses consisted of three main elements.

1. Divine appreciation of the plight of the Israelites.
2. The preparation which the Lord had made for His people.
3. The commission given to Moses to lead the people out.

First, there is appreciation in heaven of the plight of the Israelites in Egypt. The Lord told Moses that He had "seen the affliction" which they were enduring, He had "heard their cry", and He knew "their sorrows". How complete was His interest in them. He had seen, He had heard, and He knew. Not only did He know their sorrows but He also understood the depth of their anguish. He did not stand afar off looking on, feeling nothing for them in their plight. The three senses mentioned here are the same as those described by Paul in 1 Corinthians 2.9: "Eye hath not seen, nor ear heard, neither have entered into the heart of man…"; the eye to see, the ear to hear, and the heart to feel and understand. By this is indicated the full range of perception. The Lord had seen with His eye, He had heard with His ear, and He knew with His heart. Thus the Lord will have His people understand that when He looked down on Egypt He was fully aware of what was taking place.

Second, there is now preparation for life after Egyptian slavery. The answer to their plight was not an emergency measure. That is one reason why the Lord revealed himself at this time as the God of Abraham, Isaac, and Jacob. He had promised, centuries before, that the people would be brought out of Egypt back to the land that had been promised to Abraham. Now this promise, made long before the scourge of the Egyptian taskmaster was felt, would be fulfilled.

Years ago Moses thought that he should deliver them, but now he has to learn that the work of deliverance must be the work of God and not of a man alone. God declares, "I am come down to deliver them". God is omnipresent, but the expression "come down" is used to indicate times when He intervenes in an open way in the affairs of men.[†] This work will bring the Israelites out of a land where people have to force a living from the desert and are dependent on the Nile for the production of food. Despite its glory and greatness, Egypt was a restricted place in which to live. The land that the Lord will give His people has no such restrictions, and it is given a fourfold description.

1. It is a good land. Practically, it is a good land because it will supply the need of all the Israelites. Aesthetically, it is a good land because of its beauty. Spiritually, it will be the place where the Lord will dwell with His people. All this will make it a good land.

2. It is a large land where there is ample room for all the people to enter and enjoy freedom. The provision of God will be enough for all to enjoy without restriction.

3. It is a land flowing with milk and honey. Sweetness and nourishment will be readily available at all times.

4. It is, however, the land of the Canaanites, Hittites, Amorites, Perizzites, Hivites, and Jebusites. This is a warning that it is already inhabited. Moses would be aware of this, but it is made clear that this land will not be entered without a struggle. These good things will only be enjoyed by those who are prepared to dispossess those who would keep them out. Thus early there is brought before Moses the twin truths of redemption - the Lord will deliver them out of the land of Egypt, but they will need to fight to gain the possessions that the Lord intends them to enjoy. True it is that each victory won will be His victory gained by His power, but it will be necessary for Israel to fight to gain these possessions. By this they will learn dependence on God.

Third, there is the commission given to Moses. "Come now therefore, and I will send thee unto Pharaoh, that thou mayest bring forth my people the children of Israel out of Egypt." The urgency of this call must not be ignored. "Come now" indicates that the long years of shepherding in Midian have come to an end. God has work for him to do which will change the course of his life.

With the call there comes encouragement for the willing servant. Note that success is not in doubt. The Lord has said that He is come down to deliver and this will most certainly take place. Those who engage in His service are guaranteed victory no matter how dark, lonely, or difficult the days may become. But there was even more to encourage Moses in the task that lay ahead. In v.8 it is the Lord who will deliver Israel, but note that in v.10 the Lord tells Moses that he, Moses, will bring them out. It will be the work of the Lord, but Moses will be given full credit for the accomplishment of the work. In His grace towards us He gives faithful servants credit for the work to which He has called them, even although all has been done by Him. With those encouraging words the call has been made and it is time for Moses to respond.

Verses 11-12: The First Objection of Moses

The response of Moses is centred round five objections. After observing the haste with which Moses has acted in the past it may be surprising to see how reluctant he is now to take up the challenge of the call of God. We must recognise, however, that since that early day Moses has been learning, and one of the great lessons was how insignificant he really was. His objections are not signs of rebellion or of faithless reluctance. Rather there is seen in them commendable features of Moses' character which have developed over the years in the wilderness.

The first objection was on the basis of his insignificance. "Who am I, that I should go to Pharaoh, and that I should bring forth the children of Israel out of Egypt?" One would have thought that the first objection to be raised would have centred round the danger which faced him should he return to Egypt. Clearly, thought of self-preservation is not foremost. What is in his mind is a feeling that he is not worthy of the task. How can someone who has spent years in a lonely desert shepherding sheep enter the presence of Pharaoh and call for the release of a nation? He has nursed this desire for forty years, but when the day dawns to heed the call there is a spiritual reluctance on his part. How can he be able for this when he has failed already in attempting to deliver the slave nation? Yet past failure does not preclude him from present service. Failure in youth is no excuse for refusing to heed the call of God in later life. The early excesses of immature service do not bar him forever from entering again into the work that the Lord has for him to do.

The answer from the Lord indicates clearly the great difference that there is on this occasion. Forty years earlier he acted without the power and presence of the Lord. But now the promise is, "Certainly *I* will be with thee". The objection of Moses left the Lord out. He was only thinking of himself and his own deficiencies. Now he is reminded that he will not be alone and that the success of this service will not depend on his own prowess. This is another version of the mistake that he had made all these years before. Then he left God out because he trusted in his own strength, now he leaves God out because he feels that he has no strength. Any spiritual service is beyond the strength of one who seeks to act alone.

The sign that was given to Moses, that he would serve God upon this mountain after the Children of Israel had been delivered, required faith. Later signs would be given to the Egyptians, which would take place almost immediately, but this was not a sign given presently at the burning bush. Because the Lord was with him the people would serve God in a future day upon the very mountain where he was now standing. Moses must have faith in the word of God and be encouraged by the promise that the work would be successful and the people would leave Egypt and travel into the wilderness at Horeb. Just as the appearance of the Lord to Moses was real, so the fulfilment of the promise was sure.[†]

Verses 13-15: The Second Objection of Moses

Moses still considers himself unworthy of undertaking this service. This second objection is that he did not know the name of God. Inherent in this is a confession of a lack of knowledge of God. It is, he argues, not enough to tell the Israelites that the God of their fathers had sent him. They would wish to know His name. The gods of the Egyptians had names and the God of the Israelites must also have a name. Moses' question is not an indication that the people had completely forgotten that their God was the God of Abraham, Isaac, and Jacob. Even although many were practicing idolatry,[†] the history of their dealings with God was not totally eradicated from their memories. Moses is asking that he be able to tell the people something beyond what they had understood in the past. If he was to embark on this course of action he had to have something to bring to the Israelites that they had not understood previously. In asking for the name of God he wished to understand the essential nature and character of the God with whom he was dealing. In knowing this there would be a better understanding of how God acts.

When it was given, the name was "I am that I am". This name contains each tense of the verb "to be". Thus it could be translated "I was, I am and I shall always continue to be". In English it has been pronounced Jehovah or Yahweh. The name of God is indeed a revelation of His character, but what does this name tell us of God? Moses learns later (6.3) that the patriarchs had not known this name, although it is used in Genesis. For example:

1. The first record of this name is as part of the compound name Jehovah Elohim (2.4).

2. Abraham called on the name of Jehovah (12.8, JND).

3. Abimelech, Ahuzzath, and Phichol say to Isaac: "We saw certainly that Jehovah is with thee" (26.28, JND).

4. Jacob at Bethel promises, "then shall Jehovah be my God" (28.21, JND).

5.   Joseph is present at the blessing by Jacob of his sons when Jacob states, "I wait for thy salvation, O Jehovah" (49.18, JND).

In total the name of Jehovah is used alone or as part of a compound name of God on more than 140 occasions in Genesis. In what way, then, was the name not known? It would appear that the patriarchs did not have an understanding of the full significance of the name, because He had not made himself known to them in the character of Jehovah.† The significance of the name is about to be further revealed in redemption. Coates (at page 30) sums this up: "The Name Jehovah was used all through the book of Genesis, but what was involved in it was not known. Its significance did not come out until God intervened in grace to deliver His people from bondage so that He might have them for Himself. The Name Jehovah involved what God was as a Redeemer and Saviour God, His compassions for His people in their afflictions, and His pleasure in having them for Himself…as Jehovah He would make known what was in His heart". This is the "glorious and fearful name" of which Deuteronomy 28.58 speaks. Arguments have raged over the centuries as to how it should be pronounced. Two things, however, are clear.

First, the character of God in all its fullness cannot be expressed in one word of human language. There is a height and a depth that our minds cannot take in. He is too great, glorious, mighty, and wonderful to have all His attributes summed up in one name. If this is a perplexing truth, comfort comes from the second point to notice, that He is the eternally unchanging God. "I am that I am" clearly testifies to a God who does not change. Paul states, "By the grace of God I am what I am" (1 Cor 15.10). It was grace that had changed him and made him the man that he now was. This is very different from, "I am that I am". With Him there was no outside power which could change Him nor was any change necessary. All that He is He owes to Himself alone. His holiness, His love, and His righteousness all find their source in Him.

Thus, what is learned of Him by His acts in the past is true today. He is the God who can be relied on to be consistent and unchanging. What He had been to the patriarchs He will be to Israel. The centuries that had passed since Jacob came down to Egypt had seen great change, but God is constant. Behind all this there was a God who wished to reveal Himself to men and have them understand the God with whom they had to do. From the beginning in Genesis until the end, God is unchangeable. Above all creation there is God unchangeable, immutable, unswerving, unfailing, and immovable. The creation of a universe did not affect His character, the rebellion of angels did not embitter Him, the fall of man did not cause Him despair, and the failure of those who had faith in Him did not cause him to abandon His purpose. The God who will reign over the new heaven and the new earth is the same God who was before creation came into being. He is Jehovah! This name is to be " my name for ever…my memorial unto all generations" (v.15). In all His dealings with men down through the centuries God was to be known by the character revealed in the name Jehovah. He remains the same, from eternity to eternity.

The "I Am" of the Old Testament is the Lord Jesus of the New. He proclaims, "I am the door"; "I am the way, the truth and the life" etc, and claims with right that "if ye believe not that I am *he*, ye shall die in your sins" (Jn 8.24). The "*he*" is in italics, as the translators added it in an attempt to give what they understood to be the meaning of the verse. There was no need for this addition. The Lord was claiming to be "I am". That the Jews understood this is clearly seen in John 8.59 when, as a result of the statement made by the Lord, "Before Abraham was, I am", they took up stones to cast at Him. He had dared to take to Himself the name of God, and that to them was a crime worthy of death. They failed to understand that the One who spoke to them with such authority was none other than the One who had spoken to Moses.

Moses was told what he had to say to the Israelites (v.15): "Jehovah, the God of your fathers...hath sent me unto you". As Moses listened to the voice of God it must have been very clear that although he had not yet agreed to commence this great enterprise, the Lord was speaking as if his acceptance had been given. The greatness of the task was emphasised (vv.16-22) so that he was fully aware of what lay ahead. When God calls His servants He does not hide from them the difficulties lying ahead.

Verses 16-22: The Instruction to Go

Moses was the bringer of good tidings. He was to gather the elders together to tell them that God had "visited" (6485) them; unknown to them the Lord had been the unseen observer of all that was taking place. He had drawn near to them in their suffering; what a comfort that must have been. He was aware of their affliction, and would bring them out of Egypt into the land that had been given to them. The presence of enemies to be overcome had to be as plainly stated to Israel as it was to Moses. In doing this Moses was the messenger of good tidings to an enslaved people. We can imagine the scene as the elders gathered from all parts of the territory occupied by the nation in bondage; old men who had endured pain and sorrow, but yet had accepted the responsibility of being leaders of the people. Now they were to be brought together to hear the news for which they had waited for so long.

The response of the Israelites to this news is foretold. The elders will hearken to the voice of Moses. One would have thought that this messenger from Midian, who many may have known as the prince who had fled there forty years before, must have met refusal. His previous "interference" in their affairs had achieved nothing. Had he not escaped and for forty years left them to suffer while he enjoyed peace and a tranquil life in Midian? Was this attempt to help them likely to be any better than his first? There are, however, great differences in the approach of Moses now. He is not acting alone without consulting the elders, and he is now coming with a message from the Lord. This, combined with the growing oppression and a longing desire to be rid of their slavery, made them accept the word of Moses more readily. Above all this, however, God was working, and He would prepare the hearts of the people for the approach of His servant.

They were to request Pharaoh to allow them to go three days' journey into the wilderness and there sacrifice to Jehovah their God. This seemed to be a reasonable request that should only lead to the loss to the Egyptians of their slaves for a short period of time. Such a view, however, does not take into account the full implications of the petition. Pharaoh would be aware that should the slaves leave his land they would not return. Allegiance to Jehovah would spoil them for Egypt and the feast to be held in the wilderness would mark their break with their past life. The third day in Scripture is the day of resurrection; thus this feast would mark the new life which Israel was commencing.

In this first indication of a reason for leaving the land of slavery it should be noted that it was not their release that was emphasised. What they would receive was great indeed, but what the Lord would receive was of far greater importance. The feast in the wilderness would be an acknowledgement of fellowship, which could be enjoyed by the newly freed slaves and also enjoyed by the Lord who had brought deliverance.

Note the refusal of Pharaoh; he will rebuff any request to let these slaves go. Their presence was necessary for the economic health of the nation. This refusal would not be the end of the matter. It will be used by God to reveal His power over the Egyptians. The hand of the Lord will be "stretched out" over Egypt, signifying that it will be subject to the judgment of God. In Isaiah 9 and 10 the anger is seen in this action: "For all this his anger is not turned away, but his hand is stretched out still" (Is 9.21). When the Lord used Moses and Aaron in bringing this judgment on Egypt they stretched out their hand (8.6; 10.12; etc). Had Pharaoh acceded to the request of Moses his power would not have been broken and he could have again troubled Israel as they left Egypt behind. Moses need not be afraid of Pharaoh's temper, nor need he feel despair at this refusal. He has God's promise of victory and that will never be overturned. Enemies they will face as they journey to Canaan but Egypt will not be one of them. In the days that lay ahead the word, "and after that he will let you go", must have encouraged Moses to keep the charge laid upon him. It will be seen in later chapters that Pharaoh was forced to seek agreement by compromise, but this Moses resolutely refused. Little wonder, when the Lord had said that ultimately Pharaoh would let them go; with such a promise no compromise need be considered. Peter encourages those who serve the Lord today in a godless society when he writes, "But the God of all grace, who hath called us unto his eternal glory by Christ Jesus, *after that* ye have suffered a while, make you perfect, stablish, strengthen, settle you" (1 Pet 5.10). This gives confidence that, no matter what the present holds, eternal glory waits *after that.*

But what future will there be for a nation of slaves, destitute and lacking what is necessary for survival? Will they simply wander as paupers in the wilderness? No, they will not be impoverished, because the Egyptians will give them jewels of silver and gold and raiment and they will not go out empty. This wealth was but righteous recompense for the work that the slaves had carried out in Egypt over many years. The form in which this wealth will be given will enable the Israelites to put it upon their sons and daughters. As jewellery, the treasure was in a very portable form, and putting it upon their sons and daughters was not primarily to decorate them, but to enable them to carry it out of Egypt.

It must have been difficult for Moses to see how such a promise was to be kept. The use of the word "spoil" (5337) may at first glance seem to indicate an act of violent plunder. However, the verb can bear the meaning of "taking", or "recovering", and it is in this sense it is used here. By the events which overwhelmed Israel's oppressors the Lord changed the disposition of the Egyptians towards their slaves, as He had said He would, and they were willing to give them of their wealth. The Hebrew women made the demand, and the Egyptian women complied, possibly influenced by the death of the firstborn. The possibility of the Egyptians loading these slaves with such treasure and then allowing them their freedom was surely, before Moses stood before the burning bush, an impossible dream. With God, however, nothing is impossible. When He promises blessing it is not a dream, but a reality, which will come to pass. He delights to let us see that with Him impossibilities do not exist.

Despite the perceived difficulties which lay ahead one would have thought that Moses would now know his God well enough to rest on the promises which He had made and commence the journey to Egypt. However, his reluctance was not fully overcome and further objections still occupied his mind.

Notes

8 Other examples of this are found in Exodus 19.11; Psalm 144.5; Isaiah 31.4; and Micah 1.3.

12 This promise was fulfilled in ch.24 when the covenant of the Law was given and when Israel willingly offered the materials for the building of the Tabernacle.

13 Joshua confirms that many had endorsed the worship of idols when they were in Egypt: "Put away the gods which your fathers served on the other side of the flood, and in Egypt" (Josh 24.14). Not only in Egypt, but also in the wilderness, they had shown their willingness to worship idols. Idolatry would not be eliminated from the life of Israel until the Captivity in Babylon.

14 See Exodus 6.3, JND margin.

EXODUS 4

The Call of Moses (continued)

Verses 1-9: The Third Objection of Moses

This third objection is based on the unbelief of the Israelites. Despite the great promises given to Moses he continues to raise objections to the call of God. He turns from his own lack of ability to what he considers will be a lack of belief on the part of others. What authority will he have with his people? Is there an attempt here to place the blame for his failure at the doors of others? Are memories still fresh of the time when, despite his attempt to save an Israelite from the taskmaster, they had refused him? Even although he has a call from God he has no means of impressing on Israel that this message is of God, and therefore they will refuse to believe him, and, as a result, will not listen to him. For over 400 years there had been no direct communication from God in this manner, so how can these Israelites be convinced that the Lord had spoken to Moses, and that this was not merely another attempt by a man hungry for fame to make his mark on history?

His fears are now proving to be stronger than his belief in the promises of God. He is guilty of the same failings which he claims will be seen in the Israelites. It is doubtful if Moses realised the inconsistency of this as he was speaking. He, who was claiming that others would not listen to the word of God, was himself reluctant to obey the Lord. It had already been confirmed to Moses that "they shall hearken to thy voice" (3.18). This, therefore, is a direct contradiction of what the Lord had stated.

The answer Moses receives is most remarkable. He is given three signs by which he will be able to convince the people that he is genuine and that the Lord has appeared to him. These three signs have been called the first miracles in the Bible, but such an assertion is dependent on how "miracles" are defined.† What is clear, however, is that these signs were the first "miracles" which a man was given power to perform.

The first sign

The first sign involved the shepherd's crook or rod which Moses was holding in his hand. The question asked of him, "What is that in thine hand?", is designed to emphasise to Moses the "ordinary" nature of what God is about to use. Moses' reply confirms that he knew this to be a common shepherd's staff, such as he had carried all the years in Midian. What took place now had never taken place before. It was so unusual and outwith the known laws of creation that Moses fled. He had been told to cast the rod on the ground, and as he did so it became a serpent. Little wonder that he fled. But only half the sign had been performed. The serpent had to be taken by the tail, and as Moses caught it, no doubt with some anxiety, the serpent became a rod once more.

Such a sign would have a dramatic effect on any on-lookers. Its purpose was to confirm that the "Lord God of their fathers...hath appeared unto thee". What significance is there, however, in the nature of this sign? Various suggestions have been made.

1. The staff was the symbol of a calling which was regarded as an abomination to the Egyptians. Although a sign of this nature was used in the presence of Pharaoh (7.10), its primary purpose, as noted above, was to be used amongst the Israelites. In Egypt, however, they would be aware of the low esteem in which shepherds were held in that land. As they watched Moses they could understand from the sign that one from such a humble calling can, when God empowers him, do mighty works.

2. In leaving the shepherd life Moses would be exposed to dangers that were even greater than the "natural" dangers he would meet in leading Israel. These would cause him fear, but he would be empowered to overcome them.

3. When Aaron cast the rod down in the presence of Pharaoh (7.10) it became a serpent (8577), and as Egypt is called the great dragon (8577) by Ezekiel (29.3) there is a picture of all the terrors and oppression Pharaoh had laid upon them. The ease with which Moses could take hold of this shows how a man called of God could subdue such a tyrant.

4. All Israel would know that it was a serpent which had tempted Eve. They would understand that the serpent is constantly the enemy of the seed of the woman. The manifestation of the work of the serpent with which they were familiar was the oppression of Pharaoh. Being called of God, Moses was now fitted to take hold of this enemy and overcome him.

Consideration of these suggestions indicates that the fourth seems to fit the circumstances. There would be great fear of Pharaoh in the hearts of the Israelites, and the serpent would immediately signify the enemy with whom they were all too familiar.

There are, nevertheless, a number of other lessons which must not be missed.

1. Man is to be given a part in the destruction of the power of the serpent. Deliverance from Egypt could have been affected without the work of Moses, but the grace of God will allow man to have a part to play.

2. Man need not fear the power of the serpent. He must not treat it casually, and he must recognise its power, but he can overcome it if he obeys the Word of God.

3. Victory over the serpent restores power to man to carry out God's work. The rod which Moses held in his hand became the rod of God (v.20) and was used in the execution of God's judgment on Egypt.

The second sign

But lest Moses considered that one sign was insufficient to convince the Israelites, another two were given. Moses was told to put his hand into his bosom and when he withdrew it the hand was completely covered with leprosy. When he again put his hand into his bosom and withdrew it, the leprosy was gone and the flesh was clean once again. Leprosy is a picture of sin. The bosom is the place of care and affection. It is there that the lambs are carried (Is 40.11) and children find safety (Num 11.12). When the hand of Moses came out of his bosom, white with leprosy, it was an indication of the sinful nature of mankind and the nation of Israel in particular. This was not an outward condition only. The use of the bosom is intended to display the inward sinfulness of the heart. But as the hand emerged from the bosom the second time it was pure and free from leprosy. The message which Moses was to bring to the people taught them of the presence of sin, but brought the means of being cleansed from that sin. This cleansing was complete, and dealt with the inward sin which the leprosy portrayed.

The first and second signs deal, therefore, with the condition of man. He is held in the grip of fear and sin, both of which can be broken by the delivering power of God's message proclaimed by His servants. If the people would not believe the first sign they would believe the second. One sign may be explained away, but two will confirm the legitimacy of Moses' claims. How effective they were in substantiating Moses' message is seen in that these signs are credited with being a "voice" which would witness to Israel.

The third sign

The third sign was only to be performed if the people refused to listen to the first two. The water of the River Nile was to be taken and poured upon dry land where it would become blood. The river was the source of good for Egypt and its being turned into blood is a sign of the judgment of God. Israel was to be taught the lesson, that disobedience brings judgment, and later the Egyptians were to experience this (7.15-18). The fact, however, that it was Moses who was to take of the water of the river and pour it upon the dry ground indicates that he was to be given the power to bring this judgment upon the Egyptians. Even the river that gave them so much could be turned into a means of judgment. There is nothing too hard for the Lord! Keil & Delitzsch comment, "If Moses therefore had power to turn the life-distributing water of the Nile into blood, he must also have received power to destroy Pharaoh and his gods. Israel was to learn this from the sign, whilst Pharaoh and the Egyptians were afterwards to experience this might of Jehovah in the form of punishment".

These three signs cannot be left behind without pointing out that Moses, the man empowered to works signs and wonders and given power to bring judgment, is here a picture of the second man, the Lord Jesus.

1. It is the Lord Jesus who truly took hold of the tail of the serpent and destroyed his power.

2. The first man, Adam, brought sin into the world, but, as putting the

hand the second time into his bosom foreshadows, the second man, the Lord out of heaven, will bring cleansing for sin.

3. The Lord Jesus is the One to whom all judgment is committed, and for those who do not believe, this can be the only consequence.

Verses 10-12: The Fourth Objection of Moses

Despite all that the Lord had said, Moses was still a reluctant servant. This objection was based on his lack of fluency. He protested that he was not an eloquent man of words. This was so before the Lord spoke to him, and nothing had changed since he heard the voice of God. The inference is that he was not fitted for such a task previously, nor had the Lord fitted him yet, despite calling him to go. Thus, although Moses seemed to be highlighting his own lack of ability, there is behind his words the suggestion that the Lord must bear some of the blame for this in not giving him the ease of language which he considered to be necessary.

Nowhere had the Lord asked Moses to use smooth expressiveness in carrying out his task. If this was in his mind it was an erroneous assumption on his part. The work that Paul carried out was not based on "excellency of speech", nor did he use "enticing words of man's wisdom" (1 Cor 2.1,4). God does not need the sweet-lipped persuasion of the orator, clever with words. It is probable, however, that Moses had something much more basic in view. He simply felt that he could not speak publicly. He found speech difficult, not that he stammered much, but it was difficult for him to articulate his message in public.

The reply of the Lord was telling. It consisted of questions to which Moses well knew the answer, and then, a command to go. "Who hath made man's mouth?" (v.11). Did the Lord not know what ability Moses had in speech? Was it not He who had made him? How foolish did this make Moses' objection. The Lord who called is the Lord who creates and He fashions us as He will. But another question arises. Has the Lord not made the dumb, the deaf, the seeing, and the blind? Even those who have disabilities have come from the hand of God and He knows how they are. The inference is that the Lord will make no mistakes, because He understands, not just how fitted His servants are to serve Him, but also any incapacity from which they may suffer. He does not call those to serve in a way for which they are not fitted. It is worth noting that those who are disabled are considered to be of value to Him. Their lack of, for example, sight, hearing, speech does not diminish them before the Lord.

The comment of Stephen should be noted when speaking of Moses as a prince in Egypt (Acts 7.22). He states that he was "mighty in words and in deeds". This shows that the excuse which Moses was making was not valid and that he did have the ability to speak publicly.

The command was short and direct. "Go, and I will be with thy mouth and teach thee what thou shalt say" (v.12). Moses was not being called to do that for which he was not fitted. Both the ability and the message would be given to him. He must rely on the Lord for this, and, doing so, he would be able to carry out the commission. Moses must have felt that he had exhausted every possible excuse. Graciousness had marked the dealings of God with him. He had answered with patience every matter that had been raised, but there appeared to be no movement on the part of this reluctant shepherd.

Verses 13-17: The Fifth Objection of Moses

He, however, still had one more point to make. He had no excuses, and now he stated that it is the prerogative of the Lord to send whom He will. This may read like a full-hearted willingness to go, but the response of the Lord would indicate otherwise. Moses understood that the Lord could send him if He so wished, but it was clearly a reluctant acceptance. In the light of the call to go now, any enthusiasm that he might still have had for the venture before he saw the bush burning, had gone. It was no doubt good to dream about such an expedition into Egypt, but when he was now suddenly faced with the reality of it his courage had deserted him. He was willing to turn his back on the Lord and let another servant carry out the work. If the Lord had permitted him to retire at this point, he might have led a quieter life without the problems and trials that lay ahead of him, but he would eternally have been the loser.

What a contrast this is with the Perfect Servant of Jehovah whose ear the Lord had opened. Having heard the word of God and the pathway which lay ahead of Him, He "was not rebellious, neither turned away back" (Is 50.5). When faced with the present reality of the pathway that He had to travel, He did not rebel and refuse to go, and having commenced He did not turn back; He set His face like a flint (Is 50.7). How different from the attitude of Moses who may not have rebelled but nevertheless showed no enthusiasm for the commission!

At last the anger of the Lord is kindled against Moses. This is one of only two occasions when Moses is stated to have caused God anger, the other being in connection with Moses smiting the rock, rather than speaking to it as was instructed by the Lord. In referring to this incident later (Deut 1.37) he states that the Lord was "angry with me for your sakes, saying, Thou also shalt not go in thither". These words were spoken by the Lord as the waters flowed out from the rock (Num 20.12). On this first occasion Moses was guilty of seeking to avoid what the Lord required; on the second he went far beyond what the Lord required. In the first he was too backward, in the second he was too forward.

Aaron, Moses' brother, on hearing of the departure of Moses from Midian would journey to meet him. He could speak well and, due to Moses' refusal, Aaron would speak for him. With this the obdurate refusals of Moses are silenced, but at what a cost. Aaron was now to be closely associated with Moses in the work which lay ahead, and in the presence of men he, as the spokesman, would appear at times to have the more prominent part. Moses was not to be set aside as the chief of the two, for Aaron was simply his "mouth" and Moses was to be to Aaron "instead of God". The communications which Aaron had to pass on to others would not come to him directly from the Lord, but through Moses, thus emphasising the leading role which Moses played. In this way Aaron would stand in relationship to Moses as a prophet stood in relationship to God. As the prophet spoke only when given the words by the Lord, so Aaron would speak only when given the words by Moses.

In the years to come, how often would Moses reflect on this day and regret the part which he allowed Aaron to have? It was Aaron who was the leader of the people during the absence of Moses when he was up the mount with God, when the golden calf was fashioned, and the idolatrous worship from Egypt practised in the Camp (ch.32). But not only was he the leader of rebellion against God, he was prepared to go along with others who rebelled. When Miriam and Aaron murmured in jealousy against Moses it is clear that Miriam was the leader, as her name is first recorded, "Miriam and Aaron spake against Moses", but Aaron went along with her (Num 12). It appears that Aaron was not a leader, but was willing to be led by others; by the people in the matter of the golden calf and by a member of his own family in the matter of the murmuring against Moses. Leaders must be stronger than this.

But as a final instruction Moses was told to take his rod which had already been used to show the power of God. It would now be the rod of God with which signs would be performed. This looked forward to the judgments on Egypt and by this means the authority of Moses would be confirmed.

Lessons from Moses' objections

At last Moses' voice is silenced. The objections have all been voiced and answered, and the future has to be faced. There are a number of lessons which can be summarised.

1. Whereas it is not good for those who serve Him to overvalue themselves in the service of God, neither must they exhibit false humility. There is a great difference between pride and an acknowledgement of being gifted for service.

2. There must be no refusal of His call on the basis of an argument that the one called is unfit for the task. This is accusing the Lord of having made a mistake by calling us without giving us what is necessary for the work that He wishes us to carry out. When God calls it must be recognised that He will fit those whom He calls for His service. Whatever gifts He has given will not be the object of pride. It must be understood that this is not the doing of the servant, and that all has come from His hand to fit for service.

3. The Lord does not need any of us to carry out His work, but in grace He permits the privilege of serving. The power for the work is not the

servant's, as the disciples learned when the Lord was on the Mount of Transfiguration. They attempted to do the work in their own strength and, as a result, found that the power which they used so effectively in the past was no longer available (Mk 9.14-29).

Verses 18-19: Encouragement for Moses

The return of Moses to Jethro was for the purpose of asking permission to travel to Egypt. There was no reluctance on the part of Jethro to allow Moses to go. Moses did not tell his father-in-law all that had taken place; he only stated that he would return to his brethren to "see whether they be yet alive". It was after he had committed himself to obey the Lord that he received further encouragement. The Lord revealed to him that those who sought his life in Egypt were now dead. Moses had not raised this problem, and the question is, Why? Perhaps it was that the early promise, "Certainly I will be with thee" (3.12), had silenced this thought before it took words. It has also been suggested that the "late" mention of enemies in Egypt indicated that there was a period of time between Moses obtaining the permission of Jethro to leave, and the Lord telling him to go. During this time all those in Egypt who would have been a danger to Moses die, and then the Lord speaks when conditions are right. There is no indication, however, that such a period of time elapsed, and even if there was such a delay, no indication that it was for the purpose of awaiting the death of Moses' enemies. It is more likely that the Lord speaks in this way so that should fear grip Moses he has the promise of God that he will not meet those whom he knew years before and who would recall the command of Pharaoh that he should be put to death. Here is the way of God with His servants, leading them gently along the pathway of obedience and confirming each step as it is taken in faith.

Verses 20-23: The Return to Egypt

Moses must now have felt confident about his safety as he took his wife and two sons with him on the journey to Egypt. What emotions must have been in his heart as he retraced the steps which he had taken forty years earlier. There had been no instruction from the Lord to take his family but he felt that they should be together as this work was carried out. Later, after returning to Midian, the family were reunited with Moses following the departure of the Israelites from Egypt (ch.18).

As this little family group travelled along the road, Moses grasping the rod of God in his hand, and leading on foot, his wife and two sons seated upon the ass, they scarcely looked likely to cause any problem to Pharaoh. Their insignificance and obvious weakness was plain to see, and yet this was the man who was to bring judgment on Egypt. Again it can be seen that God had chosen the weak things of the world to confound the things that are mighty.

On the way the Lord appears to him again. All the signs which the Lord will give Moses to do he will carry out. This covers not only the signs that he has already performed but also all those that the Lord will bring on Egypt because of the refusal of Pharaoh to let the Israelites go free.

Two further revelations are given to Moses at this time. First, the Lord will harden the heart of Pharaoh. A heart which has been hardened can no longer be moved. It is closed to all influences and indifferent to any appeal. At times it is stated that the Lord hardened the heart of Pharaoh and at times it is recorded that Pharaoh hardened his own heart.[†] Thus the hardening of Pharaoh's heart is seen to be God's work and yet also to be his own work.

The sovereignty of God is seen in this, because it was due to this hardening that ultimately the Passover took place and the people were redeemed by blood. No matter what takes place in the human heart God will work all things out according to His purpose. Once again, before the plagues come, Moses is told that the Lord will harden Pharaoh's heart (7.3). When the plagues came and Pharaoh refused to move from his position that he would not let the people go, it is stated after the first five refusals that Pharaoh hardened his heart. It is only after the sixth plague that the Lord hardened Pharaoh's heart. Even after his magicians were prepared to acknowledge that the finger of God was in the plagues which had troubled his people he refused to bow his will to the will of God (8.19). A determined, increasingly obstinate unbelief is seen in his response to the work of God.

In the case of Pharaoh, therefore, his refusal to believe resulted in his heart being hardened. As he hardened his heart so the Lord then hardened it. In a similar fashion God gives over to the consequences of their sin, those who deliberately refuse to believe Him (Rom 1.24-28). This does not suggest that the sovereign acts of God are only reactions to the actions of men. But it does let us see the grace of God in allowing Pharaoh more than one opportunity to soften his heart and to listen to the message of God, bow his will to it, and enjoy the blessings of obedience. Rather he took a pathway which resulted in judgment for himself and for his people, ultimately leading to death in the Red Sea.

If the first new revelation to Moses had to do with the Egyptians, the second had to do with Israel. For the first time it is revealed that Israel is Jehovah's "son", His "firstborn". Israel could rejoice in a relationship so close that it is expressed in terms of sonship. Israel has been chosen for this honour out of all peoples (Deut 14.2) based on the sovereign choice of God, a choice which was first revealed when Abram was called out of Ur of the Chaldees. But more than a son, Israel is the "firstborn", a term indicating a son who has privileges and responsibilities above others.

Now a final warning is given to Moses to bring before Pharaoh. If he will not let Jehovah's firstborn go free, he and his people will lose their firstborn. It is the principle that "whatsover a man soweth that shall he also reap" put into practice. If Pharaoh will refuse to let Jehovah enjoy His firstborn as they make a feast to Him in the wilderness, the Egyptians will not be allowed to enjoy their firstborn.

Verses 24-26: The Meeting at the Inn

This remarkable incident, which is so briefly mentioned, is one of grave importance. It is clear that in the house of Moses there had been serious departure from the terms of the covenant which was established between the Lord and Abraham. One of the sons of Moses had not been circumcised. It may be that Zipporah was responsible for the omission as she carried out the act when the Lord intervened, but Moses was still responsible for what took place in his household.

Many may not regard this as anything but a trifling departure which can be excused due to the fact that Moses had so long been away from his people. It was not that he was unaware of the need to circumcise his sons, for clearly this had been performed on one of them, possibly the elder, leaving only one to be circumcised by his mother. Apart from all other considerations, the fact that Moses had been in the presence of God should have spurred him on to have this act of obedience carried out.

The action of the Lord appears to be extreme after all the grace and patience which He has shown towards His servant. "The Lord met him, and sought to kill him" (v.24). It is not revealed how this came about. It may have been through illness, accident, or attack, but he did recognise, as did his wife, that this was the hand of God. Even better to note is that they understood the reason for this having taken place. This poses questions.

1. Why did the Lord seek to slay him? Surely it was necessary that there were no inconsistencies in the life of Moses as he set out on his work. The failure to circumcise a son was a serious omission which would compromise his authority amongst the people.

2. Why was this not raised earlier? The Lord is slow to anger and Moses had been given time to repent from this sin, but he had not done so. Now, rather than have a disobedient servant, the Lord would prevent him continuing.

For us the lesson is clear. Known sin, whether of commission or of omission, is a serious issue in our lives. It compromises our service for the Lord. In this particular case the act of circumcision pictures the cutting off of the flesh. If the servant fails to do this and allows his body to control him, letting the flesh direct his actions, he will be disapproved for service. It is this issue which Paul addresses in 1 Corinthians 9. To allow his body free reign and not "keep it under" will cost him the prize at the end of the race.

It has already been observed that it was Zipporah who carried out the act of circumcision. She realised that the alternatives were either to lose Moses or to have her son circumcised. She chose the latter. Her act and her words add weight to the view that she was responsible for the failure to have the circumcision performed earlier. She may not have appreciated its importance and may have regarded it as mere mutilation. Her twice repeated words to Moses that he was "a bloody husband", and her behaviour at this time, almost indicate that she acted with some reluctance, blaming Moses for the necessity to do that from which she had previously recoiled. But why does she use such strange language, referring to Moses as a "bridegroom of blood" (RV)? Clearly she understood that she would lose her husband. The only way to have him restored to her was by the blood of their son.

It may have been this incident which prompted Moses to send his wife and children back to her father. As far as the child was concerned it would be easier for him not continue on the road to Egypt after the act of circumcision. He could also have recognised that Zipporah would have found it difficult to go through what he would have to endure in the months ahead. In this action Moses displays a care for his family and also a realisation that he could serve with greater freedom of movement when he did not have his wife and family to consider.

Verses 27-31: Return to Egypt

At last the journey to Egypt can be completed, but on the way, as the Lord had told him, he met his brother Aaron who had been instructed by the Lord to travel into the wilderness, to the Mount of God. We cannot be sure that there had been no communication between the two brothers over the forty year period when Moses was in Midian, but this must have been a most memorable meeting. Aaron listened with interest as Moses told him all that the Lord had said and all the signs which had been given, while Moses knew that it was his own obstinacy which had given Aaron a part in the great work which lay ahead.

On their arrival in Egypt Aaron immediately became his spokesman, as the Lord had ordered. The words of the Lord given to the elders of Israel and the performance of the signs before them convinced them that the Lord had sent Moses. Despite the years of oppression and the idolatry of many, there still remained in them the hope of deliverance, and at last the deliverer had come. The nation that had rejected him forty years before was now ready to accept him. The scene is solemn as the elders bow their heads and worship. No higher response can they make.

Notes

2 See Appendix 1: *The Character of Miracles in Scripture*.
21 The Lord hardened Pharaoh's heart: Exodus 4.21; 7.3,13; 9.12; 10.1,20,27; 11.10; 14.4,8.
Pharaoh hardened his heart: Exodus 7.14; 7.22; 8.15; 8.19; 8.32; 9.7; 9.34,35.

EXODUS 5

Confrontation with Pharaoh

It may be considered strange that so many chapters of the book are devoted to the confrontation which took place between Moses and Pharaoh. The nature of the issue must be understood, and then there will be an appreciation of why it is regarded as worthy of being dealt with in this detailed way.

This confrontation was not between two men, but between Jehovah and the gods of Egypt (12.12); it was between Jehovah and the Adversary. These issues are great and involve the whole purpose of God for this world. There must, therefore, be significance in how God acted. In all of the dealings of the Adversary with men the fundamental issue has been the antagonism which he displays to the Lord. His purpose is to oppose God, and men and women are used by him to achieve this end. This long dialogue between the ruler of Egypt and the leader of the Israelites is an example of the obdurate refusal of men under the power of the Adversary to yield to the Word of God. It is also an example of the grace of God in allowing Pharaoh opportunities to repent. We know that if it had been His will Jehovah could have slain the firstborn in Egypt at the first judgment, or even delivered the Israelites without Egypt having to endure the succeeding judgments which rolled over the land. This He did not do, but, sadly, Pharaoh did not understand that this was proof that Jehovah was longsuffering. He despised "the riches of his goodness and forbearance and longsuffering; not knowing that the goodness of God leadeth...to repentance" (Rom 2.4).

The comment of Edersheim is worthy of note: "The predicted trial was...to establish two facts for all ages, and to all mankind. In the sight of Egypt (7.5) and of Israel (10.2) it was to evidence that God was Jehovah, the only true and living God, far above all power of men and of gods (9.14). This was one aspect of the judgments which were to burst upon Egypt (Rom 9.17). The other was that He was the faithful Covenant-God, who remembered His promises, and would bring out His people 'with a stretched out arm and with great judgments', to take them to Himself for a people, and to be to them a God (6.1-8). These are the eternal truths which underlie the history of Israel's deliverance from Egypt" (*Bible History: Old Testament*).

Verses 1-9: Moses' First Audience with Pharaoh
The message from the Lord delivered

After a period of time, which probably was of short duration, Moses and Aaron entered the presence of Pharaoh to bring to him a message from the Lord. The Lord had assured Moses that he would come to no harm from the king, but this entrance into the palace required courage. What did Moses feel as he entered the royal portals after an absence of forty years? He had lived here as an honoured member of the court, but was returning as a despised shepherd. It may seem strange that he was not recognised. That "all the men are dead which sought thy life" (4.19) would have removed the fear which otherwise Moses may have felt is clear, and there was no attempt to hide their identity. Pharaoh addressed them as "Moses and Aaron" (v.4). Forty years may appear to be a long time, but memories of Moses would surely have been alive with some, and the mention of his name would stir these old memories again. It may be that the Lord ordered events so that this Moses was not linked with the events of a generation earlier; it may have been that the circumstances behind Moses' flight were at the time deliberately kept close so that no "dishonour" would come upon the royal house; it may be that the Pharaoh before whom Moses and Aaron stood simply regarded the events to have been so long before that they did not warrant any action after so many years. When God overrules He can do so in many different ways, and use many differing circumstances.

There were two matters which Moses wished to impress upon the king. First, the Israelites were not Pharaoh's people. He may have regarded them as such and treated them as his personal property, but he would have done well to heed the message. Jehovah called them "my people". Pharaoh was thus claiming ownership over what did not belong to him. In this he was no different from Satan, his master, who claims ownership over this world and its peoples. Second, the Lord desired that this people should be let go in order to travel into the wilderness and make a feast to Him. As they were His people He had the right to make this demand. This was the first intimation of such a request to the monarch, but the two visitors clearly stated that the message had come from the Lord God of Israel. Nothing was hidden.

When the Lord spoke to Moses the request to be put to Pharaoh was that the Hebrews should go "three days' journey into the wilderness, that we may sacrifice to the Lord our God" (3.18). These sacrifices were now seen as "a feast" to the Lord in the wilderness. Thus the sacrifices, which would consist of burnt offerings, were a feast for the enjoyment of the Lord. In Genesis, burnt offerings are the only offerings noted, and no further instruction was given regarding sacrifices until Leviticus 1. In sacrificing to the Lord, the Hebrews would express their thankfulness for their deliverance from Egypt, but the sacrifices were also a feast to be enjoyed in heaven. Salvation not only gives the saved something, but also gives the Lord that which is for His enjoyment as He receives joy and satisfaction from the thankful sacrifices of redeemed souls, who have come into the good of this great work, and express this in worship.

The reply of Pharaoh
In reply Pharaoh had two points to make. He stated categorically that

he did not know Jehovah, and as a result he would not obey Him. In this
he was completely honest, as the Lord God of Israel was not known to
Pharaoh. This was not merely because of his birth or background. Others
who were not of Israel had come to know the Lord God of Israel. Moses'
father-in-law is an example of this. The deeper reason for this ignorance
was spiritual, and, like those who today do not know the Lord, he would
not be obedient to the Lord. Coming to know the Lord God of Israel was
a spiritual matter and Pharaoh had no liking for that. As Pharaoh will endure
the judgment of God for his disobedience based on his ignorance of God,
so Paul in 2 Thessalonians sets out the same principle. The Lord Jesus will
be revealed in judgment, "In flaming fire taking vengeance on them that
know not God, and obey not the gospel of our Lord Jesus Christ" (1.8). At
this stage the quick response of Pharaoh indicated that he cared little to
give any time or attention to this trivial interruption. He did not know the
Lord God of the Israelites and he had no intention of seeking to know
Him. So, today, those who do not know the Lord do not obey Him. His
Word is set aside as irrelevant to this present age, and it is often the object
of scorn and baseless mirth.

   This lack of the knowledge of God lies at the root of all the problems
besetting the human race. Paul took this up as his cue as he preached the
gospel on Mars Hill in Athens (Acts 17.23), when he declared that he had
come to tell them of the God whom they did not know. The altar that he
saw may well have been raised as a precautionary measure. Legend has it
that it was raised because of the deliverance of Athens from a plague after
homage was made to the "unknown god". No matter what the background,
the Athenians were careful to ensure that they omitted no god in their
gallery of deities, but Paul turned this on them by preaching, "Him declare
I unto you". It is of course a wise individual who acknowledges the existence
of God as he views creation, but to know God is only possible through the
Lord Jesus Christ. Thus it is that the eternal life that He gives has as its
purpose "that they might know thee the only true God, and Jesus Christ,
whom thou hast sent" (Jn 17.3). The knowledge of God is bound up with
the knowledge of the Lord Jesus, and, as we have already asserted, it is not
possible to come to know God without knowing His Son.

Moses and Aaron continue their request
   Upon the refusal of Pharaoh, Moses and Aaron added to the request
that they had made. They speak now, not of the Lord God of Israel, but of
the God of the Hebrews. That these slaves were known as Hebrews is
clear for the exclamation from the lips of Pharaoh's daughter on seeing
the babe taken from amongst the bulrushes: "This is one of the Hebrews'
children" (2.6). The word "Hebrew" (5680) seems to be associated with a
word meaning, "the region on the other side, situated across a stream or
across the sea", or "the river crosser". It is used firstly to describe "Abram
the Hebrew" (Gen 14.13) at the time when Lot and his family had been

taken captive by the troops of the alliance which fought against Sodom and Gomorrah. By the law of first mention we see, therefore, that the title indicates separation. Abraham was the man who had left his home and had gone to the other side of the Euphrates. It was only such a man living a separated life who could deliver Lot from his captivity.

Here the use of the name by the Egyptians and by Moses and Aaron at this time showed that they were still a separated people. God does not look on them as He looks on other nations. It may be that the Egyptians used the title, through the word having been taken into their language, without any real understanding of its significance, or it may be that even they appreciated that the Hebrews were different from others. No matter what the Egyptians considered the name to mean, its use here clearly shows that, despite the long years in Egypt, this people were still the "Hebrews".

The original request made to Pharaoh is now expanded in two ways. In leaving Egypt they have to go a three-day journey into the wilderness. From the standpoint of Pharaoh this was as good as bidding them farewell. Although they were only asking for a short respite, the king knew that, having gone three days' journey, they would be beyond the reach of his power and they might not return. Having, for three days, enjoyed freedom from oppression they would not lightly come back under the yoke.

Spiritually, the number three has great significance. It was on the third day that Abraham and Isaac came to the mountain in Moriah which the Lord had told him of, and on that day he received Isaac back to life again in a figure (Gen 22). It was on the third day that the Lord Jesus rose from the tomb. This day is, therefore, the day of resurrection, the day when new life commences. Thus this feast, to be held on the third day in the wilderness, would mark the beginning of a new life for Israel.

In addition, there is now a note of warning in the words of these two messengers. If Pharaoh refused to let the people go God would fall on the *Israelites* with pestilence or with the sword (v.3). The price of their disobedience was to meet trouble and violent death. This should have been a warning to Pharaoh. If the God of Israel is so jealous of His honour that He will punish His own people for not obeying Him, no matter the reason, how much more should Egypt fear Him?

The underlying lessons to be learned from this first confrontation between the servants of God and the man who stood at the head of the greatest "world system" of the day is clear. The world was claiming the Hebrews for its own service. It demanded everything from them with the object of using them to build up the treasures and resources of Egypt. It is true that, in typical form, these people had not yet known the power of the blood to save them from death, but we can recognise that Satan, through Pharaoh, was determined to keep them under his sway in the kingdom of darkness.

Pharaoh orders the Hebrews' burden to be increased

The reaction of Pharaoh to Moses' request is to make the burdens of the Hebrews even greater. He dismisses them as "the people of the land", those who are only fit for what was regarded as lowly work. The Egyptians did not see the dignity in honest labour; these were "land people" as distinct from the ruling classes. The materials for carrying out their tasks were no longer to be given to the Hebrews. They were obviously idle when they were asking for time away from their labours. The means of driving such thoughts from their minds was to add to their oppression.

At this point a little more insight is given into how the Egyptians organised the slave labour teams. Over them there were taskmasters, Egyptians charged with obtaining the maximum effort from the slaves. They would occupy a management role in organising the work. Under them were "their officers" (writers - 7860) who were Israelites (v.14) responsible for distributing the work amongst the slaves and ensuring that it was completed satisfactorily. These clerks prepared the tally of the bricks in order to report back to the taskmasters on the quantity manufactured on a daily basis. They did not occupy a favoured place as they were beaten when the work fell short of the impossible demands placed upon them (v.14).

The edict proclaimed was to the effect that the straw used in brick making was no longer to be delivered to the slaves. They had to gather this themselves, but there was to be no decrease in the quantities of brick to be produced. It was the practice to gather the stubble left after the corn had been reaped, or the corn which was lying flat and could not be harvested. This was chopped up and mixed with the clay, giving greater strength to the bricks, which were then left to dry in the hot sun.

The designs of Satan have not changed. Where there is in any heart the seed of a desire to be gone from the kingdom of darkness into the kingdom of God's dear Son (Col 1.13) he will seek to increase the hold of the world and detain his subjects by driving from their minds all thought of freedom and worship. Ensuring that they are fully occupied with meeting the demands which the world places upon them means that they will have little or no time to consider a journey out of slavery into glorious freedom.

This means of occupying fully the minds and the time of men, and driving from them any thought of salvation, is still one of the main methods of Satan in seeking to keep his hold over individuals. The pace of life and the demands of a greedy and cold-hearted world are as real today as they were in Egypt. He attempts to prevent any time being left to the believer for prayer and the service of God, and for the unbeliever, any moments when there can be reflection on eternal issues must be thwarted.

Verses 10-19: Increased Oppression and its Result

As a result of the meeting with Pharaoh, the people were scattered throughout the land searching for straw, as the taskmasters drove them on to meet their daily tally of production. The Egyptians made little, if any, provision for them, and stubble was all that they were able to gather. We should note that before this, although the Israelites were slaves, they had time to grow some crops including leeks, onions, and garlic (Deut 11.10; Num 11.5). Now this time was severely curtailed, and the whole tenor of their lives was changed. Pharaoh asserted that the request to go three days' journey into the wilderness indicated that the Hebrews were idle and were in fact able to meet their targets with time left over. Moreover, any time spent sacrificing to the Lord was "wasted" time, just as today the world regards any time, material, or energy that is put into the service of the Lord as being wasted. "Better" could have been done with it just as "better" use could have been made of the alabaster box of ointment which Mary of Bethany used to anoint the Lord Jesus (Jn 12.5). All this is worldly thinking which displays nothing of true appreciation of what is valued in heaven.

It is clear that the taskmasters obeyed the command of the king ruthlessly. There was no sympathy for the slaves, only a cold hearted determination to punish them for their failure to meet the impossible targets given to them, such failure being regarded by their taskmasters as acts of disobedience. Despite this, the "officers", or "writers", appeared before Pharaoh to plead the cause of the people, perhaps because they did not consider that Pharaoh was aware of the harsh treatment under which they were labouring. They were disappointed. The edict was confirmed and the people were left under no illusion that Pharaoh intended their lives to be harsher.

Verses 20-23: The Hebrews Complain to Moses

There was great anxiety amongst the Hebrew slaves. Their writers met Moses and Aaron who waited for them as they came fresh from the audience with the king. The early ready acceptance by the Hebrews of the mission of Moses had now changed. The fact that the writers had approached Pharaoh shows that Moses was being challenged and this continued as they met following the audience with the monarch. The Hebrews could not see what good was coming of this and said that the Lord would look upon him and Aaron and judge whether their conduct had been right or not. What the slaves felt can be understood in measure, but how fickle they were. Rather than see that the Egyptians were ripe for judgment they stated that it was the conduct of Moses and Aaron which should be under the scrutiny of heaven.

It is of credit to Moses that in his distress he turned to God. How remarkable are the closing two verses of the chapter. These are not the irreverent words of a rebel. They voiced the genuine concerns of a faithful servant. He had carried out the task with which he had been charged, but there had been no deliverance. "Wherefore hast *thou* so evil entreated this people?", he cried, recognising that ultimately all things are in the control of the Lord, and thus he asked the question. He could not see the way ahead and was looking for an explanation as to why he had been sent. Before this turn of events he thought he understood the purpose of his mission, but now that confidence had gone. Looking at the events that followed it can be understood why Pharaoh had responded as he did, but Moses did not know what lay ahead and he was perplexed. How many servants have felt as Moses did. When events take an unexpected turn and seem to go wrong, the question, "Why?", comes quickly to our lips. How much the poorer would we have been if the Lord had put it into the heart of Pharaoh to let the people go at this time. Let us consider a number of reasons why events took this "turn for the worse".

1. Pharaoh had to be given an opportunity to repent and to acknowledge the Lord. If he had listened to the voice of the Lord it would have been an indication that his heart had been moved by the request that had been made, and that he had come to know Jehovah.

2. The true nature of Egypt had to be made plain to Israel. Their cruelty had been revealed over the past eighty years, but their complete rebellion against God, despite the many opportunities to obey, must be clearly seen. Israel's love for things Egyptian comes out in the wilderness, even although their memories were very selective, forgetting their oppression (16.3; 32.1-4), but the lesson to be learned is that things Egyptian are associated with a people who not only do not know Jehovah, but who are utterly opposed to Him.

3. The Hebrews had to be brought to a point where their situation was hopeless. By this they would be in no doubt that their deliverance, when it did come, was of the Lord. In redemption there is no place for man taking some of the credit that belongs to Him alone.

4. There was a greater picture, which Moses could not at that time see. He and the people were about to add to these things that were "written aforetime" (Rom 15.4) so that others in succeeding generations would learn the lessons concerning the judgment of God on sin, redemption by blood, and how to approach God.

5. Obeying the will of God does not always lead to kinder circumstances. Obeying the Lord when He said, "Let us pass over unto the other side" (Mk 4.35), brought the disciples into a storm which they would never have encountered if they had not followed Him. The faithful preaching of John Baptist led him to imprisonment. Doubts and fears may grip the heart when this occurs but His servants are cast on the Lord to take them through. It may be difficult to appreciate this truth but, despite appearances to the contrary, He is working out all things for our good. It was difficult for the Hebrews to see that at this time, but ultimately they would cross the Red Sea and see the armies of Egypt totally overthrown.

EXODUS 6

Promises from the Lord Restated

Verse 1: The Lord's Promise to Deliver

Such a plea as has risen from the lips of Moses will be answered, for the "effectual fervent prayer of a righteous man availeth much" (Jas 5.16). The response from the Lord is that what has taken place is not an indication that the Lord will not deliver His people. Indeed Moses will see what the Lord will do to Pharaoh. That obstacle to the release of this captive nation will be tackled at its source. They will not go out by the use of guile, nor will they have to fight battles to leave Egypt. That they will go is certain, but the description of the manner of their going must have amazed Moses after the reaction of the king. Israel will leave Egypt and it will be Pharaoh who will insist that they go. He will not do this unwillingly but will thrust them out of the land. They will be expelled from Egypt, no longer welcome there. God, therefore, will deal with Pharaoh, until he submits to the will of God and ceases his rebellion.

In dealing with Pharaoh in such a way, we see how God deals with all rebellion. There will come a day when "at the name of Jesus every knee should bow, of things in heaven, and things in earth, and things under the earth; And that every tongue should confess that Jesus Christ is Lord, to the glory of God the Father" (Phil 2.10-11). This does not mean that all will be saved, but all will acknowledge that God has to be obeyed. On that day of which Philippians 2 speaks, the manifest triumph of God will be such that there will be no other way but to acknowledge that "Jesus Christ is Lord". Those who have refused to trust Him by faith will be forced to acknowledge His Lordship by His overwhelming power.

There are times when it is not possible for His servants to see how His purpose will be accomplished. The problems seem so great and the barriers insurmountable. Circumstances in Egypt from the human standpoint did not seem hopeful, but it was the Lord who was at work, and the journey to the land promised to them would begin in the manner which He had declared. Similar impossible circumstances faced Jeremiah, not in respect of the initial possession of the land, but in relation to the land being possessed again after defeat at the hands of the Babylonians (Jer 32). He had bought a field in Anathoth, for "the right of redemption" was his to buy it. But was this not a foolish thing to do as the Babylonians had already captured that ground and Jeremiah would never be able to enjoy his purchase? He was confident, however, that the word of the "Lord of hosts, the God of Israel; (that) Houses and fields and vineyards shall be possessed again in this land" (v.15) would come to pass. Nevertheless, as he looked around it could not be seen how this could be. "Behold the mounts" (v.24), he cries; the siege engines around Jerusalem but indicate that the city will shortly fall and the Babylonian triumph. The answer of the Lord to the cry,

"Behold the mounts", is, "Behold, I am the Lord, the God of all flesh: is there any thing too hard for me?" (v.27). With Him nothing is impossible and the lesson which Jeremiah learned is one that was taught to Moses generations earlier.

So it is with Pharaoh; there is nothing too hard for the Lord. He will be given opportunity after opportunity to submit to the will of God, but, having refused to do so, he will be forced to yield by a display of overwhelming power. It is of interest to note that the display of this power in a coming day will be preceded by the wrath of God falling on a rebellious earth, followed by the deliverance of Israel. What we are about to see worked out in Egypt is the judgment of God falling on a rebellious nation, followed by the deliverance of Israel.

After this initial assertion, the Lord has some further words of comfort for Moses (vv.2-5), and then gives him the reply to bring to the people (vv.6-8). Let us look firstly at the words of comfort.

Verses 2-5: The Comfort of Past Dealings with God

To Abraham and Isaac He had appeared as God Almighty, but now He was to be known as Jehovah, the never changing One. Reference is made to the significance of this name in the commentary on 3.13-14. It is on this basis that He reminds Moses of the covenant which had been made with the patriarchs regarding the land of Canaan. Jehovah will not change his purpose because of the obstinate refusal of Pharaoh. The covenant has been established, never to change.

But Jehovah is not only the God of the covenant; He is also the God of compassion. The groaning of the slaves had been heard in heaven and Jehovah remembered His covenant. It is almost unnecessary to state that when Jehovah "remembered" there was no suggestion that He had forgotten. It indicated, rather, that the suffering of the Hebrews was not a sign that Jehovah had become indifferent. The covenant was remembered, and had been from the day when it was given.

Verses 6-8: The Sevenfold Promise of Deliverance

Now here is the message which Moses was to bring to the people. It commenced with the grand opening words, "I am Jehovah". On that basis a seven-fold promise is given to the nation.

1. *I will bring you out from under the burdens of the Egyptians.* No longer will they be slaves. They will leave Egypt behind and it will no longer be where they live.

2. *I will rid you out of their bondage.* Against the fear that the Egyptians might pursue them and enslave them in the land to which they are going, this promise is made. They will not only be redeemed out of the land of slavery, but they will be delivered from slavery itself. The bondage of Egypt will no longer oppress them.

3. *I will redeem you with a stretched out arm, and with great judgments.*

This promise tells them how such deliverance will be carried out. It will not be by their power or military prowess. The deliverance will be the work of the Lord alone and will be "great". The "stretched out arm" is a sign of the judgment of God falling on a people. It reminds us of the hand of Jehovah which is "stretched out still" against Israel, a sign that "His anger is not turned away" (Is 9.12,17,21; 10.4). So the anger of the Lord will be kindled against Egypt and His arm will be stretched out in judgment.

4. *I will take you to me for a people.* Not only is there a promise of redemption, but also there is the promise of a relationship with Jehovah. This nation of freed slaves will have a unique and special relationship with Him.

5. *I will be to you a God.* Jehovah will be their God. They will not be left abandoned after their departure from the land of their agonies, but they will have a God who will care for them and protect them. As their God He will be worthy of their homage and of their praise.

6. *I will bring you into the land.* There is an already decided destination and their arrival there is guaranteed. Just as their deliverance from Egypt was not their work, so their arrival in the land will not be by their own strength, He will bring them in, and by doing this He will fulfil the promise which was made to Abraham and which was confirmed by the Lord, lifting up His hand (AV margin) in affirmation.

7. *I will give it to you for an heritage.* In that land they will not be aliens, but they will possess it and enjoy it. From dwelling in a land where they possessed nothing they will be taken to a land that will be all for them and for their pleasure.

As at the beginning, so at the end there is the ringing pronouncement, "I am the Lord"; a promise that is encircled by the power of Jehovah. This is a reaffirmation of the promise given to Moses when the Lord appeared to him in the backside of the desert.

Verses 9-13: The Response of the Children of Israel

It is without surprise that we read of the deep distress and despair which gripped the hearts of the Israelites. With the coming of Moses they must have been filled with anticipation that, at last, the years of oppression were about to come to an end. Now disappointment had cast its shadow over them and "anguish", a feeling of anxiety that gripped them physically, is the outcome of listening to Moses.

Often the attitude of other believers to the work of the Lord can discourage those who are fervent in their service, or can give excuses to those who are seeking justification in abandoning the work. There can be a degree of sympathy for Israel labouring under increased bondage, but Moses had been given the promise of God and the statement, "How then shall Pharaoh hear me", was not worthy of one who had heard the voice of God. The reluctance of Moses to continue with the course of action declared by the Lord is clear when he argued that he was a man of uncircumcised lips. By this he declared that he was not fitted to carry out this task, again suggesting that the Lord had made a grave mistake in selecting him for such an enterprise. This description has been seen by some as confirmation that the reluctance to speak which had been expressed by Moses when the Lord spoke to him at the burning bush was due to an impediment in his speech. There is no indication at any other time that Moses had such a handicap. Jeremiah writes of an uncircumcised ear (Jer 6.10), uncircumcised hearts are mentioned (Lev 26.41; Ezek 44.7), and even uncircumcised fruit (Lev 19.23). The thought is that of being unsuitable for use. The uncircumcised heart does not submit to the Lord; the uncircumcised ear does not listen to the word of God; the claim by Moses that his lips were uncircumcised indicated that he did not regard his lips as being able to be used in the service of the Lord. Uncircumcised fruit is that of trees that are three years old and under, the trees at that stage being not mature enough for use.

Against the despair of the people, therefore, there is the determined purpose of God. Moses had to go to Pharaoh once more and repeat the demand that the Children of Israel be allowed to leave. The difference now is that there is no reference to a period of three days. It is now simply departure from Egypt.

The Lord intervenes swiftly. The time for procrastination and complaints has passed. It is now time to act. A solemn charge is given to Moses and Aaron, and they have now to put this into practice. Their allegiance to Jehovah will now be put to the test. Only obedient servants can lead others in a path of obedience.

Verses 14-27: The Genealogy of Moses and Aaron
The reason for the genealogy

What is introduced now is an interruption to the narrative as the genealogy of Moses and Aaron is traced. Two reasons at least can be discerned for such a list at this point.

1. This puts into place the last piece of the background of the two men who will lead the people.

2. The genealogy acts as a dividing point in the narrative. Shortly, the judgments of God will fall on Egypt. In a sense, up until this point it had been a day of grace for the Egyptians in which they were given the opportunity to accept the message of God. Having refused it, the character of the dealings of God with them now changed radically.

Reuben and Simeon

The names of Reuben and Simeon are mentioned before that of Levi, the son of Jacob from whom Moses and Aaron were descended. No other members of Jacob's family are included in the list. The purpose of the inclusion of the two eldest was to show the order in which Levi came in seniority amongst the sons and also to confirm that they had been by-passed, so that the leadership of the nation and the dignity of being priests did not fall to Levi by mistake, oversight, or by a presumptuous claim by Moses and his tribe. In the commentary on ch.2 it has been seen why it was that Simeon was by-passed, and that Reuben's exclusion was due to his conduct which is described by Jacob at the time of the blessing of his sons (Gen 49.3-4). This refers to the sad incident recorded in Genesis 35.22 about which, although Jacob heard of it, he said nothing until all his sons were gathered together for him to tell them "that which shall befall you in the last days"(Gen 49.1).

The four sons of Reuben and the six sons of Simeon are noted. Nothing more concerning them is recorded in the Word of God, a reminder that those whose lives are not recorded in the Scriptures are still remembered by the Lord. No life is forgotten, no matter how it is lived.

Phinehas

The last name on the list is that of Phinehas, a grandson of Aaron (6.25), who was responsible for wielding the javelin to preserve the purity of the nation at Shittim (Num 25.7ff). The list of names reveals, therefore, that this family will not only lead the people out of Egypt, but will be used to preserve them in the wilderness. Despite all their failures the list declares that God had made no mistakes in selecting His servants. Phinehas will live up to his high calling.

The name Amram is mentioned twice. In v.18 he is a son of Kohath and in v.20 he is the father of Moses. These are not two mentions of the same man, but rather two separate individuals. No better can be done than to quote Keil & Delitzsch on this point: "But the Amram mentioned in v.20 as the father of Moses, cannot be the same person as the Amram who was the son of Kohath (v.18), but must be a later descendant. For, however the sameness of names may seem to favour the identity of the persons, if we simply look at the genealogy before us, a comparison of the passage with Numbers 3.27-28 will show the impossibility of such an assumption. According to Numbers 3.27-28 the Kohathites were divided (in Moses' time) into four branches, Amramites, Izharites, Hebronites, and Uzzielites, who consisted together of 8,600 men and boys (women and girls not being included). Of these, about a fourth, or 2,150 men, would belong to the Amramites. Now, according to Exodus 18.3-4, Moses himself had only two sons. Consequently, if Amram the son of Kohath, the tribe-father of the Amramites, was the same person as Amram the father of Moses, Moses must have had 2,147 brothers and brothers' sons (the brothers' daughters, the sisters, and their daughters, not being reckoned at all). But as this is absolutely impossible, it must be granted that Amram the son of Kohath was not the father of Moses, and that an indefinitely long list of generations has been omitted between the former and his descendant of the same name".

Verses 28-30: Final Commission

With these words the narrative, which has been interrupted by the genealogy, is continued. It is probable that this is a summary of what was said when the Lord spoke to Moses earlier in the chapter, rather than a further meeting when Moses voiced the same objections once again. Implicit in these words is the right of Aaron to have a place in the leadership of the nation. It was the claim by Moses that he was not able to speak that led to Aaron being his spokesman. How much, however, is dependent on the words, "I am the Lord". All rests on the character of the Jehovah, and on that basis nothing can fail.

EXODUS 7

Plagues in Egypt

Verses 1-7: Final Instructions Before Meeting Pharaoh

The last objection raised by Moses was now completely dealt with by the Lord. Moses will be a God to Pharaoh and Aaron will be Moses' prophet. Previously (4.16) Moses had been told that he would be "instead of God" ("as God", RSV; "for God", JND) to Aaron, in the sense that it would be from Moses that Aaron would receive the communication from the Lord which he had to declare to Pharaoh and the Egyptians. Now Moses is to be a god ("I make you as God", RSV; "I have made thee God", JND) to Pharaoh in the sense that he is to have authority over Pharaoh, and thus he need have no fear of the monarch. How complete this authority will be and how little he need fear the power of Pharaoh is well expressed in Moses' becoming a "god" to the mightiest monarch on earth. It could have been said that Moses was "to have power" over Pharaoh, or that Moses "would be protected" from the anger of Pharaoh. None of that would have expressed in such a descriptive way the absolute authority which was now in Moses' hands, the total protection which he enjoyed and the promise that Pharaoh would at length acknowledge this authority. Keil & Delitzsch confirm this by writing that "Moses was a god to Aaron as the revealer of the divine will, and to Pharaoh as the executor of that will".

This authority will only be effective if Moses and Aaron bring before Pharaoh all that the Lord commands them. To say less or to add to what they have to say would destroy their power from the Lord. Only by complete submission to the Lord would they have the privilege of having a part in this great work of deliverance.

Signs and wonders in Egypt

As the signs and wonders which will lead to deliverance are about to experienced by the Egyptians, some general lessons which can be derived from them must be considered.

These signs will cause the Egyptians to know that the God of Israel is Jehovah, and they will learn His absolute power and authority. Thus it is that those who refuse to obey Him as He acts towards them in grace will at length acknowledge His Lordship. There will come a day when He will not tolerate rebellion from this world which He created and which He sustains. The longsuffering of God is mistaken by many as weakness, or as evidence that God does not exist. Such attitudes will, one day, be revealed as folly and all will confess "that Jesus Christ is Lord, to the glory of God the Father" (Phil 2.11). Pharaoh may have declared that he did not know Jehovah (5.2), but after the plagues he was very aware of the power of the Lord and he acceded to the command of Jehovah to let the people go.

There are also lessons to be learned by the Israelites. They will see how complete is the rejection by the Lord of all that Egypt is. There is nothing in that land which is exempt from His condemnation. The rivers, the fish, the cattle, the land, the people all feel the stroke of judgment. Hail comes from heaven, darkness covers the land, and at last the greatest blow of all falls when the firstborn of all, from the monarch to the lowest servant, and the firstborn of all cattle, die under the hand of Jehovah. Those who were to be brought out of Egypt will learn by the "signs" that there is nothing in Egypt that is of value to Jehovah, and, no matter how attractive it may appear to the eye, it is only fit for judgment. There will, therefore, be no regrets at leaving a world, the true character of which has been revealed by the acts of Jehovah. Only when these lessons have been forgotten will there be any longing for Egypt.

In essence this battle was between Jehovah and the gods of Egypt (12.12). It was a spiritual struggle and it had to be seen how comprehensive was the victory of Jehovah over false gods. There were idols in Egypt, but behind the idols there were spiritual powers that had risen in rebellion against Jehovah. The defeat of the whole Egyptian system was to be openly demonstrated. Its people, its commerce, and its religion were all to know the stroke of God in judgment.

In the book of Revelation there are three groups of judgments that fall on the earth. The opening of the seals, the blowing of the trumpets, and the pouring out of the vials of wrath are all for the purpose of showing that God is sovereign, that man is puny and powerless before Him, and that the world is ripe for judgment. What is seen in Egypt is but a pale shadow of what will take place before the Lord Jesus comes in glory to set up His Kingdom on earth. Warning is given here that God's grace, which had given Pharaoh an opportunity to allow the people to go, was not a sign of weakness. So, today, these events so long ago in Egypt are a warning to turn "to God from idols to serve the living and true God; And to wait for his Son from heaven, whom he raised from the dead, even Jesus, which delivered us from the wrath to come" (1 Thess 1.9-10).

After the initial personal sign to Pharaoh of Moses' rod becoming a serpent, there are nine further signs which divide into three groups of three, followed by the final and tenth sign which led to Pharaoh driving the Israelites from his land. We should note that the signs that commenced each group of three, i.e. signs one, four, and seven, were announced to Pharaoh in the morning. The signs which ended each group, i.e. signs three, six, and nine, were carried out without any announcement being made. All the other signs, i.e. two, five, and eight, as well as numbers one, four, and seven above, were declared to Pharaoh before they were carried out. With each sign there was an opportunity for Pharaoh to repent, but he did not avail himself of this.

The signs
Group One.
The reason given - "In this thou (Pharaoh) shalt know that I am the Lord" (7.17).

In this group all the land of Egypt is affected and it is Aaron who stretches forth his hand and his rod to instigate the judgment.

Sign 1   The waters of Egypt are turned to blood and the fish die.
Sign 2   Frogs cover the land.
Sign 3   Dust becomes lice throughout the land.

Group Two.
The reason given - "To the end thou mayest know that I am the Lord in the midst of the earth" (8.22).

In this group the land of Goshen is not affected and Aaron becomes less prominent.

Sign 4   The land is filled with swarms of flies.
Sign 5   A plague on all cattle.
Sign 6   Boils upon man and beast.

Group Three.
The reason given - "That my name may be declared throughout all the earth" (9.16).

In this group the land of Goshen is again not affected and Moses instigates each plague by "stretching forth his hand to heaven".

Sign 7   A grievous hail which destroys cattle.
Sign 8   Locusts invade the land.
Sign 9   Darkness over Egypt.

Final Sign.
Sign 10   The death of the firstborn.

The reaction of Moses and Aaron
Two statements are made which at first reading may appear to be superfluous. The first is: "And Moses and Aaron did as the Lord commanded them, so did they" (v.6), and the second: "And Moses was fourscore years old, and Aaron fourscore and three years old, when they spake unto Pharaoh" (v.7). The first is to emphasise that the reluctance of Moses to act, which was clear even at the end of ch.6, has now been overcome. Both he and Aaron did as the Lord commanded, with the concluding statement, "...so did they". The double mention of their obedience confirmed that any thought of delay or unwillingness was now a thing of the past.

The reference to their ages is to show that this is a crucial milestone in their lives. All that has gone before has been preparation for this moment. The fact that Aaron was three years older than Moses did not give him the leading place, for in the service of God greater age is not the prime factor in leadership. But the mention of eighty and eighty-three reminds the reader that these men were not novices. They were mature and could not be accused of setting about this great task with the enthusiasm of youth and its accompanying inexperience.

Some are called to enter into the service prepared for them by the Lord when they are young. Joseph was thirty years of age when he was raised to high office in Egypt (Gen 41.46), and it is likely that Jeremiah was in his late teens when he was called to serve (Jer 1.6), but Moses had to wait until a large part of his life was past, and at that time his greatest service lay ahead. Let this encourage all who may consider that the best years of their service for the Lord are over. There yet is service that He has for you to do, and if He gives it He will also give the necessary strength to carry it out. Many have stood, as did Moses and Aaron, at the door of opportunity which was about to open at a time when others would have declared both of them to be past starting something new. The Lord chooses His servants and chooses them in His own time.

Verses 8-13: Before Pharaoh Once More

It must have been with amazement that Pharaoh saw these two men appear before him again. This time they are asked to show a sign to confirm their authority, as Jehovah had told them. They cast the rod before Pharaoh where it became a serpent. Pharaoh is therefore the first man to see a servant of God perform a miracle.

This was a different serpent from that into which the rod turned previously (4.3). On that occasion it was NACHASH (5175), which denoted a snake or snake-like creature. Here it is TANNIN (8577) which denotes a large snake or large serpent-like creature. What took place before Pharaoh was more frightening than that which took place when Moses was alone.

The rod is stated to be the rod of Aaron. Despite the assertion by some writers (see, for example, Keil & Delitzsch) that this was Moses' rod, the rod which he held in his hand when he stood by the burning bush, it appears that the rod of Aaron and not the rod of Moses was used.

Aaron's rod was used:
1.   To be cast before Pharaoh and become a serpent (7.10).
2.   To be stretched over the waters of Egypt that they become blood (7.19).
3.   To be stretched out over the waters of Egypt to bring the plague of frogs (8.5).
4.   To be stretched out to smite the dust of the earth that it became lice (8.16).

Moses' rod was used:
1.   To smite the waters of the River Nile (7.17,20).
2.   To be held up to heaven to bring thunder and rain (9.23).
3.   To bring the plague of locusts (10.13).

4.   To divide the Red Sea (14.16).

It has been stated that, as proof of there being only one rod used, the rod of Moses, v.15 states that this was the rod which had become a serpent, and it is carried in Moses' hand. When it came time to use the rod before Pharaoh, Moses obviously passed it to Aaron. This does not, however, take into account the fact that the "serpent" referred to is NACHASH, into which the rod of Moses turned in 4.3, and not TANNIN, into which Aaron's rod turned (7.10). The rod in v.15 belonged to Moses who used it to smite the river (vv.17,20).

The "wise men" of Egypt

The men whom Pharaoh called to his aid were entitled "wise men" (2450), "sorcerers" (3784), and "magicians" (2748). "Wise men" are those who have based their knowledge on observation of the human condition and have built a body of teaching without seeking the God who is behind creation. This is the wisdom which is earthly, sensual (Jas 3.15). Attempts to find truth in any area of life are doomed to failure when God is left out. "Sorcerers" are those who engage in witchcraft and the occult. The command of the Lord to Israel concerning these was clear: "Thou shalt not suffer a witch to live" (22.18). The depths of the sin of Manasseh, king of Judah, can be measured by the witchcraft in which he engaged (2 Chr 33.6). "Magicians" were sacred scribes skilled in Egyptian writing who were engaged as priests in the Egyptian religions. There are, therefore, ranged against Moses and Aaron all the powers which were at Pharaoh's disposal. This band of occultists, idolaters, and men of human wisdom must have presented a formidable sight as they stood before their monarch. They wove their enchantments, cast their spells, uttered their curses, and invoked their gods, and by so doing held the nation in their thrall. They had been initiated into the secrets of their profession, and they guarded these secrets with their lives. Only the initiated could wield their power. We must not underestimate the enormity of the issues as these two groups of men faced each other - two men from the despised Hebrew race facing an array of the very best that Egypt could muster.

As the magicians of Egypt cast down their rods, these also became serpents. There must be no doubt as to the might at the disposal of the principalities and powers (Eph 6.12) against whom Moses and Aaron were doing battle. The serpents were similar to the large snake or serpent-like creature into which Aaron's rod turned. They, too, could work outside the "normal" laws of creation. What followed, however, showed decisively that the power of Jehovah was greater far than the power of the Adversary. Aaron's rod swallowed up their rods. The power which was at the disposal of these profane men was not only less than that which was at the disposal of the servants of the Lord, but by their open challenge to God's servants there was publicly displayed the overwhelming power of the Lord, as the serpents from the Egyptians' rods were swallowed up. Their rods were

then no longer available to them, emphasising the complete defeat that
they had suffered.

A *warning from Paul*

Paul recalls this incident as he writes to Timothy (2 Tim 3.5) warning
him against those who have a form of godliness, imitators who pretend to
be servants of the Lord, but do not know the Lord. We learn from Paul the
name of the two leaders of the Egyptian group facing Moses - Jannes and
Jambres. This desire to imitate the power of God and thus destroy the
effectiveness of the testimony is a means still in use today. The increase in
interest in mystic religions, the occult, and spiritism is designed to delude
men and women and cast doubt and confusion into the minds of those
who seek after truth. Let us remember that the power of God is greater
than the power of the Adversary. Despite such overwhelming proof,
however, the heart of Pharaoh is hardened and he refuses to listen to the
appeal to let the people go. The folly of refusing the message of God is
clearly displayed.

Believers must be warned to keep well clear of all "spiritist" activity.
There is an upsurge of this in modern society; a generation which states
its refusal to believe in the God of the Bible still seeks what "spiritism" can
give. Séances, mediums, users of tarot cards, astrologers with their charts,
and many others all claim to offer knowledge of what will take place
tomorrow, or even what lies beyond death. Communication with the dead
is one of the "attractions" which some of them offer. Much of it is the work
of opportunist charlatans, but beware, because the devil is at work and he
does have powers and will use them to delude and deceive men and
women. These black arts were well honed in Egypt, and Moses and Aaron
confronted their outstanding practitioners. The fact that they appear to
do what is supernatural does not mean that their work is of God. They are
those who "resist the truth: men of corrupt minds, reprobate concerning
the faith" (2 Tim 3.8).

Verses 14-25: The First Plague

Now the Lord will show his hand in judgment over the land of Egypt.
Moses and Aaron have to meet Pharaoh in the morning as he goes out to
the Nile. It may be that the purpose of this morning visit was to worship
the Nile deity, or it may be a visit for bathing, as was the purpose of the
visit of Pharaoh's daughter in 2.5. Whatever the reason, the Nile was
regarded as the lifeline of Egypt and the god of the annual flood was known
as Hapy.

It has previously been noted that this was the first of the opening group
of three plagues. The lesson to be learned by Pharaoh and the Egyptians is
that "thou shalt know that I am the Lord" (v.17). This was fundamental,
because it was in relation to this very fact that Pharaoh had declared on
the first visit of Moses, "Who is the Lord...I know not the Lord" (5.2).

Water turned to blood?

This first plague turned the waters of Egypt into blood. Some "expositors", when faced with such a display of divine power, have concluded that the waters did not turn into blood, but that red coloured sediment washed down from the upper reaches of the river caused it to be blood-like in appearance. It is not possible, however, to explain away such a manifestation of the power of Jehovah in this manner. Whereas it is acknowledged that even the appearance of this red sediment in the waters at exactly the moment when the rod was raised over the river would be an evidence of the power of God, this sign was an even greater act, as the water of the Nile *and all the other waters of Egypt* turned into blood.

1. The statement in v.19 is clear and unambiguous: "…that there may be blood throughout all the land of Egypt, both in vessels of wood, and in vessels of stone", and again, in v.20, "all the waters that were in the river were turned to blood".

2. The red sediment which is annually washed down the river after the rains in the highlands, where the river finds its source, does not cause the river to stink, nor does it cause the fish to die (v.21).

3. If we allow that the change in the colour of the water was not caused by the red earth, but was due to some miraculous chemical change in the water, we must ask why Scripture does not state this openly. Why not state that it was "like blood"? This is how the manna is described - "like coriander seed, white" (16.31). We do not know the chemical composition of manna, but we are told what it looked like. Such a description given to the first sign would not have diminished it in any way. The incident in 2 Kings 3 when the Moabites perceived that the water in the valley appeared to be blood is stated to be the result of the shining of the sun on that water (v.22). There is no suggestion there that the water did in fact turn into blood. It is true that the prophet Joel speaks of the sun being turned into darkness and the moon into blood (2.31). However, the context of this passage indicates that it is the colour of the moon and the sun, and not their substance, which is the point at issue. The sun will be turned into darkness, it will not be seen on earth, and the moon will be seen as blood red.

4. The washing of red sediment down the Nile would be, if not a regular event, at least a familiar occurrence to the Egyptians. It would hardly be seen as a definite indication of the judgment of God upon them. They would have experienced this in the past. It would not have been a new phenomenon.

It should also be noted that this sign was carried out "in the sight of Pharaoh, and in the sight of his servants" (v.20). It was not done in a hidden way; it was done openly so that there could be no suggestion that Moses had used some other means to "pollute" the river. Servants of God must always work in an open manner so that they cannot be accused of deviousness or even of falsehood. Paul states clearly to the Thessalonians that, when he was with them, "our exhortation was not of deceit...nor in guile" (1 Thess 2.3). The masters of Egypt observed what took place and even that did not bring about repentance.

Not only the Nile but also all the water in Egypt was affected by this loathsome condition. All the vessels of wood and of stone were filled with blood. These may have been domestic vessels as well as the conduits and the containers or any other vessels used to transport and store water for domestic or other purposes. Throughout the land the stench of blood would be in the air, dead fish adding to the foul odour. The loss of fish was, by itself, a serious setback. The Egyptians relied on them as part of their staple diet. Even the freed slaves could remember when they ate fish freely in Egypt (Num 11.5). This was an environmental and economic disaster of immense proportions. Attempts were made to obtain water by digging about the river to find wells which would provide some little supply of water to alleviate the thirst felt by everyone.

One lesson that would not escape the attention of the Egyptians was that the Nile was now fatal to the creatures that lived within it. This river, which was regarded as the giver and sustainer of life, was now a place of death, no longer able to give or support that for which it was revered.

The response of the magicians
The court magicians are now forced to display their power by imitating what Moses and Aaron have done. If they cannot, their lack of power will be displayed, so they also add to the horror. It is not clear how they could add to what had been done completely, but it may be that there were residues of water left to allow them to display this power. The utter folly of their actions, and their lack of concern for their own people is revealed. The proof of their power and the preservation of their position meant everything to them, and they cared nothing of how their own people suffered as a consequence of their actions.

The process of changing the water was not gradual. Pharaoh's heart was hardened and then he returned to his own house. As he stood beside the river in the morning light he saw it become blood, he looked on the work of the magicians, he weighed up all this evidence, and his heart was hardened.

For seven days the river of blood flowed through the land, the Egyptians laboured daily digging for water, and fish lay rotting by the river's bank. What a scene of horror this must have been for a nation, which, as has already been observed, venerated this river and saw it as the source on which they relied for the prosperity of the kingdom. The period of seven days, the same length of time which was given to the inhabitants of Jericho to repent (Josh 6.3-4), gave Pharaoh and the people time to consider what Jehovah had done, but no sign of repentance was seen. In this first plague

Pharaoh did not move his position. The pull of the gods of Egypt was too strong.

By this single act Jehovah declared His supremacy in a manner that could not be denied. He touched the life of Egypt at its source, and let it be seen that it was to Him and to no other that they owed their existence. Although there was no acknowledgement of this on their part, Jehovah was the supplier of their needs. In addition to this, the blood-filled river of Egypt confirmed that this was a dead society. It is that lesson which the Egyptians must also learn. There was no life in them, and for seven days this was clearly shown. God, who spent seven days in creating life and resting in it, here takes seven days to show that sin has made His creation a place of death.

EXODUS 8

Plagues in Egypt (continued)

Verses 1-15: The Second Plague

How much time elapsed between the end of the first plague and the second stroke to fall on the land is not known. Pharaoh may have considered that he had won a victory and that, with impunity, he had withstood Jehovah. Such thoughts, if they did exist, were soon proved to be ill-founded.

The second plague consisted of frogs which infested the whole of the land. "All the borders" were affected, each region and area bearing the brunt of this plague. Out of the river there came millions of frogs that made their way into the homes, the beds, the ovens, the storage areas, indeed into every corner of the houses and palaces. Once again the river had been the source of these unclean things; this river which was worshipped was the source of what was unclean, the source of a pestilence which made life intolerable. The Egyptians would kill as many as possible, but still they advanced, overwhelming a nation that gloried in its cleanliness. Again, the magicians of Egypt showed their lack of concern for their countrymen by imitating the work of Moses and bringing yet more frogs out of the river. If, in the first plague, it was possible to find some alleviation of the horror by digging for water, no such relief was to be found now.

The Egyptians esteemed the frog and used it as a symbol of deity. Over these days they must have come to loathe it with the slime and filth of the river which these creatures carried with them. So great is the disaster that at last there appears to be some change of heart on the part of Pharaoh. For the first time he acknowledges Jehovah: "Intreat the Lord, that he may take away the frogs" (v.8). He who had denied that Jehovah existed is now forced to turn to Him for help. This acknowledgement that Jehovah was the One who had brought the plague on Egypt was also an admission that his own magicians were powerless to control this loathsome pestilence. So desperate was he to rid the land of the frogs that he was prepared to promise that he would let the people go that they might sacrifice to Jehovah. This appeared to be the answer for which Moses was waiting, but there is no exulting on the part of God's servants.

Moses does respond, however, and gives to Pharaoh the honour of deciding when the plague will go. What confidence Moses showed here. Up until this point he had instigated two plagues, but had not been responsible for bringing them to an end. In the first plague there was no indication that Moses took any action to change the blood back to water. Here, however, he was prepared to let Pharaoh decide the actual day when the relief would come. By doing this he revealed his confidence in his God that the frog plague would go when, using the authority given to him, he ordered it to recede. By this he was also taking the opportunity of showing Pharaoh further evidences of God's power.

The first compromise offered by Pharaoh

This is the first of five compromises which are offered by Pharaoh (8.8,25,28; 10.10-11,24). This should cause no surprise, as the way of the world in dealing with differing views is to compromise and agree on a solution where every party involved sacrifices something in order to agree on "common ground". This is the stand taken by the monarch, but the solutions that he offered would either keep the people within his power, or ensure that, if they left Egypt, they would be unable to do what the Lord required of them after their deliverance. By this means, if they could not be kept in his kingdom, they would lose their ability to serve God and He would be robbed of their worship. For those who seek to obey God, compromise is not possible when the Word of God is the point at issue. That is why Moses continually and resolutely refused to heed the voice of Pharaoh. What the Lord required had to be totally obeyed.

The answer from the king may seem surprising. He did not ask for immediate relief from the plague. His request was that it should be lifted the following day and at that time he would "let the people go, that they may sacrifice unto the Lord" (v.8). Why did he allow his people to suffer for another day?

1. Was it that he considered it necessary to allow the Lord one day to clear this pestilence out of the land? Did it appear to him to be impossible for this to be done in a shorter period of time? Surely, however, the power which he had seen displayed was enough to convince him that the God who had turned a rod into a serpent, who had made the water blood, and had filled the land with frogs, could immediately rid the land of these creatures. He had seen how quickly Jehovah could work when Moses lifted up his rod and the Nile became blood. Apart from these evidences his concern for his own people should have driven him to ask that the plague be lifted immediately.

2. Was it that Pharaoh thought it necessary to allow Moses one day to intercede with Jehovah? Knowing the length of time which the Egyptian priests took in their dark arts and mysteries, it was perhaps too great a leap for his mind to take that intercession could be immediate. This also, however, is unlikely, as he had no knowledge of intercession with Jehovah and could not possibly have come to the conclusion that one day would be required.

3. It is possible that Pharaoh asked for the delay until the next day simply because he was unwilling to let the Israelites go if any means could be found to detain them in Egypt. Would something turn up to change the situation? Twenty-four hours may not seem a long time, but to a desperate man it was a breathing space to give him time to think. It did mean that he would allow the people to suffer longer than was necessary, but he had confidence that if no other power could be found, or no other plan made in the time available, the frogs would go by the next day.

This last suggestion seems to fit the circumstances. Where there is a desire in the heart of anyone to leave the kingdom of darkness, and be sheltered by the blood and the power of God, the Adversary will suggest that it be left until tomorrow. His purpose is that none should be saved today. He will suggest to us that the course of action we are considering should be given further thought and that no hasty judgment must be made. The changes it will bring, the uncertainty of the future, and the reaction of others should be weighed up carefully before we take this step. Such are the suggestions he makes today. You can go, but make it tomorrow. If we follow that advice, days will become weeks, weeks will become months, months will become years, and years will stretch into a lifetime. It may be thought that such a suggestion is folly in light of the power that Pharaoh had seen displayed, but it must never be forgotten that the actions of Satan are always based on folly. Any design of his is doomed to failure.

Moses and Aaron left the presence of Pharaoh and Moses cried unto the Lord. The use of *cried* (6817) indicates the strength of Moses' intercession. The root of the word is to call for help in times of distress. Moses will pray to God in this way on many occasions in the future. His prayers did not consist of tired platitudes and empty words. His feelings were real, and the strength of his prayer is measured by the power of his words. So he cried to Jehovah and his prayer was heard. We must observe that, even although Moses knew that he had been made a "god" to Pharaoh, and that signs and wonders would multiply by his hand, he never assumed that this power was his to use in his own way. Prayer was necessary, and the power that had been given him by the Lord had always to be used in dependence on Him. The delegated power, which was given to the disciples to cast out demons, left them when they began to assume that it was their own power and could be used in a way independent of the Master. Thus they could not cast out the demon that possessed the son brought to them by his father when the Lord Jesus was on the Mount of Transfiguration (Mk 9.14-29).

And so the frogs died and Pharaoh saw that there was respite in the land. A breathing space was given, or so he imagined, and his heart was hardened once again. This has ever been the way of natural man when faced with a crisis. Initially, there is much prayer and calling on God, but when the crisis passes the heart becomes hard and cold and God is forgotten.

We have already alluded to the lesson that came from this second plague. The river that they worshipped had produced what was unclean. This always is the outcome of idolatry. "Wherefore God also gave them up to uncleanness", is the comment of Romans 1.24 on those who, like Pharaoh, have refused to acknowledge His eternal power and Godhead.

Verses 16-19: The Third Plague

This third plague came without any warning being given to Pharaoh. The word KINNIM (3654), which is translated as "lice" in the AV, probably refers to gnats or a type of mosquito. How great an invasion of these creatures it must have been is seen in that it is the dust, or loose topsoil, of the land that becomes gnats. Throughout the land their number was as great as the dust, an overwhelming invasion of these little creatures bringing much pain and irritation. On this occasion the attempts of the court magicians of Pharaoh to imitate the power of Moses proved to be unsuccessful. This forced from them the admission that "This is the finger of God". This manifestation of power was something beyond the might of man and could only be explained as a work of God. At this point the magicians gave up the uneven struggle and retired from the contest. Defeated, they made no further attempts to imitate Moses and Aaron. Despite this, the heart of Pharaoh refused to admit to the truth and there was no response, not even the little which there had been with the plague of frogs. Again, it is not known how long this plague continued, nor is it known how it came to an end. There was no command given to Moses to end the plague, nor do we read this time of Moses praying for the power of God to be seen in ending this agony. At length, however, the plague did abate.

With this ends the first group of three plagues. There has been a pattern set which is repeated in the next two groups. The first plague is preceded with a long and detailed warning which is given to Pharaoh in the morning. The second plague is preceded with a shorter warning and the third plague comes with no warning being given.

Surely after such an evidence of the power of God it would have been thought wise to listen to the call of Moses and let the people go. This does not take place because the sinful heart will continue to rebel against God, no matter how hopeless the situation is. If observing the great work of creation does not produce in the heart an acknowledgment of the eternal character and power of God, it should not be the cause of surprise that any work of judgment that He carries out does not move the sinful heart until His work is overwhelming. Sin creates in the heart a condition through which God is not acknowledged until it is impossible to continue in rebellion. Even in the days when the wrath of God is poured out on the earth, rebellion will continue until the Lord destroys those who fight against Him with the "brightness of his coming" (2 Thess 2.8).

Verses 20-32: The Fourth Plague

Once again Moses and Aaron had to return to the Nile to meet Pharaoh on his morning visit. Now it was a plague of swarms of flies that was promised. This first of the next of the three groups gives us the second stated reason for the judgment of God falling on them in this way. It was that Pharaoh would know "that I am the Lord in the midst of the earth". This was an advance on the reason given for the first group - "thou shalt know that I am the Lord" (7.17). The lesson which they should have learned was that there was only one God and that He was Jehovah. What they had to learn now was that He was the Lord who moved in the land to bring about His purpose. He was not a distant remote God with little interest in the daily lives of His people. Those who did not believe Him could not rest secure in the knowledge that He would not intervene in their lives. This God was in the midst of the land i.e. Egypt, and would act according to His good pleasure to bring about His will. If the first group of signs proved the existence and authority of Jehovah, the second group proved that Jehovah could act in Egypt according to His will. The magicians of Egypt had only gone as far as to say that the signs were the finger of *a* god. Now they would see that He is the God of Israel.

As further proof of this, from now on the land of Goshen where the Israelites lived would not be subject to the plagues which afflicted Egypt. Up to this point the Israelites must have suffered as did the Egyptians, but now they would be protected from the oncoming disasters; "I will put a division between my people and thy people" (v.23). "Division" (6304) here means a redemption or deliverance that emphasised the difference between the Egyptian and the Israelite.

Flies entered into all the houses of the Egyptians and their servants. The Psalmist wrote that "He sent divers sorts of flies among them, which devoured them" (Ps 78.45). No one was immune from the onslaught of these insects as they devoured the people and disfigured them with sores and swelling which were the results of their bites. Plant life, animal life, and human life were all affected until Pharaoh was forced to call for Moses and Aaron and cry for respite.

The second compromise offered by Pharaoh

The promise of Pharaoh to allow the people to sacrifice to their God was conditional. He would allow them to carry out such sacrifice or feast on condition that they did not leave the land, i.e. that they did not leave Egypt. This was the second compromise solution that Pharaoh had offered, the first being to let them go "tomorrow". This latest proposal was unacceptable to Moses on two counts.

1. The command of Jehovah had been to go into the wilderness, and anything less than that would be disobedience to the Lord.

2. The worship that the Israelites would carry out was very different to anything which the Egyptian priests practised. The differences were so great that the worship of the Israelites would be regarded by the Egyptians as an abomination, and seeing this in the midst of their country would cause tension leading to the Israelites being stoned by the Egyptians.

The lesson of this is that Moses was aware that the worship of Jehovah and the religious practices of the land of Egypt could not exist together. There was such a fundamental difference that the Egyptians would feel resentment and anger at these true worshippers. So intense would be their feelings that, as has been noted, it is described as an abomination to them.[†] The lesson must be taken to heart today when the ecumenical movement advocates that all so-called "Christian" churches should come together and sink their differences in the cause of "Christian unity". Many of these purportedly Christian churches are run and supported by those who do not know salvation and, as a result, have not eternal life. The scriptural practices of the believer are foreign to such individuals and cause them to be angry that what is taught in the Word of God is not put aside as old fashioned, to give place to observances to which all so-called Christians can subscribe. The exhortation to do this is couched in language which appears to be "reasonable" and motivated by "Christian love for others". "Understanding of the sincere beliefs of your brother", are words that come from the lips of such purveyors of this poisonous teaching. The spiritual life of a believer cannot flourish in such a "church" and the exhortation to "come out from among them, and be ye separate" (2 Cor 6.17) must be obeyed before progress in the Christian life can be enjoyed. The point at issue is the authority of the Lord and of the Scriptures. The only way to please Him is to obey His Word.

Behind this suggestion was the desire of the Adversary to keep the people in Egypt. Pharaoh's compromise was that they would have freedom to do whatever they wished by way of worship if they remained in the Egyptian world. Although Pharaoh did not state it, Moses understood that this would mean adopting the religious practices of Egypt when worshipping their own God. This still remains Satan's way today - keep believers in the world and allow them to worship their God provided they compromise to conform to this age in their practices. Such a course would have resulted in no worship for Jehovah and no freedom for the Hebrews, who would have continued as slaves. Moses' reply was unambiguous. The compromise was rejected and the truth stated: "We will go three days' journey into the wilderness, and sacrifice to the Lord our God, as he shall command us" (v.27).

The third compromise offered by Pharaoh

Pharaoh now offered a third proposal: "Ye may sacrifice to the Lord your God in the wilderness; only ye shall not go very far away" (v.28). He was now forced to concede a little more, but still this was a compromise. Three days journey is what Moses again stated, but the king would have none of this. If they must go into the wilderness, make it not very far away, still within his reach, so that he could be sure that they would return. This was the compromise of leaving the world behind, but remaining so close to it that it could influence behaviour and continue to exercise control. To go any further away, the world asserts, is surely unreasonable extremism.

If the question had been put to the people there might have been some who would have argued that this offer should be accepted. They would believe that this could mean immediate "release" from Egypt yet leave them still near enough to Egypt to influence it and perhaps convert the Egyptians to the worship of Jehovah. Such would be the reasoning, but it would be very flawed. A pathway of disobedience is no basis on which to build a testimony for the Lord. Again, sad to say, this compromise is still offered today, and by some accepted. Profession of salvation is followed by living as close to the world as is possible. There has developed a world-bordering way of life that is justified by three arguments.

1. The blessings of salvation include material blessings, and therefore it is to be expected that believers will prosper in this world. This is an excuse for a worldly way of life, showing the danger which confronts those who "will be rich" (1 Tim 6.9). Scripture does not promise that salvation will bring with it material wealth. God does make some rich, and there is no fault in that, but to pursue wealth as a goal enables the Adversary to keep a degree of control over a believer who is dwelling "not far away" from Egypt.

2. Moving too far away takes away any possibility of testifying to the world and will make the believer remote and out of touch with those who need the gospel. This is an excuse to enable believers to enjoy the world. It will be possible to testify because, it is argued, time is spent with the world. By being in the places where unbelievers are to be found, particularly in their leisure time, it is possible to speak to them about the gospel and to understand the problems and difficulties which they face. As a result of this conduct, however, the world receives a false view of a Christian and the believer becomes conformed to this age.

3. "My faith and conscience are so strong that I can be close to the world and not be affected by it", is the boast that is sometimes heard. This ignores the effect that the conduct of a believer can have on other Christians and may result in some believers pursuing such a path but, as they are not "strong", they fail disastrously and wreck their testimony.

Separation from the world must not be looked on as a penalty which has to be paid by Christians as part of the cost of obtaining salvation. There must never be the thought that it is denying the believer good things that could be enjoyed, and that refraining from such associations is a loss of enjoyment. Should salvation itself not be enjoyed, the Adversary is quick to introduce such thoughts; an "easy" way of living the Christian life is the inducement. It must never be forgotten that Egypt is the land of cruel slavery, and that any association with Egypt involves such slavery. To remain near to it shows that there is a love for the things of the world; "Love not the world, neither the things that are in the world. If any man love the world, the love of the Father is not in him" (1 Jn 2.15) is an exhortation given to guard against any such compromise.

This was the first plague to show the difference existing between the Israelites and the Egyptians, as Jehovah withheld it from the land of Goshen. The three compromise solutions offered in this chapter (more were to follow) were designed to eliminate that difference and to make the Israelites indistinguishable from the world.

Moses showed great grace when he agreed to intreat the Lord for

Pharaoh, but the king was warned that he must not act deceitfully. The pestilence of flies was removed completely, but still Pharaoh hardened his heart, refusing to let the people go. The emphasis on the fact that "there remained not one" (v.31) of the flies is included to show that Pharaoh had no excuse for his refusal to let the people go. The Lord removed every trace of the plague, giving the land complete rest from this pestilence.

Notes

26 Three things are said to be an abomination to the Egyptians:
  1. Sharing a meal with the Hebrews (Gen 43.32).
  2. The Hebrews' occupation of shepherding sheep (Gen 46.34).
  3. The religious sacrifices and practices of the Hebrews (Ex 8.26).

The thought here in v.26 is not that the Israelites would offer the sacrifices that were offered by the Egyptians to their deities. This would indeed be an abomination, but Moses would hardly have described Egyptian sacrifices as *abominations* to Pharaoh. What the Israelites offered to the Lord, however, would be viewed by the Egyptians as an abomination. Lambs and sheep, for instance, were regarded in this light.

EXODUS 9

Plagues in Egypt (continued)

Verses 1-7: The Fifth Plague

The four plagues preceding this were of increasing ferocity. Pharaoh had felt "the lightening down of the heavy arm of divine indignation, without yet being brought to submit to the mandate of heaven. He consequently stands a mark for the arrows from Jehovah's quiver" (Bush). With the fifth plague Pharaoh was faced with the mortal consequences of refusing to let God's people go. Although he may have refused to accept that the announcement of plague amongst the cattle would lead to death, he soon had to face this disturbing fact. Ultimately, death is the consequence of sin and the deadly disease that affected the cattle was a foretaste of what lay ahead should Pharaoh's refusal continue.

Up to this point the signs visited on Egypt left no long-term effect when they were removed. The blood turned back to water, and the frogs, lice, and flies no longer tormented the people. Now, when death strikes, the economic life of the nation is threatened. Cattle cannot be replaced immediately, and it would take years to rebuild the herds and flocks. Keil & Delitzsch comment: "In the words *'all the cattle of the Egyptians died,'* *all* is not to be taken in an absolute sense, but according to popular usage, as denoting such a quantity, that what remained was nothing in comparison; and according to v.3, it must be entirely restricted to the cattle *in the field*. For, according to vv.9 and 19, much of the cattle of the Egyptians still remained even after this murrain, though it extended to all kinds of cattle, horses, asses, camels, oxen, and sheep, and differed in this respect from natural murrains". Even when we take into account the restrictions placed on the plagues, it remained a grievous blow to the well-being of the Egyptians, one which could not quickly be righted.

Lest it be considered by the Egyptians that this plague was simply one of the many which affected cattle from time to time, there were two features which declared this to be a direct intervention by God. First, Moses stated that the plague would begin on the day after he had made the announcement. The time was appointed by the Lord and gave Pharaoh one day in which to repent. When repentance was not seen, at the appointed, pre-announced moment the plague descended. The second evidence of the hand of God is that the plague did not affect the cattle of the Israelites. Pharaoh sent messengers to enquire and they returned reporting that the plague had not visited the cattle in Goshen. There could be no doubt now that this visitation was of God, yet still the obstinate heart of the king refused to repent.

Verses 8-12: The Sixth Plague

As with the third plague, there was no warning given to Pharaoh. Moses and Aaron were told to take handfuls of ashes from the furnace and sprinkle them toward heaven in the presence of Pharaoh. Taken from the furnaces were the dust, cinders, and ashes left over from the fire. The furnaces were limekilns or metal smelting furnaces used to produce the ornaments and buildings of Egypt. These were at the forefront of Egyptian technology and would be the source of great pride to the nation. It was from them that some of the glory of Egypt came, and now they would learn that even this could be touched by the hand of Jehovah. But more than this, what had produced their beauty was now used of God to produce judgment. There was no part of their society which was not under His control.

Both Moses and Aaron took handfuls of ashes, but it is Moses who sprinkled them towards heaven. Aaron must have handed his ashes to Moses. The same hands which would take the sweet incense (Lev 16.12) and bring it within the vail, now take the ashes which bring judgment. The first sign had commenced with an act "in the sight of Pharaoh" (7.20), and this sign commenced in the same way, with an act "in the sight of Pharaoh". The king will not be allowed to ignore the two men who are acting under the authority of heaven. He will see them at work to drive home the lesson that God is judging, and only He has the authority to bring these miseries to an end. If he had had compassion for his people he would have bowed before the will of God. The act of sprinkling ashes towards heaven conveyed to the watching king that it was the power of heaven which would visit this further plague upon them. The ashes were carried as dust over the land and became boils upon man and beast. As with the third sign, both man and beast are afflicted, but the increasing ferocity of the nature of the plagues cannot have escaped any thinking Egyptian.

The humiliation of the magicians continues. They are not immune to the boils. They cannot save themselves, and so they have clearly no power to save the nation. It would appear from the comment, "the magicians could not stand before Moses" (v.11), that it had been their practice to stand in the presence of Moses and Aaron as the signs were performed. Their purpose was no doubt to examine the means employed by the servants of Jehovah and seek an opportunity to strike back and reclaim their position and their reputations. Now, defeated, they retreat discredited, their intervention at an end. What had been achieved by their confrontation with Moses and Aaron? The manifestation of the sovereign supremacy of Jehovah over all the gods of Egypt! Their work, like the work of their master, the devil, had been used of God to reveal their inadequacies and demonstrate the greatness of His power.

Yet again Pharaoh did not repent. For the first time the statement is made: "the Lord hardened the heart of Pharaoh" (v.12).[†] The patience of Jehovah would not last forever, but Pharaoh would never be able to claim that he did not have opportunity to repent and let the people go.

Verses 13-35: The Seventh Plague

For the third time Moses is called to meet Pharaoh in the morning (7.15; 8.20). This meeting no doubt took place as Pharaoh approached the Nile for his morning religious ablutions (7.15). We have already observed that the first sign in each of the three cycles of signs is preceded by a morning encounter between Moses and Pharaoh. This message to Pharaoh commenced with the words which now must have been familiar to him. He had heard them on five previous occasions (5.1; 7.16; 8.1; 8.20; & 9.1), and once again they were voiced in his presence.

It is clear from the words of Moses that the plagues which were about to descend on Egypt were more deadly than those which the Egyptians had already endured. They would go right to the heart of Pharaoh and his people and strike a mortal blow. The obdurate refusal of this monarch to acknowledge Jehovah had now brought the nation to the point where the plagues were not only instructive but had also a punitive element in them. If there is wonder at such refusal in the face of what had taken place, consideration of the refusal of men and women to accept the gospel reveals that the human heart has not changed. The refusal of Egypt is mirrored in the refusal of mankind today to accept the message of the love of God proclaimed in the gospel.

There are two lessons to be learned by Pharaoh from this third cycle of plagues. The first is "that thou mayest know that there is none like me in all the earth" (v.14). There is none, whether man or idol, like Jehovah. He stands above and beyond all others and cannot be challenged. The second is that "my name may be declared throughout all the earth" (v.16). The triumph of Jehovah over the deities and armies of Egypt was to be published abroad. Rahab heard of it (Josh 2.8-11); the inhabitants and the rulers of the surrounding nations would hear of it (Ex 15.16); since then throughout the world the victory has been proclaimed.

Despite his determined opposition to Jehovah Pharaoh was still given space to repent. This was a constant feature of the dealings of God with this monarch. Indeed, it seems repetitious to mention it again. The grievous hail which would fall on the land would come "tomorrow about this time". He had a twenty-four hour period to reflect and repent. But no matter how repetitious this may appear it is but an indication of the grace of God extended to all men and woman, and thus is a display of that for which all should give thanks.

The hail that was to come on the morrow was something which had never afflicted Egypt since the kingdom had been established (v.18). This cannot be dismissed by the sceptic as just another natural disaster which people of simple minds attributed to Jehovah. The first sign was also a unique manifestation of the power of God, but the five that had followed could have been looked on as an extreme form of something natural. There is always an eager desire to dismiss the work of God as a "natural" phenomenon, a necessity for those who insist that there is no God. This sign, however, is not only unique in the history of the nation, but it commences at the time foretold. Not "some time tomorrow" but "tomorrow about this time". The combination of these two features, the nature of the sign and the fact that it commences at the time foretold by the Lord, confirms to any thinking individual that this is His work.

Knowing when the hail would come had another significance. It enabled those who feared the word of the Lord (v.20) to gather their cattle indoors to a place of safety. There was no possibility of saving the crops, but the cattle could be preserved if the word of the Lord was heeded. Urgency and speed must be the order of the day as the cattle "flee into the houses". There were some, even in Egypt, who had learned to fear the Lord. This does not indicate that they were believers in Jehovah in the sense of having salvation. It simply indicates that they had a fear of the Lord in their hearts and believed that what He said would come to pass. Many still "regarded not the word of the Lord".

It is difficult to visualise the frightening scale of this storm. It came at the appointed time. Its ferocity was such that man, beast, crops, and trees were destroyed. Fire mingled with the hail and ran along the ground consuming all that lay in its path. So intense was this outburst that even trees fell before it. Once again Goshen was left unscathed.

These features, together with the fact that it started exactly when Moses had predicted, ensured that there could be no doubt as to the supernatural nature of this disaster. Pharaoh was forced to admit this. His plea to Moses revealed the shallow nature of his confession, He was prepared to admit that he had sinned "this time" but there was no true repentance in his words. This was an attempt to ensure that such a storm of hail and fire did not come again to the land. It was not submission to Jehovah. Moses' reply showed that he understood the heart of Pharaoh. The end result confirmed that Pharaoh had no intention of letting the people go.

Notes

12 "He hardened Pharaoh's heart" (7.13, KJV) is better rendered "Pharaoh's heart was hardened". See JND - "Pharaoh's heart was stubborn".

EXODUS 10

Plagues in Egypt (continued)

Verses 1-20: The Eighth Plague

Once again Moses is instructed to present himself before Pharaoh in order to announce yet another plague. But lest Moses be discouraged by the refusal of the monarch to let the people go, he learns that the Lord is hardening the heart of Pharaoh and of his servants. What a warning this is to those who oppose God! The Lord deals with Pharaoh in divine government and, as a result, his heart is hardened. This is what Pharaoh desired and it has now been brought to pass. But, in revealing this to Moses, there is displayed the care and compassion of the Lord for his servant.

The hardening of Pharaoh's heart

As the Lord states here for the first time, "I have hardened Pharaoh's heart", it is suitable at this point to consider the heart of Pharaoh and how it was hardened. A hardened heart is one that is stubborn and obdurate. It is immovable and cannot be changed or moulded in any way. It indicates a fixed attitude and opinion which no reasoning will alter and which will remain fixed no matter what evidence is presented to it in order to effect a change. This is the condition of the heart of Pharaoh. This "hard" condition is referred to fifteen times in connection with eleven events.

1. *After the rods were turned into serpents.*
"And he hardened Pharaoh's heart" (7.13);
"Pharaoh's heart was stubborn"(JND);
"Pharaoh's heart was hardened" (RV);
"Pharaoh's heart is hardened" (7.14).

2. *After the first sign of turning the water into blood.*
"Pharaoh's heart was hardened" (7.22).

3. *After the second sign of frogs.*
"He (Pharaoh) hardened his heart" (8.15).

4. *After the third sign of lice.*
"Pharaoh's heart was hardened" (8.19).

5. *After the fourth sign of flies.*
"Pharaoh hardened his heart" (8.32).

6. *After the fifth sign of the plague on the cattle.*
"The heart of Pharaoh was hardened" (9.7).

7. *After the sixth sign of boils.*
"The Lord hardened the heart of Pharaoh" (9.12).

8. *After the seventh sign of hail.*
"Pharaoh...hardened his heart" (9.34);

"The heart of Pharaoh was hardened" (9.35).

9. *Before and after the eighth sign of locusts.*
"I have hardened his heart" (10.1);
"The Lord hardened Pharaoh's heart" (10.20).

10. *After the ninth sign of darkness.*
"The Lord hardened Pharaoh's heart" (10.27).

11. *After the Passover.*
"The Lord hardened the heart of Pharaoh" (14.8).

Summary of what took place during the plagues.
"The Lord hardened Pharaoh's heart" (11.10).
This does not refer to a separate incident but is the final word regarding the behaviour of Pharaoh as the plagues fell on Egypt.

The detailed recording of every occasion when Pharaoh had a hard heart teaches that the Lord takes account of every action that we perform and every sin is noted. Nothing was forgotten in the divine record. But note must also be taken that, if there is acceptance of the JND/RV rendering of 7.13, Pharaoh hardened his heart and then, in response the Lord hardened the heart of Pharaoh. It is not until 9.12 that it is stated that the Lord hardened the heart of Pharaoh. The godless monarch is responsible for the action of the Lord against him.

But there is another reason for the Lord dealing with the ruler in this way. There were further signs to be shown in Egypt, and the hardening of the heart of Pharaoh would ensure that they were carried out. These signs were important for they would be spoken of and passed down through the generations, teaching that the One who delivered them was God. The signs about to be revealed leave the reality of this fact beyond doubt and the wonder of them will never be forgotten. Israel stands on the threshold of momentous days, as God is about to work in a manner so powerful that it has never been seen before nor has it been repeated. It should not be overlooked that the mighty acts of God were more for Israel than for Egypt, and the redeemed nation must not forget what God did to effect their deliverance.

The response of Pharaoh to the plague

The charge laid against Pharaoh was that he refused to humble himself before the Lord. The word "humble" (6031) is first mentioned in Scripture in relation to the captivity of the Children of Israel: "And he said unto Abram, Know of a surety that thy seed shall be a stranger in a land that is not theirs, and shall serve them; and they shall *afflict* them four hundred years" (Gen 15.13). The monarch of the nation that had afflicted and humbled the Hebrews must now humble himself before the Lord, but refused so to do.

The refusal of men and women to humble themselves lies at the very root of the controversy which the Lord has with sinners. There will come a day when "at the name of Jesus every knee should bow...And that every tongue should confess that Jesus Christ is Lord, to the glory of God the Father" (Phil 2.10-11). That day has yet to dawn. Each time a plague descended on the land Pharaoh professed to bow before the will of God, but each utterance proved to be false. Thus it is today that sinners in their pride and self-confidence feel independent of God and live as if there was no God to whom they must give account.

The plague which was promised should Pharaoh refuse to humble himself was severe. Locusts would descend on the land and any crops or produce which escaped the plague of hail would be consumed. A plague of this extent had never before been experienced in Egypt. With this announcement Moses turned and left the presence of Pharaoh. The hearts of the servants of Pharaoh had been hardened, as was their master's after the plague of hail. Now, however, even the servants began to look for an end to this catalogue of disasters. There was no question of their repentance but they understood that some arrangement had to be made to end the plagues. Their suggestion was that the Hebrew men should be allowed to go. Keeping the wives and children in Egypt would be the means of ensuring that the Hebrews returned after they had served their Lord in the wilderness. Accommodation, compromise, and coming to a acceptable solution which meets the requirements of both sides is always the way of the world, and the servants of Pharaoh felt that they had such an acceptable solution. Without this, Egypt would be further ravaged and already they declare, "Egypt is destroyed".

Moses and Aaron were summoned back to the presence of Pharaoh to have this proposition put to them. Once again, as with all compromise, it appeared to have attractive features. The men would be able to go into the wilderness and sacrifice to the Lord but they would have to return to Egypt. However, perhaps their good conduct on this occasion would make it possible for Pharaoh to allow them all to go should they ask a second time. This is how it would appear to human reasoning, but there was to be no compromise!

The reply of Moses made it quite clear that the departure of the Israelites with their wives and children, and taking their flocks with them, was the only acceptable response to the demand of the Lord. The answer of Pharaoh, which seemed to allow such a departure, was spoken in irony, although his strong feelings came through. He considered them to be up to no good. Evil would lie before them and he would only let the men go. He claimed that this was the original request of Moses, but in this he was incorrect. The demand of the Lord had not changed, nor would it. By keeping the children in Egypt Pharaoh sought to ensure that this people would return, but even if they did not they would have no future as a nation. A complete generation of probably up to twelve years of age would be lost, dealing a heavy blow to the Israelites.

Behind Pharaoh the Adversary still worked. His wiles with Pharaoh are still those used today. If he could keep a generation away from salvation he would severely weaken the testimony. How important it is to ensure that children are brought up to know the gospel. The anger of Pharaoh was obvious as Moses and Aaron were driven from his presence. It appears that they were quickly removed, with no ceremony, from the audience chamber.

The hand of the Lord was seen in this plague in two ways. First, the wind from the east started to blow immediately Moses raised his rod. Second, the wind blew for one day and a half, showing that the locusts had been driven from a very great distance. The ferocity of this swarm was unparalleled as it covered the whole of the land. There had never been such an invasion of locusts before this nor has one been experienced since. A description of a locust invasion is given in Joel 2 which, although dealing with an invasion to be suffered by Israel, nevertheless gives a vivid account of such a plague. "Like the noise of chariots on the tops of mountains shall they leap, like the noise of a flame of fire that devoureth the stubble, as a strong people set in battle array" (v.5). "They shall run to and fro in the city; they shall run upon the wall, they shall climb up upon the houses; they shall enter in at the windows like a thief. The earth shall quake before them; the heavens shall tremble" (vv.9-10). Such a forbidding description gives some indication of how fierce this onslaught was.

It is little wonder that Pharaoh called for Moses and Aaron in haste. This locust plague could not be long endured. Egypt had suffered so much, and this latest sign from the Lord must be stayed. Before the Lord's messengers he confessed that he had sinned. Previously he had stated that he had sinned "this time" (9.27), but now he takes the matter a little further and confesses that his sin had been against "the Lord your God, and against you" (v.16). But there was nothing of sincerity about this confession. Immediately he uttered the words he followed them with, "Forgive, I pray thee, my sin only this once" (v.17). He had a very limited view of his sins. Only this one sin needed to be dealt with! His motive was that "this death" (v.17) might be taken away.

This acknowledgment of sin was not based on repentance. He saw it simply as a means of having this trouble removed, a danger which exists when the gospel is preached today. Sinners sometimes are attracted to the gospel because they have trouble in their lives which they wish to have put right, and the gospel *appears* to offer a way of life which is free of such problems as have been experienced. They may see themselves as having done something wrong, but any sense of being worthless sinners who are cast upon the grace of God is absent.

As with all such "professions" the lack of reality is soon revealed. The Lord knew the heart of Pharaoh but still drove the locusts from Egypt. This need not cause surprise. The Lord will act in a way that will never enable Pharaoh to state that he was treated unrighteously. He claimed to acknowledge his sin and the strong west wind removed the locusts, but then again he would not let the people go.

Verses 21-29: The Ninth Plague

A further plague has yet to come. Now it is darkness that descends over Egypt with the land of Goshen being untouched. To the Egyptian mind this was a defeat for *Ra* the sun god who, though he still marched across the heavens, was unable to give light. The intensity of this darkness is described as being a darkness that could be felt. For three days it lay over the land, ample evidence to convince the Egyptians that this was not a natural occurrence. In this intense darkness it was not possible to see one another or to move about; the land lay in dark unmoving silence as life came to a halt. God had withdrawn His gift of light and without it there was no enjoyment of life. Any attempt to pierce the gloom and spread a man-made light was doomed to failure.

What was seen physically in Egypt is also true spiritually. When there is rebellion against God and His message is treated with disdain the Lord will leave men and women in darkness. Without the light of the gospel real life cannot be enjoyed and man is unable to remedy the situation. But in the midst of such darkness those who believe God and acknowledge that Jesus Christ is Lord are living in enjoyment of light. Into darkness they will never be brought.

Pharaoh's compromise

Once again Pharaoh calls Moses with another compromise solution. They would be allowed to go, accompanied by their children, but they must leave their cattle behind. The increasing desperation of Pharaoh is clear, yet still he refuses to yield; still he seeks a solution which did not surrender completely to the word of the Lord. The reply of Moses is unbending. The Israelites will go with their flocks. When Moses states, "Thou must give us also sacrifices and burnt offerings, that we may sacrifice unto the Lord our God" (v.25) he is not asking the Egyptians to provide cattle from their flocks. He is asserting that Pharaoh must allow the Israelites to take their own cattle when they leave Egypt. To take some of their cattle only is also unacceptable. Not a hoof is to be left behind! Until they arrive in the wilderness they will not know exactly what animals will be necessary.

Behind the voice of Pharaoh once again there was the scheme of the Adversary. Pharaoh may have reasoned that without flocks and herds Israel would starve in the wilderness. But something deeper was also involved. If the devil could prevent Israel taking their flocks with them they would not have what was necessary for sacrifice. There would be nothing for the altar and nothing of a sweet savour would ascend to heaven; there would be no worship, and the Lord would be robbed of what was His due. This is still part of Satan's wiles; that saints may have nothing to offer in worship. A cold altar is a delight to the one who is the enemy of God. This is the last of five compromises which Pharaoh offered. In each of them we see the hand of the devil seeking to destroy this work for God.

Ref	Compromise	Significance
8.10	Tomorrow	An attempt to delay this request until tomorrow. When tomorrow comes it will still be put back to tomorrow.
8.25	Sacrifice in the land (Egypt)	Sacrifice in the land of Egypt linked with the Egyptian religious system.
8.28	Not very far away	If they cannot be kept in Egypt he attempts to keep them on his borders, near enough for him to exercise control over them.
10.11	Go now ye that are men	The children will be kept in Egypt. The hearts of the Israelites will therefore lie in Egypt. A generation will be lost to the Lord.
10.24	Let your flocks and your herds be stayed	No cattle to go, ensuring that the Israelites will have nothing to offer on the altar.

What Pharaoh offered is still being offered. The response of Moses must be the response of saints today. There must be no compromise on the teaching of the Word of God. Anything falling short of this, no matter how attractive it may appear, has to be shunned.

The words of Pharaoh indicate his anger at what he deemed to be Moses' unreasonable refusal to lower his demands. Moses has to go and never appear before Pharaoh again. Should he do so it will be in peril of his life. Pharaoh has "spoken rightly" (v.29, JND). How sad to see the servant of God declaring that he will not present himself before Pharaoh again. The opportunities that had been open to the monarch to humble himself before the Lord are now over and the narrative enters a fresh phase.

Nine plagues had descended on Egypt and with increasing force had destroyed much of the wealth and health of the land. Why did the Lord wait so long on Pharaoh? He did so firstly as a mark of His grace, offering to sinners a way of escape from their ways. He did so also to teach sinners His power, that He is a God to be reverenced and to be feared. He is longsuffering, but Pharaoh now had to learn that this longsuffering would not continue forever. But He also acted to teach Israel His power. The cost of deliverance, the power to be overthrown, the greatness of God had all been impressed on the nation. The actions of Pharaoh and his refusal to let them go was the reason for the further great display of divine power about to be seen and not to be forgotten.

EXODUS 11

The Promise of Redemption

Verses 1-3: The Promise Re-stated

These verses form a parenthesis and were spoken to Moses before his final interview with Pharaoh. They are brought in here to show Moses' authority and confidence in bringing the final appeal to the monarch. What follows, therefore, from v.4, is a continuation of the interview recorded in ch.10. Although Pharaoh had demanded that Moses leave his presence (10.28), Moses remained long enough to make the solemn declaration that one more plague had still to come.

The promise is made that this time, not only will Pharaoh allow them to go, he will thrust them out of his land. This appeared to be an impossible turn of events, but the faith of Moses grasped that, no matter how impossible a situation appears, there is nothing too hard for the Lord.

But there was another matter that had to be addressed before they went. For many years the Israelites had worked as slaves, and payment for that labour had to be obtained. The righteousness of God demanded this. The people would *ask* (see JND) of their neighbours not *borrow*. Little had Pharaoh realised, as the slaves were driven to greater effort, that every hour worked was accruing a debt that must be paid. The labour was not to be free. The disposition of the people to give the Israelites of their gold and silver may appear strange. To move from the position where they were downtrodden slaves in the land to being the recipients of wealth freely given by the Egyptians reflects a change of heart which was brought about by Jehovah as the "Lord gave the people favour in the sight of the Egyptians". "The man Moses was very great in the land of Egypt", so the reputation of Moses with the Egyptians was an issue as they realised that it was not advisable to work against this people. What Israel received at this time would, in the wilderness, constitute their ability to serve the Lord in offerings for the building of the Tabernacle.

Verses 4-8: The Plague Foretold

The dialogue with Pharaoh, interrupted by vv.1-3, is now resumed. The warning that came to Pharaoh is stark, consisting of three elements.

This last plague, a blow greater than they had yet experienced, was to be carried out by the Lord Himself. Keil & Delitzsch comment: "The *going out* of Jehovah from His heavenly seat denotes His direct interposition in, and judicial action upon, the world of men. The last blow upon Pharaoh was to be carried out by Jehovah Himself, whereas the other plagues had been brought by Moses and Aaron". The firstborn of every family in the land of Egypt would die, unless the blood was applied to the door as instructed in ch.12. Even the firstborn of the beasts would die; there would be no exemptions.

The cry that would ascend from the stricken homes would be greater than any that had gone before or that would be heard in future. This was a unique work by the Lord and this nation, which had been so favoured in the many warnings that had been given, would feel the severity of the judgment of God. This judgment was just and righteous, for He who is the Judge of all the earth always does right (Gen 18.25).

In the midst of this severe judgment the Hebrews would not be afflicted in any way. Not even a dog would bark or growl at them, an expression meaning that not the slightest harm would touch them. The difference between Israel and the Egyptians would be shown in this unmistakable manner.

The servants of Pharaoh would come to Moses and, bowing before him, would ask him to leave Egypt with all "the people that follow thee". The authority and rule of Moses over the Israelites would be acknowledged by Egypt, and the demand made to Pharaoh, from the first time Moses stood before him, would then be granted.

The solemn prophecy did not soften the heart of this proud monarch, a heart so hard that it was unmoved by the prospect of death entering the homes of every Egyptian where there was a firstborn. Such a prospect would surely move the most godless, but it failed to impress the haughty king who had withstood God in the nine plagues that had preceded this warning. No matter how great the suffering that had gone before, the Lord would act in a way that far surpassed anything they had endured. This Pharaoh, who had held them in bondage with such determination, would, however, shortly command them to be gone from his kingdom. Israel stood on the threshold of one of the most momentous events in its history, indeed, in the history of mankind!

The difference between the Israelites and the Egyptians would be plain to see. Each Israelite had to shelter under the blood and if they did so their safety was guaranteed. Although this was so, the people were not singing at this point. There was no song until the enemy had been destroyed and the saved people were over the Red Sea and in the wilderness. Those who did not apply the blood to their doors could not be saved from this danger by their own devices. They must simply obey the word of God and on that basis, and that basis alone, they would be saved from death.

Verses 9-10: The Decisive Conclusion

These are the last words of the Lord before the Passover was instituted. All the wonders had been displayed to Egypt and yet there appeared to be no progress in the pathway to freedom. The promise of Jehovah had been made but appeared to be no nearer fulfilment. It has been a long pathway for Moses since he saw the burning bush and heard the call of God. If the meeting with the Lord in the backside of the desert was a momentous turning point in his life, an equally momentous event is about to take place. At the burning bush only he was involved, now every family in Egypt, no matter what nationality, will be touched in some way. As this, therefore, is the close of one stage of God's dealings, to be followed immediately by the start of a new stage, it is appropriate to summarise the lessons which have been learned from these extraordinary events. God's dealings with a nation which is facing judgment and which has had the privilege of hearing from the lips of the servant of God how this could be avoided have unmistakable parallels with this present age.

The continual refusal of Pharaoh to listen to the plea of the servant of the Lord highlights *the patience and longsuffering of God*. He does not work in haste and is not subject to the time constraints that we would like to see in place. The number of weeks or months over which these plagues were spread is not revealed, but they were not over in a few days. "The Lord...is longsuffering...not willing that any should perish" (2 Pet 3.9) is how the New Testament puts it. That all have had the privilege of this longsuffering is clear from the words of Paul: "Despisest thou the riches of his goodness and forbearance and longsuffering; not knowing that the goodness of God leadeth thee to repentance" (Rom 2.4). Christians often look around them and wonder how it is that the Lord does not judge the evil surrounding them. How is it that godless men are allowed to continue? Part of the reason is that the Lord bears with them to give them space to repent. So it is with Pharaoh. He could never claim that he did not have the opportunity to heed the word of God, nor could he claim that he was not made aware of the consequences of his refusal to listen. There is no record in Scripture of anyone having more opportunities placed before him to listen to and obey God's word. The patience of Jehovah made Pharaoh without excuse.

During the long account of the plagues it can be clearly seen that *the purpose of God does not change*. The rebellious intransigence of the human heart does not affect the purpose of God in any way. "I am come down to deliver them out of the hand of the Egyptians" (3.8) was the statement made by Jehovah as He spoke to Moses in Horeb, and that had not altered. There were times when the elders of Israel doubted, as the pressure on them increased and the oppression of the Egyptians intensified (5.20,21). His purpose, however, still stood and was now about to be carried out. How encouraging this is to believers today. In a society that has abandoned Scripture, which denies openly the very existence of God, and which promotes practices abhorrent to God, the devil is always suggesting that God has lost the battle and that sin has triumphed. Nations ignore Him, rulers treat His Word with contempt, and false religion abounds. Yet through all this the Christian, although he may at times cry, "How long?", is confident in his faith that the Lord will triumph. His purpose, unaltered, will be fulfilled completely.

It is remarkable to consider that these events took place in order that *the power of God might be displayed* (11.9). "For the scripture saith unto Pharaoh, Even for this same purpose have I raised thee up, that I might show my power in thee, and that my name might be declared throughout all the earth", is how Paul states this (Rom 9.17), quoting the words of Exodus 9.16. It was vital that not only the Egyptians, but also the Israelites, learn of the power of God. This gave the people about to leave Egypt a foretaste of the power that would be available for them if they obeyed Him. With that they could face the wilderness and the Promised Land possessed of the knowledge that their God had defeated, not only the Egyptian potentate, but also the gods of Egypt.

But in addition to what these events have taught us about Jehovah, there are also lessons to learn regarding the chief characters in the crisis. It is of value to consider *the difference in the attitude of Moses*. At the beginning he was timid and had no confidence in his ability to stand before Pharaoh. Now he has confidence and is regarded as "very great" in Egypt (v.3). This confidence is not in his own abilities but in the promises and work of God. He has learned that the Lord will perform what He promises and the he will not be left alone to face the wrath of the king. So it is when servants are called of Him. Their strength and confidence increase as they see Him at work and as they experience His presence and power at first hand. To be called of God brings a sense of personal weakness and inability to fulfil the call. To go on obediently by faith and to see the hand of God at work gives confidence to the doubtful and strength to those who feel weakness.

This did not mean that there were no problems lying ahead and that there would be no days of doubt and despair. Moses would have to face such days. It does mean that those who trust the Lord, committing their way to Him, will get to know Him through His Word, and in the experiences, trials, and triumphs of life through which He calls them to pass.

Consideration must also be given to *the behaviour of Moses and Pharaoh*. Throughout, Moses had a calm and deliberate persistence as he made his requests and threatened punishment from the hand of the Lord. By this it is clear that, although he may not have gained the affection of the Egyptians, he had earned their respect. Never do the Egyptians threaten him personally and never do they seek to expel him from their country. His demeanour, and the fact that what he foretold took place, resulted in a good "testimony" amongst the people. The repeated, "Thus saith the Lord God of the Hebrews", showed that he claimed no power of his own. He stood as the mouthpiece of Jehovah, unflinching and unwavering, moving on with certainty and confidence. Little wonder that he was held in respect.

Pharaoh, on the other hand, proved to be crafty, unreliable, and wavering in his behaviour. For an absolute monarch to be confronted by such a man with such a message must have been a strange experience. His response, rather than having a desire to get to know the God of whom Moses spoke, was to offer compromises and make promises that he did not fulfil. "The craft of Pharaoh was ill matched against the downright straitforwardness of Moses" (Rawlinson, *Moses: His Life and Times*).

Now Moses had delivered his final message - "a message full of solemnity and dignity, suited indeed to the majesty of Him whose messenger he was" (Dennett). He had declared that the firstborn of Egypt would die. The stroke, however, would not fall that night at midnight. It is likely that some time would be allowed for Moses to instruct the people regarding the taking and the slaying of the lamb. Quite apart from that, the lamb was to be taken and kept from the tenth to the fourteenth day, so the instruction of 12.3 was given during the first month but in advance of the tenth day. During the interval, Egypt and its monarch waited. Everything Moses had said before had come to pass, so assuredly this last message would also. Here we have the final proof that the unbelieving heart, hardened against the Lord, will remain unrepentant and unmoved even when threatened with such a blow. Would they change, even at this late hour? As Moses was arranging the departure of the nation, would Pharaoh yet avert the blow shortly to fall? No voice was heard! No call was made for Moses to enter the palace! Hard hearts withstood God, and now they waited for the "midnight hour" as Israel prepared for release.

EXODUS 12

Salvation by Blood

Introduction

After the long account of the Lord's dealings with the monarch of Egypt it was now time for the deliverance of Israel to be effected. The promises, to bring them out from "under the burdens of the Egyptians" (6.6) and that God would take them to Himself "for a people" (6.7), were about to be fulfilled. The birthday of the nation of Israel dawned! It is not an overstatement to assert that this is one of the great landmark chapters of the Bible. It should be noted that what is about to take place is the Passover in reality. There was only one Passover. Every Passover celebrated in later years was a commemoration of this first feast. The lesson for today is that salvation takes place once. It need not and cannot be repeated, but it must never be forgotten.

That the Passover lambs slain in Egypt are a picture of the Lord Jesus and His death on the Cross is clearly stated by New Testament writers.

John Baptist	"Behold the Lamb of God, which taketh away the sin of the world" (Jn 1.29).
John	"A bone of him shall not be broken" (Jn 19.36 - a reference to Ex 12.46).
	"A Lamb as it had been slain" (Rev 5.6).
Paul	"Christ our passover is sacrificed for us" (1 Cor 5.7).
Peter	"...with the precious blood of Christ, as of a lamb without blemish and without spot" (1 Pet 1.19).

The word "passover" (6453) is found in its noun and verb forms 49 times in the Old Testament.[†] The number 49 (7x7) signifies perfect rest. The references are in nine Old Testament books; 9 (3x3) is the number of perfect sufficiency. The death of the Lamb of God brought perfect rest, into which those who trust Him will enter, and perfect sufficiency to cover the needs of all.

Verses 1-3a: The Announcement of a New Start

God has finished speaking to Pharaoh and now speaks to Israel. Everything changes with redemption. All things become new. The announcement is of divine provision for the deliverance of Israel from the bondage under which they had suffered. The first point to note is *where this announcement was made* (v.1). It was "in the land of Egypt". Why is this stated when any reader would already understand that Moses was there? Is it not to emphasise that there is truth associated with the fact that the announcement was made in Egypt? Of the seven Feasts of Jehovah, which Israel were instructed to keep each year (Lev 23), only the Passover took place firstly in Egypt. This Passover is for those who need redemption, and in later years it had to be commemorated by those who had been redeemed. There is no mention of an altar. Before they can approach an altar in worship they must know redemption by blood. Before they can offer to God they must receive from Him.

But in addition to where it was announced it is necessary to note *when it would be celebrated* (vv.2-3a). The month in which it was celebrated was to be the beginning of months,[†] marking the commencement of a new "religious" yearly calendar. This was the month Abib (13.4), the meaning of which is "green ears" (24), indicating that this was the time of ripening grain, commencing sometime after the middle of March, and was the seventh month of Israel's civil calendar. The long dark winter is over and this is reflected in Israel's experience. When redemption comes to an individual their long dark winter is truly over. When the beloved came to his love he exclaimed, "For, lo, the winter is passed, the rain is over and gone; The flowers appear on the earth; the time of the singing of birds is come, and the voice of the turtle is heard in our land" (Song 2.11-12). When he came he brought spring with him. After the nation was carried captive to Babylon this month was renamed Nisan (Est 3.7). But now this new start was to be marked by a completely fresh dating system, indicating the fundamental change which was to take place at this time.

The fact that this new date has to be "the beginning" indicates that for Israel the past has been cancelled out. It is not merely a new phase of life for the people; it is the beginning for them. At the time of salvation such a change always takes place. Paul writes, "If any man be in Christ, he is a new creature: old things are passed away; behold, all things are become new" (2 Cor 5.17). For the Christian, salvation cancels out the past. The same truth is emphasised to Nicodemus when the Lord stated that "Ye must be born again" (Jn 3.7). The new birth is not a new phase, but a completely new beginning.

To emphasise this change the Hebrews are called "all the congregation of Israel" (v.3) for the first time. The word "congregation" (5712) means "a gathering", "a family", or "a crowd". Now the Lord sees them as an assembled company, a family; no longer individual families but a united nation. They are viewed as the people in whose midst He will be pleased to dwell. One year after Israel's redemption, on the first day of the first month of the second year, the Tabernacle was erected (40.17). Coates comments: "The first year we learn what God is in grace *for us*...the second year we learn what it is to be *for God* as identified with the Tabernacle of testimony".

Verses 3b-5: The Selection of the Passover Lamb

Instruction is now given as to *what has to be taken*. On the tenth day of the first month a lamb was to be taken. There were ten Commandments, and the tithe was one tenth. The number ten in Scripture indicates human responsibility towards God. That dispensation has now run its course and man has failed. It is necessary for the Lord to provide the deliverance which man's failure has made essential. But another picture also presents itself in the selection of the lamb on the tenth day, the day in which the lamb came to the notice of the household for which it would die. This vital day pictures for us the day in which the Lord Jesus commenced His public ministry, and the tenth to the fourteenth day pre-figures the time span of that ministry. Before that public debut He had fulfilled all human responsibility and was presented to the nation as One who had not failed. The hidden years of the life of the Lord Jesus were pleasing to His Father who declared His delight in His Son by the public words of approval from the opened heaven (Mt 3.17; Mk 1.11).

Why was it that a lamb had to be taken? The offering of Abel had been of the "firstlings of his flock" (Gen 4.4). The word "flock" (6629) indicates sheep or goats. The only previous specific reference to a sacrificial lamb is in Genesis 22. Isaac expected that a lamb would be available for sacrifice as he asked, "Where is the lamb for a burnt offering?" (v.22). Historically, therefore, the patriarchs used lambs for this purpose. Practically, in Egypt a lamb was also a wise choice. The Israelites were shepherds when they went down to Egypt (Gen 47.3), and they had continued to pursue that occupation, as they had flocks at the time of the Exodus (10.9,24). Lambs, or even goats, would not therefore be difficult for them to obtain, and, being relatively small animals, would be of a suitable size for a family. But, in addition to the historic and practical reasons, there is typical significance in a lamb which is characterised by meekness, submissiveness, and gentleness, as is confirmed by the words of Isaiah: "He is brought as a lamb to the slaughter" (53.7).

Every man was to take a lamb "according to the house of their fathers". If a lamb was not available a kid of the goats was to be taken. There was to be one lamb for each house or family. Calculation was to be made of how much was necessary for the family: it was to be of a size to satisfy "every man according to his eating". No-one would have a portion which was too small for them; the lamb would satisfy each one and would do so completely. There would be no one in a home standing watching others partake of the lamb, but unable to partake personally because the lamb was too small. The two situations would never arise where there was no lamb for a family member, or the portion given was insufficient.

The same truth is seen in the giving of the manna. "This is the thing which the LORD hath commanded, Gather of it every man according to his eating, an omer for every man" (16.16). Once again there would be complete satisfaction for all who ate manna. Whether in relation to salvation, or to spiritual sustenance after salvation, the Lord Jesus Christ satisfies all who come to Him, and satisfies completely. The Cross has power for the redemption of all, and none can claim that redemption was lost to them because the Lamb was too small. The power of the Cross is sufficient for all sinners, from all lands, at all times, no matter what their state. When consideration is given to the number of lambs which must have been slain at that Passover feast, the fact that there is now "one sacrifice for sins for ever" (Heb 10.12) is an eternal confirmation of the value in the sacrifice of the Lamb of God. One further observation should be made here. Should the family unit be too small for one whole lamb, two families would eat of the one lamb if they were under the one roof. Thus although it has been noted that the lamb could not be too small for the house, it was possible for the house to be too small for the lamb.

The lamb to be taken was not to be worthless. It was a male, in the full strength and vigour of an animal of one year. It must not be an immature lamb, but one that had health and strength to grow to maturity. It was necessary that it be "without blemish" (8549), meaning perfect, sound, and without spot. The lamb must be fit to stand the close attention and scrutiny of all in the house, and have no visible defects and no hidden flaws. What a picture this is of the Lord Jesus. "Freedom from blemish and injury not only befitted the sacredness of the purpose to which they were devoted, but was a symbol of the moral integrity of the person represented by the sacrifice" (Keil & Delitzsch). John Baptist, as has been noted, points Him out to Israel as "the Lamb of God" (Jn 1.36), and He was indeed perfect, without defect. Men may seek to portray themselves in their best light when they come into the public eye, but here was a man whose perfections were appreciated in heaven. Born into an obscure family, the son of a humble carpenter, later to become a carpenter Himself, living a quiet life in a town which had an unenviable reputation, He nevertheless gave delight to God. The words "This is my beloved Son, in whom I am well pleased" (Mt 3.17, see also Mk 1.11; Lk 3.22) confirm that the Lamb of God was without blemish before He was publicly introduced to Israel.

John is the only writer in the New Testament, as he quotes John Baptist, specifically to refer to the Lord Jesus as the "Lamb of God" (Jn 1.29,36). In Revelation he refers to Him as the "Lamb" twenty-nine times. Yet John does not tell us of that declaration from heaven at the time of the baptism of the Lord Jesus in the River Jordan to which the other three Gospel writers refer. One might have expected such a commendation when the Lamb is introduced. However, the absence of this makes it clear that as the Lord Jesus was declared to be the "Lamb of God" the reader needs no other affirmation of His perfection. The fact that He is the Lamb of God's choosing is enough to affirm that He is "without blemish".

A further declaration of His perfection is made on the Mount of Transfiguration (Mt 17.5) after He had been rejected by Israel, proof that this rejection was not caused by any failure on His part. Even men acknowledged this truth. As He worked amongst them they said, "He hath done all things well" (Mk 7.37), and a demon declared, "I know thee who thou art, the *Holy* One of God" (Mk 1.24). The Epistle to the Hebrews states that He was "holy, harmless, undefiled" (Heb 7.26). Pilate, a man well used to sifting through evidence as he sat in judgment on the conduct of others, declared that He was a "just person" (Mt 27.24) and that he could find no fault in Him (Jn 19.4,6). He was passing comment on the actions of the Lord Jesus with which he was concerned, but nevertheless any who examined His life closely with a view to finding flaw or cause of guilt could find nothing with which He could be faulted or condemned. In all things and at all times He showed Himself to be without blemish and without spot. How necessary this was! Just as a blemished Passover lamb could not meet the need of the Israelites in Egypt so a Saviour with blemish could not meet the need of mankind. The statements, "Who did no sin" (1 Pet 2.22) and, "in him is no sin (1 Jn 3.5), written by two men who had observed Him closely and carefully over a number of years, had listened to Him, and had lived with Him, serve only to confirm that He is a worthy Saviour.

In looking therefore at what Scripture states about the lamb, the following points must be noted.

1. The first recorded sacrifice in Scripture acceptable to God was Abel's and that consisted of a lamb, "of the firstlings of his flock" (Gen 4.4).

2. The first recorded act of the Lord to Israel in effecting redemption was to instruct the selection of a lamb for each house.

3. The first public presentation of the Lord Jesus to Israel was accompanied by the invitation from the lips of John Baptist to "Behold the Lamb of God, which taketh away the sin of the world" (Jn 1.29). This was followed the next day by the further cry, "Behold the Lamb of God" (Jn 1.36). Stating this twice indicates that this is confirmed, reliable testimony.

4. In the book of Revelation, as heaven is opened to view, amidst the glory of that scene John sees "a Lamb as it had been slain" (Rev 5.6). When He takes the book out of the hand of the One who sat on the throne the courts of heaven resound with praise as the new song is sung and as ten thousand times ten thousand, and thousands of thousands join in the acclaim saying, "Worthy is the Lamb that was slain…" (Rev 5.12). The view of the Lamb caused the host to break into song.

Verses 6-7: Slaying the Passover Lamb

From the tenth to the fourteenth day there had to be *the display of the lamb*. It should be noted that the purpose of this was not to examine the lamb and ascertain that it was without blemish. This had already been carried out when the lamb was selected. The purpose of keeping the lamb in this way was twofold. During these days the household would come to appreciate the beauty of the lamb. As they gazed on it they would see perfection. But would it not also be true that the household would come to have affection for the lamb, and when it came time to slay it they would feel it all the more keenly? So, during this period there is in the home a lamb the beauties of which they were able to appreciate and for which they gained love and affection. Each day the members of the household would observe the lamb on which their deliverance depended. The beauty of the animal would be admired, its meekness plain to see, its death the cause of sorrow - yet die it must if they would be free of the oppression under which they suffered.

On the fourteenth day there was *the death of the lamb.* The "whole assembly of the congregation" was to carry out this act. No exceptions could be allowed. Every family making up the congregation had to slay their lamb in the evening. The expression "evening", or "between the two evenings", is "likely 'twilight', the time interval between sunset and darkness, in which there is a state of illumination" (TWOT at 1689a). It has often been pointed out that this is the first sacrifice in the Scriptures where blood is mentioned. In other sacrifices, Abel's, Noah's, and Abraham's on Mount Moriah, clearly blood was shed, but it was not given a conspicuous place. In this sacrifice it is prominent, reminding the reader of the importance and value of the shedding of blood in the work of redemption. A living lamb was not sufficient for their deliverance. It had to be slain! No matter how beautiful the life of the Lord Jesus, He had to be slain to effect redemption.

No blood was to be placed on the doorstep or entrance path lest it be trampled underfoot (see Heb 10.29). The placing of the blood on the lintel over the door and on the two doorposts (v.7) was not primarily to let the Egyptians see it. Some of them may have noticed and wondered what was the significance of this strange act. But this was not its chief purpose. It was not a witness to them. Enough had been done in the months past to testify to the power of Jehovah and to the fact that He was God. It was there that Jehovah might see it and "pass over" the house. It was proof that those within the house had believed the word of God as it was passed to them through Moses and Aaron. They had selected the lamb, they had scrutinised the lamb, and then they had slain the lamb. As the darkness descended on that momentous night there were only two types of house in Egypt - those without blood applied and those with blood applied. It was the blood that made the difference. There was no third condition. What stood between the Hebrew family inside the house and the "destroyer" (v.23) was the blood and that alone. Nothing else would avail. In the greatest question of life there are only two choices and only two resulting conditions; those who are saved, sheltered under the blood and ready to go, and those who have refused the message of God and who, with no blood to shelter them, will be subject to His judgment. This was a solemn night and has a message for all, ringing down the corridors of time, warning all of the folly of rejecting the offer of grace in the gospel.

Verses 8-11: Partaking of the Passover Lamb

Having placed the blood of the slain lamb on the doorposts and lintel, the family retired into the house to eat of the Passover as they awaited the call to depart. Eating the lamb was a significant act as it indicated their belief that they would partake of the blessings that would come from its death. It signified them appropriating the value of the lamb to themselves. The instructions for eating the lamb were very particular.

How it had to be prepared (vv.8-9)

It must be "roast with fire", not raw or sodden (boiled) in water. The lamb was to be subject to the flame and endure all the heat. If it were raw it would not have endured the full heat of the fire and if it were sodden in water it would have escaped the full effect of burning. The Lord Jesus was also "subject to the flame". There was nothing to alleviate His sufferings. All had to be endured in full.

How it had to be eaten (v.8)

It had to be eaten with unleavened bread. This was the start of a new life. Leaven in Scripture always speaks of sin. Unleavened bread speaks of determination to have done with sin. It is the self-sacrificing resolve to keep sin out of the life. As they left Egypt it was unleavened bread that they took with them, as they had no time to leaven the bread before their hurried departure (v.34). It also had to be eaten with bitter herbs, reminding them of the bitterness of their life in Egypt. Both of these features can also be applied to the Lord Jesus. He was sinless. He did not and could not sin. The bitter herbs bring to mind the sufferings through which He would pass at Calvary.

What had not to be done (v.9)

The lamb must not be divided. The head, the legs, and the fat must not be separated from the body. If the lamb had to be subject to the flame it must *all* be subject. No part of it could be left aside or subject to less than was necessary to roast the flesh with fire. Note the three parts:

The Passover lamb	*The Lamb of God*
1. The head	"Who knew no sin" (2 Cor 5.21).
2. The legs	"Who did no sin" (1 Pet 2.22).
3. The purtenance (inwards)	"In him is no sin" (1 Jn 3.5).

Nothing had to be left until the morning (v.10)

The lamb had to be eaten when it was fresh. It was not to be left until the morning because corruption was never associated with the Lamb of God. Even in the tomb that precious body saw no corruption. If any of the lamb was left until the morning it had to be burned. Note also that the power of the Cross of the Lord Jesus Christ never becomes "stale". There is an eternal freshness about Calvary.

Before morning came the journey out of the house of bondage had commenced, but any lamb left over from the Passover meal was not to be used for sustenance. The lamb could not be partaken of twice. Once it was eaten it could not be eaten again. When redemption blessings coming from the shedding of the blood of the Lamb have been appropriated they cannot be appropriated again. In the language of the New Testament we cannot be saved twice.

How the people had to be dressed (v.11)

This was no meal before retiring for the night. They were to have their loins girded with garments used for "outside" activity, their sandals for travel on their feet and a staff for support on the journey in their hands. They ate, prepared for immediate departure, before Pharaoh knew that they would go that night. They ate in confidence, knowing that this was the long awaited moment, and they ate with urgency, knowing that their departure would require speed.

The closing words of v.11, "It is the Lord's passover", would remind them that nothing was to be left to their own whim or design. Complete adherence to the word of God was vital if they were to enjoy deliverance. It was not Israel's Passover, it was the Lord's. This is the first mention of "Passover" (6453). It has the meaning of passing or skipping over, but the suggestion has also been made that it means "to defend", or "to protect" (TWOT at 1786a). This latter aspect is seen in v.23.

Verses 12-14: Preserved by the Blood of the Passover Lamb

The work to be done that night in Egypt will be the work of the Lord. Three things are to be noted in v.12. First, He will pass through the land. There will be no area into which He will not enter; the work will be complete and total. Second, He will smite all the firstborn. The word "smite" (5221) in this context means a "mortal blow" bringing death; it is used by the Lord regarding Cain who had a mark set upon him, "lest any finding him should *kill* him" (Gen 4.15). Not only was the coverage of Egypt to be complete but the judgment on each of the firstborn would also be completely effective. No firstborn of man or beast would escape should the blood be absent from the door. Pharaoh had set his hand against the firstborn of the Lord (4.22) and warning had been given to him about what was now about to take place (4.23). Third, the gods of Egypt will be judged. They will be revealed as impotent and Jehovah will be revealed as the Lord who has power far beyond anything that the Egyptians claimed for their gods. This will be the final humiliation of Egypt's gods. Already they have been seen to be powerless. "Each blow insults and abuses them. Serapis blushes till his Nile waters, erst so translucent, turn to blood red: Ra, the sun god, is compelled to smile on Israel and frown on Mizraim. The sacred frog and fly become objects of loathing. The bull-god, Apis, cannot protect himself nor his fellow cattle from the murrain. Seb, the earth, is covered with vermin. Osiris and Isis are extinguished in the sky; and Nepte, the vault of heaven, is covered with a shameful darkness as with a garment of mourning. The whole obscene brood are hurled headlong flaming from the ethereal sky. In hideous ruin and combustion down to bottomless perdition".†

It is true that idols are nothing (Is 41.24). They are but the work of the hands of man (Is 37.19), wood and stone with no life in them. Some may assert that, if that is so, they are harmless, and, if they seem to satisfy, what evil is in them. But behind these idols were the evil spirits controlled by the Adversary. Therein lay their evil! Here, in Egypt, the battle had been between Jehovah and the forces of the "power of darkness" (Col 1.13). In that battle the Lord will now be seen to have triumphed.

Although this was a solemn and sorrowful night for Egypt it is but a faint picture of what will yet come to pass when the judgment of God falls on this world, a record of which is given in Revelation. The words of Revelation 19.2, "true and righteous are his judgments", spoken in connection with the judgment which had befallen Babylon the Great, are equally true here.

This night was never to be forgotten. It was to be kept as a "memorial…a feast to the Lord throughout your generations…an ordinance forever". It was to be a memorial to remember, a feast giving occasion for joy, and an ordinance to obey.

This consideration of the lamb cannot be left without calling attention to the development in Scripture of the doctrine of the Lamb. The lamb is first for the individual (Gen 4.4); for the family (Ex 12); for the nation (Is 53.7); and for the world (Jn 1.29).

Verses 15-20: The Feast of Unleavened Bread

Immediately after the instructions for Passover there were given directions for the Feast of Unleavened Bread. Leviticus 23 (which gave instructions for the annual observance of these feasts) taught Israel that these were the first two of seven Feasts of Jehovah which were to be celebrated annually, beginning in the first month of Israel's "religious" calendar and ending with the Feast of Tabernacles (Booths) in the seventh month. So close was the link between these two feasts that often the Jews regarded them as being one. Luke confirms this as he writes, "Now the feast of unleavened bread drew nigh, which is called the Passover" (Lk 22.1). Mark corroborates this as he records that "After two days was the feast of the passover, and of unleavened bread" (Mk 14.1), and draws attention to "the first day of unleavened bread, when they killed the passover" (Mk 14.12). However, it is clear that they were two separate feasts, but so closely linked that it can be said of them that they are distinct yet indivisible.

What is leaven? It is yeast that is placed in dough in the baking of bread. It causes the dough to rise by creating little pockets of air within it. It has three features which are significant. First, it works internally in a hidden way. Silently and away from the gaze of onlookers it carries out its function. Second, it brings rapidity of growth with no added weight. Third, its progress is arrested by the flame. Only after the loaf has been fully baked does the work of the leaven cease.

Leaven indicates sin and how it carries out its work. In the Old Testament the meal offering had to be free of leaven (Lev 2.11; 6.17). In the New Testament there are references to leaven which define its spiritual significance.

The Gospels
Matthew 16.6,12	"Take heed and beware of the leaven of the Pharisees and of the Sadducees…the doctrine of the Pharisees and of the Sadducees".
Mark 8.15	"Take heed, beware of the leaven of the Pharisees, and of the leaven of Herod".
Luke 12.1	"Beware ye of the leaven of the Pharisees which is hypocrisy".

The Epistles
1 Corinthians 5.7	"Purge out therefore the old leaven".
1 Corinthians 5.8	"Therefore let us keep the feast, not with old leaven, neither with the leaven of malice and wickedness".
Galatians 5.9	"A little leaven leaveneth the whole lump".

The woman who took leaven and hid it in three measures of meal (Mt 13.33) does not picture the kingdom growing for the glory of God, but rather portrays the corrupting effect of sin.

With this as a background the close link between the Passover and the Feast of Unleavened Bread now becomes clear; so close, as has already been noted, that they are distinct and yet indivisible. Those who have enjoyed salvation through the shedding of the blood of the Lamb will now go on, as a result of that deliverance, to seek to live a life free from sin. It is to this that Paul refers when he writes, "Christ our Passover is sacrificed for us: Therefore let us keep the feast, not with the old leaven…" (1 Cor 5.7-8). The feast to which he refers is not the Lord's Supper but the Feast of Unleavened Bread. This may require the "purging out" of the old leaven, the sins which we practised before salvation and which we have not yet abandoned, and the purging out of malice and wickedness. The evidence of the reality of a profession to believe the gospel is not found in our words, but in our actions. The link, as with Passover and the Feast of Unleavened Bread is unbreakable. Salvation and a desire to be done with sin are, as with the Old Testament picture, distinct yet indivisible. No Christian reaches a state of "sinless perfection" in this life. Sin, however, is not expected to be the normal manner of life, but rather the exception. John recognises this when he writes, "If any man sin" (1 Jn 2.1). The emphasis is on *if*. It is not *when* that is used.

Three things are noted about dealing with leaven.

1. Leaven was to be put away from their houses (v.15). It had to be dealt with domestically. There was to be a desire to have none of it in the home. Searching was to take place to ensure that it was not present. Leavened

bread was not to be eaten (v.15). It was not to be fed on and thus be appropriated.

2. No leavened bread was to be "seen with" them (13.7). It had to be dealt with personally. It had not even to be seen in their possession.

3. No leavened bread was to be in their quarters (13.7). It had to be dealt with nationally. When excluded from the home it had not to be stored elsewhere.

The presence of unleavened bread on this first occasion of the feast was due to the fact that the Egyptians had thrust Israel out and there was no time to leaven the dough. In later times they had to follow the instructions of v.15. These are so important that they are re-emphasised in vv.18-20. The punishment for failing to obey the directions for this feast was severe. Such a man would be "cut off from Israel" (v.15), "cut off from the congregation" (v.19). He would be treated as if he were not an Israelite and thus denied all the God-given privileges enjoyed by Israelites. In the New Testament the same punishment is meted out on the individual who refuses to have his trespasses dealt with. He becomes "as a heathen man and a publican" (Mt 18.17). In the local church the same principle is still in force when one who has sinned in a grievous way is "put away" (1 Cor 5.13). Paul contemplates the consequence should he allow sin to control his body through the passions of the flesh (1 Cor 9.27). The result is that he would become a castaway, one who is disapproved for service, unable to carry on with the work of Christian testimony. A Christian will have no love of sin, and should it come into the life there will be strong desire to repent and be done with it, and a determination not to "continue in sin" (Rom 6.1)

The Feast of Unleavened Bread commenced on the fifteenth day of the first month and continued for seven days (see Lev 23.6). It is clear from v.18 that unleavened bread was eaten on the fourteenth day, the day when the Passover lamb was slain, although the feast did not commence until the next day. During the seven days from the fifteenth, unleavened bread was eaten and the first and the seventh days (fifteenth and twenty-first days of the month) were designated "holy convocations". In those two days no work was to be done except that which was necessary for the provision of food.

When Canaan was settled this was one of three occasions each year when the men of Israel were required to appear before the Lord. It should be noted that in Leviticus 23 when the word "feast" (2282) is used it is the translation of a word which is from a root meaning "to celebrate". It therefore contains the thought of joy and celebration. It is used of only three of the feasts, those which are termed the *pilgrimage feasts*, the Feasts of Unleavened Bread, of Weeks (Pentecost), and of Tabernacles, when all the males were called to appear before the Lord (23.14-17). This feast, linked so closely with the Passover, was an occasion of joy, not only for the past deliverance from an implacable foe (that is the Passover aspect), but also for the new life into which they had been brought (the Red Sea aspect). Unleavened bread was not a pleasant thing to partake of for seven days. Bread with leaven was much more palatable. So it is today: sin is palatable to the flesh and the absence of it is irksome.

Before these verses are left behind it should be observed that when the Lord speaks of Israel leaving Egypt the past tense is used (v.17). He was speaking of the future observance of this feast but the use of the past tense indicates that He saw the work as already complete. To Him they would go out as a "army", an ordered host. The world would see them as a group of fleeing slaves with little chance of success against the enemies they would meet, and little hope of being able to survive the conditions through which they would be called to pass. The Lord, however, sees them as ready for the battle. So it always is in the things of God. The world sees His people as weak, powerless, and often to be pitied. He sees them as there are in His presence - warriors, workers, and worshippers, all fitted by Him for the journey.

Verses 21-24: Further Instructions Relating to the Passover Lamb

It is clear from v.3 that the Passover was not slain on the day when the Lord spoke to Moses. Before that could take place the elders of Israel had to be called together and the Passover lamb had to be taken on the tenth day of the month. The Lord must have spoken to Moses before the tenth day at a time which allowed the meeting to take place with the elders and the selection of the lamb to be made. The lamb then had to be removed from the flock and kept separate before it was slain.

Additional information is given which is not recorded in the earlier account of the Lord speaking to Moses. This does not imply that Moses added this of his own accord. It would have been given to Moses but only now brought to our attention.

1. Hyssop was to be dipped in the blood of the lamb and the blood applied to the lintel and doorpost by that means. This is the first mention of hyssop in Scripture. It is used in the cleansing of the leper (Lev 14.4,6,51,52) and in sprinkling the ashes of the red heifer on what had to be cleansed (Num 19.18). Cleansing is linked with the use of hyssop as is confirmed by David: "Purge me with hyssop and I shall be clean" (Ps 51.7). Figuratively, therefore, the house that had blood applied through the use of hyssop had been cleansed.

2. No one had to leave the house until the morning. If they did so the blood that had been applied to their house would not cover them and therefore they would be subject to judgment if they were the firstborn of the family.

3. In v.13 Moses is told that the Lord will pass over the house when blood is applied to it, but in v.23 he states that the Lord will "pass over the door", and will not suffer the destroyer to enter. It appears, therefore, that the Lord visited every house in Egypt and when there was no blood He

permitted the destroyer to enter. When there was blood He "passovered" the house and prevented the destroyer entering.

Verses 25-28: Explaining Passover to the Next Generation

When the land is possessed the deliverance from Egypt must never be forgotten. They must "keep this service". This was a responsibility given to them to be undertaken for God as it had been ordained by God and was to be carried out for Him. As they kept it, their children would enquire to learn of the significance of the feast. Here is a good example for parents. In the home, truth should not only be taught but should also be practised. It is spiritually healthy when children ask parents why they act as they do. There is little value in teaching children the significance of truth which they do not see practised in the parents' lives. That will make no impact for God.

The value of spiritual example in the home is further emphasised by three other questions which it is anticipated children will ask. The first of these is in connection with the setting apart of the firstborn to the Lord: "And it shall be when thy son asketh thee in time to come, saying, "What is this?" (13.14). The second has to do with the Scriptures: "And when thy son asketh thee in time to come, saying, What mean the testimonies, the statutes, and the judgments, which the Lord our God hath commanded you?" (Deut 6.20). The third refers to the twelve stones which were placed on the bank of the Jordan where Israel passed over the river: "That this may be a sign among you, that when your children ask their fathers in time to come, saying, What mean ye by these stones?" (Josh 4.6). What a range of truth is involved in this. The key issues of salvation, separation to the Lord, the value and use of Scripture, and what has to be done to live in the enjoyment of the things of God are all covered. It is necessary to emphasise again that children were not taught what they did not observe around them. The questions came from the young, provoked by the lives of the parents. Note carefully that it was necessary, not only that the parents should obey the Word of God, but also that they must be able to explain to the children the reason why they lived as they did. For them this was not to be merely a preferred "lifestyle", nor a set of rules and regulations handed down from generation to generation to preserve cultural tradition. It was obedience to the Lord carried out with an intelligent understanding of why they lived as they did.

Verses 29-36: The Events of Passover Night

The death of all the firstborn during that dark Egyptian night is covered by one verse. The Lord does not delight in the work of judgment and a simple declaration of what took place, in the briefest of terms, is all that is given. As He had promised, so He performed. There were no exceptions. As the Israelites remained in their homes the cry went up all over Egypt. Those who were awake or were wakened became aware that death had entered their home, and neighbours who were roused by the grief of others soon learned that they had cause for grief also. The scope of it can scarcely be imagined. Hundreds of thousands died. The firstborn, the crown of the hopes of the people, those on whom the responsibility for the next generation would fall, the anticipated future heads of the families, all taken away in one night. Little wonder that the cry that went up was a "great cry". All Egypt learned that night that "It is a fearful thing to fall into the hands of the living God" (Heb 10.31).

In the final meeting which occurs between Moses, Aaron, and Pharaoh what seemed at one time impossible now takes place. At last Pharaoh permits them to leave and take their flocks and herds with them. There is no Egyptian requirement for a diminution of Moses' demands. They have to go as they have said. The Egyptians are now insisting that they leave, their presence no longer desired. If Moses had compromised in his demands this would never have taken place. The nation is about to take the pathway of separation from Egypt and is being urged by Egyptians to do so. The lesson for believers today is that if a clear uncompromising testimony is displayed, the world will enforce the path of separation. Christians who maintain a good testimony are not welcome company for the world. The problem of how far to go along with the world can be solved by virtue of the fact that a good testimony results in an absence of invitations to join them; the world has no wish to have the company of faithful believers. The same principle is seen in the church in Jerusalem where no unbelievers wished to join themselves to them (Acts 5.13) as they recognised that God was with the Christians. The sense of the holiness and righteousness of God, driven home by the deaths of Ananias and Sapphira, made unbelievers conscious of the fact that to "join themselves" to the assembly made them subject to the government of God. It should, however, be observed that what kept the unbeliever away did not prevent concerned souls being saved, for "believers were the more added to the Lord" (Acts 5.14). The sense of the presence and power of the Lord made the world determined that His people would not be among them and that they would not be among His people. This is not isolation from the world but separation to the Lord while living in the world.

As they prepared for the journey the Israelites took only unleavened bread with them. On a practical level there would be no time to bake leavened bread before they had to leave, but there is a lesson here. There was no short period when they could enjoy the leavened food so that they could gradually be weaned from that to the unleavened. They left carrying only holy food, that which was fit for the Feast of Unleavened Bread. The redeemed people are showing in symbol that they are done not only with the taskmaster but also with the sin of Egypt. Gospel preachers today must declare that salvation results in a new life, not commencing at some undetermined future date, but on the day of salvation. It is true that some sins which dominated unsaved days may not be dislodged immediately, but the desire and determination to change is the direct result of salvation. The truth of the unleavened bread starts at the moment of conversion.

Before they leave the Israelites "borrow" from their neighbours, silver gold and costly raiment. The word "borrow" (7592) can mean "to demand", "to ask" (JND), or "to request". Clearly the Egyptians did not resist this request. They were willing to give because the Lord gave the Israelites favour in their sight. The events of the Passover night would give the Egyptians a different view of their slaves. Rather than being a down-trodden people they were now a people whose favour was desirable. The promise had been given to Abraham that they would "come out with great substance" (Gen 15.14) and this was confirmed to Moses (Ex 3.3ff). There was no unrighteousness in this. They were not taking with them that which was not their due. For years they had worked under oppression and Egypt, as has been noted (see 11.2), now had to pay the wages which were due reward for their labour. Little did the oppressors realise that every day the Israelites worked for them was adding to the wages that now had to be paid. The word "lent" (7592) in v.36 (the same as "borrow" in v.35) is used here in the sense of giving (see JND: "they gave to them") and not in the sense of lending with the expectation of having the goods returned. To lose their firstborn and then to suffer this very severe financial loss must have been a grievous blow, not only to individuals, but also to the Egyptian state.

Verses 37-42: Departure from Egypt

Rameses was in the area of Egypt which had been given to the Children of Israel when they came down into Egypt. Later, during their oppression, they built a treasure city there. They left their homes and travelled to Succoth, the place where they now assembled together, ready for the journey. "Succoth" (5523) means "Booths", and it is likely that this was a shepherd encampment also used by travellers. Their booths would be erected from the branches of trees etc to form suitable temporary accommodation. That the Children of Israel lived in booths when they left Egypt is clear from Leviticus 23.43: "I made the children of Israel to dwell in booths, when I brought them out of the land of Egypt". It was at Succoth that this practice commenced, perhaps only during their time there, but it might have continued, with the branches taken from Succoth, until they were able to make tents, probably from goat's hair which was the usual material for this purpose.[†] Although slaves, they did live in houses in Egypt. The difference in their new domestic circumstances was very considerable. Living in booths, then in tents, and the temporary nature of each stopping place on the journey, brought a new way of life completely. Salvation touched all aspects of their lives and changed everything.

But this great number did not travel alone. A "mixed multitude" went with them. Who were these people? They were not of Israel because they are noted as being a separate company who are not "of" Israel, but "with" Israel. They were "mixed" in that they were not of one nation, but a company who wished to leave Egypt behind. They may have consisted of poor dissatisfied Egyptians and of slaves of other nationalities who had taken advantage of the haste with which the Egyptians had sent their Hebrew slaves away to obtain their freedom at the same time. They may have been others living in Egypt who, for a variety of reasons, wished to leave. As they were not of the "congregation of Israel" (12.3) their firstborn would have died. Why, then, should they leave Egypt?

Without doubt they had observed all that was taking place and concluded that their lot would be better with the Israelites than with the Egyptians. It may be that the power of God which had been displayed so openly over the months led them to believe that as God was with Israel they, too, for the sake of their own safety, should accompany them. It is sadly possible today for individuals to seek to "profess" to be saved, not because there is genuine repentance and a desire for salvation, but because Christians have a way of life which appears to have benefits worth gaining. As with the mixed multitude their true nature will be revealed by their subsequent conduct.

The company leaving Egypt was very large, numbering, apart from women and children, about 600,000 adult men.[†] Sceptics have challenged the large number, insisting that such a company could not leave Egypt in this way. This, however, is the record of Scripture, and the Lord is in control. If, on average, each of these men was married and had two children this would make the total 2,400,000. The logistics of moving such a multitude would demand order and discipline. But they were to be well led. The Psalmist writes that the Lord "made his own people to go forth like sheep, and guided them in the wilderness like a flock" (78.52). As far as the Egyptians were concerned they were glad when Israel departed "for the fear of them fell upon them" (Ps 105.38). For 430 years they had remained in Egypt,[†] It was, therefore, to a new world that they travelled, a world which they had never experienced, and a way of life completely different from all that they had known. "All the hosts of the Lord" (v.41) went out. None was left behind, another example of the faithfulness of the Lord in fulfilling His promises.

This most memorable of all nights is called "a night to be much observed unto the Lord for bringing them out from the land of Egypt" (v.42). The constant emphasis that this night and its feast must be remembered (vv.17,24) teaches believers today that what the Lord has done for Christians in delivering from bondage greater than that of Egypt, must never be forgotten. If remembering that night brought from the hearts of the Israelites thanksgiving and praise to their God, how much more should be stirred the hearts of those who enjoy the fullness of God's salvation today. It is a cold heart that does not worship when salvation is remembered.

What has been left for believers today is not an annual remembrance, but a weekly one. The Lord's Supper, celebrated on the first day of every week, is when He is remembered and when those who partake "shew the Lord's death till he come" (1 Cor 11.26). The practice of gathering for the Lord's Supper on the first day of every week is confirmed in Acts 20 when Paul was at Troas, where the believers broke bread (the Lord's Supper) "upon the first day of the week" (v.7). The word "week" is in the plural, so that literally what was written was that they gathered "on the first day of the weeks". In addition to this it is clear that Paul was anxious to be at Jerusalem by Pentecost (Acts 20.16), but despite this he waited at Troas for seven days as that enabled him to be with the disciples when they broke bread. This weekly remembrance of the Lord Jesus and His work is significant in a number of ways for those who gather.

1. To remember Him (1 Cor 11.24). Those who gather should have their hearts filled with Christ and be so drawn to Him that any less frequent remembrance would be unacceptable.

2. To show forth His death (1 Cor 11.26). "The acts of breaking the bread and drinking the cup constitute a silent proclamation of the fact, significance and efficacy of the Lord's death."†

> No gospel like this feast,
> Spread for us, Lord, by Thee:
> No prophet nor evangelist
> Preach the glad news so free.
> (E. R. Charles)

3. To be reminded of the swift passing of time and of His coming (1 Cor 11.26). It is only "till he come", and with the purpose of keeping before the hearts of the saints the fact that He is coming again. Vine again comments that "This great event of the future is, in the feast, linked with the great event of the past" (*op cit*).

4.   To teach that it is a continuous feast. The words "till he come" as well as reminding those present of the Rapture, the coming of the Lord Jesus to the air for His saints, also confirms that this feast will be celebrated until that day and not only for some years or an era during that period. Vine further comments succinctly that "The remembrance will cease when the Remembered returns" (*op cit*).

> We know Thee now exalted high,
> Ourselves in Thee accepted;
> We wait the hour which now draws nigh,
> Thy coming long expected.
> Till Thou dost come we still would be,
> With grateful hearts remembering Thee.
> (G. W. Frazer)

Verses 43-51: Further Passover Instructions

Two further matters have to be dealt with in relation to the Passover. There were certain groups who were prohibited from taking part. "Stranger" (1125, 5236) translates two Hebrew words which mean *one who was not born into the house of Israel*. A foreigner (8453) means *one who is a temporary resident,* clearly also not an Israelite. A hired servant, who was also not an Israelite, could not take part. Bondservants (5650) could only partake if they were circumcised. However, if any of the first three groups also submitted to circumcision of the males they could partake (v.48). Circumcision was a willing acknowledgement that there was permanent link between the individual and the God of Israel. It was acceptance of the covenant which had been made with Abraham. There was to be one law for Israel and the others; one standard only. All, no matter into what nation they were born, could have confidence in the God of Israel. Once again the promises of God are treated as if they are already fulfilled. "He shall be as one that is born in the land" (v.48), is spoken as if the land was already in their possession.

The second matter is the emphasis placed upon the fact that the Passover lamb was to be eaten in one house. Where a house was too little for a lamb it was to be shared with neighbours. The lamb, however, was not to be divided into two parts. The feast would take place in one house and the two families would eat in that one house. Neither the flesh nor the bones were to be broken asunder. They were to remain as one. This points us forward to the Cross. His body was not "broken".† He did not die a "broken" man. His sufferings were great, far beyond what others can comprehend, but despite that He was not "broken". No bone of Him was to be broken. How vital this was because the soldiers broke the legs of crucified men in order to hasten death. When they came to the Lord Jesus they did not require to carry out this act because He was dead already (Jn 19.32-33). Men could not, therefore, say that they had hastened His death. The precious body of the Lord Jesus went into the tomb with no broken bones. They did, however, pierce His side so that Scripture could be fulfilled - "A bone of him shall not be broken. And again another scripture saith, They shall look on him whom they have pierced" (Jn 19.36,37). The body of the Passover lamb was to be treated with dignity and respect. In relation to the Cross God overruled and the Lord Jesus was taken down with loving hands handling Him tenderly.

The detail with which the Passover is dealt is a fitting reminder that information is not given in Scripture without reason. Today it is popular to regard some Scriptures as more important than others; if there is concentration on the "main things" in dealings with other believers or with the world, other issues are not so important. But who decides what is important and what is not? All Scripture is inspired and is profitable (2 Tim 3.16); therefore it ill behoves any to judge the relative value and importance of sections of the Word of God. The details given in the closing verses of the chapter have equal weight with those given at the beginning. Scripture must be embraced in its fullness, and those who seek to serve God must be prepared to submit to all of its teaching, no matter if other believers (wrongly) regard sections of it as outdated or irrelevant to present circumstances.

The people carried out the Word of God (v.50). This was done when the taskmaster's whip was not a memory but a present reality. Many of them would have felt the scourge on their back that very day, a day which they knew would end with the Passover being eaten. As they stood and partook of the lamb they would still feel the hurt of the lash. No wonder, then, that "Thus did all the children of Israel". Salvation and deliverance to them on that day was not a hypothetical issue of intellectual interest, it was not something so far lost in history that it seemed too remote to appreciate. It was present salvation; it was real, delivering from felt hurt and oppression. It was achieving what they could not achieve themselves, and it was not because of their faithfulness to their God over the centuries in Egypt - it was despite their conduct over these long years. What an example of God's free, unencumbered grace to the undeserving. What a story of promises made centuries before, as fresh as ever, and about to be fulfilled.

Christians today enjoy a salvation far greater than that known to Israel in Egypt. These events were a picture of the great salvation now to be obtained through believing the gospel. Little wonder that believers can "joy in God through our Lord Jesus Christ" (Rom 5.11).

> And we have known redemption, Lord,
> From bondage worse than theirs by far;
> Sin held us by a stronger chord,
> But by Thy mercy free we are.
>
> (M. Peters)

Notes

Introduction The occurrences are: 6 in Exodus; 1 in Leviticus; 11 in Numbers; 4 in Deuteronomy; 2 in Joshua; 3 in 2 Kings; 19 in 2 Chronicles; 2 in Ezra; 1 in Ezekiel.

2 See Appendix 2: *The Jewish Sacred Calendar*.

12 W. Kelly, *The Bible Treasury* Vol 17, page 271.

37 On a practical level, their departure took place at the beginning of the dry part of the year which afforded them time to make their tents before weather came for which booths would not be suitable in the wilderness.

37 603,550 over the age of twenty (38.26).

41 See note in the Introduction, "The Duration of the Captivity".

42 W. E. Vine, *1 Corinthians*.

46 1 Corinthians 11.24 has "broken for you" in the AV, but the word "broken" is omitted in RV and JND.

EXODUS 13

Journeying out of Egypt

The people are still at Succoth and further instructions are given regarding the responsibilities of those who are redeemed. The words, "And it shall be when the Lord shall bring thee into the land" (vv.5,11), and, "And it shall be when thy son asketh thee in time to come" (v.14), indicate that the chapter deals with teaching for future conduct now that the Passover has been slain and appropriated. This is not the end of the dealings of the Lord with them. It is the beginning, and new teaching is given immediately after their deliverance from the "destroyer". There is no period when they can "relax" and enjoy a time of leisure after what may have been regarded as the "stresses and strains" of the previous months. Interest in the things of God, desires to please Him and to be taught by Him are features of the reality of salvation and should be seen immediately in the lives of all who profess to be saved.

The sanctification of the firstborn and the Feast of Unleavened Bread are brought before the people. The former was a new revelation given to Moses at Succoth, but the latter had been given to him previously (12.15-20). Why did the Lord leave the revelation concerning the firstborn until Israel was at Succoth, and why did Moses not reveal the Feast of Unleavened Bread until this point?

The answer is the grace of God in leading his people. He always acts with kindness and loving consideration when leading His own flock. Truth is revealed when we are ready to bear it. When we desire to go on for God He does not reveal all to us at the beginning. Growing maturity makes it possible to bear more truth. This is not in relation to dangers to be faced and difficulties to be overcome. It has to do with growth. A young baby cannot share a meal with adults. Growth and maturity are necessary before this can take place. This is no excuse for believers to remain immature or harbour sin in their lives with the excuse that they have not long been in Christ. The Feast of Unleavened Bread will dispel that notion. Here is seen the principle of revelation of truth as it can be borne and not overwhelm. Israel learns what the Lord desires for the firstborn. Further revelation of the power of God has yet to be seen, but the revelation already given is a stepping-stone to submission to more of His revealed will. Remarkably, not only did the Lord make revelation to Moses, but in the Feast of Unleavened Bread, as has already been noted, Moses makes fresh revelation to Israel. He is acting as a wise leader and teacher who, with the good of the flock in mind, knows that there is truth to be revealed and that there is the right time to reveal it.

The great example of this is the teaching of the Master, the Supreme Teacher. One instance will suffice to prove the point. He did not reveal to the disciples from the moment that they commenced a life of following

Him that He would die on the Cross. Matthew states that it was "From that time forth" that He began to "shew unto his disciples, how that he must go unto Jerusalem…" (Mt 16.21). Before that they would not have been able to bear it, and even when it was revealed it was difficult for them to understand. The teacher does not wait until his hearers will fully understand but until they are mature enough to bear what is being taught and obey it, even if they do not fully comprehend. There is no new revelation today. All truth is found in the Scriptures. As Christians grow spiritually, the significance and practical consequences of truth open up, and increasing devotion and likeness to Christ will be seen in the life.

These ordinances are to be observed when they come into the land (vv.5,11). It was due to their failure that forty years elapsed between leaving Egypt and entering Canaan. If they had obeyed the word of the Lord these ordinances would have been observed by all who left Egypt. However, they must not be forgetful even when they come into the land. When the blessings of God become the regular feature of life, those who enjoy them are prone to forget the cost involved in making them freely available. During the long wilderness years it was not possible to keep the Feast of Unleavened Bread. There were no harvests in the wilderness from which bread could be baked. Manna was their staple diet. Wilderness conditions have to be endured, but it is when the land is being enjoyed that believers will find it easier to refrain from leaven, from the sin of which it speaks. The means of guarding against the entrance of sin is to be in the enjoyment of the things of God.

Verses 1-2: The Sanctification of the Firstborn

These two verses stand as an introduction to the next seventeen. This is the second use of the word "sanctify"(6942), the first being in Genesis 2.3 - "And God blessed the seventh day and *sanctified* it". It means to make or pronounce clean, to dedicate, to purify, or to consecrate. Here it has the thought of dedicating to God and giving the firstborn over completely to Him. The firstborn were particularly delivered in Egypt. In a very vivid way they were representatives of the nation but, in addition to that great truth, they could each say that the lamb had died in their place. If no blood had been shed they would have died and never known life outside of Pharaoh's grip.

Now what are the consequences of that deliverance? First, the firstborn had been bought and therefore they belonged to the Lord and were a *purchased people*. Twice Paul reminds the Corinthians of this truth - "For ye are bought with a price" (1 Cor 6.20), and, "Ye are bought with a price (1 Cor 7.23). In the former reference it is used following the instruction to "Flee fornication (1 Cor 6.18). We are not our own as we have been bought with a price, and therefore we do not have ownership of our bodies. In the latter, it is used in the context of the exhortation not to become "bondmen of men" (JND). Because we have been bought with a price we

do not submit to the lordship of a man. This does not means that we do
not acknowledge legitimate authority in the State or in employment, but
any occupying such a position is not our supreme lord. We acknowledge a
Lord far above these as the One whom we serve. This applies equally in
the local assembly. Elders must be acknowledged, but we would not
recognise the authority of party or faction leaders who set themselves up
as men to be obeyed. For the believer there is only one Lord, supreme in
all areas of life, and it is to Him alone that we bow in complete submission.
Believers today recognise that God has rights over all men and women,
rights that are His because He created all. It is this to which Paul refers
when preaching in Athens where he states that "we are also his offspring"
(Acts 17.28). But it is also recognised that He has further rights over His
redeemed people because He has purchased them and redeemed them
with "the precious blood of Christ, as of a lamb without blemish and without
spot" (1 Pet 1.19). Recognising this, the body is not used for immoral
purposes (1 Cor 6), and is not given in total submission into the control of
other men (1 Cor 7). Christians have to be kept pure for their Lord and to
be kept free from any service or servitude which encroaches on His
Lordship.

But not only do the firstborn recognise that they are a purchased people
and thus acknowledge their position and privilege before God, this also
affects their practice. They are a *serving people*. With the words, "it is mine",
the Lord claims, rightly, complete ownership. As servants belong to their
masters and serve them, so the firstborn belong to the Lord and serve
Him. Their lives are to be totally devoted to Him. From Genesis we know
that the position of firstborn was one of honour and dignity (some such as
Esau and Reuben lost this), but in redemption the firstborn are taught
that they cannot rely for salvation on the dignified position which they
have by birth. Redemption brings in something far better by which they
are purchased by the Lord and committed to serve Him.

Man and beast were included. The firstborn of a beast would be offered
in sacrifice unless it was an unclean beast, in which case it was redeemed
(Num 18.15,17). In this way the lesson is taught that not only should the
persons of the redeemed be given entirely to the Lord, their possessions
must be dealt with in the same way. What they have is the Lord's. A vivid
example of the result of misusing possessions is found in Numbers 32.
The tribe of Reuben and the tribe of Gad intimate to Moses that they do
not wish to cross the Jordan but desire to remain on the east bank of the
river. The reason for this decision is that they have "a very great multitude
of cattle" and judge that side of the river to be a suitable area for keeping
their livestock (Num 32.1). The cattle represent the blessings of God that
they were enjoying. His blessings, held for Him and used in His service are
benefits. When they are held selfishly, to be used in self-indulgence or to
be hoarded, they become barriers to progress. Setting apart the firstborn
of the beasts for Him is giving the best to Him, and, as the firstborn of the

Children of Israel represented the whole nation, so the firstborn of the beast represents all an individual's possessions. Later they will be taught that the firstfruits of the field have to be given to the Lord (Lev 2.12-16; 23.9-14). The firstborn of man, the firstborn of the beast, the firstfruits of the field, are all to be given to Him. His due is to receive the first of all.

The significance of the "firstborn" is emphasised by the writer to the Hebrews who sums up the work of the Lord in bringing Israel out of Egypt as the act of "he that destroyed the firstborn" (11.28). Believers today are called the "church of the firstborn" (12.23). The word "firstborn" there is in the plural. In the singular it refers to the Lord Jesus. Hebrews thus confirms that what was represented typically by the firstborn of Israel is true in reality of Christians today.[†]

Verses 3-7: The Feast of Unleavened Bread
When Scripture records the Lord giving instructions to His servant and then His servant giving them to others it is not vain repetition. There is nothing superfluous in the Word of God. The reason for the careful recording of both proves the faithfulness of the servant in discharging his responsibilities. It shows that the people received the word of God accurately given. A solemn lesson this for all who teach the Scriptures! What is passed on to others must be in accord with what is received from the Book. Otherwise, wittingly or unwittingly, truth is not being taught.

The inclusion of this teaching regarding the Feast of Unleavened Bread at this point emphasises that the issue being dealt with in the sanctification of the firstborn is that of holiness. There was a danger that some might consider that, with the giving of the firstborn, their responsibility was met and no further demands were placed upon them. Not so! This feast will but remind them that there is a responsibility upon all who have been redeemed to live holy lives. Holiness is not for one class or group, it is for all. The first of five "calls" to believers in the first Epistle of Peter is a call to holiness: "…be ye holy in all manner of conversation; Because it is written, Be ye holy; for I am holy" (1 Pet 1.15-16).

In dealing with this feast in ch.12 it was observed that Moses includes two conditions which would have been given to him at that time but are not revealed until this point. The previous chapter records that leavened bread had not to be eaten and that leaven was to be put away from their houses (12.15). Now there is added that there was no leaven to be seen *with them*, nor was leaven to be in their *quarters* (1366). Leaven was not to be seen anywhere. To see something may create a desire for it. Just as Samson's marriage to a daughter of the Philistines was the ultimate outcome of "seeing" her (Judg 14.1), so desires for sin can be created by what the eyes see. The absence of leaven ensured that cravings after it would not be created by looking at it. But, in addition to this, leaven was not to be in their quarters. The word *quarters* goes beyond *houses* and means "borders" (JND), or "territory" (RSV). Leaven was not to be found anywhere in their tents, houses, living quarters, stables, or folds. Lest they consider it enough to have it out of their houses, but kept or concealed elsewhere, this instruction is given. It is possible to appear to be free of sin by not having it obviously in us or around us, but to have it in places where others are not aware that it is kept or practised. It would be as dangerous to have it around unseen as it would be to have it in view. The knowledge that it was in their "quarters" could give it an illicit attraction.

Those who seek to be holy in life must be prepared to be disciplined. Sin does not remain out of the way to allow holiness to grow. The attractions of the world, the immoral and licentious society which surrounds us, and the activity of the Adversary and his host in seeking to destroy any work for God make it necessary for Christians to be watchful and determined to do whatever is necessary to keep sin out. Taking again the example of Samson, he may have argued that there was no prohibition on a Nazarite preventing him entering a vineyard (Judg 14.5), but as a Nazarite did not drink wine he was moving too close to what he should have been avoiding.

Verses 8-10: Teaching the Family

This is the second of four occasions when the necessity of teaching the family is impressed on Israel (see 12.26; Deut 6.20-21; Josh 4.6,7). In ch.12 it was observed that the instruction there had to do with deliverance from Egypt. Here the instruction has to do with the holy life which follows. Children were to be taught that salvation and holiness of life are linked and cannot be separated. They celebrated the feast because of "that which the Lord did unto me when I came forth out of Egypt". Note the personal nature of these words. It is not "that which the Lord did unto Israel", but "that which the Lord did unto me". Each one recognised their individual deliverance which brought with it individual responsibility to be holy. They were never to forget their salvation or the effect which that had on their lives. It is possible to remember the fact of salvation but forget the changes which it brought about. Peter has this in mind as he writes his second Epistle warning that it is possible for a Christian to forget that "he was purged from his old sins" (2 Pet 1.9). When such forgetfulness grips the mind it is possible for these old sins to become re-activated. The "old leaven" of which Paul writes (1 Cor 5.7) speaks of sins which dominated the life in pre-conversion days. These have to be purged out and kept out.

The reference to this precept being a "sign…upon thine hand, and…a memorial between thine eyes" (v.9) was taken by many to instruct the wearing of mnemonic signs upon the hand and upon the forehead for the purpose of continually being reminded of what must not be forgotten. But it does not teach that Israelites must literally keep a portion of Scripture referring to this feast, and possibly the instructions regarding the firstborn (v.16) and its responsibilities, upon the hand and between the eyes. The reference to the Lord's Law being kept "in thy mouth" (v.9) clearly shows this is not to be literally carried out; it is not possible to keep the Law in the mouth of an individual. The Rabbis, however, erroneously taught from this passage that these injunctions were to be written on parchment or on linen and worn on the wrists or on the forehead. The Lord Jesus referred to these "phylacteries" when he censured the scribes and the Pharisees with the words: "But all their works they do for to be seen of men: they make broad their phylacteries, and enlarge the borders of their garments" (Mt 23.5). They were worn, as broad as they could be made to display their professed "piety", only in such a place that others would see. Piety for public declaration before men holds no attraction for heaven.

These words, therefore, are simply expressions used figuratively as an injunction to keep the precepts continually. The reference to the hand, the eyes, and the mouth may refer to the need to act in accord with Scripture, keeping it before the mind and heart to direct every act, and to be so familiar with the Word of God that it is spoken about and practised in a manner which commends it. One of the great joys of Christian life is to meet fellow believers who are so familiar with Scripture that they are always ready to speak of it intelligently. It is a sad feature of early 21st century life that this is not as prevalent as in the past. Mention of Scripture can, at times, bring to a halt a full flowing conversation, instead of being the start of discussion of the precious truths of God. "With a strong hand" the Lord had brought them out of Egypt and that should have provoked conversation and thankful discussion of such great deliverance.

Verses 11-16: Instruction given Regarding the Firstborn

What follows in these verses includes some detail in addition to that contained in v.2. The word "set apart" (5674) in v.12, which is different from "sanctify" in v.2, has the meaning of "transferring over". Strong comments that it is "used very widely of any transition". In the context it refers to the transferring over of ownership of the firstborn of the beast to the Lord. Bush comments that it "may be considered as explanatory of the term *sanctify*". All rights to the beast are, therefore, forfeit, and it now belongs to the Lord with the Israelite having no claim to it and no right of ownership in any way. When a cow, a sheep, or a goat gave birth to its firstborn it was given to the Lord in sacrifice (Num 18.17). This was the way in which they were "set apart for the Lord", and for a people for whom cattle constituted wealth this was a sacrifice that would be felt keenly. Each individual who gave over the firstborn for sacrifice paid a price. If the firstborn was of an ass, as this was an unclean beast, it was not acceptable to God as a sacrifice, therefore a lamb was slain in its place and by that means it was redeemed. It owed its life to the death of another. If it was not redeemed in this way its neck had to be broken. Without redemption it died! When dealing with the firstborn male child, the young baby was redeemed when one month old by the payment of "five shekels, after the shekel of the sanctuary" (Num 18.16), emphasising again that the young child owed its life to a redemption price having been paid.

For the second time reference is made to the fact that sons will ask their fathers the significance of what they practise. Comment has already been made on this at 12.25 where the context is the keeping of the Passover. Here it is in connection with the setting apart of the firstborn. As sons saw the firstborn of the cow, sheep, or goat being sacrificed, a lamb being sacrificed for a firstborn ass, a firstborn ass having its neck broken, and the five shekel payment being made for a firstborn male child, the question of "Why?" would be on their lips. This apparent waste of good livestock and money would puzzle those who were ignorant of the nation's history and would give rise to the inquiry, "What is this?". Again it is plain to see that these ordinances had not to be carried out in ignorance. The sons must be taught that all belonged to the Lord and that life was enjoyed because of the redemption brought about when "by strength of hand the Lord brought us forth out of Egypt".

Verses 17-19: Travelling from Succoth

There is no record of how long the Israelites camped at Succoth. There are six stopping places: Etham (13.20), Pi-hahiroth (14.2), Marah (15.23), Elim (15.27), beside the Red Sea (Num 33.10), and between Succoth and the wilderness of Sin (16.1). This period also covered the crossing of the Red Sea. The wilderness of Sin was reached on the fifteenth day of the second month after their departure from Egypt. That was one month exactly from their departure. Given the distance they travelled, the stops on the way could not have been long.

His care over them

The care and consideration of the Lord for His newly redeemed people is in evidence. They were not left to chart their own course. Moses would be aware of the location of Canaan and know the normal routes used by travellers who journeyed to that land. However, it was not left to him to decide their course, which turned out to be one which others would not take. When the Lord makes it clear that there is a goal to which He would have His servants travel, it is vital that they let Him lead the way and do not fall into the trap of mapping out their own course. The servant who said, "I being in the way, the Lord led me" (Gen 24.27), understood that the goal of finding the right wife for Isaac could only be attained if the correct pathway was followed. Help and guidance from the Lord is only possible when we are in the "Way" and do not wilfully deviate from it.

The direction which they took would appear to the onlooker to be mistaken. There was a route north-east, through the land of the Philistines and this was a direct route to their destination. They were not yet ready to face the Philistines in war. Care for His newly delivered people caused the Lord to lead them east on a more southerly route into what seemed to be impossible terrain. The comment of Matthew Henry in his *Concise Commentary* is apt: "There were two ways from Egypt to Canaan. One was about four or five days' journey; the other was much further about, through the wilderness, and that was the way in which God chose to lead His people Israel…The Egyptians were to be drowned in the Red Sea. The Israelites were to be humbled and proved in the wilderness…God's way is the right way, though it seem *about*. If we think He leads not his people the nearest way, yet we may be sure He leads them the best way, and so it will appear when we come to our journey's end".

Discouragement and sin would be the result of the "normal" pathway with the possibility of them returning to Egypt. So it is when Paul, writing to the Corinthians, takes away any excuse for sinning by stating that God "will not suffer you to be tempted above that ye are able" (1 Cor 10.13). Matthew Henry again sums it up well when he writes, "Thus God proportions His people's trials to their strength".

And so they journeyed "harnessed out of Egypt". The word "harnessed" (2571) is noted in Newberry's margin as meaning "by fifties". If this be so it is a reminder of how the Lord Jesus made the men sit down in fifties (Lk 9.14) as the means of arranging the company of about 5,000 men into manageable groups for the distribution of the five loaves and two fishes. In the three other occasions when the word is used (Josh 1.14; 4.12; Judg 7.11) it is translated "armed". JND renders it "arrayed", in the sense that they were fully fitted to meet any eventuality. Others indicate that it has the thought of being in ranks of five. If that were so there would be almost 500,000 ranks. This is hardly tenable because, as Bush comments, "…at this rate if we allow the ranks to be about three feet asunder, the 600,000 fighting men alone would have formed a procession sixty miles in length; and if we add to them the rest of the host, the line would have extended…from Egypt quite into the limits of the land of Canaan". The significance of the expression would appear to be that they left Egypt in an orderly way, fully equipped for what was before them. This large company, whom many would regard as a group of ill-equipped runaway slaves, was fully prepared and fitted for all that lay ahead. Order and discipline marked them as they left Succoth behind to set out on the great journey of discovery. They were about to learn much about themselves and they were about to have revealed on the way much about the God who had saved them. The Lord would not set them on such a course without ensuring that they had all that was necessary to face everything that they would encounter.

The same care which was seen in the preparation of the Children of Israel for the wilderness is evidenced in believers today. It is not now the pillar and the cloud which have to be followed. The words of the Lord Jesus to His disciples make clear that they have to take up the Cross to follow Him (Mt 16.24). And for that journey they are fully fitted. They, too, came out of "Egypt harnessed". They belong to a great company, the Church. They have the Holy Spirit indwelling them. They have the Word of God as their weapon to face the enemy and the armour of God to protect them (Eph 6). The Lord will not take his people on a journey for which He has not equipped them fully, and any failure that darkens the pathway is the responsibility of the follower and not of the Leader.

The bones of Joseph

With them they took the bones of Joseph. This had been his request (Gen 50.25) when he took an oath of the Children of Israel to ensure that his bones would be carried out of Egypt. By this act Joseph confirmed his confidence in the Word of God that Israel would come out of Egypt and inherit the land which had been promised to them. When he spoke in Genesis 50 there was little evidence to be seen that this promise could be fulfilled. The patriarchal family had been forced to leave the land to which Abraham had taken them. Joseph had become, not lord of that land, but of Egypt. At that time they had a land set aside for them in Goshen with the prospect of settling there. Despite all the outward evidence, Joseph still had faith in the promises of God, persuaded, as was Abraham, that "what he had promised, he was able also to perform" (Rom 4.21). Faith grasped the promise and did not let present circumstances cloud it.

Verses 20-22: The Pillar of Cloud
Cloud by day and fire by night

And so they travelled to Etham, their next stop on the journey. It cannot be ascertained with certainty where this is, but Easton writes, "...perhaps (it is) another name for Khetam, or "fortress," on the Shur or great wall of Egypt, which extended from the Mediterranean to the Gulf of Suez. Here the Israelites made their third encampment. The camp was probably a little to the west of the modern town of Ismailia".[†] It has been stated in v.17 that "God led them" but the question of how God led them has not as yet been revealed. Now the answer is given. The Lord went before them in a pillar of cloud by day and a pillar of fire by night. Note that the guidance was suited to the circumstances. Fire by day and a cloud by night would have been of little value. The cloud by day and the fire by night could be seen at all times, day and night. That the pillar of cloud led them by day and night is stated here and confirmed by other writers: "...thou leddest them in the day by a cloudy pillar; and in the night by a pillar of fire" (Neh 9.12); and, "In the daytime also he led them with a cloud, and all the night with a light of fire" (Ps 78.14). In addition to this the Psalmist writes that the cloud gave them shade from the heat of the sun: "He spread a cloud for a covering; and fire to give light in the night" (Ps 105.39). Estimates of between seven and fourteen miles across have been made for the size of the encampment. A cloud which acted as a shade to all of the people would, therefore, require to cover this very large area. There can be no complete certainty as to how this was achieved. It may not have been necessary for the cloud to be the size of the Camp, but it would need to be of such a size that it kept out direct sunlight over such an area. It would be an impressive sight as it covered the Camp and as it rose and moved ahead of the travelling column.

By night, the purpose of the fire was, therefore, to give them light. That some travelling took place at night is thus clear. This cannot have been a regular occurrence as sleep would be needed on the way. Moving such a large company of people would make it necessary to progress at the rate of the slowest member. Consideration would need to be made for the young, for those who were older, and for the rate at which animals could travel. It cannot be expected, therefore, that large distances were covered daily. The vital issue here is that the Lord went before them and there was the constant evidence of His presence day and night. He would not, indeed would never, leave them or abandon them in the wilderness.

But why was it that a pillar of cloud and of fire was used to signify the presence of the Lord? Surely it was because the cloud and the fire shrouded the presence of the Lord. Due to the impenetrable shroud of the cloud and the intense brightness of the fire Israel could not look into the cloud or into the fire. This was one of a number of ways in which Israel was taught the holiness of the Lord.

Other references to the cloud

Before the Tabernacle was erected the cloud not only guided them, but at the crossing of the Red Sea it guarded them from the Egyptian armies (14.24). When the people complained in the Wilderness of Sin regarding food, the glory of the Lord appeared in the cloud (16.10). How that took place is not revealed, but clearly the appearance of the cloud changed in a way that displayed His glory. When the Law was given at Sinai the Lord appeared to Moses in a thick cloud (19.9); when he was up the mount "a cloud covered the mount" (24.15); when he went up Sinai after he had broken the two tables of stone "the Lord descended in a cloud" (34.5). When Moses entered the temporary tabernacle which was erected until the Tabernacle was reared, after Israel had worshipped the golden calf, all the people saw the cloudy pillar descend and stand at the door of this tabernacle (33.9-10). When the Tabernacle was reared the cloud covered the tent "and the glory of the Lord filled the tabernacle" (40.34). When Israel had to move the cloud was taken up from the Tabernacle, irrespective of whether it had remained in one place for a day, a month, or a year (Num 9.21-22). The people did not know in the morning whether this was to be the day when they moved, but they had to be constantly ready to do so. The priests announced that the cloud was moving by blowing short sharp sounds on the trumpets (Num 10.1-10). Those who were closest to the Sanctuary were first to discern that the Lord was leading on. The principle remains the same today. Those who are most in the Sanctuary are better able to discern the will of God. The Children of Israel moved in four divisions according to how they camped round the Tabernacle. Those who encamped on the east, Judah, Issachar, and Zebulun, led the march; those who encamped on the south, Reuben, Simeon, and Gad, were second; those who encamped on the west, Ephraim, Manasseh, and Benjamin, came third; those who encamped on the north, Dan, Asher, and Naphtali, came fourth. Positioned between the first and second divisions were two of the divisions of the Levites, the sons of Gershon and the sons of Merari. They were responsible for the transportation of the curtains, coverings, hangings, and cords (Gershon), and the boards, pillars, bars, pins, and sockets (Merari) of the Tabernacle. After the second division of the tribes came the Levites who were the sons of Kohath carrying the Ark, the vail, the Altars and all the holy vessels (Num 10.14-28). Coming in this order, therefore, the Ark was in the middle of the column. It should be noted that the princes offered wagons to assist in carrying the Tabernacle. Two wagons and four oxen were given to the sons of Gershon, four wagons and eight oxen were given to the sons of Merari, but the sons of Kohath had to carry the holy vessels by bearing them upon their shoulders (Num 7.1-9).

The cloud shrouded the Lord when, on other occasions, He came to Israel. When the seventy elders were appointed "the Lord came down in a cloud" (Num 10.25) and spoke to Moses. It appears that this was the cloud which rose from above the Tabernacle. The Lord also came down in the cloud when Miriam and Aaron spoke against Moses and complained that he had married an Ethiopian woman (Num 12.5). Indeed, when Miriam became leprous as a result of her sin the cloud departed from the Tabernacle (Num 12.10) and doubtless was absent for a period of time, perhaps until the seven days during which she was shut out from the Camp were complete. Following the rebellion of Korah the glory of the Lord appeared in the cloud (Num 16.42). When Joshua was confirmed as the leader who would assume that responsibility after the death of Moses "the Lord appeared in the tabernacle in pillar of a cloud: and the pillar of the cloud stood over the door of the tabernacle" (Deut 31.15). Three times it is recorded that the cloud came to the door of the tabernacle: when the leadership of Moses was confirmed after the golden calf was worshipped (33.10 - this tabernacle is the temporary tabernacle to which reference has already been made); when there was an assault on Moses' leadership from Miriam and Aaron (Num 12.5); to confirm the appointment of Joshua (Deut 31.15).

The presence of the Lord today

The cloud, therefore, was a significant part of the lives of the pilgrim people. Today there is no cloud by which guidance can be received. The glory of the Lord does not appear as it did to Israel. So it may be considered that Christians have more difficulty in knowing the mind of God than did this pilgrim nation. Such a thought, however, fails to take into account the blessings that are enjoyed today by those who follow the Lord. As far as behaviour is concerned the Scriptures give us ample guidance now. Israel did not have the whole Bible which has been given us. When guidance is needed in particular circumstances, there is not only the Word of God to guide, but there is the Holy Spirit who dwells within every believer.

Emphasis must be given again to the main truth to be apprehended here. The Lord desires to dwell with His people, guiding them, protecting them, chastening them and comforting them. All this is for their good and blessing.

When the local assembly meets today the Lord Jesus states that He is in the midst (Mt 18.20). Paul reminds the Corinthians that they are "the temple of the living God", and that God has said, "I will dwell in them, and walk in them" (2 Cor 6.16). It is, therefore, the responsibility of believers to ensure that spiritual conditions exist which will allow God to enjoy being with, and walking in the midst of, His people. His presence in the midst, and the holiness which marks such a company, is the secret of power in His service and of the saints being a pleasure to Him.

Notes

2 For further notes on the "The Firstborn" see Appendix 3.
20 *Easton's Revised Bible Dictionary.*

EXODUS 14

Crossing the Red Sea

Verses 1-4: Camping before Pi-hahiroth

Having left Etham and travelled south following the cloud Israel found themselves in what seemed to be a very vulnerable situation. They camped "before Pi-hahiroth" in an area where there was a range of mountains on their right, sea to their left, and desert and mountains in front of them. It appeared to be an impossible situation should an enemy attack them from the rear.

What lessons have they learned so far about the way in which they are being guided? First, they are being taught that the pathway of following the cloud is *not the direct path*. It is a longer journey, but a journey with a purpose that can only be fulfilled if the cloud be followed. This pathway, as has been noted in ch.13, preserves them from battles which they were not yet ready to bear (13.17), will teach them their total reliance on the Lord, and prove their obedience. It will be "all the way which the Lord thy God led thee…to humble thee, and to prove thee, to know what was in thine heart, whether thou wouldest keep his commandment or no" (Deut 8.2). This pathway was to be a school where they were taught what otherwise they would never have known.

It was also *a wilderness pathway*. The wilderness was not a sandy, Sahara-type desert. There could be found in it areas where flocks could feed. Conditions, however, did not allow the cultivation of crops yielding enough to feed such a company. Their nomadic manner of life in the wilderness also made this impossible. The wilderness was a barren area of rock and earth over which wagons could be hauled. It was, nevertheless, an inhospitable landscape and was a constant reminder to them that this was not their destination. The land to which they were heading beckoned as a place of plenty to which, as pilgrims, they were journeying.

It has also been observed that this was *a misunderstood pathway*, incomprehensible to those who looked on regarding it as unnecessary and dangerous. Sad to say, events will show that for many of them leaving Egypt would prove to be *a pathway of wasted years*. When they refused to go up to the land, all who were over twenty at the time of leaving Egypt, with two honourable exceptions, were condemned to die in the wilderness, never to enjoy the blessings that the Lord had prepared for them. As a nation, only two of the forty years in the wilderness were engaged in travelling to the land. Disobedience robbed them of progress.

It was also a *pathway of careful submission*. No matter at what rate the cloud moved they were never to go ahead of it and they were never to fall behind it. Each stage of the journey was to be at the rate ordained by the pillar of cloud and of fire.

These are lessons which are still of importance today. The Christian pathway is one of pilgrimage. As Israel faced the wilderness it was clear that the Lord would ask obedience to His word and in return would give them the care, protection, and guidance which they needed. Christians are required to be obedient to the Word of God, and in return they can claim the protecting care of God. Disobedience robs of the right to claim that care, but submission to Scripture gives the right to lay hold of the promises of the Lord and to leave our protection and guidance in His hand. This is not arrogance or presumption. It is taking the Word of God and the promises therein and asking the Lord to fulfil His promises, which He will do.

The hand of God is still upon Pharaoh. It has already been observed that this is a misunderstood pathway. It was misunderstood by Pharaoh who, states the Lord, will say that the Israelites have become entangled in the land. The word "entangled" is translated elsewhere as "perplexed" (Est 3.15; Joel 1.18), indicating the entanglement in the minds of those who were in the situation. They were shut in and in a perplexing situation, not knowing where to turn.

But the pathway on which they were embarked was also a *God honouring pathway*. The Lord "will be honoured" (v.4) upon Pharaoh. At the time He will "glorify Himself" (v.4, JND). How remarkable this is. He will receive glory from the actions of men who set themselves up to oppose Him as they learn on this, their final assault against Him, that truly He is the Lord. This looks forward to a day when a greater army will determine to oppose the Son of Man as He comes in glory. Men will then bow the knee and confess that Jesus Christ is Lord (Phil 2.9-11). His enemies, like the Egyptians, will be required to honour Him and bow before Him.[†] It is an encouragement to Christians that although the pathway is one of testimony and difficulty, the end of it is that the Lord will be glorified and in His triumph be publicly acclaimed and vindicated. The Pharaoh who so boldly stated, "I know not Jehovah" (5.2), will finally see overwhelming proof of His power and will acknowledge that He is Lord.

Verses 5-9: The Pursuit by the Egyptians

When faith is absent the world soon forgets that God has spoken. "Why have we done this?", they exclaim, forgetting within days the many first-born who had died on Passover night. It always has been so. In days of national emergency in the past nations turned to God, but when the emergency was over God was forgotten. Despite the plagues and death that had been experienced, the Egyptians again showed their enmity towards the people who had been so clearly delivered by Jehovah.

Egypt had not been able to prevent the Children of Israel being sheltered under the blood, but it will now seek to prevent them from leaving Egypt. It is its purpose to keep Israel in bondage under Egyptian power. This always had been the plan of Pharaoh when confronted with Moses' demands. It is still today the purpose of the Adversary to ensure that when souls are saved they do not rid themselves of the dominance of sin. If he can ensure that the testimony of the newly born babe in Christ will not flourish, that soul will not be able to enjoy the good things that have been prepared for those who put their trust in Him. Being delivered from Egypt was the only way that Israel could enjoy the freedom that comes from having Jehovah as Lord.

The army that came after Israel was an impressive sight. Keil & Delitzsch describe it vividly: "According to v.9, the army raised by Pharaoh consisted of chariot horses, riding horses (lit. runners), and the men belonging to them. War chariots and cavalry were always the leading force of the Egyptians (compare Is 31.1; 36.9)". All the power and might of the world was amassed and only the best, six hundred "excellent" chariots, formed the vanguard. Pharaoh was determined that the "runaway" slaves would not escape. Humanly speaking it was an unequal contest, yet what he did not recognise was that Israel was leaving Egypt with a "high hand" - not the "high hand" of pride and arrogance, but the "high hand" of Jehovah. The power of the Lord was with them.

Verses 10-18: Israel's Doubts

The appearance of the Egyptian army behind them caused fear and doubt. It may seem strange to the reader that this fear gripped them so early on the journey. Despite the power of God which they had seen they had no confidence for the present. There is a sense of ingratitude in their words that they had known in Egypt that Moses' actions would only "(take) us away to die in the wilderness". It is true that they had already complained to Moses, although not quite in the terms which they set out here. That complaint did not come at the very beginning of Moses' return to Egypt, but only when their oppression was increased (5.21). The irony of their words should not be missed: "Because there were no graves in Egypt, hast thou taken us away to die in the wilderness?", is the charge which was made.

Two lessons stand out here. Courage in the pathway of obedience can quickly evaporate when the enemy opposes, and blaming those who lead is a convenient way to avoid responsibility. Israel had willingly taken the lamb, slain it, and placed the blood on the door. They had willingly left Egypt with no word of protest. Now, when problems arise, they so quickly point the finger of accusation at Moses. Leaders who courageously shepherd the children of God may have to face such a charge.

In contrast to the fear of the people, Moses is fearless. The people have not to be galvanised into action. They have to "fear...not", to "stand still", and to "see the salvation of the Lord" (v.13). The Lord will fight for them and, as a result, they have to hold their peace. This does not mean that they have to remain silent, but rather that they have to remain calm as they wait on the Lord. It is clear from v.15 that Moses had cried to the Lord, and that cry and the response of the Lord was the secret of his calm demeanour. This servant knew that the answer to the situation was only to be received from the Lord. The people had also cried to the Lord (v.10), but they linked this with complaints to God's servant. Moses cried to the Lord with no complaining spirit. There is, however, in the reply which he receives the implication that rather than cry to the Lord he should be urging the people forward. The Lord had promised to take them to the land that He had promised them, and this promise held good, no matter how ominous the present situation appeared to be.

Verses 19-22: Crossing the Red Sea

The expression "the angel of God" (v.19), or "the angel of *Elohim*" (430) differs from the expression "the angel of Jehovah". *Elohim* means the "Mighty God", and "the angel of God" is first found in Genesis 21.17 when the "angel of God called to Hagar out of heaven". That it is God Himself who speaks on that occasion is clearly seen in that He states in reference to Ishmael, "I will make him a great nation" (v.18). This work could not be claimed by an angel. The angel of God spoke to Jacob in a dream (Gen 31.11) and declared, "I am the God of Bethel" (v.13). The angel of Jehovah appeared to Gideon (Judg 6) and there is no reason for supposing that the angel of God who spoke to him (v.20) was a different being from the angel of the Lord who had already spoken (v.12). That the Lord is He who had spoken is clear (vv. 14,16). To Manoah and his wife there appeared "the angel of the Lord" who is also called "the angel of God" (Judg 13.3, 9), and Manoah exclaims, "We shall surely die because we have seen God" (v.22). The appearances of the angel of God in the Old Testament, therefore, are pre-incarnation appearances of the Lord Jesus Christ.[†]

The angel of God now moves with the cloud from in front of the Children of Israel to behind them, separating them from the Egyptians. To the Children of Israel the cloud gave light, but to their enemies it brought darkness. By this means the two peoples were kept at a distance from each other. As Moses raised his hand, holding his rod, over the sea "the Lord caused the sea to go back by a strong east wind" (vv.16,21). This differed considerably from the later crossing of the Jordan. At the Red Sea an east wind blew all night and caused the seas to retreat. At the Jordan there was no wind, but when the feet of the priests touched the water of the overflowing river the waters stood up in a heap (Josh 3.14-17). No matter how great the work that is being done, and no matter if it bears similarities to what God has done before, He is not bound to one way of working at any time.

The Children of Israel did not seek a way round this barrier - "They went into the midst of the sea" (v.22). One would have expected that the bed of a sea, even when the water had retreated, would be wet, muddy, and difficult to cross. For the Children of Israel, however, it was dry land. Only He who had opened the sea could turn its bed into a king's highway. What stretched before them was not a tangle of sea-bed vegetation, dying marine life, and waterlogged soil or sand. In front of them lay a dry, perfect highway ideally suited to be their pathway out of Egypt. Little wonder that the Psalmist writes, "Come and see the works of God...He turned the sea into dry land: they went through the flood on foot: there did we rejoice in him" (Ps 66.5-6).

No time scale is given for the crossing of the Red Sea, but there are some indications which render it possible to make a reasonable assumption. It was the cloud which went behind the Children of Israel (v.19), but the crossing appears to have been made by night (v.21). It can therefore be assumed that the cloud went behind them towards the close of the day (it was not yet a pillar of fire, which form it took at night) and the crossing commenced at the beginning of the night, about early evening around 18.00 hrs.

Verses 23-25: The Egyptian Pursuit

The Egyptians were affected by the cloud (v.20) which must have brought early darkness to them and deepened the natural darkness of the night. During that night they did not make contact with the Children of Israel and therefore they must not have been able to go down into the bed of the sea until all the Israelites had travelled some distance from the "shore" of the sea. By the time of the morning watch, which was between 03.00 hrs and 06.00 hrs, the Egyptian army was crossing in pursuit and the Israelites had entirely crossed over. In approximately a nine hour period, from 18.00 hrs to 03.00 hrs, over 2,000,000 Israelites with their goods and their flocks crossed, and the Egyptian armies entered the Sea. Unlike the crossing of the Jordan (Josh 3.16) the width of the "highway" is not noted, but it must have been very considerable.

At the time of the morning watch "the Lord looked unto the host of the Egyptians" (v.24). What did this involve? "This look of Jehovah is to be regarded as the appearance of fire suddenly bursting forth from the pillar of cloud that was turned towards the Egyptians" (Keil & Delitzsch). This caused trouble and confusion amongst them. Next, the Egyptians found that their heavy chariots were being bogged down. The work of God had ensured that the "highway" had a firm enough surface to take the weight of human feet and that of the animals. If the Children of Israel had wagons at this stage they were less in weight, even when loaded, than the war chariots of their enemy.[†] The wheels of the chariots came off and made progress impossible. This caused them to realise that the Lord was on the side of the Israelites. Thus they acknowledged the supremacy of the Lord.

Verses 26-31: The Destruction of the Egyptians

As the morning light appeared, Moses stretched out his hand over the sea and the waters rolled back, drowning the fleeing Egyptians. The chariots and the horsemen, the cream of Egyptian soldiery (vv.7-9), were in the forefront of the pursuit and they were overcome. "All the host of Pharaoh that came into the sea after them" (v.28) also perished. This indicates that some of the Egyptians did not enter the sea. It may be that these were the "support services" who would be able to return and bring news of the defeat, so complete that not one of those who entered the sea, returned to the shore. Truly the Lord displayed openly and decisively that He is "King of old, working salvation in the midst of the earth" (Ps 74.12).

Twice over it is recorded that Moses stretched out his hand over the sea (vv.21,27): when the waters opened up, and when they returned again. True it is that the Lord could have accomplished this without the outstretched hand of His servant, so why was Moses asked to do this? It is a sign of the grace of God allowing His servants the privilege of taking part in His work. God does not need the intervention of men and women to do His work, but still today in grace He allows them to have a part in it and to be rewarded for what He does through them. By this He also confirms again the leadership of Moses at a crucial time. The people can see that Moses is still in touch with God and, no matter how difficult the circumstances may be, the presence of such a servant of the Lord brings confidence.

As the sun rose, the scene that met the Children of Israel was the complete destruction of the power that had held them in bondage. From the point of view of godless man the impossible had been brought about, and these "runaway" slaves had overcome the strength and might of the most powerful nation on earth. To the thoughtful observer, however, it was clear that the God of Israel was God. News of this triumph reached far lands. In Canaan the city of Jericho heard that "the Lord dried up the water of the Red sea for you, when ye came out of Egypt" (Josh 2.10) and, forty years later, it was still remembered. The lesson taught to one of the inhabitants was a step on the road to her salvation. Rahab learned that "the Lord your God, he is God in heaven above, and in earth beneath" (Josh 2.11).

But the Children of Israel also learned lessons that day. What a fitting start this was to their pilgrim journey. When difficulties were to be faced and barriers closed their way they could look back and remember these decisive moments in Egypt and over the Red Sea when the power of God was clearly displayed in an unforgettable manner. How gracious the Lord is in this way. When He asks His people to set out on any enterprise in which faith will be tested He gives experiences of His care that will encourage in days of difficulty. Remembering all the way He has led and guided in the past strengthens faith for the present. These events, therefore, should have strengthened the resolve of the people to obey the God who had proved His faithfulness to them and His ability to preserve them.

But they also "feared the Lord, and believed the Lord" (v.31). Not only could they be encouraged by what had taken place but they also learned that the Lord is One to be feared. This is not in the sense of abject terror, but in a God-fearing spirit. To fear Him, in the sense of holding Him in awe and respect, should be in the heart of every believer today. The fact that the grace of God is seen in the gospel and that the love of God is proclaimed to all, does not alter the fact that He is not only a God whom we should love, but that He is also One whom we should honour and treat with the utmost respect. Their fear of Him and belief in Him is further displayed in their attitude to His servant Moses. If this had remained in their hearts what sadness and sorrow could have been avoided. How fittingly the Psalmist writes of their doubts and their deliverance.

"Our fathers understood not thy wonders in Egypt; they remembered not the multitude of thy mercies; but provoked him at the sea, even at the Red sea. Nevertheless he saved them for his name's sake, that he might make his mighty power to be known. He rebuked the Red sea also, and it was dried up: so he led them through the depths, as through the wilderness. And he saved them from the hand of him that hated them, and redeemed them from the hand of the enemy. And the waters covered their enemies: there was not one of them left. Then believed they his words; they sang his praise" (Ps 106.7-12).

The Spiritual Significance

Paul refers to the events of this chapter in writing to the Corinthians. "Moreover, brethren, I would not that ye should be ignorant, how that all our fathers were under the cloud, and all passed through the sea; And were all baptized unto Moses in the cloud and in the sea" (1 Cor 10.1-2). The destruction of the power of their enemy and the subsequent provision of manna and water should have ensured that they did not fail in the days ahead. Every provision was made for them to enable them to succeed in this new life into which the Lord was leading them. If they were to fail the cause lay with them and not with the Lord.

The great blessings that they enjoyed were fivefold. The repetition of "all" emphasises that none were excepted. (The latter two will be dealt with when chs. 16 and 17 are being considered).

1. All our fathers were under the cloud.
2. All passed through the sea.
3. All were baptised unto Moses in the cloud and in the sea.
4. All ate the same spiritual meat.
5. All drank the same spiritual drink.

All of Israel were under the protecting power of the cloud, that is, of Him who dwelt in the cloud, and, as a result, they all passed safely though the sea. In addition to that they were baptised unto Moses in the cloud and in the sea. They were baptised unto Moses in the sense that they were linked with Moses as he went through the sea and in following the cloud. They moved from the place where Pharaoh ruled to the place where Moses ruled. Israel disappeared behind the cloud, crossed the sea, and emerged on the other side. They were severed from Egypt and brought under the authority of Moses, just as Christian baptism is a public display of believers having moved from the place where the devil rules to where the Lord Jesus rules, and where they now are under His authority.

Thus, as Israel stands on the far side of the sea, they are in a very different situation from that which pertained when they stood on the Egyptian shore of the sea. Everything has changed. The power of the oppressor has been broken and they are beyond his reach. They stand on completely new ground and the Adversary no longer has authority over them. Egypt still has power. A new pharaoh will ascend its throne, and its armies will regroup, but as far as the Children of Israel are concerned they need have no fear. For them the power of Egypt has been destroyed. Thus, if they fail it is not because the Lord has failed them, but because they have failed Him.

As has been observed above, so it is with Christians today. Baptism is an acknowledgement of what took place at the point of salvation. They passed from being under the authority of the "power of darkness" to being under the authority of "the kingdom of his dear Son" (Col 1.13). They moved from tyranny to well-ordered rule, from disorder to order, and from fear to love. They can never again be subjects of the power of darkness. Should they allow the Adversary to control them, it is not because they are his subjects, held under his sway, but because they willingly submit to him even although he has no power to force them so to do. This is vital teaching, and to be aware of it gives confidence when facing attempts by the Evil One to gain control of those who have moved out from under his authority.

The comment of the Hebrew writer is apt at this point. The Lord Jesus took part of flesh and blood "that through death he might destroy him that had the power of death, that is, the devil; And deliver them who through fear of death were all their lifetime subject to bondage" (Heb 2.14-15). Being controlled by the devil brings with it death. By this very means, however, the Lord Jesus has destroyed the power of the devil. He has annulled it and made it inoperative in the life of a believer. In such lives the destruction of the power of the devil and deliverance from it are complete.

Therefore, as with the Children of Israel, the Christian has no excuse for failure. All that is necessary to bring about triumphant Christian living has been accomplished. Again it can be asserted that failure is the result, not of Him failing His own, but of His own failing Him, despite all that has been accomplished on their behalf.

Notes

4 Note that Israel had to be taught that Jehovah was Lord (6.6,7,8,29; 10.2; 12.12; 16.12; 20.2,5; 29.46; 31.13). Egypt had to learn this also (7.5,17; 8.22; 12.12; 14.4,18).

19 The New Testament appearances (Acts 10.3; 27.23) would seem to be those of an angelic messenger.

25 The Israelites did have wagons later (Num 7), but it is not known whether these were brought from Egypt or built after the crossing of the Red Sea.

EXODUS 15

The Song of Redemption and the Journey to Marah

Having seen the triumph of Jehovah in the destruction of the Egyptians, the first thing that Israel did was to sing. Songs are mentioned in Genesis (31.27) when Laban states that if he had known that Jacob was leaving he would have sent him away "with mirth, and with songs". This chapter, however, is the first recorded song of the Bible.

Singing differs greatly from speech. By its use it is possible to express depths of emotion, either of joy or sadness, with an intensity which normal speech cannot convey. Although others may have enjoyed listening to this song, if opportunity had allowed, the singers directed their words to the Lord. When the saints sing "psalms and hymns and spiritual songs" (Eph 5.19) today these are directed to the Lord even although others will enjoy the sentiments expressed.[†] Singing is, therefore, a form of worship. What is recorded in this chapter is an outburst of worship for the deliverance brought about.

Two other songs are referred to in the writings of Moses. When the Lord gave them water at Beer (Num 21.17) Israel sang and joy attended the giving of water. At the end of the wilderness journey Moses was instructed by the Lord to leave a song with Israel, "that this song may be a witness for me against the children of Israel" (Deut 31.19). It was a song account of the goodness of God to them which, in later years as they sang, condemned their conduct as there was brought to remembrance how much they owed Him.

There is no record in Scripture of angels singing. At the birth of the Lord Jesus the multitude of the heavenly host praised God "saying, Glory to God in the highest" (Lk 2.13,14). Again, in Revelation the voice of many angels joined together "saying with a loud voice, Worthy is the Lamb that was slain" (Rev 5.12). To the redeemed is reserved the privilege of singing to the Lord. Only they can express in song sentiments which are acceptable in heaven. The saints today can sing. "Is any merry? let him sing psalms" (Jas 5.13). This is the product of hearts knowing redemption. The deliverance which the Children of Israel celebrated was national and typical. That which saints sing of today is personal and eternal.

But here, at the beginning of their journey, there are three noteworthy features of this first song. First, they did not need to be taught to sing. Although no comment is made in Scripture regarding the quality of their singing, it was surely most melodious and tuneful. Yet there were no singing lessons. Second, they did not need to be taught what to sing. It may be that Moses sang and the men repeated the refrain, which was then taken up by Miriam and the women (vv.20-21). Third, they did not need to be taught how to sing together, almost as a choir, as they sang unitedly. The simple lesson to be learned is that there are some things which those who are newly saved do not need to be taught. True it is that Israel had now entered the school of God and had much to learn. They would be reluctant pupils and slow learners, and would never reach a stage where their education was complete. Nevertheless, there were basic things which they did not need to be taught. The joy that was in their hearts, the greatness of their deliverance and the wonder at what had taken place was expressed. As with Israel, so it is with believers today. Salvation brings with it some things that are known instinctively, and enjoyment of them will create that music in the soul of which this song is the first recorded example.

There was nothing superficial or hypocritical about the singing. Referring to this time in the history of Israel, Jeremiah writes, "I remember thee, the kindness of thy youth, the love of thine espousals, when thou wentest after me in the wilderness, in a land that was not sown" (Jer 2.2). This was the time of espousals, that brief period between leaving Egypt and the giving of the Law, which was marked by the intensity of first love. True it was that they had complained, and would do so again, but there was an underlying love for the Lord which He remembered.

The prophet Hosea refers to this youthful, vigorous love: "she shall sing there, as in the days of her youth" (Hos 2.15). When Israel is restored this first love will be recovered and again the voice of the nation will be raised in loving song to the God who has guided them and saved them.

Verse 1a: Introduction

It must have been a memorable sight as the people stood on the shore on that first morning of freedom from the tyrant. Such singing which filled the air had never before been heard. Note, first, that Moses was the leader of the praise: "Then sang Moses and the children of Israel". As he had led them on the journey so he led them in their thankful worship. Leaders will be known, not only by their trust in God displayed in fortitude in facing the enemy, but in their thankfulness for His goodness, acknowledging that the triumph is not theirs but of the Lord.

It is encouraging to observe also that, as has already been seen, Moses began and ended the wilderness journey with a song. It is good to see those who have newly started on the Christian pathway with a song in their hearts, but there is something particularly appealing about those who have been many years on the road, now approaching its end, and who still have that song in their hearts. Moses had gone through much that would have caused disappointment and bitterness to come into the hearts of lesser men. The frowardness of the people, the great disappointment of their refusal to enter the land, the constant complaining and discontent; all this would have taken the song out of most hearts, but not that of Moses. Of course the purpose of this latter song, already noted, was to keep in front of Israel the faithfulness of God and their sad record, but Moses' spirit was such that the Lord could ask him to write the song.

The failure of the people had not closed his heart to the faithfulness of God.

It is possible that disillusionment can set in caused perhaps by the conduct of others or by circumstances failing to turn out as hoped. Bitterness grows in the soul and attitudes to others become soured and difficult. The song goes from our lips and from our souls and the dark shadow of a joyless spiritual life envelopes us. Little wonder that Paul exhorts, "Rejoice in the Lord alway: and again I say, Rejoice" (Phil 4.4). The desire of all must be to start the journey with a song, to continue it rejoicing, and to end it with a song still ringing in our hearts. For this, Moses is a good example to follow.

It is emphasised that this was a song of intelligent worship. They sang and "spake, saying…". The words that they sang were intelligent and not merely a mantra. The song was a statement of spiritual truth and, as such, is doctrinally correct. It is true that in many hymns there is some allowance for the use of metaphor and "poetic licence". It is most desirable, however, that a hymn should not contain that which is doctrinally incorrect. Sad to say, much of what is sung falls down in this respect. But not only was the song an accurate account of spiritual truth using words with meaning, it was also sung in a way which made these words intelligible. The tune used for any hymn is important, but when the tune becomes the main reason for singing the hymn, and the words become secondary, the whole point of singing has been lost. The best hymns, whether they be old or new, are those that are written out of deep spiritual exercise, expressing timeless truths.

Verses 1b-10: Thankfulness for Their Deliverance
The opening praise (v.1b)

The opening words of the song in v.1, "I will sing unto the Lord", confirm that this was a song of worship directed to the Lord. The use of "I will sing" shows this to be a very personal song of praise. Moses uttered these words because the song was a personal expression of the joy of his heart. But the Israelites echoed the words; therefore it was for each of them a personal expression of what was in their hearts. Each individual raised their voice and sang, "I will sing". This was not merely taking part in a hymn which others were enjoying, it was the expression of the hearts of all. Wholeheartedly they sang, recognising that what had taken place at the Red Sea was the deliverance of the nation, but was also the personal deliverance of each individual and, in recognition of this, there had to be individual thanksgiving.

The Lord is said to have triumphed "gloriously". His was not a small victory or one gained by a narrow margin. It was a glorious victory. The word "gloriously" (1342) means "to rise, to grow up, to increase", and thus "to triumph". This victory is one which shows the power of the Lord in an increased way. The firstborn had died in Egypt and that was a mighty sign of the power of the Lord, but now the cream of Egypt's military might lay dead on the seashore, their weapons and accoutrements useless against the power of the Lord. Truly, the Lord had triumphed gloriously.

This victory was a foretaste of what will be one day when the kings of the earth will take counsel against the Lord. As the destruction of Israel was the purpose of Pharaoh, so it will be the purpose of these kings as they commit the folly of seeking to turn their weaponry against the Lord's Anointed. "He that sitteth in the heavens shall laugh: the Lord shall have them in derision" (Ps 2.4), and yet again the outcome will be the complete destruction of those who presume to "take counsel together, against the Lord, and against his anointed" (Ps 2.2).

This remarkable triumph was brought about by the "horse and his rider" being thrown into the sea. Again there is here the greatness of the triumph in that both horse and rider were destroyed. "Thrown" (7411) is "to hurl", or "to shoot", showing the power by which Egypt was overcome. The Lord hurled them into the sea with an irresistible power. This was not an accident or an act of purely natural processes. The Lord hurled the enemy into the depths of the sea with the ease with which an arrow is shot or a stone is thrown, but the power behind the act was immense. To escape was impossible and to resist was futile.

Personal appreciation (v.2)

In v.2 the singers exult in the fact that the Lord who was responsible for such a triumph is their God. This is appreciated individually. "My strength and song", "my salvation", "my God", and "my father's God" declare this exquisite truth. The God who controls the destiny of nations is the God of the individual, not too mighty to ignore the weak, not too strong to ignore the powerless. If they need power He is their strength, if they need joy, He is their song. But in addition to that His power has been seen in action, and now He has become their salvation. All is owed to Him. Nothing is of them. When He destroyed Egypt in such a powerful way He had each individual Israelite before Him. But what response should that bring from the hearts of those for whom that power has been put to work? They will acknowledge Him as their God and will prepare Him a habitation (5115). This has behind it the thought of rest, and therefore the thought of being at home. The habitation which each Israelite intended to make for Him was not merely a dwelling place. It was a home where He could be at rest. Doubtless it was of the Sanctuary which they sang, their desire to have in their midst a Sanctuary in which He could dwell amongst them. That came to pass when the Tabernacle was reared. It should be noted, however, that other translations with general agreement render this "I will glorify him" (JND); "I will praise him" (RSV). This indicates the desire of Israel to give Him the place amongst them which is His by right.

But this God had not associated Himself with Israel in this generation alone. He was their fathers' God and in past generations He was the God of Israel. Doubtless they had in mind the links which existed between the nation and Jehovah since the time of Abraham down to the present generation. He had been faithful in the past and had proved that to their fathers. Despite their disobedience and idolatry He had kept His promises, and the God who had been the God of their fathers was now their God.

Pharaoh's armies disposed of with ease (vv.3-5)

It should not be thought strange that the Lord had accomplished such a victory, for in v.3 the singers exult in the fact that "The Lord is a man of war". This does not imply that the Lord is only a "man of war". He is the God of peace, and God is love. But lest it is thought that such a loving God who joys in peace is One who can easily be overthrown it is worthy of note that He is also a "man of war". The battlefield is not a strange place to Him where unfamiliar skills have to be used. He never knows defeat. His always is the victory. When an enemy rises up against Him he will never prevail against the Lord. This is the confidence which Israel can have as they face the future. Ahead there are enemies to be faced and battles to be fought but with the God who is a man of war leading them they will know what it is to be overcomers.

What overcame the leading cavalry of the Egyptian host has been dealt with (v.1), but now the song turns to deal with the main body of the troops. The chariots and the accompanying soldiery had been cast into the sea (vv.4-5). As with the horse and the riders the Lord had simply hurled them into the sea with the ease with which an arrow is aimed and fired. For a man of war this was not a difficult thing to accomplish. The captains chosen to lead this host were the choicest in Egypt, but even they, skilled as they were in the art of war, could not turn the tide of this battle. As the waters returned none escaped and they sank to the bottom of the sea like a stone. There are materials which sink after floating for some time, or others which start to sink, but do so gradually. Not so a stone. It sinks swiftly and immediately, and thus it was with this enemy of the Lord. Their overthrow could not be resisted even for a moment.

The power of His right hand (vv.6-7)

At this point the tone of the song changes. The third person has been used but now the second person is used as the Lord is directly addressed. The change came with "Thy right hand, O Lord, is become glorious in power" (v.6). From declaring the victory to all who will hear, the nation now turned to address the God who gave deliverance. The right hand is the hand which dispenses blessing (Gen 48.13-18), but it is also the hand of power (Ps 20.6; 60.5; 89.13). The attempt by Pharaoh to pursue the Children of Israel was a rising up against the Lord (v.7). To become an enemy of God's people was to become His enemy. Would that men had understood this. It would have prevented many of the tragedies which have stained the pages of history. The words to Saul of Tarsus are apt:

"Saul, Saul, why persecutest thou me?" (Acts 9.4). In the age of the church this emphasises that the church is His body and to touch it is to touch Him. Nevertheless, the truth is timeless and overlaps all dispensations. To persecute Christians is to raise the hand against the Lord and against heaven. All who do so indulge in great folly and are only certain of ultimate defeat. Nations were raised up of God to chastise Israel by inflicting defeat on them, but even they were judged for unrighteous acts which they committed (see Hab 2).

The wrath of the Lord was directed towards the pursuing host. The word "wrath" (2740) is the first use of a form of a word (2734) which itself is first used of Cain (Gen 4.5). When the Lord is wroth, however, it is always righteous anger. Abraham feared that his continued intercession for Sodom might cause the Lord to be angry (Gen 18.30). Egypt had no such thought despite the many evidences which they had seen of the power of God. The anger of the Lord is a constant state of displeasure about sin. It is never uncontrolled. God never "loses His temper"; He does not burst out in uncontrolled rage, but judgment is carried out as a result of this anger in a controlled manner which is effective. This same anger will be seen when the wrath of God is directed towards earth as a result of the rebellion of mankind which, even today, is moving rapidly towards its climax. "The wrath to come" (1 Thess 1.10) will never be experienced by believers of the church age as they have been delivered from it. The book of Revelation reveals the extent and the intensity of the judgment of God which falls on a rebellious world, but Christians need have no fear as, before that day dawns, they will have been "caught up...in the clouds, to meet the Lord in the air" (1 Thess 4.17). Men today would be well advised to consider what befell Pharaoh. In their "wisdom" they declare this event to be but a natural catastrophe thus taking God out of it altogether. Those who have real wisdom know that this event is a warning to all who refuse to bow today and acknowledge that Jesus Christ is Lord. The powerlessness of the Pharaoh is emphasised in that his armies were consumed as worthless stubble. This adds to the picture of their overthrow being as a stone sinking under the waves. Now, as stubble is consumed so they are consumed completely with no power to resist.

What took place at the Red Sea (vv.8-10)

Now a graphic account is given of what took place that evening by the Red Sea. The rolling back of the sea was not a natural event. Search has been made for centuries to seek an answer as to what took place on that day. It has been concluded that it was either a natural event explainable by the fact that this was a shallow wet area where it was possible to find passages through the marsh, perhaps because of long rain-free periods, or because it was a natural disaster which overwhelmed Israel's enemies. Scripture, however, is quite clear that it was none of these. Unbelieving men must seek another solution as they refuse to accept any record of an event displaying the power of God. The rolling back of the waters was due to a "blast of thy nostrils". With such ease the Lord brought this about. Three statements are made. The waters were gathered together, then they stood upright as a heap, and the depths were congealed. The great walls of water which stood up on either side of the pathway through the sea "congealed". They were completely stable and did not have the unstable consistency that is associated with water. They formed a solid mass which would not fall back until the God who ordered this commanded that they should do so.

Faced with such a sight the Egyptians were undeterred (v.9). Four times in this verse Pharaoh states, "I will". "By these short clauses following one upon another…the confidence of the Egyptian as he pursued them breathing vengeance is very strikingly depicted…the soul is the seat of desire i.e. of fury, which sought to take vengeance on the enemy" (Keil & Delitzsch). His determination was unaffected by what had taken place in the months past. Truly he spoke the truth when he declared to Moses, "Who is the Lord…I know not the Lord" (5.2). The purpose of the pursuit was twofold. There was the matter of the wealth which Israel had taken from Egypt and Pharaoh desired to have that back. He will divide the spoil and satisfy his lust and desire for plunder. He also will put Israel to the sword and destroy them completely. The plagues which had befallen his realm should have moderated his passions and made him careful in his dealings with God. The effect, however, had been the opposite. Rather than moderating his feelings, his desire for Israel was not that they should be enslaved, but that the whole nation should be destroyed.[†]

Just as the gathering of the waters was an act ordered of God so likewise was the return of the waters. "Thou didst blow with thy wind (breath, JND)" is how it took place. With such ease the waters were commanded to resume their former place and, like lead, Pharaoh and his hosts were overcome.

Verses 11-19: Thankfulness that the Deliverance will be Completed
"Who is like unto thee?" (vv.11-13)

The mood of the song now changes from praise because of deliverance from Egypt to one of praise for the fact that the work will be completed and that they will not be left in the wilderness but will be taken to the land which had been promised them (v.17). If only they had remembered this in the days that lay ahead much sin and sorrow would have been avoided. The accusations that they had been brought into the wilderness to die there (16.3; 17.3) would never have left their lips. How quickly the promises of God were forgotten and fear took their place. This is not limited to Israel. Every believer knows what it is to have the bright serene atmosphere of reliance on His promises changed quickly to one of fear and doubt. But here in the brightness of that first morning out of Egypt the promises gripped their hearts. They understood that ahead of them lay the land

and the Sanctuary and that they would not be left alone on the journey. He would bring them in (v.17).

Verse 11 is an expression of the uniqueness of their God. "Who is like unto thee?", is a rhetorical question. The answer clearly is that there is no one like Him. He is glorious in His holiness in the sense that His holiness exalts Him. JND renders this as "glorifying thyself in holiness", signifying that it is His intent that this should be. The thought that holiness limits an individual, resulting in weakness and powerlessness, is thus set aside. Matthew Henry in his *Commentary* describes God as "...a God of matchless and incomparable perfection...He is glorious in holiness; his holiness is his glory...his holiness appeared in His hatred of sin, and His wrath against obstinate sinners. It appeared in the deliverance of Israel...and his faithfulness to his own promise". He is also "fearful in praises". The acts which caused praise to be rendered to Him also caused Him to be held in awe. Gratitude for what He had done did not give rise to a lack of wonder and reverence. "Doing wonders" was not a difficult thing for Him. He can accomplish that which is impossible for others. There are no limits to His power and no boundaries to His authority. Such acts are miracles.

In v.6 the right hand of the Lord has been described as being "glorious in power" and again it is spoken of in v.12. The earth swallowed His enemies when His right hand was stretched out. It is sad to note that this nation who spoke of the right hand of the Lord stretched out in judgment towards their enemies would experience that right hand stretched out in judgment against themselves and yet would refuse to acknowledge it and repent from their ways (Is 9.12,17,21; 10.4). This is a state of mind into which all can enter. It is folly to be quick to recognise that the Lord is dealing with others, but slow to recognise that He is dealing with oneself.

The expression "the earth swallowed them" causes no difficulty even although they were drowned in the sea. "The earth" (775) is found in Genesis 1.1: "In the beginning God created the heaven and the earth". It does not, therefore, refer to earth or soil as distinct from water. It indicates that they were swallowed into the depths of this earth. The use of "swallowed" simply indicates the completeness of their overthrow. When Korah and his fellow rebels were to be swallowed up, Moses stated that the earth would "open her mouth" (Num 16.30) to swallow them, the word earth (127) meaning "soil" as distinct from water (also translated "ground" in v.31). When the act took place (v.32), "the earth" (776), the same word as in Exodus 15, is used. The distinction is clear. This earth swallowed them, but with Korah it was the soil and not the water that brought this about. The same is found in the book of Jonah where the prophet states that "the earth (776) with her bars was about me forever" (Jonah 2.6) even although he was cast into the sea.

In v.13 it was recognised that the mercy of the Lord caused Him to effect their deliverance. This acknowledges that what had taken place was an undeserved act on the part of Jehovah. There was nothing in them that warranted such gracious action. This word "mercy" (2617) is first found when used by Lot (Gen 19.19): "thou hast magnified thy mercy, which thou hast shown unto me in saving my life". Now Israel had come to know the same mercy. Compassion and kindness were extended towards an undeserving people. God's mercy is expressed in His dealing with souls in the opposite way to that which they deserve because of their sin. The promise, "I will redeem you with a stretched out arm" (6.6) had been kept. Titus 3.5 affirms that the same mercy of God is extended to sinners today. It is "Not by works of righteousness which we have done, but according to his mercy he saved us".

The "holy habitation" to which they refer is Canaan (see Ps 78.54). "Thou hast guided them" is in the past tense and yet Canaan still lies ahead of them. It is seen as an accomplished fact even although it has not yet taken place. When God acts, even future events are seen as accomplished. It is certain that they will take place. The word "guided" (5095) is otherwise translated "gently lead" (Is 40.11). In the wilderness there is a foretaste of that joyful experience of which Isaiah writes, and which will be enjoyed by the nation during the Millennium when He gently leads those that are with young. As they travel towards Canaan He will not ask them to do that which is beyond their strength. He will be aware of their weaknesses and take into account their circumstances. Never will it be possible for them to claim that He is the cause of their failure.

"The people shall hear, and be afraid" (vv.14-16)

Now the song turns to the response of the world to the deliverance of Israel. The news of such an event would spread quickly. Those who travelled would bring tidings of what had befallen the feared might of Egypt. The people heard and were afraid. The inhabitants of Palestina were gripped by pain and sorrow. "Palestina" refers to the area north of the Sinai, probably where the Philistines were situated. They are mentioned first as it would appear to them that the Israelites might be travelling in their direction. The chiefs and princes of Edom were amazed and dismayed. "Edom" was the name given to Esau when he sold the birthright to Jacob (Gen 25.30). Doubtless they were not unhappy that the descendents of Jacob were slaves in Egypt. They had an ordered society and were a free nation. Kings reigned over them before there was a king in Israel (Gen 36.31). But now a remarkable change had taken place and they were dismayed by the tidings which had been brought to them. Moab was descended from the son of Lot who was born out of the incestuous relationship which he had with his daughter (Gen 19.30-38). The strong, mighty men of Moab will tremble when the news comes to them. The inhabitants of Canaan will "melt away" in the sense that their courage will dissolve. Everywhere fear and dread will be felt. Only by the work of God could slaves in Egypt create such widespread alarm, fear and dismay.

In Canaan, news of the crossing of the Red Sea came to Jericho. Rahab heard it. We do not know whether she was old enough to hear and understand it at the time, but even if she was not, the news would be passed to younger ones as they matured. As a result she stated to the two spies who lodged in her home that "your terror is fallen upon us, and that all the inhabitants of the land faint because of you" (Josh 2.9). She had heard this and believed. Faith came by hearing and Rahab the harlot became a woman of faith. It is clear that her faith did not come when she received the spies, but she took them into her home as a result of having faith. Perhaps when the news of the Red Sea crossing came, perhaps later when news arrived of the defeat of the Amorites, of Sihon, or at the time of the victory over Og, king of Bashan, we know not at what point, but we do know that she believed in the God of Israel whom she states to be "God in heaven above, and in earth beneath". She understood that the Lord had given the land of Canaan to Israel. In this way the Lord was preparing Canaan for the entrance of Israel. Later, the crossing of the Jordan had the same effect on the Canaanites. When the kings of the Amorites and the kings of the Canaanites "heard that the Lord had dried up the waters of Jordan from before the children of Israel…their heart melted, neither was there spirit in them any more" (Josh 5.1). Bush comments that "Throughout the whole context the gradations of distress are strikingly marked. First, there is fear among the people; then sorrow is to overtake the inhabitants of Palestina; next the princes of Edom are to be amazed or painfully disturbed; then the Moabites shall tremble with terror; and, finally, the hearts of Canaan shall melt away with overwhelming dread of the coming disasters".

As a result of this the people would "be as still as a stone". They would be petrified, immobile, and paralysed by fear and dread, until the purpose of God had been served, unable to oppose Israel. Even when other nations not mentioned here sought to bar their progress it would prove ineffective. Amalek was the first nation to do battle with Israel (ch.17) but that was a futile attempt to halt the progress of the people who had the Lord with them.

Israel's promised entrance into Canaan (v.17)

The "holy habitation" to which they were heading has been alluded to in v.13 but is now introduced once more. The purpose of bringing them out of Egypt was to bring them into Canaan. They would be planted in the "mountain of thine inheritance" (v.17). This indicated that in Canaan their days of journeying would be over and they would be given a firm and settled inheritance. Just as a tree is a secure fixture that cannot easily be moved, so Israel will be secure in her borders and, if obedient to the Lord, will not be moved. The same is true of a vine and it may be that it is the vine rather than a tree to which this "planting" refers. Psalm 80 refers to Israel being planted as a vine in Canaan: "Thou hast brought a vine out of

Egypt: thou hast cast out the heathen, and planted it. Thou preparedst room before it, and didst cause it to take deep root, and it filled the land. The hills were covered with the shadow of it, and the boughs thereof were like the goodly cedars" (vv.8-10). This vine was tended and all that was needed to make it fruitful was provided in abundance, but, sad to note, for the Lord it only brought forth sour grapes (Is 5.1-2). In becoming a man, the Lord came to His vineyard and, finding only sour, unripe grapes, He turned from it to the field, which is the world (Mt 13).

In these early days, however, all that lay ahead and Israel was rejoicing in the prospect of being planted in the land promised to them. In the "mountain of thine inheritance", Canaan, there was a place which was a Sanctuary. The Tabernacle was pitched at Shiloh but doubtless it is Zion to which reference is made here. This was where the Lord desired to have His house. The longing desire of Jehovah to dwell with His people is a continuing theme in the Word of God. The Sanctuary to be built on Zion will make this possible.

"The Lord shall reign" (vv.18-19)

The conclusion of the song is found in these verses. The throne of Pharaoh has been humbled and He who brought this about is the One who will reign for ever and ever. This outburst of praise is a fitting beginning to the final words of the song. The salvation of Israel, great and momentous though it may be, is not an end in itself. It is but one step in the unfolding of the purpose of God, which one day will be seen complete when the Lord does reign and is openly seen and acknowledged as supreme. The closing words sum up that which has been expressed, bringing to an end the paean of praise and worship by restating the greatness of the theme, and wonder at what the Lord has done.

Verses 20-21: The Response of Miriam and the Women

It would appear from these verses that Miriam and the women of Israel joined in the song with a refrain or chorus which consisted of the words of v.21. This is the first time that Miriam is named. In ch.2, when the child Moses was found in the Nile, it is only "his sister" who is mentioned. She is said here to be the sister of Aaron, making her also the sister of Moses. Twice she is closely linked with Aaron, here and when she and Aaron were prominent in a rebellion against Moses (Num 12), indicating that she was closer to Aaron than to Moses. This would be understandable as Moses had been in the family home as a young child, but since then had been in the palace and later in the land of Midian. Even allowing for him visiting the family there would not be the close bonds which are created by growing up together in the same home. When Moses returned to Egypt his position as leader of the nation would also set him apart somewhat from his brother and sister.

She is referred to here as "the prophetess". Although she failed badly in

Numbers 12 it must be recognised that she was a woman of godly worth. She was a prophetess in the sense that she spoke the mind of God, and may have been used to communicate this to the women of Israel in relation to matters which could not discretely be dealt with by men. Any attempt to deny the truth of 1 Corinthians 14.34 by using Miriam and other women who prophesied fails to appreciate that the instructions to the church in Corinth have to do with the gatherings of a New Testament local church. In these gatherings, as is taught there, women do not speak publicly.

Verse 22: Into the Wilderness of Shur

With the Red Sea now behind them, the Israelites' journey to Canaan commences. They have experienced a wonderful salvation which is not the end of their dealings with God. It is the beginning of their education as He teaches them His ways and how they can enjoy to the full all the many blessings which He has in store for them. With their old master defeated they start a new life, to be taught new lessons and to enjoy their new-found freedom.

Under the leadership of Moses, a leadership which has been confirmed at the Red Sea, they move into the wilderness of Shur (7793), which means "a wall". Clearly this desert was such a formidable area that it was a barrier which acted as a wall closing this border of Egypt. Travellers did not venture through here, but into this inhospitable area Israel travelled, continuing for a period of three days and finding no water. A dry barren vista stretched in front of them. Why had they been led into such a place as this? It seemed to their fainting hearts that leaving Egypt had but led them into circumstances more difficult than those from which they had come. Why was this? The answer is that there are lessons which have to be learned, the first being their complete dependence on the Lord for sustenance. In this wilderness which faced them there were not sufficient resources to sustain them. It should not have been difficult to rely on such a God as they had seen at work over the months past, but they were about to learn that when they were tested they failed. Not that this should surprise the reader! The same failure so often is found in the hearts of Christians. Having trusted the Lord for salvation it is strange that it is difficult to place trust in Him for the issues of each day. Israel will learn that there is a tendency to look at the problem and not to the Lord. Right at the beginning there will be impressed on them the truth that the way of blessing is to be totally reliant on Him.

Verses 23-26: At Marah
Bitter water

After journeying for three days without finding a water supply they come to Marah. If the wilderness of Shur was a place of drought, Marah added disappointment to this. It looked so promising that they had expected the problem of water to be solved. The reference to "three days'" journey is a reminder of the word of God to Moses that Israel was to go three days' journey into the wilderness that they might sacrifice to the Lord their God (3.18). This was repeated to Pharaoh when he offered to let them sacrifice in the land, that is, in Egypt (8.27). They have travelled the three days into the wilderness and it would be expected that they would now sacrifice to Him. This was to be a place of worship. Circumstances, however, drove all thought of sacrifice from their minds. Three days without water, and now water that is bitter and unfit to drink. How could anyone think of worship with such worry on their minds? How often is it that saints gather to worship but hearts soon became occupied with the worries of life! These press in and fill the mind that should be filled with Christ. If Israel had but cast their problem on the Lord what a difference there would have been. No murmuring would have been heard. Experience, however, teaches that this is easy advice to give to others but difficult advice to apply to our own lives.

Bitterness causes murmuring

So they murmured! "What shall we drink?" It seemed such a reasonable question, yet often a seemingly reasonable question cloaks a rebellious spirit. The verdict of the Word of God settled the issue. Their question voiced a complaint. This is the second time that they have expressed their displeasure (see 14.11-12). A sad pattern is being established which marked them whenever the road became difficult. The word "murmur" (3885) has behind it the thought of obstinacy, of something stopping over in their hearts. It indicates a complaint that is always before them, filling their hearts and causing them to murmur. As in ch.14, Moses is the object of their complaint. They have not yet become bold enough to complain against the Lord, but they feel no restraint in complaining against His servant. This was widespread, for "the people" murmured. Murmuring against Moses was, however, murmuring against the Lord since he was leading them as the Lord directed. The lesson has to be learned today. To complain against godly leaders, to murmur against godly teachers, is but to raise the voice against the Lord whom they serve. In this respect Paul experienced the same "murmuring" even from those who had come to know the Lord through his preaching. The Corinthians were turning away from his teaching on the basis of the assertion that "his bodily presence is weak, and his speech contemptible" (2 Cor 10.10). To the Galatians he has to defend his gospel against the claims that it was not in itself sufficient. Saints turned away from him when the going became hard (2 Tim 1.15). They may have insisted that they were still following the Lord, but their actions towards Paul indicated that this was not so. As with Moses, to murmur against God's servant is to murmur against Him.

It is probable that the name "Marah" (4785), meaning "bitterness", had already been given to this place, indicating that it was well-known for the bitterness of its waters. It is worth noting that coming to Marah was not a result of the disobedience of Israel. It can be that the bitter experiences of life are due to our disobedience. This is so with Naomi who, on her return to Bethlehem after years in Moab, says, "Call me not Naomi, call me Mara: for the Almighty hath dealt very bitterly with me" (Ruth 1.20). She uses the word "bitterly" to describe, in terms of taste, something that she would rather not have experienced. A bitter taste is that which is not pleasant, so she has gone through experiences that were not agreeable. However, the bitterness experienced by Israel was not due to disobedience. It came to them as a result of following the Lord, and the question arises as to why the Lord led them to bitter waters. The answer is that He would there teach them lessons that could not be taught under any other circumstances. They would learn by experience how the Lord could sweeten that which was bitter.

Bitter experiences are not always the result of disobedience. If sin and disobedience have marked the life it will be readily seen, as in the case of Naomi, that there is a link between that and the present bitterness. But if in pursuing godliness the saint has to experience this bitterness it is that there are lessons to be learned. Israel must learn that they are completely dependent on the Lord and that even that which appears to meet their need can only do so when His hand has fitted it for them. There is no escape from this state of dependence, and for the faithful follower there is no desire to escape from it. Dependence on Him is the secret of contentment and the guarantee that every need will be met.

The answer provided

The response of Moses to the murmuring of the people was to cry to the Lord. In this he showed true wisdom. To remonstrate with the people and reason with them on account of their behaviour would have achieved nothing. Moses was doing what the Children of Israel should have done. They ought to have been crying to the Lord but, in the face of their failure, Moses interceded on their behalf. His anguish is seen in that he *cried* unto the Lord. There was fervour and passion in his voice, and the reply which he received came quickly as "The Lord shewed him a tree" (v.25). There is no indication that this tree naturally had properties that extracted or neutralised the bitter elements in the waters. There has been much futile speculation as to which tree this was. Searches have been made in the area to find such a tree or bush but without success. This, however, was not a "natural" answer to the problem. The change in the waters did not take place because of the nature of the tree that was cast in. It took place because of the miraculous intervention of the Lord following the obedience of Moses in casting the tree into the waters. Although there is no note of the Lord instructing him to cast the tree into the waters, the fact that the cure came as a result of this indicates that this instruction had been given. The Lord had provision ready to effect this change. All that was necessary was that the Lord had to be brought into the problem by asking Him to act.

It cannot be without significance that it was a tree which was cast in. When the Christian reader observes this it is the Cross that comes into view. Where the Cross is put into the circumstances the bitter becomes sweet. All that is involved in the Cross - the hope which this gives the believer, the school of God into which the Christian has now been brought, and the goal for which the Lord is fitting those who are trusting in the work accomplished at Calvary - brings a different light to bear on the present bitterness. And so the waters became sweet.

But the lesson of Marah must be learned. "There he made for them a statute and an ordinance, and there he proved them" (v.25). Every blessing received from the hand of the Lord brings lessons with it. The lesson for the Children of Israel is that obedience to the Lord will result in their avoiding the plagues that fell on the Egyptians. They will not come under divine chastisement and will enjoy health bestowed by Jehovah Ropheka, "The Lord that healeth thee". By this He would prove them; He would put them to the test. This test, which they had faced at Marah is set out before them so that there can be no misunderstanding in future. Verse 26 contains the statute and the ordinance to which reference is made in v.25. Their health will depend on their obedience. This is a most solemn matter. Should they be disobedient to the Lord they will no longer be fit to bear testimony for Him. If they obey, none of the plagues that fell on the disobedient Egyptians will fall on them. If they disobey they will be subject to the chastening hand of God. The fact that the journey saw many of them "overthrown in the wilderness", that there "fell in one day three and twenty thousand", that many "were destroyed of serpents", and that "many were destroyed of the destroyer" (1 Cor 10.5-10) is a sad testimony to the fact that they did not diligently hearken to the voice of the Lord. Paul's reference to these sorrowful events when writing to the Corinthians is a warning for today. These things were written "for our admonition" (1 Cor 10.11), and it is well that the warning be heeded. Should folly make believers feel that no such failure will mark their service the sombre warning is given, "Let him that thinketh he standeth take heed lest he fall" (1 Cor 10.12). It is the responsibility of all believers to ensure that they are not "overthrown in the wilderness".

Spiritual health depends on obedience to His Word. It is also worth observing that many of the promises of God are conditional. Paul encourages the Philippians with the promise that the peace of God "shall keep your hearts and minds through Christ Jesus" (Phil 4.7). This is conditional on them "by prayer and supplication with thanksgiving" letting their requests be made known to God. No prayer means no peace. Again, he promises them that "the God of peace" (Phil 4.9) shall be with them. This will only be the case if they do the things which had been learned and received and heard from Paul, and which they had seen practised by him.

These promises even extended to their material circumstances. "My God shall supply all your need" is one of the great promises of the Bible, but it was given to those who had given of their substance to support the apostle (Phil 4.19). Giving to Him is a guarantee that needs shall be met. These many promises can only be claimed when there is obedience to His Word.

Verse 27: Elim

On leaving Marah they came to Elim. This was a very different place to Marah. Twelve wells of water and seventy palm trees were there. It was a pleasant place and if a choice could be made as to location, this would have been ideal. All they required was to be found in this oasis in the wilderness. Thus it is that the Lord who took them to Marah now leads them to Elim. Life is like that. There are days when the bitterness of Marah is experienced, but also times when the rest of Elim is found. The pilgrim will not be overtaxed. The events leading up to and subsequent to the Passover had been stressful. All had been new and they had not learned, and indeed would never all learn, the necessity of casting all their care on the Lord. But the Lord is gracious and now there are wells to be enjoyed and trees to give shade. How glad they must have been to arrive at Elim.

And yet amidst the calm tranquillity of Elim there was something missing. On this part of the journey, which culminates in the giving of the Law, Elim is the only stopping place where it appears they did not learn anything new about God. When the sun shines and no shadows are around it seems that less is learned about Him. Nevertheless, at Elim the Lord gives His people time to rest as they prepare for the next stage of the journey, that they may recognise that the Lord can lead not only to the Marahs but also to the Elims. He is a merciful God!

Notes

1 There is no scriptural authority for singing hymns with unbelievers.

9 The AV margin reads "repossess" and JND "dispossess", but most translate this as "destroy".

EXODUS 16

The Giving of the Manna

Introduction

Before dealing with this chapter it is well to consider the significance of what takes place in the light of the teaching of John 6 which was a turning point in the ministry of the Lord Jesus as, after listening to Him, "many of his disciples went back, and walked no more with him" (v.66). Following the feeding of the 5,000 the Lord had drawn a distinction between the "meat which perisheth" and "that meat which endureth unto everlasting life" (v.27). The Jews reminded Him that their fathers had eaten manna in the wilderness, but He asserted that His Father now gave "the true bread from heaven" (v.32). In stating that He was the bread of life He was rightly claiming that He was that "bread from heaven". Just as the manna satisfied Israel physically, so He satisfies the entire spiritual needs of the soul. The manna, therefore, was a picture of the Lord Jesus. He is the bread of God who came down from heaven, not only available for Israel, but for the world.

When the manna came it was "a small round thing" (v.14) which lay upon the ground. It was small, indicating the humility and lowliness of the Lord Jesus, and it was round, signifying His perfection. It was also white, as hoar frost, declaring His purity and holiness. Other men were called "holy men" (Elisha is an example of this in 2 Kings 4.9), but they were so called relatively, compared to other men. The Lord Jesus Christ was holy, not relatively, but absolutely. No sin was in Him.

The cry of the people, "Lord, evermore give us this bread" (Jn 6.34), was followed by many rejecting Him. Unbelieving hearts desire all that heaven can give, but do not accept that it is only through Him that those blessings are obtained.

Verses 1-3: Further Complaints

After Elim the Israelites journeyed and encamped by the Red Sea (Num 33.10) and then entered the Wilderness of Sin. This area is reckoned to be south of Marah and Elim, and to stretch as far as Sinai. The pleasant conditions of Elim had been left behind and once again they faced a wilderness journey. Elim was an attractive place where most would have preferred to remain, but more had to be learned and Elim was not the place for these lessons to be taught. On the fifteenth day of the second month they arrived in the Wilderness of Sin, one month since taking their leave of Egypt, during which time they had been eating the unleavened bread which they had brought from Egypt (12.39). Apart from the spiritual lessons to be learned from this diet, unleavened bread could be kept for one month and still be edible.

But now they had reached the end of their resources. The bread on which they had lived had all been consumed and there was no possibility of baking more. If they had learned the lessons of the previous month they would have lifted their voices to the Lord in supplication but the pattern which had been established in the past was still followed and they complained against Moses and Aaron. At Marah it was against Moses that the complaints were directed, here it is against Moses and Aaron. They were not content with one, but included both leaders in their murmurings as their hearts had been unmoved by the grace of the Lord towards them. Ingratitude was their response, and protest instead of prayer was on their lips. There were no exceptions to this tide of dissent; it was more widespread than that which had taken place at Marah, as "the whole congregation of the children of Israel murmured". What short memories they had!

The depth of their feelings amazes the reader. They would rather have died in Egypt than face the wilderness, and the significance of their words must not be missed. It would have been better to die at the time of Passover than to have been sheltered by the blood and redeemed out of Egypt. Memories of flesh-pots and bread eaten to the full were traded and spoken of, and compared very favourably with what they regarded as their present straitened and life-threatening circumstances. When affection for the Lord is low and difficulties press round, the world looks attractive. Nothing was said of the taskmasters, of the whips, or of the murderous activity of Pharaoh and his servants. They had forgotten the true nature of life as slaves; the burdens of Egypt were forgotten and the blessings bestowed by the Lord unappreciated.

They had not learned that it is a blessed thing to be entirely dependent on the Lord. Just a few moments reflection would have taught them that He had fulfilled every promise, overcome every difficulty, removed every danger, and met every need. None of this, however, was in their minds. Their desire was to have in their possession everything necessary to meet their needs thus removing any sense of dependence on Him. But they are about to be taught again that it is far better to rely on the Lord than on their own resources. This longing for self-sufficiency was never far from their minds. Generations later Jeremiah wrote of the nation forsaking "the fountain of living waters" and hewing out for themselves "cisterns, that can hold no water" (Jer 2.13). The desire to be independent of the Lord was still there. What blessing it is to rely on Him entirely. It may be argued today that regular employment takes away the need for this reliance in material things. An employer, not the Lord, provides the weekly or monthly pay or salary. But who provided the employment? Who provides the employer with the means to pay? The spiritual mind recognises that all this is of the Lord and that He meets all material and spiritual needs of life.

The charge, that Moses had brought them into the wilderness to kill them with hunger, was clearly nonsense. To what purpose was all that had taken place? "Such is the line along which a soul out of communion will travel. It first loses the sense of being in God's hands for good, and finally begins to deem itself in His hands for evil. Melancholy progress this!" (C. H. Mackintosh).

Verses 4-5: The Reply from the Lord

After such conduct it would not cause surprise if there had been a strong censure from heaven. A reminder of what the Lord had accomplished on their behalf and a rebuke for their behaviour is the least that could be expected, but when the Lord does speak it is to declare that He would pour blessing on them. Their obstinate refusal to appreciate His goodness is met by a promise to bestow more of heaven's bounty. Such is the grace of God. These events took place between Elim and Sinai when they were still under grace, as the Law had not been given. The Lord heard their murmurings, but there was no plague here as there is in Numbers 11 when, following their murmuring, "the Lord heard it; and his anger was kindled; and the fire of the Lord burnt among them" (Num 11.1). The Lord displayed how great was His grace, and for that there should have been thankful hearts.

The response of the Lord will be to "rain bread from heaven". The sin of Sodom and Gomorrah was met by brimstone and fire being rained down (Gen 19.24); the Egyptians had to endure hail being rained upon them (Ex 9.23). Here, in contrast, it is bread that will be rained from heaven, not sparingly but "rained" down. Natural rain cannot be controlled from earth. Men cannot turn it on and off; that is quite beyond them. They cannot claim credit for such rain coming when it is needed and for shutting it off when that is required. So the blessing will come from the Lord alone. It will come plentifully and it will come regularly and, just as rain falls from the skies, it will be controlled from heaven alone. They will be entirely dependent on Him.

But this blessing would not only come to satisfy their need, it would come also to "prove" (5254) them. To prove means to test or to try. When the Lord opened His hand to them it was for the purpose of putting them to the test to see if they would walk in His law. This aspect of enjoyment of His bounty is easily forgotten, as in the joy of receiving from Him there may be a failure to understand that the recipients are being put to the test. Responsibility follows blessing! Would they walk in His law? In context the "law" refers to the instructions for the gathering of the bread that is rained down from heaven. The important point is that obedience was to be the response to blessing as daily they would be put to the test. Today the same principles hold good. The many and varied blessings enjoyed by believers put them to the test. Is the response one of indifference or ingratitude? Is the faithfulness of God enjoyed so regularly that it is treated lightly, or does it invoke a response of devotion? Never let it be forgotten; daily blessing means daily testing!

The bread from heaven had to be gathered every day and it would be sufficient to meet the needs of each day, except on the sixth day when twice as much would be gathered. At this point no explanation of this double portion was given, as that came later (v.23). The Sabbath is not mentioned until v.23, but the seventh day was the Sabbath. No reference to the Sabbath has been made since the Fall, but here it appears again, in connection with the manna, the lesson being that there is no rest to be found apart from the Lord Jesus Christ.

The Lord gave manna, but they had to gather it, and if they failed to do so they would remain hungry. He would bestow, but they must exercise themselves to partake of what heaven had supplied, a principle still in force today.

Verses 6-10: Moses and Aaron Instruct Israel

Instructions are now given to Israel as to how the blessing will come. The purpose is that the people may know that it was the Lord who brought them out of Egypt, and that they understand that He has heard their murmurings. He had heard because their words were not merely directed against Moses and Aaron but in truth directed against the Lord. In the evening they will be given flesh to eat, and in the morning they will see the glory of the Lord and be given bread to the full.

First, therefore, the evening will bring them flesh. They have been longing for the fleshpots of Egypt, so the Lord will give them flesh. This must have seemed an improbability in such a wilderness but they will be taught that the Lord is not withholding the food of Egypt because He *cannot* give it; He is withholding it because He *will* not give it, as to supply them regularly with such food is not for their good. Their wilderness diet is not due to the powerlessness of the Lord but to His graciousness. Should believers today seek satisfaction from that on which the world feeds it is sobering to reflect that His care for us has provided something far better and it is folly to feast on another diet.

Second, in the morning they would see the glory of the Lord and be given bread. It is true that the glory of the Lord appeared in the cloud, but is that the glory to which reference is made? The glory referred to in v.7 would be seen in the morning, and there is no indication that the glory of the Lord which appeared in the cloud did so in the morning. It is, however, specifically stated that the manna came in the morning and it is the giving of the manna that was a revelation of the glory of God. Just as the turning of the water into wine was the occasion when the Lord Jesus "manifested forth his glory" (Jn 2.11), so the giving of the manna was a manifestation of the glory of the Lord. When the Lord works it is always a manifestation of His glory as it is not possible for Him to act and fail to be glorious. At the marriage in Cana there was no bright outshining of glory such as there was on the Mount of Transfiguration. Nevertheless, the miracle was a manifestation of His glory just as was the provision of manna.

But there was also a manifestation of the glory of the Lord in the cloud.

The people looked toward the wilderness where the cloud was to be seen. It had come to a halt in the direction in which it was leading them. Their murmuring had halted their progress. It is not known how the glory of the Lord was manifested. It may be that there was a bright outshining from the cloud, or the fire was seen during the day when it was normally seen in the darkness. Sufficient it is to understand that there was a change in the cloud which the people recognised as being a manifestation of the glory of the Lord. By this means He indicated that He had heard their murmurings, but despite that He had not abandoned them. His statement was clear; He was still "the Lord your God".

Verses 11-13a: The Giving of the Quails

On the evening before the manna came for the first time, the promise that they would eat flesh was fulfilled. Quails, a small bird, came in great numbers and covered the Camp. The lack of bread was for the purpose of creating in them a desire for provision of food from heaven, but it had created a desire for that which was of the flesh. The giving of the quails is a warning to all. The Lord will allow us the desire of our hearts, but if that desire is fleshly there will be no blessing in it.

> He gives to them the heav'nly wine to sup
> Whom He anoints,
> And also lets them drink the other cup
> That disappoints
> That, when they prove 'twas but a worthless waste
> They thought so fine,
> They may the more appreciate the taste
> Of better wine.†

The purpose of giving them the flesh to eat, therefore, was that they would learn the difference between the food of the world, which cannot satisfy, and the bread that was rained down from heaven which would fill them and satisfy them.

The differences between quails and manna are very marked.

1. The quails looked attractive but the manna did not have the attractiveness appreciated by the flesh. It was a "small round thing".

2. The quails required much effort, not only in gathering them, but also in preparing them for eating. Each bird yielded only a small portion of flesh, but the carcass and feathers had to be separated for disposal. The manna in its entirety could be eaten. There was nothing unfit for consumption. All was of nutritious value.

3. As has been noted, they would eat the quails, but be filled with bread. The flesh, which they so desired, could not satisfy them. Only manna could fill them.

The quails were not given each evening as it was not until the events recorded in Numbers 11 that quails were given again. The cause on that occasion was the discontent of the people with their daily diet of manna, the "mixt" multitude being in the forefront of this wave of dissatisfaction. So great was it that the people wept and spoke again of the "cucumbers, and the melons, and the leeks, and the onions, and the garlick" of Egypt (Num 11.5). In response the Lord sent a wind bringing quails in such great quantities that the ground was covered up to a depth of 2 cubits for a distance of one day's journey on either side of the Camp. This would appear to be in greater quantities than on the previous occasion. "He that gathered least gathered ten homers" (Num 11.32) compared to the one omer per man which was gathered of the manna (Ex 16.16). Judgment, however, fell on them, for as they were eating the quails the Lord smote them with a plague because by that time they had had opportunity to appreciate the manna and, more significantly, they were then under Law and not under grace. In Exodus 19 they had entered into a legal covenant with the Lord; the covenant with its demands upon them, and penalties for breaking it, had been willingly accepted and was in place. This sad event is enough to confirm that quails were not given as a regular part of their wilderness diet.

Verses 13b-15: The Giving of the Manna

The manna, however, was there when the sun burned off the morning dew. The linking of it with the dew is not without significance as dew speaks of the daily caring refreshment that comes from heaven. Isaac, in his patriarchal blessing, speaks of the "dew of heaven" (Gen 27.28), as the first of the blessings to be enjoyed. "There was a layer of dew round about the camp" (v.13, Newbury margin), and when this was gone there lay on the face of the wilderness, clearly visible, the bread from heaven. It came as silently as the dew, a sign of the tender mercies of God in providing daily sustenance. It is this which is before the mind of the prophet Jeremiah as he exclaims, "...his compassions fail not. They are new every morning: great is thy faithfulness" (Lam 3.22-23). Even as he surveyed a ruined Jerusalem, Jeremiah understood that the Lord was still, morning by morning, meeting the need of those who were faithful to Him.

This morning bounty from heaven was a constant reminder that the work of God continues, even when men sleep; His care for His people is never ending, for He neither slumbers nor sleeps. (Ps 121.4). In the stillness of the night, silently and unobserved, tomorrow's provisions were laid out, and the question which was asked by rebellious hearts, "Can God furnish a table in the wilderness?" (Ps 78.19), was answered. He *can* furnish a table, and He did, even in the face of sin and provocation.

Much useless speculation has surrounded the nature of manna. Of what did it consist, and is it to be found in the Sinai Desert? Clearly it is not to be found today, as it was not a natural phenomenon, and if it had been it would have been already known to the Israelites and to all travellers passing through the area. Until that first morning when it appeared it was unknown to man, and when Israel reached Canaan it ceased (Josh 5.12). After that the only portion preserved was that which was laid up before the Lord in a pot (Ex 16.33-34), and this was absent when the Ark was placed in the Temple (1 Kings 8.9), probably removed, together with Aaron's rod that budded, during the time when the Ark was in the country of the Philistines. To search for it today or to seek to understand its composition, as some have done, is folly.

It has already been noted that the manna was a picture of the Lord Jesus as the bread of God which came down from heaven. It is on Him that His people feed and it is necessary that they feed on Him daily, as spiritual life requires spiritual sustenance and that can only be provided by feeding on Christ. As with the manna, so with the Lord Jesus, there is nothing that appeals to the flesh. The "small round thing" which lay on the face of the earth was not attractive because of its appearance, but the fact that it came from heaven, food from the Sanctuary, was what gave it attraction to God's people. There is nothing attractive to the world in that from which Christians find their spiritual nourishment.

The humanity of the Lord Jesus was pictured in the manna. To the world He was insignificant, but feeding on Him, with prayer, meditation on Scripture, listening to the teaching of the Word of God, conversing together about the "things concerning Himself", and making the Bible the book at the centre of life make up the diet which produces spiritual growth. To the unbeliever it is most unattractive and undesirable, but to the believer it is the corn of heaven. It can only be enjoyed fully when there is no appetite for that on which the world feeds. May the cry from each believing heart be that which has already been quoted: "Lord, evermore give us this bread" (Jn 6.34)!

What was manna?

That it was the basic diet of Israel in the wilderness is clear. It was not impossible for them to have had in their possession flour, from which bread could be baked, as this was used at the consecration of the priests (Ex 29.2,40), for the shewbread (Lev 24.5), and for the meal offerings (Lev 2.1). They could, therefore, obtain some wheat, but in wilderness conditions not enough to satisfy the needs of the whole nation. It is of interest to note that the manna was never used in the sacrifices. As the supply ceased when the land was entered, it would not have been available for sacrificial use in Canaan. Clearly, as they also had flocks and herds, it would be possible to eat meat, but they could not live on that only. Such great quantities of meat would have been necessary that with regular killing their flocks would soon have been greatly diminished. It should also be noted that when the people declared their dislike of the manna (Num 11) they did not have another plentiful food source to which they could turn. Manna, therefore, was the basis of their diet, their staple diet, from one month after they left Egypt.

Manna is described in Scripture in a number of ways. When it was first seen the people exclaimed, "It is manna: for they wist not what it was" (v.15). The AV marginal reading, "What is this?", conveys something of their surprise. It is "the bread which the Lord hath given" (16.15); "the corn of heaven" (Ps 78.24); "angels' food" (Ps 78.25), which may be translated "the bread of the mighty". These descriptions all confirm that this was heavenly given food, beyond the ability of man to produce. It has already been noted that it was "a small round thing" (v.14), and it was also like coriander seed with the colour of bdellium (v.31; Num 11.7). "Bdellium is an aromatic gum…and a production originally of the land of Havilah (Gen 2.12). Some authorities suppose the word to mean *the pearl* or some other precious stone".[†] As manna has been likened to hoar frost on the ground it must have had the same lustre as is found on a pearl. Coriander seeds are the size of small peppercorns and used for medicinal purposes and as a spice. Manna came like this, in the form of little seeds coloured white and lustrous as pearls. The taste is described as "like wafers made with honey" (v.31). Wafers are thin flat cakes of unleavened bread. Manna did not come in the same form as a wafer but tasted like it; but whereas unleavened bread has little taste, manna had additionally the sweetness of honey.

Verses 16-18: The Gathering of the Manna

Moses now instructed the people how the manna had to be gathered. The men of the family gathered it each morning, apart from the Sabbath, one omer being gathered for each person in the family. When this was done the manna was measured out with an omer measuring vessel,[†] and the need of all was supplied. In what way, however, was the manna measured out to the family members? There are three views.

1. All the manna was placed in heaps and measured out to the nation. Every one then had enough to satisfy them and there was no waste. Those who gathered did not gather for their family, but to place the manna in the supply heap that would be used for a tribe, or for designated sections of the tribe.

2. The manna was gathered by family representatives for the use of their family. As there would be more than one man gathering for a family some gathered more than others. However, when the manna was measured out to the family of those who gathered there was enough for everyone to eat as the quantity gathered provided one omer for each family member. It may also be that appetites were different and some took more and some less, but there was enough for all to eat.

3. No matter how much was gathered for the family the Lord intervened in a miraculous way and, if they gathered less than was necessary for the whole family, when measured it gave just one omer per family member.

Even if more than was necessary for the family was gathered there was still but one omer for each.

The second suggestion seems to fit the text most satisfactorily. The important point is that the needs of the whole nation were satisfied daily. How much organisation would this have taken if it had been left to men to determine how manna was to be gathered and distributed? The administration required would have been considerable, but when the Lord ordered the distribution of the "bread of heaven" the correct quantity was supplied to every Israelite without exception and no one suffered from lack of nutrition.

The great quantity of manna gathered must not be overlooked. An omer measured by volume is 5.169 pints or 2.94 litres. If there were six members of a family it was necessary to gather over 17 litres of manna. To feed 2.4 million people required just over 7,000,000 litres daily, the gathering of which was a very considerable task, an enterprise not for the faint hearted, requiring dedication, devotion and discipline. To spend less time than was necessary, or even to fail to rise early to gather, resulted in an empty larder and a day of weakness and hunger. The same is true of those who seek daily to gather of that spiritual manna which is to be found in the Word of God. But it cannot escape the notice of the reader that there was no provision made for those who refused to gather, only for "those who gathered little" perhaps because of age or physical limitations.

When Paul dealt with the matter of giving (2 Cor 8.15) he took up the example of the manna as a principle to be carried out in meeting the needs of the saints. Those who have gathered more than they need should consider the needs of those who have gathered less than is required, and, just as there was enough manna to meet the needs of all, so giving will meet the needs of others. In the Camp those who gathered more had not to hoard it for themselves, but had to give to others in the family circle who did not have enough. God had given, and receiving what came from His hand ought to have created a desire to give to others. Receiving from a bountiful God creates a desire to be bountiful to others.

Verses 19-20: Leaving the Manna Until the Morning

The pattern of disobedience in the midst of blessing is once again repeated. None of the manna had to be left until the next morning (the exception being the manna gathered on the sixth day). Some, however, did leave a quantity until the next morning and "it bred worms and stank". There are two possible reasons why some left it until the next morning. First, they may have wished to hoard it, an evidence of a lack of faith, showing that they had no trust that the Lord who had given today would give on the morrow. The same attitude dictated the conduct of Israel when they "hewed them out cisterns, broken cisterns, that can hold no water" (Jer 2.13). Rather than enjoy the fresh water provided daily from the "fountain of living waters" they made cisterns where this water could be stored for future use. But, as in the wilderness they found that when they came to use the manna on the next day it was unusable, so when they went to the cisterns to obtain a supply they found that their leaking cisterns had been unable to hold the water. The lesson for today is that spiritual food is given daily and, as it cannot meet the needs of tomorrow, it has to be gathered fresh each day. By tomorrow it will not only be stale, it will be unusable.

Second, it may be that manna was left until the morrow because there was no appetite for it. It appears from the specific mention of some being left over at the end of the day that the Lord expected each day's provision to be consumed since there was not a surfeit given which would cause unnecessary waste. The supply for each family was not only sufficient to meet their needs, but was necessary to meet these needs. To leave it over, therefore, could only result in the people being under-nourished. How sad it is for Christians to have before them daily a spiritual banquet, food from heaven to be enjoyed, and yet to refuse it. Lack of appetite, resulting in lack of spiritual nourishment, leads to lack of spiritual energy and loss of spiritual health and, with spiritual strength thus weakened, work for the Lord diminishes. Little wonder Moses was wroth at the folly of refusing what the Lord had graciously given!

Verse 21: When the Manna had to be Gathered

Not only are there lessons in how the manna was to be gathered, but also in when it was to be gathered - "They gathered it every morning". This had to be done very early in the morning, because in the heat of the sun the manna melted. The question may be asked, "Why did the manna not melt away in the heat which surely would be felt even after it had been gathered?". It would appear that the gathering process ensured that the "melting" did not take place as the Lord preserved what was gathered for use during the hours for which it had been given. Gathering in the early morning that which sustains for the rest of the day is a profitable prelude to the busy hours which lie ahead. The Lord Jesus rose up "a great while before day" (Mk 1.35), during the final watch, between 03.00 hrs and 06.00 hrs, using this time to be alone and pray. Today's world is busy with pressures which make it difficult to set aside times such as this for prayer and meditation. To be up early may make it necessary to bring the previous day to a close earlier, and that can be very difficult to achieve. Nevertheless, as always, there are great spiritual benefits in seeking to follow the example of the Lord Jesus Christ and, although it may not be possible to set aside a long time each morning, even a short period will be a time of profit in which the presence of the Lord can be enjoyed, spiritual manna gathered from His hand, and preparation made for the busy hours to be faced. It cannot be done later, for, as the hours go on, the "heat" of the day's activities ensures that manna gathering cannot be carried out. Let all, whenever possible, value the early hours of each day.

Verses 22-26: Gathering for the Sabbath

On the sixth day a double quantity of manna was provided. In total, therefore, the Lord provided on the sixth day in excess of 14,000,000 litres of manna. How great is the grace and liberality of God! No manna came on the seventh day, which, as has already been observed in connection with vv.4-5, is identified as the Sabbath. This is the first occasion since the Fall that the Sabbath has been mentioned. Indeed the words "Sabbath (7676) and "rest" (7677), meaning a "Sabbatism" or "special holiday" are used here for the first time. There is no indication in Scripture that the Sabbath had been kept over these years since the Fall, indeed it is unlikely that slaves in Egypt would have been able to keep it (see Deut 5.14-15 which indicates that in Israel not only masters, but servants had to rest), but with the giving of the manna it is mentioned, and with the giving of the Law the keeping of it became a commandment. The specific mention of the fact that "the people rested on the seventh day" (v.30) confirms this. How significant are the words of Moses on the sixth day of gathering: "To morrow is the rest of the holy sabbath unto the Lord". If the seventh day had been a day of rest kept for generations there would be no reason to state that this seventh day rest had to be observed, so the first Sabbath kept since the entrance of sin was the first "seventh day" of the manna. No man was to go "out of his place on the seventh day" (v.29), but this does not mean that it was necessary for them to remain indoors. It simply indicates that they did not go out to gather manna.

The Sabbath rest of God had been broken when sin entered. The Lord Jesus stated, "My Father worketh hitherto, and I work" (Jn 5.17). Sabbath rest did not entail the cessation of all work. It was not to be regarded as a day of idleness; indeed, when God rested on the seventh day He did not cease from all work. "This rest occurred because the work of creation was complete, but after that God was always working towards and in His creation, as Paul wrote, 'by him all things consist' (Col 1.17)".[†] Necessary works (which included the holding together by God of the universe which He had created), and those that have been defined as "works of love and mercy" continued on the Sabbath. Only in Christ is rest obtained and only as a result of the death and resurrection of the Lord Jesus will God be able to rest. As the manna speaks of Christ, the bringing in of the Sabbath at this point but emphasises that the coming of the Lord Jesus to earth and the work which He carried out here is the foundation of the rest which one day will be enjoyed by God's people.

It should be observed in passing that the Sabbath is not kept by believers today, nor does the Lord's Day become the "Sabbath" of the church age. This is not a dispensation of days, feasts, and holy days as there is no instruction in the New Testament for the seventh day rest to be continued. The Lord's Day is when, in the breaking of bread, saints remember the Lord, but it is not a special "holy day" or "day of rest", for in the Christian era every day is a "holy day" to be lived in a manner which is pleasing to the Lord. In the goodness of God, for many generations, circumstances have been such that the first day of the week has been, for many, a day when the normal working routine of the week is set aside, and the time thus freed can be used in the service of the Lord, but this is a privilege which is being gradually taken away. However, in the early church period there was no such privilege, and saints would be required to work on the Lord's Day, making it necessary to break bread in the evening. The western Sunday, with freedom from normal toil, is an opportunity to be grasped and guarded, with hours to be used in His service, but do not let this be confused with the Sabbath of the Old Testament.

The fact that no manna came on the seventh day was further proof that this was not a "natural" phenomenon. With regularity over the entire wilderness years no manna came on the seventh day, and to seek to gather manna on that day was an act of disobedience to the Lord. If, however, Israel had gone hungry on the Sabbath it would have been cause (or excuse) for breaking the Law, but the Lord provided a double quantity every sixth day, and also ensured that the manna which was kept for use on the Sabbath did not "stink, neither was there any worm therein". In this Sabbath provision Israel should have seen further evidence of the presence of Lord and of His work for them.

But it cannot fail to be noticed that this was also confirmation that what the Lord asks of His people He will enable them to fulfil. Today, no one can assert that the pathway of discipleship is too hard for present conditions. He makes provision to ensure that should there be failure in obeying His Word the cause is not that the pathway is impossible, but is failure on the part of the servant to make use of the resources made available to enable His Word to be obeyed.

Mention is made of the cooking arrangements for the manna. There is no reason to believe that cooking was necessary. It could be eaten as it was given, but Moses indicates that it could be baked or seethed (boiled - 1310), enabling the manna to be served in different ways. It could be served cold or it could be served hot, making it suitable for all times of the year, no matter what the season or what the conditions, to provide a meal for the colder days of winter as well as for the warm days of summer. The practical lesson for today is that what is received from the Lord daily from Scripture, and what is given to strengthen as the day progresses, can be enjoyed just as it is received from the Lord. But "cooking" it, meditating on what has been given and extracting from it all the truth that the Lord will graciously supply, can also provide further enjoyment. As with the gathering of the manna it requires effort and diligence, but it provides a spiritual diet suitable for all times and all circumstances. Coates describes it well when he states: "The baking and cooking here seem to suggest the exercise that comes in so that grace given may be utilised to the best advantage…I take the cooking and the baking here to represent the right spiritual diligence of the soul that grace shall be utilised in the best possible way".

Notice must be taken, however, of what appeared to be a misuse of the cooking. The appetite of the Israelites for the manna soon decreased until about one year later they wept and cried, "Who shall give us flesh to eat?...But now our soul is dried away: there is nothing at all, beside this manna, before our eyes" (Num 11.4-6). The people gathered the manna and "ground it in mills, or beat it in a mortar, and baked it in pans, and made cakes of it" (Num 11.8). This apparently frenetic activity was an attempt to make the manna more palatable. This activity went far beyond seething and cooking. It was an attempt on the part of those who had lost their appetite for the bread of the mighty, the corn of heaven, to change the taste and presentation of it to suit the appetite of the flesh. There should be no surprise at this. The flesh finds that which is spiritual to be tiring and irksome, and sets about making the things of Christ to be acceptable to the flesh. This may be done today by the importation of liturgy, or of human tradition or splendour in the form of robes, hierarchies, and all that goes with these things. On the other hand the "evangelical" can also fail by bringing in a form of "worship" which models itself on the entertainment of the world. But even those who would shun such extremes can fail by introducing organisation and form which has no foundation in Scripture. How careful all must be to keep a keen appetite for the Lord; to desire to feast on Him and on Him alone. Such an appetite will not need to grind and beat that which heaven has given.

Verses 27-31: Seeking to Gather on the Sabbath
The first sin of which certain were guilty in relation to the manna was that of hoarding what should have been used. Now there is the sad record of some going out on the Sabbath to gather what the Lord had declared would not be available on that day, having a desire, fuelled by avarice, to gather more than was their due. It was not due to need, for that had been already met, so again, as with the hoarding of the manna, it can only be that there was a lack of faith that tomorrow would see the hand of God open again in giving, compelling some to seek for manna today. Fear for tomorrow brings sin today. There is a sharp warning in the words, "and they found none". The folly of their conduct is that they sought that which the Lord had stated would not be given and considered that the Lord was seeking to keep back from them on the Sabbath that which was available for enjoyment. "Disobey Him and that enjoyment will be gained" - from the entrance of sin this has always been one way in which the Adversary has sought to blind the human mind. The suggestion that the Lord was keeping Eve back from what could be gained was successful in deceiving her. She would gain so much by putting aside the "restrictions" placed upon her by a God whose intention was to keep her from realising her potential; thus the evil suggestion was made and, sad to say, acted upon. There is a similar situation here. It entered into the minds of some that there was manna to be gathered and that this could be enjoyed despite

the "needless limitation" placed upon them. The same spirit is seen today when that which the Lord forbids is viewed as something desirable, with benefits and enjoyment being denied men and women simply because of "irrelevant, petty restrictions". There was a failure then, as there is presently, to understand that all instruction from the Lord is for the profit and benefit of mankind, and that if the Word of God teaches that certain conduct is sinful, it is very much a real blessing and benefit to all who obey. The blessing that these disobedient searchers sacrificed was that of the Sabbath rest as they expended time and energy, gaining nothing and losing what could not be regained. A wasted day can never be relived.

The grace of God was seen in that no judgment fell on their heads. On a later occasion the people found a man gathering sticks on the Sabbath day. He was brought before Moses and Aaron and all the congregation (Num 15.32-36), and they put him under guard until the mind of the Lord was known. The gravity of the situation was understood and the Lord declared that he should be put to death by stoning. As was true in other examples of the first public acts of disobedience,[†] punishment was righteous so that sin might never be treated lightly. But the events of Numbers 15 took place when they were under Law; at this time they were still under grace so no judgment was carried out. How often in this section of the narrative does the reader rejoice in the goodness and grace of God! If Israel had realised how much they owed to this grace they would have refused the Law and continued to cast themselves upon the grace of God.

These verses cannot be left behind without considering the significance of the words to Moses in v.28: "How long refuse *ye* to keep my commandments". Moses had not been disobedient but he ruled over a disobedient people. Because of this he was charged with that disobedience and, as the ruler, he was bound up with his people, emphasising the great responsibility of leadership. The prophets never separated themselves from the sins of the people, crying, "We have sinned" (Neh 1.6; Jer 3.25; Dan 9.5), and not, "They have sinned".

Leadership today is no less onerous. It involves being responsible for those who are led and being identified so closely with them that at the Judgment Seat of Christ an account must be given (Heb 13.17) of the condition of the flock over whom "the Holy Ghost hath made you overseers" (Acts 20.28). The work of leading and shepherding the saints must never be looked on as a "promoted post"; nor must it be regarded as an "official position" which gives status. It is a responsibility taken up before God with love and care for the saints, desiring His glory and their blessing. It may not lead to "official" recognition as an overseer, but spiritual saints will recognise who has their well-being at heart and who has the spiritual qualifications to be recognised as leading the flock.

A description of the manna given in v.31 is dealt with in the comments on vv.11-15. At this point it is the "house of Israel" who call what God had given "manna". In v.15 it is the Children of Israel who call it "manna". This is the first mention of the "house of Israel" in Scripture. It seems to indicate a happy agreement amongst the family of Israel that this was "manna". It is good when there is such a family feeling and agreement amongst saints, but only in appreciation of the Lord can such a healthy state be found.

Verses 32-36: The Golden Pot of Manna

One pot of manna was preserved for generations following, another proof of the miraculous nature of this "daily bread". Moses was commanded to take one omer, a supply equal to that given daily for each man, and place it in a vessel. The Septuagint renders this as a "golden pot" and this is confirmed by the writer to the Hebrews who states that in the Ark was placed "the golden pot that had manna" (Heb 9.4). The purpose of this was that future generations might "see the bread wherewith I have fed you in the wilderness" (v.32). There was to be a perpetual remembrance of the goodness of God in feeding His people so that they would understand that "their fathers were neither stinted to hard fare nor to a short allowance, and could thus judge between God and Israel, whether they had cause to murmur or be grateful" (Bush).

Aaron was instructed to fill a pot with the manna and "lay it up before the Lord". Although the Tabernacle had yet to be built, these words anticipate the manna being placed inside the Ark. When the Tabernacle was reared it is only stated that Moses "put the testimony into the ark" (40.20), but it was doubtless also at that time that the golden pot of manna was placed beside the testimony in the Ark. This, however, raises another question. If the manna was placed inside the Ark, how could the people see it? Not only was it in the Holy Place into which only the High Priest could come, but it was also inside the Ark where even he could not see it.

Moses understood that this pot of manna could have become an object of interest and curiosity to future generations of the Children of Israel. They could have made it a talisman to be passed around and some might have had the boldness to seek to "sample" the manna. There were times when even the Ark was misused in this way. The instruction of Josiah to "Put the holy ark in the house which Solomon the son of David king of Israel did build; it shall not be a burden upon your shoulders" (2 Chr 35.3), indicates that it was their practice to carry the Ark about as such a talisman. To prevent misuse of this nature, the manna was laid before the Lord inside the Ark. Should the Lord have required it to be removed to display to the Children of Israel He would have so commanded, although there is no record of this taking place. Israel would be aware of its presence in the Ark and in that way it would be a constant reminder to them of the food with which their fathers had been fed in the wilderness. Matthew Henry's comments are apt: "God having provided manna to be His people's food in the wilderness…the memory of it was preserved…Eaten bread must not be forgotten. God's miracles and mercies are to be had in everlasting remembrance" (*The Concise Commentary*).

It is this manna placed in the Ark to which reference is made in Revelation 2.17: "To him that overcometh will I give to eat of the hidden manna", one of two blessings which are promised to the overcomer in the church in Pergamos. There is, therefore, a lesson for today. Calling this pot of manna "hidden manna" indicates that it was hidden from the eyes of the people in the Sanctuary. As "hidden manna" it was for the eyes of God alone and represents the features of the life of Christ which were known to God and enjoyed by Him alone. But the overcomer will be given some of this hidden manna, some fresh appreciation of the life of Christ, an appreciation which God has already enjoyed. As the manna is "spiritual meat" (1 Cor 10.3) the overcomer will be able to benefit from some of this unique spiritual provision, and for those with a desire to get to know Christ better this promise should be an incentive to be an overcomer.

The further comments of Matthew Henry express well what ought to be the desire of all who seek to serve Him: "Let us seek earnestly for the grace of the Holy Spirit, to turn all our knowledge of the doctrine of Christ crucified, into the spiritual nourishment of our souls by faith and love".

> Guide us, O Thou great Jehovah,
> Pilgrims through this barren land;
> We are weak, but Thou art mighty;
> Hold us by Thy powerful hand:
> Bread of heaven,
> Feed us now and evermore.
>
> (W. Williams)

Notes

11 I. Y. Ewan, *The Caravanserai*.

15 *Universal Bible Dictionary*.

18 A domestic vessel used for measuring dry weights.

23 J. Heading, *What the Bible Teaches: John*.

29 See Nadab and Abihu, first in the Aaronic priesthood (Lev 10); Achan's sin, first in Canaan (Josh 7); Ananias and Sapphira, first in the Acts (Acts 5).

EXODUS 17

The Smitten Rock and the Battle with Amalek

Verses 1-3: Complaints about Lack of Water

The entire congregation now continue their journey, fortified by their daily diet of manna. Although there is no mention of them here, they encamped at two stopping places, Dophkah and Alush, between the Wilderness of Sin and Rephidim (Num 33.12-13). The pattern of life in the wilderness was being established. There were places where fresh lessons were learnt, there were places where the calm conditions of Elim were enjoyed, and there were places where there is no record of either, only remembered as resting places on the way to Canaan. Life is like that. There are times of testing and trial, there are other times when the sun shines and calm and peace are enjoyed, and there are times when there is little of either, just days which take us nearer Canaan. In them all the goodness of God can be appreciated.

The pathway was determined by following the cloud. It was in this way that they journeyed "according to the commandment of the Lord". Yet again we see that the pathway of obedience leads them into further testing. Rephidim (7508) means "Reclining Places", a place where rest could be anticipated, yet for Israel it did not live up to its name. The fault did not lie with the Lord who had led them there; it lay with the people and their response to the problem of lack of water.

This problem had been faced before in the wilderness of Shur (15.22) and the Lord had met the need of the people. The events of that time must have been fresh in the minds of the Israelites as they faced the same problem once more. Surely their experience would result in faith that the Lord would again meet their need! Sad to relate, this is not what takes place. The experience of the believer ought to produce added faith in the Lord. Looking back at how past difficulties were met, and overcome, should give confidence for today. Often, however, the first reaction to a problem is to dismiss the Lord from the circumstances. The mind becomes filled with worry and the Lord is left outside.

The events which followed their arrival at Rephidim proved that, despite the remarkable and miraculous goodness of God and the fact that there had not been any lack of food or water on the journey so far, there was no faith that He would continue to bless them. Their words revealed the condition of their hearts. They cried to Moses, "Give us water that we may drink". There was no crying to the Lord, only to His servant. This is the first occasion on which it is said that they thirsted. It may be that the order of events was significant in this respect. It is after they chide with Moses that their thirst is recorded. Perhaps if they had called on the Lord first they would have avoided the thirst which gripped them. But even that thirst did not change their attitude; they still directed their words to Moses.

The accusation against the Lord's servant was that he had brought them into the wilderness so that they would die there of thirst. The indictment was that he had deliberately brought them into circumstances that would lead to their death. Three words are used to describe their behaviour. First, as has been noted, they are said to *chide* (7378) with Moses. The word means "to contend, complain, or debate". It has the thought of open strife and indicates a more aggressive attitude than they had previously displayed. It was used of the dispute that arose between the herdmen of Gerar and the herdmen of Isaac regarding the wells that Isaac's servants had dug. The well dug in Gerar was a source of strife, as the Philistines objected to refreshment being available to Isaac and his servants (Gen 26.20-22). The word is also used of the attitude of Jacob to Laban when Laban overtook him as he journeyed home (Gen 31.36). "Jacob was wroth and chode with Laban", but, sad to note, one of the charges which Laban made was true, although Jacob was unaware of this. Rebekah had stolen some of the "gods" from Laban's house and had hidden them in her tent. The background to these two incidents may make the chiding, if not approved, at least understandable. Dealing, however, with the behaviour of the redeemed nation of Israel towards Moses, this conduct is inexcusable.

Second, Israel was charged by Moses with a serious offence. "Wherefore do ye *tempt* (5254) the Lord?", he enquired of them. They were putting God to the test. The sin in this act was that the putting to the test was not on the basis of faith but of unbelief. They questioned whether the Lord was with them or not. They had seen the plagues in Egypt, had witnessed the deaths that came upon Egypt at Passover, had passed through the Red Sea as it opened up for them, had seen the flower of Egypt's army destroyed, had watched as Moses cast the tree into the bitter water at Marah, were daily enjoying the manna from heaven, and yet now they doubted whether the Lord was actually with them. The Lord, through the prophet Malachi urges the people to "prove" (to test - 974) Him by bringing all the tithes into the storehouse. In response He will open the windows of heaven and pour them out a blessing. This testing is not, however, out of unbelief, it is based on faith; putting God to the test to see His promises fulfilled. How very different from the events at Rephidim! Here, as they do not have faith that the Lord is with them, they ask for proof. Further comment on this will be made when dealing with v.7.

Third, Israel *murmured* against Moses. A "murmur" (3885) is an obstinate grudge that remains with an individual; it is a state of grumbling. The complaint was ridiculous and reveals that the sentiments that they had voiced on a previous occasion had not gone away (see 16.3). Could it possibly be accepted that Moses had brought them into the wilderness to have them die from thirst? Was this the purpose behind all that he had done since his return from Midian? If they had kept their eye on the Lord they would have understood that such complaints were outrageous, but when they lost sight of Him the outrageous soon filled their minds, with no accompanying sense of how ridiculous such thoughts were.

Ingratitude to the Lord, despite all the blessings which He gives, is a common problem. It may be that His consistency in giving makes them so familiar that they are taken for granted and are seen as a "right" rather than an expression of His grace. Indeed, the fact that they are bestowed so regularly may make it look as if they are simply natural phenomena enjoyed by everyone. As a result, when trial comes it is resented as an unwarranted intrusion rather than being seen as an opportunity of faith testing God with the objective of seeing Him meeting the need.

Verse 4: The Response of Moses

Moses now did for the people what they were unwilling to do for themselves - he cried unto the Lord, calling for His help. This was not the first time that Moses had done this. He cried to the Lord for the removal of the plague of frogs afflicting Egypt (8.12); when the Red Sea was before them as an apparent barrier to progress (14.15); when the bitter waters of Marah were encountered (15.25); and later he cried to the Lord for the removal of Miriam's leprosy (Num 12.13). He was no stranger in the presence of God and now, in the face of Israel's cries against him, he cried to the Lord. There was no one else to whom he could turn, but this was not done in desperation; he knew where the answer lay.

So strong is the feeling of the people that they are prepared to put Moses to death by stoning. Again they charge Moses with responsibility for what they consider to be a hopeless situation. They may not yet be bold enough to charge the Lord with this, but they do so by proxy, laying the blame firmly on the shoulders of His servant. At a later date, when they feared to take possession of Canaan there was a conspiracy to set another captain over them and return to Egypt (Num 14.4).

Thirst can drive men and women to extreme actions, and it is clear that Moses was in a position of real danger. This is reflected in his words, "What shall I do unto this people?", admitting that he did not know how to handle the crisis. He had no preconceived ideas of his own and did not call on the Lord as if he had already determined how to act. This servant was cast on the Lord and entirely dependent on Him. How happy a state in the midst of turmoil!

Verse 5: The Response of the Lord – "Go on before the people"

The answer comes, as it always will to those who cry to Him. There was to be a public display of the grace of God in action. Moses was instructed to take the elders of Israel and with the rod of God in his hand to "Go on before the people", leading them to the rock in Horeb. They had charged him with leading them into an impossible situation, now there would be public vindication of his leadership; the same Moses would lead them to blessing. The cloud would be in front, but Moses would be seen to be following the cloud, just as he had always instructed them. The people would be forced to confess that where Moses led them was where the Lord led them.

He had to take the elders with him. The close view they would enjoy of the events about to happen would enable them to confirm to the people what took place before the rock. The great number of people made it impossible for them all to view what was to occur at Horeb, and this was not a time for rumours to grow. Without witnesses these exaggerations and stories would run throughout the Camp, but the truth of what transpired must be faithfully declared to the people.

More significantly, as far as the people were concerned, he had to take the rod of God in his hand. This rod had been used on more than one occasion, but what are referred to here are the events surrounding the turning of the waters of the Nile into blood (7.20). At that time, it was clearly seen as a rod which brought judgment, and as Moses now walked in front of the people carrying it many would reckon that it was about to be used in judgment once again. The judgment this time, however, was due to Israel, not Egypt. They had seen it turn water into what was undrinkable, now, when the point at issue was lack of water, what awful blow would be felt? What fell upon Egypt, due to their failure to obey Jehovah, was severe, now what was going to overwhelm Israel because of the same sin? With what fear and trepidation did they watch Moses lead the way! What fierce manifestation of the judgment of God was about to fall upon them? Their conduct surely demanded it!

Verse 6a: Moses Before the Rock

The instructions to Moses are definite. The Lord will stand before the rock in Horeb. There the cloud would stop. The mention of "the rock" indicates that it was a rock already known to Moses. This was an area with which he was familiar. It was here that he had encountered the burning bush (3.1). The word "rock" (6697) means "a cliff", or "rocky wall". It was large, and a prominent feature in the landscape. This large rocky wall he was to smite with the rod. The word "smite" (5221) is very strong, meaning "to slay", "to smite fiercely", or "to kill". It is first used regarding Cain: "And the Lord set a mark upon Cain, lest any finding him should *kill* him" (Gen 4.15). The blow falling on the rock was to be one of judgment, a mortal blow that would cause death if directed towards a man.

But it did not fall upon the people; it fell upon the rock. The significance of this is explained by Paul who writes, "that Rock was Christ" (1 Cor 10.4). The rock is a picture of the Lord Jesus smitten in a judgment deserved by others.[†] The pictures of Christ in these chapters are unfolding. In the manna there is the Lord Jesus Christ come in the flesh, the bread of God which has come down from heaven, and now in the smitten rock it is the Lord Jesus Christ slain on the cross.

That the giving of this water was a miraculous act of God is without doubt. The time when it came, immediately after the rock was smitten, the place where it came, and the quantity of water which came, all made it impossible for this to be a natural event. "Horeb" (2717) means "desert", or "dryness". This was an area well known for the lack of water. The fact that Moses led his flock there in earlier years (3.1) indicates that some refreshment was available, but clearly, having been given the name Horeb, such water as could be found was completely inadequate for the needs of so great a number.

Verse 6b: How the Water Came Out

Although there is no specific account of the water coming from the rock, it is clear that it did. Two Psalms speak of this event: "Yea, they spake against God; they said, Can God furnish a table in the wilderness? Behold, he smote the rock, that the waters gushed out, and the streams overflowed" (Ps 78.19-20); "He opened the rock, and the waters gushed out; they ran in the dry places like a river" (Ps 105.41). The word translated "gushed out" (2100) in both these instances is found in no other Psalm. It is the same word which is translated "flowing" when the land is described. On more than one occasion Canaan is described as a land *flowing*, or *that floweth*, with milk and honey (Ex 3.8,17; 13.5; 33.3; Num 13.27; Deut 6.3 etc). To confirm the testimony of the Psalmist, Isaiah cannot refrain from writing of this, using the same word: "And they thirsted not when he led them through the deserts: he caused the waters to flow out of the rock for them: he clave the rock also, and the waters *gushed* out (48.21).

The water gushed out in abundant quantities. Just as Canaan would be a land of abundant provision, so the smiting of the rock turned the wilderness into a place of copious supply. Where the Lord is there is no scarcity. They need not wait until they arrive at the Promised Land to enjoy His abundant provision. As plentiful as will be the milk and honey, so was the water that came from the rock. This is in keeping with the character of the God who fulfilled His promise to rain down bread from heaven. There is no restraining His goodness to His people. He delights in giving and does so copiously, generously, liberally, and freely. Would that all His people appreciated the bountiful blessing of God. The children's chorus expresses it simply and yet accurately:

> Count your blessings; name them by the score,
> And when you have named them you'll find many more.

In a very different context, but writing of the same God, Paul states: "Now unto him that is able to do exceeding *abundantly* above all that we ask or think, according to the power that worketh in us…" (Eph 3.20). Although the power was not in them, surely Israel would be able to express the same sentiments, that the Lord had done exceeding abundantly above their wildest expectations. Every believer today knows the greatness of God's giving, having experienced that "the grace of our Lord was exceeding *abundant* with faith and love which is in Christ Jesus" (1 Tim 1.14). Again, in the parable of the Good Samaritan the same feature is seen. Meeting the need of the wounded man lying at the side of the road he bound up his wounds "pouring in oil and wine" (Lk 10.34). His giving was liberal and unstinting as he *poured* in what was required.

The Rock that followed them

And so the water came! Not in small streams or rivulets, but in a great river that created overflowing streams. But the words of Paul to the Corinthians reveal more. It has already been observed that the rock represents Christ (1 Cor 10.4). This statement is preceded, however, with the declaration that they "drank of that spiritual Rock that followed them". In what way did the Rock follow them? Some consider that the water flowing from the rock followed them for many years in the wilderness until they commenced their journey into the wilderness of Zin (Num 20.1). Whereas there may be some merit in this argument, there are two serious objections. In Numbers 20 the people do not charge the Lord with discontinuing this miraculous supply. They do not even mention that it is no longer available, which is surely an observation they would have made.

More telling, however, is the fact that Paul does not state that the water followed them; he asserts that the Rock followed them. The Rock itself did not physically move and follow them, as some of the rabbis teach. The One of whom the Rock is a picture followed them; Christ followed them with the purpose of supplying their need. At a later stage, when again they were short of water, their need was met in a miraculous way (Num 20), and at the brooks of Arnon where water was provided by obedience to the Lord who had said, "I will give them water" (Num 21.14-18), He showed that He was still with them. What Paul is teaching is that throughout the long wilderness years He followed them, caring for them, yet despite such lavish and tender consideration they still rebelled against Him.

One last point remains to be settled. What confirmation was there for the Israelites that Christ was following them? The evidence was the Lord in the cloud as a shepherd, and wherever they travelled the cloud led the way. The One who was in the cloud was none other than the Lord Jesus Christ, who is Jehovah. The verb "followed" (*190*) used by Paul is more in the sense of accompanying than of coming behind them.

But what of the water which came from the Rock? Dispensationally, this is a picture of the giving of the Holy Spirit at Pentecost. Just as the death of the Lord Jesus Christ is seen in the smiting of the Rock, so the water is a picture of what took place in the upper room in Jerusalem (Acts 2.1-4). What remarkable consistency there is about Scripture! This should cause little wonder, for although there were many writers employed in giving us the Scriptures there is only one Author.

Verse 7: Massah and Meribah

Moses now named this place Massah (4532), meaning "temptation", and Meribah (4809), meaning "strife", or "provocation". Rephidim, which should have been a place of rest as its name indicates, became a place of strife. They had tempted the Lord in that they had not believed that He was with them. So great was their sin that it was brought before them on three future occasions (Deut 6.16; 9.22; 33.8), with warnings that this must not be repeated (Deut 6.16). They had seen the grace of God at work in providing the water, but this was not an indication that their behaviour was acceptable to the Lord. God's grace is not a licence to sin nor an evidence that those who receive it are worthy of it. The question asked, "Shall we continue in sin, that grace may abound?", is given the right and forceful answer - "God forbid" (Rom 6.1-2). How sad it is that Israel should leave behind them a place bearing such a name, evidence of their sinful behaviour. The milestones of life, once erected, cannot be removed, and the warning today for those who follow Him is to ensure that days over which "Massah" and "Meribah" could be written are not left behind on the journey.

Comparison with Numbers 20.1-13

It is of more than passing interest to pause briefly and compare these events to those which took place many years later. The problem was again lack of water and the attitude of the people was once more one of strife, so that the name Meribah is applied to this location also. Problems of a similar nature can occur in successive generations.

But there are significant differences.

1. Moses was told to speak to the rock and not to smite it.

2. The rod which he took would appear to be Aaron's rod and not his rod of judgment. It was the rod that was "before the Lord" (Num 17.6-13).

3. The congregation were gathered before the rock, not the elders.

The use of the rod of Aaron brings to mind the truth of resurrection, for it was this rod that budded (Num 17.1-13). The picture is of Christ in resurrection, and that is why Moses had not to smite the rock. The Cross could only take place once and it had already been pictured at Rephidim. Moses had to speak to the rock to invoke the power of the Christ who had died and risen again.

Sad to say, Moses, marked for his outstanding meekness, gave way to anger, and crying, "Hear now, ye rebels; must we fetch you water out of this rock?", smote it twice. While there may be some sympathy for him after all the years of bearing the burden of this people, it cannot be overlooked that he disobeyed. As a consequence neither he nor Aaron led the people into Canaan.

It is not without significance that on this occasion it is recorded that the water came from the rock. The grace of God once more is seen in action, and, lest the reader consider that no water would come due to the sin of the people, or indeed the sin of Moses, the record of it coming out abundantly is there. A sobering thought is that blessing from the Lord is no proof of the obedience of those who are blessed. Should the Lord be blessing a local assembly or individual saints there should never be the thought nor the claim made that this is due to exceptional obedience or holiness. In His sovereignty God blesses, and any who enjoy that privilege must bow in His presence and worship for no one is worthy of the least of His blessings. This was something that Jacob understood when he stated, "I am not worthy of the least of all the mercies, and all the truth, which thou hast shewed unto thy servant" (Gen 32.10), and all do well to follow his example in this matter. It was also a lesson which Israel had to learn after they gained the victory over their enemies in Canaan: "Speak not thou in thine heart, after that the Lord thy God hath cast them out from before thee, saying, For my righteousness the Lord hath brought me in to possess this land: but for the wickedness of these nations the Lord doth drive them out from before thee. Not for thy righteousness, or for the uprightness of thine heart, dost thou go to possess their land" (Deut 9.4-5).

Verse 8: The Approach of Amalek

Just as the people were enjoying the liberal supply of water the enemy appeared: "Then came Amalek". The enemy attacked *then*, at the very point when the blessing of the Lord was being enjoyed to the full. Let all be aware that this is still a strategy which the devil employs with cunning effectiveness. When the hand of the Lord is open in blessing it does His people well to be on guard at that very time because the enemy is the silent observer of all that has taken place and is determined to bring blessing to an abrupt halt.

Amalekites are first mentioned in connection with the invasion of Chedorlaomer and his allies (Gen 14.7). This, however, has not to be thought of as proving that the nation of the Amalekites was in existence at that time. The name Amalek (6002) means "Valley Dweller" and could be applied to any who lived in the south of Canaan. It should be observed, moreover, that Chedorlaomer and his allies smote, not the Amalekites, but *all the country of the Amalekites*. When Genesis was written later the readers would understand the area to which this reference was made.

Amalek was a son born to Esau's son Eliphaz, by Timna, a concubine (Gen 36.12). This is the first mention of Amalek since then. A great nation has grown from this union, so great that Balaam speaks of them being "the first (or chief) of the nations" (Num 24.20). Here, then, is the first appearance of Amalek as a nation, and it is as an enemy of God's people, a character which it never lost. It may be that a certain jealousy had gripped the minds of the Amalekites. They doubtless had heard of the prosperity of the Israelites in Egypt and would have been pleased to learn of the hardships and oppression that they subsequently endured. The news that had come from Egypt of Israel's deliverance and the mighty power of God working through them would be the cause of this attack. It was their purpose to stop immediately the progress of this revival in the power of Israel.

It would appear that before the battle took place Amalek had been engaged in what would now be called guerrilla warfare. Later Israel was not allowed to forget "How he met thee by the way, and smote the hindmost of thee, even all that were feeble behind thee, when thou wast faint and weary; and he feared not God" (Deut 25.18).

As blood relations of Israel they are a picture of the flesh. In the New Testament the word "flesh" is sometimes used to denote the body in which we live (see 1 Jn 4.2-3), and sometimes the sinful desires and lusts of the body (see Gal 5.16-21). Amalek is a picture of the latter and as such is utterly opposed to that which is spiritual. The list which Paul presents in writing to the Galatians makes sorry reading: "Now the works of the flesh are manifest, which are these; Adultery, fornication, uncleanness, lasciviousness, Idolatry, witchcraft, hatred, variance, emulations, wrath, strife, seditions, heresies, Envyings, murders, drunkenness, revellings, and such like: of the which I tell you before, as I have also told you in time past, that they which do such things shall not inherit the kingdom of God".

Verse 9a: The Choice of Joshua

There were times of crisis when Moses, not knowing what to do, cried to the Lord. There were times, however, when he did not hesitate, knowing exactly what course to take. The approach of the Amalekites was such an occasion and without delay he acted. Sometimes there has to be waiting on the Lord and crying to Him for guidance. Clouds of uncertainty cover the horizon and the way ahead is unclear. At other times the issues seem to be settled quickly and actions can be taken in the confidence that these are according to the mind of God. The immediate choice of Joshua, who was of the tribe of Ephraim (Num 13.8), indicates that he was a young man who had fitted himself for this task.[†] It would appear that he was in his mid-forties at this time (Caleb, another of the spies was forty years of age - see Josh 14.7). He died, over 60 years later, when he was 110 years old (Josh 24.29). He was born, therefore, not many years before Moses made his first unsuccessful attempt to help the Hebrews (2.11-14). This is the first time that he is named in Scripture, but clearly he was well known to Moses, and over the years he had worked to prepare himself for the service of the Lord. He would not be aware of what form that service would take, but nevertheless he was intent on being ready when the day arrived, and now that that day has dawned Moses has no hesitation in putting his hand on Joshua to lead the armies of Israel in their first battle as a nation. Redemption has changed servile slaves into mighty warriors!

The Lord prepares His work for His servants and His servants for His work. There comes a day when both meet; the servant and the work come together and the fruit of years of preparation is seen. The lesson for young believers is to prepare themselves, because all have a task to carry out or service to perform, the Lord graciously providing this opportunity for His people. This preparation should not be with determined, fixed ideas of what that service is to be. Better to work in the local assembly, learn from the Scriptures, build a life of devotion and prayer committed to Him, and then He will open the door of the service which He has prepared. The vital early years must not be wasted. There is always value in serving the Lord, but if youth has not been spent in a spiritually profitable manner it will be difficult, and perhaps even impossible, to realise one's full spiritual potential. The early years are vital!

Moses did not only choose Joshua, the people accepted him as leader. When the soldiers were chosen there was no word of complaint nor was there refusal to fight under this man untried in generalship. The testimony of Joshua was such that Moses and the nation had complete confidence in him. Paul's desire was that Timothy would also be accepted as a leader amongst the saints and his words to him teach the same lesson: "Let no man despise thy youth; but be thou an example of the believers, in word, in conversation, in charity, in spirit, in faith, in purity" (1 Tim 4.12).

Verses 9b-12: The Battle with Amalek

This battle took place on two fronts, one in the valley and one on the hilltop. More is written about the battle on the hilltop than of that in the valley. The valley battle is mentioned at the beginning and the end of this brief account, but more detail is given about the activity of the men who ascended the hill.

The men on the hilltop

On the day after the appointment of Joshua as leader of the army, Moses, Aaron, and Hur ascend to the top of the hill. Hur is mentioned here, also for the first time. He was the grandfather of Bezaleel (31.2), the chief workman in the building of the Tabernacle. If Joshua is brought to the attention of the reader as a young man, Hur is introduced for the first time as a relatively older man of Moses' generation. As with Joshua, Hur was a man of godly standing to whom Moses turned without delay. So it is that some servants of God have the pattern of their service laid out before them when they are relatively young. Others, however, may find that new avenues of service open up for them in later years. Joshua assumed a more prominent role at this time, as did Hur, but the latter was years older than the former. Older and younger are all needed in the service of the Lord.

Let those of more mature years take heart, the Lord has work yet to be done!

As they ascended the hill, Moses took the rod of God in his hand. This rod had been used in striking the rock and once again it would be a rod of judgment, this time against the Amalekites. The events on that hilltop can be looked at in a number ways; first as a picture of the present work of the Lord Jesus on behalf of His people, second as a picture of the work of believers praying on behalf of others, third as the sovereign power of God over events on earth.

The three-fold picture

On the hilltop Moses pictures the Lord Jesus who has ascended to heaven and "who also maketh intercession for us" (Rom 8.34). Listed in that chapter are a number of the great blessings enjoyed by Christians. This is the climax, that at the right hand of God there is One who is making intercession for us. He is there on behalf of His own and actively helping them by interceding for them. In the midst of the battle the servant is not alone!

But these three men on the hilltop are, secondly, a study in how vital prayer is. Four features are worthy of note. They went up unitedly: "Moses, Aaron, and Hur went up to the top of the hill" (v.10). It may seem a small point, but nothing is placed in Scripture without significance and the mention of them going up together emphasises that there was unity of purpose amongst them as they set out to pray. Of the apostles it is written that they "all continued *with one accord* in prayer and supplication" (Acts 1.14) and that "they were all *with one accord* in one place" (Acts 2.1). The words of Psalm 133.1 sum it up well: "Behold, how good and how pleasant it is for brethren to dwell together in unity!".

They also approached the time of prayer with determination. They went up to the top of the hill. The thought of stopping half way, which would have made the journey physically easier, was not considered. With fortitude they set off to reach the top of the hill. Prayer is one of the most difficult features of Christian life to discipline. In the morning there is not enough time and there is so much to do, so the thought is to leave it until the evening when the responsibilities of the day have been discharged. In the evening, however, tiredness has taken over and the thought is to leave it until the morning when body and mind are fresh. Attempts in the middle of the day are overtaken by the rush and pressure of activity. There has to be determined purpose in turning aside to pray, such as these men displayed when they went all the way to the top of the hill.

As they commenced their work on the hilltop there was consideration for each other. Moses held the rod in his *hand* (singular). It would appear that he held up the hand in which was the rod, and then passed it to the other hand, then back again. From one hand to the other the rod passed, with the purpose of ensuring that it was always held up. As the hours passed the hands of Moses became heavy. It is not difficult to appreciate the pain which he would feel as he stood with an arm raised holding the rod high. Then it was that the support of his two colleagues became necessary. They put a stone under him on which he could lean, and they held up his hands. Together they accomplished what alone would have been exceedingly difficult or even impossible. As Joshua and his men fought in the valley they could look up to the hill and see that the rod of Moses was still being held high. It was like a banner prominently raised to encourage them. They knew that this was the rod, the use of which had brought the judgment of God on Egypt, and that it would have the same effect on Amalek. What a beautiful picture of mutual support in prayer. When prayer is being offered in the prayer meeting it is the responsibility of all who are present to pay attention to the prayer, and bear up in the presence of God him who is praying. When there is such common interest and consideration it breathes life into a prayer meeting.

These men continued on the hilltop "until the going down of the sun". As long as the battle was being waged they continued their intercession. No doubt there were many moments when fatigue told them that it was now a reasonable time to halt; they had done all that could have been expected of them and no fault would have been found if they came down. They knew, however, how vital was the work that they were doing and that the lifted hands of Moses had a direct bearing on the conduct of the battle. Through the long hours of that day they kept their vigil.

Like them, Christians today must keep at prayer, remembering that the going down of the sun for them is not the end of each day, but the end of their day of battle on earth. Until the gates of heaven are crossed, keep at prayer. Just as the raised rod helped the progress of the battle, so today, prayer helps. Paul knew this, as he writes to the Corinthians, "Ye also helping together by prayer for us" (2 Cor 1.11). Prayer directly helps others, and in this way it is possible for those at prayer to strengthen servants who are engage in the great battle of the service of God. This is one of the reasons why the prayer meeting is such a vital gathering.

The third picture is of the sovereign power of God. The rod held up by Moses was one of authority, as had been evidenced in its use in Egypt. Above the valley there stood one with the rod of authority in his hand, and events on earth were dependent on this. Moses tired, but in heaven God never tires and the rod of authority is never lowered. No matter how fierce was the onslaught of Amalek, they could gain no victory because of the One overlooking the conflict. The lesson that "the most High ruleth in the kingdom of men, and giveth it to whomsoever he will, and setteth up over it the basest of men" (Dan 4.17) is one which can be traced through history. Sovereign authority lies in heaven and from it He will never abdicate.

The hilltop sees the sovereign authority of God, the prayerful labours of His servants, and the intercessory ministry of the Lord Jesus all working together. How blessed when heaven and earth are in agreement, working in fellowship to bring about His will.

Verse 13: The Outcome of the Battle

It has been observed that more is written of the events on the hilltop than of the struggle in the valley. This verse and the brief comment found in v.10, "So Joshua did as Moses had said to him", are all that is found regarding the battle itself. Israel overwhelmed Amalek, winning a mighty victory, but clearly the work of Moses, Aaron, and Hur was of utmost significance. When men assess work carried out for God much credit is given to those who stood in the forefront of the battle, but in this account greater prominence is attached to those who stood on the mount. This is not to underestimate the work of Joshua, but it is a warning not to underestimate the work of the Lord Jesus, of those who pray, and of the sovereign work of God.

There may have been times when, in the heat of the battle, and when things did not seem to be going well, the hilltop would be forgotten by the warriors. So intense would be the conflict that all their energies would be taken up by the cut and thrust of combat. Such preoccupation, if allowed to continue, would have driven from their minds the comfort to be derived from the scene above them. Let us all look up. God is still on the throne!

Verse 14: The Memorial to the Battle - the Writing in the Book

The opening instruction to Moses was to "Write this...in a book". This is the first instruction to write in Scripture. It would appear that Moses had to write that the remembrance of Amalek would be utterly blotted out for other translations substitute the word "that" in place of the second "for" so that the verse reads "Write this for a memorial in the book, and rehearse it in the ears of Joshua, *that* I will utterly blot out the remembrance of Amalek from under the heavens" (JND). It should be noted that the writing was not to be in *a* book, but in *the* book. The writing would doubtless be an account of the battle with the events on the hilltop included, with the message that Amalek would be blotted out.

Why had this to be written in a book?. The reason was that it had to be rehearsed in the ears of Joshua so that it would never be forgotten by him; an event that he always had to keep in the forefront of his mind. Even although there was blood relationship between Amalek and Israel there had to be no treaty, alliance, or agreement with them. The Lord had declared that Amalek would be blotted out and God's people could have no links with such a nation. "Remember what Amalek did unto thee by the way, when ye were come forth out of Egypt" (Deut 25.17) was the solemn reminder given some years later.

1. The future of Amalek confirmed that the judgment of God was carried out.

2. Saul was ordered to smite the Amalekites after having had brought to his attention the fact that the Lord remembered "that which Amalek did to Israel, how he laid wait for him in the way, when he came up

from Egypt" (1 Sam 15.2). Saul failed in this by sparing Agag, King of the Amalekites, and the best of their flocks (1 Sam 15.20-21).

3. David, however, vanquished them while recovering all that they had taken from Ziklag (1 Sam 30.1-20).

4. A great blow against what remained of Amalek took place during the reign of Hezekiah when five hundred men of Simeon "smote the rest of the Amalekites that were escaped" (1 Chr 4.43).

5. Despite this a few survived and the final reference to them is when Haman the Agagite, known for his hatred of the Jews, and a courtier in the palace of Ahasuerus, was disgraced and hanged for his plot against the Jews (Est 7.10). He is described as "the Agagite" (Est 3.1), a descendent of Agag, king of the Amalekites, mentioned above.

It should be noted in passing that Joshua was the first man to be instructed to live by the Book (Josh 1.8). The "book of the law" was the guide for all Israel, and as the leader of the nation Joshua had to set an example of obedience to the word of God.

Verse 15: The Consequences of the Battle - Jehovah-nissi

In addition to writing the words in a book, Moses built an altar. The first altar builder in Scriptures was Noah (Gen 8.20), and Abraham built four (Gen 12.7; 12.8; 13.8; 22.9). It is likely that the form of these altars would be according to the instruction given to Moses in 20.24-26. They would be made of earth or of undressed stone. There was nothing elaborate about them. The purpose of the altars was to mark some dealing with God, and Moses determined that this battle should be so marked. The title given to the altar, "Jehovah-nissi", means "the Lord my Banner" referring back to the rod which had been held up over the battlefield as a banner. The altar recognised the fact that the rod itself did not contribute to the victory; the God who told Moses to hold it up did.

This altar is one of the milestones left behind in the wilderness. Israel would move on and it would not be possible in coming days to revisit this altar, but the events of that place would not be forgotten. Other milestones would be left on the way. Sad to say, subsequent events would determine that a cemetery was left behind them everywhere they travelled, a mark of their disobedience in refusing to enter the land. However, as the ashes of the daily burnt offerings were left outside the Camp in a clean place (Lev 6.10-11), they also left a mark of their devotion. In addition, the bullock that was offered for a sin offering was burned outside the Camp in clean place (Lev 4.12) leaving the evidence of confession of their sin. For the Christian pilgrim and stranger today the question of what milestones are left behind will be answered at the Judgment Seat of Christ.

There is no note of any offering being placed on this altar, but it would be strange to build an altar and not sacrifice. As this was the first altar built since leaving Egypt it may be the place where the instruction to sacrifice to the Lord their God in the wilderness was obeyed (see

3.18). This would explain why Moses built the altar without any specific instruction from the Lord being recorded. Having kept before him these words of the Lord, he now recognised that this was the time when it was possible to obey.

Verse 16: The Message Associated with the Altar

This verse gives the reason for the altar being built at that particular spot. Differences of opinion exist regarding the exact meaning of the words, "Because the Lord hath sworn that the Lord will have war with Amalek from generation to generation". JND renders this as: "And he said, For the hand is on the throne of Jah; Jehovah will have war with Amalek from generation to generation!". This view asserts that the hand of Amalek had been against the throne of Jah and because of that there will be war from generation to generation. Amalek has always been opposed to Jehovah and this is why that nation will be put out of remembrance. In opposing Israel Amalek raised its hand against the God who dwelt in the cloud. Another view is that the verse refers to the hand of the Lord raised against Amalek. Others feel that this is an instruction to Israel to raise their hand in war against Amalek from generation to generation with their hands lifted up to the Lord as were the hands of Moses on the hilltop. The AV translation indicates that the hand of the Lord is raised in swearing that Amalek will be destroyed. No matter which view is taken, the verse clearly indicates that the future of Amalek had been settled, as was displayed on the battlefield at Rephidim.

There were other nations which were less than friendly to Israel but it appears that the censure against Amalek is particularly strong. Why is this? There are a number of reasons. As has been noted, Amalek was a blood relation to Israel and should even have had natural feelings of affection for them. Second, Amalek was the first nation to deliberately seek to destroy Israel. Others nations later opposed them but notice must be taken of how they acted.

1. Permission was asked of the king of Edom to pass through his territories, with the promise that Israel would not touch the crops or take water from the wells. Edom refused permission and led an army to block the way. Israel then turned aside to seek another route (Num 20.14-21).

2. Arad, king of the Canaanites, came against Israel and took some of them captive. Israel fought with them and destroyed them (Num 21.1-3).

3. Sihon, king of the Amorites, refused permission for Israel to pass through his land and he gathered an army which fought against Israel. Israel "smote him with the edge of the sword" (Num 21.21-30).

4. Og, king of Bashan, fought with them and was so completely defeated that of his armies "there was none left him alive" (Num 21.33-35).

5. The king of the Moabites, in alliance with Midian, sought assistance from Balaam to curse Israel, but in this he failed. After the sad episode when the people committed whoredom with the daughters of Moab, Moses

was instructed to "Vex the Midianites and smite them" (Num 22.1-25.18). The Midianites were subsequently defeated decisively (Num 31.1-12).

The only enemy in this list who was not engaged in battle was Edom, the reason being that he did not seek to destroy Israel in this way. All the others did, even Moab and Midian who did battle by using another kind of warfare, that which was of the spirit world. To oppose Israel meant overwhelming defeat. All of these enemies, however, stood against Israel as the forty-year journey was coming to an end and Israel was travelling to Canaan. Amalek was the only enemy to attack them at the beginning of the journey and the defeat they suffered was of particular significance as a portent of what would be the end of all Israel's enemies. It is a matter of utmost gravity to persecute God's people, and the principle set out by Paul still holds today: "Seeing it is a righteous thing with God to recompense tribulation to them that trouble you" (2 Thess 1.6).

Notes

6a This is one of the many occasions in Scripture when the existence of the Lord Jesus before His birth at Bethlehem is stated as a fact.

9a Definitions of "young" and "old" have to be set against the longer life span of people living in those days.

EXODUS 18

Moses and Jethro

Verse 1: Jethro Hears the News

After the incident in the inn on the way down to Egypt, Moses had sent his wife, accompanied by her sons, back to Midian (4.24-26). During the intervening months they must have waited anxiously for news. Now, "all that God had done for Moses, and for Israel His people" had been made known to them and Jethro determined that it was time for Zipporah and her sons to return to Moses. Jethro has been introduced in ch.2 and once again he is called "the priest of Midian".† The momentous events which had taken place since that first meeting over forty years before had not diminished the faith of Jethro. He was still "the priest of Midian". The Midianites as a people were later opposed to Israel, but within that nation there were some who worshipped the Lord.

It is clear that no breach had been made in the friendship between Moses and his father-in-law. This is one important lesson learned from the inclusion of the events of this chapter. Although Jethro had replied, "Go in peace" (4.18), when Moses asked to return to Egypt, the reader may wonder if the events in the inn and the return of his daughter and grandchildren had changed his view. His desire to meet Moses again and his attitude to Moses when they met show that he still had affection and respect for his son-in-law. He was prepared to commit Zipporah and his grandchildren into his care.

Verses 2-6: Jethro Travels to Meet Moses

Moses had two sons, Gershom and Eliezer. Gershom (1647), meaning "foreigner", the oldest (see 2.22) who was named to mark Moses' exile as a stranger in a strange land, had a son, Jonathan (Judg 18.30),† who was the first priest appointed to the idolatrous image set up by the tribe of Dan. What a sad occupation for a grandson of Moses. Did he take this post because he considered the family of Moses to be set aside and this was the opportunity for "place"? No matter his motive, he set his family on a course of idolatry. The following generations continued in that office until the captivity. A better future, however, lay ahead of another branch of the family. Shebuel, also descended from Gershom, was appointed by David to the post of "ruler of the treasures" in the house of God (1 Chr 26.24).

The second son, named Eliezer (461), "God is help", commemorated the deliverance of Moses from the sword of Pharaoh. This cannot refer to the exodus as that had not taken place when Eliezer was born. It refers to the escape of Moses from Egypt after he slew the Egyptian (2.15). Eliezer had only one son, Rehabiah, "but the sons of Rehabiah were very many" (1 Chr 23.17). Descended from him was Shelomith, who was "over all the treasures of the dedicated things, which David the king…had dedicated" (1 Chr 26.26).

We do not know how far Jethro's home was from Rephidim. In that area was Horeb which was in the backside of the desert (3.1), the place to which Moses had taken his sheep. It was, therefore, within the distance that was travelled by a shepherd and his flock, although "the backside of the desert" may indicate that it was at the extremity of that distance. The fact that Moses was now out of Egypt and within travelling distance was doubtless a factor in Jethro's decision to undertake the journey. In travelling with his family Jethro showed his care, not only for Moses, but for them. He had no intention of remaining with Moses but, no matter what distance had to be covered, he wished to see Zipporah taken safely to her husband and, even although he must have been an old man at this time, he was prepared to go.

The courtesy between the two men in arranging their meeting should be noted. In v.5 Jethro does not meet Moses, as this does not take place until v.6. The family camped some distance from the tent of Moses, perhaps even from the Camp of Israel, and sent messengers to Moses announcing their arrival. Dignity, and not undue haste, marked their conduct, despite the obvious desire of Zipporah to see her husband.

Verse 7: The Meeting of Moses and Jethro
When they last parted, the future of Moses would have been regarded by many as extremely uncertain. Now he had become the leader of a great and victorious people and his time would be at a premium as the burden of rule fell upon his shoulders. However, weighty although these responsibilities were, they did not serve as a reason for failing in his family duties. Sending back his wife had not been motivated by a desire to be rid of his family, but rather to ensure their safety and save them from a road that they would have found difficult to travel. Now they are about to meet again.

Leadership amongst God's people is no reason for neglecting family life. Paul writes that an elder in an assembly must be one who "ruleth well his own house, having his children in subjection with all gravity (1 Tim 3.4), and also "the husband of one wife, having faithful children, not accused of riot or unruly" (Tit 1.6). This does not mean that the children must be believers, but that they must behave in an orderly way, commending the gospel. If Moses had left his family with his father-in-law this could have been used as a reason to attack his integrity, the charge being that he was not fit to lead Israel as he had neglected his own wife and family. It may be that this was one of the reasons why Jethro made this journey.

Despite the fact that Moses was now the ruler of this people he treated Jethro with the respect due to a father-in-law by bowing before him and kissing him, thus affording him also the courtesy of a warm welcome. Moses showed that the high office which he now occupied did not affect family relationships. His new station in life did not cause him to treat Jethro with less respect than he did when he was in his employment as a shepherd. Elevation to high rank or office must not cause a Christian to treat family or friends as now being "beneath" him or her in standing; indeed, to handle such circumstances with sensitivity, care, and dignity is a mark of spirituality.

The affection of Moses was real and not hypocritical, such as was the traitor's kiss given by Judas Iscariot to the Lord Jesus (Lk 22.47-48). This meeting was marked by genuine feelings of warmth and care, for, after the kiss, "they asked each other of their welfare" (v.7). Even with all that Moses must have had on his mind, he took time to ask after the welfare of Jethro; the meeting was not an unwanted interruption in the schedule of a busy man. They both acted as gentlemen, with Jethro returning the greeting. To show concern for others and ask after them is another mark of Christian consideration. Believers must be gentlemen and gentlewomen with nothing of the indifference and coarseness of the world about them.

Verses 8-11: The Conversation Between Moses and Jethro

Following this exchange of greetings Moses invited Jethro into his tent. The conversation between them centred on the events which had taken place. Jethro had already heard of "all that God had done for Moses" (v.1) but Moses gave him a further account. The text of v.8 does not indicate that Jethro enquired eagerly for further details, but that Moses willingly, without being prompted, started to tell the story. Once again the courtesy of Jethro is displayed. He did not meet Moses with the excited immaturity of one who had come to "get the news", or to be in possession of a "first hand account" with which he would later entertain others. Moses understood the concern Jethro had for him and wished to advise him of all that had taken place, knowing he was speaking to a man who was reliable and would not twist and turn the story.

What Jethro heard was, initially, all that the Lord had done for Israel. Moses put the Lord first and recounted all that had taken place in Egypt and since they had left the land of their servitude. But he also told him of "all the travail" (toil, hardship, weariness - 8513) that had come upon them by the way. He referred, not to the hardships that had been endured in Egypt, but to those endured since they left Egypt and which are found in chs.16 and 17. Those who had expected that life after crossing the Red Sea would be one long holiday soon found that this was not to be. The pathway of following the Lord involved trial, the purpose of which was to educate them in the ways of God so that they might come to know Him better and enjoy Him more fully. The lives of the apostles show this to be their experience, and Christians today should not be surprised to encounter the same kind of learning process. Moses acknowledged the lessons that they had learned by recounting to his father-in-law "how the Lord delivered them". If there had been no problems there could have been no memories of deliverance, memories which would help them on their journey and encourage them when further difficulties were encountered.

The response of Jethro was not to dwell on the trials but rejoice for "all the goodness which the Lord had done to Israel". He was careful to give the Lord the glory, and did not rejoice in what Moses and the Children of Israel had done. He did not flatter Moses with congratulations on what he had achieved. His heart was filled with joy and he was quick to give the Lord His place in these events. Further credit is due to him because there was no bitter feeling that he had not been there to see the work of God. He harboured no resentment, nor was he offended that the Lord had excluded him from such a momentous history. He was showing that he could "rejoice with them that do rejoice" (Rom 12.15). At times, it can be easier to weep with them that do weep than to rejoice with the joyful. When blessing comes to others a feeling of spiritual jealousy may arise in the heart which suppresses the desire to rejoice with those who have been so blessed. Jethro rose above all this and his heart was filled with gladness as he heard how the Lord had delivered Israel.

Jethro expressed his appreciation with the words, "Blessed be the Lord…". Others had blessed God, among whom were Noah (Gen 9.26), if in somewhat sad circumstances, and Abraham's servant (Gen 24.27). Paul did this as he wrote to the Ephesians: "Blessed be the God and Father of our Lord Jesus Christ, who hath blessed us with all spiritual blessings in heavenly places in Christ" (Eph 1.3). There are two blessings in this verse. Paul blessing God, and God blessing the saints. When God blesses He adds to those who are blessed. He bestows "all spiritual blessings". When His people bless Him they can add nothing to Him as it is not possible for created man to add to the Lord. Those who bless Him worship with thankfulness which is a joy to Him. Jethro, in blessing God, is expressing this thankful worship for all that He had done.

He acknowledged that "the Lord is greater than all gods". This does not indicate that up to this point he had considered the Lord to be one of many gods, on equality with all the others. It is his way of declaring the omnipotence of the Lord. What he does recognise is the true nature of the battle which had taken place in Egypt. It has previously been observed that this battle was not between Pharaoh and Moses but between Jehovah and the gods of Egypt. These gods were only so called because they sought to take that place and were acknowledged as such by the Egyptians. They did not exist, but they were a deceitful front used by the Adversary to deceive men. The power behind them had acted "proudly" in dealing with Israel. In a haughty way they had confronted the Lord and had been decisively overthrown.

Verse 12: The Worship of Jethro

How remarkable it is that in this book a Gentile makes the first recorded sacrifices to the Lord! It has been noted that Israel may have sacrificed to the Lord on the altar raised by Moses (17.15), but there is no record of that. Here the record is clear; Jethro offered a "burnt offering and sacrifices for God". What a meeting this had been! Would that all the conversations which believers have together were marked by the same courtesy, spirituality, and expressions of worship. This holy conclave comes to a conclusion with worship and the enjoyment of mutual fellowship. Of what did Jethro partake during the meal with Moses, Aaron and all the elders of Israel? Did he have the privilege of eating of the manna and thus enjoying the bounty of the bread rained down from heaven? No matter what the feast consisted of, the Lord was present and that was what made this a holy gathering.

A Millennium Picture

This is the final chapter before the Law is given in chs.19 & 20. Up to this point Israel has been under grace, but shortly they will place themselves under Law. It has been observed that the manna coming from heaven was a picture of the Lord Jesus come to earth, the smitten rock a picture of the Cross, and the water that flowed out in abundance a picture of the Day of Pentecost when there took place the baptism in the Holy Spirit. Now the order continues, for what is seen in this chapter is a picture of Millennium conditions. Every type and picture in the Old Testament falls short in some aspects, only in Christ is perfection, but the shadow of a coming day is clearly seen.

After the triumph of Israel over their enemies, the family coming to meet Moses at the Mount of God pictures two things. First, in Zipporah is seen the Gentile who was taken as a bride when Moses was rejected by his brethren. She is a picture of the Church. Second, in Jethro is seen the Gentile nations who will desire association with the triumphant Israel. Zechariah writes of this: "Thus saith the Lord of hosts; In those days it shall come to pass, that ten men shall take hold out of all languages of the nations, even shall take hold of the skirt of him that is a Jew, saying, We will go with you: for we have heard that God is with you" (Zech 8.23). As Jethro rejoiced over the goodness of God to Israel, so the Gentile nations will rejoice in tracing the hand of God with His people. The joy and fellowship between Israel and the nations is beautifully pictured in the sacrifices offered and in the meal which followed.

Verses 13-16: Moses Judging the People

The arrival of Zipporah could not halt the daily responsibilities which Moses undertook. The day following the feast, Moses sat to judge the people. This must have been an arduous task. Israel had recognised elders when they were in Egypt (3.16; 4.29; 12.21; 17.5; 18.12), and to them initially would possibly fall the task of judging issues as they arose. Some of these issues, however, had to be referred to a higher authority, and Moses then sat in judgment. The number of cases brought for consideration is evidenced by the fact that the people stood before him from morning until evening as the judgments were given.

Nations need government. This is the first occasion in Scripture where judgments were carried out in a nation subject to the Law of God, for the standard by which Moses exercised judgment was the "statutes of God, and his laws" (v.16). This ought to be the measure used in judgments carried out by civic authorities. They have a responsibility to be the "minister of God…for good" (Rom 13.4), but, sadly, governments fall far short of this standard. There is no longer the recognition that the Word of God must be the basis of legislation. Previous generations did not carry this out fully, but in many lands there was an attempt to make the Scriptures the foundation on which laws regarding moral issues, human life etc were enacted. In this present generation that principle has been completely abandoned and the standards of Scriptures are treated with derision. It is not even accepted that the ensuing sorry conditions are a result of this rejection of the Word of God.

The people came to Moses, not to hear what his view was of their dispute, but to "enquire of God" (v.15). The Law had not yet been given, but Moses did understand the statutes of God even although they had not been set out in writing. His experience in Egypt, when he saw idolatrous legislation enacted, and the long years of meditation and contemplation in Midian during which he had been alone with God, had given him an understanding of these statutes. This he did not have when he slew the Egyptian (2.12), but the intervening forty years had been well spent in the school of God.

Verses 17-27: The Advice of Jethro

The long hours of sitting in judgment appalled Jethro. He considered that this would cause Moses to "wear away". His health would be affected by the onerous duties which he undertook. He also considered that the people would wear away, doubtless referring to those who had to wait on Moses for their case to be heard. Something had to be done, for Moses was not able to bear this burden alone. Out of genuine concern for the health of his son-in-law he offered advice. The proposal made by Jethro was:

1. Moses was to mediate for the people and "bring the causes unto God".

2. He was to teach the people ordinances and laws and "shew them the way wherein they must walk".

3. Able, godly men were to be selected and an infrastructure created with ranks: some over ten, above them some over fifties, above them some over hundreds, and some over thousands. When cases could not be settled they were referred upwards and would only reach the ears of Moses if the matter was too great for even the ruler over one thousand to judge.

4. These judges were to be such as "fear God, men of truth, hating covetousness".

If Moses put this structure into place he would "be able to endure, and this people shall go to their place in peace".

How good was the advice of Jethro?
The question is, "Was this good advice?".

In favour

1. It seemed to be eminently sensible advice. One man could not possibly undertake the government of a nation of over 2,000,000 souls. Issues requiring judgment would arise daily, and Moses would soon become exhausted by the workload.

2. The advice came from a godly man. It has already been observed that Jethro was a man of high character who was "the priest of Midian".

3. Jethro appeared to suggest that his words had the approval of God when he stated "and God command thee so" (v.23).

4. The Lord did not censure Jethro for the advice that he gave. The silence of heaven could have meant that the Lord approved of what Jethro had offered.

5. The Millennium picture to which reference has already been made is now complete in that now Israel and the Gentiles are united in government.

Against

1. There is no indication that Moses had become overtired by the work. No complaint had come from him and there are no other signs of his being exhausted.

2. Although Jethro was a godly man it cannot be assumed that this was a guarantee that his advice would always be according to the mind of God.

3. Although the Lord does not censure Jethro for his advice, the silence of heaven does not necessarily indicate approval.

4. If the Millennium picture is considered, will the Gentiles advise Israel how to govern? Nothing in Scripture would support such an assumption.

5. The Lord appointed Moses, and he whom the Lord appoints is given the strength to carry out the task. It may have appeared to Jethro to be formidable, but this did not take into account the fact that the Lord enables those to whom He gives responsibility.

6. Despite the major change that was being introduced to the government of Israel neither Moses nor Jethro called on the Lord for guidance.

7. The words, "and God command thee so" (v.23), could be seen in a different context to that noted in point 3 in favour. It is possible that his words are instructing Moses that he had to seek the approval of God: "If thou shalt do this thing, and God command thee so".

The conclusion, therefore, seems to be that although this advice was well-intentioned and came from a man of integrity, it was not of God.

Against this conclusion there may be set the argument that this event is no different from that which took place when the Tabernacle was erected and the princes of Israel brought to the Lord offerings of wagons to assist in its transportation (Num 7). Surely this is also help which was not requested and for which no instructions were received from the Lord. There is, however, one main difference. As the princes brought their offerings the Lord spoke to Moses and told him to accept them (v.5). When Jethro's advice was proffered it has been noted above that the Lord was silent.

Jethro's approach is a warning not to heed the advice of others unless it is tested in the presence of God. Even the godly can be sincerely wrong. All who have taken responsibility for leadership amongst the people of God know what it is to wish that this load could be shared or even completely given over to another. Where is the shepherd who has not felt the weight of it, and at times the sorrow of it? Such circumstances cannot, however, be a reason for introducing an order which has not been received from the Lord.

It should be noted that this new order did not meet the need. The burden carried by Moses was still very great (or was this simply a feeling created by Jethro's words) and there came a time when he cried to the Lord, "Wherefore have I not found favour in thy sight, that thou layest the burden of all this people upon me?" (Num 11.11). His conclusion then was, "I am not able to bear all this people alone, because it is too heavy for me" (Num 11.14). The complaints and disobedience of the people had now caused Moses to feel the great weight of his responsibility with the accompanying feeling of being unable to continue. At that time the Lord instructed Moses to take seventy men of the elders of Israel who would "bear the burden of the people with thee". They would be fitted by the Lord for the task by being given the spirit that was upon Moses. As a result, they were able to prophesy, that is, to tell out the mind of the Lord. So furnished, they were fully equipped to share the burden of government with Moses. This did not diminish Moses' position; he still remained, under God, the leader of the nation. Dennett's comment, however, is worth noting: "Though, therefore, the Lord granted him his desire, there was no additional supply of strength for the government of Israel, but Moses was now called upon to share with the seventy the Spirit which he before possessed".

However, there is left the question: "Would the complaint of Moses that he could no longer bear the burden of the people have been made if Jethro had not put the thought into his mind?". Until Jethro spoke there was no crisis, but he created one by his words and it appears that these words lodged in the mind of Moses. When he spoke to the Lord in Numbers 11 it was to voice the very complaint which Jethro had raised.

Lessons to be learned from Jethro's advice

Two lessons have to be learned from this incident. First, do not create problems that do not exist. It would have been better for Jethro to enter the presence of God and lay the circumstances before Him. Where it seems that the strength of a servant of the Lord is being overtaxed, bring the matter before the Lord and only give advice when definite guidance has been received. Indeed, it would be better to pray that the Lord would reveal to His servants any change in service which has to take place. To do otherwise may discourage a servant by putting into his mind unhelpful thoughts and considerations which had not previously been there.

Second, care must always be exercised that the government of the people of God is subject to methods that are divinely sanctioned. The work of God and the methods employed will look inadequate when human reasoning is brought to bear. Even the preaching of the gospel is looked at in such a light. Regarding the message itself Paul writes that "the preaching of the cross is to them that perish foolishness" (1 Cor 1.18), and, "we preach Christ crucified, unto the Jews a stumblingblock, and unto the Greeks foolishness" (1 Cor 1.23). Regarding the means of spreading this message Paul declares that it is through the "foolishness of preaching" (1 Cor 1.21) that men and women are saved. This does not mean that the means used are foolish, but that it is regarded by the world as foolish. Again, when the wisdom behind the message is considered, Paul asserts that "the natural man receiveth not the things of the Spirit of God: for they are foolishness unto him: neither can he know them, because they are spiritually discerned" (1 Cor 2.14).

It is possible for believers to use human reasoning. Then the ways of God will appear inadequate and suggestions will arise as to how "improvements" may be made to "help the work". The motive may be of the best, and suggestions come from those who are genuinely concerned for the work, but all such proposals must be tested by the Word of God. In this present age there is laid out in Scripture the means by which the life of a local church will be ordered. To add or take away from this is to introduce human reasoning. Despite the changes in society, cultural and otherwise, over the centuries, the Word of God still stands and can be put into practice as fully as when it was first written. To add to Scripture in order to help the work of God or even to defend the Word of God is not God's way. Far better to leave matters in His hands and let Him show that His way is perfect (see 2 Sam 22.31; Ps 18.30).

Notes

1 For the background of the Midianites see ch.2
2 The word "Manasseh" in this verse should read "Moses" - see RSV, JND etc.

EXODUS 19

The Covenant at Sinai

This chapter introduces one of the most momentous periods in the history of Israel. The deliverance from Egypt and all that has taken place since has seen Israel under the grace of God. Despite the goodness of God, they have consistently failed, but no judgment has fallen. Each complaint has been returned by proof of God's love and compassion for them. Faced with the Egyptians behind and the Red Sea in front of them they cried, "Because there were no graves in Egypt, hast thou taken us away to die in wilderness?" (14.11). At Marah they murmured against Moses saying, "What shall we drink?" (15.24). When the bread they had taken from Egypt was consumed they said, "Would to God we had died by the hand of the Lord in the land of Egypt" (16.3). When the manna was given, some of them disobeyed and stored a quantity until the next morning (16.20), and some went out to collect it on the seventh day (16.27). When they came to Rephidim and there was again no water, despite the fact that this problem had been met before and the Lord had provided, they "did chide with Moses" and did "tempt the Lord" (17.2), backing this up by murmuring against Moses (17.3). All this had taken place in the first few weeks after leaving Egypt's bondage. This is a record that would hardly give pleasure to any who considered their behaviour since they had enjoyed the great deliverance brought about for them through the Passover. In understanding what is about to take place it is necessary to keep this background in mind.

W. W. Fereday comments that "It was a great day when Israel encamped before Mount Sinai. God was now going to put flesh to the test, for the instruction of all the peoples of the earth while time lasts...such was the self-confidence of the people, even with a bad record behind them, that they had no doubt of their ability to do all that might be demanded. It was sheer flippancy, betraying utter ignorance of the badness of the flesh and the holiness of the One with whom they had to do".[†]

Description of Sinai

They have arrived at the place where the Law would be given and it was a fit situation for such solemnity. Edersheim, quoting Dean Stanley, describes it thus: "This mountain district...forms a huge mountain-block, about two miles in length and one mile in breadth, with a narrow valley on either side...and a spacious plain at the north eastern end. That plain...known as *Er Rahah*, is computed to be capable of accommodating a host of two millions. Right beside it rises Jebel Musa, from which protrudes a lower bluff, visible from all parts of the plain. This is the modern *Ras Sufsafeh* (willow-head), and was in all probability the Sinai upon which the Lord came down, and where He spake 'the ten words'. In that case the plain of Er Rahah must have been that on which Israel stood, and the mound in front on the ascent to *Ras Sufsafeh*, the spot where Moses separated from the elders who had accompanied him so far on his ascent.

As we try to realise the scene presented at the giving of the Law, we can well understand how 'all the people that was in the camp trembled' (19.16). The vast plain of Er Rahah, and all the neighbouring valleys and glens, were dotted with the tents of Israel. No more suitable camping ground could have been found than this, the best watered neighbourhood in the whole peninsular, where 'running streams are found in no less than four of the adjacent valleys'. The plain itself is nearly 5,000ft [approx 1540 metres] above the level of the sea. Right in front, cut off by intervening valleys from all around rises the Horeb group…and from it projects into the valley, like some gigantic altar or pulpit, the lower bluff of Ras Sufsafeh, the nether part of the mount, that Sinai from which the voice of the living God was heard" (*Bible History: Old Testament*).

How must it have appeared as this great "mountain-block" quaked, with smoke emanating as fire rose up from it, as the thunders roared and the lightning flashed, and as was heard "the voice of the trumpet exceeding loud" (v.16). Adding to the solemnity and majesty of the scene, bounds had been set round the mount so that none could go up or touch it. At this location momentous events would take place. The remainder of the book of Exodus, all of the book of Leviticus, and the book of Numbers up to ch.10 all took place here. It was not until the twentieth day of the second month of the second year that they departed, following the cloud, into the wilderness of Paran (Num 10.11-12).

Verses 1-2: Arrival in the Wilderness of Sinai

The journey to Sinai was completed in the third month after leaving Egypt, in "the same day". The Jews taught that "the same day" meant the first day of the month. If that were so, it is possible to calculate the number of days that had passed since Passover. The Jews held that this was 45 days - 16 in the first month and 29 in the second. On arrival at Sinai, a further five days were to pass, the first when Moses went up to the mount (v.3), the second when he returned (v.7), and three days when the people prepared (vv.10.11). It was argued that the giving of the Law took place on the day of the Feasts of Weeks, which is also known as the Feast of Pentecost (Lev 23.15-21). This is a popular idea as it places the giving of the Law on the same day as the birthday of the Church (Acts 2.1), but there are two difficulties. It is not certain that the words "the same day" mean the first day of the month,[†] and the Feast of Pentecost was held fifty days after the Feast of Firstfruits which itself took place on "the morrow after the sabbath" following Passover (Lev 23). The expression could, however, indicate the same day in which they came out of Egypt which would be the fifteenth day of the month.

The mountain before which they camped was Horeb (33.6; see also

Deut 1.6,19; 4.10, etc). "Horeb" refers to a range of mountains, as they had already camped before the "mount of God" (18.5). They had travelled approximately 150 miles (240 kilometres) since leaving Egypt and the distance which lay ahead of them to Canaan was also approximately 150 miles. They had, therefore, covered about one half of the journey, although disobedience lengthened their sojourn in the wilderness by years. This is so for all who disobey the Word of God. Failure to obey Scripture lengthens the time in reaching the goal that the Lord has for us and may, as with the generation which was now encamped before the mount, lead to many never attaining it. Salvation, once received, is never lost, but the goals that lead to greater enjoyment of the things of God remain out of reach when submission to His will is refused.

Verses 3-4: The Message of the Lord to Israel - Promises Fulfilled
For the first time Moses goes up the mount. His dealings with God there will occupy the book until the end of ch.34, and in that period he ascends the mount on seven occasions.

	GOES UP	COMES DOWN
Initial message to Israel	19.3	19.7
Instructions to prepare for the third day	19.8	19.14
Charge to warn the people not to come near	19.20	19.25
Moses draws near after the giving of the Ten Commandments	20.21	24.3
The covenant meal. Return to the Camp is implied in vv.11-12	24.9	24.11
The two tables of stone and the charge regarding the Tabernacle given	24.12	32.15
The second two tables of stone taken up the mountain	34.4	34.29

These verses give the first declaration from the Lord to Israel since the Passover. It marks the end of the first phase of the journey. They need to be taught and, as will be seen, it brings with it a challenge. Moses went up the mountain to which the cloud, signifying the presence of the Lord, had moved. He may have been on one of the lower slopes of the mountain with the cloud higher up, and he is called upon to bring to the people the words of the Lord. What a privilege this was! The message would place before them the purpose of God in delivering them. Freedom from the yoke of bondage was part of it, but there were higher thoughts even than that.

The message is addressed to "the house of Jacob, and…the children of Israel". The name, "house of Jacob", reminded them that they had gone down to Egypt; "all the souls of the *house of Jacob*, which came into Egypt, were threescore and ten" (Gen 46.27). Their background, and the behaviour of the house of Jacob which led to their being in Egypt, must not be forgotten. As the "house of Jacob" they did not deserve the grace of God which they had experienced in salvation. It is remarkable that when the coming kingdom of the Lord Jesus is described by Luke he writes, "And he shall reign over the *house of Jacob* for ever; and of his kingdom there shall be no end (Lk 1.33). That coming glory will also be due entirely to the grace of God. They had not earned the right to be delivered, nor will they earn that right in a future day.

They were also "the children of Israel", referring to the dignity bestowed upon them as the descendants of the man who became "a prince with God". The former expression "house of Jacob" is found only once in Genesis and only here in Exodus, although it is found in total 22 times in Scripture. The name "children of Israel" is first used after the new name was given to Jacob at Peniel (Gen 32.28-32), and is included in the first verse of Exodus.

The opening words of the message to Israel refer to the past, to what the Lord has done to Egypt. He has made promises and these have been fulfilled. The judgment of God that has fallen on Egypt should give Israel confidence in the future. The Lord has displayed His power in a mighty way and fear of tomorrow will surely not dominate their thoughts. But not only had He dealt with Egypt, He had dealt with Israel in a very different way. Two things are stated. He had borne them up "on eagles' wings". The strong loving care of the Lord for His people is pictured here. The prominent features of the eagle are set out in Scripture. Two of these characteristics are relevant at this point: their flight is swift (Deut 28.49; 2 Sam 1.23; Jer 4.13; 49.22; Lam 4.19), and they mount high in the air (Job 39.27; Prov 23.5; 30.19; Is 40.31; Jer 49.16). The Lord bore them up so swiftly that none could touch them, and took them up to such a height that they were beyond the reach of any enemy, above the turmoil caused by their departure.

The purpose of this was not only to lead them into the wilderness. They had expressed this when complaining against the Lord (14.11; 16.3). There was a higher purpose behind it all, for He had brought them to Himself. He desired to have them with Him and to enjoy them. His wish was to see them out of bondage and enjoying fellowship with Him as a redeemed people, bringing them close to Himself. How great a privilege and honour this was, one that had been offered to no other nation.

But no matter how great the privilege of Israel as they left Egypt, that which is enjoyed by Christians is greater. It is still the desire of God to have His people with Him. One of the reasons for choosing twelve disciples was that they would be with the Lord (Mk 3.14), not only for their education, but that He would have them close to Himself. He also expresses His desire for His own in a coming day: "I will come again, and receive you unto myself; that where I am, there ye may be also" (Jn 14.3).

Verses 5-6: The Message of the Lord to Israel - Their Responsibilities
Privilege brings responsibility and this is where "if" comes in. Should failure enter it will be on the part of the people. A threefold promise is

made to Israel if they will obey His voice and keep His commandments. First, they will have a unique place on earth; they will be His "peculiar treasure" (5459). This word means "valued property", or "treasure". How great the grace of God! How can this people be for Him a "treasure"? He who created the worlds regarding this people as a "treasure"! This word is used eight times in the Old Testament, six of which refer specifically to the nation of Israel (Ex 19.5; Deut 7.6; 14.2; 26.18; Ps 135.4; Mal 3.17). The last reference is to the joy of a coming day when the Lord will claim those who fear Him in Israel as His own, when He makes up His jewels (His peculiar treasure). That He makes one nation His treasure does not mean that He is the God of Israel only. If that were so, the choice of Israel would be the only one available. All the earth is His, and any nation could have been the object of His choice, but it was Israel that was brought near.

The second part of the promise is that they will become a kingdom of priests and will have a king, who will be Jehovah. As priests they will have access to Him to worship and to enjoy His presence. They had known a society in Egypt where priests were a class apart, creating "mysteries" and religious forms which set them at a distance from the people and enabled them to hold men and women in bondage. Approach to their "gods" was only for the priests and in ways shrouded in mysticism. Israel is now presented with the possibility of being a nation of priests with no "mysteries" from which the majority were excluded.

This is followed by the concluding promise that they would be "a holy nation", that is, a nation which was set apart for the Lord. In this they would be unique. No other nation would enjoy such privilege and blessing. His desire was that the nation should be near to Him; a special treasure unlike all other nations. It will be seen, however, that the eagerness they displayed when they placed themselves under the Law made it impossible for that nearness to be enjoyed. They moved away from Him and entreated Him not to speak to them directly again (see Deut 5.22-27). A relationship where there is no direct communication is not a close relationship.

Verses 7-8: Moses Brings the Message to the People the First Time

Moses descended from the mount and brought the message to the elders of Israel. The words of the Lord were "laid before their faces". This is where Israel revealed that they had not learned the lessons which should have been learned from their conduct since leaving Egypt. There was a test in the message from the Lord and they failed the test. The Lord had said that they had to obey His voice and to keep His covenant. Surely this would produce deep exercise of heart before God and ensure that they would carefully and prayerfully consider all the issues involved before they replied. Wisdom would have caused them to understand the impossibility of attaining this level of obedience, and that disobedience under Law would lead to them forfeiting their right to the blessings they had enjoyed. It may be that the victory over Amalek had given them this confidence. Already they had forgotten the significances of the altar raised to "Jehovah-nissi". Their history, to which allusion was made at the commencement of this chapter, displayed clearly the sin of their hearts, yet still they made the grand claim: "All that the Lord hath spoken we will do". What self-assurance is displayed based on supreme confidence in their own works. This is the very point at issue. Israel from now on will be relying on their own works and not God's grace. "Instead of clinging with tenacity, because of their own felt impotence, to what God was for them, which is grace, they foolishly offered to make everything depend upon what they could be for God, which is the principle of law" (Dennett).

All had been of grace and no blessing enjoyed had been deserved as a reward for faithfulness. Contemplation of the past weeks should have made them cast themselves further on the grace of God, but rather they made the self-confident claim that they would do all that the Lord commanded. Such confidence in their own strength would be the cause of much suffering and disappointment.

Moses was a faithful mediator who "returned the words of the people unto the Lord". The message that he brought back was exactly what the people had said. He did not embellish it or seek to put the people in a better light. William Kelly sums up their condition at this time: "Had there been any true understanding of their own state in the sight of God they would have confessed that, however righteous the obligations to render obedience to the law, they being unrighteous, could only be proved guilty under such a proof. The test must have brought inevitable ruin. But they had no such thoughts of themselves, any more than real knowledge of God. Hence therefore, no sooner does God propose to them that they should obey His law as the condition of their blessing at His hands, than they at once accept the terms. The result soon appears in their ruin".[†]

Verses 9-10: Instruction Regarding the Preparation of Israel for the Giving of the Law

Much now changes. Israel is about to turn from grace and be put under Law. The change is noted immediately. The Lord will now appear to them in a thick cloud and the people will hear when He speaks to Moses. The manner of His appearing will confirm Moses' position of mediator, a position which will be his until the end of his life. All this indicated that there was now distance between the Lord and Israel.

Preparation for the giving of the Law commenced with the people sanctifying themselves and then washing their clothes. The process of sanctifying is noted in addition to washing and therefore involved more than that one act. "Sanctify" (6942) is to "set apart" and involved putting away all that was unsuitable for the presence of God and the cessation of all acts that would render them unclean. Moses carried out this sanctification, doubtless by his instructing the people on what had to take place, as they would not have the knowledge and sensitivity to the holiness of God to enable them to do this by themselves. How different from what had gone before. They now have to fit themselves for His presence.

The washing of their clothes was indicative of ridding themselves of all impurity. As this act is mentioned separately from sanctifying it has added significance. Sanctification was not to be merely external, but was to affect their persons. Clothes speak of character and this was also to be sanctified, pictured in the newly washed clothes. It would be possible to wash the clothes without sanctifying themselves but this would have been mere external observance which is without value before God. With both carried out, those looking on would not be able to detect any sign of defilement. Nothing in their presence or in their person was to be unsanctified.

Zechariah sees in a vision "Joshua the high priest standing before the angel of the Lord" (Zech 3.1). He "was clothed with filthy garments" (3.3). Baron comments that "'the filthy garments' in which Joshua was clad symbolised the sin with which the nation as a whole was defiled, and which he, as high priest, represented in his official capacity".[†] Clothes represented the moral condition of the nation, making it necessary for them to be washed at Sinai.

Verses 11-15: Instruction Regarding the Preparation of the Mount for the Giving of the Law

Bounds were to be set about the mount. The nature of these is not revealed but it is possible that the mount was fenced round in some way. No matter how it was done, there were clear limits set so that there was no doubt where the boundary lay. Once again the changed nature of their relationship with God is revealed to the people. Never had such an arrangement been necessary before.

The Israelites had been sanctified, but even after that act their true condition made it impossible for them to come near to God at any time. They had to learn that their own efforts could not make them clean in His presence. They had not yet learned the truth of the words of the Lord through Jeremiah: "For though thou wash thee with nitre, and take thee much soap, yet thine iniquity is marked before me" (Jer 2.22). The judgment for touching the mount was the same for man and beast; they had to be put to death. No one had to touch *it* (v.13). The reference here is not to touching the mount, but to touching the one who had gone over the boundary on to the mount. No hand had to stretch over to pull the offender back, because that would have involved the would-be rescuer reaching over on to the mount area and becoming guilty of the same sin. The means of putting the offender to death was by stoning or being shot through with an arrow, both of which could be carried out at a distance. The awful solemnity of the place was such that death was the only possible consequence of disobedience.

The people would wait until the trumpet sound was heard. This was the summons from the Lord to come up to the mount. The setting of the bounds seems to contradict the invitation to come up the mount, or was it that the bounds could be breached when the Lord gave the invitation to come? There was no contradiction! They were instructed to come *up to* the mount, but they were not permitted to go *up into* the mount. As they were now under Law, the bounds could not be breached and the invitation to go up to the mount was extended to a confident Israel so that they might have impressed on them yet again that they were unfit for His presence. This will be seen in how the people responded when the trumpet sounded.

Moses had ascended the mount in v.3, returning in v.7. He had gone up the second time in v.8 and returned in v.14 bringing the commands to wash their clothes etc, and be ready for the third day when the trumpet would sound. What frantic activity must have occupied these three days as the nation prepared for the Lord's summons. Putting away all that would defile, abstaining from what would otherwise be legitimate, washing their clothes and examining them to see that they were clean. What activity, but just a foretaste of what Law would bring into their lives and those of generations to follow.

Verses 16-19: Sinai on the Third Day

How solemn was the scene which presented itself to them on the third morning. The mount was enveloped in a thick (heavy, massive, dull - 3515), impenetrable cloud; peals of thunders sounded, and lightening flashed. Then the sound of the trumpet was heard. This was not a trumpet sounded by man. There is no indication given as to how this sound was produced, but need there be? It was a trumpet blast which the Lord had ordered and it was "exceeding loud". The effect of this awful sight and sound was to cause Israel to tremble.

In comparing the Law with the grace which they now enjoyed, the writer to the Hebrews describes the scene at the mount in a sevenfold way (Heb 12.18-21).

1. *For ye are not come unto the mount that might be touched.* Believers today have not come to a mount that might be touched, as did Israel. This does not refer to the command to refrain from touching the mount. It emphasises that Sinai was a material mountain that could be touched, although only Moses was allowed so to do. In the gospel believers come to a spiritual "mountain".

2. *And that burned with fire.* Sinai burned with fire "to the heart of heaven" (Deut 4.11, JND), the flames rising to such a height that they reached up into the heavens. Everything about this scene was designed to cause awe in the heart of the beholder. How different this is from the burning bush to which Moses was allowed to approach (3.1-6). Everything there was to attract Moses to that bush, but that was grace at work. Here it

is Law and distance, as awe and fear filled their hearts. The flames displayed the absolute righteousness and holiness of God.

3. *Nor unto blackness.* Surrounding the mount from which the flames ascended to heaven there was blackness. Gloomy obscurity stood between them and the Lord. How different from that which they had enjoyed from the God who bore them up "on eagles' wings" and brought them to Himself.

4. *And darkness.* Despite this being the morning, darkness also surrounded the mount. The use of the two words "blackness and darkness" emphasises the impenetrable nature of the darkness that separated them from Sinai.

5. *And tempest.* Storm and tempest raged around the mount. Doubtless the quaking which gripped the mount was part of the storm. There was no manifestation here of the God of Peace. Law keeping would never allow anyone to enjoy the peace of God.

6. *And the sound of a trumpet.* The sound of the trumpet was heard above the rolling peals of thunder and raging of the storm. How loud it must have been for all Israel to hear its call above such a tempest.

7. *And the voice of words.* "The voice of the words" was heard (Deut 4.12), but so fearful was the sight that the people entreated that they might hear His voice no more. Thus far had they removed themselves from the enjoyment of His presence.

So terrible was this sight that even Moses exclaimed, "I exceedingly fear and quake". There is no record in the Old Testament of these words being spoken but their inclusion in the New Testament is sufficient to confirm that he uttered them. Not only did fear grip his heart, but physically he trembled as he beheld the sight. The forces of nature had been used by the Lord to declare His majesty, holiness, power, and might. This is the God to whom the Israelites had declared that they would obey His Law, not just in part, but completely.

When the trumpet sounded the people "stood at the nether part of the mount". The bounds had been set and they could approach no further. Little wonder that all the people in the Camp trembled.

These solemn events display clearly that, without the grace of God and the work of redemption, it is impossible for mankind to stand before God. Even if a sinner seeks to approach God on his own merits the only outcome can be death and judgment. Sinners are enemies of God (Rom 5.10), and it is impossible for Him to meet the sinner on any other ground than that of the death of the Lord Jesus Christ as a substitute, bearing the judgment due to the sinner. His holy claims must be satisfied; they cannot be overlooked, and only in Christ are they met.

Verses 20-24: The Lord Speaks to Moses

The Lord called to Moses who now moved to the upper part of the mountain. It has already been observed that the instruction to the people to come up to the mount (v.13) only allowed them to approach the bounds set around it. This was to show the people that although the Lord desired their presence they could not approach Him on the basis of Law. The bounds were to protect the people, not because the Lord desired to keep them at a distance, but because approach on the basis of Law resulted in death.

Thus it was that as Moses ascended the mount the Lord directed him to return to the people and charge them that they had not to come beyond the set bounds. There might have been the temptation to draw nearer, the result of which would have been that, even if they were priests, the Lord would "break forth" (punish - 6555) upon them. The reference to "priests" cannot denote priests of the Aaronic order as that order had not yet been established. It refers to the "family priesthood" which was in place at that time and which was superseded when Aaron and his sons were consecrated to the priestly office.

All is now set for the giving of the Law. Readers who wish to look further into the purpose of the Law should read Appendix 5.

Notes

1 *Believer's Magazine*, April, 1949.
1 See Keil & Delitzsch.
8 *Lectures Introductory to the Pentateuch.*
10 *The Visions and Prophecies of Zechariah.*

EXODUS 20

The Giving of the Law

In the midst of the thunderings, the lightning, and the sound of the trumpet, God spoke. His voice was clearly heard by all Israel standing in front of the smoking mount. The scene was one of overwhelming majesty and power. In the first seventeen verses of the chapter the people listened to the voice of God, but from that point, due to the fact that they feared for their lives, they requested Moses to act as a mediator and speak with God for them. This is not the still small voice with which He spoke at other times. He was addressing a sinful people who had declared with confidence that they would keep His Law, and now the terms of that Law were about to be placed before them.

These Ten Commandments are called the "words of the covenant, the ten commandments" (34.28). Much fruitless discussion has taken place regarding how the Ten Commandments or "words" were placed on the two tables of stone that were given to Moses (31.18). That they were the essence of the Law is clear, for the Lord stated to Moses that the stones had written on them "a law, and commandments which I have written" (24.12). One view is that the "words" were divided into two groups of five, but the fact that that first group would contain many more words than the second is a problem. Another view is that the "words" were placed on the stones in an abbreviated form, but there is no indication that this was so. Other permutations have been suggested, but, as Scripture does not refer to how they were written on the stones, it is a matter of little consequence. The importance is in what was written upon the stones, not in how it was written.

That there were ten Commandments is worthy of note. Ten is the number of responsibility and this Law placed great responsibility on the shoulders of those who professed that they would keep it. The first group of four had to do with responsibility towards God and the second group of six had to do with responsibility towards others. W. W. Fereday noted of this second group that "The fifth and seventh protect our relationships; the sixth protects our lives; the eighth our property; the ninth our reputation and the tenth is designed to protect all that we have and are".[†] The answer of the Lord Jesus when He was asked, "Which is the first commandment of all", summarised the Law into these two groups when He replied, "Thou shalt love the Lord thy God with all thy heart, and with all thy soul…this is the first commandment. And the second is like, namely this, Thou shalt love they neighbour as thyself" (Mk 12.28-31).

How, then, was the Law given to Moses? It is clear that the Lord spoke to Moses (20.1,22, etc), but Stephen, in his defence before the council, states that Israel had received the Law "by the disposition of angels" (Acts 7.53). Paul confirms this when he writes that the Law was "ordained by angels in the hand of a mediator" (Gal 3.19). The mediator is Moses, as is confirmed by his words to Israel when referring to this occasion: "I stood between the Lord and you at that time" (Deut 5.5). But what part did angels have in this? Scripture does not explain exactly what they did but it may be that the tables of stone, which were written with the finger of God, were passed to Moses through angels. In this way the Lord emphasised the distance that Law introduced.

Verses 1-2: Introduction

Right at the beginning it is emphasised that all the words that were spoken were from God and none of what follows is from Moses. Their deliverance from the land of Egypt is first brought before them, reminding them that they were responsible to obey because of the great work accomplished by the Lord. It is necessary never to forget that salvation has been enjoyed. Out of the land of Egypt, out of the house of bondage they had come, as the Lord had promised, and His rights over them had been established beyond any doubt. As no other had taken part in their deliverance, these were sole rights; they owed sole allegiance to Him, and on this basis they had an obligation to submit to His word and obey His commandments. It should never be forgotten that although believers today are not under Law the obligation to obey the Word of God still holds true.

Verse 3: The First Commandment

"Thou shalt have no other gods before me".

Here is what has been called the "devastating exclusivity of biblical monotheism".† It must not, therefore, be thought that this is admitting to the existence of other gods. In dealing with ch.12 it was pointed out that idols were nothing but that there were evil spirits behind them. However, this first commandment goes beyond idols to make the absolute statement that there must be no other gods of any kind before the Lord their God. Nothing and no one has to be put before the Lord. It is possible to engage in idolatry without there being idols of wood, stone, or precious metals. During the Captivity, the elders of Israel came to the prophet Ezekiel and, although they no longer worshipped idols openly, the Lord declared to the prophet that they had "idols in their heart" (Ezek 14.3). Many are the idols which can lodge in the heart – ambition, wealth, pride, and anything which, or anyone who, is the object of our affection above the Lord. He must have first place at all times; anything else breaks the first commandment.

When the Lord Jesus was asked what the greatest commandment was, He replied, "Thou shalt love the Lord thy God with all thy heart, and with all thy soul, and with all thy mind. This is the first and great commandment" (Mt 22.37-38). He was summing up the responsibility of man towards God given in the Law and in so doing teaching that the Lord did not wish the keeping of these commandments to be on the basis of cold duty. It was to be based on love for Him. When there is genuine love and affection in this way it will not be a heavy burden to have no other gods before Him. This does not mean that there is no place in the heart for the legitimate love of others; indeed, it ensures that there will be a place for such love. Those who love God will love others, for God is love.

Verses 4-6: The Second Commandment

"Thou shalt not make unto thee any graven image, or any likeness of any thing that is in heaven above, or that is in the earth beneath, or that is in the water under the earth: Thou shalt not bow down thyself to them, nor serve them: for I the LORD thy God am a jealous God, visiting the iniquity of the fathers upon the children unto the third and fourth generation of them that hate me; And shewing mercy unto thousands of them that love me, and keep my commandments".

To the general statement that there was to be no other god before the Lord is now added the prohibition of idols of any kind. It is incongruous to think that man can manufacture an idol from lifeless material and then worship what he has manufactured. Even Israel did this when Moses was up the mount (32.1-29) as, with the cry, "Up, make us gods, which shall go before us", they made the golden calf. This prohibition would include making a representation of Jehovah. Nothing of that nature was placed in the Tabernacle. Coates comments, "The natural thought of man is that something material would be a help to worship, but any image or form simply opens the door for Satan to possess himself of that which is due to God from man. Those who worship God must worship Him in Spirit and in truth. It is a true instinct which leads people to close their eyes when addressing God; they desire to be withdrawn from the seen and material".

Isaiah graphically sets out the folly of idolatry, demanding of false gods, "Produce your cause" (41.21). They were challenged to show the things that are yet to be, that they had knowledge of future events. If they were gods they would display their ability to do this, but they proved that they were nothing (41.24). The challenge goes forth from God: "Is there a God beside me? yea, there is no God; I know not any" (44.8). The point at issue is that no such "god" would exist if the worshipper had not made it. The idol cannot rise above its maker and has no power to help or succour the one who made it; it is the creature of its maker! Utter futility is seen in the method of making the idol. The tree from which it comes is cut down and part of it used for fire with the residue being formed into the idol. The same piece of wood that was regarded as being of so little value that it was used for burning is the piece from which the idol was made, and before this worshippers bowed.

Idolatry was practised in the patriarchal ages. Rachel stole her father's images (8655) when Jacob left Laban (Gen 31.19), probably because she believed that Laban would be able to consult these "gods" to discover where Jacob had gone. These "gods" were the household deities of the family and it may also be that Rachel wished to have their protection during the flight from Padan-aram. "Strange gods" remained in the household of Jacob until the final stage of the journey to Bethel when he instructed his household to "Put away the strange gods that are among you" (Gen 35.2). Israel had been guilty of idolatry while in Egypt (Josh 24.14) and this explains why they understood what had to be done to produce the idol of the golden calf. The statement that the gods of the Canaanites would be a snare to the Children of Israel was sadly seen to be true (Judg 18.17,24). The tribe of Dan established an "official" system of idolatrous worship which was in place all of the time that the Tabernacle was pitched at Shiloh (Judg 18.30-31). The priestly caste supervising this abomination was led by Jonathan, who was a grandson of Moses (Judg 18.30, see JND, RSV).[†] Towards the end of the era of the judges, Samuel had to instruct Israel to "put away the strange gods and Ashtaroth from among you" (1 Sam 7.3). The habit continued through the reigns of the kings when ungodly men occupied the throne.

The order, "Thou shalt not bow down...nor serve" should be noted. To bow down is to worship, and whatever is worshipped will be served. Worshippers become the servants of their gods no matter how idolatrous is the object of their worship.

The statement that "I the Lord thy God am a jealous God" reveals again the desire of the Lord to have their love and affection for Himself alone. Coates comment is worthy of note: "That is the language of love. It is as much as to say, 'I cannot bear not to have your affections wholly for myself'. How God must love His people to use such language".

The final word of warning indicates that the sins of the fathers will affect the children to the third and fourth generation. The government of God is such that the sins of fathers impact on families, perhaps through hereditary features, although this is not specifically stated, or in future dealings which the Lord will have with the family. This does not exclude future generations from salvation but may affect the nature of the life and times of the family.

The mention of "thousands" indicates the great desire of God to show mercy to many, and also that many will love Him. The fact of their love for Him is proven by them keeping His commandments. In this way obedience is rewarded.

Verse 7: The Third Commandment

"Thou shalt not take the name of the Lord thy God in vain; for the Lord will not hold him guiltless that taketh his name in vain".

To take the name of the Lord in vain is to use His name for empty or worthless purposes, or to use it for witchcraft, or for false swearing (Lev 19.12). The name of God was not to be invoked for unholy and ungodly causes. To swear by His name in such an issue, or to swear by His name in that which is false, is abhorrent to Jehovah, showing a lack of reverence with no sense of awe at the greatness of God. "The name of the Lord thy God" includes every name and title that is His.

In the world today the names of God and of the Lord Jesus trip lightly off the tongue, with no sense of reverence. Most who use them in this way are not even aware of having mentioned a divine name, so trivial has it become to them. Some may regard this as a matter of little consequence, but it is not so regarded by the Lord, for He will not hold him guiltless who indulges in such folly. The emphasis here on this fact reveals the seriousness with which the Lord treats our language, and that this commandment cannot be disregarded with impunity. Such conduct displays complete indifference to God and is an evidence of a godless life. The Lord values His name and will not tolerate its being used in this way. His name should only be used in prayer, praise, appreciation and thankfulness, and when speaking in a manner which is godly and well-pleasing to Him.

When a believer is exposed to others who use this profane language, care has to be taken that it does not become so familiar that the sense of its sinfulness is lost. If it is possible, listening to such language should be avoided. The media use it constantly claiming that it is necessary to ensure that they reflect the "reality" of society, but this simply encourages its use and reveals the base nature of much that passes for "the arts", "music", and "entertainment".

Verses 8-11: The Fourth Commandment
"Remember the sabbath day, to keep it holy. Six days shalt thou labour, and do all thy work: But the seventh day is the sabbath of the Lord thy God: in it thou shalt not do any work, thou, nor thy son, nor thy daughter, thy manservant, nor thy maidservant, nor thy cattle, nor thy stranger that is within thy gates: For in six days the Lord made heaven and earth, the sea, and all that in them is, and rested the seventh day: wherefore the LORD blessed the sabbath day, and hallowed it".

This is the longest commandment of the ten. The fact that they had to "remember" the Sabbath day indicates that they knew of the six days of creation and of the setting aside of the seventh day. It does not indicate that the Sabbath had been kept. One interesting side issue is that there is no question that days of twenty-four hours are in view in the creation account.

They were to consecrate the seventh day of the week by keeping it for sacred duties and to cease from all work during its hours. The seventh day would be known by taking the first day of the first month as was introduced by Jehovah (12.2) and working from that base point. There were to be no exceptions to this requirement, the reason being that the Lord God worked for six days and on the seventh He rested, enjoying what He had created. The principle is that of working, and then resting in the good of that work. Israel had declared that they would keep all the commandments of the

Lord, and, as a consequence, under the Law they would work then rest in the good of their work. This rest, of course, was never attained by those who sought it by Law keeping. The important lesson is that this is what the Lord God did in creation, and Law keepers had to follow the same pattern. Work then rest is the principle of Law.

On the Sabbath day no work of any kind was to be carried out. This applied to all, three groups being mentioned. The first is the group of all free Israelites including sons and daughters, the second is made up of those who were servants, and the third is comprised of strangers, that is Gentiles who were resident in Israel on the Sabbath. Beyond this, cattle were also to be kept from labour. The whole nation came to a halt on the Sabbath; even the collection of manna was forbidden, although such an effort would have been useless as no manna came on the seventh day.

The word Sabbath (day of rest) is first used in connection with the giving of the manna (16.23). It has been argued that the institution of the Sabbath was at the end of the sixth day of creation (Gen 2.3), but, although God rested on that original seventh day there is no indication that there was any responsibility given to Adam to do so. There is no record in the book of Genesis of its being kept, and in Egypt there is no account of a Sabbath day or of Pharaoh being censured for preventing the Israelites observing the day. It is clear that before the giving of the Law the Sabbath was not kept, as it has a direct link to the Law. This is recognised in the words of the Levites in the days of Nehemiah: "And *madest known* unto them thy holy *sabbath*, and commandedst them precepts, statutes, and laws, by the hand of Moses thy servant" (Neh 9.14).

It must be noted that in addition to the weekly Sabbath seven separate days each year were set aside as days of rest.

1. The first day of the Feast of Unleavened Bread (Lev 23.7).
2. The seventh day of the Feast of Unleavened Bread (Lev 23.8).
3. The day of the Feast of Weeks (Lev 23.21).
4. The day of the Feast of Trumpets (Lev 23.24).
5. The Day of Atonement (Lev 23.28).
6. The first day of the Feast of Tabernacles (Lev 23.35).
7. The eighth day of the Feast of Tabernacles (Lev 23.36).

In six of these days no *servile* work was to be done, but on the Day of Atonement, as with the weekly Sabbath, no work at all was to be done. Servile work was employment, business, or labour as a servant in any way. Baron defines this as work "implying hard toil, bondage or degradation".[†] The Sabbath and the Day of Atonement were days of complete rest.

The Lord's Day, which falls on the first day of the week, is not an extension of the Sabbath into another dispensation. It is not the Sabbath moved to the first day. It has a completely different character, and is for those who are under grace. It reminds believers that grace gives rest because of peace with God and then work for God follows.

Verse 12: The Fifth Commandment

"Honour thy father and thy mother: that thy days may be long upon the land which the Lord thy God giveth thee".

The importance of the attitude of children to their parents is emphasised here insomuch as one of the Ten Commandments is given over to this subject. Issues that were only of passing importance would never have been in the Decalogue. Some of the commandments up to this point have contained warnings regarding the consequences of disobedience (vv.5,7). The fifth commandment is the first to contain a promise which will be fulfilled when there is obedience. The "honour" involved is not conditional on the behaviour of the parents. No matter what relationship exists in the family, it is not acceptable for children to treat their parents with disrespect and without ensuring that, when necessary, they are cared for. David was particular in this respect when he escaped to the cave of Adullam by placing his mother and father in the care of the king of Moab (1 Sam 22.3-4). For those who kept the commandment there was the promise of a long life to enjoy the land. "Honour" embraces more than mere obedience. It is treating another as worthy of respect and with the necessary accompanying dignity. It is possible to obey without treating the one obeyed with honour.

Paul writes of this commandment, reminding his readers that it is "the first commandment with promise" (Eph 6.2). He quotes from the book of Deuteronomy where it is stated that the blessing will be twofold. First, "that thy days may be prolonged", and second, "that it may go well with thee, in the land which the Lord thy God giveth thee" (5.16). Questions have been raised as to why he calls this commandment the "first" with promise. An indication of the answer has already been given, because, although the second commandment has a promise, it is one of judgment on those who engage in idolatry. This is the first promise of blessing. Note also that no following commandment has a promise, raising the further question of why did Paul not write, "...the only commandment with promise". The Expositor's Greek Testament makes the suggestion that the apostle has not the Ten Commandments alone in view, but the whole series of Divine Commandments, Mosaic and later".[†]

Paul is not suggesting that the Christian will live long as a result of honouring parents. He is quoting the promise of the commandment; teaching that there is blessing to be obtained by doing this and that God will bestow this on all who treat their parents with such honour. "The promise of the land is not given to the Christian, nor the promise of long life. The promise to the Christian is not prolonging of life but quality of life (1 Tim 4.8; 1 Pet 3.10-12)".[†]

Verse 13: The Sixth Commandment

"Thou shalt not kill".

With this commences the five commandments that are summed up in Leviticus 19.18 with the words: "...thou shalt love thy neighbour as thyself" (see also Mt 22.39; Mk 12.31; Lk 10.27; etc). This short, sharp commandment is based on the value of life that can only be given by God. To take life is so abhorrent to God that the scriptural response is that the life of the murderer is forfeit. No punishment is mentioned here, but in other parts of Scripture it is clearly laid out. It should be noted that suicide is included in this prohibition; it is not confined to the death of another.

The question of capital punishment has often been discussed against the background of this verse on the basis that it is killing by the State and is therefore condemned. Such an argument cannot be sustained in view of the Word of God. "Whoso sheddeth man's blood, by man shall his blood be shed: for in the image of God made he man" (Gen 9.6), is a principle that has not been set aside. The punishment of murder by the taking of the life of the guilty party is not seen in Scripture as itself being murder. That this is valid today is confirmed by Paul in the Roman Epistle when he writes of the one in governmental authority as he who "beareth not the sword in vain...the minister of God, a revenger to execute wrath upon him that doeth evil" (Rom 13.4). The mention of the "sword" is sufficient to understand that this may involve the taking of the life of the guilty.

Clearly, steps require to be taken to ensure that the accused is guilty beyond doubt, but, despite current thinking in the western world, the Scriptures teach that those who commit murder forfeit their right to life.

Verse 14: The Seventh Commandment
"Thou shalt not commit adultery".

Adultery is sexual intercourse of a husband with a woman who is not his wife, or of a wife with a man who is not her husband. With this commandment the sanctity of marriage is preserved. There can be no doubt as to its meaning, nor is there any doubt that it is a commandment which is greatly ignored in society since the teaching that sexual relations are to be confined to marriage is regarded as no longer relevant. Scripture, however, emphasises that sexual relationships are only permissible within marriage. It was never intended that they should be short term or casual, and are not merely for the gratification of physical lust. So vital is this commandment that the Law demanded death for those who were guilty of breaking it (Lev 20.10).

Verse 15: The Eighth Commandment
"Thou shalt not steal".

If the seventh commandment protects the rights of husbands and wives, the eighth protects the rights of an individual in respect of property or anything over which he has ownership. This commandment covers taking the possessions of another, whether it is openly or by stealth. It also covers retaining in one's possession that which belongs to another. To deliberately and knowingly keep an article which is given on loan is a form of stealing. Stealing may be wrongly regarded as something of no importance when it involves that which should be returned to its rightful owner.

Stealing shows itself in many other circumstances. To keep what has been found, knowing the identity of the rightful owner, is theft (Lev 6.4). It can be practised under the cover of business. To charge for goods or services more than is legitimate or has been agreed, and to pay to creditors less than is due, is dishonest. The withholding of amounts due for longer than the agreed terms of business is not being a "smart" or "astute" businessman; it is being plainly dishonest, and for the period of time when payment ought to have been made it is "stolen" because it is in the possession of one who does not own it with no permission of the owner being given for such a retention.

Time also can be stolen. An employer pays for a number of hours and when these are withheld this is also a case of breaking the eighth commandment. This may be done by a lazy attitude to work when present at the place of employment. It is also true when time is taken from work for reasons that are not genuine. The feigning of illness or creation of "reasons" for absence also amount to the breaking of the ninth commandment.

Stealing is a common practice in the world but should not be in the life of a believer. "Let him that stole steal no more" (Eph 4.28) is the exhortation given by Paul to the Ephesians. The Christian must be marked by giving not by stealing, as Paul adds, "but rather let him labour, working with his hands the thing which is good, that he may have to give to him that needeth". Going from stealing from others to giving to others is one of the evidences of salvation.

The punishment for stealing was reparation. "If a man shall steal an ox, or a sheep, and kill it, or sell it; he shall restore five oxen for an ox, and four sheep for a sheep" (21.1), is but one example of this. This thief must not profit from his crime. The trespass offering was offered by those who had taken what was not theirs (Lev 6.1-7), and in addition to the offering there had to be restored to the wronged party that which had been taken plus 20% added.

Verse 16: The Ninth Commandment
"Thou shalt not bear false witness against thy neighbour."

It may appear at first reading that this commandment has to do with bearing false witness against another when giving testimony in a legal matter. It certainly does cover this, but is much wider in its embrace. To bear false witness is to declare what is not true, no matter what the circumstances. Whenever anyone is spoken of in conversation, if it is necessary to say anything, only what is true may be stated. Exaggeration or emphasis to distort meaning to suit the purposes of the talebearer is to bear false witness.

Essentially, to bear false witness is to lie. That this must never be in the speech of a Christian is obvious. God cannot lie (Tit 1.2), and the Lord

Jesus declared that He was the Truth (Jn 14.6). In the first of the Psalms of Ascent (Ps 120) the writer looks about him at the surrounding society which was causing him so much grief and declares, "Deliver my soul, O Lord, from lying lips, and from a deceitful tongue" (v.2). That was the character of the world then and it has not changed over the centuries. The advice of the wise man must be taken to heart: "Lying lips are abomination to the Lord: but they that deal truly are his delight" (Prov 12.22). The Lord Jesus stated that it was the devil who first introduced lies into creation; "He was a murderer from the beginning, and abode not in the truth, because there is no truth in him. When he speaketh a lie, he speaketh of his own: for he is a liar, and the father of it" (Jn 8.44). Lies are his stock-in-trade and ultimately he will perpetrate the great lie (2 Thess 2.11) that a mere man is god.

Society today has accepted lying as a normal part of life. It has been given a number of other names to make it appear respectable. "Economical with the truth" is one such expression which has come to the fore in recent years. To give "spin" to a statement is often the method of making others believe what is not true, without actually voicing the lie. To tell only half the truth can lead to a false impression being given. In commerce, the lie is often seen as being a sign of shrewdness and is acceptable to the business establishment if it results in financial gain. The sons of Jacob told one lie so that Joseph's father would believe a lie which they did not voice (Gen 37.32-33).

It ill behoves a Christian to become involved in any form of falsehood. "Wherefore putting away lying, speak every man truth with his neighbour" (Eph 4.25) is an exhortation to be taken to heart while living amongst those of the deceitful tongue. Yet lies have come from the lips of men and women from whom the truth would have been expected. Abraham devised a lie when he uttered his first recorded words in Scripture as he went down to Egypt (Gen 12.10-20). Rahab told a lie when she was challenged regarding the presence of the spies (Josh 2.3-7). Peter told a lie as he was warming himself at the fire in the courtyard of the house of the High Priest (Mt 26.69-75; Mk 14.66-72; Lk 22.55-62; Jn 18.25-27). The warning is clear to all. The telling of lies is often an apparently easy way out of a difficult situation. In a group it can be used to make the speaker the centre of attention. Personal advantage or financial gain may be pursued by it. Nevertheless, Christians remember that they are followers of the One who declared, "I tell you the truth" (Jn 8.45), even when it is not accepted.

Verse 17: The Tenth Commandment
"Thou shalt not covet thy neighbour's house, thou shalt not covet thy neighbour's wife, nor his manservant, nor his maidservant, nor his ox, nor his ass, nor any thing that is thy neighbour's".

To covet (2530) is to desire something, and in the context of the tenth commandment conveys the meaning of an "inordinate, ungoverned, selfish desire".† It relates to desires that will be translated into actions that are sinful, those desires being the root from which sinful actions grow. The clear warning is to avoid the root and therefore to avoid the actions. Specific objects of covetousness are mentioned, all of which belong to a "neighbour", emphasising that the covetous individual has no right to possess any of those objects of his desire. People as well as possessions are included. To allow these desires to run unchecked may result in theft, in unrighteous dealings, and in adultery.

Take note again that this commandment does not only forbid the taking of these things, for that has been covered in the seventh and eighth commandments, but is concerned with the thoughts, lusts, and desires which will result in breaking these other commandments. This was what was born into the heart of Eve when the tempter approached her in the Garden. She saw that the tree was a "tree to be desired (coveted)" (Gen 3.6) and as a result ate of the fruit of the tree. The silver and gold taken from the idols of the nations were not to be coveted. They were to be burned with fire, including the precious metals, lest such silver and gold became a snare to the people (Deut 7.25). Confession to breaking this commandment was the sorrowful consequence of the actions of Achan when he stated, "When I saw among the spoils a goodly Babylonish garment, and two hundred shekels of silver, and a wedge of gold of fifty shekels weight, then I *coveted* them, and took them; and, behold, they are hid in the earth in the midst of my tent, and the silver under it" (Josh 7.21). The downward pathway was first to see, then to covet, and finally to take. The covetous desire for fields (Mic 2.2) was the cause of violence and oppression in the latter days of the kingdom of Israel and, ultimately, of Judah. What sorrow and heartbreak would be avoided if the teaching of Paul to Timothy were taken to heart: "But godliness with contentment is great gain" (1 Tim 6.6). The believer who does not seek satisfaction in, nor depends on, things but rather looks to the Lord is blessed indeed.

In modern society the danger of covetousness must be recognised. The advertising industry speaks of placing before the public "objects of desire". When dealing with expensive items of merchandise, whether they be cars or consumer goods, it presents the possession of them as signs of success and prosperity. The believer must be careful not to fall into this silken trap and, as a result, adopt an approach to life centred on the possessions of things. Indicators of spiritual (i.e. real) prosperity have nothing to do with possessions. God makes some materially rich and they remain pilgrims and strangers, but to make the acquisition of wealth and possessions the aim of life is opposed to all the teaching of the Word of God. A further danger lurks in coveting "thy neighbour's wife". Adding to what is written regarding the seventh commandment it should be noted that the world no longer recognises this as sinful. Beware of those who "call evil good, and good evil" (Is 5.20).

Verses 18-21: The Response of the People

As the Commandments were given, the people stood outside the bounds of the mount, as near as was permissible for them to come (19.17). But the effect of all that they saw and heard was to make them retreat to stand afar off. They are now under Law and the presence of the Lord in these circumstances is a fearful thing. He who bore them up on eagles' wings and brought them to Himself (19.4) now seems remote. The request is then made to Moses that he act as a mediator between them and the Lord. "Speak thou with us, and we will hear: but let not God speak with us, lest we die", is how they voice their fears. They understand that, now that they have agreed to keep the Law and make that the basis of their relationship with God, they are not fit for His presence. As a nation they now must fear the judgment that will follow sin.

Nevertheless, Moses tells them that they need have no fear. The purpose of all that they had seen was to prove them, to teach them that they must fear God and display this by refraining from sin. All the thunder and lightning, the sound of the trumpet, and the smoking mountain are but to teach that God cannot be ignored or disobeyed and that sin will bring judgment. As the people stand at a distance, Moses enters the thick darkness that there might be given to him the next instalment of the Law.

Verses 22-23: No Gods with Jehovah

Verse 22 commences a section which ends at 24.2. Keil & Delitzsch refer to this section as "The leading features in the covenant constitution". It may seem strange that in the midst of the giving of laws, the Lord turns the attention of the people to the question of worship, proof again that at all times this is what the Lord desires. They were told how they should not worship (v.23) and then how they should worship (vv.24-26). The former is an amplification of the first commandment. There were to be no gods before the Lord and in addition they must have no gods *with* the Lord. It is completely unacceptable to the Lord to have any other gods regarded as equal with Him or, even if not equal, to be regarded as gods fit to be in His presence. With this is emphasised what has already been described in relation to the first commandment as the "devastating exclusivity of biblical monotheism", and no apology is made for repeating that statement here. The particular gods mentioned are those made of silver or gold. The value or beauty of the image matters nothing to the Lord. The very best and most valuable that man can produce are not fit for His presence. Any object of worship placed beside Him challenges His sole rights as God.

It is possible that the context refers to the act of having images made which claim to be images of Jehovah. There is no doubt that the human heart loves images before which it can bow and to which it can offer prayers. Such images, even if they purport to be images of the one and only God are abhorrent to Him as Jehovah cannot and must not be represented by an image. In many parts of Christendom the practice of using images as a so-called "aid to devotion" is rife. The claim is made that they help in prayer and worship. For this practice the Bible has only censure. If Israel was commanded to have no such objects, there is no place for them in this day of grace. Faith does not need images; they are the products of men's hands that ultimately become the objects of their veneration.

Verses 24-26: Altars of Earth and Stone

It seems almost as if the subject which is being brought before the Children of Israel is now changed. For a few verses worship and the altar occupy the reader and the question must be asked, "Why?". The answer is that, despite the giving of the Law, the Lord still desires worship from His people, and adherence to the statutes which are being given to them does not lift from their shoulders the responsibility to express their thankfulness and devotion in worship.

A description of the altars that they must use for this purpose is given to them. They both use material which would be readily available in their journey through the wilderness, or even in the land. It must not be thought that their wilderness pathway was through a sandy desert. Although it was an inhospitable area there was enough vegetation to be found to feed their flocks. It was also possible to use wagons to carry parts of the Tabernacle (Num 7.1-3), plainly an impossible task on a surface of sand. There would be places where earthy soil, even although it may not have been of the best quality, was sufficient for the erection of an altar. The other material that could be used was stone and there would be no shortage of that as they journeyed! What lessons can be learned from these materials? The fact that no elaborate altar had to be built allowed everyone the privilege of worship in this way. There was no restriction on the poor, and there was no advantage to the rich. The altar built of earth reminded the worshipper that Adam came from the dust of the ground (Gen 2.7) - the word "ground" (127) in Genesis 2 is the same word as "earth" in Exodus 20.24. It also served to remind him of the words of the Lord to Adam after the Fall: "In the sweat of thy face shalt thou eat bread, till thou return unto the ground (earth)" (Gen 3.19). As the worshipper approached this altar there was written large the truth that approach to God displayed the grace that was being enjoyed by those who were descendants of Adam.

The other material also had lessons to teach. The stone was to be used in its natural state. No hewing of it was to take place and no tool was to seek to beautify it in any way. Intricate carvings or designs were not required to adorn this altar. The worshipper approaching is reminded that he is not there because of anything of value that has come from his hands. No human work or effort, no matter how beautiful to the human eye, could open up the way to God. No altar was itself to become the object of admiration, veneration, or worship. To carry out such "beautification" would pollute the altar and thus make it unfit for worship. Man cannot produce anything for God's delight apart from what is the product of submission to His Word.

A further requirement was that there had to be no steps up to the altar. The worshipper is reminded that he cannot ascend one single step upwards to the Lord. To do so would "uncover his nakedness"; it would be a revelation of the flesh, as is every attempt on the part of man to achieve this goal by his own efforts. Because it was impossible for man to do this, the Lord came right down to where man was. His descent, not the ascent of man, is the means by which men and woman can come into relationship with Him and, by so doing, be able to worship.

But when and where were such altars to be built? When the Tabernacle was reared there was a Brazen Altar to which sacrifices were brought, so what was the purpose of the altars of earth or unhewn stone? Altars had been built in the past; Noah built an altar after the flood (Gen 8.20); Abraham built four, at Shechem (Gen 12.7), east of Bethel (Gen 12.8), at Hebron (13.18), and on the mountain in the land of Moriah (Gen 22.9); Moses had built an altar after the victory over Amalek (17.15).

The first thing to note in answering the question, "When and where?", is that these altars were not to take the place of the Brazen Altar and thus became an alternative to the Tabernacle. This is quite clear as the instructions for making the Brazen Altar came later. But it does not appear that the erection of the Tabernacle made these stone and earth altars redundant; there was still use for them after the Tabernacle was raised up. Gideon built an altar (Judg 6.24) which he called "Jehovah-shalom", and then he built a second altar on which he offered his father's "second bullock of seven years old" (Judg 6.25-28). Manoah, the father of Samson, offered "a kid with a meat offering" upon a rock, clearly an unhewn rock, which acted as an altar (Judg 13.19-20). Samuel built an altar unto the Lord at Ramah (1 Sam 7.17); he also offered sacrifices at other times and in other places where an altar would be necessary (see 1 Sam 16.1-5). Is it not also significant that the healed Namaan took back "two mules' burden of earth" (2 Kings 5.17) to Damascus to offer burnt offerings unto the Lord? He was obeying the Word of God in his plans to erect an altar.

These altars were to be erected "in all places where I shall make my name to be remembered, I will come unto thee, and bless thee" (v.24, JND). When the Lord appeared to His servants, or manifested His presence and power in any way, provision was made for the building of an altar. Surely only worship could be the response to such a manifestation! Here was opportunity for individual devotion. Note that neither Gideon, Manoah, nor Samuel were Aaronic priests, and yet they offered sacrifices which were accepted by the Lord.

But a further word of warning must be sounded in connection with the first point made above. These altars were never intended to be a gathering place for the Children of Israel. The spiritual experiences of individuals will be the cause of rejoicing and worship but must not become the basis for creating separate gathering places. It was not God's will that the people should gather to them in place of, or in addition to, the Tabernacle. There was only one gathering place and that was where the Lord had placed His name. Great and godly men have lived and known the hand of God with them and sometimes their lives, teachings, and experiences have become the basis for the creation of another "church". The pattern for gathering in the New Testament is clearly set out and no other pattern must be allowed to take its place.

However, do not let the warning detract from the glorious possibilities that these altars provide. Particularly observe that in days when the testimony at the Tabernacle was weak and compromised, even when the Ark was missing, it was possible for faithful individuals to have dealings with their God. The corporate testimony may have failed, but personal devotion can still flourish and the promise of the Lord enjoyed, that He will "come unto thee and…will bless thee" (v.24). Take heart that in such times the Lord can still be enjoyed and His presence and blessings crown each day.

Notes

1 *Believer's Magazine*, April, 1949.
3 A. Motyer, *The Prophecy of Isaiah,* page 343.
4 The AV states that Jonathan was "the son of Gershom, the son of Manasseh", but note that "Instead of Manasseh, some would read Moses; as it is found in some MSS., in the Vulgate and in the concessions of the most intelligent Jews. But Bp. Patrick takes this to be an idle conceit of the Rabbins, and supposes this Jonathan to be of some other family of the Levites. Yet Kimchi acknowledges, that the Jews, deeply concerned for the honour of their lawgiver, to whom they thought it would be a great dishonour to have a grandson who was an idolater…changed (the name) into Manasseh" (*Treasury of Scripture Knowledge*).
10 D. Baron, *Types, Psalms and Prophecies,* page 71.
12 *Expositor's Greek Testament: Ephesians.*
12 A. Leckie, *What the Bible Teaches: Ephesians.*
17 TWOT at 673.

EXODUS 21

Judgments of the Law

The opening verse of this chapter indicates that the close of the previous chapter had been an introduction to the subject which would be addressed during Moses' time with the Lord, continuing until 24.2.

Verse 1: The Judgments

The word "judgments" (4941) covers laws and ordinances which gave instruction based on the Ten Commandments, and which had to be observed if the Law was to be kept. It indicates that these were not brought before Israel as mere suggestions as to how society was to be ordered; they were not a set of loose guidelines to be interpreted according to local conditions and customs. "Judgments" refers to laws that have legal standing and could be used by judges in cases which were brought before them. Law in Israel would not be built on precedent, resulting in changes being brought into force when new precedents were created. Nor would it be altered to reflect changing views as to what constituted law-breaking. This is how present day society has been ordered, particularly in the moral sphere, with much of what past generations rightly regarded as sinful and criminal being now accepted as normal behaviour. The Law was unchangeable, based on the word of God. The Ten Commandments and the chapters which follow set out that Law with clarity not confused by terminology unable to be understood by the "man in the street".

Each of the laws which follow, therefore, is based on the Commandments of ch.20, and is given to teach how these should be put into practice. It is not suggested that every detailed circumstance that might occur is dealt with, but what was set before them was sufficient guidance to teach how the Law should be applied. This body of judgments was inseparable from the Ten Commandments. Even in the last mention of the Law in the Old Testament the two are referred to together: "Remember ye the law of Moses my servant, which I commanded unto him in Horeb for all Israel *with the statutes and judgments*" (Mal 4.4).

Consideration of these judgments "is eminently calculated to impress the heart with a sense of God's unsearchable wisdom and infinite goodness" (Mackintosh). It also teaches the reader that there is no part of life with which the Lord does not deal. Serious matters are dealt with, and what some may regard as minor matters are included: the death of a borrowed animal (22.14-15); the forbidding of usury when lending to the poor (22.25); regulations for the taking of the clothing of a neighbour for a pledge (22.26); returning to an enemy his ox or ass that had gone astray (23.4). When the Lord reigns, righteousness must mark every act no matter how great or small and apparently insignificant.

It is clear that the purpose of these laws was to ensure that the nation lived by righteous principles. They would act as a deterrent to the would-be law-breaker, for the guilty were never to profit from their acts. The value of life, the requirement to pay for any damage inflicted on others and the need to have respect for others and their property were all found here. Such laws would be a worthy foundation for the ordering of any society.

Verses 2-6: The Hebrew Servant

The first matter dealt with is that of the Hebrew servant. The teaching of this section is often applied to the Lord Jesus and it is true that He was the Perfect Servant, with no other ever having greater devotion than He. The following comments, however, deal with what these laws meant to a Hebrew who had become a servant, and then apply the lessons to those who seek to serve the Lord today.

Why were they servants?

Before considering the conditions under which Hebrews served it is necessary to consider why they should be servants. The opening words of v.2 reveal that they were *sold* as servants, so why were they subject to such a transaction? The first cause was that if one had been guilty of theft, and could not make restitution for what had been stolen, he was to be sold in order for payment to be made (22.1-3). There was always a price to pay when guilty of theft.

The second reason was that some might find themselves "waxen poor" (Lev 25.35). In these circumstances precise instructions were given for those who had lost their inheritance. Should a neighbour fall into such circumstances he and his family were to be supported without charging him interest on any money expended or making profit out of any food given to him, the reason for this grace shown to others being that the Lord had shown grace to Israel in delivering them from Egypt. They were to deal with others as the Lord had dealt with them. If, however, circumstances were such that the man had to be sold to meet his obligations he was not to serve as a bondservant, a slave, but as a hired servant until the year of jubilee (every fiftieth year).

According to Leviticus 25 the one who was sold on account of his poverty could not be sold as a bondservant, but as a hired servant who was paid agreed wages for his service. There was, however, no such limitation placed on the man who was sold because he was a thief. It was not written of him that he could not be sold as a bondservant; a Hebrew bondservant is, therefore, one who had been sold because of his sin.

How long did they serve?

The servant was to be freed, if he wished, in the seventh year of his service. Should the year of jubilee come before the seventh year it shortened his tenure of service as he was released at that time. In Leviticus

25.40 it states that the hired servant was to serve until the year of jubilee. As this could mean up to almost fifty years of service it does seem out of step with the instruction for the release of the bondservant in Exodus 21.2. It appears, therefore, that servants were released in the year of jubilee no matter how long or short a period they had served, and the requirement to serve the whole period of six years held true if no year of jubilee intervened.

What were the conditions for release?

In the seventh year the Hebrew bondservant could leave the service of his master and "go out free for nothing". He was not required to pay a bounty of any kind to obtain his freedom. Three different sets of circumstances are dealt with.

1. If he were unmarried when he entered service he would go out unmarried.

2. If he were married when he became a servant he would take his wife and family with him. His liabilities would have been met from the purchase price that was paid for him. At the end of his term of service the master was to furnish him liberally from his flock, his threshing floor, and his winepress (Deut 15.12-18) to provide him with the means of re-entering society as a free man.

3. If he entered the service of his master as an unmarried man, and had been given a wife by his master, a momentous choice was before him. He could leave the service of his master but he had to "go out by himself" (v.4). His wife and children had to be left behind, a law that seems, on the surface, to be very severe. But, was it really so? The servant who married a wife given to him by his master had bound himself to the house of his master. As he would be familiar with the teaching of this part of the Law, he understood the implication of such a marriage. The master had blessed him abundantly and the servant now faced a decision, the result of which would be to show whether he had been serving out of duty or out of devotion. This was the point at issue! Outwardly it might not have been possible to detect whether service had been out of the necessity of duty or whether the heart of the servant had been moved in devotion to his master. That the master thought highly of his servant was clear, otherwise he would not have given him a wife, but how did the servant consider his master? He could decide to leave his service and, if that were his choice, he could not be held against his will in the house as a servant. If he departed, however, he could not take his wife and family with him; he must go out alone and leave behind him all that was dear to him. He was not only leaving a master who had cared for him and blessed him, but he was leaving behind those who loved him and depended on him. Such a choice was an irresponsible denial of the undeserved blessings which had been his, leaving behind that with which the master had enriched his life.

The other choice was to remain in the service of the master, but, if he did so, it was no longer for a stipulated period of time; he agreed to serve his master forever. With such a choice he could continue to enjoy the company of his wife and family while working for a master who cared for him and had his good at heart. A wise servant understood that life would be much better in the service of this master than it would be if he insisted on his emancipation. To serve such a master was the better choice.

The choice to remain

If the choice of the servant was to remain there was a set procedure to be followed. The "transaction" had to be carried out legally and it was of such a nature that the servant could never claim that it was done without his knowledge or under duress. First, he must state plainly that he loved his master, his wife, and his children. Take note that this decision was based on love and not on convenience or seeking for gain. The order in his statement was also significant; he placed his master first but he loved his wife and children no less. The same verb was used to cover all three, with the master having prime place. This was the plainly stated reason why he would not go out free. Second, he was taken to the judges so that his decision could be legally certified. Third, the master took the servant back to his (the master's) house where his ear was bored with an awl against the door, or the doorpost. By submitting to this he was symbolically binding himself to the house forever. This was, therefore, no hasty, ill-conceived decision made in an emotional moment. It was fully thought through, and the process carried out in a manner that left no doubt with master and servant as to the significance of what had taken place.

The significance of the act

First, the servant had declared that he loved his master. Over the years of his service he had learned not only to respect, but also to love the master who had delivered him from his poverty-stricken condition and had treated him with loving consideration.

Second, true love to his wife and children was shown by his remaining in the service of his master. This, he knew, would result in a better life for them.

Third, to choose freedom entailed him leaving his wife and children. He would go out alone and leave behind those whom he loved. To do so would display cold-hearted lack of feeling and selfish callousness.

Fourth, wherever he went the pierced ear would be seen by others, showing that he was devoted to his master. This public sign of his devotion would mark him out as a servant who had returned his master's goodness. He was not prepared to take all the blessings bestowed on him without, in return, displaying his love for his master.

Fifth, on every occasion the servant left the master's house he would be reminded by the hole in the door, or the doorpost, that he belonged to that house and had vowed his determination to remain there.

Sixth, the pierced ear and door, or doorpost, not only said much about the faithfulness of the servant, but also about the character of the master. Looking at the servant, others would observe that he had a master who was worth serving. Looking at the entrance to the house, visitors would see that its master was worthy of love, devotion, and respect. The bearing of the servant and the character of the house spoke volumes about the master who ruled the house.

It can be seen, therefore, that the conduct of the Hebrew servant who had his ear pierced through with an awl commended both him and his master. Anyone being sold as a servant could wish for no better master!

The spiritual lessons to learn

The placing of this teaching within the "judgments" of the Law is not without significance. It comes at the beginning. Having servants in the house was an opportunity for the master to show that he loved his neighbour as himself. This only would be possible if he loved the Lord his God with all his heart. But was the Lord not teaching that, despite the fact that Israel were now under Law, devotion was still what He desired from His people? Would they learn the lesson that serving Him was serving the best of masters? This is the lesson for today. To be a bondservant of Jesus Christ is not an onerous, burdensome duty, but is a delight and a privilege that should be gladly and readily acknowledged. Those who own the Lord as Master have been delivered from sin with its resultant spiritual poverty. He has paid the price to enable such deliverance to take place.

It was a blessed household where the master was given the first place and where the husband could state truly, "I love my master, my wife, and my children". This did not diminish the love that he had for his wife and children; it did not relegate it to a second rate love; it rather guaranteed that he did love them deeply and knew that their good would be served by remaining in the service of his master. A home where the Lord Jesus is loved is one where wife and children will be loved and honoured and where the marriage difficulties which are such a feature of present day society will, should they begin to arise, be settled in the presence of the Lord before they destroy the harmony of the home. A spiritual wife will be pleased to be married to a husband who puts the Lord first, and a spiritual husband will be content when his wife does likewise.

It has been noted that to leave the service of the master was to go out alone. The servant would be separated from the blessings that the Lord had bestowed upon him. For those who go the way of the prodigal a bleak future lies ahead. They have declared that they do not wish to be subject to Him, and they will learn that He will allow them what they wish. It is not a question of the possession of eternal life; it is a question of submission to Him as Lord and Master. It will soon be learned that loss and not gain is the result of such a decision.

Devotion to the Lord leaves its mark. Just as the Hebrew servant had a bored ear, the bondservant of Jesus Christ bears the marks of devotion. It is not an ear bored through with an awl; it is the manner of life manifesting love for the Lord, and is just as clearly seen as the Hebrew servant's ear. The challenge to the heart of the Christian is whether such features are present for others to see.

Such love for the Master displays to others that He is a master worth serving. He asks that we present our bodies as a living sacrifice to Him (Rom 12.1), and those who do so find that He cares for them and blesses liberally. The wise have no desire to leave His service; they are willing servants, understanding that serving Him is a privilege beyond measure.

> My Master, lead me to Thy door;
> Pierce this now willing ear once more:
> Thy bonds are freedom; let me stay
> With Thee to toil, endure, obey.
> (H. C. G. Moule)

The application of this truth to the assembly is worthy of note. The assembly has the features of the House of God and those who enjoy fellowship there should all be devoted servants. It would be a blessing to have every saint with the character of the Hebrew servant who loved his master. If, therefore, there are fifty in fellowship in an assembly there ought to be, metaphorically, fifty bore marks on the "door", every believer by his or her manner of life declaring that they have a good Master who has blessed them beyond measure. The assembly should be the house of devoted servants, none wishing to leave their Master.

Verses 7-11: Duties to Maidservants

As abuse of servants was a common practice amongst some peoples, the Law now deals with the rights of young women who were sold as servants. If a family was so impoverished that a daughter had to be sold, "she shall not go out as the menservants do", and the conditions for her release from her servant status were different from those of a male servant. A number of possible situations are dealt with.

The first possibility was that the master was betrothed to the maiden. It may be that this was the purpose of her being sold. The maiden was now regarded as the master's wife and when the marriage took place there was no need of further regulation. She had the status and privilege of a wife. But it was necessary to protect the maiden should the master, after betrothal, decide that he no longer wished to marry her. This change of heart took place because she did not "please" (7451, 5869) him. This did not indicate that there was a moral matter making her no longer acceptable to him, but rather that she was no longer attractive to him. In this situation she could be very vulnerable if not protected, but she could be redeemed, bought back out of her servant state, should there be a relative who was rich enough to pay the redemption price. The master could not sell her to a strange (foreign) nation, as a Hebrew could not be a servant to Gentiles. After the redemption price had been paid she would be free to return home.

The second possibility was that she could be betrothed to the master's son. The master was required to treat her as if she was a daughter and pay the dowry which the son would expect to receive from the father of his bride. If she was married to the master, or to his son, and then found that her husband had taken another wife, she was still to be maintained as a wife. None of the privileges and provision that she enjoyed had to be forfeited.

Where no betrothal took place, and after she had served the stipulated time as a servant, she was free to return home without any price being paid to her master. "Thus in his compassionate love, the Lord surrounds his weak and defenceless ones with laws to secure for them equitable and considerate treatment" (Dennett).

It appears that the term of service of a maidservant was similar to that of the male. She would serve for six years and be released in the seventh unless a year of jubilee had come before the seventh year, in which case she would be released early. As no further directions are given it was assumed that these conditions were similar for male and female Hebrew servants. This certainly was the practice in Israel. During the reign of King Zedekiah, the godless monarch, doubtless in "panic" piety, ordered the release from service of Hebrew menservants and maidservants, because the law regarding their service had been ignored (Jer 34.8-10). It was accepted that both maidservants and menservants were subject to the same conditions of service.

Nothing is written here regarding a maidservant who wished to remain with her master after her years of service have expired. It can be concluded that the same conditions applied there also, and she too could have her ear bored to the door. This is confirmed in Deuteronomy 15.17.

Verses 12-14: Murder and Accidental Slaying

The subject of service and liberty having been dealt with, the Law turns to the right to life. There are now introduced crimes that demanded the death penalty. In the following verses there are four of this nature: premeditated acts of murder, which are dealt with here; assault against a parent; stealing or kidnapping individuals; cursing father or mother.

When a man smote another and slew him wilfully he had to be put to death. The use of capital punishment is sanctioned in the Word of God, as the principle, first found in Genesis 9.6, has not been set aside. No alternative punishment was provided for the crime of premeditated murder. The nature of the sentence indicates the value of human life, that which only God can give and which no man or woman has the right to take away.

Where death was the result of accidental slaying, there was provided "a place whither he shall flee". If, however, the death was the result of a premeditated purpose, even fleeing to the altar, as did Joab (1 Kings 2.28-34), did not afford protection. The sentence was not to be carried out at the altar, but he was to be taken from it "that he may die".

Where death was not the result of premeditated action, the man who had caused the death could flee for safety to an appointed place. Provision was made for this in the six cities designated "cities of refuge" in the land possessed by Israel (Num 35.9-32; Deut 19.1-10). Three of these cities, Bezer in the territory of the Reubenites, Ramoth in the territory of the Gadites, and Golan in the territory of the tribe of Manasseh, all on the east bank of the Jordan, were appointed by Moses (Deut 4.41-43). The other three, all in the land on the west side of the Jordan, were not appointed until after the land had been possessed - "Kedesh in Galilee in mount Naphtali, and Shechem in mount Ephraim, and Kirjath-arba, which is Hebron, in the mountain of Judah" (Josh 20.7). These were all towns that had been given to the Levites as part of their inheritance of forty-eight cities (Num 35.6-7). When instructions were given for the selection of the cities in Canaan it was laid down that the land should be divided into three parts and one city selected from each part. It was also necessary to ensure that a suitable highway was prepared so that those who sought refuge would have no difficulty in reaching the city. The point was that it was not to be difficult for the man responsible for accidental slaying to reach the city of refuge.

On reaching a city of refuge, the man stood at its gate and declared "his cause in the ears of the elders of that city" (Josh 20.4). If the elders acceded to his request for entry he was given the right of residence "until he stand before the congregation for judgment, and until the death of the high priest" (Josh 20.6). It may be that the man, before he left his own city, had already been arraigned before a tribunal to try his case and been declared free of guilt (Num 35.24), although he had still considered it wise to take refuge from the anger of the relatives of the dead. There may even have been circumstances about the case which made the elders of the city of refuge feel that at a suitable time the man should be returned to his own city to be placed before a tribunal. If he was declared to be guiltless he was "restored" to the city of refuge as, has been noted, passions might still have been running high in the family of the dead man. The point of this was that although justice must be carried out, the hasty feelings of the avenger of blood must not be allowed to overrule righteousness of action.

Verse 15: Smiting Mother or Father

Particular attention is paid here to the respect due to parents. The smiting of a father or a mother might not lead to death, but the punishment was as severe as that which was meted out for murder. It has been observed in connection with the fifth commandment - "Honour thy father and thy mother: that thy days may be long upon the land which the Lord thy God giveth thee" - that this was the first commandment with promise. Smiting a parent broke that commandment and was the sign of an ungrateful spirit devoid of natural affection. This lack of natural kindness and family feeling was twice alluded to by Paul (Rom 1.30; 2 Tim 3.2) as a mark of those who have no love for God.

Verse 16: Stealing a Man or Woman for the Purpose of Selling them
The condition of those who became servants in Israel was not that of abject slavery. Such a condition was a denial of the dignity of man. Here the stealing of a man was expressly forbidden. Stealing would entail holding an individual against his or her will, either for the purpose of using their labour, or with the intention of selling them as servants or slaves. The serious nature of such an act was indicated by the punishment to be meted out to the offender; he was to be put to death. Even in the sinful condition of mankind today, a condition that has led to the lowest of behaviour and cruellest of acts, human life and liberty must still be honoured. Reading this brings to mind the deed of Joseph's brothers when they sold him as a slave into Egypt, an act that under the Law would have led to their being sentenced to death.

Verse 17: Cursing Father or Mother
Attention is drawn again to the relationship between parents and children. The "cursing" of parents would be punished by death. In v.15 the point at issue was the use of violence against parents, but here "cursing" parents was contempt, and the use of insubordinate language. Also included was the refusal to accord parents the respect which was their due, including ensuring that, in old age, their needs were met. This behaviour was a sign of a depraved mind, one that was not fit to live. In every way children were required to treat parents with the utmost respect.

Such disrespect was the breaking of the fifth commandment, and this was the law which the Lord Jesus used to impress on the Jews that they had substituted tradition in place of keeping the commandments (Mt 15.1-9; Mk 7.1-13). By their behaviour in this matter they proved that although they declared their devotion with their lips, their hearts were far from Him. Despite such clear instructions from the Law, the scribes and Pharisees revealed where their hearts lay as their traditions provided a way of ignoring the obligation of the Law. Should parents be in need and their family had the means of meeting that need they could simply state that what was required by the parents was "Corban", or "a gift". This gift, however, was not given to the parents, the excuse being that it had been consecrated to the Lord, and with such a sinful device this law was set aside. It should be observed that perhaps a small gift might have been taken to the altar, but there was no reason to believe that this was always done, and the declaration that what the parents required was Corban would, on many occasions, be the end of the matter. Little wonder that the Lord Jesus called them "hypocrites". The Law was broken, and lies and avarice dictated conduct.

Verses 18-19: Strife Between Men

The situation dealt with here was that of two men being in dispute, and, as a result, tempers rising, and violence being used. Should such violence lead to the death of one of the protagonists the Law had already dealt with the consequences, but what had to take place if the injured party did not die? Should the injured man recover from his injuries no action had to be taken against the other party, but responsibilities were laid upon him. He must pay for any loss of earnings suffered by the victim as a result of his injuries, and he must pay for all the medical treatment necessary to bring about recovery. If this was carried out the attacker was "quit"; he had faced up to his responsibilities, paid the price of his actions, and thus was not guilty of an offence demanding further punishment.

These laws, apart from ensuring that matters were dealt with righteously, also acted as a deterrent, holding back premeditated violence and the rise of temper that could lead to violence. All would be aware of the demands of the Law in these cases, and that the cost of such an outburst could be considerable and prolonged. In more serious cases the payments might have to be made for many years.

Verses 20-21: Smiting a Servant

The use of the rod as a means of chastising was allowed in Israel. "But a rod is for the back of him that is void of understanding" (Prov 10.13), and "a rod for the fool's back" (Prov 26.3) teach that the rod could be used when individuals did not yield to reasoned correction. It was not licence for indiscriminate use, but was intended for those who refused to bow to any other kind of instruction or discipline. When the rod was used against a servant and caused death, the servant was to be avenged. The case would be heard by the congregation and judgment carried out in view of the circumstances. Where the servant did not die for some days after the punishment it was accepted that the master did not intend to put the servant to death and that this was not a premeditated act. In such a case no action was taken as the master had suffered loss in the death of the servant, for "he is his money".

If it is thought that this law favoured the master greatly it must be understood that a servant was of great worth to a master. The fact that the servant was the "money" of the master indicates the value with which he was regarded. It was, therefore, not in the interests of the master to slay a servant, for by so doing he was diminishing his wealth. The purpose of punishing a servant was that he would, by this correction, be a better servant, not that he would no longer be able to serve.

Verses 22-25: Hurt to a Woman with Child

The respect and care that was to be given to the unborn child was the subject of this law. The woman was not part of the dispute which took place between a number of men, nevertheless when violence broke out she was injured in some way. There were two possible outcomes to this. The first was that she might give birth to a healthy child prematurely. Yet, although the mother and child had sustained no injuries, there was still a judicial process to be gone through to enable the husband of the woman to determine what punishment had to be carried out. The danger was that in anger the husband demanded a penalty in excess of what was righteous, so judges had to confirm the penalty. The punishment was in the form of a fine, and, after the husband and the judges had agreed, the guilty party had to pay.

Should there be injury to the mother or the child then the demands of the law are "life for life, Eye for eye, tooth for tooth" etc. This must be seen in light of the previous instruction that a fine had to be paid as compensation for the pain and distress suffered by the mother even when no injury followed. The teaching here was not that, whatever injury was suffered by the mother or the child the guilty party should be injured in the same way. The loss of a hand should not result in the guilty party losing a hand. That would be vengeance, but would be of little value to the victim. The principle here was still one of compensation, and there must be paid to the victim a sum, agreed by the judges, as righteous reparation for the loss that had been suffered. The compensation was directly related to the injury, taking into account all the factors including, for example, reduction of earnings, medical costs, care needed. It must be emphasised that the purpose of this law was not to ensure that some sort of revenge was carried out, but that such a course of action did not take place. Private vendettas were not to be waged; the court decided the matter.

The Jews, however, took this law to mean the opposite of what was intended. They asserted that the right to personal revenge was not only allowed but also demanded, thus using the commandment to defeat its purpose. The Lord Jesus spoke of this (Mt 5.38-42), and asserted how enmity must be met. The essence of His teaching is that there has not to be a yearning for revenge; the heart must not be filled with thoughts of vengeance. Private campaigns against any perceived to be enemies are forbidden, and care must be taken to ensure that the great purpose of the Law, that love for others must be as great as love for ourselves, is carried out.

Verses 26-27: Injuries to a Servant

Should a master smite a servant so that injury resulted, the matter was not brought before the judges. The injury in this case was not fatal, as that has already been dealt with (vv.20-21). The eye and the tooth are mentioned, but the Law goes beyond these two members which are quoted as examples. The loss of any member or the loss of the use of it was covered by Law, as would any injury resulting in the servant being unable to work. Although the judges were not called to hear the case, the master had to give liberty to the servant or maidservant who had been maimed. In this way he suffered loss of a financial nature in being deprived of the services of the servant. The principle of eye for eye, tooth for tooth had been maintained, and the compensation paid to the servant was release from his service. The deterrent effect of such a law was clear, as no master would deliberately suffer so great a loss.

Verses 28-32: Death Caused by an Ox

The owner of an ox was held to be responsible for the behaviour of the beast. The choice of an ox was possibly because the other animals in the possession of an Israelite would scarcely be capable of causing death. Doubtless, if another animal did cause death the owner would also be subject to this law.

If the ox gored a man or a woman, so causing their death, it must be put to death by stoning. There was no guilt attached to the owner because he had no prior warning from the behaviour of the ox that it was capable of such an act. Nevertheless, after the stoning of the ox, its flesh was not to be eaten because no profit was to come to the owner. Its carcass was to be treated as unclean because it had been the cause of blood being shed.

If, however, the ox had caused danger by its behaviour in the past, and this had been reported to the owner, he was held to be guilty because he had not kept the ox inside or in an area where it would not be a danger. The owner was then regarded as being guilty of the death caused and he had to be put to death. However, the judges could determine a sum of money to be paid by the owner to the bereaved family, this being in place of the death penalty. By that act he redeemed his life, that is, he bought it back as it had been forfeited. It should not be thought that this was simply an easy way out, as the sum involved could be very considerable. The law covered any death in a family, whether it be that of mother, father, son, or daughter.

Where the victim was a servant, the same law applied with the sole exception that the amount of compensation to be paid was not left to the judges to determine, but was stipulated as thirty shekels of silver. This sum was significant as the value placed on a servant. The prophet Zechariah writes of the Shepherd whom Jehovah has charged with the feeding of the flock. This Shepherd, the Lord Jesus, then challenges Israel, "If ye think good, give me my price" (Zech 11.12). He asks for his wages and Israel have to state their estimation of His value, which they determine at thirty pieces of silver. Three things should be noted of this transaction. First, it was deliberate. "They weighed for my price", indicates that this was not done without thought, but was a premeditated act. Second, it was derisory. They thought long and hard and reckoned He was only worth the price of a servant. Third, it was disapproved, as the Lord states with derision that it was a "goodly" price. In casting it to the potter, regarded as a menial trade, its lack of value was publicly displayed.

When it came time for Israel to value the Lord Jesus, the prophecy of Zechariah was fulfilled. Thirty pieces of silver was the amount decided by the bargain between Judas and the priests (Mt 26.15). Both agreed as to His value, the price of a servant, and these legal religionists, even with their knowledge of the book of Zechariah, were still set on paying the minimum possible, even although it meant fulfilling Scripture. In their hatred for the Lord they were blind to that as they paid the traitor his money.

Verses 33-34: The Loss of an Ox or an Ass

Having dealt with matters regarding life, the subject of property is now addressed. To the Israelite, his ox or ass would possibly be his most valuable possession and the loss of it a considerable blow. Where this loss was caused by the negligence of others it was necessary for compensation to be paid. The owner of a pit was required to ensure that it was not left uncovered, thus creating a danger to others. If an ox died as a result of falling into the pit, the owner of the ox was compensated for his loss by the owner of the pit, after which the carcass became the property of the latter. Righteousness demanded that Israel must be a responsible society in which individuals were accountable for their actions. How different this is from the spirit of our present age where responsibility and accountability are avoided.

Verses 35-36: The Death of an Ox

Two situations are dealt with here. The first was when one ox, never having previously been known to be aggressive, caused the death of another ox. The live ox was sold with the proceeds being divided between the two owners. The dead ox was also divided between them. The value of the two oxen was thus equally divided. The owner of the living ox suffered the same loss as the owner of the dead ox.

The second situation was when the ox that had caused the death was known previously to have acted in this manner and the owner had not kept it fenced in. In that case the owner must pay ox for ox by providing an ox in place of the dead animal, after which the carcass became his.

EXODUS 22

Judgments of the Law (continued)

Verse 1: Stealing an Animal

When an ox or sheep was stolen and killed or sold, the compensation to be paid to the owner was five oxen for each stolen ox, or four sheep for each stolen sheep. The difference reflected the greater value attached to an ox. If, however, the stolen animal was not sold or slain, the compensation was reduced to double what had been stolen (v.4). The stolen animal was returned, and, in addition, another given. The reduction in compensation was due to the fact that in the latter case there was less careful planning and prior deliberation in the theft.

The principle is that no one guilty of theft should profit from his deeds; indeed he would suffer financial loss. He who sought to reduce the worth of another found that his own worth was reduced by a greater amount than that by which he intended others to suffer.

This was in the mind of David as Nathan the prophet visited him and told the story of the stolen lamb (2 Sam 12). David was indignant and stated that fourfold compensation should be paid. This was also what Zacchaeus had before his mind when he stated that if he had taken anything by false accusation he would repay it fourfold (Lk 19.8). These words do not constitute an admission of guilt on the part of Zacchaeus, for he states, "if I have taken…", but it was an admission that restitution should be made if there had been any unrighteous dealings, even if carried out without intention to rob.

Verses 2-4: Breaking and Entering

When a thief was found breaking into the house by night and died as a result of injuries inflicted by the one protecting the property, no guilt attached to the person who caused the death. Should the events take place during daylight hours the one causing the death should be treated as a murderer. It was not expected that such force would be used in the daytime, but the conditions at night made the robber a much more frightening figure, and that accounts for the different consequences of the act. Due to the fact that a burglar would realise that the owner of a property, because of fear brought about by an uninvited nocturnal "visitor", might react by the use of force, it is attributed to the robber that he had the intention of using force, meeting the defensive activity of the house-owner with violence, even to the extent of taking life. Due to this, no criminal activity was attributed to the owner of the property as he had the right to defend himself in a situation which could have cost him and his family their lives.

The principle is that anyone has the right to self-protection when his life seems to be threatened. The burglar would be well aware of the law in this respect and understood the danger in which he was placing himself by undertaking this sinful and criminal activity at night.

"Full restitution" (7999) was to be made by the thief. The compensation to be paid was not based on the ability of the thief to pay, but on the reparation to be made. If the ox, ass, or sheep which was stolen when the property was entered illegally was recovered, it was the responsibility of the thief to return double to the owner. Doubtless this could be in the form of live animals or in the form of the recovered animals plus money to the value of the animals. Should the thief be unable to meet this obligation he was to be sold as a servant to enable the amount to be paid. The principle noted above, that full compensation must be paid to those who suffer loss through theft and that the compensation be fully met by the thief, is satisfied.

Verses 5-6: Loss of Produce

Nothing was overlooked in the Law. Such a seemingly unimportant incident as is here recorded surely cannot have the attention of heaven. But it does! All potential strife-causing events are dealt with. Where a man allowed his beast to wander into a field or vineyard belonging to someone else, the animal would eat what was available in its new-found environment. When it did so, compensation had to be paid in the form of the best of the produce from the animal owner's ground. Lest the thought occur to the owner of the beast that he could profit as a result of the action of his beast, which was not known to him, no second-rate compensation was acceptable; it had to be the best. This would also be an incentive to those who might have sought to save their own fields by placing their herd in a neighbour's field, to refrain from such conduct, as no profit would fall to them.

A further situation dealt with was where fire was started and as a result the standing corn or the stacks of corn are destroyed. Once again, compensation had to be paid by him who was responsible for starting the fire. In both cases the damage was not deliberate, but this did not excuse the one responsible or absolve him from the need to pay compensation.

Verses 7-13: Goods Lost while in the Possession of a Neighbour

Where a man had given his neighbour money or goods to keep on his behalf, and they were stolen, the thief had to pay double as compensation, but if the thief could not be found, the master of the house with whom the neighbour had deposited his goods had to clear himself of the suspicion that he himself might have taken them. Should it not be possible to do this the matter was brought before the judges, and, if the man into whose care the goods had been placed was found to be guilty of theft, he had to pay as compensation double the value of what had been lost.

In the case of a beast which had been given to a neighbour to keep on behalf of the owner, and that beast was injured, lost, or even died, and there were no witnesses, it was necessary for the neighbour into whose care the beast had been given to swear an oath that he had not stolen the beast or harmed it in any way. No compensation was necessary as the neighbour had not been guilty of carelessness or crime. If, however, the beast was stolen from him when it was kept in his house or stable, he had to pay compensation on the grounds that greater care should have been taken of the beast. Should the beast have been torn in pieces by another animal, and its carcass could be produced, it was not necessary for compensation to be paid.

Verses 14-15: Borrowed Goods

Where a man borrowed from his neighbour the Law differed from that contained in vv.7-13 because, unlike the situation when a neighbour had been asked to keep property for someone, the initiative here came from the man wishing to borrow and not from the owner of the property. In this situation the responsibility of the borrower was greater if the owner was not present. It could also be that an ox was borrowed for a specific task and the owner of the ox came along to supervise the use of his animal.

Should the animal be injured or die and the owner was not present, the borrower must make full restitution to the owner. This could involve payment to bring the animal back to health, or a payment to make up any loss suffered by the owner because the animal was no longer able to work as it had previously. Where death had taken place, a replacement, or the price of a replacement, had to be given to the owner. Where the owner was present when the injury had taken place no compensation was required as the owner was responsible for the animal at the time of the incident.

Verses 16-17: Seduction of a Young Woman

When a man seduced a young woman who was not betrothed to another man, the seducer must ask that he marry the woman. The use of the word *entice* (6601) indicates that this was not forced on the woman against her will, but that the man persuaded her. In asking for the hand of the maiden in marriage he was required to pay the dowry appropriate for the woman which was due to the father of the bride (see Gen 34.12), the amount depending on the age and status of the bride and the families involved. The custom would appear to be based on compensation for the father because his daughter would no longer be able to share the workload of the home and paid help might become necessary.

Should the father refuse to consent to the marriage the dowry was still to be paid as compensation for the shame which this act had brought on the family. It should be noted that the payment of the dowry and the marriage, if it took place, did not lift the shame of the act. When Shechem the son of Hamor the Hivite seduced Dinah, the daughter of Jacob, it was stated that he "defiled her" (Gen 34.1-2). He did love her, but his act caused her harm. In an age of lax morals it should not be regarded as a light thing to carry out an act of this nature. The gratification of lust defiles the woman even if she has been persuaded to agree. It should be noted that if the young woman involved was betrothed to another man the punishment was much more severe (Deut 22.22-23).

Verse 18: Witchcraft
Sorcery and witchcraft are first encountered in the Scriptures in Egypt (7.11). Dabbling in the occult was a practice that was completely condemned by the Word of God. The instruction here was definite; the witch must not be left alive to carry on her satanic practices. It has been suggested that the English word "witch" is related to the verb "to wit", or "to know" and conveys the idea of possessing knowledge that was not available to others. The idea seems to be that of a sorceress. The witch, therefore, professes to have knowledge of matters in the spirit world, and even to have ability to use this knowledge for the foretelling of events or to contact the dead and to cause spirits to work at her request. One purpose of these practices was to convince men and women that there was life after death, but not as is taught in the Word of God. Another was to display apparently supernatural powers by those who deny the truth of Scripture. The witch of Endor claimed that she could contact the dead, and because of this Saul visited her. The appearance of Samuel was not, however, due to her work. She was exceedingly surprised when he appeared (1 Sam 28.7-25), for she "cried with a loud voice", showing her fear.

One question that must be addressed was why a witch, and not a wizard, is mentioned. It could be that witches may have been more common than wizards; although in Leviticus 20.27 both are mentioned. Another issue was why the words, "Thou shalt not *suffer a witch to live*", are used and not the more common "shall die". It would appear that these words are used to emphasise that she will not be spared to carry on her evil work; she will no longer continue these practices. "Die" would indicate the same outcome but in a less telling manner.

Verse 19: Bestiality
Unnatural sexual activity of this nature was not to be tolerated. It is not without significance that this law comes immediately after witches have been dealt with. Evil sexual behaviour has always accompanied evil spirit activity. This great wickedness was practised by the inhabitants of Canaan (see Lev 18.23,27), one of the reasons why they were "spued out" of the land (Lev 18.28).

Verse 20: Sacrificing to a Strange God
The matter dealt with here was the subject of the first commandment. So serious was this, however, that it was necessary to specify the punishment to be carried out on those who committed this sin. The offering of sacrifices was for Jehovah alone and death was the consequence of offering to any other. Once again, it was clear that the Lord will not share

His place with any other "god" nor will He tolerate any other "god" being acknowledged.

The use of the words "utterly destroyed" (2763), which are also translated as "devoted to destruction" (JND), indicates very strong action, with a more vigorous thrust than "put to death". It emphasises not only that the life of offenders comes to an end, but also that all their works are similarly ended. "It connotes total annihilation and includes the destruction of the criminal's property." (Merrill). Nothing was to remain, and all that brought to mind memories of the offender was to be completely removed from Israel.

Verse 21: Consideration to the Stranger

The next three laws form a group concerned with the care of the stranger and the needy. The first of these deals with the "stranger", one who was not an Israelite, but was dwelling amongst them. Such individuals could be oppressed and mistreated because of their differing customs, manners, or even dress. Israelites should display a manner that commends the God whom they profess to serve and not to act in such a way that the stranger would ill regard the Lord because of the low behaviour of His people. They had been strangers themselves in Egypt and had experienced the goodness of God towards them, so, in turn, that same goodness must be displayed to other strangers. It is worth pausing to consider that the goodness and grace of God enjoyed by Christians should produce a caring, compassionate attitude to others. That is one effective way of testifying to unbelievers. In a cold world, empty of genuine compassion, it can leave with others never to be forgotten memories of how Christians live.

Verses 22-24: Widows and the Fatherless

Widows and the fatherless had the protecting care of Jehovah over them in a special way, as the absence of a father in the home exposed them to exploitation and abuse. With the loss of the breadwinner they were also faced with straitened circumstances and perhaps poverty. Provision was made in the Law (Deut 25.5-10) for a widow to marry the brother of her husband, but the purpose of this, although it would ensure that her new husband provided for her, was that the son of this marriage should "succeed in the name of his brother which was dead". Further provision for the poor was made (Lev 23.22) when the gleaning of the harvest was left for them and Ruth, the widow, made use of this when she came to Bethlehem (Ruth 2.1-3). In addition to this, however, the Lord takes special care of all who are in these circumstances, as is clearly stated in Deuteronomy 10.18: "He doth execute the judgment of the fatherless and widow", and all who consider treating them unrighteously must bear in mind that He administers justice on behalf of those who have lost the husband and father who otherwise would protect them. The same truth was emphasised by the Psalmist: "A father of the fatherless, and a judge of the widows, is God in his holy habitation" (68.5), and, "The Lord preserveth the strangers; he relieveth the fatherless and widow" (146.9). This care was demonstrated when Elijah was sent to the widow of Zarephath (1 Kings 17.8-24), and again when the needs of the widow of one of the "sons of the prophets" were met through Elisha (2 Kings 4.1-7). The Pharisees were roundly condemned by the Lord Jesus when He accused them of devouring widow's houses (Mt 23.14; Mk 12.40; Lk 20.47), taking advantage of their position and authority to take from widows and to lay claim to be beneficiaries in their wills. Compassion towards the widow was further seen with the raising of the son of the widow of Nain (Lk 7.11-15), and in the careful attention with which He noted the two mites cast by the widow into the Temple treasury (Mk 12.41-44; Lk 21.1-4).

The maltreatment of the weak was abhorrent to the Lord, and those responsible for such behaviour died by the sword, making their wives widows and their children fatherless. This was not extreme action, but an indication of how the Lord regards oppression of those who have no-one to protect them. There was no judicial process by which the perpetrators of these acts were to be tried, but they were to die "by the sword", indicating that the Lord will lead into war those who are guilty and His word will be fulfilled by that means. Clearly, if the nation did not tolerate such behaviour and dealt with the guilty this would not be necessary, but too often the affliction of those who cannot defend themselves was the product of a callous and indifferent society intent on gain at any price. Such actions bring disaster to the guilty!

Verses 25-27: Usury

The lending of money in the normal course of business with interest rates which did not exploit the borrower was not covered by this law, but the increase of the burdens of the poor by this means was forbidden. Where money was lent to the poor it was to be with a zero rate of interest, the principle being that none should gain from the troubles of others.

A striking example of the misuse of usury was practised in Jerusalem after the return from Babylon (Neh 5.1-13). The increase in the population (v.2), combined with the limited supply of food (v.3) and the payment of taxes to the king (v.4), resulted in the need for many to borrow money and to sell their sons and daughters as servants in order to buy food and meet their other obligations. This caused Nehemiah to be "very angry" (v.6), and he demanded that the practice cease. He had the moral right to do so because he had not asked for taxes to be paid to meet the cost of his household, which, as governor, he would have been entitled to do (v.11). Greedy creditors promised that the vineyards and lands which had been taken in lieu of payment were to be returned, and Nehemiah shook his lap stating, "So God shake out every man from his house, and from his labour, that performeth not this promise, even thus be he shaken out, and emptied" (v.13). The "shaking out" would result in the death of those who failed to carry out their promise.

One particular practice of the lender was covered by vv.26-27. Where a legitimate transaction had taken place and the garment of the borrower was given as a pledge, the garment had to be returned to the borrower each evening. The garment to which reference was made was the outer garment (8008) which was used as a blanket, serving as clothing during the hours of sleep. Even those with whom the lender had a business relationship had to be treated with respect and compassion. There was to be no disregard of the health and well-being of the debtor. When the morning came the garment would be returned to the lender as it was legally his until the loan was repaid.

Verse 28: Contempt for Authority

The word "gods" (430) was used of God, gods, rulers, and judges. Keil & Delitzsch state that "*Elohim* does not mean either the gods of other nations as Josephus, Philo, and others, in their dead and work-holy monotheism, have rendered the word; or the rulers, as Onkelos and others suppose; but simply God, deity in general, whose majesty was despised in every break [*sic*] of the commandments of Jehovah, and who was to be honoured in the persons of the rulers". JND translates the verse: "Thou shalt not revile the judges, nor curse a prince amongst thy people". "Judges" fits the context, but Keil & Delitzsch's point is relevant in as much as the judges were responsible for the maintenance of the Law, and, therefore, to despise them was to despise the Law and God who gave it and to whom the nation was responsible. To revile (7043) was to regard with light esteem, to hold to be of little account, to be contemptuous of or to treat as being despicable.

To show respect for authority was not limited to honouring rulers who were godly and whose behaviour merited being treated in that way, for to act otherwise would result in rebellion. Unworthy rulers would be dealt with by the Lord. When Paul, after his arrest, stood before Ananias the High Priest, who commanded that he be smitten on the mouth, he said, "God shall smite thee thou whited wall…". Those standing by protested, "Revilest thou God's high priest?", to which Paul replied that he was not aware that the man before him was the High Priest, and then stated, "Thou shalt not speak evil of the ruler of thy people" (Acts 23.1-5). He was aware of the teaching of this verse and would not have spoken as he did if he had known that Ananias was the High Priest, despite the fact that he was unfit to hold that office.

Christians today act in the same manner, remembering that, even when the holder is unfit, they honour the office and not the holder of it. The teaching of Romans 13.1 confirms this: "Let every soul be subject unto the higher powers. For there is no power but of God: the powers that be are ordained of God". When these words were written the tyrant Nero wore the purple and abused the dignity of the office of Caesar by his vain and murderous behaviour. Nevertheless, the Christians were not taught to rise and overthrow Caesar, for all authority was derived from God and it is He who raises up and puts down whom He will. To resist the government was to resist the ordinance of God. Christians are not revolutionaries, but they are not indifferent to cruelty and suffering around them, bringing it before the Lord in prayer. The power available there is far greater in effect than can be exercised through sedition. Even although Abraham would have been aware of the character of Sodom and Gomorrah he did not attempt to overthrow the rulers of these two cities when he rescued Lot from Chedorlaomer and his allies. Rather he refused any favours from the king of Sodom and left these cities in the hands of God who took dealings with them later (Gen 14.1-24; 19.1-25).

Verses 29-30: Giving the First to God

That the firstborn of man and of beast had to be given to the Lord was commanded at the time of departure from Egypt (13.1-2), and this instruction is given again with the added responsibility to bring to the Lord the first of harvests and the wine which had been produced. The "first of thy ripe fruits" means the fullness of the harvest, and it was clear that it was all the harvests to which reference was made, but the emphasis not to be missed is that there must be no delay in the offering of these firstfruits. To delay would indicate reluctance to give to the Lord what was rightly His due, revealing lack of gratitude to and appreciation of the One who had blessed them in the fullness of the harvest. It was possible to give with the wrong spirit and that was the point at issue here. He had given the former and the latter rains, and Israel's appreciation should be such that the first act would be to give Jehovah His portion of the harvest in gratitude for the liberality of a bountiful God. The same truth was taught in the New Testament for "God loveth a cheerful giver" (2 Cor 9.7), and a mean, miserly, reluctant giver brings no joy to the Lord.

The same was true of the sheep and the oxen, with the stipulation that the young were not to be taken from their mothers until they were eight days old, a tender note which tells the reader that the Lord does care even for the animals. The same care was seen when the Lord cleansed the Temple in Jerusalem as the Passover drew near (Jn 2.13-17). He entered the Temple precincts and found there a crowded concourse with oxen, sheep, and doves being traded for gain to the Temple authorities. Faced with such blatant commercialism, the Lord drove out the moneychangers, the merchants, the oxen, and the sheep, but he did not cast out the doves. These would either be tied or in cages, and to prevent undue injury to them, which would be the result of throwing them to the ground, He tells those who were trading in them to take them away. What careful consideration against a background of extreme provocation!

The giving of the firstborn of the sons of Israel was dealt with in ch.13, but is addressed again here with the emphasis on the requirement that there was to be no delay in obeying the word of God in this matter.

Verse 31: Holy Men

Here there is an apt reminder of the purpose of these Laws. They were not merely to regulate their conduct to produce an orderly society, nor to ensure that peace reigned and wrong-doing did not go unpunished, but to make them holy in their conduct and thus able to have fellowship with God. The eating of the flesh of a creature which had been slain by other beasts was forbidden as holy men must not partake of that which an animal had slain and then refused as food. If the beasts refused it, holy men must not demean themselves and deprive themselves of their dignity, by eating it. Matthew Henry in his *Commentary* writes appropriately that "...they should not eat any flesh that was torn of beasts, not only because it was unwholesome, but because it was paltry, and base, and covetous, and a thing below those who were holy men unto God, to eat the leavings of the beasts of prey. We that are sanctified to God must not be curious in our diet; but we must be conscientious, not feeding ourselves without fear, but eating and drinking by rule, the rule of sobriety, to the glory of God".

That holiness is the first demand of salvation is writ large over the Word of God. The section of the Epistle to the Romans which deals with the practical response to the gospel starts with the words, "I beseech you therefore, brethren, by the mercies of God, that ye present your bodies a living sacrifice, holy, acceptable unto God, which is your reasonable service (Rom 12.1). Peter also writes of this: "But as he which hath called you is holy, so be ye holy in all manner of conversation; Because it is written, Be ye holy; for I am holy" (1 Pet 1.15-16). The word is found 70 times in Exodus. He saved them to set them apart, they were to be holy men, for His pleasure and for His glory.

EXODUS 23

Judgments of the Law (continued)

Verse 1: Talebearing and slander

Much damage is caused by the talebearer, and while that practice is covered in this verse, the emphasis is on slanderous talk which may lead to charges being laid against the person who is the subject of the "story". To "raise" (5375) has the meaning of lifting, carrying, or taking, and signifies the one who begins the tale and those who, having heard it, pass it on, no doubt adding to it as it is retold. The use of "report" (8088) indicates that the person passing on the information is not a witness, but has heard the report or heard of alleged events on which the report is based, perhaps even creating or altering what took place in order to harm others. It was such a report which led to the imprisonment of Joseph (Gen 39.7-20), and Sanballat and Geshem, the enemies of the Jews, threatened to use this device to bring to a halt the work of rebuilding the walls of Jerusalem (Neh 6.1-9).

Should a person be called to testify to the truth of an accusation, particularly, but not exclusively, before the courts, the wicked claim of an accuser must not be corroborated, as such behaviour results in the witness sharing the guilt of the accuser. A conspiracy to bring an innocent man before the courts is in view by referring to the custom of putting "thine hand" with the wicked; this was a sign of an agreement having been reached and, as a result, the parties having entered into a binding mutual undertaking.

The most infamous example of this odious practice was the evidence brought against the Lord Jesus at His trial. Matthew writes; "Now the chief priests, and elders, and all the council, sought *false witness* against Jesus, to put him to death; But found none: yea, though many *false witnesses* came, yet found they none. At the last came two *false witnesses*, And said, This fellow said, I am able to destroy the temple of God, and to build it in three days" (26.59-61). The compact was made, the agreement sealed, and the chief priests, elders, the council, and the witnesses, supported by the Pharisees and Sadducees, laid their false charges against Him, taking His words and, by misquoting Him, building on them their lie. The accusation was that He had said, "I am able to destroy this temple", but what He had declared was, "Destroy this temple, and in three days I will raise it up (Jn 2.19). He had not stated that He would destroy *the* Temple, but that others would destroy "this temple", which was His body (Jn 2.21), and in three days He would raise it up; thus they were about to carry out what He had stated they would do. The very words that they twisted to form the basis of their lies were the words that they were having a part in fulfilling. Despite the fact that "many bare false witness against him, but their testimony did not agree" (Mk 14.56), and even as "every poisoned arrow of their carefully-provided perjuries fell harmless at His feet, as though blunted on the diamond shield of His innocence",[†] they determined to continue their foul plan to have Him put to death.

The trial of Stephen was marked by the same calumny. They "set up *false witnesses*, which said, This man ceaseth not to speak blasphemous words against this holy place, and the law: For we have heard him say, that this Jesus of Nazareth shall destroy this place, and shall change the customs which Moses delivered us" (Acts 6.13-14). Their vile methods were unchanged, for, even after perpetrating the greatest crime ever committed, there had been no repentance, only a continued hatred of the Lord Jesus and of all who followed Him. These legal religionists felt that they could break the Law with impunity and in self-righteous indignation stoop even to murder, a foul deed cloaked in judicial guise.

Verses 2-3: Impartiality in Judging Issues

Where the crowd seek to carry out that which is evil it is easy to follow, but it takes courage to stand out against the sinful designs of the multitude. Noah and his family did not follow the example set by the multitude, but Aaron, sadly, did in the matter of the golden calf (32.1-2). Not only, however, is the danger of following the views of the crowd highlighted, but also, in matters which are the subject of judicial action, the danger of giving an answer or testimony which is false in order to follow the popular view. It is the easy course to be carried away by the attitude of the majority.

Once again the most telling example is to be found at the trial of the Lord Jesus. Pontius Pilate heard the evidence and, well used as he was to sifting testimony to tease out the truth, he saw that there was nothing to warrant punishment of any kind. His verdict was, "I find no fault in this man" (Lk 23.4). On the second occasion when the Lord stood before him he again declared, "I, having examined him before you, have found no fault in this man touching those things whereof ye accuse him: No, nor yet Herod" (Lk 23.14-15), yet despite this he condemned Him to death. The cry of the many, "Away with this man, and release unto us Barabbas" (Lk 23.18; see Mt 27.20), together with the implied threat of the Jews to report to Caesar that he had released one who claimed to be King of the Jews (Jn 19.12), was enough to affect his judgment.

But if it was unrighteous to favour the crowd, it is equally so to countenance (to honour, show partiality to - 1921) the poor in his cause. Pleading on behalf of a man simply because of sympathy due to his poverty is not righteous. Knowing that this support would be available could encourage the poor to engage in unrighteous acts in the awareness that there would be sympathy for them. There must be impartiality in judgment, no showing of favour to the crowd, the rich, nor the poor, but dealing solely with the issues of the case.

Verses 4-5: Impartiality in Helping Others

Personal animosity must not interfere with doing that which is right. Should a man find an ox or an ass, which belongs to one who is his enemy (to be hostile - 341), wandering away from its pasture, he is required to return it to its owner. The same impartiality is to be exercised when a man sees one who hates him (to be hateful - 8130) with his ass which has collapsed under the weight of its burden. He must not forbear (to cease, leave alone - 2308), but is required to help his enemy loose the ass from its burden so that it can stand on its feet again.

The use of the noun "enemy" in the first case and the verb "hateth" in the second would appear to indicate that there was a different degree of antagonism. In the first it is a mutual feeling or even a feeling held only by the man who finds the wandering beast, but the second may indicate that the hatred is one-sided, on the part of the man whose ass is in trouble. In this way, all kinds of enmity are covered, leaving no excuse for withholding help when the opportunity arises.

This principle is set out by Paul when he writes, "Dearly beloved, avenge not yourselves, but rather give place unto wrath...Therefore, if thine enemy hunger feed him; if he thirst give him to drink: for in so doing thou shalt heap coals of fire on his head. Be not overcome of evil, but overcome evil with good" (Rom 12.19-21). Where issues arise it is not for the believer to seek to bring vengeance to bear on the one who is responsible for the wrong. Rather, when the opportunity arises, the believer should ensure that the other party is treated with kindness and courtesy. When the "enemy" is in need it must not be an occasion for rejoicing, but rather be seen as an occasion to display compassion, so that he will feel burning pain in his heart and conscience due to his hostility being met by love. The evil which has been done to individuals must not gain the mastery over them; rather they have to overcome evil with good.

Verse 6: Neglecting the Causes of the Poor

The situation here differs from that of v.3 where showing partiality to the poor is dealt with. The opposite is addressed now, where the case of the poor is ignored because they are poor and are regarded as being of little consequence. An example of this is the widow whose case the unjust judge refused to hear (Lk 18.1-8). The fact that she was a widow is emphasised because she had no one to take up her cause and, although it does not state that she was a poor widow, it is clear that in the eyes of the judge she was of little importance, her widowhood suggesting that she did not have great resources. In Psalm 72, which looks forward to the reign of the Lord Jesus in the Millennium, it is stated that "...he shall deliver the needy when he crieth; the poor also, and him that hath no helper. He shall spare the poor and needy, and shall save the souls of the needy" (vv.12-13). There will be no neglect of the poor and the afflicted when this King reigns in righteousness.

It is still possible for neglect to be shown towards the poor. James warns of this: "and ye look upon him who wears the splendid apparel, and say, Do thou sit here well, and say to the poor, Do thou stand there, or sit here under my footstool" (2.3, JND). The lack of influence, which is the lot of the poor, must not be a determining factor in how they are dealt with.

It is worth mentioning at this point that it was the custom of the Lord Jesus to give to the poor. When He said to Judas in the upper room, "That thou doest, do quickly" (Jn 13.27), some of the disciples thought that, as Judas kept the money, he was being instructed to buy food, to "give something the poor", and it was not thought strange that this should be done.

Verse 7: Avoiding any Evil Cause
It has been plainly stated that no false witness or evidence had to be given when issues were being judged, but a further danger is now dealt with which is equally serious - that of the possibility of refusing to give false evidence but still aiding the evil cause. Even to be seen to be associated with such a cause might give it credibility which otherwise it lacked, by virtue of the fact that a person known to be righteous appeared to be on agreeable terms with those who were pursuing a false claim. When such situations were encountered it was wise not to associate with the cause, nor to be seen to be close to it, but to make it quite clear, by remaining far from it, that there was no link of any kind with it and its perpetrators. The reference to slaying "the innocent and the righteous" indicates that judicial murder is in the hearts of those who promote the "false matter".

Verse 8: Bribery
In all areas of life bribery is an unrighteous practice. When issues have to be decided, acceptance of a bribe influences decisions, gives advantage to the rich over the poor, and makes it impossible for impartial judgments to be reached. Even if it were possible to reach a righteous judgment after the receipt of a gift, should the result be favourable to the one who bestowed the gift it would cause doubt to be cast on the judgment on the basis that the gift could have perverted the cause of justice. The human heart is such, however, that gifts do blind the eyes, even of the wise, to the truth by causing them to have favourable thoughts of the giver and "perverteth (distorts - 5557) the words of the righteous" so that they do not speak with unbiased integrity.

It was sad to record that the sons of Samuel stooped to this unrighteous practice as they "walked not in his ways, but turned aside after lucre, and took bribes, and perverted judgment" (1 Sam 8.3), resulting in the request of the people for a king. This seemingly reasonable petition was an act of rebellion against the Lord as it was the rejection, not of Samuel, but of God. The behaviour of Samuel's sons gave the people the excuse for which they were looking to express their wish to be ruled like the nations.

Verse 9: Oppressing the Stranger

It is possible for national prejudice to lead to the oppression of the foreigner, but this was forbidden on the grounds that Israel knew what it was to be a stranger, for they were strangers in the land of Egypt. They were aware of the inner feelings and sentiments of the stranger, they knew "the heart of a stranger" and were able to enter into the feelings of those who are far from home. With such a background there must be sympathy and not enmity for those who are in the same situation as they had been in Egypt. However, the main issue continues to be that of judgment, and judges had to guard against discrimination against those who were not of Israel.

One of the evidences of a heart touched by compassion is to learn from the experiences of life and to be able to sympathise with those who are enduring the same trouble and affliction. Paul shows this when writing his second Corinthian Epistle to believers who had gone through a time of trial and trouble, difficulties with which he could empathise because he had endured affliction. He had come to know the "God of all comfort; Who comforteth us in all our tribulation, that we may be able to comfort them which are in any trouble, by the comfort wherewith we ourselves are comforted of God" (2 Cor 1.3-4). Not only could he enter into their feelings but he could also comfort them in the way he himself had experienced comfort, something far more than mere human sympathy - deeper, greater and spiritual, a real help in the trial. Thus, as with Israel, he could enter into the heart feelings of those who were experiencing what he had himself endured.

Verses 10-12: Sabbaths

In addition to the keeping of the seventh day as a Sabbath, the seventh year was to be kept as a Sabbath year. During this year there was to be no sowing or reaping, with the land left to rest, and any crops which grew by themselves left for the poor. This law did not only apply to the field but also to the vineyard and to the olive trees. Leviticus 25 adds to the instruction given for this year by stating that even the grapes which might grow on untended vines had to be left ungathered and, with the crops which had grown by themselves, be left for the servant, the maid servant, the hired servant, or the stranger.

Clearly, this must have been beneficial for the land but it also brought to the attention of Israel the significance of the principle of the Sabbath day; that law entailed working and then rest as a result. The weekly observation of this could become simply a routine, the reason for which was lost or little considered. This seventh year was a change of a very significant nature to that routine, emphasising the Sabbath truth to the nation. Note also that during this "sabbath of rest" Israel would have time to contemplate the goodness of God which they had enjoyed, affording them the opportunity of deepening their appreciation of His kindness and His care.

The commencement day of the Sabbath year could not have been in the month Abib, the first month of the religious year, as sowing did not take place at that time, which was a period of reaping, first of the barley harvest and then of the wheat harvest. Sowing commenced in the eighth month, after the Feast of Tabernacles which marked the end of the season of the Feasts of Jehovah (see Appendix 2), and at that time the Sabbath year would start. Its climax, therefore, was the Feast of Tabernacles in the next year, and it was at that feast, every seven years, that the Law was read to the people as they gathered to the place where the Lord had chosen to place His name. The purpose of this was made known to the people, that they might "hear, and that they may learn, and fear the Lord your God, and observe to do all the words of this law" (Deut 31.12). On this solemn note of the reading of the Law, the Sabbath year ended.

It is a sorrowful fact that there is no record of Israel observing this law, and the neglect of it was one of the causes of the captivity of the nation. It was foretold by Moses, that should disobedience mark them and, as a consequence, should they fail to keep this year, "then shall the land enjoy her sabbaths, as long as it lieth desolate…even then shall the land rest, and enjoy her sabbaths" (Lev 26.34). They were carried away captive to Babylon "until the land had enjoyed her sabbaths: for as long as she lay desolate she kept sabbath, to fulfil threescore and ten years" (2 Chr 36.21). As Israel was in captivity for seventy years she had failed to keep the seventh year as a Sabbath year for 490 years. The Sabbath year was a great blessing to the nation and it was vitally significant.

What has been written above about this Sabbath can be summarised.

First, it lasted for one year and not for one day; the longer duration suggests its importance.

Second, its relative rarity compared with the seventh day suggests that it was something less "ordinary" and very precious.

What follows in v.12 is a repeat of the law regarding the Sabbath day, and it may be enquired why this is raised again. It brought the weekly Sabbath back to mind as the seventh year was dealt with in a way which emphasised that these two Sabbath periods were equally important, and that, even during the seventh year, the seventh day had still to be kept. It did not take the place of the Sabbath day by freeing the people from the need to remember the seventh day. That is why the weekly Sabbath is confirmed in v.12. What must not be lost sight of is that the seventh day was one of rest for the people, but the seventh year was one of rest for the land. This teaches, in the former, that the people can look forward to rest as a nation, and, in the latter, that the land can look forward to the time when the groaning creation is delivered (Rom 8.22), and with the Lord, the people and the land in harmony and still productive, will be at rest.

Verse 13: Be Circumspect

From this point to the end of the chapter, Israel is warned against going after other gods:

1. "Make no mention of the name of other gods, neither let it be heard out of thy mouth" (v.13).

2. "Thou shalt not bow down to their gods, nor serve them" (v.24).

3. "Thou shalt make no covenant with them, nor with their gods" (v.32).

Due to this danger, they are instructed on the resources that they possess to ensure that such a failure does not take place. These resources are:

1. The three pilgrim feasts when the mutual fellowship enjoyed will strengthen them in obedience.

2. The Angel who will go before them.

3. The promise of the Lord that their obedience guaranteed that their needs would be met and that the enemy would be driven out of the land so that they would enjoy the rich provision of Canaan.

But first, in everything they were to be circumspect (to guard, to exercise care over, to watch - 8104). The thought is that of keeping faithfully to what they had been taught, always vigilant lest they disobey: "And ye shall be on your guard as to everything that I have said unto you" (JND). In order to help towards this end they were not to mention the name of other gods, nor to speak of them. In the former, the instruction was that they had to ignore them completely and count them unworthy even of a mention of their name. To speak of them was to make them the subject of conversation and give them a place in their interests. To treat them as objects of curiosity or to dwell on them in any way was not for their good and could lead to greater entanglement. Such a warning is still relevant today. Whereas an understanding of some matters can be helpful in our testimony to others, the religions and cults of the world should not be a source of undue interest to God's people. Better to spend the time positively getting to know the teaching of the Bible in order to be better equipped to answer those who purvey their error.

Verses 14-17: The Three Pilgrim Feasts

The feasts which are mentioned here are three of the Feasts of Jehovah, teaching regarding which is given in Leviticus 23. Details of these feasts and the dates on which they were to be held can be found in Appendix 2. The three to which reference is made are those in which the males were to "appear before the Lord God" by travelling to the Tabernacle at Shiloh and later, to the Temple in Jerusalem. They were the Feast of Unleavened Bread, which was held from the 15th to the 21st day of the first month of the year, the Feast of Weeks (Pentecost), which was held 50 days after the Sabbath of the Feast of Unleavened Bread, and the Feast of Tabernacles (Booths), which was held from the 15th to the 22nd day of the 7th month. In Leviticus 23 three different nouns are used to describe the seven feasts, with the word from a root meaning, "to celebrate" (translated "feast" in the singular - 2282) being applied in this chapter to these three feasts, indicating that these were times of joy, celebration and gladness.

The purpose of these feasts was to commemorate the past, to be thankful to the Lord for redemption (see, for instance, Leviticus 23.42-43), and for the harvests: the barley harvest at the time of Unleavened Bread, the wheat harvest at Pentecost and all the other harvests at Tabernacles. A second reason was social in that mutual fellowship could be enjoyed, leading possibly to marriage for the young, but certainly creating bonds of friendship. Their dealings with God and all His goodness to them over the past years could be spoken of and shared, encouraging greater trust in Him. There was also a typical reason, in that the feasts were an annual chart of the nation's past and future history.

To encourage their attendance, lest there be any fear of leaving home and family behind, the Lord guaranteed that no harm would come to them while they were away: "Neither shall any man desire thy land, when thou shalt go up to appear before the Lord thy God thrice in the year" (34.24).

The reason for these instructions appearing here is, as has been noted, the encouragement which the journey to the Tabernacle or Temple would be to the people. By these means they would be strengthened, and the unique separated life of Israel be more appreciated. Gathering with others of like mind is still today a benefit to believers, with encouragement coming from the mutual sharing of the things of God. "Not forsaking the assembling of ourselves together, as the manner of some is; but exhorting one another: and so much the more, as ye see the day approaching" (Heb 10.25), is an exhortation ignored by those who live an isolated spiritual life. Attendance at the regular gatherings of the assembly is not an optional extra, it is vital for spiritual growth and stability.

Verses 18-19: Instruction Regarding Sacrifice

These two verses deal with the Passover, the requirements for the Feast of Unleavened Bread and the offering of firstfruits. The detailed instructions regarding the first two of these feasts have been dealt with in chs.12-13 but are re-stated here to emphasise that, despite all that had taken place since the departure from Egypt, and all that had been given in the Law, these initial instructions still stood and had not been diminished. Instruction for handling the firstfruits follows, although reference to it has been made (22.29; 23.16). To that which had already been given a further command is stated: "Thou shalt not seethe a kid in his mother's milk". This cannot refer to the Passover as the sacrificial animal, if it were a goat, had to be a kid of one year, and at that time it would have been weaned from its mother. The reference not only was general in nature, but in particular was concerned with the offering of the male firstborn of the beasts (13.11-13). This had not to take place before the weaning of the young, making it possible to cook it in his mother's milk, with the resultant distress to the mother in losing her young and the physical discomfort which she would suffer in being a mother in milk with no suckling. Such a meal was regarded as a delicacy, but the compassion of the Lord for the animal creation forbade such a practice.

Verses 20-23: The Promise to Bring them into the Land

The Angel to whom reference is made here is Jehovah as is ascertained from the following facts.

1. He had authority vested in Him and had to be obeyed. He would not bring to them the word of the Lord as it had been delivered to Him; it was His word and His authority, not derived from another.

2. Disobedience would provoke Him, so it was His response to sin which was vital to consider.

3. He had the authority to pardon transgressions.

4. "His voice" was heard when the Lord spoke (v.22).

These facts confirm the conclusion of Keil & Delitzsch: "The name of Jehovah was in this angel (v.21), that is to say, Jehovah revealed Himself in him; and hence he is called in ch.33.15,16, the face of Jehovah, because the essential nature of Jehovah was manifested in him. This angel was not a created spirit, therefore, but the manifestation of Jehovah Himself, who went before them in the pillar of cloud and fire, to guide them and to defend them".

The Angel will go before them, guiding them to their destination. What comfort they could derive from this. The Lord who delivered them will not direct them from a distance nor will He remain aloof in heaven while they wend their way through an inhospitable wilderness. He will be with them, going before them, so that the pathway He has prepared, into what for them (but not for Moses) is unknown territory, but selected by Him and passed through by Him before it is trodden by their feet, may be safe. As with Israel, so today He goes ahead of His people, mapping out the road and granting them the comfort of His presence.

Not only must He be followed, however, He must be obeyed. Their past record on this account was not good. They had disobeyed and they had provoked the Lord, but their future prosperity depended on having learned the lesson and obeying His voice. Obedience lies at the heart of blessing, and the rebellious soul loses because transgressions are not merely overlooked; under Law the perpetrator must pay the price of lawless actions.

Obedience to Him will bring protection from enemies with the Lord taking the place as the enemy of those who are enemies of Israel. By this means they will be brought into the land long promised to them. Their own strength and prowess in arms will not accomplish this; it will be by the Lord alone working with them and through them. So they could trust the promise made. The Angel will "bring thee into the place which I have prepared" (v.20), and "mine Angel shall go before thee, and bring thee in" (v.23). The land to which they were travelling had been prepared for them; their part simply was to obey!

Verses 24-30: The Promise to Give them the Land

But not only was the promise made to bring them to the land of Canaan, a further promise was made to give them the land.

The overthrow of their enemies

The first element in this paragraph of promise is that the nations who at that time possessed the land would be overthrown, provided Israel did not bow down before the gods worshipped by these nations. This was in keeping with the second commandment (20.5), but added that the idols of the heathen had to be broken down and utterly destroyed, and the deeds and practices of the idol worshippers had not to become part of the life of the redeemed people. Their lives were to be different from those of the nations, a principle which still is relevant today. In the Epistle to the Romans, Paul commences that section of the letter in which he is dealing with the practical effects of salvation on the conduct of believers with a clear call to be different from the world: "And be not conformed to this world: but be ye transformed by the renewing of your mind, that ye may prove what is that good, and acceptable, and perfect, will of God (Rom 12.2).

Blessing for obedience

As a result of refusing to bow down to the idols of the land, Israel would be able to serve the Lord, for this could not be done if idols were the objects of veneration. The consequences of obedience are seen in the threefold blessing that is now declared.

There will be fullness of provision with resultant bounty for all. The former and the latter rains will be given with the harvests of barley and wheat and the fruits of the land, all liberally given for the satisfaction of an obedient people. The blessings that are given today are of a spiritual character, although it is true that the Lord meets the temporal needs of His people, and submission to Him enables us to enjoy His provision all the more.

The second blessing is one of fullness of health, as sickness was to be taken away from the midst of Israel, resulting in no shortening of life but a full span for the enjoyment of the land. The promise of long life in the land had been made, in the fifth commandment, to those who honoured their father and their mother, but now the nation is promised that they will be free from physical ailments and illnesses if they obey the Lord. Mention must also be made of the promise of the Lord that was given at Marah, that if they "diligently hearken to the voice of the Lord thy God, and wilt do that which is right in his sight, and wilt give ear to his commandments, and keep all his statutes, I will put none of these diseases upon thee, which I brought upon the Egyptians: for I am the Lord that healeth thee" (15.26). With this promise, He revealed Himself as "Jehovah Ropheka" - the Lord who healeth.

The third blessing concerns fullness of life. Nothing would cast its young nor would there be any barrenness in the land, therefore there would be no life withheld or terminated before birth, nor would there be any lives terminated before they had run their course. This is not another way of stating that none would die of illness or disease, it is much more embracive, for life can also be terminated early by other causes, including accident or violence.

An obedient people in the land, therefore, need have no fear of famine, disease, or shortened lives. The blessings of a beneficent God were available to an obedient, God-fearing people. It is sad to record that these blessings were never enjoyed, as the people rebelled against the word of God and with stubborn self-will pursued a path of sin and disobedience. Famines took place, including those in the days of the judges (Ruth 1.1), during the reign of David (2 Sam 21.1), and during the ministry of Elijah (1 Kings 18.2); the people were also stricken by illness.

Their enemies driven out of the land

The nations who sought to oppose Israel in the conquest of Canaan would be driven out before them. They would be gripped by fear, not the fear of the armies of Israel, but the fear of Jehovah, and as a result they would turn their backs on Israel, in the sense that they would flee from them. The Israelites were not to concentrate their energies on training for military struggle, they were not to cultivate the arts of war or determine to be known as a nation of warriors, but rather they were to concentrate all their energies on serving the Lord and He would fit them for every situation they would meet. When met by the foe they need not fear, for these nations whose lands they had to possess would be destroyed before them and those who met them on the field of battle would turn and flee. What a promise of overcoming power!

The dealings of Israel with Jericho are an example of the Lord honouring this promise (Josh 6.1-27). It is clear that the fear of the Lord had gripped the heart of Rahab the harlot and had led to the happy result of her trusting the God of Israel. She stated that "we have heard how the Lord dried up the water of the Red Sea for you, when ye came out of Egypt; and what ye did unto the two kings of the Amorites, that were on the other side Jordan" (Josh 2.10); faith had come by hearing, as she heard and believed. In this way He had sent His fear before them and prepared Jericho for the arrival of the spies and the ultimate destruction of the city. It should be noted in passing that Rahab referred to events that took place at the beginning of Israel's journey out of Egypt and almost at its end. There is no reference to anything that had taken place during the long years after they refused to enter the land and before they commenced their journey again. These were the years during which there is recorded only one sad event, the rebellion of Korah (Num 16); during this barren time there was no testimony from Israel making its mark with the world, but when they again became overcomers Jericho heard and Jericho feared, but only one woman and her family believed.

When Israel approached the city, the Ark displayed to the enemies of Israel did not bring a change of heart in the inhabitants, and this resulted in the complete overthrow of Jericho and its people by the Lord. As the Israelites entered the city, the battle was already won. Sad to record, the disobedience of Achan resulted in a very different situation when Ai was attacked; the enemy did not turn their backs on Israel, Israel turned their backs on the enemy (Josh 7.1-26). After the judgment of the sin in the Valley of Achor, the enemy was engaged once more and they fled, but Israel had much to do to bring this about. The right to win a victory with calm dependence on the Lord alone, such as had been their experience at Jericho, had been forfeited.

In order to prepare the nations for the coming of the Israelites the Lord promised to send hornets in front of them to drive out their enemies. It may be that the reference is to literal hornets, but it is more likely that the reference is to God-given circumstances; miraculous intervention, and fears within, which drained from the enemy any desire to continue further resistance against Israel. This is confirmed by the words of Joshua when he stated that God had sent hornets before them when they defeated the two kings of the Amorites. The account of those victories contains no references to swarms of hornets going before Israel, although Joshua asserts (Josh 24.12) that God had sent the hornet before them referring to the miraculous defeat of the enemy (Josh 10.1-14). Hornets, when they attack, come in swarms and are to be found everywhere, with little relief being possible. No relief would be allowed these heathen people until they were driven out, leaving room for Israel to enter. This would not take place at one time; the nations would gradually leave the land open, but only when Israel was numerous enough to occupy and cultivate the abandoned territory, ensuring that their resources would never be overstretched. No army had ever such power or resources with which to enter and conquer a land.

The battle to possess Canaan is a picture of the battle fought by Christians today as they seek to possess all that is in the heavenlies for their enjoyment. The enemy is not flesh and blood but principalities and powers, the rulers of the darkness of this age, the powers of spiritual wickedness in high places (Eph 6.12). The battle is individual and the weapons at the disposal of the Christian warrior are more than sufficient for the task - the whole armour of God: truth, the breastplate of righteousness, the gospel of peace, the shield of faith, the helmet of salvation, and the sword of the Spirit. God has provided all these weapons and, if used, they are a guarantee of victory in the struggle.

Verse 31a: The Boundaries of the Land

These are set from the Red Sea to the sea of the Philistines and from the desert to the river. The original promise given to Abraham was of a land that would stretch "from the river of Egypt unto the great river, the river Euphrates" (Gen 15.18), and this is now confirmed. The border on the west was to comprise the Red Sea and the sea of the Philistines, which is the Mediterranean Sea, with the eastern border set as the Arabian Desert and the River Euphrates. These borders were not possessed in the days of Joshua as Israel's failure, caused by their sin, was marked by their inability to drive out all the inhabitants of the land (Judg 1.21-36). It was not until the reign of Solomon that the extent of the kingdom reached these bounds, for this mighty monarch ruled "from the river unto the land of the Philistines, and unto the border of Egypt" (1 Kings 4.21), and the kingdoms within those borders served Solomon all the days of his life. The Lord had promised them a "good land and a large" (3.8), and such extensive borders were the fulfilment of the promise.

It is sobering to consider that, despite all the promises of God to give them this land, the negative report of ten of the spies was accepted and that generation lost the right to enter the land, the opportunity to learn what it was to be overcomers, and the enjoyment of the liberal bounty of their God. Sin, as always, robbed them of the blessings prepared for them.

Verses 31b-33: Relationships with the Inhabitants of the Land

Great care had to be taken when dealing with the inhabitants of Canaan. That they were to be driven out was the purpose of God, but as they would be driven out "little by little" (v.30) there would be some years when both Israel and some of the Canaanite nations would share the land until they were dispossessed. Danger lay in the potential to form alliances and friendships which would compromise the separation of the nation and make the eventual dispossession of these people difficult because of close relationships that had been formed. No covenant had to be made with them nor their gods, and they were not to be given leave to dwell in the portions of land that were possessed by Israel. The need to remain separate from the world is emphasised to the saints in Corinth as Paul exhorts them: "Be ye not unequally yoked together with unbelievers" (2 Cor 6.14). When there is such a yoke it forces the Christian into the situation where it is not possible to act independently of the other in the yoke. It has also to be recognised that should the unbelieving party act unrighteously, the believer is partly responsible because the unbeliever is acting on behalf of both parties in the yoke.

Close relationships with the world, even if they are not based on an unequal yoke are dangerous. "Evil communications corrupt good manners" (1 Cor 15.33) is a truth of which all believers must be aware. To associate with unbelievers in sharing their pleasures and entering into their way of life is harmful to the Christian who must rather "Awake to righteousness, and sin not" (1 Cor 15.34).

The later sad record shows that Israel failed in this. In Judges 1 we find that the Canaanites were not driven out completely and continued to dwell with Israel. The Jebusites remained with the Benjamites (v.21), the Canaanites in the land possessed by the tribe of Manasseh (v.27), many others were made to be servants of Israel (v.28), and the tribes of

Ephraim, Zebulun, Asher and Napthtali are all recorded as failing to drive out the Canaanites. The result of this was that in place of the Lord sending His "hornets" amongst the enemies of Israel they were a thorn in the side of the people and their gods became a snare to the nation whose God was the Lord (Judg 2.3). Little wonder that the place where they heard the words of censure from the angel of the Lord was named "Bochim" (weeping - 1066). Judges 2 records that because of their disobedience they would became subject to poverty (v.14), powerlessness (v.14), and distress (v.15). The warning to the believer is that what appears to be an attractive proposition from the world must be considered prayerfully to ensure that there is no unequal yoke involved, nor is there any involvement in the world which would adversely affect Christian life and testimony. Should there be, the Lord will honour those who resolutely say, "No!", and leave the consequences with Him. Israel's actions reduced them from being a powerful people displaying the might of God working for them to being weak and powerless, and eventually enduring periods of subjugation by the heathen. Links with the world never strengthen God's people; weakness is always the result.

Notes

1 F. W. Farrar, *The Life of Christ*, ch.58.

EXODUS 24

The Ratification of the Covenant

At this point, the covenant, the requirements of which had been laid before Israel, is ratified. It is formally confirmed with acceptance of its terms, after which there begins that section of the book giving the instructions for the building of the Tabernacle and the institution of the sacrifices and rites forming part of the covenant. The solemnity of the ratification is clearly indicated by the events of the confirmation process.

Verses 1-2: The Command to Go up the Mount

In 20.21 it is recorded that Moses "drew near unto the thick darkness where God was", and there is no record of him having come down from the mount since then. The words, "Come up" (v.1), are linked with the previous chapter and form part of that address. Although spoken on the mount, Moses is told to "Come up unto the Lord". It was implied in this command that Moses had first to go down the mount and then return with Nadab and Abihu, the two eldest sons of Aaron, and seventy of the elders of Israel. Moses was to come near to the Lord, but those who accompanied him were not to draw nigh, but worship at a distance, and the people were to remain in the valley away from the mount. As in ch.19, it is being emphasised that the Law did not bring the people near to God, but rather introduced distance.

It is remarkable that Nadab and Abihu shared the privilege of going up the mount, even if it did not involve drawing near to the Lord. This was no doubt due to their being the eldest sons. These were the men who later would sin against the Lord in offering strange fire in the Tabernacle, a sorry event that took place immediately after the consecration of the priests; an attempt by Satan to destroy the Tabernacle worship before it began (Lev 10). These honoured men, of an honoured family, from an honoured tribe chosen out of an honoured people showed that such heights of dignity did not cleanse their hearts, as they manifested the darkness and obdurate sinfulness of the human condition. These guardians of the Law broke the Law, and their memory is forever a byword for sinful folly in the face of the goodness of God. Yet at this point all that lay ahead was known only to God who called them up to worship. Their presence on this hallowed occasion ensured that they could not argue later that they were denied the privileges and dignity of their position, even although at this time they had not been consecrated priests, nor had an indication been given that they would be so.

What a warning from the record of such men as this. Privilege, dignity, and blessing may be enjoyed to the full, but this does not prevent failure and sin when the flesh takes control of actions. Such a man as Abraham told a lie, David committed adultery, the honour of being a servant of a man of God did not prevent the covetous heart of Gehazi destroying his usefulness in service, and even Peter failed under the pressure of questioning as he warmed himself at the fire during the dark night before the day of Christ's death. The stark admonition must be heeded: "Let him that thinketh he standeth take heed lest he fall" (1 Cor 10.12).

Verse 3: Bringing the Terms of the Covenant to the People

Before the covenant was ratified all the words of the Lord were told to Israel, ensuring that there was no misunderstanding as to its terms. It has already been noted that the people had declared their confidence in their ability to obey all that the Lord had spoken (19.8), but after the terms had been laid down in some detail they were brought before them again so that they had a full understanding of the covenant into which they were entering. Never in the future would they be able to allege that they were kept in ignorance of the demands of the Law, as, without any dissenting voices they claimed again that they would carry out in full all that the Lord had given to Moses. Their behaviour since they left Egypt should have told them otherwise, but such was their ignorance of the sinful condition of their hearts that they considered themselves capable of complete obedience to a holy Law. Moses wrote all the words of the Law so that Israel would always have them in their possession, the written word ensuring that these Laws were not passed on to succeeding generations in a watered-down form. This was the book of the covenant from which he would later read to the people.

Verse 4-6: Sacrificing on the Altar

The next morning Moses built an altar under the hill (note JND - "built an altar under the mountain"), at the foot of Sinai. This altar would be made of earth or of unhewn stone according to the instruction given (20.24-26), and beside it were constructed twelve pillars representing the twelve tribes of Israel. Moses chose certain young men, and it has been suggested that these were the firstborn of their families on whom the dignity of family priesthood would ultimately fall in the era before the giving of the Law. It is not possible, however, to determine if this were so, and it is better simply to accept that all that is told of these men is that they were young. They were sent to offer on the altar burnt offerings and peace offerings, for it was vital, in order that the covenant be ratified, that blood must be shed (see Heb 9.18). The burnt offerings were for the acceptance of the people, and the peace offerings to thank God for communion with Him. Half the blood of the sacrifices was placed in basins and half sprinkled on the altar, indicating that the God to whom the sacrifices were offered was one of the parties in the covenant.

Verse 7: Reading the Book

The book of the covenant, that which had been written by Moses, was now read to the people. Time was being allowed them to consider the great issues the covenant presented to them, and that not once, but on two occasions, to the first of which reference has already been made (19.7,8). They are not being rushed into this without due time for reflection.

Verse 8: Sprinkling the Blood

The writer of the Epistle to the Hebrews adds details which are not given here, namely that water, scarlet wool, and hyssop were added, and that the blood was also sprinkled on the book of the covenant (Heb 9.19). It must not be thought that this indicates a deficiency in the Exodus record or an unwarranted addition in that of the Hebrews. Both these records are accurate accounts. The Hebrew record does not contradict that of Exodus but adds further detail that is of interest to the readers of the epistle. The additional features, water, scarlet wool, and hyssop, are also mentioned in the cleansing of the leper (Lev 14.1-7), and in the slaying of the red heifer outside the Camp (Num 19.6). Hyssop was also used to place the blood on the lintel and two doorposts at the first Passover (12.22).

The sprinkling of the blood upon the altar, the book, and the people is of deepest significance. It has already been observed that the sprinkling of the blood on the altar indicated that God was a party to the covenant, and the sprinkling of it on the people had the same significance, marking them as being the other party. The sprinkling on the book solemnised the terms of the covenant as being binding upon both parties, the use of the blood of the slain indicating that death was the penalty for transgression of the Law. There could be no claim of ignorance now as to what constituted sin, a truth confirmed by Paul: "I had not known sin, but by the law: for I had not known lust, except the law had said, Thou shalt not covet" (Rom 7.7). Dennett sums this up succinctly: "Such was the solemn position into which, by their own consent, they had been brought. They undertook to obey under the penalty of death. Well therefore might the apostle say, 'As many as are of the works of the law are under the curse' (Gal 3.10). It is the same now in principle with all who accept the ground of the law as the way of life, all who are trusting to their own works as the condition of blessing. They know it not, but they are really binding upon their shoulders the curse of the law".

But it is the happy occupation of saints today to look beyond the curse of the Law and be thankful for Him who bore that curse in their place, as is stated, again by the apostle, "Christ hath redeemed us from the curse of the law, being made a curse for us: for it is written, Cursed is every one that hangeth on a tree" (Gal 3.13). The demands of the Law were righteous, and with the giving of the new covenant these demands have not been ignored or set aside: they have been kept and One has died because the Law has been broken, not by Him but by others. The righteous claims of the Law have, therefore, been met in the Lord Jesus and His death on the Cross. The Law has been satisfied, and the sprinkling of the blood on the day when this covenant was ratified looked forward to that day when He died under the curse of the Law. None of what was symbolised here could be accomplished by the Law, as only in Christ could the demands of God be satisfied.

Peter makes reference to the sprinkling of blood in his First Epistle where he writes, "Elect according to the foreknowledge of God the Father, through sanctification of the Spirit, unto obedience and sprinkling of the blood of Jesus Christ" (1 Pet 1.2). How different this is, however, to the blood that was sprinkled by Moses. This sacrifice of which Peter speaks was made by One dying for sin. The sprinkling of the blood represents the power and value of the sacrifice applied. Only when the blood is sprinkled does the individual come into the good of the sacrifice. Under the Law the blood that was sprinkled linked them with a sacrifice that had to be repeated continually and that could not take away sin. Today the Christian is linked with a sacrifice that had to be offered only once and is capable of dealing with sin for all eternity.

The other additional features noted in Hebrews also have significance. The water speaks of the need of cleansing, and the scarlet wool of the depth of the sin that has to be cleansed. Isaiah expresses this: "Come now, and let us reason together, saith the Lord: though your sins be as *scarlet*, they shall be as white as snow; though they be red like crimson, they shall be as wool" (1.18). Both the water and hyssop are referred to by the Psalmist as cleansing agents: "Purge me with hyssop, and I shall be clean: wash me, and I shall be whiter than snow (51.7). But the hyssop was also regarded as the most insignificant and lowly of plants. Solomon spoke of it as such: "And he spake of trees, from the cedar tree that is in Lebanon even unto the hyssop that springeth out of the wall" (1 Kings 4.33). The cleansing and purging symbolised by this lowly plant speaks of the lowliness of the Lord Jesus and the cleansing He brought to others by his willingness to make Himself "of no reputation", and become "obedient unto death, even the death of the cross" (Phil 2.7-8).

The act of ratification is now over, sealed by the words of Moses: "Behold the blood of the covenant, which the Lord hath made with you concerning all these words". With ratification, the covenant is now in force, both parties having agreed to its terms; Israel is now under Law.

Verses 9-11: Communion on the Mountain

Now Moses, Aaron, Nadab, Abihu, and the seventy of the elders of Israel ascend the mount. Later Moses would be asked to go up alone (v.12), but now the favoured group with Moses see the God of Israel and partake of the covenant meal that followed the covenant coming into force. God revealed Himself later to Israel in the cloud, the glory that rose from the Holiest of All in the Tabernacle, but here this favoured number are allowed to see His glory in whatever form He determined to reveal Himself. The pavement or paved work that was under His feet was like a sapphire stone is in its brilliance, and was of a purity that was not of earth. Such a scene was solemn yet, despite the fear which the people had of the presence of God (20.19; Deut 5.25), none of these nobles was struck down; rather they took part in the covenant meal of communion. What glory and privileges they enjoyed in that elevated place, a pledge, surely, of what they would have enjoyed as a nation if they had kept the covenant.

The words of Moses at the beginning of v.12 indicate that the group returned down the mountain at the conclusion of the meal. A casual reading may indicate that Moses merely left the group where they had been dining and went further, but when he descended the mountain with Joshua, at the end of the lengthy audience with the Lord, Aaron is with the people in the Camp (32.1), confirming that he had returned at this stage.

Verses 12-18: Moses Summoned up the Mountain

The summons to Moses is for the purpose of giving him the two tables of stone on which the Law and Commandments were written, those that had to be taught to Israel. Moses is seen here as the mediator of this covenant, showing that although others had enjoyed the glory of the Lord and the covenant meal, Moses alone held the favoured mediatorial position. Korah and his accomplices (Num 16), and even Miriam and Aaron (Num 12), attacked this position in later days, jealousy consuming them, but here all can see that he alone has the right to go up the mount to receive the tables.

The words of the Law had already been given, but the tables of stone,[†] on which were now to be written the Ten Commandments (34.28) with the finger of God (31.18), were destroyed by Moses (32.19) when he saw the idolatry of the people, knowing that to bring them into the Camp would result in death for the guilty. Moses was then told to hew another two tables of stone and take them back up the mount for the Law to be written once again. These tables, the tables of the covenant (Heb 9.4), contained the Ten Commandments, the foundation principles of the Law, the extended details of which had been written by Moses in the book of the covenant (24.4,7).

Joshua was the "minister" or attendant of Moses, an honoured position, and not one of abject servility. Doubtless he was called to ascend the mount with Moses because he would, in later years, lead the Children of Israel into Canaan. Aaron and Hur were charged with the responsibility of administering the people during the absence of Moses. On the mount, Moses and Joshua waited for six days, first, because God's presence required preparation and must not be regarded lightly, and second, because the people had declared that they would obey the covenant and earn the rest which such obedience would bring, the principle seen in the six days of work and the seventh of rest. This seventh day was, therefore, a day of great privilege, as would be every seventh day, should the Law be kept.

Only Moses went into the midst of the cloud, Joshua was left behind on a lower part of the mountain. He remained there for a period of forty days.

This period of time is significant in Scripture; there are other examples.

1. At the time of the Flood the rains fell for a period of forty days and forty nights (Gen 7.4,12).

2. The Children of Israel were in the wilderness for forty years (Ex 16.35).

3. The spies who searched out the land did so for forty days (Num 13.25).

4. The Philistines, with their champion Goliath, drew near to the armies of Israel in the Valley of Elah for forty days (1 Sam 17.16).

5. Elijah went for forty days and nights journeying to Horeb in the strength given by the food prepared by the angel (1 Kings 19.8).

6. Ezekiel had to lie on his right side to bear the iniquity of the house of Judah for forty days (Ezek 4.6).

7. Jonah entered the city of Nineveh preaching the message that "Yet forty days, and Nineveh shall be overthrown" (Jonah 3.4).

8. The Lord Jesus was in the wilderness tempted of the devil for forty days and nights (Mt 4.2; Mk 1.13; Lk 4.2).

9. After His resurrection the Lord Jesus "shewed himself alive after his passion by many infallible proofs, being seen of them forty days" (Acts 1.2).

Forty, therefore, is the number which represents testing even in the temptation of the Lord Jesus, not in the sense that there was any possibility of His failing the test, but in the sense that He learned by experience what it was to be tested by the tempting of the Devil.

The period of the Law commenced with a man in the favoured position of being alone in the presence of God and enjoying that for forty days and nights, during which time he partook of no food or drink (Deut 9.9). But, as he was communing with God those forty days, the hearts of the people turned away from their God (32.1) and they sinned grievously in making the golden calf, manifestly unable to keep the covenant into which they had willingly entered. At the commencement of the public ministry of the Lord Jesus, He was also alone for forty days at the end of which He was hungry (Lk 4.1-2), but on this occasion it was with the devil, a great contrast to that which Moses enjoyed. In the wilderness, in the most unfavourable circumstances, He showed decisively that His work would not be marred by sin at its very beginning, and proved that at no time would He, in future days, fall to the wiles of the devil. It was impossible for Him so to do! Here is the contrast - on one hand, a people who had entered a covenant which they could not keep, and which they would break right at the beginning of its existence, and, on the other, a Man who had come on behalf of others, and who would overcome the Adversary; two forty day periods of contrast, one marked by failure and the other by triumph.

Moses had seen a fire burn in the midst of a bush and the bush was not consumed (3.2); he had ascended to the mount to which the Lord had descended in fire (19.18), and now he does so again. This was the third time the Lord had spoken to Him from the fire, and what revelation was about to be given!

Notes

12 See note on the tables of stone at the beginning of ch.20.

EXODUS 25.1-9

The Tabernacle[1]

Introduction

During this period of forty days and forty nights on the mountain, the Lord also revealed to Moses the pattern of the Tabernacle which would be central to the life of Israel up to the days of David the King, despite a gap of over one hundred years during which the Ark was absent,[2] after which, in the reign of Solomon, the Temple took its place. Associated with the Tabernacle there was a priesthood and a sacrificial system which was divinely appointed, and any who regard this as merely a historical development which has been superseded and has no value for today are robbed of much that is essential divine truth.

The purpose of the Tabernacle has been long recognised. Keil & Delitzsch state: "To give a definite external form to the covenant concluded with His people, and construct a visible bond of fellowship in which He might manifest Himself to the people and they might draw near to Him as their God, Jehovah told Moses that the Israelites were to erect Him a sanctuary, that He might dwell in the midst of them. The construction and arrangement of this sanctuary were determined in all respects by God Himself, who showed to Moses, when upon the mountain, a pattern of the dwelling and its furniture, and prescribed with great minuteness both the form and materials of all the different parts of the sanctuary and all the things required for the sacred service. If the sanctuary was to answer its purpose, the erection of it could not be left to the inventive faculty of any man whatever, but must proceed from Him, who was there to manifest Himself to the nation, as the Holy One, in righteousness and grace".

The Importance of the Tabernacle

Over fifty chapters in the Bible are devoted to the Tabernacle; thirteen in Exodus (chs.25-31; 35-40); seventeen in Leviticus (chs.1-10; 16-17; 21-24; 27); thirteen in Numbers (chs.1-9; 16-19), three in Deuteronomy (chs.16-18) and it is central to eight in Hebrews (chs.3-10). This far exceeds the chapters dealing with the Temple and reflects the value of the teaching which is associated with the Tabernacle. So great is this truth that although the creation of the universe is covered in two chapters in Genesis, the erection of the Tabernacle occupies a large part of the book of Exodus. The great purpose of God centred on redemption.

It was the dwelling place of Jehovah

"Let them make me a sanctuary; that I may dwell among them" (v.8), was the glorious instruction which fell on the ears of Moses as the God who had delivered them from the sore bondage of Egypt declared that His desire was to dwell in their midst. On more than one further occasion the Ark is stated to be the dwelling place of the Lord, He who dwelt between the cherubims which were upon the Mercy Seat in the Holy Place. Hezekiah spoke of it as such as he "prayed before the Lord, and said, O Lord God of Israel, which dwellest *between the cherubims*, thou art the God, even thou alone, of all the kingdoms of the earth; thou hast made heaven and earth (2 Kings 19.15). The Psalmist also writes of Him who "dwelleth between the cherubims" (Ps 80.1).[3] It is true that God cannot be contained in a temple made with hands (Acts 7.48), but He decreed that He would meet with His people in this Sanctuary, which did take place when the High Priest entered the Holiest of All as the representative of the people, so He declared that He would dwell there in the midst of His people. God is omnipresent, but in grace He was willing to make the Holiest of All the audience chamber where He was to be found.

It is vital to note that there was no image of God in the Tabernacle. Heathen temples all contained their images, man made, and purporting to be the god worshipped there. The nonsense linked with idols and idolatry is exposed by the Lord through Isaiah (44.9-20), as men fall down to worship that which is the product of their own design and manufacture. No such image was to be placed in the Tabernacle, as Israel was to make no graven image, nor any likeness of anything as an object of worship (20.4).

Dwelling in a Sanctuary in the midst of His redeemed people was a new development in the ways of God. In Eden, when man was in the garden, it was His desire to walk with them. When Israel was in the wilderness dwelling in tents He commanded that a tent be made in which He would dwell. When they settled in Canaan and were dwelling in houses He ordered that they build Him a house. This desire of God is further seen in the Person of the Lord Jesus when "the word was made flesh, and dwelt among us" (Jn 1.14), and, after the resurrection and ascension of the Lord Jesus to God's right hand, He sent the Holy Spirit to dwell with His redeemed who are now "an habitation of God through the Spirit" (Eph 2.22). Today the Lord Jesus promises that "where two or three are gathered together in my name, there am I in the midst of them" (Mt 18.20). In a future day the great voice out of heaven will declare, "The tabernacle of God is with men, and he will dwell with them (Rev 21.3). God's desire is to dwell with His people!

It was a divinely appointed order of worship

This was the first divinely given system of united public worship, and as such was a further stage in the revelation of God. Up to this point sacrifices had been offered by Abel (Gen 4.4), Noah (Gen 8.20-22), Abraham (Gen 22.13), Jacob (Gen 31.54), and Job (Job 1.5), and doubtless by many others. Now, for the first time there was a recognised redeemed nation whose God was the Lord, and therefore it was necessary to have an order, given by Him, of approach to the Lord, and of worship.

As it functioned, the Tabernacle taught necessary lessons. The holiness that must mark the House of God and those who approach Him; the importance of priesthood; the functions and the glories associated with the High Priest; the nature of the sacrifices which the Lord desired to have offered - all this was designed to teach Israel how to worship and to enjoy the presence of the Lord in the midst. It also brought with it solemn lessons in respect of the cost of disobedience and how the Lord would brook no compromise in carrying out His word.

It was central to the life of Israel
The Tabernacle and its worship was an essential part of the life of Israel. It can be asserted with confidence that there was no part of the life of an Israelite that was not in some way touched by it. The Shekinah glory which ascended from over the Holiest of All was always in sight; their journeys in the wilderness were directed by this cloud. To the gate of the Tabernacle they brought their sacrifices and offerings, and there the priests and the Levites taught them the Law. At the beginning, over 8,000 Levites[4] were engaged in its service and there, at the very centre, was to be found the Holy Place wherein was the throne of God. No Israelite could be ignorant of it or of its purpose, and any who ignored it did so at their peril.

During the years in the wilderness on the journey from Egypt to Canaan, for almost forty years, two generations camped round it, always in sight of the cloudy pillar or that of fire. After the entrance into Canaan, through the times of the judges and the reigns of Saul and David it was with them. There may be difficulty in tracing its complete history during these years, and we know that after the Philistines took the Ark (later returning it) that hallowed symbol was missing from the Holiest of All. Nevertheless, the Tabernacle was the focal point for the worship of the nation.

It was to be diffferent from all other shrines and temples
This Sanctuary was to be essentially different from the shrines and temples that were to be found in Egypt, indeed from any other places of worship. One difference already noted is that there was to be no image of God in its precincts. Israel had been delivered from a nation that had images for all their many gods. That this practice had affected them is clear, for when Moses was up the mount with God they constructed an image, a golden calf, which they had made the object of worship. "Make us gods, which shall go before us" (32.1), was their cry to Aaron, and when he bowed to their wishes they said, "These be thy gods, O Israel, which brought thee up out of the land of Egypt" (32.4). The absence of idols from the Tabernacle made this Sanctuary markedly different from all others.

All defilement was to be kept outside; it was to be free from all such influences. There were to be moral conditions for approaching God, and the immoral and dishonest conduct that marked the worship of false gods had to be absent from the dwelling place of the Lord. Even before it had been set up, the worship of the golden calf saw the people naked, engaged in debauchery and revelry; such conduct would not be tolerated around the "Tent of Meeting".

All other "deities" received from their worshippers and gave nothing in return. They never spoke and they never moved. The God of Israel, in contrast, spoke to His people. He would have done so directly, but they requested that it be done through Moses. He blessed them for their obedience and showed His displeasure at their sin. He was a God who sought to reveal Himself to them, to dwell among them, and not to wrap Himself round with impenetrable mysteries which were understood only by a favoured few initiates. He was a God who at times acted publicly, clearly displaying His power, holiness, and abhorrence of sin. His House had to be different from that erected to all other "deities", because He was different, He was the true God, the only God; He was unique.

It was constructed according to divine instructions

Everything about it was appointed by the Lord. The command to build it came from Him (25.8) as did the instructions and pattern for every part of it. The materials to be used are set out in detail (25.3-7), the workmen who were to be responsible for the work, Bezaleel and Aholiab, were not only appointed to the task, but were given the skills and wisdom necessary to carry out the work (31.1-6). Those who would take part in the construction were also given the necessary wisdom (31.6). Direction was given as to where it had to be erected, and the order in which the twelve tribes, the families of the Levites, and the priests were to pitch their tents around it was laid out. There was nothing that was left to the wisdom or ingenuity of the people; all was ordained and directed by the Lord. It was the Tabernacle that was pitched by man (Heb 8.2), but everything was of the Lord.

The great importance of the detail of the construction is reflected in the three times that it is detailed. The instruction to build is found in chs.25-30. The frequently repeated words, "Thou shalt make", indicated the importance of the pattern shown to Moses on the mount, and highlighted that it should be followed with meticulous care and attention to detail. The construction is described in chs.35-39, showing that the instructions were carried out. There is first noted how the materials were brought, and then how they were wrought. At the end of the construction "Moses did look upon all the work, and, behold, they had done it as the Lord had commanded (39.43). The erection of the whole is found in ch.40. Although the detail there is not so great as in the two previous accounts, it nevertheless re-states the items which were carefully put in place. In this can be seen that God desires His word to be carried out exactly; that is why chs.35-39 are almost a repeat of the instructions of chs.25-30. The account in ch.40 confirms, not only that everything instructed by the Lord was made, but also that, as it was put in place in the finished Tabernacle, nothing was omitted. When this was done "a cloud covered the tent of the congregation, and the glory of the Lord filled the tabernacle" (40.34). The vital lesson to be learned is that every task undertaken for God must be carried out according to His Word, and will, as a result, lead to enjoyment of His blessing.

It reflected the spiritual condition of the nation

The spiritual condition of the people was reflected by conditions in the Tabernacle. Scarcely is it mentioned in the book of the Judges - a time when devotion to the Lord was low. The sad situation at Shiloh during Eli's tenure as High Priest (1 Sam 1-4), and in the years which followed, mirrored the hearts of a nation which had divided affections and had lost its love for the Lord. The devotion of David for the Lord was clear as he determined to bring back the Ark (2 Sam 6), and although it was not given to him to build a House for the Lord, nevertheless his heart desired it.

Those who loved the Lord loved the Tabernacle! Wrote the Psalmist, "My soul longeth, yea, even fainteth for the courts of the Lord: my heart and my flesh crieth out for the living God", and, "For a day in thy courts is better than a thousand. I had rather be a doorkeeper in the house of my God, than to dwell in the tents of wickedness" (Ps 84.2,10).

It gives an understanding of later Scriptures

Without the detail of the Tabernacle it would be impossible to understand the book of Leviticus and the worship which is ordered there. Without the Tabernacle the sacrifices could not have been offered, and the priesthood could not have carried out the duties with which they were charged. The Temple, built during the reign of Solomon, does not, as has been noted, take as many pages to describe as does the Tabernacle, and it is through the latter that a greater understanding of the Temple can be gained. It was a more permanent structure, based upon the Tabernacle, the essential features of which are the same as those associated with the Tent of Meeting erected by Moses. The Epistle to the Hebrews would almost be a closed book to the reader if there were no knowledge of the Tabernacle, as the teaching is to a great extent built on the service which took place there, with particular emphasis on the Day of Atonement.

The Titles Given to the Tabernacle

Scripture contains a number of titles given to the Tabernacle. Some of the main ones are commented on below.

A Sanctuary

The first mention of the word "sanctuary" is in 25.8, and the desire of the Lord to have such a place in which He would dwell is found in the great redemption hymn of ch.15, when Israel sang of their destination where there would be "the place, O Lord, which thou hast made for thee to dwell in, in the Sanctuary, O Lord, which thy hands have established" (15.17). The word "sanctuary" (4720), means a sanctified, set apart place, holy and hallowed, which would not be for common use.

The Tabernacle of the Lord

This title is used six times in the Pentateuch, indicating that the Tabernacle was the possession of the Lord. It emphasises the holiness which marked the place; it was the Lord's House and He ordered all that was in it; the running of it, and the conditions for entrance and service were all His. It was His possession.

The Tabernacle of Testimony

This Sanctuary was a testimony to Israel as to the presence of God, the means of approach to God, and the enjoyment of fellowship with Him. It was also a testimony to the nations that the Lord was with Israel and dwelt among them.

This designation is found nine times in various forms. In Exodus 38.21; Numbers 1.50,53; and 10.11 it is given as "the tabernacle of (the) testimony". In Numbers 9.15 it is referred to as "the tent of the testimony", and in Numbers 17.7,8; 18.2; and 2 Chronicles 24.6 the title is translated as, "the tabernacle of witness". It is first used with reference to the "the things numbered of the tabernacle, the tabernacle of the testimony, which were counted, according to the commandment of Moses, by the service of the Levites, under the hand of Ithamar, son of Aaron the priest" (38.21, JND). That which is to be a testimony and witness to others must itself be faithfully prepared to ensure that all that the Lord intended is included in the construction, with no deficiencies.

It is not without significance that it was the Tabernacle of Testimony over which the Levites were appointed, including the responsibility of camping round it, taking it down, bearing it on the journey, and setting it up again (Num 1.50,53). As they marched through the wilderness they carried with them the symbols of His presence and power.

It is also of more than passing interest to observe that it was the "tent of the testimony" which the cloud covered when the Tabernacle was reared up, for His presence is an essential part of testimony (Num 9.15).

It was in the "tabernacle of witness" (Num 17.7,8) that, subsequent to the rebellion of Korah, the rods were laid up to show who had been chosen to be High Priest, the testimony being given to Israel that it was Aaron.

Testimony today should bear the same features, so that any who observe the order of the gatherings of the assembly can truly "report that God is in you of a truth" (1 Cor 14.25).

The Tabernacle of the Congregation

The use of such a title as "the tabernacle of the congregation", or "tent of meeting" (JND) was a great honour for Israel. The congregation were linked with the tent which was the Tabernacle of the Lord. This term is used more than any other, being found on 128[5] occasions (in the AV 115 times as "the tabernacle of the congregation", and 13 times as "the tent of the congregation") in the Pentateuch, first appearing in Exodus 27.21 where the people are instructed to prepare the oil for the Lamp which was to burn "In the tabernacle of the congregation without the vail, which is before the testimony". It signifies that this was the gathering place of the people, the place where they or their representatives were summoned to appear before the Lord, the centre of their lives, the place where their spiritual needs were met, where they offered their worship, and the place the maintenance of which was their responsibility.

Difference between "tent" and "tabernacle"

Reference has been made to the fact that the Tabernacle is sometimes called "the tabernacle of..." and sometimes "the tent of...". What is the difference? "Tabernacle" (4908) means a dwelling place, and "tent" (168) means a temporary tent, that in which wandering tribes would dwell.

The General Plan of the Tabernacle

The Tabernacle was not a grand edifice, but rather of relatively modest proportions. The central structure was surrounded by a court measuring 100 cubits by 50 cubits; the longer side being placed from east to west and the shorter from north to south. A white linen curtain or hanging, which was supported on pillars, surrounded the court and on the east side there was a gate measuring 20 cubits.

The central structure was 30 cubits long, 10 cubits broad, and 10 cubits high. It was situated in the courtyard with the entrance door facing eastwards and was divided into two compartments; one, the Holy Place, was 20 cubits long and the other, the Holy of Holies, was 10 cubits long making this latter compartment a perfect cube. Outwardly this central structure had little of attraction and beauty as the covering seen was of badgers' skins giving a somewhat drab appearance. The beauty was all to be found in the inside.

In the courtyard, nearest to the gate there was the Brazen Altar on which the sacrifices were offered. Between the Brazen Altar and the door of the central structure was to be found the Laver at which the priests washed their hands and feet before and after entering the Holy Place. Passing through the door into the Holy Place the priests, for only priests were permitted to enter, saw before them the Table of Shewbread, the Lampstand, and the Golden Altar of Incense. The Holiest of All was entered only by the High Priest, and that once a year on the Day of Atonement, and in there were the Ark, and the Mercy Seat with the two cherubims whose wings were spread over it. In the Holy Place the only light was that of the Lampstand; in the Holiest of All the only light was that of the glory of God.

The Tabernacle was pitched in the centre of the Camp of Israel with the tents of the tribes surrounding it: on the north, Dan, Asher and Naphtali; on the west, Ephraim, Manasseh, and Benjamin; on the south Reuben, Simeon, and Gad; and on the east, Judah, Issachar, and Zebulun. The families of the Levites were also camped round about it, and were closest to it: on the north, those of Merari; on the west, those of Gershon; on the south, those of Kohath; and on the east, before the gate, Moses, Aaron, and his sons.

The Symbolism of the Tabernacle
It was a picture of the "true tabernacle"

The writer of the Epistle to the Hebrews deals with the symbolic significance of the Tabernacle at some length. The interest of the reader is quickened when there is an understanding that what was erected in the wilderness was an object lesson in eternal realities. Indeed, it is to rob the believer of a rich mine of divine truth if it be thought that the Tabernacle, its offerings, and its priesthood are but the provision made by God for an ancient people unable to understand anything more than the simplest forms of worship, which long have been redundant. That the Tabernacle has lessons to teach believers today is clear, and the Epistle to the Hebrews expresses this plainly. The Tabernacle is an example or pattern (5262). The priests are "the example...of heavenly things", the words meaning a pattern, a representation, a figure, or a copy (see Heb 8.5; 9.23). Note four words used to describe the design of the Tabernacle.

1. It is "the shadow of heavenly things" (Heb 8.5). Vine in his Dictionary states that such a "shadow" (4639) is "caused by the interception of light...the image or outline cast by an object". It is an image cast by an object when light is shone on it. In order to create a shadow there must be a real object and there must be light. The image which is cast is a shape of reality but lacks one dimension, that of depth, and is devoid of all colour (see Heb 8.5; 10.1). It has no substance of itself, but requires the real thing to be in existence. In heaven there is the Sanctuary, and the Tabernacle which was on earth was a shadow, albeit a pale shadow, of the heavenly.

2. It is described as "a figure (3850) for the time then present" (Heb 9.8-9). Again, Vine states that this refers to "a casting or placing side by side...with a view to comparison or resemblance". The Tabernacle was, therefore, an object lesson in truth concerning what is in heaven.

3. The Hebrew writer states that "Christ is not entered into the holy places made with hands, which are figures of the true; but into heaven itself" (Heb 9.24). The word translated "figures" (499) here differs from that used in vv.8-9 of this chapter. Vine describes this as meaning "a copy of an archetype". It is a counter or corresponding pattern - that which was on earth corresponding to the heavenly.

4. Regarding the priests and their service in the Tabernacle, it is written that "There are priests that offer gifts according to the law: Who serve

unto the example…of heavenly things" (Heb 8.4-5), and "It was therefore necessary that the patterns of things in the heavens should be purified with these" (Heb 9.23). The words "example", and "patterns" are the same in Greek *(5262)* and mean "a copy".

The "real thing", of which the Tabernacle is an example, a pattern, a shadow, and a figure, is heaven itself and heavenly things. It is, therefore, a figure of heavenly things, not earthly things; it is a representation of the true. Here, in a form which can be understood by men and women, is pictured how to approach God and have fellowship with Him, the reality of which is found, not in that Tabernacle made with hands, but in the true Tabernacle above, which the Lord pitched, and not man. Anyone with a desire to learn more of heavenly things must study the Tabernacle. These Scriptures all confirm that "the Tabernacle and its furniture are meant to be studied as an object lesson illustrating deep and abiding reality. The substance is the heavenly Sanctuary where Christ ministers…it may be observed that there is every justification for concluding that in the Tabernacle we may find ample material as a prefigurement of Christ and His work for His people, the new Israel of God".[6]

Tabernacle Limitation

No sacrifice, no blood shed in the worship of the Tabernacle could take away one single sin. Day by day the sacrifices were slain, day by day the flames of the Altar rose into the sky, day by day the priests carried out their work, and yet no sin was ever forgiven by the blood shed and the sacrifices laid on the Brazen Altar. All this was but a picture, a necessary picture, to teach Israel, and to teach all people, that the shedding of blood was the basis of approach to God and the maintenance of fellowship with Him. It all pointed forward to the one perfect sacrifice that would be offered up at Calvary. Studied in this light, the truths seen in the Tabernacle come alive, enlighten the soul, and give cause for worship.

> No blood, no altar now,
> The sacrifice is o'er;
> No flame, no smoke ascends on high,
> The lamb is slain no more;
> But richer blood has flowed from nobler veins
> To purge the soul from guilt, and cleanse the reddest stains.
> (Horatius Bonar)

Verses 1-2: The Privilege of Giving

The instruction from the Lord to bring an offering for the erection of the Tabernacle is limited to His redeemed people. The privilege of giving to Him for His work and for His Sanctuary is only for those who have been redeemed by the blood of the lamb. The materials to be offered were those that had been given by the Egyptians as the people were leaving

Egypt (12.35). It was not regarded as a loss of wealth to give to the service of the Lord.

A heave offering

The word used for "offering" (8641) means "heave offering". It has the original meaning of "lifting up" in the sense of lifting up an offering on to the altar, but became simply a term for an offering, something that was lifted from one's own possessions and given to the Lord. This is the first use of the word; it indicates that those who offered would feel the weight of what they were doing. It was not to be a light thing to give to the Lord, but as they presented it there would be a realisation of its worth, felt by them as they lifted it to present it to the Lord.

Willingness to give

The offerings had to be given willingly, without regret or compulsion. The recognition of what the Lord had given to them would create in them the desire to give back to Him. This is the first use of the word "willingly" (5068) which has the meaning of "an uncompelled and free movement of the will unto divine service or sacrifice…and…describes the inner state of those contributing to the construction of the tabernacle" (TWOT at 1299). It is fitting that it is introduced as being a feature of the redeemed, for only the grace of God can produce that willingness to give to Him. Apart from its use in connection with the offerings for the Tabernacle, it is also used of the willingness of the people and the governors of Israel to give themselves to the battle of freeing Israel from the yoke of Jabin, king of Canaan (Judg 5.2,9); of the giving of the materials for the building of the Temple (1 Chr 29.6,9,14,17); of Amasiah, the son of Zichri who willing offered himself as the leader of 200,000 men in the days of King Jehoshaphat (2 Chr 17.16); of the offering of the material for the rebuilding of the Temple (Ezra 1.6); and of those who willingly offered themselves to dwell in Jerusalem (Neh 11.2). The willing offering of possessions and of persons for the building, maintenance, and preservation of the House of God is evidence of an appreciation of His grace.

This generosity of grace is seen amongst the believers in the church at Jerusalem when they sold their possessions to meet the need of others (Acts 2.45). This same willingness was a feature of the Macedonian believers as they gave for the need of the poor saints in Judea (2 Cor 8.3), not only offering their possessions, but "first gave their own selves to the Lord" (2 Cor 8.5). They were reminded that the motive behind such liberality was their knowledge of "the grace of our Lord Jesus Christ, that, though he was rich, yet for your sakes he became poor, that ye through his poverty might be rich" (2 Cor 8.9), and that a willing mind was essential (2 Cor 8.12). The sad condition of Israel recorded by Malachi is highlighted by the nature of their giving to God. They brought as sacrifices, the blind, the lame, and the sick (1.8): valueless animals, revealing their low estimation of the Lord.

Giving from the heart

The phrase, "every man that giveth it willingly with his heart" ("every one whose heart prompteth him", JND), indicates that the willingness was not based on a cold calculation, but was the result of the feelings being touched. There was to be no feigning of willingness, but the intellect and the emotions were to be involved together. Paul exhorts the Corinthians to manifest the same heart condition: "Every man according as he purposeth in his heart, so let him give; not grudgingly, or of necessity: for God loveth a cheerful giver" (2 Cor 9.7). This spontaneous, voluntary, uncompelled giving to God not only meets the needs of others, but is also appreciated in heaven (Phil 4.18).

Giving to the Lord

Everything was given, not to Moses, Aaron and his sons, or the Levites; all was given to the Lord and He speaks of it as "my offering" (v.2). He had rights over their possessions for He was the giver of them. All giving must be seen as being to the Lord, as Paul states to the Philippians in the passage referred to above, "an odour of a sweet smell, a sacrifice acceptable, wellpleasing to God". Giving to God is returning to Him what is His by sovereign right and by right of redemption.

Verses 3-7: The Offerings Given for the Tabernacle

Where the Israelites obtained the materials to offer has been the subject of much speculation. Most of it came from the Egyptians who gave them considerable wealth when they left Egypt. It has also been suggested that this was augmented by wealth that they had built up over the years in Egypt, but it is unlikely that, after the years of slavery, much of any wealth that they may have possessed would have been left. Some also have considered it possible that in the wilderness they had traded with the caravans of merchants moving to and from Egypt, but again, even if this took place, it would have been on a very limited scale as their location was not on the well-used trade routes and as insufficient time had passed for them to gain wealth in this manner. It may be conceded that some of the spoils of battle were obtained after the victory over Amalek, but it is extremely unlikely that, apart from the Egyptians, any of these supposed sources contributed materially to their riches. The great majority, if not all of it, came as payment for their decades of forced labour in Egypt. It must be remembered, however, that even although this was the payment for many years of labour, it was divinely given. If there had not been the work of God in their land, the Egyptians would never have considered imparting their wealth to slaves. Only the work of God brought it about and the Israelites could claim no credit for it being in their possession.

When dealing with the spiritual significance of what was given no one can be dogmatic. What follows is suggestive but is by no means exhaustive.

Gold

Gold is the first, and the most precious material mentioned in the Bible (Gen 2.11). In the building of the Tabernacle it was used in the construction of

1. The Ark and its staves
2. The Mercy Seat
3. The cherubims
4. The Golden Altar and its staves
5. The Table of Shewbread and its dishes, spoons, goblets and bowls
6. The Lampstand
7. The four pillars on which the vail was hung, at the entrance to the Holiest of All
8. The five pillars on which the curtains were hung, forming the door at the entrance to the Holy Place
9. The boards which made up the main structure and the bars which gave them stability.

All these vessels and boards were to be found in the Holy Place and the Holiest of All.

It was also used in the making of

1. The Ephod of the High Priest
2. The shoulder settings in which were the precious stones bearing the names of the tribes
3. The Breastplate of Judgment
4. The chains linked with the Breastplate
5. The rings linked with the Breastplate.

The word used for "gold" here (2091) means "shimmering", or "yellow". It symbolises the sun, that which is greater than all the planets surrounding it; the giver of light and the bestower of heat. Amongst all metals it stood as the most precious. Gold, therefore, in the Tabernacle is a symbol of deity; of Him who is greater than all others, the giver of light and heat (life and energy), Him who cannot be ignored by those who dwell on earth, and whose resplendent majesty and glory can be seen by all who acknowledge it.

Silver

This precious metal was used in

1. The sockets on which the boards of the Tabernacle structure sat
2. The rods connecting the pillars forming the outer court
3. The hooks on the pillars forming the outer court
4. The trumpets used by the priests.

The significance of this metal is seen in the fact that the atonement money was paid in silver coinage, half a shekel for each man (30.11-16; 38.25-27). It is therefore a symbol of atonement, the money being the "redemption money which each man of responsible age had to pay for his ransom" (Dennett).

It was this payment that was in the mind of Peter when he wrote, "Forasmuch as ye know that ye were not redeemed with corruptible things, as silver and gold, from your vain conversation, received by tradition from your fathers; But with the precious blood of Christ, as of a lamb without blemish and without spot" (1 Pet 1.18-19). The reference to gold has to do with special circumstances surrounding the numbering in Numbers 31, after the battle with the Midianites, when the money was paid by bringing the gold spoil from the battlefield.

Brass

This metal was not that which is referred to today as "brass", but is regarded as being copper. When referring to it, however, the word "brass" will be used. Brass was used in the making of
1. The great Altar which stood inside the gate of the Tabernacle and which was overlaid with it
2. The pots and shovels etc for the use at the Brazen Altar
3. The taches or clasps for the goats' hair curtains
4. The bases, or sockets, on which the pillars of the court were placed
5. The sockets on which the pillars at the door were placed
6. All the fixing pins
7. The laver and its base.

The significance of brass is that it is that metal which was able to stand the heat and flame of the Altar. It refers, therefore, to the redemption which has been purchased for others by the sufferings of the Lord Jesus on the Cross, those sufferings which only He was able to bear.

Blue

This colour was probably obtained from the cerulean mussel. The offering was of thread and material which had been dyed. Being the colour of the heavens, it denotes that which is heavenly. TWOT (at 2510) states that "...the uncertainty of the results of dyeing in those days made it almost impossible for them to reproduce colours with any degree of precision. Words [such as those which are translated 'blue' and 'purple'] denoted colours that spanned the spectrum from brilliant red through deep purple, and 'blue' is simply a conventional translation. It may well be that the ancients were more interested in richness, darkness, brilliance, and the like than in precision or tint or hue. At any rate, the best and costliest ancient dyes were the blues and violets and purples that were made from the secretions of various mollusks".

Purple

Purple probably indicates shades from deep red-black to violet. The purple signifies the regal dignity of the Lord Jesus.

Scarlet

Scarlet, sometimes known as "worm scarlet", came from the bodies of dead maggots or from the kermes insect. It is not without significance that the name Adam means "red earth". The colour, therefore, refers to the humiliation of the Lord Jesus in becoming a man and being obedient unto death. Blue, purple, and scarlet were used in the making of

1. The vail
2. The door
3. The gate
4. Together with gold, the Ephod of the High Priest.

Fine Linen

This is the second use of this word, the first being in Gen 41.42, "arrayed him…in fine linen", referring to the attire of Joseph. It is used of Egyptian white linen of exceptional quality. It represents the pure, spotless, righteous Person of the Lord Jesus, particularly as this was seen in His humanity. Note that in Revelation 19.8 when it is the attire of saints it is referred to as "the righteousness of saints". In the Tabernacle, however, it is not the saints, but the Lord who is in view.

The fine linen was used in the making of

1. The vail
2. The door
3. The gate
4. The hangings of the court.

It was, therefore, a very prominent feature of the structure. It was in the Ephod of the High Priest and the garments of the priests.

Goats' Hair

A hairy garment was the attire of prophets (Zech 13.4-5). When King Ahaziah lay dying and sent messengers to enquire of the god of Ekron as to whether he would recover, they met the prophet Elijah bearing the message that the king would die. On their return the king enquired, "What manner of man was he which came up to meet you", to which they responded, "He was an hairy man (a man clothed in a hairy garment)". The king then knew that "It is Elijah the Tishbite" (2 Kings 1.7). His dress was enough to identify him. It is also written of John Baptist that he was clothed in his "raiment of camel's hair, and a leathern girdle about his loins" (Mt 3.4). The Lord Jesus was a prophet; indeed, He was the Prophet of whom Moses spoke (Deut 18.15-19). Eleven curtains of woven goats' hair were made which formed one of the coverings of the Tabernacle, speaking of this aspect of Christ.

Rams' skins dyed red

Unlike the curtains of fine linen and goats' hair, there is no size recorded for these. They formed a part of the covering of the Tabernacle.

At the consecration of the priests two rams were brought, both of them were slain and one of them burnt upon the Altar (29.18). The blood of the other was placed upon the tip of the right ear, the thumb of the right hand, and the great toe of the right foot of Aaron and each of his sons. The ram was called the "ram of the consecration" (29.27) and the redness of the skins emphasised consecration to death; Christ was "obedient unto death, even the death of the cross" (Phil 2.8).

Badgers' skins

Again no size is recorded for these. The badgers' skins formed the outside covering of the Tabernacle and signified the Lord Jesus Christ as He is seen by the world. Isaiah writes that "there is no beauty that we should desire him" (Is 53.2), His beauty not being of the kind that is attractive to the flesh. The priests saw all the beauty of the Tabernacle as they worked inside, as did the High Priest in the Holiest of All on the Day of Atonement.

In identifying the "badger" the comment in TWOT at 2503 is of interest, suggesting that it may be the skin of the bottle-nosed dolphin which was used, as the badger is "rarely if ever seen in Sinai" and that "most recent commentators translate the Hebrew word as "dolphin, porpoise, dugong or the like". When referring to this covering, however, for consistency "badgers' skins" will be used.

Shittim (acacia) wood

The shittim tree was to be found in the wilderness and flourished in conditions that were hostile. "Mature shittim-wood trees, while retaining a full head of foliage and beautifying the desert plain with fragrant, yellow flowers, bear the appearance of having survived adverse and hostile growing conditions".[7] Its wood was used in the construction of the Ark and its staves, the Golden Altar and its staves, the Table of Shewbread and its staves, the Brazen Altar and its staves, the boards and their bars, the pillars for the door, the vail, and the gate, and the pillars which formed the outer court. This wood, which was incorruptible, represents the incorruptible, sinless humanity of the Lord Jesus.

Oil for the light

This was made by the people and used in the Lampstand which stood in the Holy Place. The Lampstand oil was replenished morning and evening, for the Lamp had always to be burning; it had never to go out. This oil, therefore, was not used in the construction of the Tabernacle, but in its daily functioning.

Spices for anointing oil

These spices were used for the anointing of the Tabernacle before it commenced to function, and for the anointing of the priests. It consisted of a mixture of myrrh, cinnamon, sweet calamus, cassia, and olive oil. The blended spices signify the beauty of the Lord Jesus.

Sweet incense

This was used in the Holy Place, morning and evening, at the time when the Lampstand was being replenished and cleaned. It was placed in a censer, with coals from the Brazen Altar, which was then put on the Golden Altar of Incense. In this way the Holy Place was always filled with sweet incense. It was also brought in a golden censer into the Holiest of All when the High Priest entered on the Day of Atonement. This incense consisted of a mixture of stacte, onycha, galbanum, and frankincense. As with the anointing oil, the sweet incense signifies the sweet fragrance of the life of the Lord Jesus.

Onyx stones

Two of these stones had engraven on them the names of the tribes of Israel, and were carried on the shoulders of the High Priest. One of the twelve stones placed on his Breastplate was onyx.

Precious stones

Twelve precious stones were carried on the Breastplate of the High Priest. These were sardius, topaz, carbuncle, emerald, sapphire, diamond, ligure, agate, amethyst, beryl, onyx, and jasper. Each stone represented one of the tribes of Israel.

Verses 8-9: The Command to Build the Tabernacle

Now the reason for the gathering of such wealth is made known; the Lord desires a dwelling place set apart amongst His redeemed people. Three things are worthy of note in this connection.

All the people are to be involved in this work, if not in the actual construction, certainly in the giving of the material. "Let *them* make me a sanctuary". It is not anticipated that any will be indifferent to the great work going on in their midst, nor that they will ignore the divine command to make the Sanctuary. The same is true today of the House of God, which is the local assembly. All who are in fellowship are expected to take a full part in the work, and there is no excuse for those who fail to engage in this and leave others to carry the responsibility which they themselves could undertake. All are exhorted to be "always abounding in the work of the Lord" (1 Cor 15.58).

Everything was to be built according to the pattern which Moses would be shown on the mount. There is no indication in Scripture of the nature of this "pattern", but Moses did see how each part had to be constructed. In the study of the Tabernacle it will be seen that there are sections about which it is not possible today to be dogmatic, as differing views are held as to the exact meaning of the written instructions. This did not present a problem to Moses as he had seen the pattern and would instruct the workmen accordingly. The purpose of these chapters is not to give such detail that the Tabernacle could be built today as it no longer has any part in the testimony of God on earth. What is given is not a building blueprint, but all that is necessary for our spiritual education in the great truths that are represented in the construction and functioning of this Sanctuary. There was no laxity allowed in the interpretation of the instruction; all had to be "according to…the pattern". Again, the same principle is seen in the local assembly. There is a pattern laid down in the New Testament and this must be followed. The Acts of the Apostles and the epistles of Paul give vital teaching as to the composition and gatherings of the local assembly, and regarding the behaviour and practices of the Christians when they gather. Sadly, over the centuries, the traditions and systems of men have been introduced, resulting in the confusion, sects, and denominations existing today. Better far to get back to the Book and put into practice what is found there. No one can improve on the Scriptures.

The third noteworthy feature is that, not only was there a pattern for the structure, there was also a pattern for "all the instruments thereof". There was nothing too small to be included in the plan; no instrument was of such insignificance that the details of it were omitted from what Moses saw. In the Tabernacle, as in the assembly today, *nothing* is left to man to devise, and nothing is *insignificant*.

Notes

1 Ilustrations of the Tabernacle and its furniture are given in Appendix 6.
2 The 20 years until the revival under Samuel, the years of Samuel as judge, the 40 years reign of Saul, the 7 years of David's reign over Judah, and the years of his reign over Israel until 2 Samuel 6.
3 See also 1 Samuel 4.4; 2 Samuel 6.2; 1 Chronicles 13.6; Psalm 99.1.
4 Total Levites between 30 and 50 yrs (Num 4.34-49): Kohath 2,750, Gershon 2,630, Merari 3,200 - 8,580.
5 A further use of the title in Exodus 33.7 refers to a temporary tabernacle which Moses erected and which was pitched outside the Camp.
6 A. Borland, *Believer's Magazine*, 1967.
7 T. Ratcliffe, *Bible Plants, Fruits & Products*.

EXODUS 25.10-22

The Ark and its Mercy Seat[†]

To Israel this was the most sacred of all the Tabernacle vessels, because it was the place where Jehovah dwelt. It was a place of government, because it was a throne, a place of grace because of the blood sprinkled on and before it, allowing man to approach, and it was a place of glory because the Shekinah glory hovered over it. It occupied the centre position in the Tabernacle and in the Camp. Israelites could look to the Tabernacle and to where the Holiest of All was situated and know that the Lord was there, the cloud rising from it confirming that fact. The Mercy Seat was the lid, which sat on top of the Ark, and the two cherubims rose above the Mercy Seat. These items of Tabernacle furniture were inseparable. They signify, for believers today, the Lord Jesus Christ in the midst of His people.

"Let us approach with deepest reverence, put off our shoes, for if any place surely this we now tread is holy ground", writes Brown in his introduction, and follows this by describing the Ark as "The Ark of the Covenant, the chief and most sacred of all the objects connected with the dwelling, and for which the Tabernacle itself, with all its brazen and golden furniture was made subordinate, and to which all the ministrations and ritual associated with them had reference". Henry Law writes, "Reader, come near to see the chiefest wonder of the wondrous Tabernacle. It is the Ark. For this the holy tent was reared. For this the holiest place set apart. This is the richest jewel in the sacred casket - the topstone of the hallowed pile".

The Construction of the Ark

The Ark was marked as being the first of the furnishings of the Tabernacle to be described, confirming its precedence over all other items. It was a box, or chest, which was placed in the Holiest of All. It measured $2^{1}/_{2}$ cubits long, $1^{1}/_{2}$ cubits broad, and $1^{1}/_{2}$ cubits high, was made of shittim wood, and was overlaid with pure gold within and without. The shittim wood, therefore, could not be seen under the pure gold covering. On each of the four corners there was a ring of gold and through these were fitted the staves, two in number, which were used in the carrying of the Ark. These staves were made like the Ark: shittim wood overlaid with gold. The top of the Ark was uncovered as over this was placed the Mercy Seat. Round the top there was a "crown", or moulding, or rim of gold, the purpose of which was to ensure that the Mercy Seat sat securely and could not be dislodged.

The Contents of the Ark

Into the Ark was placed the testimony, the two tables of stone containing the Ten Commandments (40.20). The first two tables of stone, which were written with the finger of God, were those taken down from the mount by

Moses (31.18). After Moses destroyed these tables (32.19), he prepared another two, on which God wrote again the Ten Commandments (Deut 10.1-4).

At later stages two other items were added - the golden pot of manna and Aaron's rod that budded (Heb 9.4) - but these two additional items were no longer present when, in the reign of Solomon, the Ark was placed in the Temple (1 Kings 8.9; 2 Chr 5.10), perhaps having been removed when it was returned from the land of the Philistines (1 Sam 6-7).

The Location of the Ark

The Tabernacle was constructed to be the dwelling place of God, but more particularly the Holy of Holies was that part of the sacred building where He was pleased to dwell. It is therefore with a spirit of worship that the subject of the Ark is approached, that which sat, with the Mercy Seat and cherubims above, in that sacred spot within the vail, in the Holiest of All. This innermost shrine was a perfect cube, each side measuring 10 cubits, in which there was no artificial light, no natural light, and no light borrowed from another compartment; the glory of the presence of God lit the place. The Ark formed the base of the throne of God, for the Psalmist writes that "The Lord reigneth; let the people tremble: he sitteth between the cherubims" (Ps 99.1). Into this throne-room Aaron, as a result of the failure of two of his sons on the first day of their service in the Tabernacle, could enter only once a year on the Day of Atonement (Lev 16.1-2,34). The wording of v.22 suggests that Moses was also allowed that privilege.

How solemn is all this. There was to be taught to Israel the lesson to be learned by all who seek to approach God, no matter the dispensation. It is no light thing to come before Him. Holiness is His and that standard cannot and will not be lowered. On a later and sadder day, the two sons of Aaron, who dared approach with strange fire, that which He had not sanctioned, found to the cost of their lives that Jehovah will not tolerate standards lower than those which He has set. As this study is pursued, it must be with unshod feet, with bowed hearts, and in a worshipping spirit. Here God was to be found; here holiness resided; here man found his highest privilege.

The Titles of the Ark

The following is a selection of the main titles given to the Ark in Scripture.

The Ark of the Testimony (25.22)

The Tabernacle of Testimony was so called because it contained the Ark of the Testimony. "The testimony" consisted of the two tables of stone placed in the Ark by Moses. Here was the divine standard, the supreme Law, and the demands of absolute holiness.

The Ark of God (1 Sam 3.3)

This title was first associated with the Ark in the days of Eli and was used at a time when it was little regarded. The last use was when David placed it in the temporary tabernacle which he erected at Jerusalem (2 Chr 1.4). It signified, in these dark days, that the Ark was His possession and could not be misused and mistreated without serious consequences.

The Ark of the covenant of the Lord (Num 10.33)

This emphasises that the Lord is a covenant keeping God, and also that Israel had entered into a covenant to keep the Law. Note must be taken of Jeremiah 3.16: "In those days, saith the Lord, they shall say no more, The ark of the covenant of the Lord: neither shall it come to mind: neither shall they remember it; neither shall they visit it; neither shall that be done any more". In the millennial kingdom, Jerusalem will be called the throne of Jehovah and the presence of the Lord will make the Ark unnecessary. Sometimes the words "of your God" (2 Sam 1.22) or, "of God" (Judg 20.27) are employed in place of "of the Lord".

The Ark of the Lord, the Lord of all the earth (Josh 3.13)

This is used with reference to the Ark being carried by the priests as they stood in the waters of the Jordan when the Children of Israel passed over into Canaan. As with the use of "of all the earth" in v.11 it was the omnipotence of the Lord that was the point at issue; everything is under His sure control. It is His earth and He can move nations at His will.

The Ark of the Lord God (1 Kings 2.26)

This was used in the reign of Solomon, and signified the desire of God to be in fellowship with His people. This double name, first used in Genesis 2.4, is one of the main titles of God in the Old Testament.

The Holy Ark (2 Chr 35.3)

This is a title which occurs only once, in the reign of Josiah. The instruction from the King, "Put the holy ark in the house which Solomon the son of David king of Israel did build; it shall not be a burden upon your shoulders", seems to indicate that the Ark was being carried about, perhaps almost as talisman, as it was when the sons of Eli had it carried to the battlefield. "The holy ark" impressed on the people the holiness of God at a time when the king was preparing the nation for the re-introduction of the Passover. In the days preceding the reign of Josiah this holiness had been ignored and forgotten as the nation fell into deeper departure and idolatry.

The Ark of Thy strength (Ps 132.8)

This Psalm is the only one in which the Ark is mentioned. It is David's desire at the removal of the Ark to Jerusalem that the strength of the Lord will be seen when it is placed again in the midst of the people.

The Ark of the God of Israel (1 Sam 5.7)

This was the title of the Ark used by the Philistines. It indicates that they recognised that the God of Israel did exist, although they considered their God, Dagon, to be supreme, a fact which was demonstrated to be false when Dagon fell before the Ark.

His footstool (Lam 2.1)

The judgment of God on Jerusalem is the subject when this title is used. That which had been His footstool, the place before which His people would fall in worship, was no longer remembered. Keil & Delitzsch write that "It is further implied, in the fact that God does not think of His footstool, that the Ark itself was destroyed along with the temple and the city".

The Significance of the Ark
The Ark itself

As has already been observed, the fact that the Ark is mentioned first indicates that the order of revelation will be from the presence of God outwards towards the people. It is clear that the desire of the Lord was not only to dwell with His people, but also to reveal Himself to them. Thus, He started with the place where He would dwell and, moving out from there, would teach Israel the way by which He had chosen to reveal Himself to them, which, in reverse, was the way of approach for them to Him.

The gold of the Ark signified the deity of the Lord Jesus Christ (see page 306); it was pure gold, emphasising that His becoming a man did not detract in any way whatsoever from His deity. This gold was as bright inside the Ark as it was outside. That which was inside was seen only by God, teaching that there are aspects of His deity which are even beyond His saints to understand, that which is enjoyed only in the Godhead.

The shittim wood speaks of the incorruptible humanity of the Lord Jesus. This wood could sustain the attacks of pests and of the diseases to which other trees succumbed. The holy life which the Lord lived showed clearly that He could not sin and that the enemy who so effectively caused Adam and Eve to fall had no power over Him whatsoever. But the shittim wood of the Ark was hidden from view under its gold covering and speaks therefore of that sinless purity which was for the enjoyment of His God and Father.

The High Priest saw what was outside, but it must be remembered that he took with him into that Holiest of All a censer on which were burning coals and sweet incense: "And he shall put the incense upon the fire before the Lord, that the cloud of the incense may cover the mercy seat that is upon the testimony, that he die not" (Lev 16.13). He would see the Ark through the cloud of incense as it evaporated from the heat of the censer. The Ark would then be enveloped in the fragrance that spoke of Christ. The Priest carrying the censer would also be touched by that fragrance, and, for the pleasure of God, the fragrance of Christ would fill the place. With this, and with the blood, the Priest found acceptance.

The Testimony

It has already been noted that the two tables of stone were placed within the Ark. These two tables contained God's righteous demands of man, demands which it was impossible for man to meet. The Law, therefore, brought death to man, because if its demands could not be met death would be the result. Paul describes it a "the ministration of death, written and engraven in stones" (2 Cor 3.7). But there was one Man who did keep it! The desire of Jehovah for Israel was that they might "magnify the law, and make it honourable", but rather they were "robbed and spoiled"; they fell far short of what was required of them (Is 42.21,22). What the nation could not do, He accomplished, and magnified the Law in His perfect keeping of it. Prophetically it was truly written of Him that He could say, "Thy word have I hid in mine heart, that I might not sin against thee" (Ps 119.11), and, "I delight to do thy will, O my God: yea thy law is within my heart" (Ps 40.8). The two stones in the Ark are an unmistakable picture of Him in whom the Word of God resided; who could be exposed to the full demands of the Law and yet not be subject to death; He of whom it could be written that "His delight is in the law of the Lord; and in his law doth he meditate day and night" (Ps 1.2).

But placed in the Ark these tables of stone are out of the sight of Israel. Moses understood the need for this because he broke the first two stones as, returning from the mount, he saw the sin that was in the Camp. To expose these stones to the view of Israel subjected the people to death. Thus it was that the second two tables of stone were placed in an ark, or chest, which Moses made before he went up the mount on the second occasion (Deut 10.1-3). Israel was not, therefore, exposed to the demands of the two tables on which God had written.

The golden pot of manna

Comment has been made regarding this when dealing with 16.32-36. The command of the Lord to put a pot of manna in the Ark was given by Moses to Aaron. Although no mention is made here of it being a golden pot, we owe that information to the Epistle to the Hebrews (9.4). Vital truths are represented in this manna.

Christ is the bread of God come down from heaven (Jn 6.33) who is the food of His people. To feed on Him is the spiritual privilege available for every Christian, and indeed spiritual health is dependent on doing so. Reference to this is also made by the Lord when addressing the church in Pergamos (Rev 2.17): "To him that overcometh will I give to eat of the hidden manna". This manna was unique because it was not subject to corruption, (unlike any other manna that was kept beyond the days for which it was given), and therefore represented the glorious fact that He did not see corruption in the grave, nor will He ever be subject to it.

Again, the "hidden" nature of this manna has sweet lessons to teach. It is true that, with reference to believers, Paul writes, "your life is hid with Christ in God" (Col 3.3), but here it is seen that the food of the believer is also hidden. Only those who have been to the Sanctuary can feast on it. Enjoyment of Christ is not delayed until heaven is entered; there are precious foretastes now for all who seek the Sanctuary.

How remarkable it is that within the Ark, resting side by side, were to be found that which brought death to man in his sinful condition and that which sustained the spiritual life of man. This food had been provided without any lowering of divine standards.

Aaron's rod that budded

The event that led to Aaron's rod budding was the rebellion of Korah (Num 16.1-50). It is sad to note that this is the only recorded incident involving the nation in the years between the refusal of the people to enter Canaan and the commencement of the journey to the land (Num 20.1). It is a solemn thing when all that can be recorded of a period of life is disobedience; a warning to all of the possibility of wasted years. Korah, with willing accomplices in the persons of Dathan and Abiram (On, the third conspirator, seemed to have abandoned the plan early), rose up with 250 princes of the congregation to confront Moses and Aaron with the complaint that they were lifting themselves "above the congregation of the Lord" (v.3). Their claim was that there was no need of priests as "all the congregation are holy" and had equal rights to come before God. This was only pretence as their motive was to have a prominent, if not the sole, place in the priesthood themselves (v.10).

The matter was resolved by laying up in the Tabernacle a rod for each of the tribes of Israel, with the name of Aaron being written on the rod of Levi. The following morning saw the rod of Aaron with buds, blossoms, and almonds, and by this remarkable display the right of the family of Aaron to be priests was confirmed. How significant is all of this! The almond tree is the first to blossom, in January, and indicates here the precedence of the Aaronic family in the matter of the priesthood. But it cannot escape notice that from a dry, dead rod there came forth an abundance of life - the bud, the blossom, and the fruit, and that all in one night. It is a glorious picture of resurrection, the rich fullness of the almond blossom declaring the richness and beauty of resurrection life. Inside the Ark, therefore, there was that which signifies the resurrection of the Lord Jesus. Aaron had been appointed High Priest, a shadow of a coming Great High Priest who now serves in resurrection, having entered the true Tabernacle with His own blood, not that of animal sacrifices.

The staves

The staves were kept in the golden rings until the Ark was placed in the Temple, when they were drawn out (1 Kings 8.8; 2 Chr 5.9). The presence of the staves indicated that this was a vessel that was to be carried through the wilderness by the Levites. There was a specific order given for the march, with each group of tribes travelling in the order in which they pitched their tents round the Tabernacle.

> Leading group: Judah; Issachar; Zebulun.
> *Gershon: carrying the curtains, coverings, hangings, cords.*
> *Merari: carrying the boards, bars, pins, pillars, sockets.*
>
> Second group: Reuben, Simeon, Gad.
> *Kohath: carrying the Ark, vail, holy vessels.*
>
> Third group: Ephraim; Manasseh; Benjamin.
>
> Fourth group: Dan; Asher; Naphtali.

It can be seen, therefore, that the Kohathites, who were charged with carrying the sacred vessels, journeyed in the centre of the march with six tribes in front of them and six tribes behind them. It must be observed, however, that in Numbers 10.33 the order is changed: "And they departed from the mount of the Lord three days' journey: and the ark of the covenant of the Lord went before them in the three days' journey". The cause of this appears to be the appeal by Moses to his father-in-law that he should accompany them on the march as he knew the area well and could help them in seeking places to camp. The Lord will not give His place to another; He has promised to lead them and it is clearly stated that "the ark of the covenant of the Lord went before them in the three days' journey, to search out a resting place for them". The services of Moses' father-in-law, no matter how willingly offered, were not required! How much better to have the "Shepherd of Israel, thou that leadest Joseph like a flock" (Ps 80.1) going before. Truly they were "thy people and sheep of thy pasture" (Ps 79.13), and they enjoyed being led beside the "still waters" (Ps 23.2). The word "still" (quietness, or rest - 4496) is the same as is translated "*resting* place". What care and consideration He showed towards Israel as He fed "his flock like a shepherd", gathered "the lambs with his arm", carried them "in his bosom", and gently led "those that are with young" (Is 40.11). The pilgrim journey would not be travelled alone!

The Ark at last came to rest (1 Kings 8.6; 2 Chr 5.7) when Solomon built the Temple in Jerusalem and it was taken there in solemn, yet joyful procession. In the innermost Sanctuary it was placed under the outstretched wings of two cherubims made from olive wood. These cherubims were 10 cubits high, half the height of the Sanctuary. Entrance into the Sanctuary was through the vail and then through two doors made also of olive wood. The account in 1 Kings 8.8 states that "they drew out the staves, that the ends of the staves were seen out in the holy place before the oracle, and they were not seen without". It is difficult to understand what this means. The suggestion most often given is that the staves were only partially withdrawn from the Ark, and because of this their ends made indentations in the vail, which could be seen from the Holy Place. The main objection to this is that the two doors, which were inside the vail, would make this impossible. Another suggestion is that the staves were left partially in place to guide the High Priest to the Ark when he entered the Sanctuary on the Day of Atonement, and that they were situated so that immediately he entered the Sanctuary the staves were at the door. The difficulty about this is that there is no indication in Scripture that this was the purpose of the staves being left in that position. It appears that the staves were partially withdrawn and that they were so placed that they could be seen when the Sanctuary was entered. The true explanation seems clear. The presence of the staves would be a constant reminder that the Ark had been in the Tabernacle, had traversed the wilderness, and had crossed the Jordan. The journey to the land would not be forgotten, a truth that would be appreciated by those who entered the Sanctuary. Believers today enter the true Sanctuary, appreciating as they do so the good hand of God that has led them into blessing. In the glory at the end of life's pilgrimage, this journey and the faithfulness of the God who led us will not be forgotten.

The overall picture

The Ark, therefore, pictures the Lord Jesus; He who is God and became a man; who lived on earth loving the Law of God and perfectly keeping it; who rose from the dead in triumphant power, and serves now as Great High Priest. As the Ark was the centre for Israel in their life and worship, so He must be the centre of the life and worship of His people today.

The Construction of the Mercy Seat

The Mercy Seat was a slab of pure gold measuring $2\frac{1}{2}$ cubits long and $1\frac{1}{2}$ cubits broad so that it fitted exactly on the top of the Ark, held in place by the crown of gold which was around the border of the open top of the Ark. There are no measurements given for the thickness of the slab of pure gold. The Mercy Seat was, therefore, the lid of the Ark. There was no shittim wood used in its construction indicating that the work of which it speaks was carried out by One who is God, the pure gold emphasising the righteousness of God.

The Significance of the Mercy Seat

The Mercy Seat (3727) means "covering". It was the place where God and man met. Of such importance is this that the Holy of Holies is called "the place of the mercy seat" (1 Chr 28.11). On the Day of Atonement, which took place on the 10th day of the 7th month, the High Priest entered the Holiest of All and sprinkled blood, once on and seven times before the Mercy Seat, for his own sins. He re-entered and again sprinkled blood as he had done on his first entrance, but on this occasion it was for the sins of the people (Lev 16.14-15). It is, as the hymn writer has stated, a "blood stained Mercy Seat".

On that annual feast, the blood on the Mercy Seat made atonement for the sins of the High Priest, his household, and all the people. The Mercy Seat was the place of atonement. To atone for sins was not merely the covering of them to be dealt with finally after Calvary, but the satisfying of divine righteousness as far as they were concerned. By "atoning", the blood placed on and before the Mercy Seat satisfied God and sins were dealt with.

When the Mercy Seat is referred to in the New Testament (Heb 9.5; Rom 3.25), the Greek word that is used is *hilasterion* (2435). It is the word used in the Septuagint in 25.17 and is the Greek translation of the Hebrew word KAPPORET (3727). The reference in Hebrews is made when the items of furniture in the Holiest of All are listed, but that in Romans refers to the Lord Jesus, "Whom God hath set forth to be a *propitiation*". He is the One who makes it possible for God and man to meet together. Propitiation is that act by which it is possible for a righteous God to have his anger against sin satisfied and thus to forgive.

The blood sprinkled on the Mercy Seat displayed before God that judgment had been carried out on sin. The claims of righteousness had not been compromised but had been met. Sins had not been swept under the carpet or put out of the way to be brought back at a future date; they had been judged, the punishment had been borne, and God was satisfied. His anger against sin had been expressed in the death of the victim.

When considering the work of the Lord Jesus in this respect it must be emphasised that His death did not just deal with sins which were committed after the Cross. The work of the Cross was effective before the event took place, and past sins were not overlooked, but those with faith had their sins forgiven and fully dealt with in view of that death of the Saviour that would take place. In this God was righteous (Rom 3.25-26).

Looking into the Ark

When the Ark, returning from the land of the Philistines (1 Sam 6) with the beasts pulling the cart on which it was placed, arrived at Beth-shemesh, the men of that place looked into the Ark and, as result, many died. An important principle is seen in this sad incident. No doubt it was curiosity which moved these men to lift the Mercy Seat and gaze on the two tables of stone, the opportunity of looking on what had come down the mount in the hands of Moses being too great a temptation to resist. But this act of folly exposed them to the Law without the protection of the Mercy Seat. It exposed them to the righteous demands of divine holiness without the work of propitiation coming between, and death was the consequence. Christians today enter the presence of God, and without the work of the Lord Jesus Christ this would result in immediate judgment, but the fact the God "sent his Son to be the propitiation for our sins"(1 Jn 4.10) enables them to do so with confidence. The Mercy Seat is in place; the golden crown ensures that it will never be dislodged.

Coming at this time in the history of Israel this tragedy reminded the nation that, although their sin had caused the Ark to be taken captive by their enemies, the holiness associated with it had not been diminished; the Ark had not been compromised in any way.

The Making of the Cherubims

There were two cherubims, one on either side of the Mercy Seat; "one cherub on the one end, and one cherub on the other end" (v.19). Their wings reached upward meeting above the Mercy Seat and their faces were towards each other looking down towards the Mercy Seat (v.20). Keil & Delitzsch write, "…the cherubs were to spread out their wings in such a manner as to form a screen over the *kapporet*, with their faces turned towards one another, but inclining or stooping towards the *kapporet*". They were made of gold that was beaten out, a process requiring very considerable skill. They were at one with the Mercy Seat in that they were beaten out on the same golden block. In that way they were as secure as the Mercy Seat, forming part of it. No measurements or other descriptions are specified, but, given the dimensions of the Ark and the Mercy Seat, they could not have been of great size.

There has been much conjecture regarding the appearance of these cherubims, and the description given to the living creatures in the vision of Ezekiel 1 is often applied to them. These creatures there had "the likeness of a man" (v.5); they had four faces, of man, lion, ox and eagle, and four wings (vv.6,10); they had feet and hands on their four sides under their four wings (vv.7,8). In Ezekiel 10 they are identified as cherubims (v.1), but there is nothing to indicate that the cherubims standing above the Mercy Seat were similar in appearance. Indeed, in Exodus, the fact that "their faces shall look one to another" would appear to indicate that each had one face and not four as in Ezekiel's account. There may be cherubims of differing appearance or it may be that they manifest themselves in different ways. From what is written in the Exodus account, a full description of the two cherubims cannot be given, the writer to the Hebrews confirming this by stating, "And over it the cherubims of glory shadowing the mercy-seat; of which we cannot now speak particularly" (Heb 9.5). Wuest makes this even clearer in his Expanded Translation: "…concerning which things we cannot now speak in detail".

The Significance of the Cherubims

After the Fall, the Lord God "drove out the man; and he placed at the east of the garden of Eden cherubims, and a flaming sword which turned every way, to keep the way of the tree of life" (Gen 3.24). They were there to keep man out of the presence of God, but now, in the Tabernacle, they looked at the Mercy Seat and saw the blood that allowed man to approach God. There was no flaming sword in their hand; the blood made this unnecessary. Feinberg comments that "Cherubim, wherever found in Scripture, are related to the holiness of God. They do not represent a likeness to God, which was forbidden by commandment. They are instruments of His government".[†] The holiness of God is not affected by sinful man approaching Him when the shed blood has dealt with his sin, righteous demands having been fully and eternally satisfied.

It has already been observed above that the Hebrew writer refers to them as the "cherubims of glory" (9.5). This may refer to their being cherubims to whom bright glory belongs, or to their being the cherubims which have to do with His glory. The latter appears to be more appropriate. They are the bearers of the divine glory.

The number "two" in Scripture signifies reliable, confirmed testimony, and the presence of two cherubims confirmed that the blood had been shed and no judgment need fall on the High Priest as he approached. It is not without significance that Matthew records that it was to two women, Mary Magdalene and the other Mary, that the Lord appeared on the day of resurrection (Mt 28.1-10). Mark indicates that Mary Magdalene, Mary the mother of James, and Salome (Mk 16.1-8) found an empty tomb. Luke states (24.1) that "they", that is the women who came with Him from Galilee (23.55-56), amongst whom were Mary Magdalene, Joanna, and Mary the mother of James (24.10), were at the tomb that morning. John points out that Mary Magdalene brought the news to Peter and John (Jn 20.1-10) who ran and entered the tomb and found the linen grave clothes and the napkin which covered His head, but He had gone. In each case, and more could be cited, there was more than one witness, confirming accurate testimony to the fact that they found an empty tomb. The same principle holds good in regard to the resurrection appearances of the Lord Jesus to others. Matthew states that the eleven disciples saw Him in Galilee (28.16,17); Mark that He "appeared in another form to two of them, as they walked, and went into the country" (16.12), and then that He appeared to the eleven as they sat at meat (16.14); Luke that He appeared to two on the road to Emmaus, doubtless the same incident referred to by Mark (24.13-32), and to the eleven (24.33-49); John that He appeared to his disciples on the evening of the first day of the week (20.19-23), and then one week later (Jn 20.26-29). No attempt is made here to show how these accounts reconcile, they are brought together to emphasise that the principle of at least two witness was upheld as firm evidence of the truth of one of the vital foundation doctrines of the Christian faith.

"There I will meet with thee"

There now had been laid before Moses the design for the Ark, on which were the Mercy Seat and the two cherubims with outstretched wings and faces directed towards each other, but looking down on the blood on the Mercy Seat. This was where the Lord said that He would "meet with thee, and…commune with thee" (v.22). He decreed that this would be "from between the two cherubims which are upon the ark of the testimony". The glory, therefore, resided immediately above the Mercy Seat, between the cherubims. Asaph wrote of this: "thou that dwellest between the cherubims, shine forth" (Ps 80.1). The unknown author of Psalm 99 (whom many consider to be David) rejoiced in it: "he sitteth between the cherubims; let the earth be moved" (v.1). The Ark was known as "the ark of God the Lord, that dwelleth between the cherubims, whose name is called on it" (1 Chr 13.6). There are altogether seven references to this - 1 Sam 4.4; 2 Sam 6.2; 1 Kings 19.15; 1 Chr 13.6; Ps 80.1; Ps 99.1; Is 37.16.

Note that the Lord stated to Moses that there "I will meet with *thee* and I will commune with *thee*". It appears, therefore, that Moses had access to the Holiest of All and there the Lord would speak to him.

The Throne of Grace

For the High Priest, approaching the Ark and Mercy Seat was a solemn, annual event, limited because of the sin of the priestly family. Each year there must have been some fear in his heart. Had all of the commandments of the Lord been carried out? Was everything in order to enable him to approach? Because of failure to do this, would he be exposed to the judgment of God? The people would share this fear until the day was over and all was well. But, if all had been carried out according to the word of God there would be no reason for fear in their hearts. Christians need have no such anxiety. The throne before which they come is a throne of grace, not a throne of judgment (Heb 4.16), where they "may obtain mercy, and find grace to help in time of need". The great privilege given to Aaron and Moses is one that all believers today enjoy. At any time, in any place, under any circumstances, it is possible to come boldly to the throne of grace. He has done all the work and therefore it has been done perfectly.

Notes

10 An illustration of the Ark and its Mercy Seat is given in Appendix 6.

18 *The Prophecy of Ezekiel*, ch.1.

EXODUS 25.23-30

The Table of Shewbread[†]

Having dealt with what was placed in the Holiest of All, the Lord now gives instruction for the vessels which had to be located in the Holy Place, the Table of Shewbread being first described (vv.23-20). It stood in the Holy Place on the north side (40.22).

The Construction of the Table

This is the first mention in Scripture of a "table". The Table of Shewbread was made of the same materials as the Ark - shittim wood overlaid with pure gold. It measured 2 cubits long by 1 cubit broad by $1^{1}/_{2}$ cubits high. It was the same height as the Ark but shorter in length and breadth. Round its top there was a crown of gold, and on the outside of this crown was a border that measured a handbreadth. On the outer edge of this border there was another crown of gold. It had four legs, and four rings made of gold were fastened to these legs at the top, close to the border. Staves were made, also of shittim wood overlaid with gold, and these were used for carrying the Table. The dishes and utensils for use with the Table were made of pure gold: dishes (7086) on which was placed the Shewbread; spoons (3709; cups, JND) for the sweet spice incense; covers (7184; goblets, JND) for pouring out the drink offering libations; bowls (4518) for offering the drink offerings, for they were "to cover withal", or "with which to pour out" (JND), or it may be that they were to receive the drink offerings poured out from the goblets. The border, measuring one handbreadth, was for holding securely the goblets, spoons, and bowls. This would always be necessary, particularly when they were travelling.

The Shewbread
How the bread was prepared and presented

It is not until Leviticus 24.5-9 that instructions are given in respect of the Shewbread, but a study of the Table without mention of the Shewbread would be less than complete. Each week twelve loaves were baked, and on the Sabbath set in two rows, six in a row, upon the Table. Each loaf consisted of 2 tenth deals of fine flour: in excess of six lbs (2.7 kilos) in weight. Given the size of each loaf, therefore, and of the size of the Table, it would not be possible to place these loaves, six side by side, in two flat rows. The loaves would be baked in a round shape, and each row would have six of them placed one upon the other. Strong confirms that the loaves were of considerable size: "Five of them were sufficient for hungry David and his companions, perhaps for several meals" (1 Sam 21.1-6). Frankincense was put on each row, and after the new bread had been placed on the Table the bread that had been there for the previous seven days was for the use of the priests; "And it shall be Aaron's and his sons', and they shall eat it in the holy place" (Lev 24.9).

The names given to the bread

A number of names are given to the Shewbread, each bringing out truth associated with it.

Cakes. The name "cakes" (2471), used of the Shewbread, is also used of the meal offering (Lev 2.4), at the consecration of the priests (Ex 29.2; Lev 8.26), in the offerings of the Nazarite (Num 6.15), and in the offering of the firstfruits in the land (Num 15.20). The word means "pierced cakes", the piercing being carried out probably to ensure that the cakes were baked in a shorter time. The spiritual significance, however, cannot be overlooked. The Lord Jesus was pierced, suffering for others, even although there was in Him a beauty and fragrance which the world had never before seen or experienced. The beauty, however, could only be enjoyed by those who entered the Sanctuary.

Bread of the Presence (25.30, JND margin). This has also been translated "Bread of the Face", the point being that this bread was set before the face of God. It was there for His enjoyment and pleasure, and also that He might constantly look on that which fed His people, sustaining their priestly exercise.

Continual bread (Num 4.7). These twelve loaves were never hidden from God, as the Lord Jesus is always before His face. Neither was this bread ever absent from the Table. While they journeyed it was emphasised that a cloth of blue was to be spread over the Table "and the continual bread shall be thereon". Even as they were moving through the wilderness the Shewbread was on the Table.

Hallowed bread (1 Sam 21.4). This is how Ahimelech the priest referred to the Shewbread when David and those who were with him came to the Tabernacle at Nob, asking for five loaves of bread to feed him and his men. This bread was hallowed, set apart for priestly use, yet Ahimelech willingly offered it to David. It has been suggested that this was an example of the law of loving your neighbour taking precedence over that which is ceremonial. That may be, but David was very conscious of the absence of the Ark. Psalm 132 indicates that as a youth in Bethlehem he had heard of it, and in later life, when on the throne, his desire was to build a house for it. He therefore recognised that the ritual being carried out in the Tabernacle was meaningless. Without the Ark there was no substance in what took place, nor is it recorded that there was any desire on the part of the priests or the people to have the Ark returned to the Tabernacle. Perhaps the presence of the Lord in the midst of His people was too demanding for them. With no Ark present, only an empty form of ritual was carried out, and honesty demanded that this be recognised when David and his followers had need of bread.

What a warning to this generation! Is the presence of the Lord too demanding for His people? Is it preferable to lower standards and live in a make-belief world of empty ritual?

Loaves to be set in rows (1 Chr 9.32, JND). The orderliness of the presentation of the bread is indicated here. Everything about the Lord Jesus is ordered in a way that is pleasing to heaven.

Exposition of the loaves (Heb 9.2, JND). This again has the thought of being set out before God and is the New Testament equivalent of "Bread of the Presence".

The Significance of the Table
The fellowship of the Table

It has already been observed that this is the first mention of a table in the Word of God. A table is a place at which meals are taken and at times is used to signify a meal: "Thou preparest a table before me in the presence of mine enemies" (Ps 23.5), and, "Can God furnish a table in the wilderness?" (Ps 78.19). The purpose of God in erecting the Tabernacle was not only to provide Himself with a dwelling place, but also to provide a set table at which His guests could partake and be satisfied. White comments: "Upon it the eye of Jehovah could rest with satisfaction and delight, whilst His priests were nourished and strengthened by its hallowed bread". The table, therefore, is a place of food and fellowship, for only those who are at one can sit at ease and without disturbance at the same table. Particularly it is only those who are in fellowship with the host who can partake at his table. It was the absence of David from the table of Saul (1 Sam 20.24-27) which indicated that David, because of the enmity of the king, no longer regarded Saul as one with whom he should sit at table.

The food of the Table

Of what then does the Shewbread speak? Some see it signifying the twelve tribes of Israel that are constantly before the Lord, but would that which signified His people be the food of priests? Most unlikely! Priests do not feed on the people of the Lord; they feed on the Lord Himself. The Shewbread, therefore, signified the Lord as the food of His people. Lessons have already been learned from the manna which was the food of Israel in the wilderness and which spoke of the Lord Jesus Christ. The Shewbread, however, is in the Sanctuary; it is Christ, the food of His people, enjoyed in the Sanctuary.

These loaves were made of fine flour indicating the spotless perfection of Jesus, the Son of God; there was no unclean or impure grain, no husk had been ground into the flour, no chaff of any kind had marred the ingredients for these loaves. Here is manhood absolutely free from all traces of sin, as holy as is God. The flour could be run through the fingers and all was felt to be fine, pure, and perfect, with a smoothness leaving a sense of satisfaction that no roughening grain was there; manhood with no roughness but in every way fine and even. None of the coarseness that was seen in others, even in the most faithful of God's servants, was to be found in Him. There was no leaven present, for sin was absent from Him, and it was impossible for the Son of God to commit sin of any kind.

Yet this fine flour had to be pierced, as has been noted, and then subjected to the heat of the furnace. He had to endure temptations at the hand of Satan, sorrow at sin and its consequences, so clearly seen around Him, rejection by sinners and derision heaped upon Him by evil tongues, the plots of the Jews to put Him to death, and ultimately the buffets and blows of coarse, uncouth men as they vilified Him. Through all this He remained pure, the fine flour as fine at the end as it had been at the beginning. He delighted to do His will and His ear was open to His God morning by morning (Is 50.4-5).

In the Sanctuary the priests were able to partake of the loaves, and figuratively feast on Christ. The manna gave energy for the wilderness; the Shewbread gave energy for the Sanctuary. But it is vital to understand that the bread on which the priests fed had been enjoyed by God for seven days. For as long as He took to create a universe, He gazed on that which spoke of Christ as the food of His people. Priestly appetites were satisfied with that which satisfied heaven. Nothing else could meet the needs of those who ministered in the holy things.

Each Sabbath these loaves were changed. They were never allowed to become stale, but were always fresh in the presence of God. Never will there be anything stale about the Lord Jesus Christ. What He is and what He endured is clothed in an eternal freshness. Frankincense was placed upon each row "for a memorial, even an offering made by fire" (Lev 24.7). Keil & Delitzsch's comment on "memorial" (AZKARA - 234), in respect of the meal offering in Leviticus is pertinent. "*Azkarah*...is only applied to Jehovah's portion, which was burned upon the altar in the case of the meat-offering (Lev 2.9,16; and 6.8), the sin-offering of flour (Lev 5.12), and the jealousy-offering (Num 5.26), and to the incense added to the shew-bread (Lev 24.7). It does not mean the prize portion, i.e. the portion offered for the glory of God...still less the fragrance-offering...but the memorial, or remembrance-portion...inasmuch as that part of the *mincha* [the offering] which was placed upon the altar ascended in the smoke of the fire on behalf of the giver, as a practical *mememto* ('remember me') to Jehovah". Strong considers that the frankincense referred to was placed in vessels from which it was taken for burning on the Golden Altar. "Frankincense appears to have been deposited not directly upon the loaves themselves, but in vessels for that purpose, where it could be conveniently renewed as fast as it should be consumed by the daily ministrations at the altar of incense". This frankincense, however, could not be used for the daily ministrations upon the Golden Altar of Incense because the sweet incense used for that purpose consisted of stacte, onycha, galbanum, and frankincense blended together (30.34-36). But yet this frankincense, which was placed on the loaves as they were set on the Table of Shewbread is said to be, as has already been noted, "an offering made by fire unto the Lord" (Lev 24.7). The procedure carried out by the priests therefore appears to be that after the frankincense was placed on the bread, the remainder of it was burned on the Golden Altar, the sweet fragrance which arose being that of the same frankincense which was upon the bread. Thus the loaves are brought before Jehovah for His pleasure and enjoyment.

Today, Christian priests partake of this holy food; it accompanies them on the pilgrim journey and sustains them as they travel. It is a feast that cannot fail to satisfy, and which never grows stale. To feast on Christ Jesus, the true Bread of the Presence, is to enjoy provision that will give all the variety of diet required; a banquet that meets the need of every part, and never fails to amaze in its diversity.

Notes

23 An illustration of the Table of Shewbread is given in Appendix 6.

EXODUS 25.31-40

The Lampstand[†]

The purpose of the Lampstand was to provide light in the Holy Place, and it was positioned on the south side, directly opposite the Table of Shewbread. It provided the only light in the Sanctuary where the priests ministered. Henry Law comments: "Reader, in holy thought enter the holy Tent. You pass a curtain rich in richest hues. Then what a scene appears! Light in its loveliest gleams around. The pure-gold sides, the pure-gold vessels, the sparkling canopy, the cherubed vail cast back resplendent rays, Whence flows this tide of day? The orbs of heaven lend not their aid. No sun-gleam plays, no moon-beam sleeps, upon the radiant walls. A Candlestick alone lifts high a seven-crowned head: and night is no more known".

The Construction of the Lampstand

The Lampstand, like the Ark, was made of pure gold, and was beaten out according to the pattern that had been given to Moses. The weight of gold employed was one talent (v.39) or, according to Newberry's tables, approximately 116 lbs (52.16 kilos). It was made with a centre shaft which sprang from the base on which the Lampstand sat. From the centre shaft there came six branches, three on either side. Each of these branches, and the centre shaft, were decorated with bowls, knops, and flowers. It is difficult to be certain about the appearance of these three pieces of ornamentation. Some suggestions, however, can be made.

The decoration on the branches

Bowls (1375). These are made like almonds (v.33), "the nut, not the blossom, for which this term is never used" (Strong).

Knops (3730). There is some difficulty in coming to an understanding of how these were formed. It appears that they were ornamented swellings somewhat like "a capital on top of a pillar...a knob or bulb on the lampstand" (TWOT at 1029). Strong states that this was like a "double-flaring circlet, like the capital of a column.

Flowers (6525). These would appear to be in the form of buds bursting into bloom.

It should first be observed that the centre shaft is described as being the shaft and the other six branches as "his branch" (v.31, Newberry margin). The words translated "branches" in the AV is in the singular. JND renders this as "its base and its shaft". This sets the centre shaft as being apart from the other branches. It was decorated differently and was the main part of the Lampstand; all the other branches came from it.

The centre shaft or branch was decorated with four bowls, each with a knop and a flower. Each of the six other branches had three bowls, but only one knop and one flower. On the top of each of the seven branches there was a lamp, in the shape of an almond flower into which was placed a receptacle for its oil, as there was no central reservoir for the oil.

No detail is given as to the height of the Lampstand. As the High Priest was responsible for cleaning and refilling the bowls it is reasonable to assume that the height was such that this task could be carried out without climbing up to reach the bowls. They must, therefore, have been within the reach of a man, and Jewish tradition, which Josephus confirms, puts it as being 5 feet (1.54 metres) high and $3^1/_2$ feet (just over 1 metre) wide, but this cannot be confirmed from Scripture.

The Lampstand was made by beating it out from the pure gold, a task which required considerable skill and energy. It was to be "one beaten work" (v.36). It is of more than passing interest to observe that the oil for the light was beaten (27.20; Lev 24.1-4), as was the sweet incense for use in the Holy Place (30.36).

Tongs and snuffdishes

No indication is given as to the number of pure gold tongs and snuffers which had to be made.

Tongs (4457). The tongs, or tweezers, would be used to clean the lamps by taking away the deposits that gathered in them, and for dealing with the spent wicks. Without this being done, the Lamp would not give its light as it should, and smoke would rise from it as it burned.

Snuffdishes (4289). These were trays, firepans, or dishes into which the deposits taken from the lamps were placed. There were also used to carry the fire with which to light the lamps after they were cleaned.

The Significance of the Lampstand
The light

Once again, in the pure gold there is seen the deity of the Lord Jesus Christ. He is the light of the Sanctuary. It is not here the Lord as the light of the world, for this light was not seen outside of the Sanctuary, it is Christ as the light of His people as they come before God. He meets every need in the Sanctuary: the food to sustain priestly exercise and the light by which priests can minister are of His supply.

In the wider context, all light finds its source in God for "God is light, and in him is no darkness at all" (1 Jn 1.5). No matter, therefore, what light is required He is the giver and sustainer of it. The first spoken words recorded in the Scriptures are, "Let there be light" (Gen 1.3), and light came into being, even before the sun was in the heavens. He is, therefore, the giver of natural light. John wrote of the Lord Jesus Christ that "In him was life; and the life was the light of men. And the light shineth in darkness; and the darkness comprehended it not" (Jn 1.4-5). The light to which this refers is not natural but spiritual.

The purpose of light is to reveal, and without it all is obscurity. Thus, without spiritual light all is darkness and ignorance. This is the state in which the Adversary holds those who are under the "power of darkness" (Col 1.13). Added to ignorance, darkness brings fear, but when the Lord Jesus comes into the life all this changes as Peter explains: "But ye are a chosen generation, a royal priesthood, an holy nation, a peculiar people; that ye should shew forth the praises of him who hath called you out of darkness into his marvellous light" (1 Pet 2.9). Before salvation came they were in darkness because "the god of this world hath blinded the minds of them which believe not, lest the light of the glorious gospel of Christ, who is the image of God, should shine unto them" (2 Cor 4.4). But, when the gospel was believed, what a change came about, "For God, who commanded the light to shine out of darkness, hath shined in our hearts, to give the light of the knowledge of the glory of God in the face of Jesus Christ" (2 Cor 4.6). So, light is inseparable from God and His desire is that His people should enjoy that spiritual light which He can give.

Returning to the Lampstand in the Holy Place, Soltau† observes that there are three reasons given for its being there.

1. The light was to be lit "before the Lord" (40.25). It shed its light in God's presence. It lit up the Holy Place.

2. The Lampstand was placed opposite the Table of Shewbread (26.35) and would, therefore, cast its light over the Table.

3. The Lampstand lit up itself: "Speak unto Aaron, and say into him, When thou lightest the lamps, the seven lamps shall give light over against the candlestick" (Num 8.2). "One chief object of the light was to illumine, and thereby display, the Candlestick itself".

Beaten gold

The fact that the gold was beaten must not escape the attention of the reader, for this is a feature of deep significance. Before any oil could be placed in the Lampstand the gold had to be beaten (as did the oil - see 27.20-21), and it is with the greatest of reverence that this "beaten" gold is considered. "He is…a man of sorrows, and acquainted with grief" (Is 53.3), and, "Is it nothing to you, all ye that pass by? behold and see if there be any sorrow like unto my sorrow, which is done unto me, wherewith the Lord hath afflicted me in the day of his fierce anger" (Lam 1.12), are all words that can be truly attributed to Him.

He wept as He looked over Jerusalem; at Bethany tears flowed from His eyes as He looked on the havoc wrought by death; He sighed and was burdened. Men sought to put Him to death, the One who had told them the truth.

The bowls

The description of the ornamentation of the central shaft and the six branches first mentions the bowls that were like almonds (vv.33-34). The precedence given to them here indicates that they were of prime importance, and they are, therefore, a key factor in understanding the meaning of the Lampstand. A two-fold significance is seen in the almonds.

The first mention of almonds in Scripture indicates that they were regarded as being amongst the choicest of fruits: "And their father Israel said unto them, If it must be so now, do this; take of the best fruits in the land in your vessels, and carry down the man a present, a little balm, and a little honey, spices, and myrrh, nuts, and almonds" (Gen 43.11). Now note the word of the Lord that came to Jeremiah asking, "Jeremiah, what seest thou?", to which the answer was given: "I see a rod of an almond tree". The Lord replied, "Thou hast well seen: for I will hasten my word to perform it" (Jer 1.11-12). "The idea of watchfulness which is basic to the root affords the key to the explanation of the Hebrew name for the almond tree" (TWOT at 2451). The almond tree blossoms in January before any other tree and is seen as watching over the spring as it comes in. In that way Jeremiah learns that the Lord is watching over Judah.

Aaron's rod that budded yielded almonds (Num 17.8). The laying up of the rods before the Lord followed the rebellion of Korah against Moses and Aaron. One of the aims of this rebellion was that Aaron and his sons should share the priesthood, probably leading to the rightful priests being displaced. In order to confirm who should be priests the Lord asked that one rod for each tribe be laid up before Him, and the rod that budded would reveal the will of God on the matter. It was Aaron's rod that "budded, and brought forth buds, and blossomed blossoms, and yielded almonds". Such abundance of life coming from a dead, dry rod is a picture of resurrection. The fact that almonds blossomed, and that they were the first to bud, speaks of "Christ the firstfruits" (1 Cor 15.23) in resurrection.

There is one other mention of the almond that cannot be ignored. When the preacher writes of old age he states that it is the time when "the almond tree shall flourish" (Eccl 12.5), a reference to the white hair of those who are older as pictured in the white blossom of the almond tree. This combination of resurrection, and the long years of those who have hair like almond blossom, brings to the attention of the reader the fact that, having risen from the dead, Christ is alive for evermore. "I am he that liveth, and was dead; and, behold, I am alive for evermore" (Rev 1.18), were the words heard by the aged John as he fell at the feet of the Lord who declared Himself to be "Alpha and Omega" (Rev 1.11).

In addition to emphasising the One who liveth "for ever" (Heb 7.17), that is "to the ages", this also reminds the reader of Him who is the "Ancient of days" seen by Daniel in the night visions. This is He to whom the "Son of man came with the clouds of heaven" (Dan 7.13). The unity of the Godhead, three Persons in one, gives the assurance that He who came from heaven to be the Saviour of the world is also eternal - He has been from before all ages.

Bringing these two factors together it can be seen that the almond pictures the Lord Jesus Christ in resurrection, caring for and safeguarding His people. In the Sanctuary He carefully watches over His own, providing the light for them to be there, and lovingly cherishing them as they worship. The fact of His resurrection reminds every servant of His that the Lord has said, "I will hasten my word to perform it". In the context of the lesson already referred to in Jeremiah 1.12 it is a work of judgment that is in view, but for believers today the resurrection of Christ is the living confirmation that His work will be hastened; there will be no delays; He will perform it completely. That is one of the blessings that come from being in the Sanctuary. The world forces false values upon believers, but in the Sanctuary what is true is enjoyed, His resurrection being a token of His certain triumph. This is what Asaph experienced; "The ungodly, who prosper in the world" (Ps 73.12) caused him great exercise of heart. How is it that the godly may be "plagued, and chastened every morning" (v.14)? But when he "went into the sanctuary of God", he declared, "then understood I their end" (v.17). Greater even than such knowledge is that of the glory which is "the end" for the Christian. The almonds, Christ in resurrection, are a constant reminder that glory is to follow.

The knops

The Hebrew word used (3730) is, as has already been observed, indicative of a decorative capital, or encircling ornament, as the top of a column. "Apparently (it is) derived from the name of Crete, as the place from which such ornamentations were first imported" (TWOT at 1029). The knops, therefore, indicate the majesty, glory, and dignity that is associated with the resurrection of the Lord Jesus and the fact that one day He will be seen to be "King of kings, and Lord of lords" (1 Tim 6.15).

The flowers

The intricate workmanship necessary to create the beauty of the flowers demanded great skill. Flowers coming into bloom denote a beauty that is fresh and fragrant, vigorous at the time of growth. So it is that the Lord Jesus in resurrection has beauty, freshness, fragrance, and vigour that will never be diminished; it will never fade, He will never be weakened.

The seven lamps

The seven lamps shining continually in the Holy Place teach the perfection of the light that was burning. The number seven is the number of a perfect work in which God can rest and take delight, for He rested on the seventh day of creation. On the sixth day He had seen that the whole creation was "very good" (Gen 1.31), and with such work completed in perfection He could enjoy rest. All aspects of the life and work of the Lord Jesus are perfect, and in them God can take delight, as is pictured here in the One who sheds His perfect light in the Holy Place.

The prophet Zechariah saw in his fifth vision a lampstand "all of gold" (Zech 4.1-14). This differed from the Lampstand in the Tabernacle in that it had a bowl upon the top of it and pipes ran from the bowl to the lights. Two olive trees stood beside the bowl, one on the right and one on the left. Two pipes or spouts ran from the two olive trees carrying the olive oil to the bowl. This vision pictured the responsibility of Israel to be the Lord's light bearer to the world (Is 42.6). Sadly, the nation did not fulfil the responsibility with which it was charged, but one day the light will shine when the Lord comes to Zion (Is 60.1-3). This is not the place to consider that vision in detail, but it cannot be left without learning the lesson of the two olive trees. The oil speaks of the Holy Spirit and the olive trees of the unending and sufficient supply available to Israel to let the light burn. Any failure in this respect does not lie with the Lord, but with the nation. It also teaches that power for the service of the God does not come from human sources. "Not by might, nor by power, but by my spirit, saith the Lord of hosts" (Zech 4.6), confirms that the sum of all mental, intellectual and physical strength is impotent in His service. Only the work of the Holy Spirit through His servants can accomplish God's work.

The apostle John saw the Lord Jesus "in the midst of the seven candlesticks" (Rev 1.13) which "are the seven churches" (Rev 1.20). If the lampstand in the prophecy of Zechariah is a picture of Israel as the light-bearer, this vision reveals that local assemblies now are charged with that responsibility. Here there are seven separate lampstands, emphasising the autonomy of each assembly. It should never be forgotten that in the darkness of this present age assemblies must shine as lights in the gloom of a godless society.

Tongs and snuffers

In the Holy Place the lamps required attention each morning and evening (27.21). It must be understood, however, that no such cleaning was necessary with the Lord Jesus. He did not require the attention of tongs and snuffers, for His light always shone brightly. The lesson to be learned, however, is that Aaron was responsible for ordering the lamps, ensuring that that they were burning brightly "before the Lord continually" (Lev 24.3). This the Lord Jesus does in that Sanctuary which He entered when He ascended in triumph. Continually the light will burn; continually He will ensure that there is no darkness there; continually He will so order it that it is possible for those who are now priests to enter the Sanctuary and worship there. The glad and glorious truth is that no tongs or snuffers are necessary to make this possible. The light shines, but no other hand is necessary to keep it bright.

The necessity of the Lampstand

Henry Law again provides a fitting close to this study. "Without this inmate, where is the Tabernacle's splendour? Its brilliant colours are all colourless. Its golden walls are a dark blank. All form, all shape, all rays are the blank sameness of a loathsome vault. The eye looks round on undistinguishable night". Without Him of whom the Lampstand speaks all glory is gone, all beauty is dimmed, all light is absent.

Notes

31 An illustration of the Lampstand is given in Appendix 6.
31 *The Holy Vessels and Furniture of the Tabernacle.*

EXODUS 26

The Structure of the Tent[†]

Having dealt with the furnishings of the Holiest of All and of the Holy Place, God now gives instructions to Moses in respect of the coverings of the Tabernacle. These are usually described as the "curtains", and consist of
1. A curtain of fine twined linen
2. A curtain or tent made of goats' hair
3. A covering of rams' skins dyed red
4. A covering of badgers' skins.
These four sets of "curtains" formed the covering of the Tabernacle, although note must be taken that three different words are employed to describe them. It has to be said, however, that the AV does not always make this distinction clear.

Curtain (3407): "Moreover thou shalt make the tabernacle with ten *curtains* of fine twined linen..." (v.1); "And thou shalt make *curtains* of goats' hair" (v.7). This is, therefore, used of the curtain of fine twined linen and of the curtain of goats' hair. It indicates that the "curtain" hangs down as a drape.

Tent (168): "And thou shalt make curtains of goats' hair to be a *covering* upon the tabernacle" (v.7). This is used only of the curtain of goats' hair. The meaning is of a temporary dwelling, a tent or home for nomadic people.

Covering (4372): "And thou shalt make a *covering* for the tent of rams' skins dyed red, and a covering above of badgers' skins" (v.14). Strong comments that these two coverings were "a twofold blanket of skins on the outside of the walls, like a weather boarding".

Verses 1-6: The Curtains of Fine Twined Linen
The form of the fine twined linen curtains

There were ten of these curtains, each measuring 28 cubits long by 4 cubits wide; two sets of five curtains each were sewn or "coupled" together (v.3) to form two larger curtains, each measuring 28 cubits long by 20 cubits wide. Cherubims were embroidered on the curtains using the threads of blue, and purple, and scarlet. Against the pure white background of the fine linen this must have been an impressive sight. The work in embroidering these two cherubims is called "cunning" work in the sense that it was exceedingly skilful in execution. The two curtains were then formed into one, 28 cubits wide by 40 cubits long, by making fifty loops of blue on the edge of each curtain, and joining them together with fifty taches or clasps of gold.

The door, the gate, and the vail[†] were all made of fine twined linen and their description is given as being of "blue, and purple, and scarlet, and fine twined linen". This curtain differs in that it is described as being "of fine twined linen, and blue, and purple, and scarlet". It appears, therefore, that the dominant colour on this curtain was the white of the linen, whereas on the others it was blue.

The significance of the fine twined linen curtains

Fine linen is a outstanding feature of the Tabernacle and it will be encountered on a number of occasions. It was prominent in the garments of the High Priest, being found in his ephod (28.6), in his coat and mitre (28.39), and in his girdle (39.29) and breeches (28.42). Likewise, in the garments of the priests it was found in their coats, girdles, and bonnets (28.40; 39.27ff), and in their breeches (28.42). The vail (26.31), the door (26.36), the gate (27.16), and the hangings surrounding the court (27.9-15) were also made of fine twined linen. It was, therefore, not possible to be in the Tabernacle without being aware of the presence of this material; it was a major part of its structure and of the clothing of the priests.

Fine linen speaks of righteousness, confirmation of which is found in Revelation 19.8: "And to her was granted that she should be arrayed in fine linen, clean and white: for the fine linen is the righteousness of saints". In the Tabernacle curtains it is the righteousness of the Lord Jesus that is pictured in the fine linen. He it was who answered the refusal of John Baptist to baptise Him with the words, "Suffer it to be so now: for thus it becometh us to fulfil all righteousness" (Mt 3.15). Holiness and righteousness marked Him all the days of His life on earth.

The cherubims have already been seen, in connection with the Ark, to be the guardians of the presence of God. On the fine linen curtain they appear again, still guarding the holy righteousness of His presence. Embroidered on the curtains, they reminded all who looked on them that the presence of God had not to be taken lightly or to be treated with less than the reverence which He is due. These cherubims were jealous guardians of His presence, as they were when they were placed with a flaming sword at the east of the Garden of Eden "to keep the way of the tree of life" (Gen 3.24). Now, although they looked down on the Mercy Seat, in the Holiest of All, on the blood that now allowed man to approach Him, their very presence on the curtains emphasised that what marked the Holiest of All was true of all work in the Tabernacle, for no matter where a priest was within the tent he could look up and see the skilfully worked cherubims.

The dimension of the curtains, 28 cubits long by 4 cubits wide signifies a perfect work (seven), which is for all the world (four). The work of the Lord Jesus is indeed perfect and it is certainly for the entire world.

The number fifty, which was the number of the clasps of gold joining the two curtains, is significant.

1. If looked at as being the sum of forty and ten it signifies a time of education (forty) and the responsibility to put the lessons into practice

(ten). Forty years of education in Egypt, followed by forty years of education shepherding sheep was the experience of Moses. Ten is the number of responsibility: there are ten Commandments, ten fingers are given for work, and ten toes to give a balanced walk. The perfect righteousness of the Lord Jesus is an education from which all who are His servants must learn, and having learned, accept the responsibility of putting the lessons into practice.

2. When regarded as being seven times seven plus one it refers to perfect rest and a new beginning. On the seventh day of creation God rested, and thus the multiple of seven times seven speaks of perfect rest. In the Lord Jesus there is to be found perfect rest, and with Him a new beginning is enjoyed.

All this glorious beauty was for the eyes of the priests alone. No-one else ever saw this inner curtain; it was a privilege to be enjoyed only by those who had been born into the priesthood. The dominant colour of white, with the intertwined threads of blue, purple, and scarlet would be a fitting background for the light of the Lampstand. Only in the Sanctuary is there appreciation of the beautiful righteous life of the Lord Jesus; only there can there be an understanding of His sinlessness. But note that priestly eyes could not miss this; it was not avoidable! So, as believers bow before Him, there can be no escaping the fact of His righteousness. Just as the Sanctuary revealed to Asaph the true nature of the human heart and its end (Ps 73.17), so it opens to the heart of the worshipper the purity of the Lord. Who could be unaffected by such a revelation?

Verses 7-13: The Covering of Goats' Hair
The form of the goats' hair covering

The goats' hair here was not goats' skins with the hair still attached. It was material made from the spinning together of the hair of goats to form a smooth, dark, cashmere-like cloth (see 35.26). This material was used by the nomadic people as a covering for their tents, and reference is made to it when the bride-to-be in the Song of Songs states, "I am black, but comely, O ye daughters of Jerusalem, as the tents of Kedar..." (Song 1.5), likening her beauty to the black goats' hair coverings of the tents.

The covering of goats' hair consisted of curtains measuring 30 cubits long by 4 cubits wide. Each curtain was, therefore 2 cubits longer than the curtains of fine twined linen. The goats' hair would be carefully woven to make each curtain; in total eleven were made. Five of these curtains were sewn together to form one curtain measuring 20 cubits wide by 30 cubits long. The other six were sewn together to form one curtain 24 cubits long by 30 cubits wide. The two large curtains were then joined together by making fifty loops on the edge of each curtain and connecting them with clasps of brass. The sewing of them together and the means by which the two curtains were joined by clasps was similar to that employed in the fine twined linen curtains, with two exceptions. First, the loops are not said to be of blue, indeed no colour is given, and, second, the clasps are of brass and not of gold.

The significance of the goats' hair covering

Garments of goats' skin were recognised as being the dress of the prophet or the man of God: "they wandered about in sheepskins and goatskins (Heb 11.37). It was a rough garment as was seen when Jacob's mother put the skins of goats on the hands of her son so that Isaac would be led to believe that it was Esau to whom he was speaking (Gen 27.16). But it must not be overlooked that it was not goatskin but the woven hair from the goat that was used for the Tabernacle. It was, therefore, not rough but of exceeding fineness.

The lesson is that the goats' hair speaks of the Lord Jesus as the Prophet of God, of One who had no roughness about Him, but with a fineness of character and words that were unique to Him. Even although He was rejected and His teaching regarded as being of no consequence, His steps dogged constantly by men who sought to slay Him, His words derided and despised, His fine character was never roughened.

Note that no one would see this curtain. Underneath it was the linen curtain and on top of it was placed the rams' skins dyed red. There are some features that are for the eye of God and cannot be appreciated by worshippers. The faithfulness of this Prophet and all that this involved is pictured here.

Verse 14: The Covering of Rams' Skins and Badgers' Skins
The form of the rams' skins and badgers' skins coverings

Little is written regarding these two coverings. No dimensions are noted and there are no instructions for the sewing of them together. The simple statement is made that "Thou shalt make a covering for the tent of rams' skins dyed red, and a covering above of badgers' skins". Two features, however, can be discerned. First, the two coverings must have been of a size to cover the structure of the Tabernacle, and, second, the rams' skins dyed red were placed under the badgers' skins.

Doubt exists as to the exact meaning of the word "badger" (8476), and it has been suggested that the reference could be to an antelope or even a porpoise (see the note on 25.5). The point is that it was a skin that was able to protect the Tabernacle structure from the rains, for even in Sinai the rains came. The outer skin, therefore, had to be weather-proof.

The significance of the rams' skins and badgers' skins coverings

The ram speaks of consecration. When the priests were consecrated into their office, the ram of consecration was slain and the blood was placed upon the tip of the right ear, the thumb of the right hand, and the great toe of the right foot of Aaron and his sons (29.20; Lev 8.22-24) indicating that they were completely consecrated to the service of God. Looking at the covering of rams' skins, therefore, there is seen the consecration of the Lord Jesus, the red dye speaking eloquently of consecration that was to death. Paul writes of this when he states that Christ Jesus "humbled himself, and became obedient unto death, even the death of the cross" (Phil 2.8). Isaiah also confirmed this when he wrote of Him: "I was not rebellious, neither turned away back. I gave my back to the smiters, and my cheeks to them that plucked off the hair: I hid not my face from shame and spitting" (Is 50.5-6).

Once again, as with the covering of goats' hair, this curtain was hidden. The consecration of the Lord is also something that is beyond human understanding. There was with Him devotion and consecration which was for heaven alone.

The outer covering was dark, possibly black or dark brown. This is what the onlooker saw. None of the beauty of the interior, or of the beautiful curtains of fine twined linen would be visible; all that was seen was an apparently small insignificant looking structure that had no outward ornamentation to give it beauty. This also speaks of the Lord Jesus. An appreciation of His glory and of His beauty is only possible for those who can enter in the Holy Place as priests. In this present day of grace all believers are priests, and therefore all believers can enjoy His beauty - but only if they take time to enter the Holiest and engage in worship. What is stated prophetically as the response of Israel to the One who would come, "...when we see him, there is no beauty that we should desire him" (Is 53.2), shows that it was not His way to appeal to the outward senses. Only those who knew Him as Lord could appreciate the great beauty which is His. The dark outward covering of the Tabernacle did not appeal to natural senses, but the interior beauty overwhelmed the worshipper.

The placing of the curtains

How the curtains were placed over the structure of the Tabernacle has lessons for the reader. In order to appreciate them, however, it is necessary to understand the nature of the structure that was underneath these curtains. Consideration of how the curtains were placed is given after the section dealing with the hanging of the vail (vv.31-33).

Verses 15-30: The Boards
The construction of the boards

The inside structure of the Tabernacle consisted of boards made from acacia wood. Each board was 10 cubits high and $1\frac{1}{2}$ cubits broad but no note is given of their depth. Each of them was overlaid with gold (v.29). On the south side of the Tabernacle twenty boards were to be erected (v.18); on the north side twenty boards (v.20); on the west side six boards with two additional corner boards (vv.22-23). There were no boards for the east side as this is where the entrance to the Tabernacle was and pillars supported the structure on that side. In total, therefore, there were forty-eight boards, all overlaid with gold.

On the base of each board there were two "tenons" (3027). The meaning behind the word is that of a hand, indicating that the base of the boards had two peg-like joints fitting into the sockets forming the foundation on which the structure stood. Differences of opinion exist as to how the corner boards, which were at the rear of the Tabernacle, were fitted. Bush notes regarding vv.23.24 that "These two verses are involved in an obscurity which we have endeavoured in vain to penetrate". The different views are examined in Appendix 6.

The length of the Tabernacle structure was 30 cubits, being twenty boards each of $1\frac{1}{2}$ cubits. Nowhere is the width of the structure stated. On the west side, however, there were six boards of $1\frac{1}{2}$ cubits, making 9 cubits in total, plus the two corner boards which, if they were placed alongside the six boards, would make eight, giving a total width of 12 cubits. This does not, however, take into account the joining of the boards at the corners, and it appears to be a reasonable supposition to make, taking the undernoted points into consideration, that the means of joining the corners reduced the inside width to 10 cubits.

1. The thickness of the side boards, or however else they were joined together, would reduce the inside dimensions.

2. A width of 10 cubits would make the Holiest of All a complete cube.

3. The Holiest of All in Solomon's Temple was a complete cube, 20 cubits in length, breadth, and height.

Appendix 6 contains further consideration of how the rear boards were fitted and how this affected the width of the structure.

The sockets

Under each of the boards there were two sockets making a total of forty on the north side, forty on the south side, and sixteen on the west side. These sockets were made of silver which the people gave as atonement money and which was to be used "for the service of the tabernacle of the congregation" (30.16). The sum of the Children of Israel was to be taken, and each numbered soul was to give half a shekel "to make an atonement for your souls" (30.11-15). The total numbered was 603,550 (Num 2.32), and therefore the total value of silver paid as atonement money was 301,775 shekels. From this silver were cast the sockets for the boards and the sockets on which stood the pillars supporting the vail. Each socket weighed one talent (38.27). It was necessary to have sockets of sufficient substance to bear the considerable weight of the boards and the coverings. On this foundation depended the strength of the whole structure! Further details regarding these sockets is given when dealing with 30.11-16.

The bars

In order to give added stability to the boards, bars made of shittim wood overlaid with gold were placed through gold rings fitted to the boards. Five bars were made for the three sides of the Tabernacle, north, south, and west. On each side, the middle bar reached from end to end, but the other four bars appear to have been of half length and thus two were placed above and two beneath the middle bar.

Some consider that the middle bar was hidden from view, running through a hole drilled in the boards. The view of the writer is that the middle bar, like the other four ran through rings on the outside of the boards.

The significance of the boards, sockets, and bars
All agree that the silver socket foundation on which the Tabernacle stood speaks of redemption. The payment of the atonement money by currency of silver confirms this fact; the work of God in salvation is firmly based on the principle of redemption. Fellowship with God rests on the redemption purchased at the Cross. Discussion of the atonement money and its significance is dealt with in 30.11-16.

The boards are typical of the Lord Jesus Christ, being made of shittim wood overlaid with gold. They came into contact with the sockets of silver and "mercy and truth are met together; righteousness and peace have kissed each other" (Ps 85.10). Again, as in the Ark, the humanity of the Lord is seen in the incorruptible shittim wood: He who is the seed of the woman, the second man, the Lord out of heaven; He who was made in the likeness of sinful flesh and yet incorrupt and incorruptible.

The gold is typical of His deity: He who is the "Mighty God", the One in whom dwelleth all the fullness of the godhead bodily; Immanuel, God with us; He who in becoming a man lost nothing of His deity and before whom Thomas stood and rightly said, "My Lord and my God" (Jn 20.28). Blessed indeed are those who have not seen but have believed in the resurrection of the One who is both God and man.

The corner boards, the details of which are discussed in Appendix 6, provided the needed stability to the rear of the structure. They cannot be regarded as having the same significance as the "chief corner stone" (Eph 2.20), for the structure in view there is a stone building, but nevertheless they can be regarded as being essential to the strength of the Tabernacle. This is typical of the fact that there is no weakness in Him, nor is there any possibility that He could fail. Nor can His work fail. That which is founded on the firm rock of redemption is, for all eternity, an unfailing work.

The bars, which also contributed to the strength of the structure, bound it together. All the truth in Scripture concerning the Lord Jesus stands together, and to deny any of it weakens the total. His deity, humanity, work of redemption, and all else taught in the Word of God must be accepted completely. It stands bound together!

The structure, therefore, is typical of the Lord Jesus, for it is only through Him and His work that worshippers can approach God. It is true that in the day of grace believers are seen as "lively (living) stones...built up a spiritual house" (1 Pet 2.5), but the fact that the boards are made of shittim wood overlaid with gold tends to the view that in the Tabernacle they speak of the Lord who maintains the whole structure for the glory of God and the blessing of His people.

Verses 31-33: The Vail
The place and appearance of the vail
In these three verses there is given the detail of the vail, one of the most significant items to be found in the Tabernacle. The word vail (6532) means "curtain". It acted as a divider or "that which separates". It formed the division between the Holy Place and the Holiest of All. This was the third of three entrances, the first being the gate at the entrance to the court, the second being the door at the entrance to the Holy Place, and the third being the vail. This beautiful curtain was made of fine twined linen and embroidered with blue, and purple, and scarlet thread. The embroidery included cherubims, although there is no indication of how many were portrayed. No dimensions were given for the vail, but, accepting that the width of the Tabernacle was 10 cubits, the vail would measure 10 cubits square (the boards were 10 cubits high). Four pillars of shittim wood overlaid with gold were made on which the vail was hung. These pillars sat, not on two sockets of silver as did the boards, but each on one single socket. The reason why only one socket sat under these pillars, whereas two were under each of the boards, is that the pillars would not be as broad as the boards. The vail was hung on the pillars by means of golden hooks.

The pillars were placed so that the vail was hung "under the taches" (v.33). This refers to the taches which joined together the two curtains of fine twined linen, made from ten smaller curtains, forming the inner lining of the Tabernacle roof (26.2-6). These curtains were 20 cubits long, 40 cubits in total, and, as the Tabernacle was 30 cubits in length and 10 cubits high, the taches joining the two curtains would be positioned 20 cubits from the door of the Holy Place and 10 cubits from the rear, with the remainder of the curtains, a further 10 cubits, falling down the rear. By this means, it is established that the Holiest of All was 10 cubits in length as the vail was hung under the taches of gold joining the two curtains.

Those who made the vail were to do so with "cunning" (skilful) work, an ability that was given to them for the purpose. The ten curtains were made with the same skill (26.1), and it would result in work of great beauty seen only by the eyes of the priests who ministered in the Sanctuary.

When it was time to move and follow the cloud, the vail covered the Ark. It would not be permissible to look on the Ark, only the High Priest ever enjoyed that privilege and only on the Day of Atonement, so the vail was taken down and the priests advanced towards the Ark holding the vail in front of them so that the Ark was not seen. It would then be placed over the cherubims and be draped over the Mercy Seat and the Ark. As has been noted, the vail was 10 cubits square and there would thus be ample material to cover an Ark which was $2\frac{1}{2}$ cubits long and $1\frac{1}{2}$ cubits broad. While it is granted that no height is given for the cherubims, the size of the Ark would indicate that they were not of great size, but would be in proportion to it. The other Ark coverings which were placed over the vail were a covering of badgers' skins and a top covering of blue cloth (Num 4.5-6).

The significance of the vail

It has been observed that the vail was the last of three barriers marking the way into the Tabernacle. It was, therefore, a constant reminder that, although the Holiest of All was where God was, entrance into His presence was not open to all. Passing through the vail was the prerogative of the High Priest and that only annually, on the Day of Atonement. This was a lesson being taught throughout the history of the Tabernacle, the teacher being the Holy Spirit, and the lesson being that the way into the Holiest was not yet open: "The Holy Ghost this signifying, that the way into the holiest of all was not yet made manifest, while as the first tabernacle was yet standing" (Heb 9.8). All that was to be found in the Tabernacle, the Brazen Altar, the Laver, the Altar of Incense, the Lampstand, the sacrifices, the Aaronic priesthood, and all the feasts which were celebrated could not open up the way into Holiest of All. Men were unable to unlock this door; no actions of theirs could permit them to enter, and one king who sought even to enter the Holy Place was stricken by leprosy till the day of his death (2 Chr 26.16-21). This barrier was not to be treated lightly, and all that Uzziah had achieved in his reign did not bestow on him the privilege of entering the compartment situated immediately on the other side of the vail.

What kept man out? Sin was the reason! All the service of the Tabernacle looked forward to Him who would meet the need and enable man to enter, but, as the Hebrew writer states, the way into His presence was *not yet* made manifest. What joy to read *not yet* and not the awful words *not ever*. The Tabernacle was a picture and a parable but, although its service could not gain worshippers access to His presence, it pictured a coming day when access to the presence of God would be open.

But the vail was rent (Mt 27.51; Mk 15.38; Lk 23.45)! Matthew and Mark record that it was "rent in twain from the top to the bottom". As the Lord Jesus "yielded up the ghost" (Mt 27.50) that great vail in the Temple built by Herod was completely torn asunder. It was not torn from the bottom to half way up, or from the top to part way down. Neither was the rending horizontal, for any of these would have indicated a partial access to His presence. The vail was completely torn in two proclaiming that the way into His presence had been made manifest. All the types and shadows of Temple worship no longer had any part to play. Shadow had given way to substance.

But in addition to this, there is one other momentous fact emphasised by the rending of the vail - the Holiest of All was empty, there was no Ark in the Temple. Edersheim writes that "A heavy double vail concealed the entrance to the Most Holy Place, which in the second Temple was empty, nothing being there but the piece of rock, called the Ebhen Shethiyah, or Foundation Stone, which according to tradition, covered the mouth of the pit, and on which it was thought, the world was founded" (*The Life and Times of Jesus the Messiah*). An empty Sanctuary manifested the bankruptcy of the whole system of Judaism and the falsehoods perpetrated by those who claimed the presence of God. True it is that the Temple built after the return from the captivity had no Ark, but these returning pilgrims did not put forward the great claims which were made in respect of Herod's Temple. This empty, ruined system was now finished!

The Hebrew Epistle deals with this great privilege: "Having therefore, brethren, boldness to enter into the holiest by the blood of Jesus, By a new and living way, which he hath consecrated for us, through the veil, that is to say, his flesh" (Heb 10.19-20). The reader must first understand that "boldness" is not arrogance, nor is it casualness. The fact that the way is now open may lead to unacceptable behaviour, if not to an arrogant approach, or, equally shamefully, to a casual attitude. "Boldness" (3954) has the thought of "freedom", "confidence", and "assurance". It indicates that there need be no doubt as to right of entrance, a right purchased by Another.

It has been argued that the vail represents the life in the flesh of the Lord Jesus. "But as the vail stood locally before the holiest in the Mosaic Tabernacle, the way into which lay through it, so Christ's life in the flesh stood between Him and His entrance before God, and His flesh had to be rent ere He could enter" (*Expositor's Greek Testament*). There is a beauty about this, that no matter how lovely was the life of the Lord Jesus, and no matter what blessing came from His hands, these were not sufficient to open up the way. He had to die and endure all the agony of the Cross, and then, and only then, was the vail rent in two.

The difficulty presented by this view, however, is that the writer of Hebrews does not deal with the Temple, but with the Tabernacle, and there is no record of the vail in the Tabernacle being rent. The mention of the vail, therefore, cannot be to the fact that it was rent from the top to the bottom. What, therefore, is he teaching? The vital point to grasp is that it is the "new and living way" that is referred to as "his flesh". By His becoming a man and enduring the Cross, He has not only opened up the new and living way, He is the new and living way. It is through Him that worshippers enter the Holiest of All. Just as it was not possible to see the glory in the Holiest unless the vail was passed, so, today, worshippers cannot see into the third heaven, into that heavenly Sanctuary. But it is possible for them to move from the seen into the unseen, from the earthly to the heavenly. He is the new and living way, and by Him those who approach God enter into the Holiest "by the blood of Jesus".

But the writer of Hebrews has more to say about the significance of this vail. He states that believers have a hope "which...we have as an anchor of the soul, both sure and stedfast, and which entereth into that within the veil" (Heb 6.19). Christians have a hope which is completely secure and which never will be lost. This is a hope of enjoying all the glory that is associated with the Lord Jesus Christ; it is the eternal glory to which all believers are travelling. The picture presented is that of the rough, boisterous passage of life, like a storm tossed boat, but a boat with an anchor, one that is firmly fixed in glory, within the veil. This anchor is imbedded, firmly settled, and incapable of slipping, one on which complete reliance can be placed.

But where is "within the veil"? It is where the Lord Jesus Christ has already entered. The anchor is where He is, for He is the anchor and the guarantee that believers will enter where He has gone. He entered there as a forerunner. The High Priest of Israel entered the Holiest of All, but not as the forerunner of Israel, for access there would never be opened to all the people. He entered representing the people, but the Lord entered, not only to represent, which He does as the Great High Priest, but also as One who is in advance of others who will follow. Note that "the forerunner is for us entered, even Jesus, made an high priest for ever after the order of Melchisedec" (Heb 6.20), the use of the name "Jesus" emphasising that it is a man who has entered.

Thus, today, the believer rejoices in two things. First, that entrance into His presence is freely available now. "Let us therefore come boldly unto the throne of grace" (Heb 4.16) is the exhortation to be heeded. No barrier exists now. Second, that this present access is but a foretaste of the day when, after death or rapture, the believer will enter His presence, following the forerunner - He who has blazed the trail and gone before. In times of sorrow, when loved ones have passed through death, it is a comfort to remember that the Lord has travelled the pathway, and that believers but follow Him right into the glory of His presence.

A vital lesson from the rent vail

Men enjoy "religion" with its robes and vestments, its incense and altars, and its priesthood and enthronements. They love the church buildings, abbeys, and cathedrals with their glorious stained glass windows and soaring galleries. They relish the altar with its railings and gates, designating the altar area as being only for the "priests", with entrance barred to the laity. All this appeals to the flesh, and is guarded jealously by those who are ordained into such "high calling and privilege". But the vail has been rent! All believers now have access. The religious trappings of such systems are meaningless and empty, just as empty as the great Temple standing in Jerusalem in the days of the Lord. True, there are believers who maintain their links with these systems, but that does not make the rituals which they follow scriptural. There are no vails now, no railings around altars, no ground on which only "ordained priests" can walk, and no places where the feet of laity cannot stand. Such practices and symbolism are worthless, denying the great truth that the way is now manifest and all can come boldly to the throne of grace.

The significance of the pillars

As already seen, the pillars were made, as were the boards, of shittim wood overlaid with gold, and sat on sockets of silver. This signifies the deity and humanity of the Lord Jesus, and their holding up the vail showed that it was He who upheld this part of the structure just as firmly as did the boards. The silver sockets again proclaim that everything in redemption depends on the Person of Christ; what He is and what He became are vital truths. It has been rightly said, "Withdraw His deity and His blood cannot atone, withdraw His humanity and there is no blood to atone".

Four pillars held up the vail. Four, being the number of universality, signifies that God would "have all men to be saved, and to come unto the knowledge of the truth" (1 Tim 2.4). It is His desire that all creatures should have fellowship with Him and come to know Him and enjoy His presence.

The placing of the curtains

The order in which the curtains and coverings were placed on the Tabernacle can be ascertained from the wording of 26.1-14. The innermost curtain was that of fine twined linen embroidered with cherubims. Over that was placed the curtain of goats' hair, on top of which was the covering of rams' skins dyed red, with the last, and outer, covering being the badgers' skins.

The curtain of fine twined linen, as has been noted, was made of ten curtains sown together to make two large curtains which were then joined by taches of gold and loops of blue. The total length of the complete curtain was 40 cubits (two large curtains of 20 cubits each) and its breadth 28 cubits. The Tabernacle structure was 30 cubits long and 10 cubits high; the Holy Place was 20 cubits long and the Holiest of All 10 cubits. When this fine linen curtain was placed over the boards, therefore, the taches of gold and the loops of blue would be positioned exactly above the vail. The curtain would cover the Holiest and down the back of the Tabernacle; the length hanging down would be 10 cubits, less the thickness of the boards. This would result in the bottom of the rear curtain being just short of ground level. At the sides the 28 cubits width of the curtains would result in their being 1 cubit, plus the thickness of the side boards, short of reaching the ground.

The curtains of goat's hair, at 44 cubits long with loops and brass taches which joined the six curtain piece to the five, was longer than the fine linen curtain and at 30 cubits wide it was broader. Due to the fact that the front curtain was doubled back on itself (v.9) this curtain was 2 cubits longer than the inner one in length and breadth. The curtain was to be so placed that 1 cubit of the extra length was over the back resulting in the curtain reaching to the ground and 1 cubit would overhang the front as a kind of gable.

Over these two curtains were placed the rams' skins dyed red and the badgers' skins of which no detail is given. It is clear, however, that they would be of sufficient size to cover the Tabernacle so that only the covering of badgers' skins would be seen.

Verses 34-35: Instructions for the Mercy Seat, Lampstand, and Table of Shewbread

These two verses seem almost to be an interruption in the flow of the text. They are situated here, however, so that the placing of all the items inside the Tabernacle can now be brought to a conclusion before instructions are given for the door. The Altar of Incense is not mentioned, even although it was in the Holy Place with the Lampstand and Table of Shewbread, because it is not introduced until ch.30.

There is no detail of the Tabernacle which is insignificant. When the Lord instructs, no doubt is left as to His requirements and nothing can be disregarded. So it is here that the positions of the Lampstand and the Shewbread Table are stated; the Table to be on the north and the Lampstand on the south, opposite the Table.

Verses 36-37: The Door
The door described

The door of the Tabernacle was made of blue, purple, scarlet, and fine linen. These are the same materials with which the vail was made, but it has already been noted that with the vail, fine linen is mentioned first. Here it is blue that is given the first place, indicating that this is the dominant colour, but the embroidery on the door was not of cherubims. This door separated the Holy Place from the court of the Tabernacle. The priests, the sons of Aaron, after their service in the court, passed through this door when entering into the Holy Place.

According to the dimensions of the Tabernacle, the door measured 10 cubits by 10 cubits, but the gate measured 20 cubits by 5 cubits - the same area for both although of different dimensions. It was hung on five pillars made of shittim wood overlaid with gold, with hooks of gold at the top to hold the door curtain in place. These five pillars sat on five sockets, not of silver as with the boards and the pillars for the vail, but of brass, as did the pillars supporting the hangings surrounding the outer court (27.10). One additional detail revealed later (36.38) is that each of these pillars was surmounted by a "chapter" or "top piece".

The significance of the door

Each entrance in the Tabernacle, the gate, the door, and the vail, represented stages in approaching God. In the court, seen in the Brazen Altar and the Laver, there was an appreciation that the shed blood was the only way in, and that it was necessary to be clean. The sacrifices on the Brazen Altar were indeed acts of worship, but passing through the door was moving further in. The purpose of the door was to permit worshippers to enter; the purpose of the vail was to prohibit their entrance into the Most Holy Place. One was an invitation; the other was a prohibition. The priests, moving from the court through the door, signify greater intimacy of worship, an intimacy which today is not limited to one priestly family. "The nearer we approach to God, as His priests, the more intimate our fellowship with Him in heavenly places; the more shall we discern the glories of Christ, and realise his power, majesty and strength".†

The absence of cherubims on the door was striking. Within the Holy Place they were always in sight, whether on the fine linen curtain overhead or on the vail, but on the door and on the gate giving access to the court they were not to be seen. The cherubims, as has been observed, were guardians of the presence of God, they jealously cared for His holiness. The closer the worshipper approaches God, the greater awareness there is of His holiness. In the court, grace dominates; no cherubims, but an Altar and a Laver. Moving closer, having washed at the Laver, there is an increasing awareness that He is holy and that the demeanour and conduct of the worshipper must reflect an appreciation of His holiness. The word "holy" (6944) is first used at the burning bush when Moses is told, "Draw not nigh hither: put off thy shoes from off thy feet, for the place whereon thou standest is holy ground" (3.5). Moses had to realise the holiness that marked the presence of God.

The pillars on which the door was hung signify responsibility. There were ten Commandments declaring the responsibility of God's people towards God and towards their neighbour. Here the five pillars have been looked at as signifying the responsibility of the worshipper to observe the Word of God as the Sanctuary is entered, but the fact that they were made of shittim wood overlaid with gold indicates that they speak of the Lord Jesus Christ. Consistency of interpretation demands this. What is seen in the pillars is the One who fulfilled all His responsibilities to God and man. He kept the Law; He was obedient and prepared to go to death; He finished the work which was given Him to do. Entering in through this door there was an awareness that such a privilege was only enjoyed because of the One who fulfilled every responsibility which He was given to undertake. All of God's purpose - the redemption of mankind and indeed of the whole universe, the defeat of the forces of evil - the fulfilment of all this was laid on Him and He triumphed and triumphed gloriously.

The brass of which the sockets were made was also used for the Brazen Altar. It signifies that which can withstand the heat and flame of the Altar.

This the Lord Jesus did when He died on the Cross, and the brass, therefore, speaks of the One who purchased redemption when He went through the flame and heat of Calvary. Brass speaks of the work itself and the silver sockets of the price that was paid to accomplish that work.

Notes

1 An illustration of the Tabernacle is given in Appendix 6.
1 In the context of this study of the Tabernacle, the AV spelling *vail*, though now obsolete, will generally be used in the interests of uniformity.
37 Soltau, *The Tabernacle, the Priesthood and the Offerings.*

EXODUS 27

The Brazen Altar and the Court of the Tabernacle

Verses 1-8: The Brazen Altar†

The worshipper approaching the Tabernacle and looking though the gate would have his view arrested by the Brazen Altar dominating the court. It was nearest to the gate and could not be avoided or ignored. To approach God cognisance had to be taken of the Brazen Altar. Of all the items in the Tabernacle for which measurements are given this was the largest. There was no possibility of anyone ignoring it or failing to take account of it. In many ways it was a terrible and awe-inspiring sight. The fire on the Altar, consuming the sacrifices which had been placed thereon, flamed up into the sky, and at night lit up the darkness. The smell of burning flesh, the heat radiating from that awful fire, the sight of priests preparing further sacrifices to be added to the flames, the blood shed by the victims, the ceaseless activity of those who attended upon the Altar; all these things made an unforgettable scene, impressing upon the onlooker the absolute, vital, necessity of the shedding of blood.

Without this Altar no progress into the presence of God could be made, even by priestly men. It stood at the gate, inescapable, unavoidable. Its demands could not be ignored; this Altar could not be bypassed. Continually, without respite, the smoke rose, the flames consumed the sacrifices, the victims were slain, and the blood was poured out; death had its stamp on everything. No sacrifice approaching that Altar escaped its grip. Slaying, pouring out blood, flaying carcasses into their pieces, casting them into the flames; all this was the daily occupation of those working at the Altar.

It was a not a place for casual comfort, nor was careless sloth to mark those busy priests. It was not a place to be approached lightly by worshippers who brought their offerings. They were giving of their best and parting doubtless with animals for which they had affection. They were bringing of their wealth, giving to their God the choicest of their possessions. The world looking on would see this as waste; consigning to the devouring flames of the Altar that which was worth much in the currency of earth, but little realising the eternal worth placed on it by heaven.

And so, hour after hour, day after day, week after week, year after year, the Altar continued. It is beyond the ability of any mathematician to compute how many sacrifices burned on the Brazen Altar and that of the Temple which superseded it; to calculate how often the carcasses were consigned to the flames was outwith the capability of any of the sons of Aaron. Yet what says the Scripture of this impressive sight: "And every priest standeth daily ministering and offering oftentimes the same sacrifices, which can never take away sins" (Heb 10.11). Over it all are stamped the words, "*never* take away sins". No matter how long they laboured, no matter how often the worshippers approached, no matter how devoted their hearts, "*never*", is the declaration from heaven. So why then all this? Because it points out the need of One to come who will deal with sin, looking to "the offering of the body of Jesus Christ once for all" (Heb 10.10), so that today worshippers can joy in the great fact that "this man, after he had offered one sacrifice for sins for ever, sat down on the right hand of God" (Heb 10.12).

It is a cause of worship to consider this issue as the writer of the Hebrews sees it: all the sacrifices on the Brazen Altar were past, and never again would it be necessary to approach in the manner which had been the practice for generations. He who died at Calvary did so once and only once.

1. "Who needeth not daily, as those high priests, to offer up sacrifice, first for his own sins, and then for the people's: for this he did *once*, when he offered up himself" (7.27). The emphasis here is on the value of His sacrifice. It was necessary that it be offered once only because it was the offering up of Himself.

2. "Neither by the blood of goats and calves, but by his own blood he entered in *once* into the holy place, having obtained eternal redemption for us" (9.12). The emphasis is on the eternal redemption obtained. The reference is to the Day of Atonement when the High Priest entered into the Holiest once a year. The Lord Jesus entered in only once and the salvation which He obtained was not good just for a year, but was eternal.

3. "For then must he often have suffered since the foundation of the world: but now *once* in the end of the world hath he appeared to put away sin by the sacrifice of himself" (9.26). The emphasis is on the sufferings through which He passed. The point here is that the sufferings of the Lord Jesus are over; there was no need for Him to suffer often. So great was the cost of Calvary, so vast was the price paid, so deep were His sufferings that they did not need to be repeated.

4. "So Christ was *once* offered to bear the sins of many; and unto them that look for him shall he appear the second time without sin unto salvation" (9.28). The emphasis is on the many who come into the good of His work. To take up and carry away the sins of many, the Lord Jesus died once. It is appointed that man should die once, and when He became a man He did not seek to return to heaven without dying. He went through with all that was involved in becoming a man, and died. But what a death!

5. "By the which will we are sanctified through the offering of the body of Jesus Christ *once* for all" (10.10). The emphasis is on the One who was submissive to the will of God. There was no pleasure for God in the sacrifices and offerings of the Brazen Altar, inasmuch as they could not deal with the problem of sin. There came One, however, who said, "I come

to do thy will, O God" (10.9), and who, on earth, carried that out to the full, and in so doing went to die.

The Use of the Altar

The vital importance of the Brazen Altar is seen in its use. The claim that it was an integral part of the life of the nation is clearly substantiated by consideration of how often it featured in the daily life of the people. To demonstrate the importance of the Altar, several of the offerings brought to be slain or offered there are noted below, although some of them were not wholly burned there. For instance, the bullock offered for the sin offering for the priest was slain before the Lord, its blood sprinkled seven times before the vail of the Sanctuary and put on the horns of the Altar of Incense in the Holy Place, after which the blood was poured out at the bottom of the Brazen Altar. The fat of the bullock, its two kidneys, and the caul above the liver were burned upon the Brazen Altar and the remainder of the animal, its skin, flesh, head, legs, inwards, and dung, were carried outside the Camp to a clean place and were burned there. The Brazen Altar was, however, still vital in this sacrifice. The offerings referred to above were:

1. The sweet savour offerings: burnt offerings, meal offerings, and peace offerings (Lev 1-3).

2. The non sweet savour offerings: sin offerings and trespass offerings (Lev 4-5).

3. After the birth of a child and when the "days of her purifying (were) fulfilled", a mother brought an offering of a lamb of the first year for a burnt offering and a young pigeon or a turtledove for a sin offering. If she was not able to bring a lamb she could offer two turtledoves, or two young pigeons, "the one for the burnt offering, and the other for a sin offering" (Lev 12.6-8).

4. When a leper was declared by the priest to be cleansed from his leprosy a number of actions had to be carried out, included in which was the offering of a he lamb for a trespass offering, a he lamb for a burnt offering, and a meal offering. If it was not possible for the leper to bring two lambs because he was poor, it was allowed that he could bring two turtledoves or two young pigeons "such as he is able to get; and the one shall be a sin offering, and the other a burnt offering" (Lev 14.1-32).

5. After the cleansing of running issues "out of his flesh", the man who had been cleansed would bring two turtledoves or two young pigeons to be offered by the priest for a sin offering and for a burnt offering (Lev 15.13-15). In similar fashion, a woman who had been healed of an issue of blood would also bring to the priest two turtledoves or two young pigeons to be offered as a sin offering and a burnt offering (Lev 15.28-30).

6. The slaying of oxen, lambs, or goats was to be carried out at the door of the Tabernacle (Lev 17.1-7). "No private person in Israel was to slaughter any such animal anywhere in the camp or out of it, except at the door of

the tent of meeting".[†] Keil & Delitzsch, referring to Leviticus 17, emphasise this by stating that, "The Israelites were not to slaughter domestic animals as food either within or outside the camp, but before the door of the tabernacle". If they were slaughtered elsewhere they still had to be brought to the Tabernacle. These animals were to be offered as peace offerings in which case part was placed on the Altar to be "the food of the offering" (Lev 3.16) for the enjoyment of God, the breast and the right shoulder were given to the priests (Lev 7.31-32), and rest was to be given to the offerer (Lev 7.16-17). It would appear from this that in the wilderness eating meat was not a regular occurrence, due doubtless to the nutritious nature of the manna.

The construction of the Altar

The Brazen Altar was made of shittim wood overlaid with brass or, more likely, copper. In this study "brass" will be used. The Altar was foursquare; it was 5 cubits long and 5 cubits broad, with a height of 3 cubits. There were four horns, made also of shittim wood, overlaid with brass, each horn rising out of the top of the four corners. No indication is given of the shape or size of these horns, but they were of sufficient size for the blood of the sin offering to be applied to them (Lev 4.25,34). There would be little value in putting horns on each corner if they were not clearly seen.

The implements for use at the Altar were made of brass and consisted of:

1. Pans to receive ashes: these were used for the ashes of the offerings.
2. Shovels: necessary equipment for handling ashes or whatever had to be taken from the Altar.
3. Basons: for the blood of the sacrifices.
4. Fleshhooks: for handling the carcasses of the offerings.
5. Firepans: for dealing with the fire of the Altar.

A grate or network of brass was made, on the four corners of which rings were formed. This network was placed "even to the midst of the altar". Staves, again made of shittim wood overlaid with brass, were placed through the rings to enable the Altar to be carried. Appendix 6 contains further notes on the construction of the Brazen Altar.

The materials used

The shittim wood speaks here, as it has when used in other items of furniture, of the incorruptible humanity of the Lord Jesus Christ. This wood was from a tree which grew in inhospitable conditions. Ratcliffe comments: "Mature shittim-wood trees, while retaining a full head of foliage and beautifying the desert plain with fragrant, yellow flowers, bear the appearance of having survived adverse and hostile growing conditions. Was this not exactly the experience of the Lord Jesus when here on earth as dependant man?...The wood is naturally resistant to disease and attack by pests".[†] The wood of the Altar had already withstood these conditions, just as the Man who hung on the Cross had moved through the desert of this world, holy, harmless, and undefiled. No matter the form or ferocity of the attack, he emerged victorious without a stain on His perfect Person.

The dimensions of the Altar

It has already been observed that this Altar dominated the court of the Tabernacle, not only by virtue of the fire and sacrifices upon it, but also by virtue of its size. At 5 cubits long, 5 cubits broad, and 3 cubits high it was the largest of all the items for which measurements are give. Five is the number of responsibility, and at the Altar is seen the work of the One who met every responsibility which was His, in living a perfect, holy life, in completely fulfilling all that was prophesied concerning Him, and in finishing the work that was given Him to do. There was no failure! But this Altar is foursquare, presenting the same dimensions to north, south, east, and west. His life and work is equally available to all, no matter who, no matter where. No one is excluded because of any shortcoming in respect of the Altar, for it has none, and no one is excluded because it is inaccessible. They can come from all sides, but they all must enter at the one gate.

The position of the Altar

This Altar stood, as has been noted, immediately inside the gate of the Tabernacle, declaring the fact that there is no approach to God apart from the Cross. There was no other gate and no other way of coming before Him. Without the shedding of blood, entrance into the presence of God was impossible. This strikes a death-blow at any teaching based on an approach to God without the Cross. This lesson has been eloquently expressed since the first sacrifice was slain. Ridout comments: "…never did blood flow from a sacrificial animal that was not divinely intended to show the atoning death of the Lamb of God" (*Lectures on the Tabernacle*).

Over the years, thousands of sacrifices would be offered on this Altar, each one reminding the worshipper that if it was the shedding of blood that delivered from Egypt, it was also the shedding of blood that allowed the worshipper to approach God.

The fire on the Altar

The fire on the Altar was never to be put out; "The fire shall ever be burning upon the altar; it shall never go out" (Lev 6.13). Throughout the daylight hours and during the hours of darkness there were always to be flames rising from this Altar. It was never to be cold and dead. How different this was from the altar which the tribes of Reuben and Gad, together with the half tribe of Manasseh, built to remind the generations following of their links with the Tabernacle. Living on territory on the east bank of the

Jordan it was possible that they would loosen their links with the Brazen Altar. (Josh 22.21-34). The altar which they built, and which they named "Ed", was an altar, "not for burnt offerings, nor for sacrifice"; it would give nothing to God, and it would cost them nothing. No offering of any kind would ever lie on it, and fire would never flame up into the heavens. This was an altar of human invention!

What a contrast between this and the Brazen Altar. Each morning and evening a sacrificial lamb was placed on its flames; Israelites brought their burnt and meal offerings; peace, sin, and trespass offerings burned in its fire. All this speaks of the Cross - the Altar itself declaring the One who endured the flames and was not consumed by them, the shittim wood encased in brass, preserved without charring or burning; the sacrifices telling out the fact that His death at Calvary was accepted in heaven, that through and from the flames there came that which was for God. All the demands of the righteous throne of God were met, and provision was made for all the deeds of guilty, fallen man.

And so the fire must never go out. After the subterfuge of the Gibeonites was uncovered it was given to this people to be "hewers of wood and drawers of water for the congregation and for the altar of the Lord" (Josh 9.27). To them fell the responsibility of ensuring that a supply of wood was constantly available to fuel the Altar fire; in a later sad age, dealing with the rebuilt Temple in Jerusalem, one of the desires of Nehemiah was that he should be remembered for the wood offering, again that which was for Altar fuel (Neh 13.31). There is revealed at that late stage in the book that one of the motives, indeed perhaps the prime motive of Nehemiah in rebuilding the walls of Jerusalem was that there might be conditions suitable for the Altar worship to continue.

Let it be stated again that this great Brazen Altar with flames rising from it declared the fact that One would come and endure death for others. This profound, solemn fact was never to be forgotten; the Cross will eternally be remembered, the power of it never diminished, and the enjoyment of God in all that it accomplished never decrease. It is the central act of all history and the central theme of all eternity.

The responsibilities of the Altar

If this large Altar speaks of the One who fulfilled every responsibility, it also reminded Israelites of the responsibilities laid on them. It was given to them to ensure that provision was made for the priests to place the morning and the evening sacrifice upon the Altar. There was placed before them in the opening chapters of Leviticus instructions for bringing their offerings to the Lord; the leper who was cleansed brought his offering to be offered by the priest (Lev 14.10-14). All of these offerings, and others, ensured that Israel was aware that the Altar was a central part of their lives. They could not exist without it.

Their responsibilities were, first, to show appreciation to the Lord for all His goodness towards them, and second, to ensure that they were kept clean. The freewill, sweet savour offerings of Leviticus 1-3 would be a delight to the Lord as the smoke ascended up to heaven. Here was the expression of the gratitude of redeemed people for all that the Lord had accomplished, the enjoyment of which was now theirs. The other necessary offerings, the non sweet savour sin and trespass offerings, showed that the offerer appreciated the seriousness of sin and the necessity of shed blood to deal with it.

For the believer today the same responsibilities have to be discharged - to show by prayer and action our appreciation and thankfulness for the goodness of God; to confess sin and bring it before Him, realising how damaging it is to our relationship with Him; to approach Him conscious of the defilement of this world which makes the work of the Cross necessary to cleanse us. The need of the Cross is not limited to the day of salvation; it is required constantly, right through life's journey. The responsibility faced by looking at the Altar is not just to understand that He gives that which believers need to keep themselves close to Him, which He has done, but also that He has given believers the opportunity of giving to Him voluntarily, thus showing how deep is their love for Him. The Altar is a display of how much He has done, and the measurement of how much those who have been blessed are prepared to do in return.

In the book of Malachi, the altar to which reference is made is that which was in the Temple rebuilt at the end of the captivity. Nevertheless the character of that altar is similar to the Altar of the Tabernacle and it is of more than passing interest to note that it is, on two occasions, referred to as the "table of the Lord" (Mal 1.7,12). A table in Scriptures is a place of food and fellowship. Here it was that the Lord enjoyed what His people set before Him and here it was that He fed on what they brought, as it speaks of Christ, and enjoyed their fellowship as they approached Him, for through this Altar that fellowship was able to continue, no matter what may have come in to disturb it. It is sad to observe that in the days of Malachi those who approached it were declaring by their actions that they treated it with contempt. They were bringing offerings which were worthless - the blind, the lame, and the sick - and presenting to the Lord that which was of no value. They were weary of coming to the altar; even those who vowed to give of their best were bringing that which was blemished (Mal 1.14). What a solemn warning for today! The Lord was not able to feed on what they brought, nor was He able to enjoy their fellowship.

The journeys of the Altar

When journeying, the Altar was covered with a purple cloth over which was placed a covering of badgers' skins (Num 4.13,14). This was the only item which was wrapped in the purple colour, the emblem of royalty, showing clearly the link between "the sufferings of Christ, and the glory that that should follow" (1 Pet 1.11). It expresses the fact that the suffering

One will yet be the reigning One. The thief, dying on a cross, by the eye of faith, pierced the badgers' skins and beheld the purple when he said, "Lord, remember me when thou comest into thy kingdom" (Lk 23.42). The suffering Son of Man will yet reign as the glorified Son of God with His brow encircled with many diadems. The badgers' skins hid the purple cloth, for the time has not yet come for that glory to be revealed. The dying thief was not alone in his perception - Nathaniel beheld the purple when he exclaimed, "Rabbi, thou art the Son of God; thou art the King of Israel" (Jn 1.49).

The rebellion of Korah

Numbers 16 records the rebellion of Korah which was directed against the priesthood. Those involved sought to usurp the priestly office and approached the Tabernacle with brass censers containing fire and incense. The Lord could not tolerate such disobedience and He caused the earth to open and swallow up the rebels. Two hundred and fifty princes of the congregation who joined them in offering incense were consumed by fire.

Following this, the censers which had been used were made into broad plates and fixed as a covering for the Brazen Altar, a reminder to all who approached that presumptuous rebellion and disobedience bring grave consequences. It was no light thing to enjoy the privilege of approaching the Altar.

Verses 9-19: The Court of the Tabernacle
The construction of the court

Surrounding the Tabernacle there was a court in which stood the Brazen Altar and the Laver. Hangings of fine twined linen marked the boundaries of this court and its dimensions were 100 cubits on the north and south sides and 50 cubits on the west and east sides. The fine twined linen hangings were fixed to twenty pillars on the north and south, ten on the west, but only six on the east as this was the side where the gate was situated. Each of the pillars sat on a brass socket and the hangings were attached to the pillars by means of silver hooks. Chords that were fastened to pegs driven into the ground supported the pillars. No mention of these is made until 35.18. There is no reason to believe that these were only on one side of the hangings; it is probable that they were placed on both sides. The uniform height of all the hangings was 5 cubits. According to TWOT at 773b, "All the pillars around the court shall be filleted with silver" (v.17), may refer to rings fitted round the pillars. Another view is that it indicates that there were silver rods connecting the pillars which prevented any of them leaning towards the other.

The gate, on the east side, was 20 cubits in length and, as with the other hangings, 5 cubits high, with the hangings on each side being 15 cubits long. It consisted of fine twined linen with embroidery of blue, purple, and scarlet. Four pillars set on sockets held up the hanging of the gate.

The width of the gate may cause surprise; it appears to be very large for the size of the building.

The court enclosures were, therefore, very securely in place. The brass sockets, the silver fillets, or connecting rods, and cords reaching from the silver hooks down to the brass pins driven into the ground ensured that the whole surrounding hangings and gate were very firmly anchored.

There is no indication given of where the tent of meeting was placed within the court, whether it was close to the west side, in the middle or nearer the gate. As the Brazen Altar was inside the gate it is reasonable to assume that the tent was towards the rear, or west side.

The purpose of the court

This court area separated the Tabernacle from the surrounding tents. It made a clear distinction between the dwelling place of the Lord and the dwelling place of the people. The Levites camped immediately outside it on three sides, and the priests on the east side, outside the gate. Inside this court the work of the Tabernacle was carried out: to the gate the people brought their offerings; inside the gate sacrifices were slain and prepared for the Altar; the priests washed at the laver and could be seen entering and leaving the Holy Place.

All this activity, however, was hidden from casual prying eyes. The 5 cubit height of the hangings ensured this; no one could look inside without coming to the gate. What took place in the court was not to be treated lightly; it was only for those who came to give to the Lord. Even these souls, however, could not see into the Holy Place or the Holiest. The court could be viewed by the High Priest, the priests, and the offerers, the Holy Place by the High Priest and the priests, and the Holiest of All by the High Priest alone, and that only on one occasion each year. By this means the holiness of the Tabernacle and its functions was clearly displayed.

For those inside the court, the hangings ensured that they could not see the activity outside, so that they could not be distracted from the work in hand. How easy it would be to have one's attention occupied with what was taking place outside.

> Shut in with Thee, far, far above
> The restless world that wars below,
> We seek to learn and prove Thy love,
> Thy wisdom and Thy grace to know.
> (Alexander Stewart)

The significance of the gate

There could be no entrance to the court save by the gate situated on the east side. This is the place from which man comes - see Genesis 4.16. There is only one approach to God for the worshipper and that is through the Lord Jesus. "There is one God, and one mediator between God and men, the man Christ Jesus" (1 Tim 2.5), is a very clear statement. There is no question of the way of approach being the subject of human choice; there is not a variety of ways, nor are there gates which are of human design. Those who have been saved out of Egypt had one way of escape, and they have but one way of approach to the God who had saved them. Take note that the Tabernacle was not for any to approach; it was not the gate for the sinner looking for salvation, it was the gate for those who had known the saving power of the blood to approach the God who had saved them. There may be principles which can be applied to the former, but the lessons are for the latter.

The four pillars from which the hanging of the gate was fixed declare that all who have known redemption are invited to draw near. The vail and the door of the Tabernacle were both of one size, 10 cubits square, but the gate was 20 cubits long by 5 cubits high. This was the same area as the vail and the door, but longer in length and only half the height. This longer length, in addition to the fact that the hangings were suspended from four pillars indicates that the Lord desires His people to draw near. Four is the universal number, and His will is that they should all, without exception, come to Him in worship. The gate is not too small, the invitation is not restricted, and the way is clearly marked.

The colours in the gate were in contrast to the white linen which marked the hangings surrounding the court. There could be no mistaking the gate and it did not require a search to identify its position; it stood out plainly. These colours are the same as those on the door and the vail except that, in the latter, cherubims were embroidered. In all three the glories of the Lord Jesus Christ are displayed; the blue picturing the Man from heaven, the purple His regal splendour, and the scarlet His sufferings and humiliation.

Just as there are four Gospels, the four pillars also signify the full life of the Lord Jesus, so that those who draw near are occupied with all that He is and all that He accomplished. It is of note that two of the Gospel writers, Matthew and John, were primary witnesses to what took place, and two of the writers were secondary witnesses, obtaining the material which they included from others. Luke explains how he did this in the opening section of his Gospel. This combination of those who were present and those who, although not present when the events took place, nevertheless were alive at that time and obtained their material, examined and studied it to check its accuracy, all writing as moved by the Holy Spirit, has given in the Scriptures a perfect account of the life of the Lord Jesus. To those moving towards the gate the four pillars speak of that vital and accurate record.

The colours have been linked with the characteristics of these four Gospels. Matthew brings before the reader the purple, the Royal One; Mark is occupied with the red, the Serving One, obedient unto death; Luke writes of the fine twined linen, the Righteous Man; John deals with the blue, the eternal Heavenly One.

The significance of the hangings of the court

The fine twined linen of which these were made surrounded the sacred dwelling place of God. White states: "The snow-white curtains which surrounded the House of God symbolise the holiness which becometh the habitation of the Most High". All who looked from the outside saw these white hangings telling out that holiness marked all that had to do with this House. The grace of God is seen in what took place in the Tabernacle, but His grace is not extended at the cost of His holiness; grace does not endanger His righteousness.

This was a testimony to the onlooker, even to those who were not of Israel but saw the Tabernacle from the outside. What was seen in His dwelling place should be seen in every gathering which claims Him to be "in the midst". From the outside, holiness and righteousness must be what is seen. In a world where these features are absent it is the responsibility of all believers to ensure that in their individual lives and local assembly testimony they display that holiness and righteousness which will mark them as different from others. The righteousness that is displayed is not that of the Pharisees; it is that of the Lord Jesus Christ.

The significance of the pillars and their attachments

The pillars signify stability. The Lord Jesus gives stability to all of the structure, but that which separates it from what is outside is as stable as the boards. This house is set apart and the hangings will not fall or fail. The difference between God's dwelling place where He meets with His people and all else will always be preserved. The brass sockets signify the atonement brought about by Him who was able to stand the fires of the Altar; the silver connecting rods and hooks signify atonement, that which was paid for the ransom of the individual. The strength of the structure is to be found in the work of the Cross.

Note also that the pillars held the white linen at a uniform height around the court. It was not lower at some points - the Lord's righteousness was constant.

Verses 20-21: The Oil for the Light

The Lampstand situated in the Holy Place was to be fed with oil supplied by the Children of Israel. This oil was prepared from olives, which were bruised and beaten to rid them of all impurities so that it would be "pure oil olive". Enough of this oil was to be on hand so that the Lamp would be able to burn continually. Each morning and evening Aaron and his sons were responsible for ensuring that the seven lamps were tended. Further instructions are given regarding this in 30.7-8.

The purpose of the Lampstand has been dealt with in 25.31-40, but it is only at this point that instruction is given in respect of the oil. The olive tree was noted for its fatness. In the parable of Jotham (Judg 9) the trees are seen as deciding to anoint a king over them. The olive tree, the fig tree, and the vine are all asked, but refuse to accept, each giving a good reason. That given by the olive tree is, "Should I leave my fatness, wherewith by me they honour God and man, and go to be promoted over the trees?" (9.9). Olive trees yielded a rich harvest of olives and these in turn gave fulsome quantities of oil.

But the olives had to be beaten. Without that they would not be suited for their task; they could never have supplied the light that was necessary for the Holy Place; they would have failed! And so they were beaten. No effort was spared in this work, no half measures could be tolerated. They were pounded and beaten until the oil was extracted; they were crushed until all that was of value for the light had been extracted from them. Anything less would result in a light that was not pure. Beaten down, crushed to the finest, they were able to give a pure clear light. Only then was the oil ready for the Holy Place.

The significance of this is plain. The Lord maintains the light in the Sanctuary and there is fullness in Him to meet all the demands placed on Him. The light will never go out; priests will always be able to minister there. He is also so pure that there is nothing in Him to cloud that sacred tent; nothing to dim that sacred light. But pause to consider the beating which He endured, not to take impurities from Him, but to display the lustre of the purity that always marked Him. Gill comments, "...and this must be pure and free from lees and dregs, and must be beaten with a pestle in a mortar, and not ground in a mill, that so it might be quite clear; for being bruised and beaten, only the pulp or flesh of the olive was broken, but being ground in a mill, the stones were broken and ground, and so the oil not so pure".[†]

But it must not be forgotten that what brought this pure light that is Christ Jesus into the Holy Place was the oil, that which signifies the Holy Spirit. There was, as has been seen, a fullness in the oil and plenty of it as daily the lamps were tended. John alludes to this when he writes, "For he whom God hath sent speaketh the words of God: for God giveth not the Spirit by measure unto him (Jn 3.34). Through the Holy Spirit that light is shed, pure and clear, filling that sacred compartment with His light, ensuring that darkness cannot reign in God's dwelling place.

Notes

1 Illustrations of the Brazen Altar are given in Appendix 6.
1 S. H. Kellogg, *Studies in Leviticus,* p 378.
6 T. H. Ratcliffe, *Bible Plants, Fruits & Products.*
20 *Exposition of the Old and New Testaments.*

EXODUS 28

The Garments of the Priests†
With this chapter, the attention of the reader moves from the Tabernacle, its structure, contents, and vessels, to the garments of the priests who served in it. It must not, however, be thought that this is the commencement of a new subject. Without the priests there would be no purpose in the Tabernacle; they are so closely associated with it that they are brought in here as part of it. Indeed, if proof is needed of this, the instructions for making the Incense Altar, the Laver, and the sweet spices are given in ch.30, after the priesthood has been dealt with, and this in turn is followed in ch.31 by the appointment of Bezaleel and Aholiab to be the skilled craftsmen responsible for construction. The Tabernacle and the priesthood are inseparable. The importance of these garments is reflected in the fact that fully 43 (19%) of the 225 verses in chs.25-30, which deal with the Tabernacle, are devoted to this subject.

The importance of garments
It is worth pausing at this point to consider the importance of garments in the Word of God. Clothing denotes character, and the book of Genesis is sufficient to bring this to the attention of the reader. The following examples, although not all the references to garments in the book, serve to illustrate this fact.

The garments of Adam and Eve
After the Fall, the eyes of Adam and Eve "were opened, and they knew that they were naked; and they sewed fig leaves together, and made themselves aprons" (Gen 3.7). This is not an indication that the human body had changed physically due to the Fall; it is that what had been beautiful and to be enjoyed was now seen through sinful eyes, contemplated with a sinful heart and mind, with the differences between male and female requiring a covering because of the effect of their attitudes due to their spiritual nakedness before God. The garments which they made were not just to cover parts of their bodies from the gaze of the other, they were to cover their nakedness before God. This fig-leaf garment did not, however, cover them before God, and when He walked in the garden, they hid themselves. Man is completely incapable of fitting himself, by his own work, for the presence of God, a fact to be kept before the reader when the garments of the priests are considered. The garments manufactured by the fallen couple only show the shamefulness of sin.

But the grace of God shines through this discreditable scene when, "Unto Adam also and to his wife did the Lord God make coats of skins, and clothed them" (Gen 3.21). These are the first garments designed by God for the use of man. They are garments of salvation, whereas the garments of the priests are garments of priestly service. The provision of this covering made it necessary to involve the death of the animal(s) providing the skins, teaching that the answer to the sin that had entered was based on the death of a victim. By this means their shame, and the sin that caused it, were covered.

The garment of Noah

This garment also deals with the question of nakedness (Gen 9.18-27). Noah was in a drunken condition, and lay naked. Ham, who "saw the nakedness of his father, and told his two brethren without" (v.22), was exposing the fact of Noah's shame to others. Shem and Japheth took a garment, and after they had laid it upon their shoulders they moved backwards into the presence of Noah and covered his nakedness. This garment was not given by God, as were those provided for Adam and Eve, but nevertheless it achieved a righteous goal. A very practical lesson is seen here, that, rather than spread the news of the shame of another, these two men sought to provide a God-given solution before the situation escalated. These were not garments of salvation, but they were garments of compassion, given to one whom they were required to respect. The good character of Noah, damaged by the incident, was protected from further harm.

The consequences of what Ham did were far reaching. Just as his act had dishonoured his father, so the acts of his son, Canaan, would dishonour him. Amongst others, the inhabitants of Canaan were descended from him. But the practical lesson must not be missed. The faults and sins of others, even of those who are respected and held in esteem, must not be the topic of conversation and gossip. There may be occasions when it is necessary to bring the actions of some to the notice of those who are concerned, as can be seen when Joseph informed his father of the behaviour of his brothers (Gen 37.2), but when such talk is but tale-bearing it is inexcusable. When Peter writes, "And above all things have fervent charity among yourselves: for charity shall cover the multitude of sins" (1 Pet 4.8), he was not excusing sin which had to be dealt with publicly, but he was teaching that the faults of others must not be spread.

The seriousness of the actions of Ham is all the more highlighted when consideration is given to the fact that it was his own father who was involved. The filial respect which should have been his is conspicuous by its absence.

The garments of Joseph

When the garments of Joseph are considered, the point at issue is not dealing with the sin question, but rather with the dignified character of one who was chosen of God for service. They also signify the character of the One who would come, completely deal with sin, and reign over this world. The coat of many colours (Gen 37.3) points out Joseph as the chosen one, the one who was the delight of his father. The garment which he left in the hand of Potiphar's wife (Gen 39.15-16) reveals him to be the overcomer who did not succumb to the attack of the devil. The prison garments (Gen 41.14) show him as the suffering one, and the garments bestowed by Pharaoh display the fact that he is now the exalted one (Gen 41.42). The parallel with the life of the Lord Jesus cannot be missed, but there is a practical lesson; at all times and in all circumstances Joseph retained his good character, and the garments of his exaltation teach that God blesses those whose life pleases Him. Today it is not material blessings which are promised, but spiritual blessings, which have far greater worth.

Genesis, which early sees man with garments of exclusion sewn together by the fallen couple in the Garden of Eden, ends with a man wearing garments of exaltation. This is the history of mankind; excluded by sin from the presence of God, but by His grace ultimately restored to honour and dignity. Garments in Scripture, therefore, are not merely items of clothing to keep the wearer warm and to show his or her wealth, they proclaim the character of man as sin brought him low, and as God raised him up.

Verse 1: Aaron and his Sons Set Apart for the Priesthood
The background of Aaron

As Moses was the mediator of the covenant, it is to him that Aaron and his sons had to draw near in order to be appointed to the priesthood. Note that there is emphasis placed on the fact the Aaron was Moses' brother. He had been called this at the beginning of ch.7 and will be on a number of occasions after this, but at this crucial point where he is about to become the High Priest of Israel he is called "Aaron thy brother". No doubt the godly mother who reared Moses as his nurse brought up her older son, and their even older sister Miriam, in a similar manner; there was not special treatment for Moses because he was to be placed in Pharaoh's court. What a commendation this is to Jochebed that all three of her children made their mark for God. The relationship between the two brothers is an important factor. Since returning to Egypt Aaron had been Moses' closest associate.

1. Due to his eloquence he was chosen by the Lord to be the mouthpiece for Moses in his dealings with Pharaoh (4.14).

2. He acted in that capacity as they both met the Children of Israel on Moses' arrival in Egypt (4.29-31).

3. Both Moses and Aaron were given the charge "to bring the children of Israel out of the land of Egypt" (6.13).

4. He accompanied Moses when they appeared in the presence of Pharaoh (chs.5-11). The Egyptians, however, always regarded Moses as the leader, for "the man Moses was very great in the land of Egypt, in the sight of Pharaoh's servants, and in the sight of the people" (11.3).

5. The different roles of the two brothers in their dealings with Pharaoh were defined by the Lord as He spoke to Moses: "See, I have made thee a god to Pharaoh: and Aaron thy brother shall be thy prophet" (7.1).

6. The crucial instructions regarding the Passover were given by the Lord to Moses and Aaron (12.1).

7. The whole congregation murmured against Moses and Aaron in the wilderness of Sin and both men brought the response of the Lord to the people (16.1-10).

8. When Israel engaged in battle with Amalek, Aaron and Hur held up the hands of Moses on the hilltop (17.8-16).

9. Aaron and all the elders of Israel came and ate bread with Jethro, Moses' father-in-law (18.12).

10. When the covenant was ratified Moses, Aaron, Nadab, and Abihu, with seventy of the elders of Israel went up the mountain and saw the God of Israel (24.9).

11. The first indication that Aaron and his sons would have responsibilities in the service of the Tabernacle was when they were charged with ensuring that the Lampstand was always lit (27.21).

Despite this, there appear to be good reasons why Aaron was not suited to be High Priest. In the idolatry of the golden calf he played a prominent part. The people approached him with their discontent and he readily received their gold and, with a graving tool, made a molten calf (ch.32). He showed himself to be weak willed, not possessed of the leadership qualities of Moses. Later he and Miriam were involved in the shameful rebellion against Moses, using the pretext that he had married an Ethiopian woman (Num 12). The mention of Miriam's name first and the fact that only Miriam, and not Aaron, was stricken with leprosy, indicated that she was the leader. In the former incident he followed the people, in the latter he followed his sister. Whatever his motive, and possibly some jealousy of Moses was in evidence, he displayed weakness in leadership and the propensity to be led rather than leading.

Why then was this man chosen to be High Priest? One reason was that he could not claim that it was his outstanding qualities which gave him the right to occupy such an office; he could not glory in that and claim any right to serve as High Priest; he could only be thankful that one so unworthy had been given such sacred responsibility.

This brief history of the background of Aaron cannot be left without attention being drawn to his wife, who is only mentioned once in Scripture. He "took him Elisheba, daughter of Amminadab, sister of Naashon, to wife" (6.23). She was of the tribe of Judah, and her brother Naashon (sometimes written as Nahshon), who is noted as having been one of the "renowned of the congregation, princes of the tribes of their fathers" (Num 1.7,16), was declared to be captain of the tribe of Judah (Num 2.3). When the princes of Israel brought their offerings to the Lord on the day that the Tabernacle was set up, the first mentioned as doing so was Naashon (Num 7.12). Aaron's wife, therefore, came from one of the leading families of the nation, but this family had even greater dignity than that, an honour that surpassed all others. Matthew 1.4 shows them to be in the family line from which the Lord Jesus was born.

The history of the priesthood

The word "priest" (3548) means "one who draws near", referring to the fact that the priest draws near to God. Priestly acts are to be found from the earliest days. The first recorded act of the sons of Adam and Eve was priestly when Abel brought of the firstlings of the flock to offer to the Lord. The first mention of the word "priest" is with reference to Melchizedek, when he is called the "priest of the most high God" (Gen 14.18).

There had been a number of different phases of priesthood which should be noted.

1. At the beginning there was individual priesthood. As has been noted, Cain and Abel approached God with their offerings. Adam did not, as the head of the family, approach on their behalf; they did so individually, on their own behalf. It is most significant that there was in the human heart from the very earliest times, the realisation of sin and that an offering had to be made to God to deal with this. The fact that the first death in the Scriptures was that of the animals slain to provide the coats of skin which clothed Adam and Eve would be known to their family.

2. After the Flood there was family priesthood, where the head of the family acted before God as a representative of the other members. Noah offered sacrifices (Gen 8.20), as did Job, Abraham, Isaac, and Jacob.

3. With the deliverance of the Children of Israel from Egypt the nation was to be a kingdom of priests: "And ye shall be unto me a kingdom of priests, and an holy nation" (19.6). This right was, however, renounced by Israel when they asked Moses to be the mediator between them and Jehovah: "And they said unto Moses, Speak thou with us, and we will hear: but let not God speak with us, lest we die" (20.19).

4. The tribe of Levi was chosen to provide the priests. The right of Reuben to have this privilege, which may have been expected as he was the "firstborn" of Jacob (see Gen 49.3), was forfeited due to his immoral behaviour (Gen 35.22). Simeon forfeited the right due to his murderous and dishonourable conduct in the matter of Dinah and Shechem (Gen 34). Levi, the third son of Leah, Jacob's wife, was also involved in the shameful events of Genesis 34, but was selected to be the tribe of the priests. This choice had been made many years before the exodus, in the family of Amram and Jochebed of the tribe of Levi (2.1). This Levite family would provide Israel's deliverer and Israel's priests. Why was Levi chosen? It has been argued that their response to the call of Moses at the time of the worship of the golden calf, "Who is on the Lord's side? let him come to me" (32.26), was the deciding factor, but the command of the Lord to take Aaron and his sons to be priests was given while Moses was up the mount, before he descended and witnessed the idolatry that was taking place. If features are to be sought which justified the choice of Levi it is better to go back to the time of Israel's bondage and see in Exodus 2 that it was a husband and wife of the tribe of Levi who desired to see a leader arise who

would deliver Israel from Egypt. This may indicate that Levi had repented of the sin perpetrated in the alliance with Simeon. Above all this, however, there is to be seen the sovereign choice of God.

5. Today, as Peter reminds his readers, all believers are priests: "Ye also...are...an holy priesthood" (1 Pet 2.5), "But ye are...a royal priesthood" (1 Pet 1.9), and their Great High Priest (Heb 4.14) is the Lord Jesus. Priesthood is no longer limited to a select few or to a sacerdotal class who have been "ordained into the priesthood". The privilege of approaching God is given to all who have been saved by virtue of the blood shed on the Cross at Calvary. In view of this, the study of the Levitical priesthood is necessary for those who seek to understand their privileges and responsibilities as priests.

Verses 2-4: The Instruction to Make Holy Garments
The character of the garments

Garments in Scripture, as has been seen, signify character. The garments to be made for Aaron were "holy garments". The holiness was not to be found in the materials of which they were made, but in the purpose for which they were made, which was to set Aaron apart from all others, to consecrate him, thus signifying the holiness which must mark any who approach God. They were garments for the presence of God and therefore they must be "holy".

Holiness had been the mark of God's dealings with Israel since Moses was told that the ground on which he was standing was "holy ground" (3.5). A "holy convocation" (12.16) was the character of the gatherings to mark the Feast of Unleavened Bread, the Lord is declared to be "glorious in holiness (15.11), He would bring Israel to His "holy habitation" (15.13), and they were to be "holy men" unto Him (22.31). Now the High Priest who would enter the Holy Place and the Holiest of All must be seen to bear that holy character.

These garments were "for glory and beauty". "Glory" (3519) indicates splendour, glory, and dignity. "Beauty" (8597) conveys the thought of being fair to behold and honourable. Bringing these two words together it can be seen that the garments of the High Priest were to mark him out as a man quite apart from all others in Israel. His clothing made his office to be distinctive; it was one of dignity, and he was worthy to be held in respect. These garments were also lovely to behold, so that beauty marked him as he went about the work of serving in the Tabernacle. The garments of Aaron, however, gave him a glory which he did not possess of himself. Without them he did not have that glory. The glory and beauty of the Lord Jesus was His essentially with no need of garments to bring it about. He was marked by dignity and honour in all that He did, and there was loveliness in every action He performed and word that He spoke. Truly, it can be said of Him that He was marked by glory and beauty. Aaron's garments were unique to him; none other wore them. None would deny that the character displayed by the Lord Jesus is unique to Him; none other can aspire to such holiness nor display such unique composure and dignity. Soltau comments that "The office added dignity to Aaron: whereas Christ dignifies the office".[†]

The workers to make the garments

It was given to Moses to "speak unto all that are wise hearted" to engage in making these garments. In 31.1-6 Bezaleel and Aholiab are appointed to oversee the work and doubtless make much of it themselves, but this verse, together with 31.6, reveals that others were involved. Discernment would have been given to Moses so that he could select the wise hearted. Unsuitable workers would not have produced items of suitable quality for the Tabernacle.

There had been "wise" men in Egypt, and they sought to interpret Pharaoh's dreams (Gen 41.1-8); wise men sought by their enchantments to equal the signs which Moses performed (7.11). The wisdom with which the Tabernacle workers were endowed, however, was of a very different nature. It was wisdom given from the Lord, for He states that He had filled them with the spirit of wisdom. The wisdom possessed by the magicians of Egypt was that which was "earthly, sensual, devilish" (Jas 3.15). For this work, those whom Moses would select had been filled with "the wisdom that is from above" (Jas 3.17), and with that they would be able to carry out the work exactly according to the instructions received by Moses. Note that the "wisdom that is from above" always acts in obedience to the Word of God. That is true wisdom! Work for God cannot be accomplished using the wisdom of the world. That leads to self-reliance and lack of confidence in the Scriptures.

Those who work for God today cannot, and indeed, must not, rely on the wisdom of the world. His servants are given "gifts" with which to carry out His work, and in this way are fitted for the task. In a local assembly it is these gifts which are used. They are spiritual endowments given to carry out spiritual work with the purpose of achieving spiritual ends (see 1 Cor 12-14; Eph 4.7-16; Rom 12.6-8). In this way Christians have been fitted to carry out the work with which they have been charged. Some are evangelists, some teachers, and some helps etc. There is no sense of "promotion" in the giving of these gifts; all Christians have one or more of them and are responsible to the Lord for how they are developed and used. As with Christians today, so with those who would make the priestly garments; they were fitted by God with the necessary skills and wisdom, and to them was given the responsibility of preparing the garments that would be worn in the presence of God. Intricate detail and the use of the finest of materials made it necessary to show the greatest of care in all that was done. Instructions had to be followed in full, no worker could add his or her embellishments or "improvements"; no careless or shoddy work would be tolerated; all was to be of God, all for glory and for beauty.

The garments listed

The garments which had to be made consisted of a breastplate, an ephod, a robe, an embroidered coat, a mitre, and a girdle: six in number. To this has to be added the plate of pure gold (v.36), and linen breeches (vv.42-43). It cannot fail to be noted that no mention is made of shoes. These were not worn by the High Priest or by the priests, for the Tabernacle was holy ground, and even Moses had understood from his experience at the burning bush (3.5) that on holy ground no shoes were to be worn. It has been observed in connection with ch.3 that removing shoes was an act of respect shown by a guest as he entered the home of his host. The Tabernacle was the place of God's dwelling and thus shoes were not worn as an act, not merely of respect, but of worship.

Comments on each of these garments will be left until consideration of the verses where their detail is given.

Verses 5-8: The Ephod

The ephod, with the shoulder pieces and the breastplate which were attached to it, formed the most costly and beautiful of the garments of the High Priest, and it became regarded as his official garment. Such a glorious vesture would be the first to attract the attention of those looking on, as the precious stones glistened in the sun, and, in the Holy Place, in the light of the Lampstand. The background of gold thread woven through the material would add a setting of lustre.

The garment consisted of two pieces of fine twined linen which were joined together at one end of each piece by two shoulder pieces, allowing a hole for the head to pass through. Bush writes that "commentators are for the most part agreed in considering it as approaching the form of a short double apron having the two parts connected by two wide straps united on the shoulders". There is no record of the length of the garment although it is reasonable to suppose that it extended as far as the waist, and possibly to some way below the hips. A girdle, which was "upon" (v.8) the ephod, joined to it in some way, gathered it, probably round the waist; the purpose of this was to bind the two parts of the garment to the body. This "curious girdle of the ephod" (v.8) is different from the girdle of needlework which was for the High Priest's coat of fine linen (v.39). Over the ephod there was worn a breastplate which was attached to the shoulder pieces by chains of gold.

This garment became a symbol of the priesthood and it appears that with the passing of years it became a custom for the priests to wear a linen ephod, even although there is no instruction for that in this chapter. Samuel wore a linen ephod (1 Sam 2.18) when he was a child. He was not of the priestly family, but the mention of this garment indicates that he did have priestly features. The eighty-five priests who were slaughtered at Nob are all stated to have been wearing an ephod (1 Sam 22.18), and David wore an ephod when he danced before the Ark as it was being taken from the house of Obed-edom to the city of David (2 Sam 6.14). Sad it is to note that ephods were used for idolatrous purposes (Judg 17.5; 18.14 etc). Even Gideon fell into the trap of making an ephod (Judg 8.24-27), which the Children of Israel used as an object of idolatry. Because the ephod with the shoulder pieces and breastplate was such a unique garment, counterfeits were used to give credibility to false claims of priesthood and worship.

The significance of the ephod

The materials used to make the ephod were similar to those used in the vail and in the gate, except that gold was added. The colours all signify features which are to be found in the Great High Priest, the Lord Jesus. Blue signifies His heavenly character; purple, His royal dignity; scarlet, His humiliation and sufferings; and fine linen, His spotless righteousness. But to these is added gold, which was beaten into thin plates and "cut…into wires, to work it in the blue, and in the purple, and in the scarlet, and in the fine linen" (39.3). What skill was required to accomplish this! The golden thread, so formed, was then interwoven into the embroidered material, so that there was no part of the ephod from which gold did not shine out. As the High Priest moved in service in the Tabernacle, whether he was in the court, or in the Holy Place, he stood apart from all other priests in this; none other had garments interwoven with gold. Indeed, in the court of the Tabernacle, this was the only gold to be seen. The deity of the Lord Jesus stamps all His work, and He is unique in this. As the gold was inextricably woven into the garment and could not be extracted, so it is impossible for Him to be considered apart from deity. Eternally God, it is an essential truth that His deity can never be separated from Him, and this glorious fact shines through continually.

But let it not be overlooked that all the other colours were similarly woven together. No cherubims were to be found in the design, but the colours were all present, just as the characteristics which they signify are all to be found in the Lord Jesus, so closely intertwined that they also cannot be separated. There was perfect balance in His attributes and features, which in Him present a beautiful, striking, glorious whole.

> In Thee, most perfectly expressed,
> The Father's glories shine,
> Of the full Deity possessed,
> Eternally divine!
>
> True image of the Infinite,
> Whose essence is concealed;
> Brightness of uncreated light,
> The heart of God revealed.
> (Josiah Conder)

Verses 9-14: The Stones for the Shoulderpieces

The shoulder pieces were where the two pieces of the material of the ephod were joined together to form one garment. Strong states that the word means "a lateral projection, designating the top or ridge of the shoulder, in distinction from the back part or shoulder blade, for which a different word is employed". Where the joining took place would be at the area where the material at both sides was longer than in the middle, thus forming the hole for the head to pass through. These pieces were the parts of the ephod which lay on the shoulder of the wearer. Keil & Delitzsch comment: "These shoulder-pieces were not made separate, however, and then sewed upon one of the pieces; but they were woven along with the front piece, and that not merely at the top, so as to cover the shoulders when the ephod was worn, but according to v.25...reaching down on both sides from the shoulders to the girdle". Scripture does not explain exactly how the shoulder pieces joined the two parts of the ephod together, but a description is given of two onyx stones which were placed on the shoulders of the High Priest, clearly on top of the shoulder pieces, almost like epaulettes on a uniform.

It is not possible to be certain as to the identity of the onyx stone. It is first found in Genesis in the description of the land of Havilah, "where there is gold; And the gold of that land is good: there is bdellium and the *onyx stone*" (Gen 2.11-12). Job, when speaking of wisdom states that "It cannot be valued with the gold of Ophir, with the *precious onyx*, or the sapphire" (Job 28.16). It is included with the precious stones of the king of Tyrus: "Thou hast been in Eden the garden of God; every precious stone was thy covering, the sardius, topaz, and the diamond, the beryl, *the onyx*, and the jasper, the sapphire, the emerald, and the carbuncle, and gold" (Ezek 28.13). It was, therefore, regarded as being a stone of great value. Strong's description does not help: "from an unused root probably meaning to blanch...probably onyx, chrysoprasus, beryl, malachite". What can be asserted is that the two stones were of considerable size, enabling six names of the children of Israel to be engraved on each.

These names were placed on the stones "according to their birth". This is generally accepted as being the order in which they are placed in Genesis 29, 30 and 35.[†] The stones would, therefore, have the names from right to left, as the Hebrews wrote.

RIGHT HAND STONE

Naphtali	Dan	Judah	Levi	Simeon	Reuben

LEFT HAND STONE

Benjamin	Joseph	Zebulun	Issachar	Asher	Gad

The names, however, may have been written in a row with each name underneath the preceding name, with, for instance, on the right hand stone, Reuben at the top, Simeon underneath etc.

Whether the above list is completely accurate is not the point at issue which is that they were listed in order of birth. It will be seen later that on the breastplate they were placed in a different order, "according to their names...everyone with his name shall they be according to the twelve tribes" (v.21).

These two stones were then placed in "ouches of gold". Strong suggests that these were golden "netted sockets"; Keil & Delitzsch that they were "gold twists", or golden ornaments. Again the exact description is not known, but they were clearly beautiful golden settings which also attached the stones to the shoulder pieces. Aaron bore them upon his shoulders as "stones of memorial" and "for a memorial", so that the tribes would be remembered in the presence of Jehovah.

The significance of the shoulder stones

The shoulders are recognised as being the place of strength and power; it was there that the shepherd placed the sheep that had been lost (Lk 15.5). As the High Priest moved about in the service of the Tabernacle he had the names of the tribes on his shoulders, bringing them before the Lord constantly. They were never forgotten; the Lord at all times had them in remembrance. With what confidence, therefore, could they go about their daily business knowing that even when the burdens of life pressed down on them and drove from their minds any thought of the Sanctuary, the High Priest, with their names upon his shoulders, was bearing them up in the presence of God.

How was it that they had such a privilege not enjoyed by others? The answer is seen in that they were engraved on the shoulder stones in the order of their birth. This was the vital factor which brought them into such a favoured place; it was their birth which placed them upon his shoulders. There is no difficulty in recognising the parallel with the present day. Our Great High Priest bears on His shoulders in the presence of God the names of His people; they are there because of their birth, that which took place when they believed the gospel and were born again. What a contrast this is with the idols on which Babylon relied. They had to bear their idol upon their shoulders (Is 46.7) in order to set it upon its place. This lifeless, sightless, mindless, powerless piece of wood or metal could do nothing of itself. The God of Israel, however, lives, and the High Priest carried every Israelite upon his shoulders.

The strength which has been noted as a feature of the shoulder ensures that these names will never be let fall to the ground. The High Priest will not fail in his responsibility and allow these precious stones, all the more precious because of what is engraved on them, fall to the dust of the court, or even to the earth of the floor of the Holy Place. They will always occupy an elevated place, shoulder high, clearly seen, with nothing to obstruct the view of heaven. Being there "for a memorial" did not simply mean that their names alone were before God. In the names were to be seen their circumstances, problems, anxieties, failings, and victories. How Christians today can rejoice in this fact! Not just the fact of being born of God, but that all their circumstances are before Him continually, and the Great High Priest will never let one of His own fall to the ground, never consign them to obscurity, never be forgetful of them. Let the Christian reader take heart; He has you on His shoulders!

Verses 15-29: The Breastplate

There are now given the instructions for the most prominent and precious part of the dress of the priests, the breastplate which was worn over the ephod. Strong states of the word (2833): "lit., it would seem, for the root is found in no other word, a *glistening*, used only of this particular ornament; often with the epithet, 'of judgment', because oracular decisions were obtained by its means". TWOT at 772 states that "Arabic cognates indicate that the word means 'beauty' pointing to its value and importance among the holy garments of the high priest". That this was the most glorious of all the garments there can be no doubt. It was made of the same material as the ephod - gold, blue, purple, scarlet, and fine twined linen - and was folded over to form a pocket or pouch measuring one span square. This is reckoned to be one half of a cubit and therefore would make the breastplate measure approximately 9 inches (22.8 cms) square, a suitable size to be worn on the breast of the High Priest. Golden rings were attached to the breastplate into which were fitted chains of gold by which it was attached to the shoulder pieces (vv.22-25). At the bottom there were another two gold rings and through these were threaded a "lace of blue" attached to gold rings on the ephod. By this means the breastplate was securely fixed, but in such a manner that there was freedom of movement for the wearer. The great detail which is recorded regarding the fixtures (vv.22-28) is explained by the fact that the security of this precious item of clothing was of vital importance to Israel. It must not, it could not be allowed to fall! To let it fall was to let them fall.

To the front of the breastplate there were fixed gold settings to which were attached precious stones. These settings would be fixed in such a manner that they would not limit the movements of the High Priests nor form an uncomfortable encumbrance. The precious stones were fixed in four rows, each row with three stones. The Hebrew script read from right to left, and, as each stone represented a tribe, and as the tribes were placed in order according to the twelve tribes, it would appear that they were placed in order of their encampment round the Tabernacle. It is likely, therefore, that they were placed on the breastplate in the manner described below.

3. Zebulun	2. Issachar	1. Judah
6. Gad	5. Simeon	4. Reuben
9. Benjamin	8. Manasseh	7. Ephraim
12. Naphtali	11. Asher	10. Dan

This was also the order in which the tribes marched, divided into four groups, each bearing the name of the leading tribe of the group - the camp of Judah, of Reuben, of Ephraim, and of Dan (see Num 2 & 10). Each of the stones had on it the name of a tribe, placed there "like the engravings of a signet" (v.21). The stones fixed to the breastplate are as shown below. Judah would thus be the name on the sardius, Issachar on the topaz etc.

3. Carbuncle	2. Topaz	1. Sardius
6. Diamond	5. Sapphire	4. Emerald
9. Amethyst	8. Agate	7. Ligure
12. Jasper	11. Onyx	10. Beryl

The significance of the breastplate

The precious stones signify that the tribes of Israel were precious to the Lord. In like manner today, Christians are precious to Him. The shoulder is the place of strength but the breast is the place of affection. So, not only are they precious, they are held close to His breast, indicating that they are close to His affections. What a precious fact this is. He loves His people so much that He holds them to His breast. As our Great High Priest moves in that true Tabernacle He has the saints close to His affections, the object of His love. But not only so, they are constantly before the eye of God, always in His presence, never to be forgotten. Even the youngest and the weakest of His own are held there, the privilege not being because they are able to hold on to Him, but because He holds on to them. The individual naming of the tribes emphasises the individuality of remembrance, so that, even today, individual believers are on His breast.

On the shoulder, the names of the tribes would not be clearly seen by those who were in front of the High Priest, but they could be seen from above. The breastplate, however, was very clearly seen, not only by the Lord, but also by those before whom the High Priest stood. How precious this is. Looking down from heaven God looked on the shoulders with the two stones and the twelve names. From the majesty of His high place of power He looked on those who were held up on the powerful shoulders of the High Priest.

An onlooker, however, could not fail to notice the different colours in the precious stones; no two of them were alike, each had its own beauty and splendour. In this there is displayed the great truth that the different character of each tribe was known to the Lord and that in His eyes each had its own beauty. In like manner, the different characteristics of each believer are displayed by the Lord Jesus as He ministers above, and in each individual He sees a unique beauty.

Verse 30: The Urim and the Thummim

Inside the pocket formed by the ephod there was placed the Urim and the Thummim. There has been much speculation regarding these. Did they consist of a white stone and a black stone; was it two other precious stones; were two precious pieces of metal placed into the pouch on the ephod? No answer to this can be given as there is no record of what constituted the Urim and the Thummim, but it is known that Urim (224) means "lights" and Thummim (8550) means "perfections". This is expanded by Keil & Delitzsch to include the meaning of "illumination" or "light" for Urim, and "inviolability" for Thummim. In understanding their purpose it has to be noted that the breastplate is known as the "breastplate of judgment" (v.15), and that when Aaron ministered before the Lord he was bearing the "judgment of the children of Israel upon his heart before the Lord continually".

When reference is made to Numbers 27.21 it can be seen that the purpose of the Urim and the Thummim was to guide the Children of Israel. Although they did have the Law, the full revelation in the Word of God which is available today was not given to them and they required illumination to guide them in their walk and actions. Whenever such illumination was required the High Priest could seek it through the Urim and Thummim. How answers were given is not revealed, but clearly this was a means by which the mind of the Lord could be ascertained with complete confidence. When Joshua was appointed to succeed Moses it was stated of him: "he shall stand before Eleazar the priest, who shall ask counsel for him after the judgment of Urim before the Lord" (Num 27.21). The Lord had spoken directly to Moses but Joshua would be commanded through the Urim. In later days Saul sought to receive counsel of the Lord but "when Saul enquired of the Lord, the Lord answered him not, neither by dreams, nor by Urim, nor by prophets" (1 Sam 28.6). There were two occasions when David consulted at the Urim and Thummim. The first was when Saul was conspiring against him and David wished to know if the men of Keilah would deliver him into the hands of Saul. He "said to Abiathar the priest, Bring hither the ephod" (1 Sam 23.9). Having made his request, the Lord responded by telling him that they would. The second occasion was when the Amalekites burned Ziklag and took the women captive. Again David called for Abiathar to bring the ephod and he enquired of the Lord "Shall I pursue after this troop? shall I overtake them?". The answer came, "Pursue: for thou shalt surely overtake them, and without fail recover all"

(1 Sam 30.7-8). There is no further record of its use during the reigns of the kings who followed David. When, after the return from Babylon, it could not be verified that certain who claimed to be priests had the necessary genealogy, Ezra decreed that they were not to be regarded as priests "till there stood up a priest with Urim and with Thummim" (Ezra 2.63; Neh 7.65), until there was a High Priest who was able to wear the breastplate with the Urim and Thummim in the pocket close to his heart, and was therefore able to discern the mind of the Lord in the matter. This indicates that at that time the Urim and the Thummim had not been recovered and there is no record of them having been used at a later date.

The significance of the Urim and the Thummim

The basis for understanding the present day significance of the Urim and the Thummim is to appreciate that it was the means by which the word of God was imparted to the enquirer. When guidance was sought, God would speak, or make known his truth in a way that has not been disclosed in detail. As the full Word of God has now been revealed, it is from the Bible that guidance now has to be found. It cannot be emphasised too much that a decision that is contrary to the Word of God does not have His approval. Many have claimed that a pathway that they have adopted, although it may be contrary to Scripture, has nevertheless been revealed to them by the Lord. This cannot be! He cannot deny Himself or His Word.

But is there not also significance in the fact that the Urim and the Thummim were held close to the heart of the High Priest? What does this mean? First, the counsels and purposes of God are to be found close to His heart. As Scriptures are read and guidance is sought, it is necessary also to draw near to Him as we seek His direction. To pursue His Word in a cold, clinical manner, using it simply as any instruction book is used, is not His way. Neither is guidance to be found in scanning through the Book seeking a verse that suits what the reader already has determined to do. That, also, is not His way. Guidance will be given to those who prayerfully, with devotion to Him, and seeking His will alone, read the Word of God and draw near to Him. Truly, guidance is to be found close to His heart. His desire is that His people should not be left in a cold world, unable to find help and unsure that their pathway has His approval. His wish is to have His own near to Him and His desire is to reveal His will to those who seek and enjoy His presence.

But more can be yet discerned. His counsels are close to His heart, close to the place of love and affection. All His purposes are based on His love and affection, and thus they are held close to His bosom. Let no servant of His fail to understand that all that He has planned for His own is for their good and eternal benefit, based on the great love that He has for them. No mean motive has formed His way, no loveless heart has planned, no cold design has come from Him; all of His own are enveloped in His love, and at the centre of that unequalled affection His will is to be found. Here it is that His people are carried in the Sanctuary on His breast and here it is that they can know His will.

Yet more should be understood. Why is it that the means by which the revelation was made known is not disclosed? We know that the Lord spoke to David when he enquired at the ephod, but we do not know in what manner He spoke. The wisdom of God is here displayed. There is no single "formula" for the Lord speaking to His people. If such a thing existed it would be open to abuse, with claims being made to support any notion which took the fancy. God speaks in many ways - through the Word of God, through circumstances, through impressing a desire on the heart of His servant. Mostly it is in a number of factors coming together, but there is no singular way by which His mind can be discerned. One essential factor is the primacy of the Word of God. Circumstances or other factors being taken into account must be in accord with Scripture and seen in the light of Scripture, never separate from it. They must never be considered in isolation, without consulting Scripture. Nor is His way revealed to the lazy or indifferent saint. Desire for help and guidance must be linked with time spent in His presence and with His Word.

It is also true that often the revelation of His will is of such preciousness that the one so blessed feels that it has to be kept close as a matter between the servant and the Lord alone. It is not for sharing; it is for personal enjoyment and satisfaction; it is so precious that it has to be kept in the heart. When it is the revelation of His will in a pathway of service, and in later days when the pathway may be rough and the Adversary whispers that it is time to give up, the servant of the Lord remembers the call received and is encouraged by the fact that God was prepared to speak to him in such a decisive way.

Verses 31-35: The Robe of the Ephod

Following the description of the ephod and the breastplate there is given instruction for the making of the robe of the ephod. This robe was made of blue material and, although no length is given, it is supposed that it went down to the lower part of the leg. It consisted of one piece of cloth with a hole being made so that it was put on over the head of the High Priest. Round this hole there was "a binding of woven work" so that the material did not tear. The uncovering of the head of the High Priest, or the tearing of his clothes, was not permitted (Lev 21.10), showing that Caiaphas, the High Priest, was disobeying the Word of God when he rent his clothes while declaring of the Lord Jesus, "He hath spoken blasphemy" (Mt 26.65). The false accusation came from a man who had no concern to submit to Scripture. The distinctive name which it was given, the robe of the ephod, indicates that it was worn close to the ephod, probably immediately under it. Round its hem there were woven pomegranates of blue, purple, and scarlet, and between them bells of gold, bells which would be heard as the High Priest moved about. It should be noted in passing that this is the only garment of the High Priest that is stated to have a hem. Pomegranates seem a strange introduction, but they are also mentioned in the Temple at Jerusalem. There, they were on the "chapters upon the two pillars" that stood in the porch of the House (1 Kings 7.20).

The significance of the robe of the ephod
The blue colour of the robe would be the first feature to catch the attention of the on-looker. Blue signifies that which is heavenly, and denotes the heavenly character of the Great High Priest and of the work which He carries out. The breastplate was placed directly on the ephod as His people are linked with One who ministers in a heavenly Tabernacle.

The bells and pomegranates could not be missed. Pomegranates (7416) were to be found in the fruits which the spies brought back from their tour of Canaan (Num 13.23) together with grapes and figs. This indicates that they were brought back as three "sample" fruits to show the great fertility of the land, these three fruits being leading examples of this fruitfulness. The fig tree and the fruit of the vine signify the nation of Israel. The pomegranates' great fruitfulness, the seeds being in number beyond that of many other fruits, signifies the fruitfulness of the gospel and its effect in the lives of those who believe it. Ratcliffe points out that "unlike any other fruit, every seed within a mature pomegranate is contained within a separate sac of red fluid. God would have all Israel to remember that their redemption from Egypt was not through any merit of their own, but as a whole, due to the sprinkled blood of an innocent victim…The most unusual crown-like calyx of the fruit would tell us that our Redeemer is now crowned with glory and honour (Heb 2.7,9), and that we are with Him in spirit (Eph 2.6)".[†] The embroidered colours of these pomegranates denote, as in their use in other parts of the Tabernacle, His heavenly character, His royalty, and His perfect humanity with the suffering which He bore.

The significance of the bells
But what of the bells which were also to be found on the hem of the ephod? This ephod was not worn when the High Priest entered the Holiest of All on the Day of Atonement, but it was worn at all other times when he was engaged in his duties. It is true that those who were not in the Holy Place would hear the sound of the bells as Aaron ministered there. They could not see him, but they could hear him. Similarly, today, the Lord Jesus cannot be seen moving as the Great High Priest, but His people can hear the sound of the bells, the evidences of His activity. To see His hand in circumstances, to hear His voice from His Word, to feel His joy in the soul are all evidences of work; they are all the sound of the bells.

However, the reason given for the bells was that "when he goeth in unto the holy place before the Lord, and when he cometh out, that he die not" (v.35). A number of suggestions have been made regarding the significance of this statement.

1. It was necessary for Aaron to announce his arrival in the way that an audience is gained with a great king. The ringing of the bells was the request for such an audience.

2. To announce to heavenly hosts that a man was about to come into the presence of God, enabling them to look on with wonder at such a scene.

3. To indicate that he was properly dressed as he served in the Sanctuary. With this suggestion, the words "it shall be upon Aaron to minister" must refer to more than just the bells as these could be worn with other parts of the official dress being missing. The suggestion is that if he were not properly robed for service he would die either when he entered or when he came out of the Holy Place.

These suggestions have varying degrees of merit but a little further consideration may be necessary. The bells were part of the robe of the ephod, a part of the dress which bears the name of the ephod and which is, therefore, closely linked with the ephod, the shoulder pieces, and the breastplate with its precious stones and the pocket in which was held the Urim and the Thummim. It has already been noted that the ephod was regarded as the main "official" part of the dress. The ringing of the bells was, therefore, noted at the end of the section dealing with the ephod and the other items closely linked with it. Thus, did these bells not act as a reminder to the High Priest that he must never enter the presence of God without the ephod and the names of the people upon his shoulders and upon his breast? To do so would be a failure to bear up the people with him as he served, and a priest with no interest in the people is no priest. It could be argued that no such reminder should have been necessary, but failure can come in remarkable ways. Who would have thought that Nadab and Abihu would fail so grievously at such an early stage after the consecration of the priests (Lev 10.1)?

It is also worthy of note that these bells are stated to be heard "when he goeth in...and cometh out" of the Holy Place. At that time "his sound" was heard; the other priests, and also those of the people who were at the gate of the Tabernacle to offer their sacrifices, heard them. This would be an encouragement to them that as the High Priest went in he was about to bear them before the Lord, and as he came out, that he had been doing so.

And so the great High Priest serves above, bearing His people up before the Lord. Those who enjoy this privilege know that there is no possibility of Him dying. He has conquered death and never again will enter into it. Death obeys Him, and will not and cannot control Him.

The glorious declaration of the Epistle to the Hebrews remains forever true: "Wherefore he is able also to save them to the uttermost that come unto God by him, seeing he ever liveth to make intercession for them" (Heb 7.25).

Verses 36-38: The Mitre

On his head the High Priest wore a mitre, which probably was turban-like in shape, and was made of fine linen (v.39). Mitre (4701), may be connected with a word which also means "blossom or flower", and this could indicate that it was styled in some such manner. On the front of this mitre, attached to it by a ribbon or lace of blue, was a golden plate on which were inscribed the words, "HOLINESS TO THE LORD". This was never to be absent from his forehead "that Aaron may bear the iniquity of the holy things, which the children of Israel shall hallow in all their holy gifts" (v.38). It was a "holy crown" (29.6), denoting the dignity which marked the holiness of the High Priest, a crowning final indication that he was apart from and above all the other priests who served in the Tabernacle.

The mitre with its golden plate indicated that Aaron bore the iniquity of the holy things which were offered by the people. Even these sacrifices and offerings were marked by iniquity and defilement because they had been prepared by human hands. The High Priest bore that iniquity and was a mediator who atoned for all the sins of the people. Only through him, therefore, was any offering acceptable to God.

The significance of the wording on the golden plate must not be missed. "HOLINESS TO THE LORD", declared that everything over which the High Priest officiated was marked by holiness. Anything less was abhorrent to God as was clearly seen in the judgment which befell any who sought to besmirch that holiness. This was the feature that was to stamp the Tabernacle and all who served in it. But note that this holiness was "to the Lord"; it was for His pleasure and for His satisfaction. He who is holy demands holiness in His house and in His sacrifices. Nothing less will do and the High Priest wore this on his forehead. This is the place of intelligence, signifying that he understood this truth and was fully aware of what that holiness involved. The condition of things in the Sanctuary and the demands of the Lord to keep them according to His word were known to the High Priest who had an intelligent grasp of the truth involved.

Why were the priests' heads covered?

The question which has to be addressed is, "Why were the heads of the High Priests and the priests (they wore linen bonnets - v.40; 39.28), covered, while the heads of the males have to be uncovered, and the head of the woman covered, when the assembly meets today? This seems, at a cursory glance, to be inconsistent, and indeed has been used as part of the argument for the abandonment of the scriptural practice of covering the heads of the women when the assembly is gathered together. Such an assertion reveals a failure to grasp the fundamental difference between the Tabernacle and the Christian assembly.

The first difference to note is that women did not serve as priests in the Tabernacle. It was Aaron and his sons who were appointed to this honoured occupation and thus only males appeared there. In the Christian age, believing women serve as Christian priests as do Christian men, and that priesthood functions, not only when the assembly gathers, but also at other times. The fact that the Scriptures also teach that women have to remain silent in the church does not detract from the reality of their priesthood.

With the presence of women in the assembly it is now possible to show the full creatorial order of which women, men, and the Lord have a part. What an honour it is to display a sign which shows that one is part of this great order of headship in God's creation, an order which should be understood by those have come to know the Lord Jesus. In the assembly the Lord is known and His relationship in the Godhead is also understood.

The Tabernacle, however, differs, and it is not a picture of the assembly. As has been noted, no women served there, and the truth of the Lord Jesus and His relationship in the Godhead was not at that time revealed. It was a question then of mankind and God. In this relationship *man* showed his submission in that he covered his head. In daily life the woman wore the veil over her head, but in the Tabernacle man did so; he was subject and the covered head publicly declared this.

Only when the great truths of the New Testament were revealed was it possible in the Christian assembly to show by public sign that the man is the head of the women, Christ is the head of the man, and the head of Christ is God. That truth had always been, but only when it was revealed could it be publicly enjoyed in the assembly.

Verse 39: The Coat of Fine Linen

Apart from the note that the mitre was to be made of fine linen, this verse contains instructions regarding the linen coat and its girdle. The High Priest wore under the robe of the ephod a linen coat, gathered round the waist by a girdle (73) which was a belt of needlework. Tradition has it, although there is no scriptural warrant for such an assumption, that the girdle was long enough to wind a number of times around the body, leaving the ends to hang down to the feet. Even leaving that aside it can be seen that the girdle would require to have the length necessary to act as a secure belt for the linen coat. The coat was of linen, and, although it is stated that they should "embroider" it, the absence of any mention of needlework would indicate that it was not embroidered with coloured thread, but rather that the linen was "woven in checks or cubes" (Keil & Delitzsch). The girdle was, however, one of "needlework" indicating that it was embroidered with the same colour of threads used elsewhere, that is of blue, purple, and scarlet. This is confirmed in 39.27-29 when a description is given of the making of these linen garments for Aaron and his sons. They are "coats of fine linen…and a girdle of fine twined linen, and blue, and purple, and scarlet, of needlework".

The significance of the coat of fine linen
The coat was the garment over which all the others were placed and was, therefore the foundation on which the High Priest's garments rested. Fine linen has consistently signified the righteousness and spotless humanity of the Lord Jesus and is no different in this case. His holy, righteous life is the basis of the work which He has carried out. The Hebrew writer underlines this truth when he states, "For we have not an high priest which cannot be touched with the feeling of our infirmities; but was in all points tempted like as we are, yet without sin" (Heb 4.15). He was a High Priest who did not need, as did Aaron and other High Priests of the Aaronic order, to offer a sacrifice for Himself. He did not and could not sin, and therefore all that He did was righteous and, for the first and only time, there walked on earth a man who was completely holy and righteous. This was a secure foundation for His work.

The girdle which bound the coat to the priest was many coloured. This righteousness of the Lord Jesus was surrounded by His regal dignity, His heavenly character, and His sufferings. These were all so closely bound to Him that they were inseparable from Him. How lovely that this comes in at the end of the description of the garments. It is almost the last glorious confirmation of His holiness and all the other features which have been marked by the garments; a final emphasis on these beautiful attributes of the Lord Jesus Christ.

But, one final thing must be noted. As this was the innermost garment much of it would be hidden from the sight of others. Some of it would be seen, but the coat of blue, the ephod, the breastplate, and the shoulder pieces all sat on top of it. Much of that which was righteous in the life of the Lord Jesus was not seen by human eyes. There were times when He was alone with God, and even when He was with others, the heart and devotion of the Lord, and the full righteousness of all that He did, were not comprehended by those around Him. It was not all done for public view, but for the pleasure and satisfaction of God the Father. He was as righteous and holy in what was not seen by others as He was in those things which were open to the human gaze.

Verses 40-43: The Garments of the Sons of Aaron
The garments which were to be worn by the priests are not described in as much detail as those of the High Priest. Each priest wore a linen coat, a girdle, and a bonnet. In the following verses it is also noted that, in

addition to what had been described, both Aaron and his sons wore linen breeches. But there is also a striking fact that is clear to the reader: although the garments of the priests are much simpler than those of the High Priest, they nevertheless are still described as being "for glory and for beauty".

The significance of the garments of the sons of Aaron

As the garments of the High Priest denote the dignity and character of his office, so likewise do the garments of the priests. It was an honour to be a priest! But as there are features in the dress of the High Priest which are not found in that of the priests, so there are features of the Lord Jesus which are unique to Him and cannot be shared with other priests. Thus the sons of Aaron wore no ephod, there were no precious stones on their shoulders or on their breasts, they bore no Urim and Thummim, they had no coat of the ephod, and no golden plate on their heads. The High Priest was unique as our Great High Priest is unique.

But what was common to both was that they wore linen garments, speaking of righteousness. The fact that the High Priest wore such a garment and that the priests are noted after Aaron suggests the lesson that they must have this characteristic feature as he has it. There had to be likeness to him in certain things, while recognising also his uniqueness. This principle is clearly set out by John: "And every man that hath this hope in him purifieth himself, even as he is pure" (1 Jn 3.3). Those who follow the Lord will have a desire to be like Him, and to come into the presence of God must seek holiness. Nothing less is demanded of those who approach Him. Where sin has been committed it will be confessed, but pursuing a sinful course is not worthy of those who seek the Sanctuary. It may be argued that believers today have imputed righteousness, but any intelligent reader of the Word of God knows that this must be answered by a daily practical response.

The importance of this is emphasised by the fact that these garments had to be worn when they served at the Brazen Altar, or when they entered the Tent of the Congregation, else they would die. Similar language had already been used in connection with the High Priest (v.35), but the priests were now included. There could be no exceptions. The Lord may not work in such a manner today (although 1 Corinthians 11.30 suggests that believers may suffer physically should they eat and drink "unworthily"). The vital point is that all who seek His presence must do so with clean hands and a pure heart (Ps 24.4). The closing words of the chapter impress on the reader that these conditions are not temporary, nor must the standard lower with the passing years. They will remain forever and are as unchangeable as the holiness of God.

And so instructions have been given for the garments of the priests, but the making of those garments did not fit Aaron and his sons for priestly service. Merely donning the garments was not enough; such would constitute usurping the priestly office. They had to be consecrated to this holy responsibility and privilege. The next chapter teaches how this was to be done.

Notes

1 An illustration of the High Priest is given in Appendix 6.

2 Soltau, *The Tabernacle, the Priesthood, and the Offerings*, p 191.

9,10 The order given above cannot be guaranteed to be right. Certain facts *can* be verified, for instance, that Reuben was born first. It has to be noted, however, that in the lists in Genesis 29, 30 and 35, the sons are listed according to their mothers.

33 T. H. Ratcliffe, *Bible Plants, Fruits & Products.*

EXODUS 29

The Consecration of the Priests

The consecration of the priests was a most solemn moment in the history of Israel. The instructions given to Moses were carried out in Leviticus 8. Without a priesthood, even with the garments of the priests prepared and the Tabernacle ready, no one could approach God.

Verses 1-3: The Introduction

The ceremony instructed in this chapter was carried out as the congregation gathered together at the door of the Tabernacle (Lev 8.4), with Aaron and his sons also there, inside the gate, in the court. The gathering of the people in this way indicated the solemn nature of what was to take place and also that all Israel had an interest in the proceedings. There would be later a rebellion against this priesthood (Num 16), but what took place when the priests were consecrated, the whole congregation seeing them inaugurated into their office, is confirmation that the Aaronic priesthood was instituted by God.

The interest of the people, however, must have been all the greater because the priests were those who would handle their sacrifices, and, in the person of the High Priest, deal with their interests in the presence of God. It was, therefore, vital that they understood the legitimacy of this priesthood and that they saw clearly that Aaron was competent to discharge this responsibility in a satisfactory manner. Should there be doubts about the High Priest the whole priesthood was affected and there could be no confidence that what took place was effective before God for the whole congregation.

Emphasis is given to the fact that it was Moses who was to consecrate the priests: "And this is the thing that thou shalt do unto them". It was not given to individuals to appoint themselves to this office as the Hebrew Epistle confirms: "And no man taketh this honour unto himself" (5.4), thus ensuring that the priesthood was not gained by self-seeking individuals. Henry Law comments, "No human mind selects the priest. No self called man usurps the work. The service is ordained by God. The sacred order has a door, which none can pass, but by divine command".

Their priests were to be "hallowed" or "consecrated" into their office. The word "hallow" (6942) means "to set apart as sacred". It is first used in relation to the seventh day of creation (Gen 3.2), where it is translated "sanctified". The priests were to be completely given over to the service of God and were "to minister" to Him. The expression "to minister unto me in the priest's office" has been used four times in ch.28 (vv.1,3,4,41), and will continue to be used in this chapter. Priestly service is directed towards God, and, although it is for the good of the people, it is a Godward service.

The whole consecration ceremony took place in the court of the

Tabernacle, and only after it was fully completed were the priests able to enter the Holy Place. Until that point was reached they were not priests and therefore were unable to enjoy the privileges and fulfil the responsibilities of the priesthood.

There could be no consecration without sacrifice, and one young bullock, two rams, and a basket containing unleavened bread, unleavened cakes tempered with oil, and unleavened wafers anointed with oil had to be made ready.

Verse 4: Washing

The first act carried out on Aaron and his sons was Moses washing them with water. It will be necessary for them to wash at the Laver as they engage in their service, but this washing, which was only carried out once, was done for them by Moses. This initial act signifies that defilement has been got rid of and that they are in a clean state, fit to serve God. Paul alludes to this when, writing to the Corinthians, he states, "And such were some of you: but ye are washed, but ye are sanctified…" (1 Cor 6.11). Washing from the defilement of sin takes place at salvation as Paul, again, writes to Titus: "…according to his mercy he saved us, by the washing of regeneration" (Tit 3.5), that is, the washing which took place at the time of regeneration, the moment of salvation. Having been washed at salvation it is the responsibility of every believer to maintain that spiritual cleanliness.

There is, however, a Great High Priest who did not need to be washed in order to remove defilement. The Lord Jesus, although He lived on earth amongst men, was not defiled in any way, always living a holy life; there was no need of cleansing from sin. Faced by unbelieving enemies who sought to kill Him because he spoke the truth (Jn 8.40), men who were desperately seeking a reason to carry out this vile deed, He asked, "Which of you convinceth me of sin?" (Jn 8.46).

Verses 5-7: Aaron is Clothed and Anointed

How solemn must have been the moment when Aaron was robed for the first time. It has already been observed that this distinctive clothing gave him honour, beauty, and dignity. It was the outward sign of his honoured place and of his great responsibility. The garments are detailed to confirm that all had been made according to the instructions given to Moses and to ensure that none of them was omitted when Aaron was clothed.

Having been clothed, Aaron was then anointed with oil, the instructions for the making up of which are to be found in 30.22-25. Anointing in Scripture set an individual apart for the service of God and signified that the necessary competency to carry out the responsibilities involved had been conferred. In addition to the High Priest, kings were anointed (1 Sam 16.13). It should be noted that the priests were not anointed as was Aaron, but rather the anointing oil was sprinkled on them.

This act signified that the Holy Spirit had anointed the High Priest. In the life of the Lord Jesus the Holy Spirit was active. When He commenced His public ministry it is recorded by Luke that He was "full of the Holy Ghost" and that He was "led by the Spirit into the wilderness" (Lk 4.1). Peter, when preaching before Cornelius stated, "God anointed Jesus of Nazareth with the Holy Ghost and with power" (Acts 10.38).

The question, however, must be asked, "Why did the anointing of the High Priest take place before the anointing oil was sprinkled on the priests?". Nothing in the Word of God is without significance, and to dismiss this issue as of no account does not do justice to the Scriptures. The answer is in observing that the blood of the bullock and the blood of a ram (vv.10-18) were shed before the anointing oil was sprinkled upon the priests, reminding the reader that they could not come into the good of this anointing until the blood was shed. In Acts 2 the Church was baptized in the Spirit and at that time, which was after the blood had been shed, the Spirit descended upon them.

Verses 8-9: The Clothing of the Sons of Aaron

The previous chapter has described the difference between the garments of the High Priest and those of the priests. It is necessary, however, that the people see not only the robing of the High Priest, but also of the priests. The clothing bestows dignity and honour and it is well that believers today, who are Christian priests, do not lose sight of the fact that dignity must mark them at all times. The clothes were what others saw, signifying the character of the priestly wearer, which was displayed to those who looked on. This must be the character of righteousness, as pictured in the linen of these holy garments. Note that emphasis is placed on the fact that the priest's office is theirs "for a perpetual statute". This cannot and will not be altered at any time in the future, as long as the Aaronic priesthood is in being.

What must it have been for Israel to see the priesthood with their garments of glory and beauty, ready to serve in the Tabernacle! Their minds would go back to the days in Egypt when Egyptian priests played a dominant part in society, holding sway over the people with their mystique and black arts. The multiplicity of gods, which they regularly added to and changed, treating animals and monarchs as gods, enabled them to hold a grip over men and women by fear and superstition. Israel had now come to know another God, the true God, One who spoke and promised; One who kept His word and never failed them; One who now showed that He delighted in the company of His redeemed people; One who had declared they would inherit the land long promised. This was their God and the consecrated priesthood allowed them to draw near.

Verses 10-14: The Sin Offering for the Priests
Unique features of this sin offering

Following the robing of the priests, a bullock was brought to the door of the Tabernacle, to be a sin offering; Aaron and his sons could not serve as priests if sin was not dealt with. Although they had been redeemed from Egypt they still sinned, and the offering of the bullock was to meet this need.

It is well to consider at this point some of the features of the sin offering so that what takes place as the priests are consecrated can be understood. Of the five offerings which occupy the opening chapters of Leviticus, greater space is devoted to the sin offering than to any of the other four. This reveals the great compassion in the heart to God to see that the need of His people is met, as it is in the work of the Lord Jesus on the Cross. There are four classes of the offering: for the priest, for the entire congregation, for the ruler, and for the common people. In the offerings for the priests and the congregation the blood of the offering is sprinkled seven times before the vail, the fat is burned on the Brazen Altar, and the remainder is burned outside the Camp. In the offerings for the ruler and the common people the blood of the offering is not sprinkled seven times before the vail, but the fat is still placed on the Altar and the remainder becomes the food of the priests.

One important difference is seen at the consecration of the priests. The bullock, which is what is offered in the sin offering for a priest, does not have its blood brought into the Holy Place to be sprinkled before the vail, and yet the remainder of the offering procedure is that which is laid out for a priest (Lev 4.1-13; 6.24-30). The detailed accuracy of Scripture is displayed here, because neither Aaron nor his sons were fitted to enter into the Holy Place until the consecration was complete.

It is worthy of note also, as far as the sin offering is concerned (Lev 4.1-5.13), that the higher the standing of an individual, the greater is the appreciation of sin. The priest who attended at the Sanctuary was expected to have a greater consciousness of sin and its consequences than that felt by the common people. The greater the privilege, the greater is the responsibility to appreciate divine truth.

In Genesis all the offerings are burnt offerings, and it is not until the Tabernacle is set up that sin offerings are offered; only then are instructions given for them. The first sin offering specifically noted in Scripture as being brought to God is, therefore, the bullock for the priest. It was the first to be placed on the Brazen Altar, something that was totally unnecessary for our Great High Priest.

Procedure for presenting the sin offering

After the bullock had been brought to the door of the Tabernacle, Aaron and His sons placed their hands upon the head of the bullock. By this act they were identifying themselves with the sacrifice; they were stating publicly that what was to be done to the bullock was carried out because it was a substitute for them; they deserved to die because of their sin, and this bullock would die in their place.

The bullock was then slain "before the Lord". He saw what took place, just as at Calvary all was "before the Lord" as the Saviour died for sinners. The blood of the bullock was then applied by the finger to the horns on the Brazen Altar, with the remainder of the blood being poured out at the bottom of the Altar. The horns of the Brazen Altar are the highest recorded items in the Tabernacle; the blood was at this high point of the Altar and at its base. On the horns it was to be seen in heaven and at the bottom of the Altar it was seen by the priests. The greater amount was at the bottom; a smearing of the blood on the Altar was sufficient for it to be fully appreciated in heaven, but the amount of it poured out at the foot of the Altar was necessary for it to be appreciated by the priest, and, even with that, their appreciation would be low at best. Following this, the fat of the bullock and "the caul that is above the liver, and the two kidneys, and the fat that is upon them" were burned upon the Brazen Altar. The remainder of the flesh was burned outside the Camp.

The significance of the sin offering

The sin offering for the priests but emphasises again that the priests after the order of Aaron were sinners who required the sin offering to make atonement for their sins. In like manner the High Priest on the Day of Atonement first offered a sin offering for himself before he could offer one for the people. Israel stood always in danger of having a High Priest who could fail, but Christians have no need of such fear because the Great High Priest will never fail, since He is "consecrated for evermore" (Heb 7.28).

The burning of the remainder of the flesh outside the Camp signifies the solemn judgment which was carried out on sin when the Lord Jesus Christ was made sin. The events of the Cross, with the three hours of darkness and the cry of the Saviour, "My God, my God, why hast thou forsaken me?", impress on the reader the awful judgment that fell on Him. Coates' comment is searching: "A large apprehension of Christ in sin-offering character lies at the basis of all priestly service. There is no priestly service - no true note of praise to God - if that is not great in the soul".

Those who would handle the sacrifices brought by others showed in the offering of the bullock that they were fully persuaded of the power of the sin offering to deal with the question of sin, fully, completely, and forever.

Verses 15-18: The Burnt Offering

Following the sin offering one of the two rams was taken and again Aaron and his sons placed their hands upon the head of the offering. It has to be noted that the word used to describe the actions of Aaron and his son, "put" (5564), which is also used to describe the similar act carried out with the bullock of the sin offering, means "to lean on". They pressed all their weight down on the head of the animal signifying that this was not merely a passing casual touch, but a complete and unconditional identification with the sacrifice. It has been noted that with the bullock the identification was with the one who would die as a substitute in place of the worshipper; that they deserved to be treated as the bullock was about to be treated. In the case of the ram for the burnt offering it is identification with the excellence of the one about to die. It is not possible for the one who offers the sacrifice to be in a condition where everything in his life is a delight to God, but the sacrifice is taking his place.

The difference in the two offerings is clearly stated by Paul when writing to the Corinthians: "For he hath made him to be sin for us, who knew no sin; that we might be made the righteousness of God in him (2 Cor 5.21). The sin offering aspect of the death of the Lord Jesus Christ is seen in that "he hath made him to be sin". He did not, and could not, sin, but at the Cross He was dealt with as a sinner should be, so that the sinner might be dealt with as a completely righteous person should be. In the sin offering all that is offensive to God has been removed, but that is not sufficient in itself, for what is delightful and a joy to God has to be brought in, and that is the burnt offering. As the ram was cut into its pieces and laid on the Altar, all its perfections were laid bare so that they could be enjoyed in heaven, and by the priests. The lesson for today is that the excellence of the beauty of the Lord Jesus is a sweet savour to God, a beauty that is not only outward, but also inward; there was no difference between the two.

Verses 19-28: The Ram of Consecration

At this stage the second ram was taken to be offered as a peace offering. Rams were offered as peace offerings by the people at the dedication of the priests (Lev 9.4-18), by the princes as part of their peace offerings at the time of the dedication of the Altar (Num 7), and by the Nazarite who had completed his vow (Num 6.14-17). The offering of this ram, however, was carried out in a unique manner.

It is called "the ram of consecration" (v.22). The word "consecration" (4394) has the meaning of being full. TWOT at 1195 comments: "To fill one's hand (with sacrifices) is to consecrate one's service". To place the blood on the ear, the thumb, and the great toe of each of the priests, and to have them eat of the ram are symbolic of their being entirely consecrated to the service of the Lord.

Once again, for the third time, Aaron and his sons placed their hands, and by so doing leaned their weight, upon a sacrifice. On this occasion it was not to show their identification with one who will die for their sins, nor to show identification with the perfections of one who will die in their place; it was to show their identification with the total consecration of the sacrifice about to die. This ram signified the total devoted consecration of the Lord Jesus, He who "humbled himself, becoming obedient even unto death, and that the death of the cross" (Phil 2.8, JND). How beautifully

Luke brings to the attention of his readers the devoted consecration of the Perfect Man. As a lad of twelve years of age He stated to Joseph and his mother, "Wist ye not that I *must* be about my Father's business" (Lk 2.49). Even at such a young age He was conscious of his devotion to His "Father's business", a devotion that never wavered in the years ahead. After a time of intense activity, when many were healed, the Lord Jesus departed into a desert place and the people followed Him. Doubtless they were trying to hinder Him and keep Him with them, but he stressed that He "*must* preach the kingdom of God to other cities also: for therefore am I sent" (Lk 4.43). When the opposition of the Jews was reaching new heights the Pharisees came to Him and declared, "Get thee out, and depart hence: for Herod will kill thee" (Lk 13.31). The reply of the Lord Jesus showed that there was no possibility of Him abandoning His work: "I *must* walk today, and tomorrow, and the day following: for it cannot be that a prophet perish out of Jerusalem" (v.33). He declared His determination to be true to his service, to be fully occupied in the great work which was His, and to finish the course. His consecration shone through, no matter what were the surrounding circumstances. As He entered and passed through Jericho, Zacchaeus was summoned from the tree where he had gained a vantage point to see the passing Saviour. "To day I *must* abide at thy house" (Lk 19.5), He declared to Zacchaeus showing the same determined, devoted consecration to service when only one individual was involved. Other references by Luke to His consecration, expressed in what He ought to do, are found in Luke 9.22; 17.25; 24.26,44,46.

The blood placed on Aaron and his sons (v.20)
The slaying of the ram was followed by its blood being put on the tip of the right ear, the thumb of the right hand, and the great toe of the right foot of Aaron and his sons. In this manner, by having the blood applied to these three extremities of the body, the priests were declared to be consecrated to the service of their Lord. Their lives would be totally filled with this service, with no time left for that which was less worthy. The consecration that marked the ram, going all the way to death, had now to mark their service. The ear indicates that all the faculties of the head will be devoted to Him, the thumb that all actions performed will be devoted to Him, and the toe that all footsteps taken will be devoted to Him. Here is total consecration, total separation to His service alone. This is the devotion shown by Paul when he writes, "This one thing I do, forgetting those things which are behind, and reaching forth unto those things which are before, I press towards the mark for the prize of the high calling of God in Christ Jesus" (Phil 3.13-14). For him the one consuming passion of life was the Lord Jesus Christ and all else fell away in his pursuit of his goal; it was total consecration. So it was also with the five men who stood before Moses to have the blood of the ram of consecration placed upon them. For the service of God He was consecrating them, but they would have the

responsibility of living up to the great dignity and privileges of the service upon which they were now embarking. The blood was then sprinkled upon the Brazen Altar, showing that the blood that had consecrated them was that which was offered to God.

The blood and anointing oil sprinkled upon Aaron and his sons (v.21)

At this point the blood was taken from the Altar and, together with anointing oil, it was sprinkled upon Aaron and his sons. Emphasis is placed on the fact that it was also sprinkled upon their garments, those garments for glory and beauty about which so much detail had been given. Looking at them one would see that these glorious garments were blood stained where the sprinkled blood had marked them. One would wonder why such garments of beauty should be so "marred".

The act of this dual sprinkling of blood and anointing oil not only conveys privilege upon the priests, but also brings an obligation. The value of the work of the shed blood of Calvary is applied and the anointing oil speaks of the work of the Holy Spirit in doing this. The blood on their persons and garments points forward to the truth enunciated by Paul when he writes that believers are "dead with Christ" (Rom 6.8). Believers have a responsibility to live in a manner consistent with this standing.

The offering placed in the hands of Aaron and his sons (vv.22-24)

The fat, the rump, the right shoulder, and the inwards of the ram were then taken and, together with a loaf of bread, a cake of oiled bread, and a wafer from the basket of unleavened bread (v.3), were placed in the hands of Aaron and his sons who waved them for a wave offering before the Lord. The significance of the hands being filled cannot fail to be noticed. There was room for nothing else in these hands but that which speaks of the Lord Jesus Christ. It was total occupation with Him, His Person, and His work. Nothing less worthy is suitable. It is also significant that the right shoulder was brought, emphasising the strength of the sacrifice, a strength with which the priest must be occupied, a strength which he must have if he would do God's pleasure and make full use of his priestly office.

But there is further significance in the filled hands of the priests. It indicates that these men were being consecrated to offer sacrifices. Should there be any complaints in future that they had taken too much upon themselves there was displayed the fact that the Lord through Moses conferred the dignity upon them, and priestly hands had handled that which was placed upon the Altar.

This offering was then waved before the Lord to display to heaven the beauty and value of the sacrifice. All that the priests will do will be carried out in view of that sacrifice. When believers today exercise their priestly office it is accepted because of what they are in Christ. As they are in the Sanctuary so they are seen in view of the great sacrifice made on their behalf.

The significance of the wave offering (v.24)

As this is the first mention in Scripture of an offering being waved before the Lord, it is a suitable point at which to consider the significance of waving (5103) an offering in this way. The offering was taken and waved before the Lord. The expression "wave offering" is used at times in a general sense. It is used in the original Hebrew of the tribe of Levi (Num 8.11), of the offering of gold for the Tabernacle (Ex 35.22), and of the brass also (Ex 38.29). It is clear that the Levites, the gold, and the brass could not be literally waved before the Lord, and it is therefore used figuratively in these instances.

There were, however, instances where the offering was actually waved before the Lord.

1. The breast of the peace offering was waved before the Lord (Lev 7.30). The breast was not burned on the Altar but was for the use of Aaron and his sons. It is significant that the wave breast of the peace offering was waved before the Lord after Nadab and Abihu had died when they offered "strange fire" to the Lord (Lev 10.14-15). In this way there was emphasised to the priests that, despite the judgment of God which had fallen upon the two who were rebellious, the value of the peace offering had not been destroyed by their folly; it was still effective, and peace and fellowship with God could still be enjoyed. The significance of the waving of the breast of the sacrifice was that this was the portion for the priests, and therefore the portion that would not be consumed upon the Altar. The waving was the symbolic presentation to the Lord of that of which the priests would eat. All of the sacrifice was, therefore, offered.

2. When the land had been entered, a sheaf of the firstfruits of the harvest had to be waved before the Lord (Lev 23.11). The significance of this act was that the sheaf would not be burned on the Altar and it was by this means symbolically offered.

3. At Pentecost, or the Feast of Weeks, two loaves which had been baked with leaven were waved before the Lord (Lev 23.15-21). These were offered with seven lambs, one young bullock, and two rams for a burnt offering along with their meat and drink offerings. Again, however, the two wave loaves were not placed on the Altar but were to be "holy to the Lord for the priest" (v.20). The same principle is seen in that what is not placed on the Altar is symbolically presented to the Lord by waving it.

4. When the Nazarite completed his vow he brought to the door of the Tabernacle his sacrifices which included a ram for a peace offering, the breast and shoulder of which was waved before the Lord, the portion which was "holy for the priest" (Num 6.13-21).

The principle of waving, therefore, in the offerings above is that the portion that was not placed on the Altar was waved as it was symbolically offered to the Lord. Although the offerings at 1, 3 and 4 above were partaken of by the priests, they were still a sacrifice and had to be offered to Him.

Priestly exercise was, therefore, maintained by that which was fit to be offered to the Lord and had been offered to Him.

There were, however, other occasions when what was waved before the Lord was also burned on the Altar, and each of these instances has a precious lesson to teach.

1. At the ceremony of the cleansing of the leper (Lev 14.1-32) the priest took one he lamb with a log of oil and waved them before the Lord (vv.12,24). This is the only occasion when a trespass offering was waved in this manner. After the waving, the trespass offering was placed upon the Altar. Thus the offering was not only presented symbolically by waving, but also in reality upon the Altar. There was a double presentation of it to the Lord signifying the double joy which He received at this time, a joy based on the fact that a leper had been cleansed. There is always joy when a sinner is cleansed and the leper is a picture of this taking place. Let it be emphasised that there is no joy in heaven over sin, but there is over a sinner who is cleansed.

2. When a wife was brought to the priest because her husband suspected that she had been unfaithful to him a jealousy offering was waved before the priest. This consisted of the tenth part of an ephah of barley meal. It was the only offering in which there was barley meal, and no oil was poured on it or frankincense put on it (Num 5.11-31). Following the waving of the offering it was placed upon the Altar. The significance of this double presentation is that the test to which the woman was put was one of such utmost importance that the offering was presented in this twofold manner to the Lord so that, as there was to be a public test of her fidelity, there had to be a very public display of the offering.

The offering over the burnt offering (v.25)

That which had been placed in the hands of Aaron and his sons was now put on the Brazen Altar to be burned "over the burnt offering" (JND). The burnt offering had already been offered (v.13), and this offering for the consecration of the priests was taken from their hands and was burned upon it. The burnt offering is the Lord Jesus Christ presented to God for His pleasure and delight, but now there was this added offering which was placed upon that which had given God joy, and it had come from consecrated hands. Is there not something here of the added joy to God when the appreciation of the Lord Jesus comes from such consecrated hands? Is it not that God delights in receiving from His people that which they have appreciated of the Lord, an appreciation which is the result of their consecration to Him? This is what is before the reader in these precious verses. As Moses received the sacrifices from their hands and placed them on the Altar it but added to the delight of heaven that those who were devoted to Him had presented these offerings; it was a sweet savour unto the Lord.

A further wave offering (vv.26-28)

Now Moses took the breast of the ram and waved it before the Lord as a wave offering. At the consecration of the priests this was to be Moses' part of the sacrifice. If the right shoulder speaks of the strength of the sacrifice, the breast speaks of the affections, and whenever a peace offering was brought to the Lord the breast and the shoulder were to be given to the priests after having been waved before the Lord (Lev 7.28-34). By this means were signified the priestly appreciation of the affection of the Lord towards His people and their enjoyment of the peace which He had brought about.

The shoulder of the sacrifice was to be heaved before the Lord, a symbol of placing it upon the Altar but emphasising the priestly energy and vigour that was necessary to "heave" it up and onto the Brazen Altar. When priests were functioning, this energy would come through feeding on the offerings, and their ability to "heave" the sacrifice would be directly linked to their diet. The spiritual energy required to engage in worship today is directly linked to how much the worshipper has been feeding on the Lord Jesus Christ; the more of Him, the more energy to "heave" the sacrifice.

Verses 29-30: The Garments of the High Priest

These two verses bring the reader back again to a subject which has been dealt with in detail in the previous chapter. It is not, however, a mere repetition of what has already been addressed. The high priestly garments were to be passed on to the son of Aaron appointed as High Priest and to be worn by him when he was anointed and consecrated into that sacred office. These verses cannot mean that the new High Priest was only to wear the garments for an initial period of seven days when he carried out the functions of his office. These garments would be worn by the High Priest whenever he served, with the exception of the Day of Atonement when he entered the Holiest of All wearing linen garments.

The significance is that the period mentioned, seven days, is that during which the new High Priest at his consecration was "not to go out of the door of the tabernacle" until the days of his consecration were ended (29.35; Lev 8.33). For those seven days he was seen to be fully occupied with the things of the Lord, serving in the Tabernacle with nothing else to occupy his attention, all as part of his consecration into the office.

Immediately before the death of Aaron, his garments were stripped from him and put on Eleazar, his son (Num 20.25-29). It was a symbolic act, indicating that there was a new High Priest, but that the character and dignity of the office was not diminished as a result. The glory and beauty that had marked the High Priesthood of Aaron was also to mark that of Eleazar. During the seven day period the people would be assured that, despite the death of Aaron, the high priestly service continued uninterrupted. Today there is no such passing over to another the position of High Priest. He, who in glory fills that office, is "a priest for ever" (Heb 7.17,21), who "continueth ever" (Heb 7.24), and who "ever liveth to make intercession" (Heb 7.25). He will never be stripped of His garments to pass them on to another. There need to be no succession fears as far as He is concerned, for no one can take His place; He is "consecrated for evermore" (Heb 7.28).

Verses 31-35: Eating the Ram

Now the wave breast and the heave shoulder of the ram were taken by Moses who was told to "seethe the flesh in the holy place". The word "seethe" (1310) means "to boil", and the "holy place" was at the door of the Tabernacle, doubtless just outside the door (Lev 8.31). The act of seething, as far as the priests were concerned, signified the preparation which had to be made before the value of the sacrifice could be practically appropriated by them. Until it was carried out they could not partake of the ram. Following this, Aaron and his sons partook of the flesh of the ram, together with the unleavened bread that had been brought in a basket (vv.2-3). This was to be done for seven days (see also Lev 8.31-33), and over that period the offerings were brought daily and the priests ate of the ram daily; any surplus that was left over until the next day had to be burned with fire. No "stranger" was to be allowed to partake of this priestly food. A "stranger" is, at times, someone who is not of Israel, but here it refers to the priestly nature of what took place, and that any who were not of the family of Aaron could not partake.

The seething of the ram was necessary, just as today it is necessary for Christians to "seethe" the sacrifice, that is, to meditate on it, to keep it before the mind. This is all part of practical consecration. The question which must be asked is, "Why was it necessary for the priests to do this, and why over a period of seven days?". These offerings had been placed in the hands of Aaron and his sons (vv.22-24) and the relevant parts laid upon the Altar, so why eat them? The answer is that it is one thing to have the hands filled, but quite another matter to partake. To have the hands filled indicates total occupation with that which is in the hands, but to partake of the offering is to obtain energy from it and, indeed, to make it part of the priest. Assimilating it by eating it signified that the consecration which marked the ram had now become part of the priest and his life. It was inseparable from him. Consecration to His service must be daily seen, not only with the filled hands denoting full occupation, but also with the eating, denoting that this was no mere outward show, but was part of the consecrated servant of the Lord. This is the result of daily occupation with, and meditation upon, Him who has been offered up. The period of seven days signified a full course of time; consecration is for life!

The Children of Israel would see that during this period of seven days the priest did not leave the court of the Tabernacle (Lev 8.33), and they would have confidence that those who would handle their offerings were men of the Sanctuary, living close to it, and eating of that which had been

offered to God. What gave Him pleasure was what they fed on; a diet that
included unleavened bread, that which was free from leaven, free from
the contamination of sin.

In this way Aaron and his sons were consecrated (4390), their hands
were filled and sanctified (6942), and they were declared to be clean and
fit to serve in the Sanctuary. Moses had been commanded to do "all the
things" which the Lord had commanded him. There was to be total
obedience to His word, with no man-made variations to the divine order
of consecration.

Verses 36-37: The Offering of a Bullock for a Sin Offering

Priests work at the Altar, and without an Altar there can be no priestly
activity. Over the seven days when the priests were in the court of the
Tabernacle and eating of the priestly food, daily offerings of a bullock were
to be made as a "sin offering for atonement". In this way the Altar was to
be cleansed and "an atonement" made for it. The priests had to be fit to
serve at the Altar and the Altar had to be fit for the service of the priests.

It should be observed that "whatsoever toucheth the altar shall be holy".
This means, first, that any thing that was laid on the Altar was fully for God.
That which had been given to God could not be placed on the Altar and
then parts of it, or even the whole of it, removed for the use of the priests
or the offerer. Once placed on the Altar it could not be withdrawn. The
Altar was "most holy", meaning that it was fully given over to the service of
the Lord and would be used for no other purpose. In like manner the
offerings placed on it were for Him alone and could not be taken off to be
used for any other purpose.

But it has also been suggested that the "whatsoever" can bear the
meaning of either "whatsoever", or "whomsoever". The latter indicates
that the priest who handled the offerings and placed them upon the Altar
was also "holy". He, too, was fully given over to the service of the Lord and
could not withdraw from this for any other purpose, no matter how
honourable that purpose might have been. The lesson is simple to grasp.
That which is dedicated to His service must not be taken back again for
use in any other way. This must be seen when the words of Romans 12.1
are read: "I beseech you therefore, brethren, by the mercies of God, that
ye present your bodies a living sacrifice, holy, acceptable unto God, which
is your reasonable service".   Having been presented and placed on the
altar as a sacrifice they cannot be withdrawn. The Altar is "most holy" and
what is placed on it is likewise "holy", so holy that everything and everyone
who touches it is set apart for His service alone. The Lord claims completely
what is on the Altar.

Verses 38-42a: The Daily Burnt Offering

Having given instruction as to how the Brazen Altar was to be sanctified
and made fit for offerings to be placed upon it, the Lord now brings before

them the offering that must be placed on the Altar daily. Two lambs were to be offered each day, one in the morning and one in the evening. Both of these were to be, like the Passover lambs (12.5), "of the first year", at the very peak of their health and fitness, prime specimens of the flock. With the lambs was to be offered a meal offering consisting of "a tenth deal of flour mingled with the fourth part of an hin of beaten oil". On top of this was to be poured a drink offering consisting of a "fourth part of an hin of wine". Morning and evening this was to be carried out continually.

The Altar fire, therefore, was never to go out; the Altar was never to become cold; there never was to be a day when there was no lamb upon it; there never was to be a night when their hours of sleep were marked by a sleeping Altar. How telling all this is to the enquiring soul! The Lord desires to receive the fragrance of worship from His people continually. Any day without this was a day of disobedience; worship in the morning was to thank Him for the blessings of salvation, to bring again to heaven the appreciation of redeemed souls for all that they had been brought into. Worship in the evening was for the same purpose, equally important because He is a God who does not slumber nor sleep (Ps 121.4).

The practical lesson cannot be missed. The lives of His people today must be marked by worship, the daily rendering to Him of their best as thanksgiving is made for His goodness and grace in delivering them and preserving them. Morning and evening, week after week, month after month, year after year the Altar fires flamed into the sky reminding the priests and the people of their deliverance and of their obligation to the One who had set them free from the house of bondage (Lev 6.13).

The burnt offering with the attendant meal offering denotes the Lamb of God slain at Calvary; the meal offering signifies the pure, perfect life of the One who went to the Cross. It was a daily reminder to Israel of the fact that their acceptance by God was based on the excellence and worth of the sacrifice, that in which the Lord saw the character of the offering of the Lord Jesus Christ. It was on this ground, and on this ground alone, that the Lord met with and dwelt amongst His people.

The obligation placed upon the people was to be completely consecrated to His service. Just as the burnt offering was totally consumed, so the Israelite was to be totally consecrated. It is significant that the encouragement to their consecration was that which spoke of the consecration of the Lamb, He who was obedient "even unto death" (Phil 2.8, JND). There is nothing more likely to encourage such devotion as occupation with the Devoted One. Those who follow the One who early in the morning took time to engage in prayer, and who in the evening turned again to be alone with His Father, would do well to be engaged in the same manner. The morning and evening sacrifice teach that these are the times when it is His delight to have His people turn to Him for thanksgiving and prayer for what lies ahead.

But just as the burnt offering would be flayed into its parts for its beauty to be displayed, so it is profitable at those times of prayer to turn the mind to some of the beautiful features of the Lord Jesus and to thank God for them. There is no higher exercise in worship than that of speaking to God about His Son, and such occupation with Him will produce its effect. The skin of the burnt offering, that part of the offering which was seen before it was slain for the Altar, was given to the priest. He carried away with him that outward part of the sacrifice (Lev 7.8). So, in like manner, those who are occupied with the Lord Jesus Christ in worship, presenting Him and all His beauty to God, will come away with something of His features on them. It is impossible for it to be otherwise; that is why those who are Christ-like in their behaviour are but revealing that they are no strangers to the Sanctuary, and that time spent in occupation with Him in the presence of God is, for them, well-trodden ground.

The importance of "morning and evening"

But not only does the Lord have an interest in the mornings and evenings of His people; He is not alone in His desire to be with them at that time. The Adversary also seeks to draw near. It was at these times that Goliath of Gath drew near to the armies of Israel: "And the Philistine drew near *morning and evening*, and presented himself forty days" (1 Sam 17.16). The word "morning" in this verse (7925) indicates that it was early in the morning. It is the desire of the Devil to command the time of the worshipper from the very beginning of the day, to dominate those precious moments that should be given to Him. In the evening also he draws near, on both occasions, not to give the believer the victory, but to ensure that the mornings and the evenings are marked by defeat. Thus for forty days the armies of Israel were defeated morning and evening, and instead of daily worship there was daily defeat. Let all believers beware; the enemy will draw near morning and evening, and should he succeed in robbing God's people of their precious times with the Lord he has gained the victory; the Christian has been defeated.

Hezekiah well understood the value of these offerings: "He appointed also the king's portion of his substance for the burnt offerings, to wit, for the morning and evening burnt offerings, and the burnt offerings for the sabbaths, and for the new moons, and for the set feasts, as it is written in the law of the Lord" (2 Chr 31.3). He set a good example to the people in that he appointed the king's portion so that the daily sacrifices could be carried out. Here was a man who displayed spiritual leadership.

The returning exiles understood the importance of these sacrifices for the first offerings that were placed on the rebuilt altar were the morning and evening sacrifices (Ezra 3.3). The life of this returning remnant could not be blessed if the altar fires were not alight. At that time "fear was upon them because of the people of those countries" and the answer was not to arm themselves for battle, but to give the Lord His place in their midst.

The ashes of the burnt offering

How the ashes of the burnt offering were to be dealt with is found in Leviticus 6.9-13. A priest was to be seen attending to this every morning. In the midst of the busy activity of the Camp, as the manna was being gathered and as the people were preparing for the activities of the day, he could be observed carrying his burden through the Camp. Some say the Camp was three miles (4.8km) across, some say that it was even seven (11.2km) or more; no matter what the distance it was a long road that lay ahead of him, his destination being outside the Camp, to be followed by the long journey when he retraced his steps.

Although dressed in the normal garments of the day, those who were discerning knew that this man was of the line of Aaron; this solitary figure, carrying that which was committed to his charge, was a priest coming from the Sanctuary. The Tabernacle, situated in the middle of the Camp was the starting point of the journey, just as it would be his ultimate destination.

That morning, as with every morning, the priests gathered at the great Brazen Altar which stood in the court of the Tabernacle. Lying amidst the flames of the Altar were the remains of yesterday's burnt offerings. To the natural eye this was but the detritus of the previous day's activities, the debris that now had to be removed and consigned to the rubbish heap. But priestly minds knew better; the word of God instructed a more excellent way. One of the priests was charged with this sacred duty, a solemn responsibility which had to be carried out. Clothed in priestly garments, he removed the ashes from the Altar, laid aside his priestly garb, clothed himself with other apparel, took up the ashes, and commenced the long journey to a clean place "without the camp". There the ashes were reverently laid and there they remained.

Why such care with ashes? Only ashes! Nothing of worth; the fire had destroyed anything useful to man, the fierce heat of the Altar consuming completely any value to be found in the offering; and now, only ashes. But these were ashes valued in heaven! They were the remains of yesterday's sacrifice. They were all that was to be seen on earth of that which only the day before had caused fragrance to ascend to heaven, that which had brought delight to the heart of God, that which had been an expression of the love, devotion, and submission of those whom He had redeemed out of the house of bondage. Yes, only ashes, but what ashes! Long after the sacrifice which was made to provide the burnt offering was forgotten, long after the offerer had no remembrance of the day when the offering was made, years after the Altar fires had burned, consuming what he had brought, generations later the eye of God was still on the ashes, the heart of God was still enjoying what had ascended to Him. That is why they were carefully taken to the clean, the undefiled place.

Let His servants take heart from this morning scene, calling on us to view sacrifice, not as the world sees it and not as the waste of which Judas spoke so disparagingly. What was sacrificed in the past, perhaps long forgotten, remembrance of which can no longer be brought to mind - the act of kindness, the time spent, the work carried out, the material possessions sacrificed - at the time costly indeed, but now long past, was not waste.

The beauty of this must not be lost. God remembers, and what was done all these years ago is not forgotten. The sweet savour, the joy, the delight and the pleasure felt in heaven is appreciated by Him today as much as it was when the act was carried out, when the sacrifice was made. The God who no more remembers our sins (Heb 10.17) is the God who never forgets our sacrifices.

Christians at times can feel discouraged. The Adversary is not slow to point out the "futility" of that in which we are engaged; swift to remind us of the apparent lack of results, the "obvious" lack of success, the waste of it all, and the better use to which our energies and possessions could be put. But be not deceived, what is done for Him is never wasted, what is given to Him is never unappreciated, and what is devoted to Him, He never forgets. Yesterday's sacrifices may today be but ashes, but in heaven they are precious and in heaven they still give delight.

But that is not the sole significance of these ashes. God ensured that the precious holy body of the Lord Jesus was taken down from the Cross by those who loved Him and placed in a "clean place", a new tomb, a fit resting place for Him. Two men, Joseph of Arimathaea and Nicodemus, took His body and wrapped it in one hundred pounds weight of myrrh and aloes,[†] and, having wound it in linen clothes, placed it in the garden sepulchre. The record of their actions has the mark of devoted care about it. There was no undue rush, nothing done secretly, for Joseph had approached Pilate to have permission to take His body. There was nothing cheap about the mixture of myrrh and aloes, nor was it used stintingly. There was care in the winding of the linen clothes and gentleness about the words, "There laid they Jesus" (Jn 19.42). He would be in that tomb until the morning of the first day of the week when He rose from the dead.

Verses 42b-46: The Promise of His Presence

These closing verses confirm three things to Israel. First, it was at the Tabernacle that the Lord would meet with them and through Moses He would speak to them. How different this was from anything they had known in Egypt, or anything that the other pagan nations had experienced. When these gods "spoke", the "god" replaced the personality of the one used to declare the message. The pagan god "possessed" him and used his faculties.

Moses and the other prophets who declared verbally and wrote the Word of God, did not lose their personalities, nor were they used in robotic fashion. Their faculties were not suspended; they did not lose control of themselves but acted in a calm rational manner and were aware of what they were saying.

Second, Israel (it is suggested that "the tabernacle" in v.43 refers to the nation) would be sanctified, as would be the Tabernacle, and the Altar, and Aaron and the priests. All would be made fit for the presence of the Lord, provided there was obedience to His word, for this promise, placed where it is, is conditional on all the instructions being faithfully carried out.

Third, Jehovah would dwell among them and be their God. In this way they would know that He was the Lord their God who had brought them out of the land of Egypt. The great matter of their deliverance from the house of bondage was never to be forgotten, and showed that the purpose of that mighty act was to enable Him to dwell among them. The Lord acted in Egypt that "the Egyptians shall know that I am the Lord, when I have gotten me honour upon Pharaoh, upon his chariots, and upon his horsemen" (14.18). But for Israel there was something far more precious than the knowledge that He was Lord. That they had learned in the past. When the manna was given the Lord declared, "At even, then ye shall know that the Lord hath brought you out from the land of Egypt" (16.6), and that lesson was always to be with them, with the additional emphasis on the fact that He was the Lord *their* God. Twice over in the closing verse this is stated, confirming the promise made many generations before: "And I will give unto thee, and to thy seed after thee, the land wherein thou art a stranger, all the land of Canaan, for an everlasting possession; and I will be their God" (Gen 17.8). Thus, that which marked Israel out as being different from all other nations - the Lord dwelling in the midst of them, with the Tabernacle and the cloud that marked His presence - was unique.

Today the presence of God is still promised to His people. The godly order of the gathered saints, and the teaching that falls on his ears, should convict the observer so much that he declares, "God is in you of a truth" (1 Cor 14.25). This is what should make the assembly different from all other gatherings; it is still His desire to dwell with His people and it is still the responsibility of His people to ensure that their obedience to His Word brings about conditions where He is pleased to be in their midst.

Notes

42a The modern equivalent is reckoned to be about 75lbs/34 kilos.

EXODUS 30

Further Tabernacle Requirements

Verses 1-10: The Altar of Incense[†]
The closing verses of the previous chapter may lead the reader to consider that the description of the Tabernacle is now complete with the declaration that it was the place where the Lord would dwell among them. Further detail, however, is still required, and this chapter gives instruction regarding the Altar of Incense, the Laver, the anointing oil, and the sweet spices. This raises the question, "Why were these items left until after the consecration of the priests had been dealt with?". The significant fact is that they do come after Moses sets outs the order for priestly consecration.

All that had been previously dealt with described what was necessary for man to approach God. True it is that this is given from the Holiest of All outwards towards the worshipper, but with the consecration of the priests all is now in place for the worshipper to approach. But how has this to be maintained? The priest understands that he will place the offerings of the worshipper upon the Brazen Altar, he knows that there is a Table of Shewbread in the Holy Place signifying the One who is the food of priests and worshippers. But when the Golden Altar and the Laver are dealt with it is the maintenance of the Tabernacle which is in view. "We see in type the divine system in Exodus 25-29. The next thing is to see what characterises it and how it is sustained, and Exodus 30 gives us this" (Coates). It is, therefore, placed where it is because, after dealing with the priests, there is unfolded the vital ministry which would be theirs in the Holy Place.

The description of the Altar of Incense
The Altar of Incense measured 1 cubit square and was 2 cubits high. Although not a large piece of furniture, it stood higher than the grate of the Brazen Altar and half a cubit higher than the Table of Shewbread. Note also that it was also half a cubit higher than the Ark and the Mercy Seat. As there are no dimensions given for the Lampstand, which also stood in the Holy Place, it is not possible to state with confidence its height for the purpose of comparison. It cannot fail to be noticed, however, that while this Altar has the smallest top surface area of any of the Tabernacle furniture, its surface is higher than any other (if we regard the grate of the Brazen Altar as its "surface").

The materials used are now familiar to the reader: shittim wood overlaid with gold. Horns were placed on it, as on the Brazen Altar, and under a crown that was placed around the surface were fitted two rings into which, when travelling, were placed staves. All of this was made of shittim wood overlaid with gold.

The Altar was placed in the Holy Place "before the vail that is by the ark of the testimony, before the mercy seat that is over the testimony, where I will meet with thee" (v.6). It was placed before the vail and opposite the Mercy Seat, that is, it stood in the Holy Place, between the Lampstand, which was on the south, and the Table of Shewbread, which was on the north. It is not without significance, however, that its positioning is related to the Mercy Seat and not to these other items in the Holy Place.

Carrying the Altar of Incense

It is strange to note that only two rings were fitted to the Altar for it to be carried. If there had been four rings, one in each corner it would have been a seemingly straightforward arrangement, but two rings seem to be somewhat irregular and even out of place. Whatever the Lord decrees must have a purpose and there is design in the use of two rings. The Altar was only 1 cubit square and therefore if there had been four rings it would have been positioned "square on" to those who carried it. That would have resulted in a distance of 1 cubit between each of the staves and it would then have been possible for two men to carry it with the ends of the two staves resting on their shoulders. The suggestion of Raven is interesting in this respect. "As there were only two rings on the altar, on diagonally opposite corners, then it must mean that the altar had to be carried diagonal-wise between the two poles. This would mean that the altar would no longer fit comfortably on the shoulders of two men, for the poles would now be 25 inches [63.5 cm] apart, the obvious inference being that although the altar was not heavy in man's eyes, yet God required four men to carry it because although small it was very weighty before God." When the cloud moved and Israel followed, the Golden Altar was covered with a cloth of blue and over that a covering of badgers' skins.

Sweet incense for the Altar

This Altar was remarkable in that no blood sacrifice was ever to be offered on it. Even when blood was brought into the Holy Place it was not placed on this Altar, except once a year on the Day of Atonement. Aaron entered the Holy Pace every morning and evening with a two-fold purpose; he tended the Lampstand to ensure that the light did not go out, and he burned incense upon the Golden Altar. Other priests were also allowed the privilege of placing the incense on the Altar as Deuteronomy 33.10 reveals: "*they* shall put incense before thee" (before thy nostrils, JND). Clearly an Altar overlaid with gold was not constructed to bear the heat of the sacrificial fire, nor was the Holy Place, an enclosed space, suitable for such flames.

Coals from the Brazen Altar were, nevertheless, used. They were placed in a censer into which was put the incense, the coals releasing its fragrance. It was thus the coals, the flames of which had engulfed the sacrifice, which were used to bring out the sweet fragrance that filled the Holy Place. It was this incense, with a fragrance released by the flame, which was put on the Altar.

In addition to the daily burning of the incense, it was also taken into the Holiest of All on the Day of Atonement. "And he shall take a censer full of burning coals of fire from off the altar before the Lord, and his hands full of sweet incense beaten small, and bring it within the vail: And he shall put the incense upon the fire before the Lord, that the cloud of the incense may cover the mercy seat that is upon the testimony, that he die not" (Lev 16.12-13).

The composition of the incense is given in vv.34-38, but the clear instruction in v.9 is that no "strange incense" was to be offered thereon, as well as the injunction that no burnt sacrifices, meat offerings, or drink offerings were to be placed on this Altar. There must be no deviation from the clear recipe for the spices; yet another example of the attention to detail which is found in all the requirements of the Lord. Man is left to none of his own devices; it must all be His plan and His design.

It should be noted that the instruction for burning the incense is very precise. The first half of v.8 is almost a repetition of v.7; a human hand would have combined the two with one short sentence by adding "and evening" to the words "burn thereon sweet incense every morning" in v.7. But greater accuracy is demanded, and the morning and the evening duties are separately described.

The significance of the Altar of Incense

Morning and evening the sweet incense from the Golden Altar ascended to heaven, a fragrance that constantly permeated the atmosphere of the Holy Place. It would not be possible to enter without being aware of it, and its fragrance would cling to the garments of those who entered. What lessons can be learned from it?

First, it was not possible to hide the fact that a priest had been in the Sanctuary. There was about him a fragrance that could be gained nowhere else. It could not be achieved by using other ingredients to form a false batch of "sweet spices"; the counterfeit would be noticed. The pure sweet spices could not be applied elsewhere because such a use was prohibited (v.37). Only in the Sanctuary could the atmosphere of the Sanctuary be enjoyed. But if the mark of the Sanctuary was on those who entered, the absence of it revealed that the Sanctuary had not been entered. Today there are saints and the mark of the Sanctuary is on them. By their demeanour and deportment, their conversation and interests, it is possible to enjoy the spiritual fragrance that comes from them. The Sanctuary atmosphere has permeated their lives, and is added to daily as they enter again and again. These saints must be valued for the worship that they render and for the prayers they present on behalf of others. The desire of all should be that those with whom they come into contact do not sense the lack of the Sanctuary character, but rather depart carrying with them some of that fragrance which has been passed on by one who has been alone with God.

In later years, when the priests ministered in the Temple, the choice of the priest to be charged with the responsibility of burning the incense was made by lot, and those who carried out this duty were only allowed to do so once. This was a man-made device, but nevertheless an indication of the importance of the day in the life of Zacharias when he entered to "burn incense in the temple of the Lord" (Lk 1.9).

Second, the priest who approached the Golden Altar was at the point in the Holy Place nearest to the Ark in the Holiest of All. Every day, when the incense was being placed on the Golden Altar, the priests were as close to God as it was possible for them to be.

Third, what took place at this Altar represented the prayers of the saints (Rev 8.3). Although it is a future day to which reference is made, the allusion to the "golden altar which was before the throne" indicates that this is not limited to that time. John, the writer of Revelation, states: "And another angel came and stood at the altar, having a golden censer; and there was given unto him much incense, that he should offer it with the prayers of all saints upon the golden altar which was before the throne. And the smoke of the incense, which came with the prayers of the saints, ascended up before God out of the angel's hand" (Rev 8.3-4). It was not the angel who added fragrance to the prayers; it was the incense that did so.

To all the prayers and intercessions of the saints the Lord Jesus adds His incense, speaking of the sweetness of His Person and work, and this makes them suitable for presentation to God. Without that, the prayers offered up would be without value; only He can make them acceptable in heaven. The Holy Place was continually filled with this incense signifying the continual enjoyment by God of the prayers of His saints, which are only acceptable to Him because they are presented to Him through the Lord Jesus Christ.

An understanding of this is an incentive to an active prayer life. Such is the value in heaven of the prayers of the saints that the Lord Jesus, as the Great High Priest, is constantly occupied with them. If He regards them as being worthy of such attention, so ought the saints who offer them. What fragrance must have arisen from the prayers of Paul and his fellow-workers; from the short prayer of Nehemiah as he stood in the presence of the king (Neh 2.4); from the somewhat longer prayer of Daniel as he understood the significance of the writings of Jeremiah (Dan 9.1-19); from the prayers of David with which the Psalms are interlaced; all these were heard because of that fragrance which He added to them as they were offered up.

> Much incense is ascending
> Before the eternal throne;
> God graciously is bending
> To hear each feeble groan.
> To all our prayers and praises
> Christ adds His sweet perfume,

And love the censer raises
Their odours to consume.
                                                   (M. Peters)

Blood on the horns of the Altar of Incense

On the Day of Atonement the High Priest went out from the Holiest of All. "And he shall go out unto the altar that is before the Lord, and make an atonement for it; and shall take of the blood of the bullock, and of the blood of the goat, and put it upon the horns of the altar round about. And he shall sprinkle of the blood upon it with his finger seven times, and cleanse it, and hallow it from the uncleanness of the children of Israel" (Lev 16.18-19). The bullock was the sin offering for Aaron and his sons and the goat was the sin offering for the people. Such is the character of man that his presence in the Tabernacle demanded that atonement be made for it, as it was defiled by the presence of men. The Hebrew writer refers to this when he states that "it was therefore necessary that the patterns of things in the heavens should be purified with these; but the heavenly things themselves with better sacrifices than these" (Heb 9.23). If the blood was necessary to ensure that the purity of the Sanctuary was maintained, in like manner the heavenly Sanctuary is to be kept clean. It may be that the writer has in view the defilement that would come from the activity of Satan and his forces, but this hardly is seen in the Tabernacle. As it was the presence of men that could defile, is this not also what Hebrews has in view? The preservation of the heavenly is all dependent on the blood and there is no danger of those who are Christian priests entering there and defiling it; all has been dealt with at the Cross.

As the incense arose from the Altar it passed by the horns on which the blood had been placed. The acceptance of the prayers of the saints, and the fragrance which the Lord adds to them, is based on the blood alone.

Verses 11-16: The Atonement Money

Following the reference to making atonement for the Golden Altar, the issue of the atonement money is now addressed. Whenever the people were numbered "a ransom for his soul" was to be paid for each man from twenty years old and upwards, so that "there would be no plague among them". This ransom was set at "half a shekel after the shekel of the sanctuary". It was not to vary according to the financial situation of the individual, the rich were not to offer more nor were the poor to offer less. This money was set aside for the "service of the tabernacle of the congregation". How vital this was is emphasised by reference to "every man" (v.12), and "every one" (vv.13,14); there was no allowance for exceptions.

The significance of the atonement money

It may seem strange to introduce the subject of the atonement money at this point. But the consecration of the priests and the details regarding the Golden Altar of Incense throw light on why it is now mentioned. The work of the priests at the Golden Altar was only available to those who had come to know atonement, and every time that they were to pass before the Lord to be numbered they were reminded of this and the obligation which it placed upon them.

So, as they were numbered they passed before the Lord individually and there was brought again to them their condition before God and their need of atonement. Man requires a ransom for his soul and God, who recognises their guilt before Him in grace makes provision for their condition.

The atonement money served two purposes. First, that there would be no plague among them (v.12). Second, it was to be used for the service of the Tabernacle (v.16). What took place when the atonement money was not paid when the people were numbered is seen during the reign of David. God allowed him to number the people (2 Sam 24.1-2), but it was Satan who was behind this for he "stood up against Israel, and provoked David to number Israel" (1 Chr 21.1). David, lifted up with pride, regarded the strength of his kingdom, the prowess of his armies, and the greatness of "his" achievement, and ordered Joab to number the people. Even Joab was uneasy about this enterprise, but he submitted to the wishes of David. There was no instruction given to collect the atonement money. Numbering of the people had only to be at the command of the Lord and not at the whims of men, no matter how great they were. The number of the people was not to be a cause of self-satisfaction to the ruler.

As the command had not come from the Lord, and as the atonement money had not been paid, David was given the choice of seven years of famine, three months of fleeing from his enemies, or three days of pestilence in the land. He chose to cast himself upon the mercy of God and asked for the three days of pestilence. Seventy thousand men died before the plague was stopped at the threshing floor of Araunah the Jebusite (2 Sam 24.16). How solemn all this was! The failure to pay the atonement money was a satanic attempt to have the people deny the necessity of atonement.

The second reason for the payment of this atonement money, that it should be used for the service of the Tabernacle, reminds the reader of the sockets on which it rested. There were 100 sockets in total, 96 for the boards and 4 for the pillars of the vail (36.20-30). The total atonement money collected was 301,775 shekels. Three hundred thousand shekels were used for the sockets, resulting in each socket containing 3,000 shekels, the atonement money for 6,000 men. As there were two sockets under each board the atonement money for 12,000 men supported one board (see 38.25-27). The whole foundation of the Tabernacle rested on the silver of atonement. Fellowship with God can only be based on redemption.

Verses 17-21: The Laver[†]

The Laver of brass is now brought before the reader. No dimensions are given for it and in the books of Moses which follow Exodus it is only mentioned once (Lev 8.11). The purpose of the Laver was that Aaron and his sons could wash their hands and feet when they went into the Tabernacle and when they approached the Brazen Altar to place an offering upon it. This was to be a statute forever; the need for washing would never be set aside and they must do so "that they die not". The reference in Leviticus 8 is to the anointing by Moses of "the laver and his foot". This would seem to indicate that the base also held water, to enable the priests to wash their feet.

The material used for the construction of the Laver was the looking glasses of the Children of Israel (38.8). It was placed in the court of the Tabernacle "between the tent of the congregation and the altar" (40.30), making it necessary to pass it when moving in and out of the Holy Place.

The significance of the Laver

At the consecration of the priests Moses washed Aaron and his sons with water (Lev 8.6). At that point another was washing them, but at the Laver they washed themselves. To serve God with hands that were dirty and feet that were not clean would bring death. When individuals are saved they are "sanctified in Christ Jesus" (1 Cor 1.2), but it is also necessary to ensure that they are practically sanctified - they must "wash at the Laver" by applying the Word of God to themselves.

The materials used were the mirrors that the women of Israel used for self-contemplation. As they looked into them they saw themselves, but after they had been formed into the Laver it was the priests who looked into them and saw what was necessary for the preservation of their cleanliness in the service of God. Their view was no longer self centred but Christ centred.

Verses 22-33: The Anointing Oil

The anointing oil was used for two purposes.

1. To anoint the Tabernacle. All the items in the Tabernacle are mentioned specifically, a reminder that none of them must be omitted. By this means they became "most holy", that is, they became fit for the service of God. The work of man's hand cannot be fit for His service until it is anointed, just as believers become fit to serve when they receive the unction or "anointing" (1 Jn 2.20) from the Holy Spirit.

2. To anoint the priests when they were consecrated. They were anointed once, just as the Holy Spirit was only given once.

So precious was this anointing oil that it was not to be poured on any other but the priests, nor was it to be made for any other purpose. So grave a sin was this that he who did it was to be cut off from his people.

The ingredients to be compounded together were 500 shekels of pure myrrh, 250 shekels of sweet cinnamon and of sweet calamus, and 500 shekels of cassia. These were to be mixed with a hin of olive oil.

Liquid myrrh

This is an aromatic resin which comes from a small bush which grows in inhospitable, desert regions. It is therefore a picture of that which brings fragrance through righteous suffering and endurance. The myrrh was obtained through cutting an incision in the trunk, boughs, and branches of the bush, and was used in the anointing oil as the first of the "principal" or "best" of the spices. As the first mentioned it is the base and foundation of the oil. On the Cross it was God who "incised" and brought forth the myrrh, but men also did much during His life. In the anointing oil it speaks of the fragrance arising to God through the sufferings of the Lord Jesus.

Other mentions of it are noteworthy:

Psalm 45.8: All the garments of the king smelled of myrrh. Even in regal splendour the fragrance of suffering is present.

Song of Songs 1.13: Her beloved is a bundle of myrrh unto her. During the night of his rejection his own love him and hold him near. He enjoys her affections but she enjoys the fragrance that he brings. See also Song of Songs 3.6; 4.6,14; 5.1,5,13.

Matthew 2.11: Myrrh was brought by the wise men to the Lord. It was an anticipation of His sufferings.

Mark 15.23: They offered Him myrrh on the Cross but He would take nothing to alleviate the pain.

John 19.39: Nicodemus brought 100 pounds† weight of myrrh and aloes to anoint His body.

Revelation 2.8 Smyrna means "myrrh" and symbolises the suffering of the church in that town.

Myrrh was always valued - it was among the commodities taken by the merchants down to Egypt (Gen 37.15), and also formed part of the gift which Jacob sent to Joseph (Gen 43.11).

Cinnamon

This plant grows to a height of 6-10 metres. The inner bark is separated from the core and is dried, contracting into rolls as it does so. The fragrance is extracted by distilling this bark. It speaks of the fragrance of the Lord Jesus which can only be enjoyed when there is an appreciation of the things that are not seen outwardly. It takes time and exercise to "strip the bark" and, in the presence of God, distil the fragrance of what can not be seen by those who only look at the outside and never seek to get beyond this.

Cinnamon is one of the spices to be found in the "garden inclosed" - "Spikenard and saffron; calamus and cinnamon with all trees of frankincense; myrrh and aloes, with all the chief spices" (Song 4.12,14). The sweetness of his beloved is described in this way.

Calamus (Sweet myrtle, JND)

Calamus comes from reeds which grow in the Jordan valley and are cut down before they come to flower. The calamus oil is obtained from the centre, from the pith of the plant. The reeds which are not cut down grow and, amongst other uses, become measuring reeds. This represents the deepest thoughts of the Lord Jesus Christ, His deep emotions and compassion. See Ezekiel 42.16 ff for use of the word as "measuring reeds".

Cassia

This spice comes from one of the evergreen laurel trees. The bark is stripped when the tree is five to seven years old, the outer bark is removed and the fragrant oil is distilled. Cassia was used as a treatment for many illnesses, the oil warming the body. It speaks of the healing which the Lord brings with Him. It is one of the fragrances on the garments of the king (Ps 45.8), and was a product traded in the markets of Tyre (Ezek 27.19).

Olive oil

This tree is reputed by some to be the longest living of all trees. The olives are harvested by beating the trees, and the fruit is pressed in the olive press. This speaks of the suffering of the Lord Jesus and the Holy Spirit who came consequent to these sufferings. The pure "oil olive" was the major ingredient in the anointing oil.

Verses 34-38: The Sweet Incense

The use of this sweet incense has been explained when dealing with the Golden Altar, and here its composition is described.

Stacte

Stacte (5198) has behind it the meaning of "drops" and signifies that which oozes out and falls to the ground in globules. Ratcliffe comments that "Stacte is one of the few plant products of the Bible about which doubt remains regarding its source...the general feeling is that the resin came...from the storax plant".[†] It gives off a fragrant odour and is used in perfume production. Who can lose the significance of this as it speaks of the Lord Jesus. He shed tears as He looked on the pitiful condition of man subject to the grip of death, and as He gazed down on the city of Jerusalem, knowing the judgment that would fall on it because of its rejection of Him, tears again flowed from His eyes (Lk 19.41). He was "a man of sorrows, and acquainted with grief" (Is 53.3), a grief that was real and deeply felt. The tears that came from His eyes were not the false tears of counterfeit sorrow.

Onycha

Onycha (7827) was the second ingredient. TWOT at 2363 states that "Besides incense of plant origin, aromatic ingredients were produced from fauna. In this latter category we would included onycha, to be connected perhaps with the shell of a mollusk (snails, clams, oysters for example) which when burned omits a pleasant odour". Ratcliffe comments with considerable justification that "For many years, I have been uneasy in my conscience about accepting that the substance 'onycha' came from a sea mollusc".[†] This unease, shared by many, is due to the fact that all shellfish, mussels etc were unclean and it is unlikely that these would be used in the making of a fragrance that speaks of the lovely beauty of the Lord Jesus. It is perhaps best to recognise that the source of this ingredient is still a matter of doubt, just as there are aspects of the loveliness of the Lord Jesus that are beyond us to appreciate to the full. We may be able to enjoy the thought of them and the fragrance of them as we linger in worship, but how they could be is beyond our understanding.

Galbanum

The third ingredient is galbanum (2464). TWOT at 652 simply states that this is "a kind of gum", but Ratcliffe provides a full description: "Galbanum is a resin obtained from the giant fennel, a member of the parsley family, with elegant, fern like, deep green foliage".[†] It appears to have been used to cool a fever and reduce agitation. Is this not another beautiful picture of the work of the Lord Jesus? He cooled the fever that gripped Peter's wife's mother (Mk 1.29-31); He calmed the anxious hearts of the disciples as He said, "Peace, be still", to the raging sea after He had rebuked the wind (Mk 4.35-41); and He brought peace to a man tormented by demons (Mk 5.1-13). No matter where He was there was the enjoyment of the calmness which possessed Him, even in the darkest hours as He faced the Cross.

Frankincense

To these three were added frankincense (3832). This is the first mention in Scripture of this substance. TWOT at 1074d states that this is "A resin from the bark of trees of the genus Boswellia. As the amber resin dries, white dust forms on the drops or tears of frankincense…". Ratcliffe writes that this tree is "a shrubby, multi-branch evergreen tree, bearing spikes of white, five petal flowers. The plant naturally exudes the fragrant resin through its leaves, twigs and papery bark…The fragrance of burning frankincense is recognised as the finest in the world".[†] It was this ingredient which produced the smoke that filled the Holy Place and the Holiest of All.

Making the incense

Three points are made regarding the making of the sweet incense. First, the ingredients had to be of equal weight, meaning that there had to be equal quantities of each, giving a perfect balance. The significance of this is very obvious. In the life of the Lord Jesus there was the perfect balance of every beautiful feature. No single one could be said to be dominant; they were all equal in their beauty. In this way the sum of the whole, uniquely balanced in His lovely life, resulted in a fragrant beauty that has been seen in no other man.

The second point is that they had to be blended together. They did not work against each other; the fragrance of one did not destroy that of another. They were perfectly at home together, the sum of the total creating a sweet odour which the ingredients could not produce on their own. What beauty was seen in Him: the lovely features which He displayed complementing each other with no inconsistencies.

But to create this beautiful substance it was necessary for the ingredients to be beaten small. The greater the beating, the purer was the incense. That which brought the perfumed atmosphere into the Sanctuary had first to be beaten small. How true this is of the Lord Jesus in all that He suffered, and it is this fragrance, as has been observed when dealing with the Golden Altar, which He adds to the prayers of the saints as they ascend to heaven.

This incense was to be kept in the Holy Place, not in the Holiest of All, for it was on the Golden Altar that it was burned morning and evening.

Warning about counterfeit

Just as it was not permitted to make the anointing oil for any other purpose, nor to make any like it (vv.32-33), so the sweet incense was for exclusive use in the Sanctuary. The judgment for failure to observe this was, as with the anointing oil, that the person responsible should be "cut off from his people". Only a sin of severe gravity could warrant such a punishment entailing being cut off from Israel and put outwith the sphere of the covenant, losing all the privileges and blessings which had been enjoyed.

If one should wonder why such severity is used, it must be understood that both the anointing oil and the sweet spices were used to anoint the Tabernacle and the priests and the sweet spices were used to give fragrance in the Sanctuary. These were holy matters, and reverence for God, His House and priesthood, and the sanctity of His presence demanded that they were treated with utmost respect. To demean them by making counterfeits and using them or the same ingredients for other less worthy uses was a display of irreverence and disrespect for Jehovah that was completely unacceptable. To allow it, or to make it subject to a mild censure, would fail to display the vital importance of the unique privileges and responsibilities involved in approaching Jehovah.

With these details the instructions for the building of the Tabernacle are now complete. Let it be emphasised again that what has been given in Scripture is not a detailed building plan. The purpose was to give all that was necessary for the spiritual lessons to be learned. Now the next chapter turns to the question of who will be responsible for carrying out the work.

Notes

1 An illustration of the Altar of Incense is given in Appendix 6.

17 An illustration of the Laver is given in Appendix 6.

23 The modern equivalent is reckoned to be about 75lbs/34 kilos.

34 T. H. Ratcliffe, *Bible Plants, Fruits & Products* (4 references).

EXODUS 31

The Workmen and the Sabbath

Verses 1-2: The Appointment of Bezaleel

Now that directions had been given for the construction of the Tabernacle, Jehovah appointed the workmen charged with the responsibility of carrying out the work. It should be noted that He did not only give the detailed instructions but He also determined who would be His workmen. The call was very specific; there was no possibility of misunderstanding for the two men are named. "I have called by name", says Jehovah. The word "call" (7121) means "to summon", "to invite", or "to commission". When He calls it is a gracious invitation, but it also is a summons to obey and a commission to fulfil.

The need for workmen

This may seem a very obvious point to make, but the service of God requires workmen. Having been given the plans, there would be little value in Moses only poring over them and enjoying their beauty on the mount; there would be no progress made if they were only the subject of debate and discussion. It was necessary for the work to be carried out and God had determined that His servants would be given the privilege of having a part in this work. It should not be forgotten that the God who alone created the universe was capable of bringing the Tabernacle into being without any part being given to Israel in its construction. To be given responsibility in this work was not an onerous burden to be reluctantly undertaken; it was a great privilege, always to be regarded with a sense of wonder, that mortal man should be allowed involvement in His work. So it is today! Yet it is possible to spend time reading the Scriptures, enjoying with other believers the beauty of the Word of God, and yet failing to be engaged fully in the work.

The work to which believers are called today includes that of labouring in the local assembly. Just as the Tabernacle was the Sanctuary which was His dwelling place, so the assembly is the place where the Lord is to be found when the saints meet together. It is necessary that all are workers, for, as with the Tabernacle, it is an honour to be involved in His work.

Gideon, the son of Joash, was threshing wheat when the angel of the Lord appeared to him and addressed him as a "mighty man of valour". "If the Lord be with us", exclaimed Gideon, "why then is all this befallen us?". Little did he realise that the problem he highlighted did have an answer, and that he was the answer (Judg 6.11-14). At times God's servants can identify the problem but fail to realise that there is an answer, and it may be that the one who recognises the need is the one whose work it is to meet that need.

So, let the lesson be stated again. God can do all that He desires without the involvement of His people, but He chooses to use workers so that they will learn the joy of His service and gain rewards for faithful work carried out.

The necessity of divine appointment

However, in the work of God it is not left to His servants to decide who is fitted for specific tasks or areas of service. He appoints and He fits those whom He has appointed. Two men, Bezaleel and Aholiab, are named as those who would superintend all the work. In giving Israel the great privilege of building the first House of God to be erected by human hands, these two men are named as leaders in the construction.

The same principle had been seen at work when Moses was chosen (ch.3), and later would also be observed when the disciples were chosen (see Mk 3.14-19). Today, in the assembly, God still fits His servants and calls them to His service. It should not be thought that when He does not call an individual to a task which is public and appears to yield much fruit for God it results in loss of reward for that individual. There is no one in His service who is overlooked in this way, and it falls to each to ensure that the work, no matter how public or otherwise, to which they are called is carried out fully and faithfully.

Bezaleel

The first of the two men called is Bezaleel, the son of Uri, the son of Hur, of the tribe of Judah. The reader has already been introduced to Hur in ch.17 where, together with Aaron, he helped Moses hold up his hands on the hilltop as the battle against Amalek was raging in the valley (17.8-16). These two were also charged with the responsibility of the administration of Israel when Moses was up the mount (24.14). Jewish tradition claims that Hur was the husband of Miriam, but there is nothing in Scripture to substantiate this. Note also that care must be taken not to confuse Caleb, the son of Hezron, who was the father of Hur, with Caleb the son of Jephunneh, the spy who, together with Joshua, urged the people to enter the land (1 Chr 2.18-20; Num 13.6). It can be seen, therefore, that Bezaleel had a good family background and it may be thought that this fitted him for the responsibilities given to him. Such, however, was not the case. No matter how fitting his family connection it was necessary for him to receive the call of God and to submit willingly to carrying out the work given him by the Lord.

"Bezaleel" means "In the shadow of the God". His parents, in so naming him, expressed the desire that he would live close to God and that he would enjoy His protection. In that shadow he would be sheltered from the glare and heat of the sun; he would enjoy the cool shade of His presence in the midst of the heat and pressures of daily life. In order so to do it would be necessary for him to remain close to God; at a distance he would be far from His shadow. To be there is to be close enough to hear His call.

The shadow of His wings (Ps 36.7; 57.1; 63.7), the shadow of the Almighty (Ps 91.1), and the shadow of His hand (Is 49.2) are all places of His care. Clearly, Bezaleel had fulfilled the desires of his mother and father, living close to his God and now called to His service.

Verses 3-5: Bezaleel Fitted to Serve
Filled with the Spirit of God
Bezaleel was "filled…with the spirit of God". Before the coming of the Holy Spirit at Pentecost, He came to individuals to fit them for specific tasks. Examples of this are when the Spirit of the Lord came upon Gideon (Judg 6.34), Jephthah (Judg 11.29), and Samson (Judg 14.6,19; 15.14). Here, however, it is stated, not that the Spirit of God would come upon him, but that he would be filled with the Spirit of God. In this Bezaleel is unique in the Old Testament. He would be enabled to carry out the work, with complete absorption in it; all his faculties controlled by the Spirit as he worked on the construction of the Tabernacle. This task could not be undertaken by using human intellect and understanding alone, it required the Spirit to do God's work.

The comparison cannot fail to be drawn that the Spirit of God who "moved upon the face of the waters" (Gen 1.2) was the Spirit who filled Bezaleel. The One who was occupied with creation was also occupied with the building of the Tabernacle, another indication of the importance of Bezaleel's task.

The work of the Israelites in Egypt was harsh, as their slave labour was used in the fields and on the building sites. It is likely, therefore, although it cannot be asserted with certainty, that Bezaleel and Aholiab were engaged in working with wood, gold, and silver in Egypt. If they were, those skills alone were not sufficient without the provision which comes with the Lord's call.

The attributes with which he was equipped
Bezaleel would not be given a trial run in building the Tabernacle. Although the people were generous in their giving (36.5), and the materials available were sufficient for the work, it is unlikely that provision was made for "practice" pieces. The materials were also of great value. To ruin them would not only be wasteful but would empty the store which the people supplied. Thus it was that the skills necessary had to be present from the start and had to be of the very best. To achieve this goal the abilities given to Bezaleel were described in a threefold manner.

The first of these is *wisdom* (2451). TWOT at 647a states that this covers "the whole gamut of human experience", but here it is limited to the skill necessary for the construction of the Tabernacle. It was required in the making of the garments of the High Priest where the workers were "filled with the spirit of wisdom" (28.3). It also would give a sense of the fear of the Lord in undertaking this great commission. Clearly, great wisdom would be required in translating the plans given to Moses into the Tabernacle building and furnishings. This wisdom, therefore, would doubtless be used in two areas of his work. First, he would be given the wisdom to understand divine requirements, and second, he would have the wisdom necessary to guide and lead the team of workers. This latter would be of great importance, no less than the former.

The second attribute is that of *understanding* (8394). This has behind it the thought of discernment and insight. Bezaleel would be able to see behind the raw material given to him and have an appreciation of how this was to be used and of how the instructions given to Moses were to be interpreted. Understanding the materials with which he was working and the ways in which they could be made and moulded were vital to create items with the quality required for such a project.

The third is that of *knowledge* (1847). This covers the technical knowledge of construction necessary in a building project. From this it can be seen that Bezaleel would not act as a mindless functionary, merely following instructions. This was not God's way with His servants then and it is not today. His wish is that His servants should have an understanding of the work to which they are called and possess the necessary skills to undertake that work successfully.

The threefold ability covered "all manner of workmanship". He would be able to work with gold, silver, brass, and wood, in the manner of a superb craftsman. There was no part of the construction for which his skill was unfitted.

Therefore, whether he had been employed in building in the past is, as we have seen, not known, but the lesson to be learned here is that, no matter the background, each servant must be completely fitted by the Lord for His service. The ability to speak publicly does not make a gospel preacher or a Bible teacher. The skills acquired in business to manage people do not make a shepherd of the sheep. The Lord prepares His servants and fully fits them out, sometimes using the skills that they have learned as He has led them through life. Moses' experience in the palace and then in the wilderness were all used in the making of a servant of the Lord.

The work which Bezaleel had to do

The ability given to Bezaleel was to be directed to devising "cunning works". TWOT at 767 states of "cunning" (4284) that "the basic idea of the word is the employment of the mind in thinking activity. Reference is not so much to 'understanding', but to the creating of new ideas". This involved bringing all his skills to bear on the building work, using the information given to him by Moses, to create what the Lord had instructed. Doubtless, this would involve him enquiring of Moses at times, and then planning and executing the work. What a responsibility was laid on his shoulders. Not one mistake could be allowed to mar the structure.

It is worthy of note that so little is written in Scripture about this man. He is hidden behind his work and showed no interest in receiving any credit himself. There is no record of anything that he said, no note of how he worked, or how he felt. As with every responsibility there would be times when he would feel burdened, times when anxiety would grip him, and times when he would feel the great weight of the task. Yet nothing is said of any of this. He quietly took up the work and completed it. He was indeed a "workman that needeth not to be ashamed" (2 Tim 2.15). He did not waste the resources given to him, as did the unjust steward (Lk 16.1-12); he was not lazy and negligent; he was diligent and used all the powers at his disposal to do a work that matched exactly the divine pattern with which he was entrusted. No petty disputes were allowed to intervene, pride was absent, and personality differences did not hinder. What an example to those who work in His service today. The pattern of their service is plainly laid out in the Scriptures, and as "labourers together" they seek to build "God's building" (1 Cor 3.9) of which they form a part.

Verse 6: Aholiab

The skills of Aholiab covered metal work, weaving, and embroidery (38.23). He appears to have been subordinate to Bezaleel in the work, as his name is always placed after that of Bezaleel. In addition, therefore, to the qualities suggested in connection with Bezaleel, it is seen in Aholiab that there was no jealousy or desire to usurp the place given to the other man.

Aholiab was of the tribe of Dan, which may appear to be a strange choice. In the marching order of the tribes, Judah, of which tribe was Bezaleel, came first and Dan came last (Num 10.25). When the land was apportioned between the tribes, Dan was the last to be given a lot (Josh 19.40ff), and in the tribal genealogies of 1 Chronicles 2-9 was omitted. In the list associated with the 144,000 in Revelation 7.4-8 the reader looks in vain for any mention of Dan. They set up a centre of idolatry when they captured and moved to Laish (Judg 18.30), and the idolatrous worship instituted by Jeroboam was set up at Bethel and in the territory of Dan (1 Kings 12.29).

It can be seen from this that there is a great contrast between the kingly tribe of Judah and the tribe of Dan. Even in the blessing of his sons Jacob refers to Dan as "a serpent by the way, an adder in the path, that biteth the horse heels, so that his rider shall fall backward" (Gen 49.17), showing that any victory gained would not be done in a majestic way. The lesson is clear to see. The choice of one man from the tribe of Judah and one from the tribe of Dan teaches that the background of an individual neither qualifies for nor excludes from the work of God. To belong to a family known for faithfulness in service does not qualify any member of that family for spiritual work, nor does membership of a family weak in spiritual things automatically exclude from this service. The individual and his relationship with God are the issues, as the call of God comes to the individual and not to the family.

The other workers

But Bezaleel and Aholiab could not carry out this work alone, so other workers had to be fitted to enable them to engage in this great enterprise for God. These workers were filled with the "spirit of wisdom" but not given all the understanding and knowledge with which Bezaleel was endowed. The Lord will fit some today to be leaders and give them the necessary "spiritual gifts", others He will fit for other tasks, but never will He fit for a service to which an individual is not called. The range of crafts to be used included weavers, workers in skins and leather, embroiderers, carpenters, metalworkers, goldsmiths, and silversmiths, all working together in co-operation with one common aim. As with Bezaleel and Aholiab it is likely that skills learned in Egypt were now used in a higher service.

Working in the service of the Lord requires the desire to "work together" under the care and direction of spiritual leaders. The Tabernacle would never have been reared according to the divine pattern if the workers had added their own ideas or altered what the Lord had set out to "improve it" or to make allowance for "contemporary conditions".

Verses 7-11: The Items Defined

For the removal of all doubt, the items to be made are listed. The complete list will be the responsibility of the workers who have been chosen by the Lord. It may be asked why this is necessary. Has it not been clearly defined in the instructions given to Moses? That is true, but to confirm the scope of the task entrusted to the workers, and to prevent any thought that others may have the right to a part of this work, the list is set out.

Verses 12-17: The Sabbath

Why it is introduced

It may appear strange that the Sabbath is introduced at this point. It was last referred to in ch. 20 in the giving of the Law and it appears again now at the end of the instructions in respect of the Tabernacle. This is not without significance. That of which the Tabernacle was a picture concerned a work in which ultimately God will enjoy His rest and, therefore, the seventh day of the week is emphasised once again. The workmen had the opportunity of putting the revealed will of God into practice; they would be able to show complete submission to His will and total obedience to His commands. It has also been suggested that the people were reminded of the Sabbath lest, in their enthusiasm to complete the work, they failed to observe it, on the basis that the importance of the work gave them liberty to work on the seventh day. The simple lesson is that no work for God justifies disobedience to Scripture. "To

obey is better than sacrifice, and to hearken than the fat of rams"
(1 Sam 15.22), was a principle that held good even before the words
were spoken to Saul.

The Sabbath as a sign

To what was given in the Law regarding the Sabbath is now added the
fact that it was a sign "between me and you throughout your generations"
(v.13); it was to be a "sign between me and the children of Israel for ever"
(v.17). This is the second sign that had been given to Israel as a token of
their relationship with Jehovah. The first was that of circumcision when
the Lord said to Abraham that "it shall be a token (sign) of the covenant
betwixt me and you" (Gen 17.11). Circumcision was a sign not outwardly
seen, but at this point, as a nation, they were given a sign that was very
visible. That it was a sign between the Lord and Israel was clearly stated,
and this was its prime purpose, but it was also a sign that was visible to
others.

The sign reminded the nation that it was the Lord who had set them
apart, distinguishing them from all other nations and giving them a unique
privilege. On the seventh day the noise and clamour of the work place was
hushed to silence. If they were travelling, the rigours of the journey gave
way to rest, and in the quiet peace of Sabbath they were able to contemplate
the goodness of God who had delivered them from bondage and preserved
them since that day. Without this day the constant pressures of life would
perhaps close the mind to His grace and mercy.

No other nation had such a day. Others would look on and wonder at
the "waste" of the hours when valuable work could be done. They would
regard as folly this setting aside of time that could be given over to
commerce. But faithful Israelites would know, and would have learned by
experience, that what was given to God was never wasted, a lesson
that was forgotten by disciples who looked on the very precious
ointment being poured on the Lord Jesus and said, "To what purpose
is this waste?" (Mt 26.8).

Warnings regarding failure to keep the Sabbath

The importance of keeping the Sabbath is further emphasised in the
warnings given relating to the punishment inflicted for breaking it. These
are clear: "every one that defileth it shall surely be put to death" (v.14),
and, "whosoever doeth any work in the sabbath day, he shall surely be put
to death" (v.15). Breaking the Sabbath put the guilty party outside the
terms of the covenant, for the act was in defiance of the sign of that
covenant, and anyone guilty was to be "cut off from among his people".
They were no longer part of the covenant people and, as they were
regarded as having forfeited the right to live, they were put to death.

This may appear to be a punishment out of proportion to the sin, but to
hold that view is to fail to understand the nature of the sin. It was open

defiance of God and a refusal to bow to His rule and authority, striking at
the very basis of the relationship of the covenant.

The first example of this punishment being carried out was in the
case of the man who was found to be gathering sticks on the Sabbath
(Num 15.32-36). The man was "put in ward", probably to give time for
the case to be considered, not because Moses was reluctant to obey
the word of God, but to ensure that nothing was done rashly and only
after due consideration had been given to all the issues. After the Lord
had spoken to Moses, the congregation stoned the guilty man to death
outside the Camp.

In six days the Lord made heaven and earth

The reason given in v.17 for the keeping of the Sabbath is that "in six
days the Lord made heaven and earth, and on the seventh day he rested,
and was refreshed". This confirms that the days of Genesis 1 were days of
twenty-four hours duration, a view based, among other considerations,
on the fact that these days are defined as having evenings and mornings.
In creation, the Lord rested on the seventh day because He could look
back on a completed work that was done perfectly and see that it was
"very good", and now the nation had to do as He did.

It must not be missed that the Sabbath, therefore, did have a secondary
significance in that those who rested on that day should have been able to
look back over six days of work well done. Here was an incentive to refrain
from lazy, poor quality work, for to rest after that was merely a sham. Better
to be able to rest in the knowledge that the days past had been filled with
work that was fitting to have come from the hands of one who claimed to
have a covenant relationship with Jehovah.

But it must also be remembered that the spiritual rest of which the
Sabbath spoke could not be obtained under the Law. The efforts of man to
please God by the works of his own hands were futile; his striving but
drove home to him the lesson that he was incapable of attaining that goal
by his labour, and that it had to be gained by another means, that of divine
grace alone.

Verse 18: The Two Tables of Stone

Reference has already been made to these two tables of stone in ch.24
where the Lord promised Moses that He would give him "tables of stone,
and a law, and commandments which I have written" (v.12). It has also
been noted when dealing with the giving of the Ten Commandments in
ch.20 that much discussion has taken place as to how these were written
on the two stones. "Early Jewish and Christian interpreters suggested that
five declarations were incised on each tablet; however, this would create
an imbalance - one tablet would contain 146 Hebrew words and the second
only 26. Others have suggested that the first tablet contained the Godward
commands (1-4) and the second contained the manward commands (5-

10). Still others have surmised that each tablet contained the entire Decalogue" (Merrill).

What must not be overlooked is that the tables were of stone, indicating the changeless nature of the Law. No man must alter its terms, take away from it, or add to it. It is an unchangeable Law, the terms of which are still true.

These tables were also stated to be written with "the finger of God". When David looked up into the night sky what he saw caused him to exclaim, "When I consider thy heavens, the work of thy fingers, the moon and the stars, which thou hast ordained; What is man that thou art mindful of him?" (Ps 8.3-4). He saw in the heavens the intricate work of God described as requiring the delicacy and skill of His fingers. The Egyptian magicians, when referring to the third plague - that of lice, also used the expression, in stating that the catastrophe was clearly the work of God (8.19). TWOT at 1873 states that the expression "refers to the handiwork of his creative power". With particular reference to the tables of stone Merrill states that it refers to "the mechanism by which God wrote His commandments…".

The point is that the writing of the Commandments was not the work of Moses. Other prophets would write the Word of God, but the fundamental nature of this work was displayed in the fact that God wrote it Himself. Much had yet to come from Moses' pen, but not this! These were the tables of the covenant (Deut 9.9), the terms of which Israel had agreed to obey. Israel had heard them when the Lord had spoken to them out of the midst of the fire on the "the day of the assembly" (Deut 9.10).

The time for Moses to descend the mount has now come. He has been forty days and nights without bread or water (Deut 9.9), yet no complaint has passed his lips. Now, with the righteous Law of God in his hands, he has to go down to the people. His later comments in Deuteronomy tell the reader what is not revealed here, that before He descended the Lord told him that the people, during his absence, had corrupted themselves by making a molten image. Although they did not yet have the tables, they had heard the voice of God declaring the Law (ch.20), so that they were without excuse. They had declared confidently, "All that the Lord hath spoken we will do" (19.8), despite their past record showing how prone they were to sin. Their claim will now be revealed to be hollow since, even before the giving of the Law is completed, they have sinned in a most grievous way, breaking the first of the Ten Commandments. To such a people Moses descended holding in his hands the holy Law.

EXODUS 32

The Golden Calf

When God is working, the Adversary is never far away. How quickly he entered the Garden of Eden; with what subtlety did he approach Sarah with the suggestion that Hagar was the answer to the problem; as has been observed, he left the people little time to enjoy the water from the smitten rock before he brought Amalek to oppose them. There is no work for God that he does not oppose, and those who serve the Lord must not be ignorant of his devices. His lies and deceit are well crafted and honed by constant use. The temptation will be formed with expert skill to meet the fears and weaknesses of those against whom it is directed. Let all beware of his wiles and be watchful for his activity! He observes our behaviour and probes our character, looking for our failings. He enjoys no periods of inactivity and his motives are always for the ill of those with whom he has to do. Lies are the tools of his trade and counterfeit is his speciality.

Verse 1: The Demand From the People
The suggestion made

So, while Moses was enjoying the presence of God and receiving from His hand the Law requested by Israel, the devil was busily engaged in the valley. How different it was when, in the battle against Amalek, there was harmony between the hilltop and the valley, the result of which was decisive victory for the nation. Now, when that harmony no longer existed, and when the people rose to the alluring suggestions of the tempter, disaster loomed before them.

How long they waited before they came to Aaron with their demands is not known. The approach was made some time prior to the expiry of the forty days because there was time for them to gather the gold and make the calf before Moses descended from the mount. The issue which gave rise to the suggestion was that "Moses delayed to come down out of the mount". It was not merely impatience at the absence of Moses, but a feeling, planted by the tempter, that they had been abandoned.

This was quite in accord with the method he employed when he confronted Eve. The suggestion then was that God did not have the good of Adam and Eve before Him, and that they would benefit by disobedience. Now he suggested that the Lord, who had led them out of Egyptian bondage, no longer had their good at heart; He had proved unreliable and had left them leaderless in the wilderness. Perhaps the fire on the mountain had consumed Moses! How absurd this would have appeared to the thoughtful Israelite. After all the evidences of His care He would not now leave them alone, but, nevertheless, with increasing success the enemy planted the seeds of rebellion, and the absence of Moses seemed, superficially, to justify their doubts.

Waiting on God has often been a time when His people are vulnerable. The thoughts that were placed in the hearts of Israel are still those used by the adversary today. "You have mistaken His intentions"; "He does not answer in the way you expect Him to - you have got this wrong"; "Life is too short to wait, He means you just to act now", are all ideas that are forced through the mind. Israel waited, listened to the subtle voice of rebellion, and fell!

But Moses had made them a promise, and had he ever failed? To the elders he had said, "Tarry ye here for us, until we come again to you" (24.14). Aaron and Hur, into whose hands Moses had placed the administration of the people during his absence, were amongst those to whom the statement was made. The people and the leaders were without excuse. Moses had spoken!

The demand was not made by a disaffected few. The people "collected together to Aaron" (JND), showing that this was a "popular" movement, and, as all such gatherings do, it fed off the communal frenzy. Since, in their view, Moses appeared to have gone from them, they asked Aaron to "make us a god" (JND), despite the fact that they acknowledged that Moses had led them out Egypt. Once again the two features that had marked their dealings with God since their release from the house of bondage came strongly to the fore. First, the absence of Moses from the Camp was a test for Israel, and again they failed. Second, despite all the goodness of God enjoyed, His provision for them, and the victory which He gave them over Amalek, they still had no sense of gratitude and no confidence in Him. How quickly they were prepared to turn to another "god".

Let us make gods

The people requested that "gods" in the plural should be made. Merrill comments: "The use of the plural noun...may indicate that the construction of the golden calf was an act of abandoning Yahwistic monotheism in favour of Egyptian polytheism". The desire was to leave aside the worship of the One God and replace Him with a number of deities, as was the custom of the Egyptians. Added credibility is given to this view by the words of the people after the calf had been made: "These be thy gods, O Israel, which brought thee up out of the land of Egypt" (v.4). It is possible that the cry, "These be thy gods", indicates that they considered the golden calf to represent Jehovah, the plural being used, as it is in reference to Him (see Gen 1.1). The holding of a feast to the Lord (vv.5-6) may have been an attempt by Aaron to reconcile the two. Despite this, however, what was about to take place was nothing less than disobedience to the commandment, and cannot be excused in any way, neither on the grounds of the wait for Moses, nor on the basis that the idol was to be a "help" in their worship.

Verses 2-4: Making the Golden Calf

The weakness of Aaron is revealed. There is no record of him remonstrating with the people, no reminding them of the goodness of God to them or of the first and second commandments. Rather, there is a ready and immediate acceptance of the will of the people. Aaron did not possess the leadership qualities of his brother, but the question of why he failed so quickly and so completely must be answered. It may be that, like all weak leaders, the pressure of the crowd swayed him, or perhaps he viewed this as an opportunity to show that he was as great a leader as his brother, and to show this by a decisive action whereby he would leave his mark on the history of the nation. Whatever his motive, the result was disastrous. He failed his God and he failed Moses. How often have weak men, in the absence of strong leaders, led God's people down pathways of disobedience!

It has been argued that the call of Aaron for the people to "break off the golden earrings" and bring them to him was an attempt on his part to calm the fervour of the people and discourage them from the course of action on which they had set themselves. There is not, however, any evidence that this was Aaron's motive in making the request: indeed, there was an unseemly haste in his response. The people were willing to give that which was of value, as today many are prepared to give of their substance to causes that are opposed to the work of God. Note that they were instructed to "break off" the earrings, and "all the people" did this; there was no coercion.

What was required from them was less than was necessary for the building of the Tabernacle, but, nevertheless, it was given. It may be that the Adversary had in mind the instruction that would be given to Israel to give their gold for the construction of the Tabernacle, and this was a way to diminish what was available for that service. The more of our resources he can turn to his use, the less is available to be devoted to the Lord.

Aaron was the workman and the result was a golden calf the design of which was based on the Egyptian "god" Apis. It has been noted above that the cry, "These be thy gods, O Israel, which brought thee up out of the land of Egypt", gives cause to believe that they considered this to be a visible representation of Jehovah. How quickly the teaching of the word of God was disregarded. The whole nation had heard from the mount the words, "Thou shalt not make unto thee any graven image…that is in heaven above, or that is in the earth beneath, or that is in the water under the earth" (20.4), and that included making an image of Jehovah.

Whether this idol was a solid piece of gold, or whether it was a wooden structure with golden plates fixed to the outside of it has been the subject of speculation but adds nothing to the lessons to be learned. Aaron's later claims as to how it was made would suggest the former. Likeness to the nations, and to Egypt, was their desire, and it now appears that the desire had been satisfied. They had their "god", visible and material. To be like the nations would continue to be a desire that would cost Israel much. It was this which was behind their call for a king (1 Sam 8.5). The comment of Stephen is worthy of note: "And they made a calf in those days, and offered sacrifice unto the idol, and rejoiced in the work of their own hands" (Acts 7.41).

The Psalmist reveals a little more of what was in the hearts of the people: "They made a calf in Horeb, and worshipped the molten image. Thus they changed their glory into the similitude of an ox that eateth grass. They forgat God their saviour, which had done great things in Egypt" (Ps 106.19-21). How quickly they had forgotten and how quickly they had "changed their glory". This glory was the unique fact that God was with them, but this they discarded in favour of an idol.

Verses 5-6: Worshipping the Idol

Now, around the idol the trappings of worship have to be placed. An altar was built and the day following was proclaimed to be a feast to the Lord, Aaron's apparent intention being not to displace Jehovah as the God of Israel, but rather to mould Jehovah into a god of their making, after their own design, and worshipped according to their own devices. In all this there is the work of the Adversary seeking the ill of the people. Having failed to prevent the exodus, he is now desiring to destroy the relationship between Israel and their God.

What a scene unfolded on the day following. There was no delay in the idolatrous acts of worship, for the people rose up early in the morning. Burnt offerings and peace offerings were laid upon the altar. These could not be as they were to be offered in the Tabernacle, for instruction in respect of these was not given until the early chapters of Leviticus. This was worship founded on fleshly principles and in flagrant disobedience to God's commands.

Added to their offerings there was the feast, which clearly was a time of self-indulgence and merriment. The Camp was filled with the noise of singing (v.18) and the people were naked (v.25), so what was taking place was drunken revelry, no doubt imitating some of the Egyptian feasts. There was a complete loss of self-control and they acted as if all restraint could be cast aside in the guise of worship. Such behaviour has been repeated in cult ceremonies even in this present age with the justification that the "worship" which is being carried out allows individuals to "be themselves" and not subject to ancient and irrelevant restrictions. Keil & Delitzsch write: "Nevertheless the making of the calf, and the sacrificial meals and other ceremonies performed before it, were a shameful apostasy from Jehovah, a practical denial of the inimitable glory of the true God, and a culpable breach of the second commandment of the covenant words".

Lest the reader consider that such behaviour ought not to blight the life of a believer, Paul writes, "Neither be ye idolaters, as were some of them; as it is written, The people sat down to eat and drink, and rose up to play"

(1 Cor 10.7). Having lusted after the food of Egypt (1 Cor 10.6), they now lust after its forms of worship, a warning to believers to refrain from seeking to worship the true God by means that are of man's devising. If such a course is pursued, the behaviour and standards of the world will soon displace godliness.

Verses 7-8: The Command to Moses to Go Down

The Lord knows what is taking place in the Camp; nothing is hidden from Him. What occurs in the following verses shows that the test of waiting, in which Israel had failed so grievously, had now to be followed by Moses' being tested. Note that the Lord refers to His people as "*thy* people, which *thou* broughtest out of the land of Egypt". The link between Moses and the people is emphasised, together with the part that Moses had played in their deliverance. This is followed by reference to the speed with which they had "turned aside…out of the way", an expression of surprise that they who had known so much of God's goodness were swift to forget Him and His commandments. The sad fact is that blessings enjoyed today are no guarantee that the recipient will be faithful today or tomorrow.

In their folly the people had "corrupted (7843) themselves". The verb indicates anything that has been corrupted so completely that it is fit only for destruction. Their behaviour put them in the position that was suitable only for the judgment of God. This revealed the magnitude of the sin that had been committed and of the crisis faced by the nation. They had declared confidently, not so many days earlier, "All that the Lord hath spoken we will do" (19.8), but now their words had a hollow ring. What a lesson for all in guarding our lips from making great claims of abiding faithfulness. Those who do so should look first into their own hearts, and what they see there will cause them to realise that rather than making vaunting claims they should be declaring their dependence on Him to keep them faithful, ensuring that they cast themselves upon Him in their weakness.

Verses 9-10: The Response of the Lord

The Lord described Israel as "this people" who are "stiffnecked" (7186), an expression which was used of the necks of oxen bearing the load of the yoke. The muscles of the neck would be powerful and unyielding, and this is the factor that is emphasised. The hearts of the Israelites were unyielding and stubborn, refusing to bow to the Commandments. In view of this the Lord states, "Let me alone". The judgment to be carried out on Israel is a solemn act in which Moses has no part to play, nor has he to intervene to change or delay the intervention of God. He has to stand aside and let righteous judgment be carried out.

To lesser men the words of the Lord would come with attractive force: "I will make of thee a great nation". The proposition which was being put to Moses was that Israel would be destroyed and in its place a nation would arise from his family. This was a test indeed! Was Moses a fit mediator for the people, even when they had been guilty of such gross sin? Would he be turned aside from the great calling which was his by the "attractive" offer made to him by the Lord? To take the place of Abraham at the head of a great nation must surely be the greatest offer that could be made to any Israelite. Could it be that the great privileges enjoyed by Moses in coming into the presence of God alone would cause him to consider that he was worthy of such an honour?

Verses 11-14: The Perception of Moses

The answer given by Moses revealed, not only his humility and meekness, but also his deep understanding of the ways of God and of the issues involved. The entreaty of the servant of God here reminds the reader of the plea of Abraham to the Lord in respect of Sodom (Gen 18.23-33). Both these men showed the strength of their faith and their intimacy with God as they pled on behalf of others.

There were three points around which Moses based his reply, although it should be noted that he did not seek to excuse the conduct of the people.

1. Israel had been redeemed out of Egypt by the power of the Lord and "with a mighty hand". His past dealings with them in delivering them from slavery displayed how great His power was, and therefore they belonged to Him and were His people enjoying the deliverance which He had effected.

2. If the Israelites were to be destroyed, the Egyptians would simply state that the purpose of the Lord in taking them out from their power was to cause them harm, an evidence of the fact that God did not have their good at heart. It would be argued that He had put them into an impossible situation and then destroyed them. It would give the Egyptians great pleasure, and enable the enemies of the Lord to misrepresent His character. It is clear from this assertion that Egypt followed the progress of their freed "slaves" with keen interest.

3. The Lord had made promises to Abraham, Isaac, and Israel that their seed would be multiplied and that they would inherit the land to which they were now travelling. Note that the name "Israel" is used and not "Jacob", as Moses brings before the Lord the name which He had given the patriarch. The Lord cannot go back on His promises. They were not dependent on the behaviour of the people and cannot be changed now. What He had promised He must fulfil. Any argument that Moses was of the seed of Abraham, Isaac, and Israel, and that his seed could be looked on as the legitimate heirs to the promise, did not enter his mind. To restrict the promise to the seed of Moses would leave it only partially fulfilled, a compromise emphasising that the Lord had been unable to keep His word. Quite apart from that, this "new" nation would bear the name of Moses, which was quite unacceptable to him.

Moses did not make any claims about the future conduct of the people by perhaps suggesting that they would learn their lesson if, for example, they were chastised in a lesser way. His argument is based solely on the faithfulness of God and not on the faithfulness of Israel. The Lord had placed the future of the people in the hands of Moses and he showed that their interests were of greater value to him than his own exaltation. He had displayed the character of a true mediator whose sole concern is the good of those for whom he intercedes. Keil & Delitzsch write: "And Moses stood the test. The preservation of Israel was dearer to him than the honour of becoming the head and founder of a new kingdom of God. True to his calling as mediator, he entered the breach before God, to turn away His wrath, that He might not destroy the sinful nation (Ps 106.23)".

Believers today should pause before this account and be thankful for the Mediator who works on their behalf. All that is enjoyed in Christ is because of His faithfulness, an enjoyment that is eternal. It must never be forgotten that eternal joy will also depend on His faithfulness; no other basis for their glory exists. He will always honour His promises.

Verses 15-18: Descending From the Mountain

Moses descended from the mountain and rejoined Joshua who had been waiting for him (24.13), and together they continued towards the Camp. Unlike the people, Joshua had waited quietly and patiently for Moses. He had not returned to the Camp to declare that Moses had gone missing. The sin of the nation serves to emphasise the faithfulness of Joshua. In his hands Moses carried the two tables of stone on which, written with the "writing of God", were the Ten Commandments. These were the words that the people had vowed to obey.

It is clear that Moses had not told Joshua of the communication that he had received from the Lord, that the people had corrupted themselves in the making of the molten calf. It may be that Moses had determined to wait until Joshua heard the sounds coming from the Camp, or that he had the hope that when they entered the Camp the people had repented of their sins. In view of what had taken place on the mountain as Moses acted as intercessor this was a forlorn hope.

Joshua misunderstood the noise coming from the Camp. His thought was that it was the noise of war, a noise with which he was familiar, as he had led the nation in the battle against Amalek (17.8-16). It may be that he considered himself to be needed in the Camp, to direct the warriors in their struggle. The thought of any lesser cause did not occur to him, but Moses understood. This was neither the voice of victory in a battle, nor was it the voice of those who were being overcome; it was the voice of singing. What a contrast with the holy atmosphere on the mountain!

Verses 19-20: The Anger of Moses

As they approached the Camp what a sight met the eyes of the two men. They saw the revelry and the dancing of the people as the golden calf was worshipped. Moses understood the significance of what was before them and his anger was hot. What course of action could he take? To carry the tables of stone into the Camp would surely have meant death to the idolaters.

The two tables were cast to the ground and broken before the eyes of the people (Deut 9.17). What was the significance of this act?

1. It was a sign of the displeasure of Moses. He was the meekest man on the face of the earth, but there was no contradiction of this in the anger which he displayed at the sin of the people. To be angry about sin is to regard it as God does.

2. It was a sign, not only of the anger of Moses, but also of the anger of God. He who broke the tables was the servant of God into whose hands they had been committed, and he was acting in this capacity as he cast them to the ground.

3. It was an indication to the people of the seriousness of their actions. Lest they thought that this was a minor error or a sin that could be excused, they would have impressed on them the dark folly of what they had done.

4. It showed, in memorable fashion, that they had broken the covenant so soon after it had been ratified. They were unfit to be a party to it, the broken tables revealing that their avowal of obedience was empty.

There was nothing wrong or failing in the Law. Paul writes that "the law is holy, and the commandment holy, and just, and good" (Rom 7.12). It was holy, as is God, it was just, in that its demands were not unfair or unrighteous, and it was good, in that to keep it was beneficial. The fault did not lie with the Law, but with the people. Now that it had been given, there could be no excuse of ignorance; sin now became transgression. Each of them would now learn the sad and solemn truth that "in me (that is, in my flesh,) dwelleth no good thing" (Rom 7.18).

The golden calf was taken, burned in the fire, and ground to powder that was scattered on water, which Israel were then made to drink. Moses described his actions in Deuteronomy 9.21: "I took your sin, the calf which ye had made, and burnt it with fire, and stamped it, and ground it very small, even until it was as small as dust: and I cast the dust thereof into the brook that descended out of the mount". This ensured that the gold which had been used to make the idol could be used for no other purpose. It was not fit to be used in the construction of the Tabernacle.

The drinking of the water was an act which was reminiscent of the trial of jealousy (Num 5.11-31) where the woman undergoing the trial had to drink the bitter water. Here the people drank of the stream into which the dust had been cast, symbolic of the fact that the sin was their own; they were part of it and had to bear the consequences of it.

Verses 21-24: Confronting Aaron

The excuse offered by Aaron was shameful, revealing his weakness and lack of strength of character. The blame he placed squarely on the shoulders of the people, refusing to take responsibility for his own actions. The call to Moses to "let not the anger of my lord wax hot" appears to refer to the anger of Moses against him. Moses, he claimed, should have understood why he had acted as he did, for the people "are set on mischief". His argument was that Moses had previously experienced this on a number of occasions, and should have recognised the pressure under which he (Aaron) had been placed.

His failing as a leader was revealed, as it would also be later when Miriam and he spoke against Moses (Num 12.1). He took some of the facts and omitted others. The people had approached him in the manner described in v.1, but he omitted the fact that he had "fashioned" the calf with a graving tool. He spoke accurately of the sin of the people, but overlooked his own major part in it. Rather, he stated, "I cast it into the fire, and there came out this calf". It was an attempt to claim that he could not be faulted for seeing this event as the work of God. The lack of response from Moses shows the contempt with which he treated this excuse.

Verses 25-29: The Challenging Call of Moses
No matter what excuses were offered, the Scriptures reveal the extent of Aaron's sin. Not only were the people naked, but also Aaron had encouraged this shameful behaviour whereby all restraint was cast aside. It has been argued that the term "naked" simply means that they had cast away their gold ornaments, or that they had abandoned their swords and defences, but it is unlikely that the expression can be limited to this. Their condition made them a "shame" (8103) among their enemies, causing them to be treated with scorn and contempt.

Days of crisis are also days of opportunity. Moses stood in the gate of the Camp and issued the challenge, "Who is on the Lord's side?". It was not a call to those who were on Moses' side, but to those who were prepared to stand with the Lord. The tribe of Levi responded to the call. There is no indication that they had stood aloof from the worship of the golden calf, indeed, there is nothing in the narrative to encourage such an assumption. It has already been noted that the opening verses of the chapter indicate that all were involved. The fact that Moses was of the tribe of Levi may have played a part in their decision, but there must also have been repentance for their sin. If their relationship with Moses had been the only factor they would have been rallying to Moses' side and not to the Lord's side. Levi here displayed the features which made the tribe fit to be chosen for the high privileges later enjoyed. What should not be forgotten, however, is that the sovereignty of God is also seen in the marriage of Amram and Jochebed over eighty years previously (see the introductory comments on ch.2).

But this willingness to stand beside Moses was about to be put to the test. It is quite one thing to make such a gesture as Levi made, but quite another to put it into practice and pay the price for the stand which has been taken. To the tribe of Levi now gathered round him, Moses issued the command that they take up their swords and "go in and out from gate to gate throughout the camp" meaning that they had deal with the whole Camp and leave no part untouched. Their purpose was to slay "every man his brother, every man his companion, and every man his neighbour". Three thousand died!

A number of issues are raised by this action. First, why was such a severe punishment meted out? To understand the reason, one has to appreciate the depth of the sin that had been committed. Reference has already been made to this, but the reader must not fall into the trap of considering God's judgment too severe. After the blessing which they had enjoyed, the wonder of the deliverance which had been effected, and the graciousness and bounty of the provision which had met their needs since leaving Egypt, to await Moses' return for forty days was not an onerous demand. Their descent into idolatry with its accompanying scandalous behaviour could only warrant the severest of judgment under the Law which they had willingly accepted, particularly when they had been given the opportunity to repent and declare that they were on the Lord's side. They had to learn the dire consequences of breaking that Law.

The second issue is why just 3,000, and not all of them, were slain. There are a number of possible reasons for this. It could be that the judgment fell on those who were the prime movers behind this idolatrous worship. It was quite possible for 3,000 to persuade the nation, and work on the feelings of concern felt by others. In these days of waiting, during which faithless anxiety may have gripped the hearts of some, here were men who gave them some project in which to become involved, which could be claimed was an act of worship to Jehovah. The second possible reason is that these 3,000 were the most recalcitrant, whereas the others at least had shown some signs of sorrow and repentance. Of these two explanations the former appears to fit the circumstances better, with those who were slain being chosen by the sovereignty of God acting though Levi.

But why did the people not resist? It is probable that they felt weak before Moses and there was no will to resist. He, and the tribe of Levi, had seized the initiative and the people were leaderless as Aaron had denied the part he had played.

In their actions the Levites were to show no partiality. Family relationships were not to be considered, friendships were not to be taken into account, neighbours were to be treated as others. Peter saw clearly that God is no respecter of persons in the bestowal of blessing in the gospel (Acts 10.34), and Paul taught that in His judgment God does not respect persons (Rom 2.11; Col 3.25). This principle the Levites practised as they entered the Camp, it having been emphasised by the words of Moses: "Consecrate yourselves to day to the Lord, even every man upon his son, and upon his brother" (v.29). On this verse Keil & Delitzsch comment: "...it is much better to understand it as indicating the object, 'that every one may be against his son and against his brother;' i.e., that in the cause of the Lord every one may not spare even his nearest relative, but deny either son or brother for the Lord's sake". It cannot be supposed that the Levites entered upon their task with relish; sorrow must have filled their hearts and, doubtless, tears would flow as they bowed to the will of God. God has no pleasure in the death of the wicked (Ezek 33.11), and His servants would have felt likewise. But sin must be judged and this first open rebellion against the Law so recently given was dealt with in a manner which allowed no one to underestimate the attitude of God to sin.

Verses 30-35: The Mediation of Moses

Following the judgment being carried out, Moses now goes up "unto the Lord" with the purpose of making an "atonement" for their sin. This does not mean that Moses considered that any act of his could pay the price for their sin, but rather that he would mediate before the Lord that His anger might be satisfied. The man who called for the Levites to "slay every man his brother" now goes before the Lord to pray for the people.

There is no contradiction between these two stands. The mediator is a righteous man and it was he who commanded that the golden calf be burned and ground to powder; it was his decision to call for those who were on the Lord's side to stand with him and slay the guilty. There is no record of the Lord specifically asking for this action, but Moses understood the action that had to be taken and did not flinch from its execution. It was in accord with the mind of God, else he would have been censured for his "folly". But folly it was not! How good it is when the servants of God are in harmony with the mind of God and act accordingly, no matter how difficult the action proves to be.

Now, however, the other side was seen. The man who ordered the use of the sword now interceded on behalf of the people. So it must be. The believer who stands for truth, and is not prepared to compromise, will also have a heart of love and care for those who oppose. The extent to which he was prepared to go reveals his heart. He confessed their sin and did not minimise it, rather describing it as "a great sin". His desire was that the Lord would forgive their sin. His words show the depth of his feelings: "Yet now, if thou wilt forgive their sin—; and if not...". The sentence is broken off and this is significant, as if he wished to voice quickly the alternative to further punishment being meted out to the people. This alternative was that Moses, and not the people, should be blotted out of God's book. Thus far he was prepared to go, and the statement was sincere. It was not a clumsy attempt to make a good impression; he knew His God better than that. He had walked with Him and talked with Him since He spoke to him out of the burning bush. He was sincere, feeling so deeply for the people that he was prepared to suffer what was due to them that they might continue on their journey in fellowship with their God.

But what did being blotted out of God's book mean? The word "blot" in the Hebrew is first found in Genesis 6.7: "And the Lord said, I will *destroy* man whom I have created from the face of the earth", and its second occurrence is in Genesis 7.4: "For yet seven days, and I will cause it to rain upon the earth forty days and forty nights; and every living substance that I have made will I *destroy* from off the face of the earth". In Numbers 5.23 it is used of in the sense of wiping clean: "And the priest shall write these curses in a book, and he shall *blot them out* with the bitter water". Thus, blotting out is the taking away of the life of an individual with all remembrance of him being removed. In this the sovereign power of God over life and death is seen. This was the length to which Moses was prepared to go, and no further could any mere man go!

But the Lord would not have Moses blotted out. The people would still be required to suffer, but the Lord took account of Moses' appeal and would permit the people to commence the journey to Canaan. Their sin, however, could not be overlooked and it would be visited on them in the days that lay ahead. When judgment fell the Lord would take their sin on this occasion into account. The closing verse of the chapter, "And the Lord plagued the people, because they made the calf, which Aaron made", may refer to a specific plague which was visited on them, or to the judgment of God which fell upon them as they journeyed through the wilderness. Even in this last comment, the accuracy of Scripture can be seen. The responsibility is placed squarely on the shoulders of the people and on those of Aaron, for it was the calf that "Aaron made".

EXODUS 33

Moses Continues to Mediate

Verses 1-3: The Command to Go

The people had not been brought back into the enjoyment of the privileges which they had forfeited through their sin. They were still in the position into which they had brought themselves, having broken the conditions of the covenant. The mediation of Moses had been effective in that the Lord now commanded His servant to take the nation into Canaan; He will fulfil the promises that were made to Abraham, Isaac, and Jacob, and will give them the land flowing with milk and honey. There was, however, one significant change. The Lord will not go with them! If He did so, their conduct would result in their being consumed in judgment. They were not fit for His presence. He will send an angel to lead them and will drive out the enemies who oppose them; the promises will be kept, but the choicest privilege has been lost. The distance that now separates them from the Lord is emphasised by His words to Moses: "…the people which *thou* hast brought up out of the land of Egypt".

Let this not be underestimated. It may be argued that because they will enter Canaan and enjoy the milk and honey of that bountiful land little had been lost. Such an argument misses the vital point that the presence of the Lord in their midst was the greatest honour which they enjoyed. This was the purpose of their deliverance, not just that they would enjoy the good things which He would bestow upon them, but that they would have the power of His presence, the privilege of close fellowship with Him, and would give Him the delight of their love and fellowship. But just as the Lord Jesus "ordained twelve that they should be with him" (Mk 3.14), so the Lord desired that Israel should be with Him, and, should this not be, He would lose that fellowship with them that He sought to enjoy. Their failure, therefore, would not only rob themselves, but would rob Him.

The importance of this must not be lost on the reader. It is possible to be saved but to pursue a manner of life that causes the loss of close fellowship with the Lord. Careless of such a loss because of the knowledge that salvation is enjoyed and guaranteed is a poor response to the One who has brought salvation. What loss can be seen in the life of "just" Lot (2 Pet 2.7), who, although he "vexed his righteous soul from day to day" (2 Pet 2.8), and was preserved from losing his life in the overthrow of Sodom and Gomorrah, nevertheless ended his days in ignominy. He did not enjoy the close fellowship with the Lord which Abraham knew. That fellowship is the most precious blessing possessed by a believer, and it is delicate flower. Losing it can be the result of an act of impulse carried out in a moment. Because recovery is possible for the Christian does not mean that such a loss should be taken lightly.

Verses 4-6: The People Mourn

The realisation that the Lord would not be with them caused the people to mourn. Coates comments: "If God's people find that He is not with them it is well to mourn. To take the low place is always open to them, and it is the first step to blessing". Now they had taken that first step. It is a cause of sorrow to be guilty of sin and yet to refuse to take the low place, as there is no sin committed which does not require humility and confession before the Lord.

No ornaments (5716) are put on; this is not a time for decoration or festivity; it is a time for mourning and repentance. The command to do so came from the Lord and they obeyed. They had taken some of these ornaments and used them in the making of the golden calf, but what is referred to here goes further than their earrings etc. All the trappings of decoration in their dress had to be put aside as there was nothing that could make them more attractive to the Lord. They had to be before Him as they were! Today the principle holds good. In the presence of God decorations of any kind are irrelevant. Any attempt to be attractive to the Lord on the basis of the outward decorations of the flesh, no matter what form that takes, is unacceptable to Him.

But putting off the ornaments was accompanied with mourning (56). This is the second use of the word in Scripture, it first being used of Jacob's mourning for Joseph: "And Jacob rent his clothes, and put sackcloth upon his loins, and *mourned* for his son many days" (Gen 37.34). The use of it in describing the condition of Israel as they stood, bereft of their ornaments, before the Lord, is a figurative way of describing the deep sorrow of their hearts. Due to a short time of godless idolatry and licence they had lost the presence of the Lord who had given them so much. So they stand waiting His judgment. Dennett comments: "It is a striking, if solemn, scene - the people stripped of their adornments, awaiting the judgment pronounced in bitterness and sorrow of heart; and the Lord pausing before the blow is struck".

The words of the Lord must have come to them with fearful force. His reason for not going with them was that their conduct was so sinful that His judgment would be bound to fall upon them if He was present in their midst. The withdrawal of His presence would mean that the glory cloud and fire would no longer be with them; an angel would lead, but the very existence of such a guide would be a constant reminder of this dark event and the loss which they had suffered.

Verses 7-8: A Tabernacle Pitched

Two things must be noted regarding the tabernacle which Moses now pitched outside the Camp. First, this is not the Tabernacle, the pattern of which was given to Moses when he was up the mount, for that had not yet been made. Speculation that this passage is placed at this point out of chronological order is clearly unacceptable. This tabernacle was a tent erected by Moses to be a meeting place between God and those of Israel who sought Him. Second, this tabernacle was pitched outside the Camp, whereas the Tabernacle which would later be erected was placed in the midst of the Camp. Moses is sensitive to the position in which the nation has placed itself. He remembered well the words of the Lord as the instructions for the Tabernacle were given to him: "…let them make me a sanctuary; that I may dwell among them" (25.8). Now it was not possible for Him to dwell among them and this tabernacle must be pitched outside the Camp.

They were not now to enjoy being the Lord's people grouped round His dwelling place; no longer to have Him as the centre. Those who sought Him must do so now individually and to do so they must go outside the Camp, outside a Camp that has been defiled by sin. Those who travelled outside the Camp to seek the Lord were moving out in separation to Him. Where they stood revealed their condition; only outside was He to be found.

And so those who sought Him went out to the tabernacle pitched outside the Camp. It would appear, however, that not many did so because when Moses went out to the tabernacle, "all the people rose up, and stood every man at his tent door". Israel were now divided into two distinct groups, those who were prepared to go outside the Camp, and those who remained in the Camp by their tents, even although they had a desire to worship.

There is a solemn warning to be heeded. Here there are people who have enjoyed the presence of the Lord and have now been given, through Moses, teaching regarding the building of the Tabernacle to be His dwelling place in the midst of them. Unspeakable blessing indeed! But this privilege they have forfeited, and the Camp is no longer fit for His presence. The sad possibility is that it is possible to belong to a group of Christians who gather as a local assembly, but who lose the enjoyment of His presence in the midst. Let all take heed. If the happy condition exists that there is a sense of the presence of God in the gatherings let that be jealously guarded, and let all beware of the subtlety of the Adversary who will seek to bring about conditions where He cannot dwell.

One final point cannot be missed. What of the people who remained in the Camp? What a scene it must have been as Moses left the Camp and went out to the tabernacle. The whole Camp watched in expectation; they stood at their tent doors watching the departing figure as he entered the tabernacle. They had an interest in divine things and wished to see what would take place. Some of them may even have been fearful as to what the Lord would now do. They had all mourned and put away their ornaments, but their affection for the Lord was not strong enough to attract them "outside the camp". Where they stood revealed their heart condition. No matter what claim they might make, their actions spoke louder. Once again, let all take heed. To be saved by His grace and power, to enjoy the blessing which He bestows and yet not truly to seek His presence is a sad condition which yields no joy. Thus they stood, still inside the Camp.

Verses 9-11: The Lord Speaks to Moses

As Moses entered the tabernacle a cloudy pillar descended and stood at the door, signifying the presence of God. In the Camp of Israel the meaning of this was clearly understood and everyone bowed and worshipped. Those standing at their tent doors may not have gone outside the Camp to the tabernacle, but they did understand that the Lord was present there, and they worshipped.

Inside the tabernacle the Lord spoke with Moses "face to face, as a man speaketh unto his friend". There is no record in Scripture of any other occasion when the Lord spoke to a man like this. "Face to face" indicates that the Lord did not speak from a distance; He did not call out of heaven, but rather He came right to where Moses was and spoke as one would speak to a friend. To other prophets the Lord would speak in a vision, in a dream, and in dark speeches, but to Moses "mouth to mouth" (Num 12.8). By referring to this the Lord declared to Miriam and Aaron, at the point when they spoke against their brother, the unique position enjoyed by Moses. To the people who stood by their tents on this solemn occasion it would but emphasise the privileges forfeited by their conduct. When the Lord did speak to Moses in this way He appeared to him in the "similitude of the Lord" (Num 12.8). Moses did not see the essential glory of the Lord for "no man hath seen God at any time" (Jn 1.18), but he did see the form in which the Lord chose to reveal Himself.

After Moses returned to the Camp Joshua remained in the tabernacle. This may indicate that the tent was divided into two sections and that Moses had gone into the inner section to speak to the Lord, while Joshua remained in the outer. This reveals three things about Joshua. First, he had been one of those who had gone outside the Camp with Moses to seek the Lord. Second, the fact that he remained behind indicated that he wished to enjoy the presence of the Lord, not in as close and intimate a manner as that enjoyed by Moses, but nevertheless his desire was to be where the Lord was to be found. Third, his purpose may have been to act as a guard so that the tabernacle would not become an object of curiosity. It is of interest that Joshua is noted here as being a young man, showing that it is possible for those who are young to love the presence of God and be aware of the responsibilities which are linked with that. How young he was is not stated, but Caleb who was one of his fellow spies in the journey into Canaan was forty years of age at that time, which was probably about one year after the golden calf incident, and it is likely that Joshua would be of a similar age group.

Verses 12-23: Moses Mediates Further

It is generally supposed that what took place here between the Lord and Moses occurred after Moses left the tabernacle, returned to the Camp, and then went out again to the tabernacle where was the waiting Joshua. While that may be, it appears to the writer more likely that this was what took place between the Lord and Moses when he entered into the tabernacle (v.9) and the Lord spoke with him face to face. Having completed the account of that visit the narrative now turns to consider what took place inside the tabernacle.

Moses' entreaty (vv. 12-13)

The first issue brought before the Lord by Moses was that he had been told to bring the people into Canaan and yet the Lord had not revealed to him who the Lord would send with him. It had already been told him that the Lord would not go with them and that an angel would accompany them (vv.1-2), but Moses sought more than this. This was despite the fact that the Lord had stated that He knew Moses by name, a declaration by the Lord which had not been previously revealed in Scripture, and that Moses had found grace in His sight. The first of these statements revealed that Moses had been recognised by the Lord as His and had been set apart for a special service. It was recognition of the intimacy of the relationship that existed, a relationship that allowed him the privilege of having greater insight into what the Lord intended for the journey to Canaan. But the Lord had also stated that Moses had found grace in His sight, and that He had acted on this basis in the past in the service that He had committed to him and in the revelation that he had been given.

Moses' entreaty is now made on this basis. In the intercession in ch.32 the ground on which Moses appealed was the promises of God to Israel and the relationship which He had established with the nation. Now he entreats on the basis of his own relationship with the Lord. The argument was that since he had found favour in the sight of the Lord would He now reveal to His servant the way by which he would travel to Canaan? If the Lord had raised him up to be His servant and the leader of the people could He now reveal to him the pathway ahead? This nation was the Lord's; they were His people, and He must, therefore, lead them and guide them. In this way the Lord would show that Moses had still found grace in His sight, and he states that by this he will "know" the Lord. To "know" the Lord is to see Him working; to see His promises being fulfilled and His purpose being worked out; this would be evidence of the favour of God to His servant and proof of the reality of what the Lord had said.

The reader will be struck by the boldness of Moses' words. They were not spoken in arrogance, nor were they voiced in the demanding tones of defiance. They were the words of a servant to his master, taking up what the Lord had said, asking Him to fulfil His word.

What lessons there are here for the intercessor! The first necessity is to know the Scriptures and have an intelligent understanding of the promises of God. No excuses were made for sin, no attempt was made to justify failure, but the Lord would receive the plea based on His promises to His own and He will fulfil these promises. To the people there were no soothing words; their sin was judged but their faithlessness would be met by His faithfulness.

The promise of God (vv.14-17)
To Moses the words now spoken by the Lord must have been sweet indeed. The Lord will go with them and will give them rest by bringing them into the land promised to Abraham. Moses would rather that there was no movement of the people if the Lord was not with them. Better not to travel than to travel alone. If they went alone there would be no evidence of the people having found favour in His sight. With the Lord they will be a unique people, separated out from all other nations, the only people blessed in this favoured way.

It must not be thought that the intercession of Moses was necessary because the Lord was reluctant to go with Israel and had to be persuaded to change His plans. Moses did not argue so persuasively before the Lord that He agreed to fulfil the promise which He had decided to set aside. The process was, rather, a test for Moses in which he displayed the true nature of intercession. It was an opportunity for him to show what understanding he had of the Lord and of His word. Moses understood, and the people must understand, that the presence of God in their midst was not because they deserved it, nor because of their faithfulness to Him, but because of His grace to the undeserving in keeping His word.

Show me thy glory (v.18)
But Moses desired to see more: "Show me thy glory". Did ever one ask for more; did ever one yearn for more than this? To see in all its eternal and essential beauty the glory of the Lord and behold what man had never seen before! "I beseech (4994) thee", he cried just as he had done before: "I pray (4994) thee...show me now thy way" (v.13). Of his God there is nothing that he does not want to know, and to see that glory would be an honour indeed. Law writes, "The suppliant here is Moses. He thirsts for a clearer knowledge of God. He has seen much, and therefore burns for more. He cries, 'I beseech Thee, shew me Thy glory'. It is a large desire. But gracious souls crave all that God can give".

But God is the One "dwelling in the light which no man can approach unto; whom no man hath seen, nor can see" (1 Tim 6.16). Keil & Delitzsch write: "No mortal man can see the face of God and remain alive; for not only is the holy God a consuming fire to unholy man, but a limit has been set, in and with...the earthly and physical body of man, between the infinite God, the absolute Spirit, and the human spirit clothed in an earthly body...which...renders a direct sight of the glory of God impossible. As our bodily eye is dazzled, and its power of vision destroyed, by looking directly at the brightness of the sun, so would our whole nature be

destroyed by an unveiled sight of the brilliancy of the glory of God". Some
English versions of the Septuagint read: "Show me Thyself". This is what
was involved in the request of Moses; he wished to see the Lord Himself,
not as He chooses to reveal Himself, but as He is essentially. Moses' desire
is that without veil and without similitude he should see the Lord Himself
as He is.

All my goodness (vv.19-20)

In response the Lord told Moses, first that he would see His goodness.
It should be recognised that this did not take place until ch.34. In reading
of what the Lord would reveal it must be confessed that it is not possible
to put into words what was seen on that day. It was a sight of perfect
beauty; an unfolding of absolute moral purity. It was a visual summing up
of all that God is which had been directed for the good of His creatures.
Moses would not see the glory of God but he would see, in a manner
determined by the Lord, His goodness, which had been enjoyed by His
people. To Moses He would also "proclaim the name of the Lord". In this
way there would be seen all His attributes as Jehovah, again in a manner
not here described, but determined by the Lord. The use of "proclaim"
indicates that as the goodness of the Lord is passing before Moses the
Lord will declare His name, so that Moses will hear the word of God
declaring what is involved in the name, Jehovah.

Having revealed to Moses what He will do, the Lord now declared,
"I…will be gracious to whom I will be gracious, and will shew mercy to
whom I will shew mercy". It should not be thought strange that this is
introduced here, because it is not only one of the attributes of the Lord to
act as He will, it is also in this particular situation the reason why Moses
will be allowed to see His goodness. In general, therefore, the Lord will be
gracious and show mercy to whom He will. In His sovereignty the cause is
not in anyone or anything else, but in Himself. This is quoted by Paul (Rom
9.15) when dealing with the question, "Is there unrighteousness with God?"
in showing mercy and compassion to some. There is not, for what God
determines in His sovereignty cannot be unrighteous.

With regard to Israel, what Moses would see of the mercy and
compassion of the Lord is here explained. The grace extended to this
people is not because of their worth, and the fact that the Lord has declared
that He will go with them in accord with the intercession of Moses is not
because they have earned this grace.

What cannot be allowed is for Moses to see the face of God, for no man
can do this and live. God is a spirit and when He speaks to Moses of "my
face" it is expressing for man what cannot be expressed otherwise. To see
His face is to see Him closely, to be before someone with nothing between
which prevents a full view. To see His face would be to see His glory. This
differs from God speaking to Moses "face to face" (v.11) where, as has
been noted, it is God speaking directly and not through visions or dreams.

There it is direct communication, but with no thought of a full view of God. Here it is a full, direct view of God's glory that has been requested, something that Moses did not see when he spoke to God "face to face", and which no man can see.

In the cleft of the rock (vv.21-23)

Now the Lord tells him how He will show him His glory. Care must be taken here, because the glory that will be shown to Moses is not that which he initially requested. "All His goodness" is here described as "my glory". There is no inconsistency in this because the Lord is glorious and that glory is in every feature and attribute. But even that which Moses had the privilege of seeing could not be viewed without Moses being placed safely in the cleft of the rock. To stand in full view of what the Lord was about to reveal was not possible.

Moses was to be protected in two ways. He was to be placed in the cleft of a rock, and when the glory passed before him the Lord would cover him with His hand. Only the "back parts" were to be seen. Merrill states, "Though Moses was not allowed to see directly the full undiminished glory of God (His face) - because he was positioned within the cleft of the rock (v.22) - he did see the so called afterglow of the divine splendour - the 'back' view of God".

Seeing God

The desire of Moses is one that has occupied the hearts of many of the servants of the Lord down through the ages. What a joy it is, therefore, to read the words of John that "the only begotten Son, which is in the bosom of the Father, he hath declared him" (Jn 1.18). It was not possible for Moses to see the face of God, but the book of Revelation reveals that "his servants shall serve him: And they shall see his face" (22.3-4). The glory of God could not be seen in the cleft of the rock, but again John writes, "(and we beheld his glory, the glory of the only begotten of the Father,) full of grace and truth" (Jn 1.14). God is revealed in the Lord Jesus, who is co-equal with the Father, eternal in His being, the uncreated Christ. Through Him God is revealed in all His fullness, for "it pleased the Father that in him should all fullness dwell" (Col 1.19), and "in him dwelleth all the fullness of the Godhead bodily" (Col 2.9).

> Thou art the Everlasting Word,
> The Father's only Son,
> God manifestly seen and heard,
> And heaven's Beloved One.
>
> Worthy, O Lamb of God, art Thou,
> That every knee to Thee should bow.
> (Josiah Conder)

EXODUS 34

The Covenant Renewed

Verses 1-3: The Call to Ascend the Mount

Effectively the Lord had agreed to the renewal of the covenant at 33.14 when He stated that His presence would go with them. Now the renewal takes place. Moses is told to hew two tables of stone similar to those given to him by the Lord (24.12). These tables, unlike the first two, which were prepared by the Lord and given to Moses, have to be hewn by Moses and brought up to the mount. This does not indicate that the Lord was displeased with Moses and, as a result, demanded that he make good what he had destroyed. The anger of the Lord was directed against the people, not against His servant Moses. Rather, the hewing of the two stones by Moses seems to indicate that as he had successfully interceded with the Lord on behalf of the people he would have this part to play in bringing the terms of the covenant back to the people. This did not constitute a censure of his behaviour; rather it was an added privilege because of his faithfulness.

It should be noted that the word "hew" (6458) does not indicate a roughly hewn stone. It is used of the process of carving or shaping with a graving tool and would create a well-produced stone suitable to show clearly the words that would be written on it.

What would be written was that which had been written on the first two. The behaviour of the people had not lowered the standards of the Law. It is not negotiable, and does not change in response to the whims of sinful hearts. There are times when the lawmakers of nations change their laws, not because a particular law is faulty, but because it is not possible to impose it, due to its being disregarded by so many. God's Law is not like that; the worship of the golden calf did not change the commandment, "Thou shalt have no other gods before me" (20.3).

On the morning on which Moses was to present himself before the Lord he was to come alone with no other man on the mount and the flocks and herds were to be kept well back. Here Moses would be alone with God. The solemnity of the giving of the Law the first time was to mark it also on this occasion. If there was no lowering of its terms, there was no less solemnity about its giving. These lessons the nation must learn.

Verses 4-7: The Lord Proclaims His Name

Did the people view Moses as he hewed the two tables of stone? Scripture does not give an answer to that question, but, if they did, what thoughts were in their hearts? Would they be anxious that the Law might have changed, not to reduce its claims, but to increase them. However, if the standards of His Law cannot be reduced, neither can they be increased. "The law is holy, and the commandment holy, and just, and good" (Rom 7.12); there can be no higher standard of holiness.

There was no reluctance on the part of Moses as he rose early in the morning and went up Mount Sinai, his obedience noted by the words, "as the Lord had commanded him". On the mount "the Lord descended...and stood with him". Note the beauty of this touch. The Lord stood with Moses, almost as if to give him confidence that the disobedience of the people and the re-institution of the covenant did not affect the closeness with the Lord enjoyed by Moses.

Now the Lord passed before him. This is what the Lord had promised in ch.33; He will proclaim His name (see 33.19). The name to be proclaimed was "Jehovah", and in that proclamation the attributes revealed by the Lord in that name were spoken. It is worth quoting all that was proclaimed: "The Lord, The Lord God, merciful and gracious, longsuffering, and abundant in goodness and truth, Keeping mercy for thousands, forgiving iniquity and transgression and sin, and that will by no means clear the guilty; visiting the iniquity of the fathers upon the children, and upon the children's children, unto the third and to the fourth generation".

Jehovah

The mention of the name twice does not constitute a double name. The first mention of Jehovah is as a heading to what follows. The significance of this name has been dealt with when considering 3.14, but it is worth adding the comment of Law concerning this name: "Jehovah. Oh! Wondrous sound! It casts the mind back through the ages of eternity gone by; it bears it forward through eternity to come. It loudly tells that through the past, the present and the future, One is...It robes Him in all the majesty, dignity, and grandeur, and boundlessness of changeless unity. It exhibits Him, as the sole fount of every stream of life. O my soul, such is your Lord".

The Lord God

This is the name "El" (410) added to "Jehovah". "El" is first used in connection with Melchizedek: "And Melchizedek king of Salem brought forth bread and wine: and he was the priest of the most high *God*" (Gen 14.18). TWOT at 93a comments: "A study of the various accompanying descriptions of El where the name occurs in Scripture leads to the rather solid conclusion that, from the beginning of the use of this term in Scripture, it was intended to distinguish the true El (God) from all false uses of that name found in other Semitic cultures". But this God is not a remote deity, distant from men and women. He is El Bethel, the God of Bethel (Gen 31.13); the God (El) of thy father (Gen 49.25). The name is found over 230 times in the Old Testament.

Merciful

"Merciful" (from 7355) has in it the thought of compassion, pity, love, and care for the individual. Merrill comments that it "has a wide range of meanings: parental love/affection towards one's children, pity shown to the orphan, compassion for those in need, and mercy for those who deserve judgment-the most appropriate nuance here...The unrepentant and the obstinate are not shown compassion, but are judged". Israel would enjoy the benefit of this attribute because the sin that had been committed deserved the judgment of God. The intercession of Moses and the repentance of the people, however, enabled God to be compassionate towards them. This compassion is described by the Psalmist, writing of the days of Israel in the wilderness: "But he, being full of *compassion*, forgave their iniquity, and destroyed them not: yea, many a time turned he his anger away, and did not stir up all his wrath" (Ps 78.38).

Gracious

"Gracious" (2587) is often linked together with "merciful". Of the thirteen times it is used, only once does it stand on its own without the link with "merciful". TWOT at 694 states that "The verb (from which this adjective comes) depicts a heartfelt response by someone who has something to give to one who has a need... the verb describes an action from a superior to an inferior who has no real claim for gracious treatment". It is clear, therefore, that those who are privileged to enjoy the gracious acts of God can claim no right to be so treated. Their actions make them deserving of judgment, but God, because of His own character, displays His grace to them. Merrill adds that the gracious acts of God "are (1) acts done gratuitously (2 Sam 24.24; 1 Chr 21.24), (2) without taking compensation (Gen 29.15: Ex 21.2,11)...(3) without cause, undeservedly (1 Sam 19.5; 25.31)".

It is not possible to consider this word without thought being given to the grace of God found in the New Testament, extended to undeserving sinners. "For the grace of God that bringeth salvation hath appeared to all men" (Tit 2.11). The greatest expression of this grace was the coming into the world of the Lord Jesus and His death on the Cross. It is this grace that has brought salvation to all men, and has made it available to all, but note that Paul adds, "Teaching us that, denying ungodliness and worldly lusts...". Salvation has been made available to all men but only those who respond to the grace of God are taught. Others fail to respond and therefore do not learn.

Longsuffering

The two words which make up "longsuffering" (750; 639) mean literally that God is "long of nose". They are also found in Numbers 14.18 and Psalm 86.15. Merrill states that "An angry person often expresses himself through flared or blood flushed nostrils...When used of divine anger 'nose, nostril' is clearly anthropomorphic, picturing God flaring His nostrils, breathing out fire. In keeping with this imagery, the oft repeated idiom 'long nostrils' refers to someone who restrains his anger rather than being quick to anger, hence 'slow to anger'…This idiom describes…divine patience".

It should not be thought that the longsuffering of God is due to the fact that He overlooks sin, or that He is weak in judgment. It is exercised to allow men and women time to repent from their sins because the Lord is not hasty in judgment. Ultimately, to the unrepentant sinner that judgment will come, but it will never be able to be claimed that there was no opportunity to repent from sin.

This longsuffering is seen in many ways. The years that were given to a rebellious world when Noah preached (Gen 6.3) right through to, and beyond, the "space to repent" given to "that woman Jezebel" in the church at Thyatira (Rev 2.21), are markers of a line of God's longsuffering forbearance which stretches through the Word of God. To the sinner today who refuses the grace of God in the gospel, that same longsuffering is extended, and let no one think that the judgment of God will not fall because it seems to be long in coming. Longsuffering is not a sign of divine weakness; it is a sign of God's grace.

Abundant

This word (7227) is used to describe the goodness and truth of the Lord. God is never miserly in His giving, nor are His attributes possessed in mean quantity. He is an abundant God who gives liberally. The word is used in the Psalms of the mercy of God (86.5,15; 103.8). This abundance of His goodness is seen in the parable of the Good Samaritan who "poured" oil and wine into the wounds of the injured man (Lk 10.34). That which was necessary to ease the pain and heal the wounds was not given in a grudging manner. The "pouring in" denotes an abundance of giving which was also seen in his dealings with the host at the inn, leaving sufficient to cover all bills but promising more if it was necessary.

Further examples of the abundance that marks Him are the baskets which were filled after thousands had been fed, and the liberal giving to all men of which James writes (Jas 1.5). So rich and beneficent is He that it can truly be said that those who enjoy His bounty are overwhelmed by His abundance.

Goodness

The word for "goodness" (2617) has been translated in a number of ways including, for this verse, "steadfast love" (RSV), and "kindness" (YLT). It describes stability, reliability, and dependability that are constant, not changing at any time. Those who trust Him can rely on this - as that which they enjoy of His attributes is dependable in a world that lacks that quality. The Psalmist puts it well when he writes, "the *goodness* of God endureth continually (Ps 52.1). The translation used often is "mercy", and it is this which Psalm 136 notes with the repetition on twenty-six occasions that this mercy "endureth for ever". Micah delights in it when he writes, "Who is a God like unto thee, that pardoneth iniquity, and passeth by the transgression of the remnant of his heritage? he retaineth not his anger for ever, because he delighteth in *mercy*" (Mic 7.18).

The use of the word here certainly includes the thought of that goodness which pardons, as Israel would understand following the golden calf idolatry.

Truth

Truth (571) denotes faithfulness, verity, and reality. Merrill states, "In contrast to fickle humans whose faithfulness is transient and fleeting (Hos 6.5-6), God's faithfulness is enduring and steadfast - permanent, certain and everlasting. The faithfulness of God endures forever". Truth is that which is by its nature unchangeable, for what is true today is true tomorrow. Paul, writing to Titus, who was resident on the island of Crete (Tit 1.5), emphasises that the hope of eternal life, which is in the gospel, comes from "God, that cannot lie" (Tit 1.2). This is particularly important as Titus was working in a society which in these days was marked by the absence of truth: "One of themselves, even a poet of their own, said, The Cretians are always liars…" (Tit 1.12). The Lord Jesus stated that He is the truth (Jn 14.6), and the Holy Spirit is named as the Spirit of Truth (Jn 14.17; 15.26; 16.13). Speaking to the Father, the Lord Jesus says, "Thy word is truth" (Jn 17.17).

Keeping mercy

Keeping (5341) "is the concept of guarding with fidelity" (TWOT at 1407), and mercy (2617) is kindness that is linked here to the forgiveness of the sins of the people. It should be noted that this mercy is not limited to a few but is directed to "thousands". Let Law speak of this: "O my soul, hearken unto the melody of this sweet note. The thought may sometimes rise, that mercy visits but a favoured few; - that the rare gift enriched but rare souls. Nay, mercy's arms are very wide. Mercy's heart is very large. Mercy's mansions are very many. It has brought saving joy to countless multitudes. It has saving joy for countless yet".

Forgiving

The concept behind this word is that of bearing as a burden. Merrill notes that "When a person is the subject, it means 'to bear one's sin', that is, to incur guilt, bear the responsibility, or suffer the punishment of sin…However, when God is the subject it means 'to take away sin', that is, to forgive sin". As a result of the intercession of Moses, God would take away the sin of many in Israel, although the leaders of this shameful idolatry would be required to bear the consequences of their own sin. It must be kept before the reader that this forgiveness is based on the repentance of those who, although they have sinned, love Jehovah - "shewing mercy unto thousands of them that love me, and keep my commandments" (20.6).

Iniquity

This word is linked with transgression and sin as comprising that which Jehovah forgives. It is not, therefore, unreasonable to conclude that the three words make up the total body of actions which are sinful and for which sinners will bear judgment unless they repent and enjoy the forgiveness of God. Iniquity (1577) has the meaning of distorting, bending, or twisting. By such actions the Law was twisted, perverted, or distorted and the person responsible was required to bear the guilt which was a consequence. It is this that is visited on the children of the third and fourth generations of them that hate Him (20.5).

Transgression

Transgression (6588) has the meaning of rebellion, of breaking a law, or of revolt against authority. Every act of transgression, therefore, is an act of rebellion against God; it is the breaking of His Law and refusal to acknowledge His authority. It reminds the reader that men and women are not free agents owing no allegiance to a higher authority. In this present age, where all forms of authority are challenged and rebellion against rule is rampant, mankind refuses to acknowledge the ultimate authority of God, for there is no-one higher than He.

It is worth noting in passing that the wide-spread acceptance of the Theory of Evolution is partly based on the fact that it gives no place to God, allowing man to deny the existence of a higher authority to whom he is responsible. Where there is no authority there is no law-giver, no law claiming man's obedience, no upholder of that law, no judgment for breaking it, no possibility of transgressing, and no court to face. Man can do as he will as he is the most intelligent of the "evolved" species and answers to no-one but himself. Happy are those who spurn such ignoble teaching and gladly acknowledge that "The Lord reigneth" (Ps 93.1). As He reigns He has authority, and blessed are those who acknowledge this truth.

Sin

Sin is the word most used in Scripture to denote disobedience to God. It bears the meaning of missing the mark, or missing the path and by doing so to travel by another way. It should not be thought that this is merely an unintentional missing of the mark, or missing the path due to ignorance or lack of directions. It is a deliberate act that is offensive to God. TWOT at 638 states that "The verb has the connotation of breach of civil law, i.e. failure to live up to expectations", and, "In so acting, man is missing the goal or standard God has for him, is failing to observe the requirements of holy living, or falls short of spiritual wholeness".

That will by no means clear the guilty

Lest what has gone before causes the reader to think that grace annuls all guilt unconditionally for all, this statement confirms that the guilty will not go unpunished. The question is, "Who are the guilty?", because all have committed sin. It must be read, however, in light of what has gone before, that the Lord will forgive iniquity, transgression, and sin. His judgment, however, will fall on those who refuse to repent. To "clear" (5352) has the meaning of being clean and pure. TWOT at 1412 states that "The release from obligation or from guilt/punishment...is often presented as being determined by the Lord". Thus what is in view here is the release from the guilt and punishment due because of sin.

Visiting the iniquity of the fathers...

This warning was clearly given in the Law (20.5). Note was taken there as to its significance, but it is of value to re-state it. The children, and the children's children will experience the effects of the sins of the fathers. This may be seen in the circumstances through which the family passes, it may be seen in hereditary features and characteristics, it may result in material loss; the Lord does not state how this will be brought about, but is warning that He will deal in this way. This is not a question of salvation - the opportunity to be saved is not withheld because of the sins of previous generations - but it does mean that the consequences of the actions of fathers and grandfathers may reach down to succeeding generations.

Verses 8-9: The Response of Moses

Little wonder that Moses bowed his head and worshipped. The name "Jehovah" had been declared to him and once again he acted as an intercessor on behalf of the people. "Let my Lord, I pray thee, go among us". The Lord had stated that He would go with Israel (33.14) and it may appear that here Moses is repeating the request that the Lord go with them, looking for further confirmation on the basis of what had been revealed to him. If the Lord is a forgiving God, let Him be with this stiff-necked people. That may be true, but it appears that there is more to this request. The word "among" must be noted. The last time it was used the Lord had said, "I will come up *into the midst* of thee in a moment, and consume thee" (33.5). Among them, because of their sin, He would judge them. Now Moses does not only wish to see the Lord *with* them, he wishes to see Him *among* them. He could be with them but not in the midst of them. Moses entreats the Lord to come amongst them, in the midst of them, central to their life, testimony, and worship.

But Moses is careful to say, "Let my Lord, I pray thee, go among *us*". He is particular not to separate himself from the people, even although they were rebellious. This true intercessor identifies himself with Israel, even although he had been absent when the golden calf was made. They were indeed a stiff-necked people, but the declaration that he had heard assured him that the Lord could forgive. Note that it was *our* iniquity and *our* sin which required forgiveness; again there is identification with the people. In the presence of God he made no attempt to prove himself holier than they were, but with humility used the word "our". The Lord knows the hearts; He understood that Moses was not party to what had taken place, but nevertheless He would be content that His servant did not have a high regard for himself.

The appeal ends with the request that Israel be taken as the inheritance of Jehovah. This does not refer to the possession of Canaan, but to the fact that the nation itself was to be His inheritance - see Deuteronomy 9.26: "I prayed therefore unto the Lord, and said, O Lord God, destroy not thy people and thine inheritance".

Verses 10-17: The Covenant Renewed

The intercession of Moses has brought about the desired effect and the Lord confirms the terms of the covenant. There are two issues addressed, the first of which is found in these verses, and deals with the relationship between Israel and the Canaanites. The promise of the Lord is that He will do marvels such as had not been done on earth before in that he will drive out the inhabitants of Canaan before Israel. These nations were not weak, ineffective, primitive tribes. They were powerful peoples, exemplified by the strong fortifications at Jericho. They were a commercial people, trading with nations such as Babylon. It was a Babylonish garment that attracted the attention of Achan at the fall of Jericho (Josh 7.21). Their wealth was confirmed by the silver and gold vessels which were found in that city. Yet these nations were to be driven out by a people who, on leaving Egypt, may have been regarded by some as unruly and rebellious slaves. Subsequent events, however, caused even Jericho to fear Israel (Josh 2.9-10).

There was to be no covenant made with the inhabitants of Canaan for this would constitute a severe danger to Israel. To leave any of these peoples amongst them would be a snare, or a trap, to Israel and would lead to the worship of the gods of the Canaanites. Just as there had been no compromise in the great struggle that had taken place between Jehovah and the gods of Egypt, so there must be no compromise between Israel and Canaan. It was this command that was broken when "a league" was made with the Gibeonites (Josh 9.1-21) who approached Israel under false pretences. Nevertheless, the agreement had been made and could not be broken. In making them hewers of wood and drawers of water Joshua was, amongst others things, seeking to reduce their influence in Israel to a minimum.

It should be noted that, although the gods of Egypt had been defeated and their weakness publicly displayed, another idol system had to be met in Canaan. No matter how great the victory won, the devil will marshal his forces to attack again. He is relentless in his pursuit of God's people and in his determination to destroy their enjoyment of the Lord.

To defeat this new danger the altars and idols of Canaan were to be completely destroyed, their images and groves to be removed. To have them there would eventually lead to them developing into objects of worship, and Israel would become like the Canaanites, inter-marrying with them and destroying the unique identity of the nation. This idol worship is called "a whoring after their gods" and Keil & Delitzsch comment that "The use of the expression 'go a whoring' in a spiritual sense, in relation to idolatry, is to be accounted for on the ground, that the religious fellowship of Israel with Jehovah was a covenant resembling the marriage tie; and we meet with it for the first time, here, immediately after the formation of this covenant between Israel and Jehovah". It is against that background that the Lord declares that He is a jealous God, as Israel in worshipping idols would be guilty of spiritual adultery.

The final command in this connection is that they should make no molten God. This they had done with the golden calf, and lest they seek to justify idolatry by refraining from the worship of the idols of Canaan and yet make their own, this warning is included. They had come from Egypt still retaining in their minds thoughts of Egyptian deities, proving this as they cried to Aaron, "Make us gods" (32.1). In future, that conduct must not be repeated. It should not be overlooked, however, that until they were carried captive to Babylon the worship of false gods was a recurring problem in Israel. Let all believers today heed the warning of John: "Little children, keep yourselves from idols" (1 Jn 5.21).

Verses 18-26: Further Terms of the Covenant

Having dealt with the first issue, which was that of their relationship with the Canaanites, the Lord now turns to deal with their responsibilities under the covenant. These have already been laid out but are brought before Israel again to emphasis that the standards of the Lord have not been lowered. They have not been compromised because of Israel's failure.

The Feast of Unleavened Bread (v.18)

It is remarkable that the Passover is not mentioned, but the Feast of Unleavened Bread is brought to their notice. Israel, however, would associate the Passover with this feast. It has been observed (12.15-20) that unleavened bread pictures the presence of sin. It may be that there was the danger of Israel remembering the great event of their deliverance out of Egypt, but forgetting the responsibilities which were theirs as a result of this. The same danger exists today and is highlighted by Peter when he writes of the possibility of the believer forgetting "that he was purged from his old sins" (2 Pet 1.9). He does not write that he had forgotten "that he had been delivered from the penalty due to his sins". The fact of salvation had not been forgotten, but the impact that it had on the life may have been.

Further Laws (vv.19-26)

These have been dealt with previously in the Scripture passages noted below.

The Firstborn - 13.11-13.
The Sabbath - 20.8-11.
The Feast of Weeks and Ingathering - 23.16.
The requirement to appear before the Lord - 23.14-17.
No leaven to be in the offerings - 23.18.
The Passover lamb not to be eaten the following morning - 12.10; 23.18.
The bringing of the firstfruits to the Lord - 23.19.

It should be noted in connection with the Sabbath that "in earing time and in harvest thou shalt rest". These were the busiest times of the year, the times of ploughing, sowing, and reaping. It could be that they were tempted to overlook their duties at these seasons, claiming pressure of work as a reason for this neglect. The direct reference to the need to observe the Sabbath indicates that, even in these busiest of times, there is benefit in heeding the Word of God.

What is additional is the guarantee given that the Lord will "cast out the nations" of Canaan and "enlarge thy borders", ensuring greater protection for them from their enemies. In addition, the further guarantee is given that no one would seek to take possession of their lands when the males went up to "appear before the Lord God, the God of Israel". The thought of leaving wives and young families behind might have encouraged some to decide that the journey should not be undertaken, but the Lord had made provision for this. They could go without fear; Jehovah would care for those who have been left behind. The three feasts at which the males were to "appear before the Lord God" by travelling to the Tabernacle at Shiloh or to the Temple in Jerusalem were the Feast of Unleavened Bread which was held from the 15th to the 21st day of the first month of the year, the Feast of Weeks (Pentecost) which was held 50 days after the Sabbath of the Feast of Unleavened Bread, and the Feast of Tabernacles (Booths) which was held from the 15th to the 22nd day of the 7th month. Without any fear of danger to their loved ones the males could travel with confidence to come before the Lord.

There is a second practical lesson for believers today. The feeling can arise that attendance to the things of the Lord is denying others the time and care which they should enjoy. It is true that no family should be neglected, but a spiritual husband and wife will determine before the Lord that His interests come first and agree how this should be carried out. What is clear is that the Lord cares for those who put Him first. To fail to attend the gatherings of the assembly out of lethargy, lack of interest, or the desire to accumulate wealth is treating lightly a privilege which cost the Lord Jesus all that He endured on the Cross. To give Him the first place ensures that those who do so can leave their interests in His control.

Verses 27-28: The "words" Written on the Tables

For forty days and nights Moses was up the mountain, and at the end he was instructed to write "the words". This does not refer to the Ten Commandments for these were written by the Lord (34.1). It refers to the words that the Lord had spoken to Moses and which had to be kept for the people. In this way the fact that the covenant had been restored is confirmed to the people. The restoration of the covenant had taken forty days and nights, a lesson to all that sin may be quickly embraced and practised, but it takes longer to restore fellowship with the Lord. The latter is a precious privilege and must not be undervalued.

Verses 29-32: Moses' Face Shone

As a result of being in the presence of God and seeing the glory of God, even if it was but the back parts, the face of Moses shone. As he descended the mount with the two tables of testimony in his hands he was not this time met by an idolatrous people. He was not aware of the shining of his face, but when Aaron and the people saw it they were afraid to approach him. However, when he called they came near and he gave them the Commandments that had been received on the mount.

Verses 33-35: Moses Veiled his Face

When Moses was speaking to the people he put a veil on his face, but when he went in before the Lord to speak with Him he took it off, replacing it again when he came out. This would indicate that Moses enjoyed the privilege of going in before the Lord in the Tabernacle, at which times he veiled his face. It is noteworthy that Aaron, the High Priest, did not do this when he ministered to the Lord in the Holy Place, nor when he went into the Holiest on the Day of Atonement. It shows that Moses did have a unique relationship with the Lord and enjoyed unique privileges when he spoke with Him.

Paul refers to this when writing to the Corinthians (2 Cor 3.13-18), comparing the glory of the New Covenant with that of the Lord. Moses covered his face to enable the people to approach him and hear what he had to say to them. Furthermore, they were not allowed to see the glory gradually fade from the face of Moses. It must not be thought that the reason for this was to spare Moses the embarrassment of them seeing the departing glory. The point at issue was they were not allowed to see the end of that manifestation of glory. From this Paul teaches that Israel still faces such a veil and cannot see or understand that, just as the glory departed from Moses' face, so the glory had departed from the Law. When Israel considers the Law there is a veil preventing them understanding its purpose. Only when they turn to the Lord Jesus is that veil taken away.

But the privilege that was uniquely Moses' is no longer limited to one man. "But we all, with open face beholding as in a glass the glory of the Lord, are changed into the same image from glory to glory, even as by the Spirit of the Lord" (2 Cor 3.18). Today that glory is contemplated as we consider the Lord Jesus, not with our eyes, but with our minds and in our hearts. It is "as in a glass" inasmuch as the full contemplation will not be ours until the day when we see Him, but nevertheless such contemplation as we do enjoy changes us. The glory of this covenant does not fade, but is "from glory to glory". That of the Law was a fading glory; that of the New Covenant is one that increases, and consequently increasingly changes those who behold it. The change is clearly that of reflecting His glory, which for us is seen in displaying Christ-likeness, so that the longer we know Him the more we should be like Him.

EXODUS 35

Preparation for the Construction of the Tabernacle

With the completion of the reinstatement of the covenant, it is now possible to commence the work of building the Tabernacle. It may be the view of some that there is much that is needless repetition in these chapters but that is not so. The importance of the Tabernacle is such that it must be clearly seen to have been constructed exactly according to the instructions given, and to the pattern which Moses saw on the mount. Any deviation from this is unacceptable to the Lord.

Two lessons of great value can be learned here. The first is that Moses passed on accurately the charge that he had been given, a lesson for all who seek to teach the Word of God. There were no "improvements" added, nor were any of the more difficult parts of the structure overlooked, or the work minimised. The second lesson is that alluded to above in that the workers obeyed the words of Moses. He did not deviate from the Lord's word and they did not deviate from his, the result being that the word of God was carried out.

Verses 1-3: The Sabbath Day

Further emphasis is given to the keeping of the Sabbath. The fact that Moses prefaced his instructions with a reminder of this commandment indicates that he was aware of the danger of working on the Sabbath to enable the construction of the Tabernacle to be carried out with greater haste. The specific instruction that no fire was to be kindled indicated that this would usually be done by those who were working, perhaps to be used in making some of the items, or perhaps for the disposal of scraps of material that were left over.

The point is one of importance, namely that disobedience to the Word of God cannot be justified by claiming that such actions are helping His work. He takes into account the impact that obedience to the Scriptures has on His people, and ensures faithfully that the work and the workers do not suffer because of their submission to His Word.

One further issue may be involved in this instruction. On this day, the heart was to be totally occupied with Him.

Verses 4-19: The People Told to Gather the Materials

With great precision Moses now lays before them the requirements for the building. All who were willing hearted are to bring, and those who are wise hearted are to engage in the work. Now they learn how they have to use the materials which they brought out of Egypt, that which the Egyptians gave them and which was their due for the many years of labour endured under the taskmasters. They came out of Egypt a wealthy people and now they can use that wealth to build a dwelling place for Jehovah.

The call to believers today is no less telling. It is that all resources should be used in ways that build the work of God, and that no regret should be voiced in carrying this out. The willingness of that past generation must be mirrored today in working for Him.

Verses 20-29: The Materials Brought to Moses

The hearts of the people were stirred up and their spirits made willing. This was not merely an outward show; it came from the heart. Note the emphasis on their willingness and their stirred up hearts (vv.21,22,26,29). The willingness displayed was not just an external façade. Paul describes it: "If the readiness be there" (2 Cor 8.12, JND). They had come to know a God who was bountiful in His giving, and they responded by being bountiful in what they returned. There was no one in the Camp who had the required materials and hid them, refusing to offer them. Note that every one who possessed blue and purple, scarlet and fine linen, goats' hair, red skins of rams, badgers' skins, gold, silver, brass, and shittim wood brought of their substance to Moses.

But it cannot fail to be noticed that there was unity in this work. The men and women wrought in harmony and the people and the rulers were united in the task. Would that it was always like this in the service of God. Every great work for God must have this feature. Despite the fact that there were some who "put not their necks to the work of the Lord", the rebuilding of the walls of Jerusalem was marked by a remarkable unity of purpose (Neh 3). The truth of the body (see 1 Cor 12) results in every member being dependent on the others, with each individual working for the one common objective of honouring the Lord Jesus. Psalm 133 also is concerned with the unity of the people of God. It is "like the precious ointment upon the head, that ran down upon the beard, even Aaron's beard: that went down to the skirts of his garments" (v.2).

Verses 30-35: The Appointment of Bezaleel and Aholiab

The Lord, and not Moses, made these appointments (31.2-6). The only further comment to be added here is to note that it was given to them to teach others the skills necessary for the work. They were not to exclude others, as it would not have been possible for these two men to carry out all the work themselves, but they were to ensure that those who laboured in the work were fully instructed.

At times, in assembly work, there can be a tendency for those who have been gifted in a particular way to discourage others gifted in the same way from following them. Their fear may be that others overshadow them, but they fail to appreciate that the work needs the help of all who are able and willing to be involved. To act otherwise discourages those who are excluded, and may result in them never developing the gift that they have been given.

Bezaleel and Aholiab did not fall into the temptation of working selfishly with a view to their names alone being associated with the work. There was recognition that the Lord had called for others to be involved, that their services were necessary, and that to include them would give them the opportunity of serving the Lord.

The range of skills listed is most impressive. Comment has already been made in dealing with ch.31 that it is probable, although it cannot be determined with certainty, that Bezaleel, and other Israelites, were engaged in this type of work as they built the treasure cities of Egypt. What is certain is that the particular work to which they set their hands was based on a pattern that was unknown to the Egyptians, the pattern that was revealed to Moses on the mount. Instruction regarding this had to be passed on to the workmen; they were taught and then they wrought. And so it is today. The local assembly is based on a pattern that is unknown in the world. It is not an impressive sight by the standards of this godless age: a few people gathering with none of the accoutrements of religion. The very simplicity is against everything that worldly ambition seeks. Those who work in the building of it, however, have found the pattern in the Word of God and use all the skills at their disposal, all the gift that has been given to them, to ensure that the work is faithfully carried out.

EXODUS 36

The Work Commences

Verses 1-4: Bezaleel and Aholiab Lead the Workers

Three matters are worthy of further note. First, *"all* manner of work" was covered by the skilled workers; there was nothing missing from the range of skills required. The Lord always provides the means for His work to be carried out at His time and according to His pattern. Second, the work was carried out faithfully, because it was done "according to *all* that the Lord had commanded". Third, they received from Moses *"all* the offering" which had been given for the work.

Account must be taken of the detail which is observed by the Lord, as nothing escapes His searching gaze. The integrity of Moses is observed in how he handled the resources that had been put at his disposal, just as the lack of honesty on the part of Ananias and Sapphira was noted as they approached the assembly at Jerusalem with what they claimed was the proceeds of the sale of their ground (Acts 5.1-11). Morning by morning the offerings were brought. It was not merely the one-off emotional reaction of the people to their deliverance from the folly of worshipping the golden calf, it was the deliberate, considered actions of willing hearts, whose willingness did not fade as quickly as it had come. Just as the manna was given every morning, so they responded every morning.

Verses 5-7: Their Abundant Giving

So willing were the people to bring that more than enough was given for the work. At that point Moses called for the giving to cease. It is a principle in the work of God that although it is a responsibility to give, there must be no waste in this service. Even the crumbs that remained were gathered up after the feeding of thousands (Mk 6.43; 8.8). The same abundance was seen in the giving of the people during the reign of Hezekiah. The tithes which they brought were so great in number that Azariah the chief priest declared that "we have had enough to eat, and have left plenty" (2 Chr 31.10). When the goodness and grace of God is recognised it unlocks the hearts and the pockets of God's people. The principle is clearly enunciated by the Lord Jesus: "freely ye have received, freely give" (Mt 10.8).

It is good to see that those who had fallen into the temptation of worshipping an idol were now prepared to give of their substance in abundance to the Lord. This was the result of His dealing with them; to bring them to the point where they were caused to appreciate something of His goodness and express it in this way. When the Lord is forgotten, as He was when Moses was up the mount, the result is disaster, but when His people look at their own hearts, realise their failure and sin, and then turn their attention to the Lord, seeing how unworthy they are and how worthy

He is, their hearts are touched. The grace of God extended to the people in the renewing of the covenant, which they surely understood was an undeserved blessing, opened their hearts in appreciation.

The same principle is seen in Zacchaeus who, having met the Lord, declared, "Behold, Lord, the half of my goods I give to the poor; and if I have taken any thing from any man by false accusation, I restore him fourfold" (Lk 19.8). Again, he had been touched by the grace of God. Paul saw this also in the churches of Macedonia where, despite their "deep poverty" they had displayed "riches of...liberality" (2 Cor 8.2).

Verses 8-38: The Curtains and Structure

Little can be added to what has been written in the previous chapters. The detail included here has already been given, but it is recorded again to show the faithfulness of the workers in the discharge of their responsibilities. The particulars of the work should be noted: the length of the curtains, the numbers of the loops and taches, the dimensions of the boards, the numbers of the sockets etc. No aspect escapes Him; surely an encouragement to faithful servants who seek to obey the Word of God. It cannot be said that any instruction is unimportant and these workers are an example to all who follow. Paul wrote that he had been a "wise masterbuilder" (1 Cor 3.10), one who had faithfully followed the pattern. His instruction to Timothy was that he should be "a workman that needeth not to be ashamed, rightly dividing the word of truth" (2 Tim 2.15). Rightly dividing (3718) has the thought of ploughing a straight furrow, cutting a stone accurately, building a straight wall, and even baking a good loaf. It involves work well done that will not be a cause of shame to the workman, and in the case of Timothy refers particularly to handling the Scriptures.

EXODUS 37-39

The Construction of the Tabernacle

These chapters contain further details of the construction of the Tabernacle. There are several additional items of information which are worth noting particularly.

Chapter 38.8: The Laver

The brass of the looking glasses of which the laver was made came from the women who assembled at the door of the "tabernacle of the congregation". As the Tabernacle itself had not been constructed, the reference is to the temporary tabernacle erected by Moses (33.7). These must, therefore, have been godly women, assembling to assist in the service of the Lord. They assembled (6633) like troops ready for service. They were not there to loiter or wait to hear the gossip and news of the day, it was not their purpose to see who came to the tabernacle and why; they were there with godly motive to help in any way possible. In this they were a good example, not only to women, but to all who seek to serve Him. Anna was in her own day a member of the godly remnant (Lk 2.36-38) as she "departed not from the temple, but served God with fastings and prayers night and day". It is sad to observe that in the days of Eli, his sons used women gathering round the Tabernacle for immoral purposes (1 Sam 2.22).

Chapter 38.21-31: The Materials Used

The information concerning all the weight of the metals used reveals that the Lord takes delight in everything that is given to Him and in how it is used for His glory. As the workmen laboured in their tasks they were creating that which spoke of the Lord Jesus, a lesson for all who are engaged in this service. That this was delightful to the Lord is emphasised by the repetition in these chapters. He does not tire in contemplating what His servants have done faithfully for Him. Wood, hay, and stubble give Him no delight, but gold, silver, and precious stones (1 Cor 3.12 - this is not a reference to the materials in the Tabernacle, but simply denotes what is lasting and what is not) are not only of enduring value for those who give them, but are of great joy to the Lord.

Chapter 39.32-43: The Work Completed

The work is now finished and the people bring it to Moses. All has been carried out according to all that the Lord commanded him. It has already been noted in the introduction to the Tabernacle that creation occupies the first and part of the second chapters of Genesis, but the making of the Tabernacle requires thirteen chapters of Exodus. The creation of the stars occupies one phrase (Gen 1.16), but the Tabernacle takes up 32.5% of

Exodus (by chapter). It is a wonder to behold creation and see in it "his eternal power and Godhead" (Rom 1.20), but He is more taken up with the work of redemption, a work that should cause us even greater wonder than observing the magnificent beauty and exquisite detail of what He has made.

Moses "did look upon all the work", doubtless examining it in detail to see that it was carried out according to the pattern. What he saw followed the pattern accurately. There was no need to send some of it back for correction; there is no record of any workman being ashamed of his work. Just as these workmen waited on his verdict as to the accuracy and quality of the work, so Christians will await the Lord's verdict on their work at the Judgment Seat (Rom 14.10). At that time there will be no opportunity to carry out any of the work a second time.

As a result Moses blessed them. What a privilege to receive this from his hand. The principle is clear; blessing follows faithfulness. He rewards the true and faithful; it is His joy to bless.

There is more to be done. The Tabernacle cannot lie empty; it must be used, and the book of Leviticus gives instructions regarding this. Further tests lie ahead, but just at this moment they have completed a great work for the Lord and can pause and rejoice in the goodness of God that had taken them from building the treasure cities of Egypt, to building the House of the Lord their God (see 23.19). Let every Christian reader rejoice that they too have been delivered "from bondage worse than theirs by far" and ensure that when they serve the Lord, they do it "as the Lord had commanded". Then the blessing will be enjoyed.

EXODUS 40

The Tabernacle Reared

Once again the importance of the Tabernacle is emphasised; the instructions have been given, the work has been completed to the satisfaction of Moses, and now it is necessary in the final chapter to record how Moses set it up. Bezaleel, Aholiab, and their workmen had carried out the work, but the setting up is recorded as being the work of Moses. Doubtless he directed others to erect and place the articles of furniture, but the responsibility fell to him.

Verses 1-33: Moses Responsible for the Work

This was carried out on the first day of the first month of the second year after leaving Egypt, that is fifteen days short of one year since their deliverance from the house of bondage. What a year that had been. They had seen the armies of Egypt stricken at the Red Sea, they had travelled into the wilderness of Shur and had seen the hand of God in turning sweet the bitter waters of Marah, the manna had rained down from heaven daily for over ten months, the smitten rock had provided their water supply, and Amalek had been defeated at their hands. Yet the days had been stained by memories of their discontent and complaints culminating in the worship of the golden calf. It was a story of the abundant goodness and grace of God and the selfish failure of Israel. Yet still God was faithful!

They had arrived at Horeb in the third month after their deliverance (19.1-2). In the time since, Moses had been on the mount with God for two periods of forty days, the first for the initial giving of the Law (24.18), and the second after the golden calf idolatry (34.28). It must, therefore, have been a work of about six months duration to construct the Tabernacle, an amazing feat when the magnitude of the task is considered. All the items are listed.

	The Instruction	The Work Completed
The boards, bars, sockets and coverings	v.2	vv.18-19
The Ark	v.3	vv.20-21
The Vail	v.3	v.21
The Table of Shewbread	v.4	vv.22-23
The Lampstand	v.4	vv.24-25
The Golden Altar	v.5	vv.26-27
The Door	v.6	v.28
The Brazen Altar	v.6	v.29
The Laver	v.7	v.30
The Court	v.8	v.33
The priests are clothed	vv.12-16	No mention - but see Lev 8

The actual clothing of the priests is not noted here because that was carried out after the Lord gave instruction to Moses for the offerings (Lev 1-7) and called to him out of the Tabernacle (Lev 8.1). As with the workers, where the instruction is given by the Lord and their faithfulness in carrying it out is noted, so here, both the instruction and Moses' faithful discharge of his responsibilities are recorded. Note that he placed the Shewbread on the Table (v.23), lit the lamps (v.25), burned sweet incense before the Golden Altar, and offered a burnt offering and a meat offering. The priests did not do this because they were not yet consecrated to their service.

Verses 34-38: The Glory Fills the Tabernacle

What a climax to the book as the glory filled the Tabernacle! Even Moses could not enter. Jehovah is now dwelling in the midst of His redeemed people, He to enjoy them and they to enjoy Him. The cloud will guide them, leading them when it is time to move and remaining still when it is time to stop. As the teaching of Leviticus unfolds they will learn even more of how central the Tabernacle is to their lives.

The moving of the cloud taught them more of their God. It is a lesson for today in how the Lord leads His people into a greater knowledge of Him and His ways; He is the guide to spiritual progress. As this study comes to an end, the great questions with which all Christians are faced are, "Are we making progress? Do we love the Lord Jesus as we should, and are we getting to know Him better, or is life simply a catalogue of self and failure?". Today God still dwells in the midst of His gathered people in the assembly (1 Cor 3.16). Let the privileges be enjoyed, and may the responsibilities be faithful discharged.

What a story has occupied the reader: from slavery to worship, from bondage to liberty, from defeat to triumph, the pathway of getting to know their God, living on the resources which He provided, following the way in which He guided, and anticipating the fulfilment of the promises which He had made. There is more to learn, and Leviticus will continue the story. This is appropriate, for in this life, and in that which is to come, there will always be more to learn. His greatness, grace, and glory are inexhaustible, and the Book of Exodus has but pictured in "things written aforetime" what He has for the saints now and what will occupy them in eternity.

APPENDIX 1
THE CHARACTER OF MIRACLES
IN SCRIPTURE

At times in history acts have taken place which cannot be explained by the normal laws of creation. These acts have been termed "miracles" and have caused fear, brought comfort, confirmed the authority of God's servants, healed the sick, and changed the course of human conduct. In Exodus 4 we read for the first time of power being given to a man to perform such acts.

The Different Nature of Miracles

When miracles are considered superficially we conclude that they are acts performed by men which do not abide by the laws of science to which the Creator has decreed that His creation will be subject. But this does not adequately cover the range of miracles in Scripture. There is a sense in which all of nature is miraculous. Each birth is a miracle, for it is beyond the power of man to create life. The glory of the lily and the beauty of the mountains cannot, from nothing, be created by man. When honestly contemplating all the wonders around him man has to confess that there is that which is beyond his ability to call into being and to sustain. In that creation God has ordained certain laws of nature. Trench comments however that "The miracle is not a *greater* manifestation of God's power than those ordinary and ever-repeated processes; but it is a *different* manifestation" (*Notes on the Miracles of Our Lord*). It is within His power to act outwith these laws and at times He has given men the power to do this, and the miraculous acts can be divided into a number of categories.

1. Works, such as we have already outlined, which men are given power to carry out and which are outwith the limits permitted by normal circumstances. Examples of this are the signs given to Moses to perform in Egypt, the smiting of the rock by Moses to produce water (17.6), and the raising of the son of the Shunammite by Elisha (2 Kings 4.32-35).

2. Wonders which God performs without any human agent being involved, but which also are clearly outwith the normal laws of creation. Examples of this are the fall of the walls of Jericho (Josh 6), the turning back of the sun dial by ten degrees during the reign of Hezekiah (2 Kings 20.11), and the birth of Isaac when Sarah was old (Gen 21.1-2). Although in the case of Sarah she conceived the child, neither she nor Abraham were told to do anything which would give her the ability to conceive.

3. Acts which in themselves are within the normal laws of creation, but are deemed to be miraculous because of the time at which they took place.

In this category are included the torrential rain which resulted in the defeat of Sisera (Judg 5.20-21), the slaying of the prophet by a lion (1 Kings 13.24), the death of 185,000 men in the course of one night (2 Kings 19.35), and the death of Ananias and Sapphira (Acts 5.5-10).

4. The miracles performed by the Lord Jesus. These are a unique group, and differ from others in at least two vital ways. First, they differ in their profusion. The Lord Jesus performed more miracles than any other person. Despite claims that He did this when a child, we know from Mark 6.2-3 that those who had known Him as He grew up were amazed that such mighty works were wrought by His hands. He was not known in Nazareth as a miracle worker. During His public ministry he did perform miracles in profusion. Well over thirty are recorded in the Gospels where individuals or small groups were blessed, apart from the many crowds who came to Him and left cured of their diseases. They differ, secondly, in how they were performed. In the Old Testament, God's servants had to be told what to do, but the Lord Jesus acted of His own volition and carried out the work with ease. The difference was that the power of prophets etc was given to them for specific acts, whereas the power displayed by the Lord was His own.

5. The miracles performed in the early days of the church. The power to do this was the result of some being gifted with the power of healing. This power was delegated to them and could be used by them on more than one occasion. In the Old Testament the power to heal was given rarely, but when the Holy Spirit came in Acts 2 this gift was given permanently to some. It was one of the "sign" gifts which confirmed the authority of this "new" message. The characteristics of its use can be seen when Peter and John used it in Acts 3 to heal a lame man. It was a public act, carried out in one of the busiest places in Jerusalem. It was a prompt act, for the man was healed immediately. It was a perfect act, because he was completely cured. It was a proven act, as all the people saw him walking and leaping. A detailed examination of the "sign" gifts of the New Testament is outwith this present study, but we should note that these gifts are not with us today. Gradually they ceased, and even Paul had to leave Trophimus at Miletum sick. (2 Tim 4.20).

The Names Used to Describe Miracles

There are three names used to describe miracles. The first of these is "signs". The Hebrew word ÔT (226) has the same meaning as the Greek *semeion*. This is what miracles given to Moses were to be to Pharaoh. In John's Gospel the miraculous works of the Lord Jesus are described as "signs", and in Mark 16.20 the word which was preached by the disciples was confirmed by "signs" following. These acts were, therefore, an indication that God was working. They were used to confirm the authority under God of those who performed them. At critical times it was necessary to establish the authority of God's servants, and this means was used to confirm that God was working through them. When used of the Lord Jesus, it confirmed that God Himself was working.

Not every sign, however, is of a miraculous nature. The stars are signs (Gen 1.14), and the finding of the babe wrapped in swaddling clothes, lying in the manger, was stated to be a sign to the shepherds (Lk 2.12). The birth of this child was indeed miraculous, but finding Him in this way was not in itself miraculous.

The second name given to miraculous acts is "wonders". It is in this way that the acts to be performed in Egypt are described (3.20). This refers, not so much to the act itself, but to the effect which it produces in the heart of man. There is a recognition that the act is beyond the capability of man himself. Were wonder alone, however, the only reaction to a miraculous act, this would fall short of the purpose of carrying out the act. "The ethical meaning of the miracle would be wholly lost, were blank astonishment or mere amazement all which it aroused" (Trench, *op cit*). Because of this, the name "wonder" is often used together with the name "sign". A wonder, therefore, is designed to startle men and women so that their understanding may be opened to truth which is being presented to them.

The third name given to miracles is "mighty works", or "powers". It is used in the New Testament, and by this name our attention is directed to the cause of the miracle, the power which belongs to God alone.

Miracles Performed by Men

The performance of miraculous acts by men was the not the main method of bringing God's message to others. If we consider the approximate times when these were carried out we see that for the greater part of history this power was not available.

From Moses going down to Egypt until the conquest of the land	60 years
During the ministry of Elijah and Elisha	20 years
During the early days of the Acts	20 years
	<u>100 years</u>
If we include the public ministry of the Lord Jesus	3 years
	<u>103 years</u>.

This demonstrates the confirmatory nature of miracles. It was not the normal means of God working though His servants. Even now there are those who claim that miracle working is carried out in the present day, and that without it there is no evidence of the work of God. This shows a misunderstanding of the subject and of the teaching of the New Testament regarding the "sign" gifts.

APPENDIX 2
THE JEWISH SACRED CALENDAR
EXODUS 23; LEVITICUS 23; NUMBERS 28-29; DEUTERONOMY 16.1-16

Month	Day	Feasts of Jehovah	Harvests etc	Jewish Feasts
1. Abib (Nisan) Spring Equinox March/April	1 14 15-21 16	New Moon **PASSOVER SLAIN** **UNLEAVENED BREAD** **FIRSTFRUITS**	**Latter rain** **Malkosh** Barley Harvest	
2. Iyar April/May	1 15	New Moon 2nd (little Passover)	**Latter rain** Wheat harvest	
3. Sivan May/June	1	New Moon **PENTECOST** 50 days after Firstfruits	**Dry season** Vines tended	
4. Thamus June/July	1	New Moon	**Dry Season**	
5. Ab July/August	1	New Moon	**Dry season** 1st Figs Summer fruit	**9** Fast - Fall of Jerusalem.
6. Elul Aug/Sept	1	New Moon	**Dry season** Summer fruit Grape/ fig harvest	
7. Tishri Sept/Oct	1 1 10 15-22	New Moon **TRUMPETS** **DAY OF ATONEMENT** **TABERNACLES**	**Dry Season** Grape/fig harvest Ploughing	**3** Fast - Murder of Gedaliah
8. Marcheshvan Oct/Nov	1	New Moon	**Former rain** **(Yoreh/Moreh)** Olive harvest Grain planting	
9. Chisleu Nov/Dec	1	New moon	**Former rain** Grain planting Spring growth	**25** Feast of Dedication (Candles) (7 Days)
10. Tebeth Dec/ Jan	1	New Moon	**Winter rain** Spring growth Rains continue	**10** Fast - Siege of Jerusalem
11. Shebat Jan/Feb	1	New Moon	**Winter rain** Spring growth	
12. Adar Feb/Mar	1	New Moon	**Winter rain** Flax harvest Rains continue	**14/15** Purim

Other Days
The Weekly Sabbath
The seventh day of every week was a Sabbath.

Monthly Days (Num 10.10; 28.11-15)
The new moon at the beginning of each month was the occasion for offerings.

The Seventh Year (Lev 25.1-7)
Every seventh year was a Sabbath of rest to the land. There was to be no sowing, pruning of the vines, or harvesting. Even that which grew by itself was not to be harvested. But what of food for the next two years? The answer is given: "And if ye shall say, What shall we eat the seventh year? behold, we shall not sow, nor gather in our increase: Then I will command my blessing upon you in the sixth year, and it shall bring forth fruit for three years. And ye shall sow the eighth year, and eat yet of old fruit until the ninth year; until her fruits come in ye shall eat of the old store" (Lev 25.20-22).

The Year of Jubilee (Lev 25.8-17)
After seven Sabbath years (49 years) the fiftieth year was to be a year of Jubilee. "This most extraordinary of all civil institutions, which received the name of 'Jubilee' from a Hebrew word signifying a musical instrument, a horn or trumpet, began on the tenth day of the seventh month, or the great day of atonement [of the 49th year], when, by order of the public authorities, the sound of trumpets proclaimed the beginning of the universal redemption. All prisoners and captives obtained their liberties, slaves were declared free, and debtors were absolved. The land, as on the sabbatic year, was neither sowed nor reaped, but allowed to enjoy with its inhabitants a sabbath of repose; and its natural produce was the common property of all. Moreover, every inheritance throughout the land of Judea was restored to its original owner" (Jamieson, Fausset, and Brown).

The Seasons of Rain
There were two distinct seasons of rain that are of interest in this study: early or former, and latter. The giving of the early and the latter rains assured an abundant harvest: "I will give you the rain of your land in his due season, the first rain and the latter rain, that thou mayest gather in thy corn, and thy wine, and thine oil" (Deut 11.14).

Malkosh - the latter rain
This fell from March into April. These spring rains brought the grain to maturity making it ripe for harvesting (Prov 16.15; Jer 5.24; Hos 6.3; Joel 2.23; Zech 10.2). These rains were needed for the spring harvest. The use of this expression by Job in relation to his miserable comforters is a telling

figure of speech (Job 29.23). If this rain failed it was a mark of the displeasure of the Lord towards Israel (Jer 3.3; Amos 4.7).

Yoreh (or Moreh) - the former or early rain

This fell from late October/early November and continued for a space of about two months (Joel 2.23; Hos 6.3; Jer 5.24). The word has in it the thought of casting forth, shooting, or sprinkling. It is the rain which is necessary preparation for the shooting of the seed which is sown. Probably, therefore, it indicates that it came before the sowing just as the latter rain came before the harvest.

The season of rain continues through to the first/second month but there is still need of the latter rain which brings the greater rain necessary to ripen the crops for harvest.

The Feasts which Demanded the Presence of the Males

The presence of all the males was necessary at the place where the Lord placed His name for the Feast of Unleavened Bread, the Feast of Pentecost (Weeks), and the Feast of Tabernacles. "Three times in a year shall all thy males appear before the Lord thy God in the place which he shall choose; in the feast of unleavened bread, and in the feast of weeks, and in the feast of tabernacles" (Deut 16.16).

When they came they were to bring the offerings that were instructed. "And they shall not appear before the Lord empty: Every man shall give as he is able, according to the blessing of the Lord thy God which he hath given thee" (Deut 16.16-17).

"Three times thou shalt keep a feast unto me in the year. Thou shalt keep the feast of unleavened bread…And the feast of harvest, the firstfruits of thy labours, which thou hast sown in the field: and the feast of ingathering, which is in the end of the year, when thou hast gathered in thy labours out of the field. Three times in the year all thy males shall appear before the Lord God" (Ex 23.14-17).

The Feasts Initiated by the Jews

There were a number of feasts initiated by the Jews quite apart from the Feasts of Jehovah. The feasts listed here are not inclusive of all. Further feasts were added, but those listed are the main feasts which are of interest.

5th Month, 9th Day - The Fall of Jerusalem

The city and the Temple were destroyed by fire on the 10th day of this month in the 19th year of the reign of Nebuchadnezzar (Jer 52.12-13; 2 Kings 25.8-9). The latter reference gives the 7th day as the day when this took place, but the city was ablaze from the 7th to the 10th day. This feast is regarded by the Jews as second only to the Day of Atonement in solemnity.

7th Month, 3rd Day – The Murder of Gedaliah

This commemorated the murder of Gedaliah, the governor appointed by Nebuchadnezzar over the small remnant left in Judah (2 Kings 25.25-26; Jer 41.1).

9th Month, 25th Day – The Feast of Dedication

This Feast lasted for eight days. In the first, one candle was lit, in the second two etc. It commemorated the dedication of the Temple and the restoration of the Temple services by Judas Maccabaeus.

10th Month, 10th Day – The Siege of Jerusalem

On this day the siege of Jerusalem commenced in the 9th year of King Zedekiah (2 Kings 25.1).

12th Month, 14/15th Day – Purim (Lots)

This observed the deliverance of the Jews in the times of Esther, and was a time of joy. It was instituted to commemorate the lot cast by Haman, the enemy of the Jews (Est 3.7). This was cast in the first month of the year, and gave the thirteenth day of the twelfth month (Adar) of the same year for the execution of Haman's plans to destroy all the Jews in Persia. The feast is held on the 14th and 15th days of Adar to celebrate the deliverance of the Jews and the ruin of Haman (Est 9.14).

APPENDIX 3
THE FIRSTBORN

The death of the firstborn at the time of the Passover, and the sanctification of the firstborn, recorded in ch.13, marked them out as being of particular significance. What, then, does Scripture teach in respect of the first male child to be born into a family? As far as Israel were concerned the Word of God is clear as to the position, privileges, and responsibilities of the firstborn, and an understanding of these throws further light on the fact that Passover was particularly the deliverance from death of the firstborn of each home where the blood was on the door posts and on the lintel.

It is clear that by the time Esau and Jacob were born the firstborn privileges were known as the "birthright" (Gen 25.31), as at this point they are initially so called. But what was involved in the birthright? First, there were privileges, given to the firstborn of every family, which gave him a leading place in that family. Second, there were privileges given uniquely to the family of Abraham, passed on through the firstborn, that had to do with the promises given to him by the Lord. This latter group would be regarded as of little value to men who lacked interest in spiritual matters. Esau had no concern for the birthright at the time when he sold it to Jacob (Gen 25.29-34), seeming to discard it with no thought as to the consequences. Later, however, his wish was to have it.

It should be noted that the male born first into a family did not always inherit the dignity of firstborn. There were exceptions, some of which will be considered below, when it passed to a junior member of the family.

Blessings to the Firstborn of Every Family

It was not within the prerogative of the father of the family to select the one on whom the firstborn birthright would fall. Even if a man had two wives and the mother of the firstborn was "hated" the father could not pass the birthright to the "son of the beloved" (Deut 21.15ff). There was to be no question of favouritism in this matter. It would appear also that the birthright did not pass without formal recognition of this taking place. Isaac, concerned that the day of his death might be drawing near, although in fact he had many years to live, directed Esau to embark on a hunting expedition and bring the venison to him to mark the formal occasion when he would "bless" his older son (Gen 27.1-4). In this way Esau was to be recognised as heir to the birthright, which gave the following privileges.

Chief of the family

Due to the deviousness of Rebekah and Jacob, Isaac blessed his younger son unwittingly. "Be lord over thy brethren, and let thy mother's sons bow down to thee" (Gen 27.29), he stated. With these words there was given to Jacob the chieftainship of his family. The branch of the family that was descended from Jacob would be the senior branch, and that from Esau the junior. This was not merely a nicety of a genealogical chart. It gave the firstborn priority over his brothers and made him the chief, not just of his immediate family circle, for he would be that in his own home regardless of whether he was the firstborn or not, but over the whole extended family.

This was not only a place of dignity and of honour, but it was position of responsibility. The maintenance of the reputation of the family, peaceful relationships within the family, and the care and well-being of all members of the family were matters of concern to the firstborn.

Involved in this was judicial responsibility. The fact that his mother's sons would bow before him indicated that he did have authority over them, and that being chief of the family was not merely an office of a powerless figurehead. Thus, when there were disputes which demanded that the issues be judged, the chief of the family would be the arbiter, ensuring that the rule of law was enforced in the family.

A double portion of the inheritance

Reference has already been made to the "son of the hated" inheriting the birthright (Deut 21.15-17). This was acknowledged by the father in giving him "a double portion of all that he hath". If there were two sons, the elder would receive two thirds of the estate and the younger one third. If there were four sons the eldest would receive two fifths and the other three one fifth each. This, therefore, was a very practical way in which the firstborn was acknowledged on the death of his father. This was not, of course, simply to make him richer than the others. There were two good reasons for this division of the estate.

1. As the head or chief of the family, the firstborn had to maintain a household of some dignity. It was necessary for the honour of the family that he be known as a man of some substance, well able to support his own house.

2. He should have enough substance to meet any crisis in the more extended family. His brothers would not expect to live off his charity, but, should emergencies arise, as the head he would have responsibilities. The greater portion, therefore, was not to enable him to enjoy luxury, but to ensure that he was able to maintain an honourable house and guard the good name of the family.

An interesting footnote to this can be seen in reference to the prodigal son (Lk 15.11-32). The younger son demanded his inheritance before the death of his father, and, as the younger, he would be entitled to one third of the estate, his older brother being due the double portion. On the return of the prodigal the father does not give him a further inheritance. He will be received into the home and enjoy the loving embrace and warm welcome of the father, but sin had cost him. The father states to the elder son, "all that I have is thine" (v.31), perhaps because the son feared that some of his double portion would be given to the younger son, but this would not be done. As the firstborn, his right to that portion would not be violated. The lesson to us is that although the forgiving, loving hand of the Lord is always opened to those who confess their sin and turn away from it, there still is loss suffered by the sinner. Wasted time, resources, and opportunities for serving the Lord remain so, whatever may take place thereafter. Sin never gives anything of value; it always robs.

Family priest

The spiritual well-being of the family also lay with the firstborn, but as the priest of the family he would also enjoy privilege. Right at the beginning Cain gave the lead in bringing his offering to the Lord, showing leadership even although his worship was unacceptable to Him. There is no distinct reference in the book of Genesis to the firstborn being the priest of the family. After the exodus the Levites took the place of the firstborn as the priestly tribe (Num 3.12) since the firstborn were set apart for the Lord because they were saved from death on Passover night. While this is true, it would appear sound to assume that the practice had been to set the firstborn aside for priesthood.

The fact that Abel, with spiritual discernment not possessed by Cain, brought the *firstlings* of the flock (Gen 4.4) indicates that he was aware that the Lord claimed the firstborn as His own.

Easton comments: "A peculiar sanctity was attached to the firstborn both of man and of cattle. God claimed that the firstborn males of man and of animals should be consecrated to Him, the one as a priest, representing the family to which he belonged, the other to be offered up in sacrifice" *(The Revised Bible Dictionary)*.

Blessings Which Were Unique to the Family of Abraham

These blessings were the privilege of the family of Abraham because that family was chosen by God to be the channel through which blessing would come, not only to the nation which sprang from this family, but to the whole world. The firstborn of this family would be in the line of the One promised, coming as the Ruler appointed by the Lord.

The line of Messiah

What a privilege and honour it was to be in the line of the family from which Messiah would come. But the firstborn of every generation would not be the One in whom the promises were fulfilled. It is this point that is emphasised by Paul when, writing of the promise made to Abraham he states, "He saith not, And to seeds, as of many; but as of one, And to thy seed, which is Christ" (Gal 3.16). The blessing to come was not through the total seed of Abraham but through One from among them. Nevertheless, let it be emphasised again how great was the privilege in being one of the line through which He would come, who would be:-

THE RULER OF ALL NATIONS

All nations will bow before Him. Jacob sees that there will be a day when his words, "Let people serve thee and nations bow down to thee" (Gen 27.29) will be fulfilled. It has already been noted that the place of firstborn did not always pass to the eldest male. This is seen when Jacob blessed his sons (Gen 49). The eldest male was Reuben but he forfeited the right because of his immoral behaviour (Gen 35.22). The next two sons, Simeon and Levi, forfeited the right because of their deception and disreputable conduct over the matter of the proposed marriage of their sister Dinah to Shechem, the son of the prince of Shechem (Gen 34). At this point the birthright passed to Judah and it was from that tribe that there would come One who would be the lawgiver and the gatherer of the people. It is of more than passing interest to note that the first proper name given in Scripture to this coming One is here noted: that of Shiloh, the Rest Giver.

The choice of the tribe of Levi for the priesthood is an evidence of the grace of God, but it also was to bring about the separation of kingship and priesthood. The attempt by one monarch to usurp the priestly office led to disastrous results (2 Chr 26.16-21). Only in the Lord Jesus will the two offices be united: "Even he shall build the temple of the Lord; and he shall bear the glory, and shall sit and rule upon his throne; and he shall be a priest upon his throne" (Zech 6.13).

THE KING OF ISRAEL

When Jacob blesses Judah he states that "The sceptre shall not depart from Judah, nor a lawgiver from between his feet, until Shiloh come; and unto him shall the gathering of the people be" (Gen 49.10). Until Shiloh come the royal sceptre, the staff of command, will be held by Judah, with the power, authority and dignity of kingship. "Until" (3588) must not be regarded as indicating that when Shiloh comes the kingship will pass to another tribe. Smith states: "Judah's capacity for rule would extend up unto Shiloh and beyond. Judah's leadership would climax in a ruler who would be able to achieve real rest for God's people".

The royal sceptre came to the tribe of Judah when David was anointed king (1 Sam 16). Even after the division of the kingdom during the reign of Rehoboam, the successors of David continued to reign in Jerusalem until Zedekiah was taken captive to Babylon. Smith comments again: "The sceptre and the ruler's staff should not be restricted to royal power...In the post exilic community, however, from 538 to at least 516 BC Judah was governed by Zerubbabel of the tribe of Judah. During the intertestamental period the entire land was called Judea after the name of the tribe. The political power of Judah came to an end when Judea was made a Roman province in AD 6". It was at this time that Jesus of Nazareth was growing to manhood. He was "Shiloh" but he was rejected by Israel.

However, the blessings of Jacob on Judah will be seen in all their fullness when He reigns in the millennial Kingdom. Truly then the day of peace and plenty to which the aged patriarch refers when he states that He will bind "his foal unto the vine, and his ass's colt unto the choice vine", when He will wash "his garments in wine, and his clothes in the blood of grapes" (Gen 49.11), will be enjoyed by the nation of Israel and by the whole world. This King will bring the nation into the land that had been promised to Abraham and they will live there with their claims to it undisputed. Never again will they be carried away, and never again will Gentiles expel them from this land.

The Firstborn in Egypt

The position of the firstborn having been established, the question of why it was the firstborn who died in Egypt can be addressed. As has been noted, the Lord had a special claim on the firstborn. They were His on the basis of the fact that giving the first to the Lord was an acknowledgment of His claims; it signified agreement that all belonged to Him, and that it was His right to receive the first. In Egypt it was indicative of the claims of the Lord to possess all of Egypt. It was not Pharaoh's possession; the gods of Egypt had no claim over the land or over the living. It belonged totally to Jehovah, and in taking the firstborn he was taking what was His by right.

The deliverance of the firstborn of the Hebrew slaves was further indication that they belonged particularly to Him. As the "first" they were the representatives of the whole nation and they also confirmed that the Lord had first claim on all living. In their deliverance they were now due to acknowledge that right, not solely on the basis of creation, but also on the basis of redemption. With the words, "Sanctify unto me all the firstborn, whatsoever openeth the womb among the children of Israel, both of man and of beast: it is mine" (13.2), they were set apart for the service of God. This separated position was transferred to the Levites (Num 8.5-22).

The government of God can also be seen in death of the firstborn. Pharaoh had set his heart on destroying Israel, the people to whom Jehovah refers as "my firstborn". The nation that sought to destroy Jehovah's firstborn suffered the loss of their own firstborn (4.22-23). What they sowed, they reaped.

APPENDIX 4
RECORDED PASSOVERS

The Passover took place initially in Exodus 12, but it was to be remembered by Israel annually. The events of that night were never repeated; there was only one Passover, but it was not to be forgotten and annual commemoration was to take place. The Exodus account strongly emphasises this.

"Ye shall keep it a feast by an ordinance forever" (v.12).

"Ye shall observe this thing for an ordinance to thee and to thy sons forever" (v.24).

"When ye be come to the land…ye shall keep this service" (v.25).

"It is a night to be much observed unto the Lord…of all the children of Israel in their generations" (v.42).

Noted below are the memorial Passovers to which reference is made in Scripture.

The Passover at Sinai (Num 9.1-14)

This took place in the first month of the second year after leaving Egypt. It was, therefore, the first commemorative Passover, taking place after the erection of the Tabernacle. The problem which occurred was that there were men who had been defiled by touching a dead body. Since the Lord dwelt amongst His people, all who were unclean had to be put out of the Camp (Num 5.2), the period of defilement lasting for seven days (Num 19.11). Thus, these men were unable to partake of the Passover, and they asked Moses what could be done to remedy the situation.

The answer from the Lord covered both the defiled and any who were away on a journey at Passover time. There was to be a second or, as it became known, a "little" Passover which was to be held on the fourteenth day of the second month. There was to be strict adherence to the conditions for the Passover, and this second Passover was not to be used as an excuse for unnecessarily failing to keep the first month Passover.

Not only does this stress that the Passover was not to be treated carelessly, but the grace of God is seen in making provision for those who were willing to commemorate the Passover in the God-given way, but who were unavoidably unable to do so. Let it be emphasised again that this grace of God was not to be used as an excuse for deliberate disobedience.

The Passover at Gilgal (Josh 5.10-12)

This Passover was the first celebrated in the land. Israel crossed the Jordan on the tenth day of the first month (Josh 4.19), the day when the Passover lamb was to be selected. After the circumcision of the people, the Passover took place on the appointed day - the fourteenth day of the first month. What a Passover this must have been! There is no record of any being kept during the years since the events of Numbers 9 although it cannot be stated with certainty that no Passover had been celebrated. With this feast the wilderness had been left behind and the conquest of the land was about to begin.

The unleavened cakes and parched corn of which they partook, according to the instructions in respect of the Feast of Unleavened Bread, would be eaten on the 15ᵗʰ day and the firstfruits offered on the 16ᵗʰ day. These firstfruits consisted of the old corn of the land, the harvest that had been planted months previously by the Canaanites. Once again the grace of God is seen in that they enjoyed that which they had neither planted nor harvested.

After this, the manna, which speaks of the humanity of the Lord Jesus, ceased, and their diet now included the old corn of the land, speaking of Christ in resurrection for, "Except a corn of wheat fall into the ground and die, it abideth alone" (Jn 12.24). The fruit of harvest declares the truth of resurrection of which He is the firstfruits (1 Cor 15.23).

The Passover of Hezekiah (2 Chr 30.1-27)

Although there is no record of a Passover taking place since that which was celebrated at Gilgal, it cannot be held that none had taken place. The reference, to be noted later, to the Passover which was held in the reign of Josiah, states that there had not been held "such a passover from the days of the judges that judged Israel..." (2 Kings 23.22), and indicates that there had been Passovers at that time. Jerusalem had not seen a Passover like Hezekiah's since the time of Solomon, so Passover was celebrated during his reign, although it is not known when or how often this took place.

This Passover was central to the reforming work carried out by Hezekiah, this great and good king of Judah. He "did that which was right in the sight of the Lord, according to all that David his father had done" (2 Chr 29.2). It is unlikely that it took place in the first year of his reign because by the time the message went out to all Israel to come to Jerusalem the Assyrians had taken the people of the northern kingdom of Israel captive (30.6,7,9), and this did not take place until the 6ᵗʰ year of Hezekiah's reign (2 Kings 18.10).

It was not possible to hold the Feast during the first month because the priesthood was not free from defilement (2 Chr 30.2-3) and the people had not gathered to Jerusalem. The desire of Hezekiah was to see all those of Israel who had not been taken captive gather, so messengers were sent throughout the land from Beersheba to Dan, from the south to the north, calling the people to assemble. Many "laughed them to scorn" (30.10), but many "humbled themselves, and came to Jerusalem" (30.11).

Due to ignorance, there were "a multitude of the people" (30.18) from the northern tribes who ate the Passover despite the fact that they were not ceremonially clean. These people had prepared their hearts to seek God and were genuine in their desire to be fit for Passover. Hezekiah brought them before the Lord in prayer and the Lord "healed the people" (30.20), making them fit to participate.

Such was the joy of this occasion that the "the whole assembly took counsel to keep other seven days" (30.23). The Feast of Unleavened Bread was extended from seven to fourteen days, and this without any reluctance on the part of the people. It was their desire to continue the feast and they did so without reluctance and "with gladness" (30.23).

There were three ways in which no Passover since the time of Solomon had been like this.

1. The invitation to come had gone out to all Israel. Representatives of all tribes gathered to Jerusalem. Since the division of the kingdom and the setting up in the north of the idolatrous system of worship by Jeroboam this had not taken place.

2. There had not been such richness and variety of offerings.

3. There had not been a fourteen-day feast. In Solomon's time this consisted of two feasts, the Feast of Dedication for the Temple and the Feast of Tabernacles (1 Kings 8.65-66; 2 Chr 7.9-10). The reference to Solomon sending the people home on the eighth day is to the eighth day of the Feast of Tabernacles.

One of the consequences of this Passover was the cleansing of the land from the images and groves which polluted it. Not just the people of Judah, but also those of all Israel, set about this task "until they had utterly destroyed them all" (31.1). In such a spirit of revival this Passover, which had seen the king seek to bring all of Israel together in obedience to the Word of God, ended.

The Passover of Josiah (2 Kings 23.21-23; 2 Chr 35.1-19)

Josiah was the last godly king of Judah. He ascended the throne when he was eight years of age and died tragically at the age of thirty-nine. This Passover is the last recorded act of the king before the events which led to his death, although it took place in the eighteenth year of his thirty-one year reign (2 Kings 23.23). It is the climax of Josiah's reforms. Earlier that year Hilkiah the priest had found the book of the Law in the house of God (2 Chr 34.15) and, although there is nothing in the text to confirm this, it may be that this Passover was held as a result of reading the book.

The account also contains the last historic mention in Scripture of the Ark of the Covenant (35.3): "Put the holy ark in the house which Solomon the son of David did build; it shall not be a burden upon your shoulders", is the instruction of the king to the Levites. Some commentators consider that during the reigns of Manasseh and Amon the Ark had been taken from the Temple; others understand this to indicate that Josiah had removed the Ark when the Temple was being repaired; yet others state that the Ark was being carried about as a talisman, just as it had been when it was captured by the Philistines (1 Sam 4.3). The view of Keil & Delitzsch is that the Ark had not been removed from the Temple and that the exhortation simply is to the Levites to ensure that the Ark remained where it had been put in the days of Solomon. It does appear, however, that it had been removed, and that the desire of Josiah was to see returned into its place the symbol of the presence of the Lord amongst His people.

That it was a memorable occasion is made clear twice: "Surely there was not holden such a passover from the days of the judges that judged Israel, nor of the kings of Judah" (2 Kings 23.22), and, "there was no passover like to that kept in Israel from the days of Samuel" (2 Chr 35.18).

This Passover, therefore, was marked by Josiah's desire to have the Lord in the midst of His people. This is an encouragement to all who seek to see the truth of God recovered in last day conditions. It required formidable spiritual determination for "there (was) no king before him, that turned to the Lord with all his heart, and with all his soul, and with all his might, according to all the law of Moses" (2 Kings 23.25).

Jeremiah commenced his work in the reign of Josiah and the king must have been aware of his prophecies. Chapters 2 and 3, for instance, were publicly proclaimed in Jerusalem during his reign. It may be that Jeremiah influenced the king. Despite the dark clouds on the horizon, Josiah determined to work in his own generation and not to let prevailing conditions and the bleak future prospects lessen his determination to leave his mark for God in a day of godlessness, spiritual indifference, and rebellion. The people did not share his love of the Lord, but none of these things deterred him. How pleasing it is to observe that in the closing days of the kingdom it was possible to enjoy conditions, even for a short space of time, which had not been enjoyed since the days of Samuel.

The Passover of Haggai (Ezra 6.19-22)

The work of rebuilding the Temple in Jerusalem had come to a halt. The adversaries of Judah and Jerusalem had offered the returned remnant an alliance that would have allowed them part in the rebuilding (Ezra 4.1-3). When this was rightly refused they then "weakened the hands of the people of Judah, and troubled them in building" (4.4). To add to the problems facing the builders, the adversaries then hired counsellors to frustrate the work, finally writing a letter to king Artaxerxes which resulted in a royal decree that the work should cease. For about fifteen years the Temple foundations lay open, a testimony to work that had been started but not brought to completion.

During that time the discouraged workers turned their attention to other projects. They were not idle and were still building, but their efforts were aimed at erecting their own houses and not the House of the Lord. Their dwellings displayed their wealth - houses with inlaid woodwork covering the inside walls. If challenged as to why their efforts should be so misdirected they would reply that it was clearly not yet time to build the House of the Lord. Circumstances, they would assert, proved the truth of that. It was not time for His power and glory to be manifested so it was not time to work on the Temple.

Haggai and Zechariah the prophets raised their voices to encourage the people to continue the work. Their call was for the people to consider their ways (Hag 1.5,7). They were to turn from building their wealth to building the House. The voices of these men seem to sound down through the centuries with a message for today. So often complacency is excused by citing present-day conditions, and the energies of many saints in the so-called "developed" world are directed to wealth building rather than assembly building.

One encouraging feature is the presence of Zerubbabel with Haggai as the call is made. Zerubbabel is named as one of the leaders of the people when the work of rebuilding commenced (Ezra 3.2,8). He was, therefore, amongst those who ceased from building, although he may not personally have agreed with such a decision. There is also no indication that during the interval he had been building his own luxurious house. The fact that he stood with Haggai would seem to indicate that he had stood aloof from all such activity. The encouragement is that although he had been part of a work that had faltered, this did not debar him from leadership in its recommencement. Let all take courage who have seen the work of God falter. Remain distant from worldly pursuits; do not fill hours that should have seen united workers busy, with that which is unworthy. Wait on the opportunity to lead again a willing and working people.

As a result of this call to the work, the building of the house was completed on the third day of the month Adar (Ezra 6.15). As Adar was the twelfth month of the year it was some weeks before Passover, and the returned captives now had the opportunity to keep this feast. Emphasis is given to the fact that the priests had purified themselves making themselves fit to undertake their responsibilities.

Little wonder that Ezra confirms that they "kept the feast of unleavened bread seven days with joy: for the Lord had made them joyful" (6.22). After seventy years in Babylon, and the frustrations and delays since their return to Jerusalem, the Temple worship had recommenced.

The Passover in the Millennium (Ezek 45.21-24)

The vision of which this forms a part was given to Ezekiel, who was of the priestly line, on the tenth day of the first month, the day when the Passover lamb should have been selected. Captivity conditions disallowed this. The vision occupies the closing nine chapters of the book, and details the millennial Temple (chs.40-42), the millennial worship (chs.43-44), the millennial administration (chs.45-46), and the millennial land of Israel (chs.47-48). The glorious future awaiting the nation of Israel is set out!

The Temple in Jerusalem will have a priesthood, and sacrifices will again be offered. The question often asked is, "Why should there be sacrifices?". After the Cross was the sacrificial system involving animals not brought to an end? That is so for the church age, but Ezekiel teaches that they will again take place. Feinberg, writing in *The Prophecy of Ezekiel,* states that in the past there had been "offerings and sacrifices which spoke of Him prospectively", but that the offerings of which Ezekiel writes "will yet testify to Him retrospectively in a day yet future". These offerings, therefore, commemorate the Cross. One other reason may be added. Death will take place in the Millennium, but will be rare. The death of these animals will bring to the hearts of the people the enormity of death and the great cost paid by the Lord Jesus in dying.

In this Passover there is no mention of a lamb being slain, for the Lord Jesus is no longer the submissive lamb. A bullock is offered for a sin offering representing the strength of devotion which marks Him.

The Passover in Jerusalem When the Lord was Twelve Years of Age (Lk 2.40-52)

When Joseph went up to Jerusalem to keep the Passover there was no requirement for Mary to accompany him, but she did so to show unity with her husband in his devotions. Those who were pious Jews would remain for the full seven days of the Feast of Unleavened Bread, and this was the practice of Joseph and Mary. In the crowds who left Jerusalem at the end of the feast was this family from Nazareth, but at the end of the first day of the journey the Lord Jesus was not to be found, even among the "extended family" and their friends.

It became necessary, therefore, for Joseph and his wife to return to Jerusalem to seek Him. The journey back would occupy up to one day (although they probably returned immediately and with haste) and the search two/three days. There must have been great anxiety in their hearts as they looked for Him in the streets of the city without avail. At last, He was located in the Temple sitting with the "doctors" (v.46), and when they found Him He spoke His first recorded words: "How is it that ye sought me? wist ye not that I must be about my Father's business?". These words could be placed over His life; He was always "about His Father's business". There is a beautiful winsomeness about the Lord as he sat with the teachers. He was not impressing on them how much He knew; rather He was found "hearing them, and asking them questions" (v.46). The discussion required that there were questions which He had to answer and repeatedly these learned men were amazed at His answers.

Clearly, at twelve years of age, the Saviour knew the purpose of His coming to earth. There are about His early years mysteries which have not been revealed to us, and it is not profitable to seek answers which Scripture does not give. This important insight reveals that He understood who His Father was and why He had come to be born in Bethlehem. The response of Joseph and Mary, that "they understood not the saying which he spake unto them" (v.50) shows that they still did not have an understanding of all that was involved in the Incarnation. Mary, however, "kept all these sayings in her heart" (v.51); she kept pondering the events surrounding His birth, and now what had taken place in Jerusalem. She had much to reflect on as there was graciously revealed to her the magnitude of what had taken place with the birth of her firstborn.

The Passover When the Lord Cleansed the Temple (Jn 2.12-3.21)

The Passover was now termed "the Jew's passover". There was no joy for the Lord in it. The nation had rejected Him and all the religious observances in Jerusalem were nothing but ritualism without reality. Nevertheless, the Lord went up to Jerusalem because failure to do so would lead to the charge that He was neglecting His responsibilities under the Law. This was fulfilling "all righteousness" (Mt 3.15). Having gone into the Temple the Lord found there that which had to be cast out. Just as leaven had to be put out of the houses of Israel in preparation for the Feast of Unleavened Bread, so this uncleanness had to be put out of this House. This He did by making a scourge of small cords and driving out the sheep and the oxen. The care which He exercised in this act is seen in how He treated the doves. These would be in cages and He did not overturn them but told the merchants to take them out.

One evening during this Passover season the Lord Jesus was visited by one of the Pharisees, Nicodemus, a teacher of some note. Discussion had taken place between this man and his friends regarding this remarkable stranger from Nazareth. The miracles which He had performed had led some to the conclusion that He was a teacher come from God, but Nicodemus had a desire to get to the truth of the matter. Thus there took place the remarkable interview which is recorded in John 3. Nicodemus asked his first question in the form of a statement, for surely such an eminent rabbi needed not to ask questions of this "untaught" man. It is of interest to note that his last question was an admission of lack of knowledge as he asked, "How can these things be?" (Jn 3.9). The answers which he received from the Lord taught him the necessity of the new birth. Here in Jerusalem, at a time when the people were commemorating the birth of their nation and rejoicing in their own birth as Jews, Nicodemus heard that all this was of no avail. Just as, with the commencement of a new calendar, the first Passover in Egypt taught Israel that a new start was necessary, so the new birth had to be experienced to give that new start in the lives of those who sought the kingdom of God. It is a happy circumstance to note that Nicodemus believed what he was told (see Jn 7.50; 19.39).

The Passover with no Record of the Lord Attending (Jn 6.4)

This Passover is mentioned as the background to the miracle of the feeding of the five thousand and the subsequent teaching of the Lord. There is no record of the Lord going to Jerusalem at this time but, although He was in Galilee, a brief visit to Jerusalem for the feast cannot be excluded. Indeed, it is unlikely that the Lord failed to go to Jerusalem three times in the year as the Law required.

The reference to the Passover is followed immediately by the miracle of the loaves and fishes which shows that there is a link between them. The Lord who had fed Israel with manna in the wilderness is the One who will now feed thousands on the mountain. This is the only event, apart from His last visit to Jerusalem, which is recorded by all four Gospel writers (Mt 14.13-21; Mk 6.30-44; Lk 9.10-17; Jn 6.5-14).

On the following day, the Lord Jesus taught in the synagogue in Capernaum. This was a turning point in His public ministry because after it "many of his disciples went back, and walked no more with him" (Jn 6.66). He referred to the manna but claimed that He was the "true bread from heaven" (Jn 6.32), the bread of life. Just as the manna sustained the physical life of the nation, so the bread of life gives and sustains the more important part, the spiritual life of His people. The manna was not living bread, therefore it could not give life, but He does.

The Passover at the Time of the Crucifixion (Mt 26.2; Mk 14.1; Lk 22.1; Jn 13.1)

It is not within the scope of this brief survey to consider all the issues which are raised regarding this Passover. It is worthy of note that the Lord now moved openly towards the city. There was no fear of man before His eyes and no attempt to disguise His purpose. He knew that "his hour was come that he should depart out of the world unto the Father" (Jn 13.1).

Some years later Josephus reports that at Passover 256,500 lambs were slain (*The Wars of the Jews*, Book 6, ch. 9, sect. 3). When consideration is given to the great quantity of blood that flowed and that none of the sacrifices slain under the Law could take away sin (Heb 10.11), it is solemn to consider that He offered one sacrifice for sins forever (Heb 10.12).

> No blood, no altar now,
> The sacrifice is o'er;
> No flame, no smoke ascends on high,
> The lamb is slain no more.
>   (Horatius Bonar)

As the Jews gathered for what would be the last Passover, little did they realise that the true Passover Lamb was about to be slain outside the walls of Jerusalem. Shadow would become reality, "For even Christ our passover is sacrificed for us" (1 Cor 5.7).

The Passover When Peter was Under Arrest (Acts 12.1-4)

"Passover" is not mentioned in connection with these events but the reference to "the days of unleavened bread" (v.2) confirms that they took place at the Passover season. Herod, the grandson of Herod the Great, who had James the brother of John put to the sword, arrested Peter and had him held in prison proposing to bring him out for trial after Passover. The king had authorised the arrest because it pleased the Jewish authorities, and to ensure that he kept in their favour he would arrange that the trial would not take place during the Passover and the Days of Unleavened Bread which followed. On the evening immediately before the day when Peter was to be publicly arraigned he was released from prison by the angel of the Lord.

Peter had learned lessons from the past. He who raised the sword to defend his Lord against arrest refrained from this course of action when he, himself, was arrested. At this point in the Acts the ministry of Peter was about to be less prominent and that of Paul to come to the fore. Yet the Lord still had valuable work for Peter to carry out, not the least of which was the writing of two epistles.

The power of the king is pitted against the prayers of the saints and the truth proved the words of John: "Ye are of God, little children, and have overcome them: because greater is he that is in you, than he that is in the world" (1 Jn 4.4). Note that the apostle who wrote those words was the one whose brother, a comparatively young man, had been slain by Herod. This experience did not cause him to doubt the truth of what he later wrote.

How sad is this last mention of what should have been a week of holy convocation. The leaven, rather than being removed, was abundant and encouraged, yet the work of God continued and a new phase in the spread of the gospel was about to commence.

APPENDIX 5
THE PURPOSE AND EFFECT
OF THE LAW

For almost 1,500 years the Law dominated the life of the nation and yet it could not impart eternal life to a single soul. Some consider that the Law can be divided into two sections, moral and ceremonial. While it is admitted that there are moral as well as ceremonial elements in the Law, the Scripture never divides it in this way. The Law stands as one body of teaching containing moral instruction and a ceremonial, symbolic element.

The Law did not annul or change the covenant which had been made with Abraham. That covenant promised blessing to the seed of Abraham, and once a covenant has been made no man can change its terms or have it cancelled (Gal 3.15); the terms still stand. The Law cannot, therefore, change a covenant which was made 430 years before Israel stood at Sinai. Even during the tenure of the Law salvation was still by faith and not by works.

The Purpose of the Law
The Law reveals sin
The Law was "added (*4369*) because of transgressions" (Gal 3.19).

It was brought in to reveal sin. With the Law in place, sin became the transgression of commandments given, and was seen to be disobedience to God. It is this same principle at work to which Paul refers when he writes, "I had not known sin, but by the law: for I had not known lust, except the law had said, Thou shalt not covet" (Rom 7.7). Paul is possibly here identifying a sin which he was prone to commit. Covetousness filled his heart, but without the Law he would have failed to recognise it as sin. Now he could recognise that which the Law declared to be sinful. However, before the Law was given sin should have been recognised: conscience should have spoken and anyone who lived in fellowship with God would have recognised sin as being that which was offensive to Him. But with the Law, sin was clear to everyone and any who may have claimed ignorance could no longer do so.

The Law deals with immaturity
"The law was our schoolmaster to bring us unto Christ, that we might be justified by faith" (Gal 3.24).

Paul illustrates this in two ways in writing to the Galatians. First, to be under the Law was to be as a child under a guide. The "schoolmaster" (*3807*) was not a teacher, but a slave who was charged with the responsibility of supervising the lives of the sons of rich families. It was he who saw to it that the son was educated in the appropriate manners and customs to which he would adhere, and in the moral code by which he would be expected to live. The care and safety of his charge was also his responsibility. From the age of 6 years the son was subject to this supervision, but when he reached 16 years he was no longer under the "schoolmaster".

The Law serves this purpose, not "to bring us to Christ" in the sense of bringing us to salvation, but "until Christ", that is, until Christ came. Those who are under Law, therefore, are in a state of immaturity, still being educated in the fundamental lessons for life.

The second illustration is of a minor who is on the same level as a slave: "The heir, as long as he is a child, differeth nothing from a servant, though he be lord of all" (Gal 4.1). The immaturity of the child puts him in the same place as those who are not born into the privileges that are his. He has position and privilege but is not in the enjoyment of them.

Those who were seeking to bring the Law in alongside the preaching of the gospel were troubling the assemblies in Galatia. Their argument was that the gospel was good, but after salvation it was necessary to keep the Law. In doing this, they claimed, the Galatians would manifest spiritual maturity. Paul's argument shows the opposite to be true. To go back to the Law was to regress to a state of immaturity, losing the enjoyment of the blessings of grace.

The Effect of the Law
The Law brings a curse

The principle of Law is diametrically opposed to the principle of grace. Law gives the principles by which it is necessary to live and please God. It insists that these instructions be obeyed, and failure brings censure and judgment. "Cursed be he that confirmeth not all the words of this law to do them" (Deut 27.26), is a clear affirmation that to put oneself under Law brings a responsibility to keep that Law with rigorous penalties for failure. That there are no exceptions to this is made clear by Paul when, quoting from Deuteronomy, he writes, "For as many as are of the works of the law are under the curse: for it is written, Cursed is everyone that continueth not in all things which are written in the book of the law to do them" (Gal 3.10).

Sin is activated

"But sin, taking occasion by the commandment, wrought in me all manner of concupiscence. For without the law sin was dead. For I was alive without the law once: but when the commandment came, sin revived, and I died" (Rom 7.8-9).

Strange though it may appear, sin used the Law as the base for its operations. How could this possibly be when the Law was holy and came from God? The answer is that sin took occasion by the commandment. When the Law was given, sin used it, in the sense that there was born into the heart a desire to do what God forbade. Man is so rebellious against

God that the moment he learns what God forbids, that is what he desires to do. Sin used the Law as the starting point. Note that it did not use the Law as the starting point of an occasional sin. It wrought in Paul all manner of concupiscence, that is, all manner of coveting. Now it can be seen that instead of suppressing sin and bringing it to a halt, the Law had the opposite effect. Sin, rather than decreasing with the Law, increased. The Law roused it to greater activity. This is what Paul means when he writes that without the Law, sin was dead. He does not mean that it ceased to exist without the Law. He did not mean that it was not present. He does mean that without the Law sin was not roused to activity. There were sins that he might not have committed, but when he knew the Law, the desire to commit these sins was activated.

Death is the result

"And the commandment, which was ordained to life, I found to be unto death. For sin, taking occasion by the commandment, deceived me, and by it slew me" (Rom 7.10-11).

What a disappointment was to be found in the Law. Those who embraced it expected it to lead to a state of happiness and felicity. Those who observed it believed that it would lead to a greater knowledge of God. In this they were deceived. The Law, rather than leading to greater happiness and a fuller knowledge of God, led instead to death, that is it led to sin which cuts us off from God. Instead of a fuller life, there is a life at a greater distance from God. What a disappointment the Law proved to be to those who hoped it would lead to a life that satisfied God's demands. The "blessed man" of Psalm 1 delighted in the Law of the Lord, but he did not depend on it (v.2).

Sin is revealed as exceedingly sinful

"Wherefore the law is holy, and the commandment holy, and just, and good. Was then that which is good made death unto me? God forbid. But sin, that it might appear sin, working death in me by that which is good; that sin by the commandment might become exceeding sinful" (Rom 7.12-13).

It has already been observed that the Law reveals sin, but in these verses this is taken further. If in Romans 7.7-8 the Law reveals the existence of sin, in these verses Paul observes that the darkness and depth of sin, its foul nature, are revealed also. The point being made by Paul here is that the Law is holy, there is no fault in the Law. He states three of its characteristics..

1. It is holy. It is in keeping with the character of God.
2. It is just. It is righteous, and not unfair in its requirements.
3. It is good. It is beneficial in its results.

Now, if all this is true of the Law, how is it that it leads to greater sin in those who are under it? If it is holy and righteous, and good, why does it result in making men and women sin to a greater extent than they did when they did not know the Law? How can such a thing possibly be?

This is what Paul tackles when he asks the question: "Was then that which is good made death to me?". The answer is an emphatic: "God forbid". That which was good, the Law, did not work death in me. It could not because it is holy, and righteous, and good. But then the question still remains: if that which was good, the Law, did not work death, how is it that the Law aroused passions of sin?

The answer is that sin worked "death in me" by using that which was good, the Law. We see here the exceeding sinfulness of sin, which can take that which is holy, and righteous, and good, and make me sin more than I previously did. So dark is sin that it will even use what comes from God to further its progress. Sin exceeded, sin grew greater, sin grew deeper, because of the Law, and thus sin revealed just how dark it really is in using what was holy, and just, and good to further its progress. So it is not the Law which works death, it is sin which works death. The Law cannot be charged with this; sin is the guilty culprit.

The Law Reveals its Powerlessness (Rom 7.14-25)

Does the Law empower those who live by it to keep its commandments? This section of the Epistle to the Romans deals graphically with the condition of those who seek to live by the Law and who find that seeking to please God in this way leads to a battle developing. The Law is spiritual, as it comes from God, but, writes the apostle, "I am carnal" (v.14), under the dominion of sin. This is true of anyone who is seeking to please God without understanding the teaching of Scripture which has been laid out in previous chapters of the epistle. Those who put their trust in their ability to keep the Law are under the dominion of sin because they are relying on their own resources to please God. What are the features of this conflict?

The first feature is that the character of what is being done is not recognised. Thus he states that what he does he allows not, that is, what he does he does not truly know (v.15a). He is not aware of the true character of his actions, and thus is not equipped to live the life which he would seek to live.

The second feature is that he does not do what he would like to do. "What I would that do I not" (v.15b), is how Paul puts it. So no matter what good resolutions he makes he is unable to carry them out.

The third feature is that the things he seeks to avoid are the very things he finds himself doing. "What I hate, that do I" (v.15c), describes one who not only cannot live as he would like, but who continues to practise what he knows to be sinful and abhorrent to God. He hates the things which he does. This is a proof of the fact that the Law is good and makes sin a hateful thing to those who seek to avoid doing that which is sinful. So here we have a man who admits to the fact that the Law is good, but is unable to comply with it.

Paul lays out his argument in a very orderly way. He divides it into two parts, each commencing with something that we know. In v.14 he states that *"we know* that the law is spiritual: but I am carnal, sold under sin". In v.18 he states that *"I know* that in me…dwelleth no good thing". Both of these parts end with the same conclusion where Paul asserts in both verses "sin dwelleth in me" (see vv.17,20).

In the first part (vv.14-17) he is dealing with the complete contrast between a Law which is spiritual and an individual who is dominated by sin. It is not possible to be obedient to a spiritual Law, when I myself am carnal. Thus it is that I cannot do what I would wish and I hate the things which I do. In the second part (vv.18-20) he deals with the contrast between the will and the flesh, the body. He has a will to do that which is right, but he cannot find in himself what he needs to bring this about.

The double verdict which he reaches in both parts is that it is sin which is working in him and not he himself. He is one who has not managed to stop sin being his master. He has not been able to put the teaching of Romans 6 into practice. Here we are simply learning that this man still is subject to sin, and, as such, he is unable to please God, and unable to practise that which He would wish to see carried out. The Law has been powerless to help anyone to keep its commands. It makes its demands but does not give the power to put them into effect. It brings about no spiritual change in the lives of those who practise it.

Redeemed From the Curse of the Law

"Christ hath redeemed us from the curse of the law, being made a curse for us: for it is written, Cursed is every one that hangeth on a tree" (Gal 3.13).

Everyone, therefore, who is unable to keep the Law is under the curse falling on the disobedient. Human effort cannot remove this curse and can never give the ability to keep God's Law. The curse must be borne! For the believer the grand truth is that deliverance from the curse of the Law has been brought about. This curse has been carried out and the Lord Jesus has borne it on behalf of others.

The Law itself declared that everyone who was hanged on a tree was cursed (Deut 21.23). The Jews did not carry out death by crucifixion, but all who were guilty of a sin worthy of death were hanged on a tree after the sentence had been carried out. The purpose of this was to show publicly the shame of the criminal. To be branded as a "hanged one" was the deepest ignominy to which anyone could be subjected. Dishonour, humiliation, disgrace, and shame were associated with such a death and it was this that the Jews sought to heap on the sinless Saviour.

His death was also payment of the ransom price, by which means believers have been redeemed through being bought out of the slave market of sin. No other way was possible.

APPENDIX 6
THE CONSTRUCTION OF
THE TABERNACLE

When Moses was given instructions for the building of the Tabernacle he was told to do so "according to all that I shew thee, after the pattern of the tabernacle, and the pattern of the instruments thereof, even so shall ye make it" (25.9). Reference to this is found on another three occasions.

1. "And look that thou make them after their pattern, which was shewed thee in the mount" (25.40).

2. "And thou shalt rear up the tabernacle according to the fashion thereof which was shewed thee in the mount" (26.30).

3. "Hollow with boards shalt thou make it: as it was shewed thee in the mount, so shall they make it" (27.8).

Moses, therefore, in a manner which is not known, had revealed to him exactly how each of the parts of the Tabernacle was to be made, and this information is not available to today's reader. The reasons for this are threefold. First, there has been revealed all that is necessary to teach lessons which have to be learned from the Tabernacle. All the spiritual truth to be assimilated can be done from the revelation given. There is nothing missing which it is necessary for the believer today to know and understand.

Second, the purpose of this revelation is not to provide a builder's blueprint for the construction of another Tabernacle. Many have engaged in such a project, but builders or model makers cannot be completely sure that what they have put together is exactly as it was in the wilderness.

Third, on the more positive side, the questions which are raised can usefully employ the minds of those who have an interest in these things. There is enough in the Word of God to absorb the attention of Christians, and in being so occupied, not just to learn "construction facts" but to learn spiritual truth, they will uncover much that is greatly for their benefit. There is no need to have a void mind when the Word of God always has unexplored avenues waiting to be travelled, which, although they may not provide all the answers to how the Tabernacle looked, will nevertheless exercise the mind in the Scriptures and open up other truths that will be for the glory of God.

The difficulties which face the present day reader did not present themselves to Moses, nor to Bezaleel or Aholiab, as Moses had seen the pattern while on the mount and would be able to pass on to the builders all that was necessary for them to complete their work exactly as the Lord intended.

The purpose of this appendix is to explore some of these issues and lay out a number of the solutions that have been offered. Let it be emphasised again that this is not to satisfy idle curiosity, but to stimulate the minds of those who desire to examine as much as possible of the construction of the Tabernacle, always keeping in mind that what is being dealt with is a shadow, a picture of the true, and that believers today are not living in the day of shadow, but in the day of substance and reality.

In these times when the Word of God is constantly under attack it is well to remember that the fact that all is not fully revealed does not constitute a failure of Scripture, nor is it an indication that the Word of God is fallible. It is not mere repetition to state again that God has revealed all that is required and that these Scriptures under consideration are, as is all Scripture, inspired of God.

Was the Tabernacle Flat Roofed?

There are two vital verses regarding this issue which read: "And the remnant that remaineth of the curtains of the tent, the half curtain that remaineth, shall hang over the backside of the tabernacle. And a cubit on the one side and a cubit on the other side of that which remaineth in the length of the curtains of the tent, it shall hang over the sides of the tabernacle on this side and on that side, to cover it" (26.12-13).

Details of a flat roof construction

The traditional view is that the two curtains, one of fine twined linen and one of goats' hair, and the two coverings, one of rams' skins dyed red and one of badgers' skins, were placed over the boards with the fine linen curtain on the inside, the goats' hair curtain placed next, followed by the rams' skins and then the badgers' skins which constituted the outer covering. Four coverings were, therefore, over the structure, supported by the boards at the sides with the "roof" section of the coverings held in place by the four pillars from which the vail was hung and the five pillars from which the door was hung.

The length of the fine linen curtain when the parts were coupled together was 40 cubits by 28 cubits, and the Tabernacle structure was 10 cubits high, 10 cubits broad, and 30 cubits long. The linen curtain would run from the door to the rear wall, 30 cubits, and then down the rear wall, 10 cubits, making the 40 cubits of the curtain length. The breadth of the curtain was, however, only 28 cubits, and, as 10 cubits of this was taken up by the breadth of the Tabernacle, this only left 18 cubits - or 9 cubits to hang down each side. This resulted in the linen curtain reaching to the ground at the back of the Tabernacle but reaching only to 1 cubit above the ground at the sides.

The goats' hair curtain placed over the linen curtain was, at 44 cubits long by 30 cubits broad, 4 cubits longer and 2 cubits broader. The two verses quoted above, it is claimed, show how this extra length was used. At the front of the Tabernacle 4 cubits of the curtain hung over the entrance. This was doubled back on itself and 1 cubit of it was used as an overhang at the front. The remainder of the curtain was, therefore, 1 cubit longer than the fine linen curtain and would be placed in the same way, but would be 1 cubit longer down the back. The breadth of the curtain at 30 cubits was 2 cubits greater than that of the linen curtain resulting in it reaching down to the ground at the sides. No dimensions are given for the other two coverings, so the assumption is made that these were positioned in the same manner as the goats' hair curtain. Keil & Delitzsch write of the goats' hair covering (note that Keil & Delitzsch use "broad" where these notes use "long" and vice versa): "This tent-cloth was two cubits longer than the inner one, as each piece was 30 cubits long instead of 28; it was also two cubits broader, as it was composed of 11 pieces, the eleventh only reckoning as two cubits, as it was to be laid double. Consequently there was an excess (that which is over) of two cubits each way; and according to 26.12 and 13 this was to be disposed of in the following manner: '*As for the spreading out of the excess in the tent-cloths, the half of the cloth in excess shall spread out over the back of the dwelling; and the cubit from here and from there in the excess in the length of the tent-cloths* (i.e., the cubit over in the length in each of the cloths) *shall be spread out on the sides of the dwelling from here and from there to cover it.*' Now since, according to this, one half of the two cubits of the sixth piece which was laid double was to hang down the back of the tabernacle, there only remained one cubit for the gable of the front. It follows, therefore, that the joining of the two halves with loops and clasps would come a cubit farther back, than the place where the curtain of the holy of holies divided the dwelling. But in consequence of the cloth being a cubit longer in every direction, it nearly reached the ground on all three sides, the thickness of the wooden framework alone preventing it from reaching it altogether."

Objections to a flat roof construction

The objection to a flat roofed Tabernacle is based on two main points.

1. A flat roof is not suitable for dealing with rain, which would gather on the roof and cause it to sag. It is true that in the Sinai Desert rain is not a constant problem and there are long periods when no rain actually falls. There can, however, be downpours from time to time. Strong comments: "The rainfall during the showers in winter on the Sinaitic peninsular is often prodigious, and snow occasionally falls to the depth of several inches in the valleys about Mt. Sinai. In March 1874, the author, with his party, was overtaken by a snow storm at Mt. Sinai, of such severity as to compel them to take refuge in the convent there for several days. Writers who think only of the dry season have little knowledge in the case".

2. The wording of 26.12-13, it is claimed, demands that it be a peaked structure, otherwise it would not be possible to carry out these instructions.

Details of a Peaked Roof Construction

There are no dimensions given for the pillars which held up the vail and the door (26.32,37), allowing it to be claimed that it was possible for them to have been of differing lengths, resulting in a peaked roof. This view understands 26.12-13 to mean that the goats' hair curtain was hung over a peaked roof, resulting in there being a 1 cubit overhang on both sides. This peak would be of a size necessary to bring the side of the goats' hair curtain high enough to have only 1 cubit overhanging the sides.

Objections to a peaked roof construction
The main objection to a peaked roof construction is that there is nothing to suggest that the Children of Israel erected tents with "A" shaped peaked roofs. As far as can be ascertained tents were erected in a manner somewhat similar to the desert tents of today.

Although allowance had to be made for rain, there were other ways in which this could be done. It may have been part of the responsibilities of the Levites to ensure that the water was not allowed to lie on the roof. Another possibility is that there was a slight increase in the height of the pillar towards the centre giving enough of a slope for the rain to run off, but not the large peak envisaged in this theory.

Were the Boards Solid?
Much discussion has taken place as to whether the boards were solid or made of an open ladder-like structure. Two arguments are advanced in support of the theory that the ladder-like structure was necessary.

1. The weight of solid boards, no matter how thick they were, would make handling them very difficult and cumbersome.

2. The acacia tree was a relatively small tree, and would not provide planks of sufficient size to form boards 10 cubits by $1\frac{1}{2}$ cubits.

The benefits of the "framework" structure
The ease of handling to which reference has already been made is the prime benefit of such a means of construction. When consideration is given to all that was involved in erecting and dismantling the Tabernacle this is clearly a matter of some importance. The load to be placed on the wagons for transporting the boards would be much reduced.

It has also been claimed that the nature of these "framework" boards would enable them to be used as ladders. When erecting and dismantling the structure the Levites could climb up and fix or release the vail from the golden hooks on the pillars from which it was hung.

The internal fine twined linen curtain embroidered with cherubims would, if the boards were solid, only be visible on the roof. All the side drop of the curtains would be hidden behind the solid boards. If, however, the structure consisted of an open framework, these would be visible on the sides.

Objections to the "framework" structure
The word "board" (7175) does not give a final answer as to which method

was employed. TWOT at 2079a merely defines it as "board, boards", and Wilson writes of it: "…as used of the boards of the tabernacle, made to be compact or fastened together, which is probably the primary meaning of the root" (*Old Testament Word Studies*). Gesenius in his Dictionary states that it means "a board or a plank". These all seem to favour a board rather than an open structure, without completely dismissing the latter.

The argument that the side-wall portions of the linen curtains would not be seen by the priests is not conclusive. There were other items in the Tabernacle which were not seen: for instance, the contents of the Ark, the curtain of goats' hair, and the covering of rams' skins dyed red. These two coverings were placed between the covering of badgers' skins and the inner curtain of fine twined linen. However, as has been observed, the roof portion of the linen curtains could be seen. It also must not be forgotten that even although there were things which could not be seen by Aaron and his sons, they were before the eye of God.

Regarding the possibility of the shittim tree providing planks large enough to form the boards, Ratcliffe observes: "There seems little doubt that when the Israelites reached the Sinai desert, following their deliverance from Egypt, the shittim wood trees would have been far more substantial in height and girth than anything found growing there today…Down through the centuries charcoal producers have decimated the Sinai peninsular of mature shittim-wood trees" *(Bible Plants, Fruits & Products)*.

The argument then comes down to the point as to whether planks were too heavy and bulky to handle. While there can be no doubt that they would be weighty, consideration must be given to the fact that there were four wagons given to the sons of Merari to carry the boards (Num 7.1-9), and that there were 3,200 of these men to take the load (Num 4.42-44).

How Were the Rear Corner Boards Fitted (26.15-25)?

It was observed in the study of these verses that there were twenty boards, each 10 cubits high by $1\frac{1}{2}$ cubits broad on the south and on the north sides of the Tabernacle. At the rear, on the west side, the description of the boards is: "And for the sides of the tabernacle westwards thou shalt make six boards. And two boards shalt thou make for the corners of the tabernacle in the two sides. And they shall be coupled together beneath, and they shall be coupled together above the head of it unto one ring: thus shall it be for them both; they shall be for the two corners. And they shall be eight boards" (vv.22-25). A restatement of what was written in the notes on ch.26 will be useful at this point. "The length of the Tabernacle structure was 30 cubits, being twenty boards each of $1\frac{1}{2}$ cubits. Nowhere is the width of the structure stated. On the west side, however, there were six boards of $1\frac{1}{2}$ cubits, making 9 cubits in total, plus the two corner boards which, if they were placed alongside the six boards, would make eight, giving a total width of 12 cubits. This does not, however, take into account the joining of the boards at the corners, and it appears to be a reasonable supposition to make, taking the undernoted points into consideration, that the means of joining the corners reduced the inside width to 10 cubits.

1. The thickness of the side boards, or however else they were joined together, would reduce the inside dimensions.

2. A width of 10 cubits would make the Holiest of All a complete cube.

3. The Holiest of All in Solomon's Temple was a complete cube, 20 cubits in length, breadth, and height."

At the rear, however, there were eight boards in total, and, if placed together, they would form a wall 12 cubits long. How, therefore, were they joined?

Solution 1

This solution, which has been widely favoured, is based on the view that the boards were 1 cubit thick. The eight back boards would, therefore, be put in place and the side wall would butt directly on to these back boards. This would reduce the inside measurement of the structure to 10 cubits. In order to join the sides and the rear together they were to be "coupled together" beneath and above, that is there may have been a ring which was placed round the rear side board and the side board which butted on to them, or else there was some other ring attachment to achieve this.

The problem which this presents is that boards of 1 cubit thick would be extremely heavy and cumbersome. Viewing the boards as being made of a framework, rather than being of solid construction may overcome this objection. (This is discussed in the section, "*Were the boards solid?*", above). It is, however, a relatively simple solution which would give a 10 cubit internal width.

Solution 2

Strong is the advocate of this solution, which depends on the view that the boards were $\frac{1}{6}$ of a cubit thick (four finger-breadths), as is stated by Josephus in *The Antiquities of the Jews,* Book 3. The first solution above is dismissed by Strong due to the excessive thickness of the boards. To form the corners, the rear corner boards were divided into two sections, one of $\frac{2}{3}$ of a cubit wide and one of $\frac{5}{6}$ of a cubit. These two parts were then joined together to form a board with a rectangular corner. When the side boards were placed inside the back boards it would leave the back board with an internal length of $\frac{1}{2}$ of a cubit. In this way the internal width would be made up of the combined width of each of the six back boards, which was 9 cubits in total, plus the $\frac{1}{2}$ cubit in both side boards, adding a further cubit and totalling 10 cubits.

The claim is made that "This clears up the obscure phraseology employed (v.24) concerning these corner planks". It means that the two boards which have been divided were joined together and fastened to the side boards by using the rings through which the bars were placed.

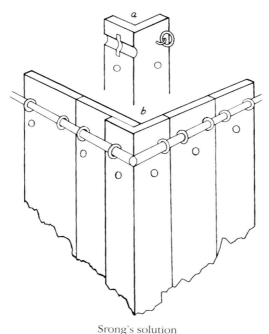

Srong's solution
Corner plank of the Tabernacle (N.W. angle) a. Separate b. Combined

This also is an attractive solution and appears to be a neat answer. It rests on the assumption that the corner boards were divided in the manner indicated although there is no direct reference to the boards being so formed. Whether or not the construction was exactly as Strong states, an answer like this has much to commend it.

A somewhat similar approach (that of corner boards being made by dividing a board) is adopted by Keil & Delitzsch, except for the dimensions of the boards involved. The idea that the boards were 1 cubit thick is dismissed because it would make "simple boards into colossal blocks, such as could never have been cut from acacia trees, nor carried upon desert roads" but the thickness is claimed to be greater than that suggested by Strong, possibly by joining together planks from the acacia tree. No detailed sizes are given to support this, nor is any indication given as to the dimension of the two pieces of the boards which are joined at right angles to form the corner.

How Did the Rings in the Boards Affect Their Transportation?

If there were rings on the outside of the boards did this create a problem when the boards were placed in the wagons for transportation? It would be difficult to place these boards flat, and the rings could well be damaged with the weight of the boards on top of them.

A number of solutions have been suggested.

1. The rings were removed when the boards were being transported. This is possible and a perfectly feasible solution.

2. There were no bottom boards in the wagons and the boards were placed face down, resting on ledges along the front and back of the wagon. This would make it necessary to have only one layer of boards in each wagon and there would not be enough wagons for such an arrangement. If there were more than one layer, the problem of the top boards resting on the rings of the boards underneath would still be present. This is answered by the suggestion that the second layer of boards would be placed with the inside (the side with no rings) downwards and then cloths or skins placed over these to protect the rings which would be facing upwards, so that the upper boards rested on the cloths or skins, and not on the rings of the boards underneath. Such an arrangement is possible, even if the bottom planks rested on a solid base with the rings facing in the upward position.

3. The boards were placed in the wagons resting on their sides. This would be a viable means of stowing the boards on the wagons.

The Brazen Altar (27.1-8)

Three questions are presented by the directions for the building of the great Brazen Altar which dominated the court of the Tabernacle.

1. How was the "grate of network of brass" incorporated into the Altar?

2. As the Altar was 3 cubits high how was it possible to lift up the sacrifices and place them on it? Was there an earthen ramp, or even steps up to the Altar to make it possible to place the sacrifice on the fire?

3. How did the shittim wood, which was sheathed with brass, resist the flames?

How was the network of brass incorporated into the Altar?

"And thou shalt make for it a grate of network of brass; and upon the net shalt thou make four brasen rings in the four corners thereof. And thou shalt put it under the compass of the altar beneath, that the net may be even to the midst of the altar" (vv.4-5).

The word "compass" (3749) means "the edge", and refers to the "ledge of an altar" (TWOT at 1038a). The word "midst" (2677) means "half", or "middle". So this network of brass was to be placed under the edge of the Altar and at the halfway point, which would be $1^1/_2$ cubits both from the ground and from the top of the Altar.

This question is inextricably linked with that of how the fire was placed on the Altar and how the ashes of the fire and the sacrifices were cleared. Three solutions have been suggested.

SOLUTION 1

This is the solution which is adopted by Strong. He writes regarding the positioning of this brass network that it was made up of "the grate, consisting of a copper network, movable by a copper ring in each corner (v.4), and placed below the top of the altar, halfway down the inside (v.5)". He continues: "It appears that there was no cover for the altar at all, and probably no bottom, but only the grating, evidently for the fire, across it at the middle. This latter was supported by sliding through slits in the opposite sides of the altar, the rings projecting outside".

This suggestion is that the fire was placed on the network of brass, and when it was necessary to clear the fire area and remove the ashes the rings were gripped and the network grate pulled though a slit on the side of the Altar, thus making it easy to clear and clean the fire. The other aspect of this solution is that the network was pulled out only half way on occasions and at the other side of the Altar this gave the priests access to clear the ashes which had fallen to the ground inside the Altar.

The question of how air gained access to the fire to create the draught necessary is dealt with by the fact that a sufficient supply of air would come in over the sides for ordinary purposes of combustion, but that if necessary the current of air could be increased by excavating openings under the sides of the Altar which could be closed when required by covering them with a stone.

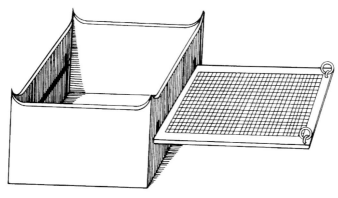

Altar of Burnt Offering, with the grate drawn out

The first difficulty presented by this solution is that there is no instruction for slits being in the side of the Altar. It is also difficult to see how this was a practical solution. If the brass network was drawn out as is suggested, most of what was on the Altar would be unable to pass through a slit and would therefore be pushed off the brass network and fall to the ground inside the Altar. Similarly, when wood for the fire or the carcass of a sacrifice was placed on the brass network when it was in the "pulled out" position it would not be possible to return the network to its place without dislodging the contents. The second difficulty is that the practice of pulling the network out halfway seems exceedingly cumbersome, particularly with the care required to return to the grate any part of the sacrifice which accidentally fell to the ground inside the Altar.

The question of air supply is one which must be answered in each solution. The excavation of holes around the Altar, covered by stones when the extra draught was not required, is not in Scripture and does appear to be a rather crude solution to the problem.

SOLUTION 2

This solution is adopted by Brown and others. He writes that "the compass was probably a rim or border encircling the upper part of the altar…The grate of network extending, in our opinion, like a shelf or a ledge from the middle of the altar on the outside, served as a platform for the priests, standing on when offering up sacrifices. Ashes falling accidentally off the altar would escape through the meshes of the grating, while fuel and pieces of sacrifice would be caught". In this solution the brass grating is not where the fire is placed. Brown writes that "Earth, therefore, of which the hollow of the altar must have been filled, would form the surface on which the fire burned (Ex 20.24)".

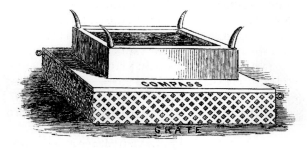

Brown's Brazen Altar

A variation of this suggestion is that the "compass" was the shelf or ledge on which the priests stood and the brass network was what supported this. Keil & Delitzsch support this view: "The altar was to have a *grating, net-work*, i.e., a covering of brass made in the form of a net, of larger dimensions than the sides of the altar, for this grating was to be under the 'compass' of the altar from beneath, and to reach to the half of it (half-way up, 27.5); and in it, i.e., at the four ends (or corners) of it, four brass rings were to be fastened, for the poles to carry it with…'compass' signifies a border, i.e., a projecting framework or bench running round the four sides of the altar, about half a cubit or a cubit broad, nailed to the walls (of the altar) on the outside, and fastened more firmly to them by the copper covering which was common to both". They conclude that the brass network was fixed to this shelf and reached down to the ground: "The copper grating was below this bench, and on the outside. The bench rested upon it, or rather it hung from the outer edge of the bench and rested upon the ground, like the inner chest, which it surrounded on all four sides, and in which there were no perforations". In this way the lower half of the Altar was broader than the top half. The priests stood on the shelf when they attended to the Altar. Support for this is claimed from the fact that Aaron "came down" from the Altar after he had offered sin offerings, burnt offerings, and peace offerings at the time of the consecration of the priests (Lev 9.22).

SOLUTION 3

This is an intriguing proposition and provides one suggested answer to the problem of how the priests were able to handle sacrifices on an Altar which was 3 cubits high. This problem is the greater when it is accepted that the sacrifice was placed *inside* the Altar on a brass grate which was positioned halfway down the interior. The suggestion of Meyer and others is that the Altar was filled with earth.

There are, however, a number of difficulties. First, there is no suggestion in the text that the Altar was filled with earth. It is believed that this is necessary because the brass covering of the Altar was only on the outside. To support this Meyer states: "The sides…within the altar were not overlaid with metal. The text merely says, referring to the outside, 'thou shalt overlay it with brass' (Ex 27.2), whereas when both outside and inside of any articles were to be covered with metal, the text distinctly says, 'within and without shalt thou overlay it' (Ex 25.11)". Clearly, with such a solution it was not possible to have the fire inside the Altar as even wood of such durable qualities as shittim wood would be consumed in the flames. It is true that it does not say of the Golden Altar of Incense or of the Brazen Altar that they were to be overlayed within and without. It is of the Ark that this is stated. It does, however, state that the Brazen Altar was to be hollow (27.8), an emphasis which may indicate that the inside and outside were to be treated similarly.

The second issue to consider is whether it was practical to have the fire laid on earth and level with the top of the Altar. An earthen floor of this nature would not provide enough draught for the fire unless the fire was raised up with the wood forming an elevated structure to allow sufficient air to be drawn into the flames. Present day bonfires are constructed in this way. The fire would, therefore, be considerably above the rim of the Altar with more than a little debris falling over the side. It is doubtful if the idea of ashes falling though the mesh of the grill, and the pieces of the sacrifices being caught by it, is practical. As the inside of such an Altar was of wood it would require constant scrutiny by the priests to ensure that the level of earth was always sufficient to cover all of the wood as, otherwise, it would be subject to charring and burning around the top.

The third difficulty is that to support the idea of earth inside the Altar reference is made to 20.24 as proof that it was filled with earth. The altar described there, however, is not the Brazen Altar (see notes on ch.20 for more details).

A fourth difficulty is the fact that the shelf on which the priests had to stand was half way up the side of the Altar, a height of $1^1/_2$ cubits. This made a step of very considerable height and to climb up on to it with no support of any kind would be difficult, if not impossible. The answer given to this objection is: "For even if the height of the altar, viz., three cubits, would be so great that a bench half-way up would be too high for any one to step up to, the earth could be slightly raised on one side so as to make the ascent perfectly easy; and when the priest was standing upon the bench, he could perform all that was necessary upon the top of the altar without any difficulty". There is, however, no instruction given for such an earthen ramp to be put in place (see, *"Was there a ramp of earth, or steps, up to the Altar?",* below).

SOLUTION 4

This solution is suggested by Raven in *God's Sanctuary*. He describes the Brazen Altar as "a hollow square box made of brass covered boards. In the middle and half way down inside the box is a grating made of brass". With that description, so far, Strong would agree. After that, however, their opinions diverge. Where this view differs substantially is that the boards that constituted the sides of the Altar are seen to be removable in order to gain access to the fire, and to clear out the ashes. The problem identified by Raven is one that is inherent in the two previous solutions: "The problem is that the altar is three cubits high, almost shoulder height for the average man. The sacrifice was half way down in the altar on the brazen grate, or some $1^1/_2$ cubits below the top of the altar. The priest could not approach too close for the altar would be very hot and wood smoke and the acrid smoke of burning flesh would act as an effective barrier to the priest trying to put his head over the edge of the altar".

The answer to this, asserts Raven, is to consider what is behind the description of the Altar as being "hollow with boards". These boards, he writes, ran horizontally as "if vertical they could serve no useful purpose". Thus the priests could remove the boards on the top half on one side of the Altar and they would with ease be able to place sacrifices on it and to deal with keeping the fire alight. For this purpose the height of the brass network was at a comfortable working height: "How easy it would be for two priests to lift the sacrifice on to this grate, push it into position with the fleshhooks and replace the boards".

The "pans to receive his ashes" and "his firepans" (27.3) would be placed in the Altar on the ground under the brazen grate, and there the ashes which fell though the grate would lie. "The ashpan will obviously be the lowest so that we can place that on the floor. If we are going to have a firepan it must mean that the fire must go in this and presumably the sacrifice must have been burnt on the grating of the altar, and the fire, in the firepan, would come between the grating and the ashpan. This would make an ideal arrangement for there would be no danger of the fire being extinguished when a whole, wet, freshly slain lamb was placed on the altar". The fire would therefore not be laid on the brazen grate, but in the firepan. In order to remove it the priests would lift all the boards from one side of the Altar, remove and empty the pan, and replace it.

To give sufficient draught to the fire, boards would be removed. "A great deal of care and skill would be required to keep the fire at such a level that it was sufficient to consume the sacrifice but not melt the grate or the firepan. By removing boards from the bottom of the altar the priest could control the access of air to the fire in much the same way as we use a damper in a modern boiler. Indeed, if he took the bottom board away all round the altar he would create a miniature blast furnace".

Raven's Brazen Altar

A great deal of detailed thought has gone into this solution, but there still remain some questions to be answered.

First, how were the boards removed? Would not the boards of the Altar be too hot to touch? It will be seen, however, when dealing with the question of how the shittim wood withstood the flame that it is argued by Raven that the outer boards would be cooler than one would think possible.

Second, how were the boards fixed to the Altar? There would be a need, as can be seen in the illustration, for a pillar at each corner of the Altar to which the boards were fixed. They could not slide down a slot in the corner pillars as it would not be possible to remove only the bottom boards and keep the top boards in place, as is suggested for control of the air flow to the fire, unless there were fixtures of some kind to make this possible. It is more likely that they were attached to the corner pillars by being placed on the pillars and held by fixtures for that purpose.

Third, the position of the firepans. As for the fire being placed under the brazen grate the question is, "Would this be sufficient to completely consume the sacrifice when the sacrifice was not placed directly on the fire?".

Conclusion

Each of the solutions has commendable features and has been proposed by godly men. In so doing they stimulate interest in the Word of God. It is not possible to claim with complete confidence that any one answer is correct, although the suggestions given in the fourth solution have fewer difficulties and answer a number of questions in an easily understood manner.

Was there a ramp of earth, or steps, up to the Altar?

Because of the height of the Altar and the place of the brazen grate halfway down the inside, some believe that there were steps or a ramp of earth leading up to it. This certainly would make access to the Altar and to the fire much easier. It has already been noted that an Altar with a height of 3 cubits would almost reach the shoulders of an average man and to deal with a fire that was $1^1/_2$ cubits within the Altar would mean leaning over the fire. Apart from that, the height of the Altar would make the placing of sacrifices onto it a difficult task, as 3 cubits is not a convenient working level for a standing man.

The placing of a shelf or ledge round the Altar, as noted in some of the solutions above, could deal with this problem, but a step of $1^1/_2$ cubits is very high and would itself require a ramp or steps for access.

The difficulty in this is twofold. First, there is no instruction for placing steps or a ramp up to the Altar, and, second, there is an instruction not to have steps up the altars of earth or hewn stones which the Children of Israel were commanded to build. The altar referred to in 20.26 is not the Brazen Altar, but nevertheless it would be unlikely that what is disallowed in such clear terms in the construction of the altar of earth or stone would be welcome in the building of the Brazen Altar. "Neither shalt thou go up by steps unto mine altar, that thy nakedness be not discovered thereon", revealed that the absence of steps ensured the preservation of the dignity of the priesthood. Certainly no ramp of earth is mentioned in this prohibition, but the danger associated with the steps was also present when a ramp was used.

It has been argued that as there are no dimensions given for the altars of earth it was possible to make them of such great height that the presence of steps would make the "nakedness" of the priests easy to see, whereas with the 3 cubit stipulated height of the Brazen Altar this was not possible. It is doubtful, however, that builders of altars of earth or stone would make them deliberately so high that it was necessary to have a considerable number of steps put in place to reach the altar. The reasoning behind these altars was that they were not difficult to build and to add such height to no purpose was but wasted, unnecessary effort.

This still leaves the problem of what is meant by Aaron coming "down" from the Altar after the consecration of the priests (Lev 9.22). This may lend weight to the view that there was a ledge or shelf round the Altar and that when Aaron completed the offering he "came down" from that ledge.

How did the shittim wood survive the flames?

The fire of the Altar would be very hot and the question has been raised as to whether the shittim wood, which was sheathed in brass, would be able to survive the constant heat. Even wood as incorruptible as that from the shittim tree does burn, and it is possible, but not probable, that the brass covering hid the charred and blackened remains of the wood.

Raven has gone to a great deal of effort to show that this was not so, and it is worth considering his conclusions. He states that brass (copper) has a greater coefficient of heat transfer than most metals, and is a great conductor of heat; that is why there are copper kettles and copper-bottomed pans. "The centre of the fire might possibly exceed this temperature because the heat would rise and the firepan would tend to dissipate the heat very quickly. Similarly, the heat on the grate might occasionally exceed the optimum because the wet carcass and the heat dissipation of the grate would help. If the centre of the fire had to be kept to this limit then the outer portion of the grate must be well below this, and as brass is such a good conductor of heat it would mean that the walls of the altar would be cooler still. In fact the altar would act as one gigantic heat sink, dissipating the heat as fast as it was generated; and the wood in the boards? - absolutely untouched. Experiments have been conducted on this and a blowtorch temperature well in excess of 1,000 degrees [F] applied to as close as 6 inches [15.25 cms] to the corner of the altar leaves the internal wood absolutely untouched". Raven's argument, therefore, is that the heat dissipating quality of the metal ensured that the shittim wood never had to bear temperatures which would cause it to char.

Conclusion

Let it be stated again, as it was at the beginning of this appendix, that these views on the construction of the Tabernacle are not presented to suggest that the record of Scripture is obscure or incomplete. All that needs to be known has been revealed to us, but the interested reader may wish to examine these ideas in greater depth to ascertain if there is any spiritual gold to be mined from such a study.

The Tabernacle is a rich seam of truth from which to gain blessing, and those who seek to explore it to the full may wish to use these brief notes as the basis for further investigation.

TABERNACLE ILLUSTRATIONS

The Tabernacle in the Wilderness

The Tabernacle with its coverings rolled back

The Ark of the Covenant

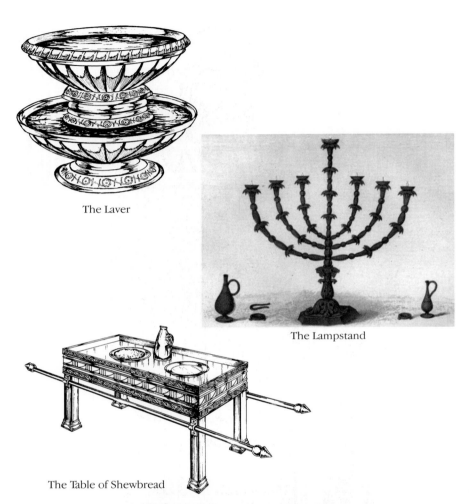

The Laver

The Lampstand

The Table of Shewbread

The Altar of Incense

The High Priest